Core Questions in Philosophy

Core Questions in Philosophy

—A Text with Readings—

Elliott Sober

University of Wisconsin—Madison

MACMILLAN PUBLISHING COMPANY
New York

COLLIER MACMILLAN CANADA, INC.
Toronto

MAXWELL MACMILLAN INTERNATIONAL PUBLISHING GROUP
New York   Oxford   Singapore   Sydney

Editor: *Helen McInnis*
Production Supervisor: *Charlotte Hyland*
Production Manager: *Sandra Moore*
Text and Cover Designer: *Patricia Smythe*
Cover illustration: Copyright 1990, C. Herscovici/Art Resource, NY. Magritte, "Ceci n'est pas un pomme."

This book was set in Meridien by V&M Graphics, and printed and bound by R.R. Donnelley & Sons Company. The cover was printed by Phoenix Color Corp.

Sources appear on pages 559–560, which constitute a continuation of the copyright page.

Macmillan Publishing Company
866 Third Avenue, New York, New York 10022

Collier Macmillan Canada, Inc.
1200 Eglinton Avenue East
Suite 200
Don Mills, Ontario M3C 3N1

Library of Congress Cataloging-in-Publication Data

Sober, Elliott.
  Core questions in philosophy: a text with readings/ Elliott Sober.
  p. cm.
  Includes bibliographical references.
  ISBN 0-02-413151-2
  1. Philosophy—Introductions. I. Title.
BD21.S615 1991
100—dc20

90-30738
CIP

Printing: 1 2 3 4 5 6 7   Year: 1 2 3 4 5 6 7

—For Aaron—

·P·R·E·F·A·C·E·

The philosophical problems investigated in this book concern fundamental facts about our place in the universe. Many of us were brought up to believe that God exists, that there is a real difference between right and wrong, that we can freely choose what sort of lives to lead, and that it is possible for us to gain knowledge of the world we inhabit. A major goal of philosophy is to discover whether these opinions can be rationally defended or are just comfortable illusions.

Core Questions in Philosophy emphasizes the idea that philosophy is a subject devoted to *evaluating arguments* and *constructing theories*. This is not the same as describing the history of what various philosophers have thought. Although I discuss historical texts, I do so because they are rich sources of ideas pertinent to answering philosophical questions. The point is not to say solemn and respectful words about worthy figures now dead, but to engage them in dialogue—to grapple with the theories they have proposed, to criticize these theories, even to improve upon them.

Besides proposing answers to philosophical questions, I also try to make clear which questions I have *not* answered. I hope that the reader will approach what I say the way I have approached the philosophical texts I discuss. This is a book to argue with, to dissect. It is not my goal to have the reader accept without question the conclusions I reach.

This work is a combination *textbook with readings*. The text part (which I call "lectures") is followed by a group of related readings (drawn from Plato, Aristotle, Aquinas, Anselm, Descartes, Hume, Kant, Mill, and others). The lectures flow together so that the main areas covered—philosophy of religion, epistemology, philosophy of mind, and ethics—are connected to each other to make a coherent whole.

The lectures are intended to be *launching pads* from which readers can pursue issues on their own. I believe that students are best able to think about philosophy if they first are provided with some basic tools and concepts. It is the purpose of the lectures to provide these *core ideas*.

Following the lectures in Parts II through V, there are a number of readings; these are drawn mainly from historical texts, although a few are by contemporary philosophers. The lectures often discuss these readings, but the area of overlap is far from total. Many lectures contain material that is not touched on in any reading, and the readings raise a wealth of issues that the lectures do not address. The lectures are intended to stand on their own as well as to provide points of entry into the readings.

Each lecture is followed by Review Questions and by Problems for Further Thought. These should help readers to consolidate their understanding of what I have said and to think creatively about related problems. The lectures each include a number of "boxes"; these boxes provide a nutshell restatement of a main idea or a brief discussion of a related matter that may interest the reader. A list of the boxes immediately follows the table of contents. Each main part of the text includes Suggestions for Further Reading. And there is a glossary at the end of the book that provides simple definitions of the main concepts used.

Besides covering a number of traditional topics, this book also takes up some contemporary theories and problems, both from philosophy and from other disciplines. Creationism and evolutionary theory are hotly debated now. The issues they raise are continuous with a tradition of argument in philosophy of religion that goes back (at least) to Aquinas, Hume, and Paley. The relation of mind and body is as old a problem as philosophy engages; but the ideas of Freud and Skinner get a hearing along with those of Descartes. In ethics there has long been a debate as to whether ethical truths are discovered or created. Plato and Sartre are separated by more than 2,000 years, but both speak to this issue. The problem of free will raises the question of whether every event is caused. Here the contributions of modern physics must be brought into contact with a perennial problem of philosophy. Philosophy is not the same as biology, psychology, or physics. But the problems of philosophy cannot be isolated from the sciences. One aim of this book is to connect philosophical problems with ideas derived from a wider culture.

The etymology of the word "philosopher" is *lover of wisdom*. This does not guarantee that all philosophers are wise or even that each individual philosopher is devoted to the attainment of wisdom. Philosophers *should* strive for wisdom; whether they do so, and whether they attain it, are separate questions.

Wisdom involves understanding—seeing how things fit together. When the pieces of a puzzle are fitted together, one attains a sense of wholeness. Current philosophy is embedded in a historical tradition of philosophical discourse. It also is connected with problems in the sciences, the other humanities, and the arts. This book aims to give the reader a sense of these multiple connections.

· ACKNOWLEDGEMENTS ·

My debts to my colleagues in philosophy here in Madison are enormous. A fixed point in my work week has been discussions of the ideas and techniques that go into presenting central problems of philosophy to new students. My philosophical outlook, as well as the view I have of teaching, have been shaped by these conversations.

It is a pleasure to thank Michael Byrd, Claudia Card, Fred Dretske, Ellery Eells, Berent Enc, Malcolm Forster, Paula Gottlieb, Andy Levine, Steve Nadler, Terry Penner, Mark Singer, Dennis Stampe, Daniel Wikler, and Keith Yandell. They were generous enough to suffer my trespasses onto philosophical terrain that was more theirs than my own. Some read parts of this book and gave me comments; others listened patiently while I tried out what I thought was a new angle.

Writing an introduction to philosophy has been a challenge. I had to reconstruct what a problem or idea would sound like to someone who had not studied the subject before. There was difficulty in this task, but also exhilaration. The project was a kind of return to the beginning—to fundamentals. I hope that what I found by beginning again will be useful to those who set themselves the project of beginning for the first time.

·C·O·N·T·E·N·T·S·

I. Introduction   1

Lectures

    1. What Is Philosophy?   2
    2. Deductive Arguments   8
    3. Inductive and Abductive Arguments   18

Suggestions for Further Reading   33

II. Philosophy of Religion   35

Lectures

    4. Aquinas' First Four Ways   36
    5. The Design Argument   49
    6. Evolution and Creationism   56
    7. Can Science Explain Everything?   68
    8. The Ontological Argument   75
    9. Is the Existence of God Testable?   83
    10. Pascal and Irrationality   92
    11. The Argument from Evil   100

Readings   106

Saint Thomas Aquinas *Five Ways to Prove That
  God Exists*   106
William Paley *The Design Argument*   108
David Hume *Critique of the Design Argument*   111
Saint Anselm and Gaunilo *The Ontological Argument*   118
Alfred Jules Ayer *The Meaninglessness of Religious
  Discourse*   121
Ernest Nagel *Defending Atheism*   126

Suggestions for Further Reading   134

III. Theory of Knowledge   137

Lectures

    12. What Is Knowledge?   138
    13. Descartes' Foundationalism   147

14. The Reliability Theory of Knowledge — 160
15. Justified Belief and Hume's Problem of Induction — 171
16. Can Hume's Skepticism Be Refuted? — 178
17. Beyond Foundationalism — 185

Readings — 191

Plato *Knowledge Is Something More Than True Belief* — 191
René Descartes *Meditations on First Philosophy* — 196
David Hume *Induction Cannot Be Rationally Justified* — 236

Suggestions for Further Reading — 245

IV. Philosophy of Mind — 247

Lectures

18. Dualism and the Mind/Body Problem — 248
19. Logical Behaviorism — 258
20. Methodological Behaviorism — 268
21. The Mind/Brain Identity Theory — 276
22. Functionalism — 281
23. Freedom, Determinism, and Causality — 289
24. A Menu of Positions on Free Will — 299
25. Compatibilism — 308
26. Psychological Egoism — 318

Readings — 327

Bertrand Russell *Other Minds Are Known by Analogy from One's Own Case* — 327
J.J.C. Smart *Mental Processes Are Physical* — 330
A.M. Turing *Computing Machinery and Intelligence* — 334
David Hume *Of Liberty and Necessity* — 356
C.A. Campbell *Has the Self "Free Will"?* — 370

Suggestions for Further Reading — 382

V. Ethics — 385

Lectures

27. Ethics—Normative and Meta — 386
28. The Naturalistic Fallacy and the Is/Ought Gap — 390
29. Observation and Explanation in Ethics — 398
30. Conventionalist Theories — 407
31. Utilitarianism — 416
32. Kant's Moral Theory — 431
33. Aristotle on the Good Life — 440

Readings   450

    Plato   *Critique of the Divine Command Theory*   450
    Jean-Paul Sartre   *Existentialism*   463
    John Stuart Mill   *Defence of Utilitarianism*   471
    Immanuel Kant   *Ethics Founded on Reason*   506
    Aristotle   *Morality and Human Nature*   527

Suggestions for Further Reading   549

Glossary   551

Sources   559

Index   561

·B·O·X·E·S·

1. Conditionals   14
2. Begging the Question   15
3. Deducing that a Theory Is True   26
4. No Surprise / Surprise   28
5. An Investment Swindle   30
6. Humans from Nonhumans, Life from Nonlife   64
7. "But How Do You Explain God?"   69
8. *A Priori / A Posteriori* and Necessity/Contingency   78
9. Neptune and Vulcan   87
10. The Expected Value of an Action   93
11. Necessary and Sufficient Conditions   140
12. Is Skepticism Self-Refuting?   145
13. Indubitability   149
14. The KK Principle   165
15. What's Relative About Einstein's Theory of Relativity?   169
16. Sense and Reference   254
17. Pain Without Pain Behavior?   266
18. Minimum Explanation Versus Deep Explanation   272
19. Newton on Parsimony   279
20. The Birthday Fallacy, Again   284
21. Positions on the Mind/Body Problem   287
22. Transitivity   290
23. Two Uses of Probability   294
24. The Normative Problem of Freedom   302
25. What is Coercion?   315
26. Apportioning Causal Responsibility   325
27. Emotivism   391
28. Values in Science   403
29. Liberalism and Conservatism   426
30. Good Versus Green   442

Core Questions in Philosophy

PART I
Introduction

·L·E·C·T·U·R·E·S·

Lecture 1

What Is Philosophy?

Philosophy is a peculiar subject. If you asked biochemists "What is biochemistry?", they would not have much trouble telling you what their subject includes. Different biochemists might provide slightly different answers. But biochemists probably would not think it is terribly important to get clear on which answer is "really" correct.

Asking philosophers what their subject includes elicits a very different response. It is difficult to answer the question "What is philosophy?". And the fact that philosophers produce different answers to this question is often taken to show that they disagree in fundamental ways about the aims and methods of their subject.

Although biochemists do not spend much time developing theories about what biochemistry really is, some philosophers have developed theories about the nature of philosophy. Often, these theories have been regarded by other philosophers as controversial and even misguided. Unfortunately, "What is philosophy?" is a philosophical question.

I'll discuss this question from two angles. First, I'll give a sketch of some of the main philosophical problems that will be examined in this book; that is, I'll describe some _examples_ of philosophy. But giving examples does not really answer the question. If you asked "What is a mammal?" and I showed you a human being, a chimp, a dog, and a cat, that might give you a _hint_ about what a mammal is. But citing examples is no substitute for saying what it is to be a mammal.

This is why there will be a second stage to my discussion of what philosophy is. After giving some examples of philosophical problems, I'll present some theories about what philosophy is. I believe that these theories have some merit, though none is fully adequate. These preliminary efforts to say what philosophy is will be enough for now. A better answer to the question will be available to you after you have read this book to the end, not here at the outset.

Examples The first philosophical problem we will consider is whether God exists. Some philosophers have constructed arguments that attempt to establish that God exists; others have tried to show that there is no God. I shall evaluate some of the more influential arguments and try to see whether they work.

The second problem we will consider concerns knowledge. It is fairly clear that belief and knowledge are different. Some people long ago thought the earth is flat. They *believed* this, but they didn't *know* it, since it isn't true. Of course, they *thought* they knew it, but that's different.

It also is fairly clear that true belief is not the same as knowledge. If you believe something for no reason at all, but happen to be right by accident, you have true belief, but not knowledge. For example, think of a gullible gambler at a race track who believes for no good reason that the first horse in every race will win. Occasionally, this person will be right—he will have a true belief. But it isn't plausible to say that he knew, for those races about which he turned out to be right, that the first horse would win. So having knowledge involves something more than having a true belief.

The philosophical problem about knowledge splits into two parts. First, there are the questions: What is knowledge? What makes knowledge different from true belief? Second, there is the question: Given some clarification of what knowledge is, do human beings ever have it? One philosophical position we will consider says that we human beings don't know anything. Sure, we have beliefs. And granted, some of our beliefs are true. But knowledge we never have. We don't even know those things we take to be most obvious. This position is called *philosophical skepticism*. We will consider arguments for skepticism and arguments that attempt to refute it.

The third philosophical problem on the agenda is the so-called mind/body problem. You have a mind; you also have a brain. What is the relationship between these items? One possible answer is that they are identical. Although "mind" and "brain" are two words, they name the same thing, just like the names "Superman" and "Clark Kent." An alternative position in this area is called *dualism*; it says that the mind and the brain may be causally connected, but they are two distinct things. We will consider other theories that have been advanced about the mind/body problem as well.

The next topic on the agenda is human freedom. Each of us has the personalities we have because we inherited a set of genes from our parents and then grew up in a sequence of environments. Genes plus environments make us the sorts of people we are. We did not choose the genes we have or the environments we experienced in early life. These were thrust upon us from the outside.

We perform certain actions and abstain from performing others. This pattern of what we do and don't do results from the personalities we have. Can we be said to perform actions freely? Is it really in our control to perform some actions and abstain from others? Perhaps our actions are not freely chosen because they are the results of factors that were totally outside of our control, namely, our genes and environment.

Of course, we talk in everyday life about people doing things "of their own free will." We also think of ourselves as facing real choices, as exercising control over what we do. The philosophical problem of freedom asks whether this common way of thinking is really defensible. Maybe it's just an illusion in which each of us indulges. Maybe we tell ourselves a fairy tale about our own freedom, because we can't face the fact that we are not free. The philosophical problem will be to see whether we can be free if our personalities are the results of factors outside of our control.

The last problem area I'll address is ethics. In everyday life we constantly think that some actions are right and others are wrong. The philosophical problem about this familiar attitude divides into two parts. First, we'll want to consider whether there really are such things as ethical facts. Maybe talk about ethics, like talk about freedom, is just an elaborate illusion.

Consider a parallel question about a science, physics, for example. In every science, there are questions that are controversial. For instance, physicists may have different opinions about how the solar system began. But most of us think that there is something else to physics besides opinions. There are facts about what the world is really like.

Clashes of opinion occur in what I'll call the *subjective realm*. Here we find one human mind disagreeing with another. But facts about physics exist in the *objective realm*. Those facts exist independently of anybody's thinking about them. They are out there, and science aims to discover what they are.

The question about ethics is whether both these realms (subjective and objective) exist in ethics, or only one of them does. We know that people have different ethical opinions. The question is whether, in addition to those opinions, there are ethical facts. In other words, does ethics parallel the description I have just given of science, or is there a fundamental difference here?

	Subjective Realm	Objective Realm
Science	Physical opinions	Physical facts
Ethics	Ethical opinions	Ethical facts

The idea that there are no ethical facts, only ethical opinions, I will call *ethical subjectivism*. We'll consider arguments supporting and attacking this position.

The second question that arises in ethics is this: If there are ethical facts, what are they? Here we assume a positive answer to the first question and then press on for more details. One theory we'll consider is *utilitarianism*. It says that the action you should perform in a given situation is the one that will produce the greatest happiness for the greatest number of individuals. This may sound like common sense, but, in fact, I will argue that there are some serious problems with this ethical theory.

Three Theories About What Philosophy Is

I have just described a menu of five central philosophical problems: God, knowledge, mind, freedom, and ethics. What makes tham all *philosophical* problems? Instead of giving examples, can we say something more general and complete about what distinguishes philosophy from other areas of inquiry? I will offer three theories about what is characteristic of at least some philosophical problems.

Several of the problems just described involve *fundamental questions of justification*. There are many things that we believe without hesitation or reflection. These beliefs that are second nature to us are sometimes called "common sense." Common sense says that the senses (sight, hearing, touch, taste, and smell) provide each of us with knowledge of the world we inhabit. Common sense also says that people often act "of their own free will." And common sense holds that some actions are right while others are wrong. Philosophy examines the fundamental assumptions we make about ourselves and the world we inhabit and tries to determine whether those assumptions are rationally defensible.

Another characteristic of many philosophical questions is that they are very *general.* In the problem of knowledge, we are not asking whether human beings know how old the earth's crust is, or whether they know why inflation occurs. These questions about knowledge are specific to geology and economics. Rather, the philosopher wants to know whether human beings know *anything.*

Here's another example that shows how philosophical questions can be more general than questions in specific sciences. Physicists have asked whether there are electrons. Biologists have investigated whether genes exist. And geologists have sought to find out if the continents rest on movable plates. But none of these sciences really bothers with the question of why we should think that there are physical objects. The various sciences simply *assume* that there are things outside the mind; they then focus on rather specific questions about what those things are like. In contrast, it is a characteristically philosophical question to ask why I should believe that there is anything outside of my own mind. The idea that there is nothing in the world but my mind is called *solipsism.* Philosophers have addressed the question of whether solipsism is true. This is a far more general question than the question of whether electrons, genes, or continental plates exist.

The third view of what philosophy is holds that philosophy is the enterprise of *clarifying concepts.* Consider such characteristic philosophical questions as: What is knowledge? What is freedom? What is justice? Each of these concepts applies to some things but not to others. What do the things falling under the concept have in common, and how do they differ from the things that do not fall under the concept?

We must be careful here, since many questions that are not especially philosophical sound somewhat like the examples just given. Consider such characteristic scientific questions as: What is photosynthesis? What is acidity? What is an electron? How does the first batch of questions differ from these?

One difference between these questions concerns the ways in which *reason* and *observation* help answer them. You probably are aware of the fact that philosophy courses do not include laboratory sections. Philosophers usually do not perform experiments as part of their inquiries. Yet, in many sciences (though not in all of them), laboratory observation is quite central.

This does not mean that observation plays no role in philosophy. Many of the philosophical theories we will consider begin by making an observation. For example, when we consider the question of whether human beings have knowledge of the world, we will want to consider the following fact: Human perception is sometimes subject to illusion and hallucination. The thing I want to call your attention to is that this fact is something we know by looking at the world we inhabit.

Here's another example. In Lecture 5, I'll consider an argument for the existence of God that begins with the following fact: Organisms are complicated things that are remarkably well adapted to the environments they inhabit. Again, the thing to notice now is that this fact is something we know by observation.

So philosophers, as well as scientists, rely on observations. But still, there is something distinctive about how observations figure in a philosophical inquiry. Usually, the observations that are used in a philosophical theory are familiar and obvious to everyone. A philosopher will try to show by reasoning that those observations lead to some rather surprising conclusions; that is, although philosophy involves both observation and reasoning, it is the latter that in some sense receives the "heavier weight." As you will see in what follows, philosophical disputes often involve disagreements about reasoning; rarely are such disputes decidable by making some observation.

Each of these ways of understanding what philosophy is should be taken with a grain of salt (or perhaps with two). I think there is something to be said for each, even though each is somewhat simplified and distorting.

The Nature of Philosophy Has Changed Historically

One reason it is difficult to say "what philosophy is" is that the subject has been in existence at least since the time of the ancient Greeks and has changed a great deal. There are many problems that are just as central to philosophy now as they were to the ancient Greeks. But there are other problems that have broken away from philosophy and are now thought of as purely scientific. Ancient Greek philosophers discussed what the basic constituents of physical things are. Thales (who lived around 580 B.C.) thought that everything is made of water; many other theories were discussed as well. Today such questions might be thought of as part of physics, not philosophy. Similarly, until the end of the nineteenth century, academic departments in universities typically put philosophy and psychology together. It is only rather recently that the two subjects have been thought of as separate.

In short, many of the problems that we now regard as philosophical are problems that have not broken away from philosophy and found their way into the sciences. Perhaps there are problems that are today taken to be philosophical, which future generations will not regard as such. The shifting historical nature of what counts as philosophy helps make it difficult to say anything very precise about what that subject is.

Philosophical Method

Having tried to say something about what philosophy is, I now want to say something about what philosophy is *not* (at least not in this book). You may have the impression that "doing philosophy" involves lying under a tree, staring up at the sky, and making deep pronouncements off the top of your head that sound very mystical but are hard to make sense of when you try to think about them clearly. I call this the mystical guru model of philosophy. Your experience reading this book will not correspond to this impression.

However, there is another experience you've probably had, which comes closer. If you took a high school geometry course, you remember proving theorems from axioms. If your geometry course was like the one I had, the axioms were given to you with very little explanation of why you should believe them. Maybe they looked obvious to you, so you didn't wonder very much about their plausibility. Anyhow, the main task was to use these axioms to prove theorems. You started with the axioms as assumptions and then showed that if they are true, other statements must be true as well.

Philosophers tend to talk about "arguments" rather than "proofs." The goal is to try to reach answers to important philosophical questions by reasoning correctly from assumptions that are plausible. For example, in Lecture 4, I'll examine some attempts to prove that God exists. The idea here is to start with assumptions that practically anybody would grant are true and then show that these assumptions lead to the conclusion that there is a God. This line of thinking resembles what you may have done in geometry: Starting with simple and supposedly obvious assumptions, you were able to establish something less obvious and more complex—for example, that the sum of the angles of a triangle equals two right angles (180 degrees).

Sometimes the philosophical questions we'll consider will strike you as difficult, deep, even mysterious. I won't shy away from such questions. However, I will try to address them with clarity and precision. The goal is to take hard questions and deal with them clearly, which, I emphasize, should never involve trying to pull the wool over someone's eyes by making deep-sounding pronouncements that mean who-knows-what.

In this lecture, I have presented three views about what philosophy is: the view that philosophy addresses fundamental questions of justification; the view that philosophy addresses questions of great generality; and the view that philosophy engages in the clarification of concepts. All have some truth in them, but none is as precise as one might wish. I have also said that discussing philosophical ideas is more like doing geometry than like being a mystical guru. In the next lecture, I'll develop some tools for evaluating arguments that will be used in the rest of the book.

Review Questions

1. What is the difference between objective and subjective?
2. If you want to say what philosophy is, why isn't it enough to list some examples of philosophical problems?

A Problem for Further Thought

1. In describing different ideas about what philosophy is, I listed some characteristics that the subject shares with mathematics. Which characteristics do the two fields have in common? How are they different?

Lecture 2

Deductive Arguments

Philosophy involves constructing and evaluating arguments. In this respect, philosophy is no different from any other rational activity—mathematicians do this, as do economists, physicists, and people in everyday life. The distinctive thing about philosophy is not that philosophers construct and evaluate arguments; what is distinctive is the kinds of questions that those arguments aim to answer. In the previous lecture, I talked about what makes a question philosophical. The goal in this lecture is to develop some techniques that can be used to tell whether an argument is good or bad.

Arguments An argument divides into two parts: the premises and the conclusion. The premises and the conclusion are statements; each is expressed by a declarative sentence. Each is either true or false. When people argue that a given statement is true, they will provide reasons for thinking this. The reasons are the premises of their argument; premises are asumptions. The statement to be established is the argument's conclusion. In high school geometry, you talked about axioms and theorems. Axioms are assumptions (premises); the theorem (the conclusion) is what is supposed to follow from those assumptions.

In geometry you may have spent little or no time asking whether the axioms are true. Not so for the philosophical arguments discussed in this book. We'll want to see whether the premises are plausible. We will also want to see whether the premises, if they were true, would provide a reason for thinking that the conclusion is true as well. I will pose these two questions again and again.

Good I want to talk about different kinds of "good arguments." What does "good"
Arguments mean? A good argument is _rationally persuasive;_ it gives you a good reason to think that the conclusion is true. Salespeople and politicians sometimes use arguments that trick people into believing what they say. These arguments may be persuasive, but they do not always provide good reasons.

Good arguments can be divided into two categories, and one of those categories can be divided into two more:

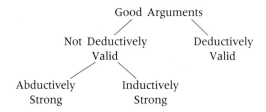

Here I treat the three categories (deductively valid, inductively strong, and abductively strong) as *mutually exclusive*. If an argument belongs to one category, it can't belong to the others. At the end of Lecture 3, I'll slightly modify this scheme of classification.

You may have heard some of this terminology before. Deduction is what you do in a mathematical proof. Induction involves sampling from a population to decide what its characteristics are. "Abduction" may be a less familiar term. It has nothing to do with kidnapping. The word was invented by the nineteenth-century American philosopher Charles Sanders Peirce. Philosophers sometimes use the longer label "inference to the best explanation" to describe what Peirce meant by abduction.

I consider deduction in this lecture, induction and abduction in the next. The goal in each case is to describe some of the considerations that are relevant to deciding whether an argument is good or bad.

The following two deductive arguments have something in common, even though their subject matters do not overlap at all:

Logical Form

All fish swim.　　　　　All particles have mass.
All sharks are fish.　　　All electrons are particles.
_____　　　　_____
All sharks swim.　　　　All electrons have mass.

These arguments have the same *logical form*. What does that mean? Think of each argument as the result of substituting terms into the following skeleton:

All Bs are Cs.
All As are Bs.
_____
All As are Cs.

You can think of A, B, and C as blanks into which terms may be substituted. Take a minute to see how the arguments just stated can be obtained from the previous skeleton by substitution—by "filling in the blanks."

I now can say something about deductive validity. An argument is valid or invalid solely by virtue of the logical form it has. The subject matter of the argument is irrelevant. From this fact it follows that the argument about fish and the argument about electrons are either both valid or neither is. They have the same logical form, so they are in the same boat.

Deductive Validity

As it happens, both arguments are valid. Indeed, each and every one of the millions of arguments you can construct by substitution into the previous skeleton is valid as well. So the following argument, being formally just like the first two, also is valid:

All plants have minds.
All ladders are plants.
_____
All ladders have minds.

"Validity"
Is a Technical
Term

You can see from this example that what philosophers and logicians mean by "valid" does not have much in common with what we mean by "valid" in ordinary English. In everyday life, we say that an idea is valid if it is plausible or true. But the technical use of the term differs from ordinary usage in two ways. First, we never say that a *statement* or an *idea* is valid or invalid. Validity is a property of *arguments* and of arguments only. Second, an argument can be valid even if the statements it contains are wildly implausible. A valid argument can have false premises and a false conclusion. The argument about ladders is an example.

Validity
Defined

I now will define deductive validity:

> *A deductively valid argument* is an argument that has the following property: *IF* its premises were true, its conclusion would have to be true.

I have capitalized the word **IF**. I'd print it in bright colors if I could, because it is important not to forget this two-letter word. *A valid argument does not have to have true premises.* What is required is that the conclusion would have to be true IF the premises were true.

Take a minute to look at the argument about ladders. Convince yourself that the argument is deductively valid. If the premises were true, then it would have to be true that all ladders have minds.

Invalidity

The definition of validity tells you what a deductively *in*valid argument will be like. If there is even the smallest possibility that the conclusion could be false when the premises are true, then the argument is deductively invalid.

The ladder argument is valid, though all the statements it contains are false. Is the reverse situation possible? Can an argument be *in*valid, even though all the statements it contains are true?

The answer is *yes*. Here's an example:

Emeralds are green.
_____
Lemons are yellow.

The premiss is true and so is the conclusion. So why isn't the argument deductively valid? The reason is that the definition of validity says that the premises in a valid argument provide an *absolute guarantee* that the conclusion is true. But the fact that emeralds are green does not guarantee that lemons must be yellow. The color of lemons is not entailed by the fact that emeralds are green. Validity concerns the *relationship* of premises to conclusion, not the question of whether the premises and the conclusion each happen to be true.

Sometimes it is not so obvious that an argument is invalid. The previous example is rather blatant—the premiss has nothing to do with the conclusion. But what do you think of the following argument? Is it valid or not?

If Jones stands in the heavy rain without an umbrella, then Jones will get wet.
Jones is wet.
_____

Jones was standing in the heavy rain without an umbrella.

Imagine that all three of the statements in this argument are true. Imagine that Jones is now standing before you soaking wet and that Jones just came in from the rain.

Even though all the statements in this argument are true, this argument is invalid. It is just like the argument about emeralds and lemons. The relationship between premisses and conclusion is not the one required by the definition of validity.

How can we see this more clearly? I said before that all arguments that have the same logical form are in the same boat. This means that if the argument about Jones is invalid, so is each and every argument that has the same form. Let's begin by isolating the argument's logical form. Here it is:

If P, then Q.
Q
_____

P

What do P and Q stand for in this argument skeleton? You can substitute any statement (declarative sentence) you please for these letters to obtain an argument with this logical form. Notice that the letters in this skeleton differ in their function from the letters in the previous skeleton. There, A, B, and C are blanks into which terms denoting kinds of things ("fish," "electrons," etc.) can be substituted.

Anyhow, we now have the logical form of the argument about Jones. If it is invalid, so are *all* arguments that have the same logical form. This means that if there is even one argument that has this logical form, in which the premisses are true and the conclusion false, then the argument form is invalid. This will mean that the initial argument about Jones is invalid as well.

Here's an argument with this logical form that settles the question:

If Sally lives in Wisconsin, then Sally lives in the USA.
Sally lives in the USA.
_____

Sally lives in Wisconsin.

The premisses of this argument are true, but the conclusion, I assure you, is false. The Sally I'm talking about lives in California.

Testing for Invalidity

Here's a strategy to use if you want to know whether an argument is invalid: First, ignore the content and isolate the logical form (the "skeleton") of the argument. Get rid of the distracting subject matter since that is irrelevant; what you want to focus on is the logical form. Second, see if you can invent an argument that has this logical form, in which the premisses are true and the conclusion is false. If you can find even one rotten apple of this type, you are finished. If there is even one argument with this property, then *every* argument of that form is invalid.

When an argument has true premisses and a false conclusion, it is quite obvious that the truth of the premisses does not guarantee that the conclusion must be true. The premisses can't be guaranteeing this, since the conclusion is false. But this tells you something general. It tells you that each and every argument of this form will be such that the premisses do not guarantee the truth of the conclusion.

So far, I've presented some examples of arguments. I have explained that a valid argument need not have true statements in it and that an argument comprised solely of true statements need not be valid. This should make you wonder whether there is any connection at all between the question of whether an argument is valid and the question of whether the premisses and conclusion are true.

There *is* a connection. It is illustrated by the following table. If an argument is valid, it can exhibit three of the four following combinations of true or false premisses and true or false conclusion:

Premisses

		True	False
	True	Possible	Possible
Conclusion	False	Impossible	Possible

This table indicates that a valid argument can't have true premisses and a false conclusion. However, the fact that an argument is valid leaves open which of the other three cells the argument occupies.

What can be said of an invalid argument? If an argument is invalid, are any of the four combinations impossible? I leave this to you to figure out by consulting the definition of validity.

When you find an invalid argument, you may want to ask if the argument can be repaired. Is there anything that can be done to an invalid argument to make it valid? There is. By adding premisses, you can make a deductively invalid argument into a valid one. Consider the following argument:

Smith lives in the USA.
_____

Smith lives in Wisconsin.

This is invalid, but it can be made valid by adding a premiss:

Smith lives in the USA.
Everyone who lives in the USA lives in Wisconsin.
_____

Smith lives in Wisconsin.

Notice that the conclusion now follows from the premisses. The trouble is that the second premiss is false.

In the previous pair of arguments, fixing the defect of invalidity just substitutes one problem for another; instead of having to criticize an argument's invalidity, you have to criticize its premisses for not being true. The following argument pair is different. Here one can repair the defect of invalidity and obtain a perfectly fine argument.

Notice first that the following argument is not deductively valid:

> Smith lives in Wisconsin.
> _____
> Smith lives in the USA.

The argument can be repaired, however, by adding a premiss:

> Smith lives in Wisconsin.
> Everyone who lives in Wisconsin lives in the USA.
> _____
> Smith lives in the USA.

This argument is valid and has true premisses as well.

You can see from these two pairs of arguments that invalidity is easy to fix. Just add premisses. What is harder is to add premisses that not only make the argument valid, but are true as well.

This idea will come up repeatedly when I discuss various philosophical arguments. I sometimes will claim that an argument is invalid. When this happens, you should ask yourself whether the argument can be repaired. Often, the price of making the argument valid (by adding a premiss) is that you have to supply a new premiss that you think is false. In making this addition, you are trading one defect (invalidity) for another (false premisses). If you can't repair the argument so that it is both valid and has true premisses, then you should consider the possibility that there is something fundamentally flawed about the whole line of argument. On the other hand, sometimes an invalid argument can be replaced by a valid one merely by supplying a true premiss that maybe you neglected to mention because it is so obvious. In this case, the defect in the original argument is not so fundamental.

So far, I have emphasized two questions that we will want to ask about arguments:

(1) Is the argument deductively valid?
(2) Are the premisses true?

If the answer is *yes* to both questions, the conclusion of the argument must be true.

Arguments are tools. We use them to do things. When the goal is rational persuasion, a good argument will provide a good reason to think that the conclusion is true. If an argument is deductively valid and has true premisses, is that sufficient to make it good? To see why validity and true premisses are not enough, consider the following argument:

Conditionals

If/then statements are called conditionals. Conditionals have other state-ments as components. For example, the statement "If pigs fly, then grass is green" is a statement of the form "If P, then Q," where P and Q are themselves statements.

In the statement "If P, then Q," P is called the antecedent and Q is called the consequent. A conditional does not say that its antecedent is true; the statement "If Joe drinks arsenic, then Joe will die" does not say that Joe drinks arsenic. A conditional does not say that its consequent is true; "If there is a nuclear war, then Washington will be attacked" does not say that Washington will be attacked.

Conditionals can be rewritten without changing what they say. Consider the statement "If you live in Wisconsin, then you live in the USA." This is equivalent in meaning to saying "If you do not live in the USA, then you do not live in Wisconsin." The conditional "If P, then Q," is equivalent to "If not Q, then not P," no matter what P and Q happen to be. Here's a piece of terminology: "If not Q, then not P" is the contrapositive of the conditional "If P, then Q." A conditional and its contrapositive are equivalent.

Consider the following two conditionals: "If P, then Q" and "If Q, then P." Are they equivalent? That is, do they mean the same thing? The answer is no. "If you live in Wisconsin, then you live in the USA" is true, but "If you live in the USA, then you live in Wisconsin" is false. These two if/then statements cannot mean the same thing, since what the one says is true while what the other says is false. "If Q, then P" is termed the converse of the conditional "If P, then Q." A conditional and its converse are not equivalent.

Lemons are yellow.

Lemons are yellow.

Here the conclusion merely repeats what the premiss asserts. This argument is valid and the premiss is true. But there is something defective about this argument. What is it?

Circularity, or Begging the Question This argument is *circular*; it *begs the question*. Suppose you did not know whether to think that lemons are yellow. The previous argument would not help you resolve your uncertainty. The argument would be useless in this regard: *If you don't already know whether the conclusion is true, this argument would not help you answer the question.*

Good arguments are tools that help answer questions about whether their conclusions are true. A good argument should give you a reason to accept the conclusion if you do not already believe that the conclusion is true. So besides checking to see if an argument is deductively valid and has true premisses, you also should see if the argument begs the question.

One other idea needs clearing up before we leave the topic of deductive validity. You'll notice that the definition of validity makes use of the idea of truth. What is truth?

Truth

There are deep philosophical questions here, most of which I will skirt. My goal is to describe the concept of truth used in this book. It is beyond the scope of this book to defend this choice or to fully develop its implications.

To begin with, whether a statement is true is an entirely different question from whether you or anybody believes it. Whether someone believes the statement "The Rocky Mountains are in North America" is a psychological question. If beings with minds had never populated the earth, I suppose no one would have thought about the location of this mountain range. But this does not affect the question of whether the statement is true. There can be truths that no one believes. Symmetrically, there can be beliefs that are not true.

"True for Me"

You'll see from these remarks that the expression "It's true for me" can be dangerously misleading. Sometimes saying that something is true for you just means that you believe it. If that's what you want to say, just use the word "belief" and leave truth out of it. However, there is a more radical idea that

---

Begging the Question

To understand what makes an argument question-begging, it is useful to examine some examples.

Suppose you were trying to convince someone that God exists. The argument you give for thinking that this is true is that the Bible says there is a God. Would this argument convince someone who did not already believe that there is a God? Probably not. Anyone who doubts that there is a God probably does not think that everything the Bible says is true.

Here's a second example. Someone is very suspicious about the reliability of consumer magazines. You try to convince him that Consumer Reports is reliable by pointing out that Consumer Reports ranks itself very highly in an article evaluating the reliability of consumer magazines. Probably your argument will fail to convince.

In these two examples, identify the premisses and conclusion in each argument. Then describe what it is about the argument that makes it question-begging.

might be involved here. Someone might use the expression "true for me" to express the idea that each of us makes our own reality and that the beliefs we have constitute that reality. I will assume that this is a mistake. My concept of truth assumes a fundamental division between the way things really are and the way they may seem to be to this or that individual mind. This is what I meant in Lecture 1 by distinguishing the objective realm and the subjective realm.

Wishful Thinking

Closely related to this distinction between objective and subjective is a piece of advice: *We should avoid wishful thinking.* Most of the things we believe are not made true by our believing them. That the Rockies are in North America is a fact that is independent of our thought and language. We don't bring this geographical fact into being by thinking or talking in the way we do.

Self-Fulfilling Prophesies

In saying this, I am not denying that the thoughts we have often affect the world outside the mind. If I think to myself "I can't hit a baseball," this may have the effect that I do badly in the batter's box; here my believing something has the effect that the belief is made true. This is the idea of a "self-fulfilling prophesy." Notice how this causal chain works:

Thought	*Action*	*Truth*
I think that I won't hit the baseball. $\longrightarrow$	I swing too high. $\longrightarrow$	I don't hit the baseball.

I have no problem with the idea that various statements may be caused to be true by individuals thinking thoughts to themselves. What I do deny is that the mere act of thinking, unconnected with action or some other causal pathway, can make statements true. I'm rejecting the idea that the world is arranged so that it spontaneously conforms to the ideas we may happen to entertain.

Later in this book, I'll investigate whether there are any exceptions to the principle that says to avoid wishful thinking. Maybe there are some statements that become true just because we think they are. Here are some philosophical claims we'll consider:

Mathematical statements and definitions are made true by our regarding them as such; for example "2 + 3 = 5" is true just because we choose to define our terminology ("2", "+", etc.) in the way we do (Lecture 4).

Some statements about the contents of my own mind (for example, "I am in pain") are made true just by my believing that they are true (Lecture 13).

Ethical statements are true just because God, society, or some individual agent thinks they are (Lecture 30).

I'm mentioning these here without tipping my hand as to whether I think any of them are plausible. If any of them were correct, they would count as exceptions to the pattern I've just described. For the moment, though, I'm merely noting that belief and truth are *generally* quite separate questions.

So far I've emphasized that truth is an objective question, not a subjective one; it concerns how things really are, not whether anybody thinks that the world is a particular way. There is another feature of the concept of truth that I want to state, one that should help demystify it.

Redundancy

When I say that a certain sentence has the property of being true, what am I saying? Consider the English sentence "The Rocky Mountains are in North America." When I say that this sentence is true, am I attributing some mysterious property to it? Not really. All I'm saying is that the world is the way the sentence says it is. When I say that that sentence is true, all I'm saying is that the Rocky Mountains are in North America. So in a way, the concept of truth is often "redundant." Sometimes when I use the concept of truth, I could say the same thing without using that concept.

In high school English, your teacher may have told you to avoid redundancy. If you hand in an essay containing the sentence "Oscar is an unmarried bachelor," the essay might come back with "unmarried" crossed out and the marginal comment "avoid redundancy." The word "unmarried" is redundant because "Oscar is an unmarried bachelor" means exactly the same thing as "Oscar is a bachelor." Adding the word "unmarried" is to spill useless ink.

The Redundancy Theory of Truth claims that the word "true" is redundant, in just this sense. "It's true that the Rockies are in North America" says exactly what the sentence "The Rockies are in North America" asserts. This helps show why truth is not a mysterious property. If you believe a statement *P*, you also believe that *P* is true. So, if you have any beliefs about the world at all, you should be quite comfortable applying the concept of truth to those beliefs.

Review Questions

1. When is a statement or idea valid? (a trick question)
2. Define what it means to say that an argument is deductively valid.
3. Invent an example of a valid argument that has false premises and a true conclusion. Invent an example of an invalid argument that has true premises and a true conclusion.
4. Can a statement be a premiss in one argument and a conclusion in another? If you think so, give an example.
5. Which of the following argument forms is valid? Which is invalid? For each of the invalid ones, construct an example of an argument with that form in which the premises are true and the conclusion false:

(a)
$$\frac{\text{If } P, \text{ then } Q.\ \ \ P}{Q}$$

(b)
$$\frac{\text{If } P, \text{ then } Q.\ \ \ Q}{P}$$

$$\text{(c)} \quad \begin{array}{l} \text{If } P, \text{ then } Q. \\ \text{Not } P \\ \hline \text{Not } Q \end{array} \qquad \text{(d)} \quad \begin{array}{l} \text{If } P, \text{ then } Q. \\ \text{Not } Q \\ \hline \text{Not } P \end{array}$$

6. A sign on a store says "no shoes, no service." Does this mean that if you wear shoes, then you will be served?

7. What does it mean to say that truth is objective, not subjective?

it concerns things how they really are not what is believed to be

Problems for Further Thought

1. The Redundancy Theory of Truth may seem as plausible as an account of what the following sentence means:

It's true that the Rockies are in North America.

Does it work as well as an explanation of what the following sentence means?

Some truths have not been formulated yet.

2. Consider the following argument:

I release an otherwise unsupported apple from my hand a few feet from the earth's surface.

_____

The apple falls to earth.

Is this argument deductively valid? What is the logical form of this argument?

Lecture 3

Inductive and Abductive Arguments

Deductive Validity a Limitation

In Lecture 2, I explained the idea of deductive validity. In a deductively valid argument the premisses provide an *absolute guarantee* that the conclusion is true: If the premisses are true, there is no way in the world that the conclusion will be false.

This feature of deductive arguments may sound like a virtue. It's a good thing when an argument provides this sort of strong guarantee. However, this virtue can also represent a kind of limitation. Granted, a deductively valid argument that has true premisses cannot have a false conclusion; but it also is a property of such arguments that the conclusion cannot say anything that was not already contained in the premisses.

To see what this means, consider what you could validly deduce from the result of some opinion survey. Suppose you were interested in finding out what percentage of registered voters in a county are Democrats. You don't feel like contacting each of them and asking, so you open the phone book and make, let us say, a thousand telephone calls.

Suppose the result of your survey is that 60% of the people called say they are Democrats. What you want to know is the percentage of Democrats in the whole county. Could you make a deductively valid argument here? Can you deduce that (about) 60% of the voters are Democrats from a premiss that describes the result of your survey?

The answer is *no*, for two reasons. The fact that 60% of the people called *said* they are Democrats does not deductively guarantee that any of them are. And even if 60% of the people called were Democrats, you can't validly deduce from this that (about) 60% of the voters in the county are Democrats. That is, neither of the following arguments is deductively valid:

60% of the people called said they are Democrats.
_____
60% of the people called are Democrats.

60% of the people called are Democrats.
_____
About 60% of the voters in the county are Democrats.

Why can't you deduce these things validly? The reason is that in a deductively valid argument, it is impossible for the conclusion to be false if the premisses are true. But it *is* possible that everyone you called in your survey lied. And it is possible, in addition, that the percentage of Democrats in the whole county is only 25%, even if nobody lied in your phone survey.

In saying this, I am not saying that the people you called actually lied. And I'm not saying that the real percentage in the whole county is only 25%. I'm just saying that these are possible, given the result of your phone calls. The result of your telephone survey does not absolutely rule out these possibilities, so you can't deduce the percentage of Democrats in the whole county from what the 1000 people said on the phone.

You can't deduce what is true about the whole county from the information you have about your sample. So the absolute guarantee that a deductively valid argument provides has this limitation: Insisting that an argument be deductively valid prohibits you from reaching conclusions that go beyond the information given in the premisses.

It would make sense to insist that an argument be deductively valid if you wanted to avoid even the smallest risk of having a false conclusion with true premisses. But often we are willing to gamble a little more than this. For example, we might think that the result of the phone survey does provide information about the composition of the county. We might think that the result of the survey gives us a pretty good reason for concluding that about 60% of the county voters are Democrats. In saying this, the "good reason" is not a deductively valid one.

Nondeductive Inference— A Weaker Guarantee

We have here a fundamental characteristic of nondeductive inference. Suppose we conclude that about 60% of the voters in the county are Democrats, based on the premiss that 60% of the people called said they were Democrats. In this case, the premiss does not provide an absolute guarantee that the conclusion is true. However, there is a lesser kind of guarantee that this premiss may provide. If the argument is a strong one, the premiss makes the conclusion *probable*; it provides a *good reason* for thinking that the conclusion is true; it makes the conclusion *plausible*. Instead of an absolute guarantee, we have here a weaker guarantee. You're running a risk of being wrong about your conclusion, even if your premiss is true. But this risk might be a reasonable one to take; the conclusion might be a good bet, given that the premiss is true.

Two Gambling Strategies

The language in the previous paragraph suggests that you can think about the difference between deductive and nondeductive arguments in terms of ideas about gambling. Consider two sorts of gamblers. The first I'll call *the extreme conservative*. This sort of individual will refuse a wager, unless winning is a sure thing. The second individual I'll call the *thoughtful risk taker*. This sort of individual at times enters into risky gambles hoping to win.

Notice that each strategy has its virtue and its limitation. The virtue of the conservative strategy is that you will never lose a gamble. Its limitation is that there will be gambles you will decline to consider that you could have won. The limitation of thoughtful risk taking is that this strategy can lose you some money. Its virtue is that it can lead you to win wagers by taking risks.

Limiting yourself to deductive arguments is a conservative strategy. You avoid the risk of reaching false conclusions from true premisses. The limitation is that you decline to say anything that goes beyond the evidence. Nondeductive arguments are riskier. The gain is that you can reach true conclusions that go beyond what the premisses say; the risk is that you may reach a false conclusion from true premisses.

Predictive Beliefs

In science as well as in everyday life, we make nondeductive inferences all the time. We often are prepared to take risks. Each of us has beliefs about the future. But these are not deduced from observations we have made in the present and past.

Universal Laws

Science is a risky business in another way. Scientists often try to reach conclusions about *universal laws*. An example is Isaac Newton's (1642–1727) universal law of gravitation, which you may have studied in high school. This law says that the gravitational attraction between two bodies is proportional to the products of their masses and is inversely proportional to the square of the distance between them. This law was intended to describe how much gravitational attraction there would be between two objects, no matter where those objects are located and no matter when those objects exist. Newton's law is universal in scope — it describes what is true anywhere and at any time. This is not an isolated example. In lots of sciences, there are universal statements that scientists say are well supported by evidence.

Could Newton have deduced his law from the observations he made and the experiments he conducted? No. His law is universal in scope. But his observations were conducted in a rather narrowly limited range of places and times. Newton did not go backward in time to check if his law held true in 3,000,000 B.C., nor did he send a space ship to a distant galaxy to do the required measurements. When scientists conclude that a universal law is true or probably true, based on premises that describe the observations they have made, they are not making a deductively valid argument.

Science is a very ambitious enterprise. Science ventures beyond what is strictly observed in the here and now, just as the conclusion in a nondeductive argument ventures beyond the information strictly contained in the premisses.

Detective Work

I said before that nondeductive arguments are constantly used in both science and everyday life. Newton was my scientific example. The calculations of Sherlock Holmes furnish an example that is more a part of everyday life.

Holmes was constantly telling Watson that he figures out detective problems by "deduction." Now there's no doubt that Holmes was a very good detective. The question, though, is whether he solved his puzzles by strictly deductive methods.

My view is that he did not. Holmes did not observe the crimes he was later called upon to investigate. What he did observe were clues. For example, suppose Holmes is trying to solve a murder. He wonders whether Moriarty is the murderer. The clues Holmes gathers include a gun, a cigar butt, and a fresh footprint, all found at the scene of the crime. Suppose that the gun has an "M" carved in the handle, that the cigar is Moriarty's favorite brand, and that the footprint is the size that would be produced by Moriarty's ample foot.

Could Holmes deduce from these clues that Moriarty was the murderer? No. Although the above information may make that conclusion plausible or probable, it does not absolutely rule out the possibility that someone else did the dirty deed.

I have been emphasizing that in a strong nondeductive inference, the premises make the conclusion plausible or probable; they do not absolutely guarantee that the conclusion must be true. I now will discuss the difference between two sorts of nondeductive inference — inductive and abductive.

Induction

I'll begin with some properties of induction. Inductive inference involves taking a description of some sample and extending that description to items outside the sample. The voter survey discussed before provides an example:

60% of the county voters called are Democrats.

About 60% of the county voters are Democrats.

Notice that in this example the vocabulary present in the argument's conclusion is already present in the premiss. Although the conclusion goes beyond what the premiss asserts (that's what makes the argument nondeductive), no new concepts are introduced in the conclusion.

Two Factors Influence Inductive Strength

In the case of deduction, I said that an inference is either deductively valid or it is not. Validity is a yes/no affair. It's like pregnancy. But inductive strength is not a yes/no matter; inductive arguments are either stronger or weaker. Inductive strength is a matter of degree.

Two factors affect how strong or weak an inductive argument is. The first is sample size. If you called a thousand individuals in your phone survey, that would make the conclusion stronger than if you had called only a hundred.

The second factor is the representativeness or unbiasedness of the sample. If you called a thousand individuals drawn at random from a list of voters, that would make the resulting inference stronger than if you had called a thousand members of labor unions. The percentage of Democrats in labor unions is higher than that in the population as a whole. If so, you are biasing your sample by drawing it exclusively from a union membership list.

By making a telephone survey, you are failing to contact people who do not have phones. Is this a problem? That depends. If the percentage of Democrats with phones is approximately equal to the percentage of Democrats among registered voters, no bias is introduced. However, if people with phones are disproportionately Democrats or disproportionately Republicans, your phone survey will have introduced a bias.

How do you avoid having a biased sample? Sometimes this is done by "randomization." If you have a list of all the county voters, drawing names "at random" means that each name has the same chance of being selected. However, this process of selecting at random can fail to ensure an unbiased sample. For example, suppose it turns out that by drawing names at random, all the people you contact happen to be women. If women are disproportionately Democrats or disproportionately Republicans, your sample is biased.

I don't say that random draws from the voter list will *probably* result in this sort of bias. My point is just that randomizing does not absolutely guarantee that your sample is unbiased.

I won't say more here about how you can avoid having a biased sample. This fine point aside, the basic idea is this: Inductive arguments are stronger or weaker according to (1) the sample size, and (2) the unbiasedness of the sample.

Abduction

I now move to abduction—inference to the best explanation. I will begin with an example of an abductive inference that was important in the history of science. After saying what is distinctive about this form of inference, I'll describe two principles that are relevant to deciding whether an abductive inference is strong or weak.

Gregor Mendel (1822–1884) was an experimental biologist who worked in a monastery in Czechoslovakia. He is credited with having discovered genes — the particles in living things that allow parents to transmit characteristics to offspring in reproduction.

The first thing to note about Mendel's discovery is that he never actually saw a gene (or an "element," as Mendel called them). Although more powerful microscopes made this possible later, Mendel never saw a one of them. Rather, Mendel reasoned that the observations he made could be explained if genes existed and had the characteristics that he specified.

Inferring What Is Not Observed

Mendel ran breeding experiments in the monastery's garden. He crossed tall pea plants with short ones and noted the proportion of tall and short plants among the offspring. Similarly, he crossed plants with wrinkled peas and plants that had smooth peas, noting the mix of wrinkled and smooth plants among the progeny. He then crossed some of those offspring with each other and saw the proportion of various characteristics found in the next generation.

Mendel observed that when plants of certain sorts are crossed, their offspring exhibit characteristics in very definite proportions. Mendel asked himself a question that never figured in my discussion of induction. He asked *why* the crosses produced offspring with characteristics distributed into such proportions.

This why-question led Mendel to invent a story. He said: Suppose that each plant contains particles (genes) that control the observed characteristics of tall and short, wrinkled and smooth, in certain specific ways. He conjectured that each parent contributes half its genes to the offspring and that this process occurs in accordance with definite rules. The whole invented story had this property: If the story were true, that would explain why the breeding experiments had the results that Mendel observed them to have.

It should be quite clear that Mendel's theory of the gene went beyond the observations then available to him. He never saw a gene, but his theory postulates the existence of such things. I noted before that it is a general feature of nondeductive inference, whether inductive or abductive, that the conclusion goes beyond the premisses. But we see here a respect in which abduction differs from induction.

If Mendel had made an inductive inference, he simply would have claimed that the observed results of the experiments he ran in his garden would also occur anywhere the experiment was carried out. His experiment was made in Czechoslovakia at the end of the nineteenth century. An inductive extension of the description true of his experiment might conclude that the same results would occur in twentieth-century North America as well.

Abduction Differs from Induction

Had Mendel limited himself to this suggestion, no one would remember him now as the father of genetics. His important inference was abductive, not inductive. He didn't simply claim that the experiment could be replicated. Rather, he offered a theoretical mechanism that explains *why* the results occurred. Mendel's inference was to conclude something about the world he did not see (genes) to explain something that he did see (the results of the experimental crossings).

Let us attend to Mendel's inference more carefully. The following is *not* a deductively valid argument:

Experimental crosses in the pea plants were
observed to exhibit such-and-such results.
_____
There are genes and they obey laws L.

Remember: You can't validly deduce a theory from a set of observations.

Why can't you do this? Basically, the previous argument attempts to infer a theory about the cause from the observation of its effects. But there are lots of possible causes that might have been responsible for the observed effects. The previous argument is deductively invalid for the same reason that the following argument is also invalid:

A pistol with an "M" on the handle, an El Supremo cigar ash, and a
size 12 footprint were found next to the murder victim's body.
_____
Moriarty was the murderer.

The clues are telling ones, as Holmes well knows. Even though Moriarty may be the most plausible suspect, the clues, in themselves, do not guarantee that he is the only possible one. Mendel and Holmes were making an inference about what is *probably* true, given the observations. They were not inferring what is *absolutely guaranteed* to be true by the observations.

If a set of observations does not deductively imply a theory, then perhaps the reverse is true: Maybe a theory deductively implies some observations. This corresponds more closely to what Mendel did. He saw that his theory of the gene implies that certain experimental results ought to occur. He then saw that those predictions came true. He concluded that the truth of the predictions was evidence that the theory is true.

So a better representation of Mendel's inference might go like this: The theory entailed a prediction. The prediction came true. Hence, the theory is probably true. What we now need to see is that the following form of argument is *not* deductively valid:

If there are genes and they obey laws L, then experimental crosses in
the pea plants should exhibit such-and-such results.
Experimental crosses in the pea plants were observed to exhibit such-
and-such results.
_____
There are genes and they obey laws L.

This is deductively invalid for the same reason that the following argument is too:

> If Jones lives in Wisconsin, then Jones lives in the USA.
> Jones lives in the USA.
> ───────────────
> Jones lives in Wisconsin.

Note that these two arguments have the same logical form.

Scientists often test their theories by seeing whether the predictions made by the theories come true. There is nothing wrong with doing this. However, the point is that the truth of the theory does not follow deductively from the truth of the prediction. Scientists are reasoning *nondeductively* when they decide that a theory is plausible because its predictions have come true. We might summarize the point by saying that *successful prediction is not absolutely conclusive proof that the theory is true.*

On the other hand, if the predictions entailed by Mendel's theory had come out false, that would have allowed him to deduce that the theory is mistaken. That is, the following argument *is* deductively valid:

When the Prediction Turns Out To Be False

> If there are genes and they obey laws L, then experimental crosses in the pea plants should exhibit such-and-such results.
> Experimental crosses in the pea plants did not exhibit such-and-such results.
> ───────────────
> It is false that there are genes and they obey laws L.

We might summarize this point by saying that *a failed prediction is conclusive proof that the theory implying the prediction is false*.

Let's generalize these points. Let T be a theory and P be a prediction that the theory makes. If the prediction comes out true, we cannot deduce that the theory is true. However, if the prediction comes out false, we can deduce that the theory is false.

How True Predictions and False Predictions Are Interpreted

Invalid	*Valid*
If T, then P	If T, then P
P	Not P
───────	───────
T	Not T

The difference between these two arguments—one deductively valid, the other not—suggests that there is an important difference between the way scientists argue that theories are true and the way they argue that theories are false. It is possible to reject a theory just on the basis of the false predictions it makes, using a deductively valid argument; but it is not possible to accept a theory just on the basis of the true predictions it makes, using a deductively valid argument. I'll discuss this difference again in Lecture 8.

INDUCTIVE
AND ABDUCTIVE
ARGUMENTS

Deducing That a Theory Is True

Recall from Lecture 2 that a deductively invalid argument can be turned into a valid one by adding premisses. I now will exploit this fact to show how the truth of a theory can be deduced from the fact that it makes a successful prediction, if you make certain further assumptions.

Suppose we wish to design an experiment that tests two theories. Here the problem is not one of evaluating a single theory, but of seeing which of two theories is more plausible. To test one theory (T_1) against another (T_2), we try to find a prediction over which they disagree. Suppose T_1 predicts that P will be true, while T_2 predicts that P will be false. If we can assume that one or the other theory is true, we can find out whether P comes true and then deduce which theory is true:

Valid	Valid
T_1 or T_2	T_1 or T_2
If T_1, then P.	If T_1, then P.
If T_2, then not P.	If T_2, then not P.
P	Not P
T_1	T_2

Both these arguments are deductively valid. The reason the truth of the prediction (P) allows you to deduce that a theory is true in this case is that you have assumed that one or the other theory is correct.

As an exercise, construct an example of this sort.

So far I've explained how a deductively valid argument can lead a scientist to reject a suggested explanation. But how do scientists ever interpret observations as providing strong evidence in favor of the explanations they consider? This must involve a nondeductive inference. What are the rules that govern such inferences? I now will present two ideas that are relevant to evaluating abductive arguments. These I call the *Surprise Principle* and the *Only Game in Town Fallacy*.

The Surprise Principle: When Does Successful Prediction Provide Strong Evidence?

I have argued that you can't validly deduce that a theory is true just from the fact that some prediction it makes comes true. But maybe only a small modification of this idea is needed. Perhaps all we need to say is that a theory is made highly probable or plausible when a prediction it makes comes true. I now want to explain why this reformulation also will not do.

An unconscious patient is brought into the emergency room of a hospital. What is wrong—what would explain the fact that the patient is unconscious? The doctor on duty considers the hypothesis that the patient is having a heart attack. How should the doctor test whether this hypothesis is true? Well, the hypothesis predicts that the patient will have a heart (after all, if someone is having a heart attack, he or she must have a heart). The doctor verifies that this prediction is correct—the patient, indeed, does have a heart. Has the doctor thereby obtained strong evidence that the patient is having a heart attack? Clearly not. This is an example in which you do not obtain serious support for a hypothesis just by showing that one of its implications is correct.

You go to the gym and someone tells you he is an Olympic weight lifter. You reason that if he is an Olympic weight lifter, he should be able to pick up the hat you are wearing. You offer him your hat; he lifts it without difficulty. Have you obtained strong evidence that he is an Olympic weight lifter? Clearly not. Once again, the hypothesis under test is not strongly supported by the fact that one of its implications turns out to be correct.

What has gone wrong in these two cases? In the first example, the presence of a heart is not strong evidence that the patient is having a heart attack. The reason is that you would expect the individual to have a heart, even if he were not having a heart attack. In the second example, the man's lifting the hat is not strong evidence that he is an Olympic weight lifter. The reason is that you would expect him to be able to do this, even if he were not an Olympic lifter.

What should you look for, if you want to test the hypothesis that the patient has had a heart attack? What you want to find is a symptom that you would expect to find if the patient were having a heart attack, but would not expect to find if the patient were not having a heart attack. Suppose an erratic EKG (electrocardiogram) almost always occurs when there is a heart attack but rarely occurs when there is no heart attack. This means that the presence of an erratic EKG would be strong evidence that the patient is suffering a heart attack.

What sort of test should you propose if you want to see whether the man in the gym really is an Olympic weight lifter? Suppose Olympic weight lifters (of this man's weight) can almost always lift 400 pounds, but people who are not Olympic lifters can rarely do this. This means that his managing to lift 400 pounds would be strong evidence that he is an Olympic weight lifter.

Think of the unconscious patient and the weight lifter as posing *discrimination problems*. The problem is to find evidence that strongly discriminates between two hypotheses. In the first example, the competing hypotheses are:

H_1: The patient is having a heart attack.
H_2: The patient is not having a heart attack.

An erratic EKG strongly favors H_1 over H_2; the mere fact that the patient has a heart does not strongly favor H_1 over H_2.

The same holds true for the second example. The problem is to find evidence that discriminates between the following two hypotheses:

H_1: This man is an Olympic weight lifter.
H_2: This man is not an Olympic weight lifter.

The fact that the weight lifter can lift 400 pounds strongly favors H_1 over H_2; the fact that he can lift a hat does not.

The Surprise Principle describes what it takes for an observation to strongly favor one hypothesis over another:

THE SURPRISE PRINCIPLE: An observation O strongly supports H_1 over H_2 if both the following conditions are satisfied, but not otherwise: (1) if H_1 were true, O would have been expected, and (2) if H_2 were true, O would not have been expected.

Let's apply this principle to the first example. Consider the observation that the patient has an erratic EKG. If the patient were having a heart attack (H_1), we would expect him to have an erratic EKG. And if the patient were not having a heart attack (H_2), we would not expect him to have an erratic EKG. This explains why the erratic EKG is strong evidence of a heart attack — the EKG strongly favors H_1 over H_2.

Now consider the observation that the patient has a heart. If the patient were having a heart attack, we would expect him to have a heart. But we would expect him to have a heart even if he were not having a heart attack. This explains why the presence of a heart is not strong evidence that the patient is having a heart attack — the observation does not strongly favor H_1 over H_2.

We were looking for an explanation of why the erratic EKG provides telling evidence, whereas the presence of a heart does not. They key is to be found in condition (2) of the Surprise Principle.

Take a few minutes and apply the Surprise Principle to the example of the weight lifter. Make sure you see how the principle explains why being able to lift a hat is not strong evidence, whereas being able to lift 400 pounds is.

In the examples of the unconscious patient and the weight lifter, H_2 says only that H_1 is false. But in other abductions, H_2 may say more than this. Suppose a doctor wants to tell whether Sam has chicken pox or measles. In this case the competing hypotheses are:

No Surprise/Surprise

The Surprise Principle involves two requirements. It would be descriptive, though more verbose, to call the idea the No Surprise/Surprise Principle.

The Surprise Principle describes when an observation O strongly favors one hypothesis (H_1) over another (H_2). There are two requirements:

(1) If H_1 were true, you would expect O to be true.
(2) If H_2 were true, you would not expect O to be true.

That is, (1) if H_1 were true, O would be unsurprising; (2) if H_2 were true, O would be surprising.

The question to focus on is not whether the hypothesis (H_1 or H_2) would be surprising. The Surprise Principle has nothing to do with this.

To apply the Surprise Principle, you must get clearly in mind what the hypotheses are and what the observation is.

H_1: Sam has chicken pox
H_2: Sam has measles.

Suppose the doctor assumes that one but not both of these is true. This assumption means that if H_1 were false, H_2 would be true.

What would count as strong evidence that H_1, as opposed to H_2, is true? The fact that Sam has a fever does not discriminate between these hypotheses, since both hypotheses predict fever. But if Sam has a rash of red bumps on each of which there is a white dot, that is more telling. The reason is that H_1 leads us to expect such a rash, whereas H_2 does not. The Surprise Principle tells us that the presence of the rash strongly supports H_1 over H_2.

Whether an observation provides strong evidence for a hypothesis depends on what the alternative is to the hypothesis considered. In the previous example, Sam's fever does not strongly support the chicken pox hypothesis (H_1), since the chicken pox hypothesis competed with the hypothesis of measles. But now imagine that the doctor assumes that the alternative to H_1 is H_3:

H_3: Sam has poison ivy.

That is, the doctor assumes that if H_1 were false, H_3 would be true.

In this case, the fever *does* tell in favor of H_1. The reason is that if H_1 were true, we'd expect Sam to have a fever, whereas if H_3 were true, we would not expect this. The presence of fever strongly favors chicken pox over poison ivy.

This brings out an important fact about how the Surprise Principle applies to abductive inferences. *If you want to know whether an observation strongly supports a hypothesis, ask yourself what the other alternative hypotheses are.* For an observation to strongly support a hypothesis is for it to strongly favor the hypothesis over the others with which it competes.

The point of the examples about the unconscious patient and the weight lifter was to show why successful prediction does not necessarily provide strong evidence. If someone is having a heart attack, that predicts that he will have a heart; but the presence of a heart is not strong evidence that the person is having a heart attack. If someone is an Olympic weight lifter, that predicts that he will be able to lift a hat; but lifting a hat is not strong evidence that the person is an Olympic weight lifter.

There is a scene in the Monty Python movie "The Life of Brian" that illustrates this idea. The setting is a marketplace. Around the perimeter of the market are assorted prophets, soothsayers, and religious nuts. The camera pans from one to the other. We see that in each case, the prophet holds a crowd of people in rapt attention. The first prophet predicts that tomorrow a purple monster will rise out of the desert and devour three villages. The crowd is amazed at these predictions and no doubt will conclude that the prophet has special powers to foresee the future if the predictions come true.

After showing us a few prophets of this sort, the camera comes to an individual who very calmly makes the following predictions: Tomorrow, many people will get up early. Others will sleep longer. Some people will decide to have breakfast, while others will postpone eating until later in the day. And so on. The joke is that the crowd in front of this guy is just as awestruck as the crowds were in front of the more outlandish prophets.

There is a lesson here. How would you test the hypothesis that someone has special powers to foresee the future? If he predicts events that people without special powers can easily predict, it is not very impressive that his predictions come true. However, if he predicts events that normal people are not able to foresee, and then these surprising predictions come true, we are more impressed. The Surprise Principle explains why the success of "safe" predictions provides less compelling evidence than the success of "daring" predictions.

Here's a related example of the Surprise Principle in action. Many people think that the astrologer Jean Dixon has special powers to predict the future. After all, she predicted the Kennedy assassination and several other events that no one could have guessed were going to happen. If Jean Dixon played it safe and only predicted events that everybody knows are going to happen, we would not be impressed. But aren't we being sensible in reasoning that she probably does have special powers, since this and other daring predictions have come true?

An Investment Swindle

Suppose you received a letter every month for a year from an investment firm. In each letter, a prediction was made as to whether "the stock of the month" would increase or decline in value during the next 30 days. You kept track of what happened to the stocks described each month. Each prediction came true. Would you conclude from this that the investment firm has a method for reliably predicting stock market events?

A few years ago an "investment firm" sent out such letters, but the mailing was a swindle. The firm began with a list of 10,000 investors. In the first month, 5,000 investors received letters predicting that stock A would go up; the other 5,000 received letters saying that stock A would go down. The firm then waited to see which prediction came true. During the second month, the firm sent letters to the 5,000 people who had received true predictions during the first month. In the second month, 2,500 investors received letters predicting that stock B would go up; the other 2,500 received letters saying that B would go down. The process was repeated, so that by the end of the year a small number of investors had received 12 letters, each containing a successful prediction.

The company then wrote to those people, asking each to invest a large sum of money. Many people did so. The company then absconded with the funds.

The investors who were swindled thought they were making a reasonable abductive inference on the basis of the company's track record. Describe the premiss, the conclusion, and the reasoning that led the investors to think that the conclusion was highly plausible. Were the investors making a strong inference?

Although this reasoning may seem to conform to the Surprise Principle, it does not. The thing that people tend to forget is that Jean Dixon makes thousands of predictions and most of them come out false. It isn't at all surprising that some handful of these should come out true. Although Jean Dixon predicted the Kennedy assassination, which surprised (practically) everyone when it happened, it is not at all surprising that someone with no special powers should be lucky a few times every thousand tries. The Surprise Principle, properly understood, tells us why we should not take Jean Dixon's few successes as strong evidence that she has special powers.

In summary, the Surprise Principle gives advice on what a hypothesis must do if it is to be strongly supported by the predictions it makes. First, the hypothesis should not make false predictions. Second, among the true predictions that the hypothesis makes, there should be predictions that we would not expect to come true if the hypothesis were false.

When we ask whether an observation O strongly supports some hypothesis H_1, the Surprise Principle requires that we specify what the alternative hypotheses are against which H_1 competes. It may turn out that O strongly favors H_1 over H_2, but that O does not strongly favor H_1 over H_3. The example of chicken pox, measles, and poison ivy illustrates this point.

I turn now to a second principle for evaluating abductive inferences. Suppose you and I are sitting in a cabin in the woods. We hear a strange rumbling sound in the attic. You ask, "I wonder what that could be?" To which I reply, "That's the sound of gremlins bowling in the attic."

The Only Game in Town Fallacy

You, being a sensible person, reply, "I really don't think that there are gremlins in the attic." I then challenge you to produce a more plausible explanation of the noises. You reply, "Gosh, I really don't have any idea why those noises occurred. I just think that your story is implausible."

To this humble admission on your part, I give this rejoinder: "Look, my story, if true, would explain why we just heard those strange noises. If you don't want to accept my explanation, you must produce a more plausible explanation of your own. If you can't, you have to accept my explanation of the noises."

What I just did was commit an abductive fallacy (mistake in reasoning), which I'll call the *Only Game in Town Fallacy*. The fact that you can't think of a more plausible explanation of the noises does not oblige you to accept the story I constructed. There is an alternative, which is simply to admit that the noises are something you don't know how to explain.

Abduction is sometimes described loosely as follows: If a theory explains some observation and if no rival account is available that can do a better job of explaining it, then you should accept the theory. Although this description of abduction is roughly correct, it makes the mistake of sanctioning the Only Game in Town Fallacy. The fact that no rival account is better than the explanation I construct does not show that my explanation is even minimally plausible. My gremlin theory is pretty silly, although maybe there is nothing now available that is clearly superior to it.

I won't try to fine-tune the idea of abductive inference any further. Induction is less well understood than deduction, but abduction is even less well understood than induction. We now have before us the basic idea of inference to the best explanation. We've seen that it is an important part of the scientific method. And I've described two principles that are reasonable guides to evaluating whether an abductive inference is strong or weak.

Review Questions

1. What is the difference between deductive validity and inductive strength?
2. What is the difference between induction and abduction?
3. What factors affect how strong an inductive argument is?
4. A given observation can discriminate between two hypotheses, while a second observation can fail to do this. How does the Surprise Principle explain when this will happen? Construct an example, different from the ones presented in this lecture, illustrating the point.
5. The Surprise Principle explains why an observation can strongly favor H_1 over H_2, but can fail to strongly favor H_1 over H_3; that is, it explains why an observation can succeed in discriminating between some pairs of hypotheses but fail to discriminate between others. Construct an example illustrating this point that is different from the ones presented in this lecture.
6. What is the Only Game in Town Fallacy? What does it mean to call it a "fallacy"?

Problems for Further Thought

1. Suppose you wanted to find out what percentage of the adults in your county are vegetarians. You obtain a list of unmarried adults in the county and contact them to do a survey. Is this sample a biased one?

2. Although induction and abduction were described in this lecture as separate kinds of inference, they have a good deal in common. The Surprise Principle was introduced as applying to abductions, but it applies to inductions as well. Suppose an urn is filled with 1000 balls, each of them either red or green. You reach into the urn, sampling at random, and bring out 100 balls. Your sample contains 51 red balls and 49 green ones. Here are some hypotheses to consider:

   H_1: All the balls in the urn are green.
   H_2: 75% of the balls are green.
   H_3: 50% of the balls are green.
   H_4: 25% of the balls are green.

   Suppose you thought that H_1 and H_2 are the only possibilities. Does the observation strongly support one over the other? Which? How does the Surprise Principle apply to this question?

Suppose, instead, that you thought that H_2 and H_3 are the only possibilities. Does the sample strongly support one over the other? If so, which?

Suppose, finally, that you think that all four hypotheses are possible. Which is best supported? Why?

3. Why think that any of the beliefs you have about the world outside your own mind are true? An example of this philosophical question might ask why you now are entitled to think that there is a printed page in front of you. Presumably, you believe this on the basis of sense experience (sight, touch, etc.). Construct an abductive argument whose conclusion is that there is a printed page in front of you. Make sure that your inference obeys the Surprise Principle. Does this abductive argument answer the philosophical question?

4. At the beginning of Lecture 2, I presented deductive validity, inductive strength, and abductive strength as mutually exclusive categories. This means that if an argument belongs to one category, it does not belong to any of the others. This is generally correct, but not always.

Here is an inductive argument that is not deductively valid:

I've observed 1000 emeralds and all have been green.

All emeralds are green.

However, by adding a premiss, I can produce a deductively valid argument:

I've observed 1000 emeralds and all have been green
If there are over 500 emeralds in the universe, they will all have the same color.

All emeralds are green.

Both the above arguments are inductive; both involve drawing a sample from a population and reaching a conclusion about that population. Therefore, some inductively strong arguments are also deductively valid.

The same point holds for abductively strong arguments. Usually, they are not deductively valid. But sometimes they are. Construct a strong abductive argument that obeys the Surprise Principle. Show how it can be made deductively valid by adding or modifying a premiss.

Suggestions for Further Reading _____

On the Nature of Philosophy:

The essays in Charles Bontempo and S. Jack Odell (eds.), *The Owl of Minerva: Philosophers on Philosophy.* New York, McGraw-Hill, 1975.

Bertrand Russell, "The Value of Philosophy," in *The Problems of Philosophy.* Oxford, Oxford University Press, 1950.

On Different Forms of Argument:

Monroe Beardsley, *Thinking Straight.* Englewood Cliffs, New Jersey, Prentice-Hall, 1975.

Irving Copi, *Informal Logic.* New York, Macmillan, 1986.

Robert Fogelin, *Understanding Arguments.* New York, Harcourt Brace Jovanovich, 1978.

Ronald Giere, *Understanding Scientific Reasoning.* New York, Holt, Rinehart and Winston, 1984.

Merrilee Salmon, *Logic and Critical Thinking.* San Diego, Harcourt Brace Jovanovich, 1984.

PART II
Philosophy of Religion

·L·E·C·T·U·R·E·S·

———————— *Lecture 4* ————————
Aquinas' First Four Ways

Saint Thomas Aquinas (c. 1224–1274) was an enormously accomplished theologian and philosopher. In his masterwork, the *Summa Theologiae*, he presents five proofs that God exists (Aquinas called them "the five ways"). I'll discuss the first four now and the fifth in the next lecture. Each of Aquinas' arguments is abductive. Each begins with some simple observation that is supposed to be obvious to everyone. For example, the first argument begins with the observation that physical objects are in motion. Each argument then proceeds through various other premises to the conclusion that the explanation of the initial observation is that there is a God.

In Lecture 3, I stressed that most of the hypotheses that scientists are interested in testing cannot be deduced from observations. For example, Mendel could not deduce the existence and characteristics of genes from the observations he made on his pea plants. The same is true in Aquinas' arguments, as he fully realizes: You can't deduce the existence and characteristics of God just from the sorts of simple observations with which his arguments begin. The existence of motion does not, all by itself, deductively imply the existence of God. Aquinas' arguments always include additional principles. It is these principles that are intended to show that the existence of God is the only possible explanation of the observations with which Aquinas begins.

The Concept of God   Before describing Aquinas' arguments, I need to say something about what he means by "God" and how I will use that term. Aquinas took God to be a person—one who is all-powerful (omnipotent), all-knowing (omniscient), and entirely good (omnibenevolent). We might call this, give or take a nuance, the traditional Judeo-Christian conception of God. So when Aquinas tries to prove that there is a God, it is an entity of this kind he wants to show exists.

I will assume provisionally that God has the characteristics just mentioned. If we don't start with some preliminary picture of what God is, we won't know what we're talking about when we try to prove or disprove God's existence. However, it is important to recognize that this conception of God is only one among many possibilities. It is parochial to assume that God has got to be just the way this single historical tradition says he (or she) is. Other religious traditions have had different pictures, and even the Judeo-Christian tradition contains a variety of ideas that have changed through history. Indeed, in Lecture 11, I'll consider an argument that suggests that God, if there is such a being, can't be all-powerful, all-knowing, and all-good. So we have to recognize that God might lack one or more of the traits I just mentioned. We have to leave this open. This is why the traditional definition I'll be using will be a temporary expedient.

Another caveat I should mention is that my versions of Aquinas' arguments will not be accurate in all respects. It is often a subtle historical question what this or that philosopher had in mind in a given text. In this case and later in the book, when I discuss the ideas of other philosophers, I often will examine somewhat simplified versions of the arguments they constructed.

You may well ask: Why is it worthwhile studying a simplified version of a great philosopher's arguments? Admittedly, there is a loss, but there also is a gain. The main point to be made here at the beginning of an introductory text is that it is useful to evaluate these simpler arguments before more subtle arguments are addressed. At any rate, there is ample philosophical material to think about in the arguments I'll describe, even if these arguments do not capture the thoughts of various great thinkers with total accuracy and completeness.

Aquinas' first argument for the existence of God is the argument from motion. Here it is, formulated as a deductive argument:

The First Two Arguments: Motion and Causality

(I) (1) Objects are in motion.
     (2) If something is in motion, then it must be caused to be in motion by something outside of itself.
     (3) There can be no infinite chain of movers/movees.

     (4) So, there is a first, unmoved mover.

     (5) Therefore, God exists.

This argument is very similar to Aquinas' second argument, which is the argument from causality. Notice how this second argument parallels the structure of the first:

(II) (1) Some events cause other events.
      (2) If an event happens, then it must be caused by something outside of itself.
      (3) There can be no infinite cause/effect chains.

      (4) So, there is a first, uncaused cause.

      (5) Therefore, God exists.

What does premiss (3) mean in the previous arguments? Let's begin with an object (O_1) that is in motion now. Since it is in motion, there must be an earlier object—call it O_2—that sent it in motion. If O_2 was itself in motion, O_2 must trace back to a previous mover, O_3. And so on. In the second argument, the subject is causality, not motion, but the idea is basically the same.

Premiss (3) says that there cannot be a chain that extends infinitely far back into the past; cause/effect (or mover/movee chains) leading from the present back into the past have finitely many links. The arrow in the following diagram represents the relationship of causality:

$$\textit{Past} \qquad\qquad \textit{Present} \qquad \textit{Future}$$
$$O_f \longrightarrow \;\cdots\; \longrightarrow \quad O_3 \longrightarrow O_2 \qquad O_1 \longrightarrow \quad \cdots$$

The principle does not say whether chains beginning at O_1 and extending into the future have a finite number of links. The question of whether the universe had a beginning finitely long ago differs from the question of whether the universe will ever come to an end.

I'll begin with two specific criticisms — one aimed at argument I, the other aimed at argument II. After that, I'll lump the two arguments together and make some objections that apply to both.

Aquinas thinks (premiss I-2) that if an object is in motion, it must be caused to move by something outside itself. Aquinas got this idea from Aristotle's physics. Aristotle (384–322 B.C.) held that if an object continues to move, its motion must be sustained by a force that keeps it in motion. If you remove the force, the object stops moving.

This idea did not survive into modern physics. You may remember from high school physics that Newton, in the seventeenth century, held that an object remains in motion unless acted on by a force. Recall that one of Newton's laws of motion is $F = ma$. This means that if an object of mass m is acted on by a force of value F, it will accelerate to degree a.

This Newtonian law says that an object that is not acted on by a force will not accelerate, which means that it will remain at rest *or in uniform motion*. Newton's laws say that an object can remain in motion forever without there being any outside force that sustains its motion. Newton's laws do not exclude the following possibility: The universe contains just one physical object which always moves in uniform motion without any forces ever acting on it. Of course, Newton's laws don't say that the universe we live in is like this. Our universe obviously contains more than one material object. My point, though, is that Newton's theory of motion was different from Aristotle's, and so was different from Aquinas'. Aristotle and Aquinas thought that motion requires an outside force; Newton and more modern physical theories hold that it is acceleration, not mere change in position, that requires an outside force.

Now for the objection aimed at argument II. Notice that premiss (2) contradicts proposition (4). If *every* event has a cause outside of itself, there cannot be an uncaused cause.

I turn now to some problems that the two arguments share. First, it is important to see that proposition (4) — that there is an unmoved mover or a first cause — does not guarantee the existence of God, where this is understood to mean a person with something like the traditional properties of omnipotence, omniscience, and omnibenevolence. After all, a first cause might just be a giant explosion — a "big bang" that set material objects into motion. A physicist might accept a big bang hypothesis and still deny that there is a God.

Another problem arises when we ask whether the argument shows that there is *precisely one* first cause, or instead shows only that there is *at least one*. Suppose we grant that each causal chain has a beginning—an uncaused cause. Does it follow that there is a single uncaused cause that is the origin of all causal chains? *The Birthday Fallacy*

No it does not. Of the following propositions, the first is different from and does not deductively imply the second:

> Every event traces back to an uncaused cause.
> There is an uncaused cause to which each event traces back.

The difference here parallels the logical difference between the following two propositions, the first of which is true and the second false:

> Every person has a birthday—a day on which he or she was born.
> There is a single day that is everybody's birthday.

I want to give a name to the mistaken idea that the second proposition follows from the first. I'll call it the *Birthday Fallacy*.

So one problem with arguments I and II is that they do not show that there is exactly one first cause or unmoved mover; at best, they show that there is at least one. To think otherwise is to commit the Birthday Fallacy.

Aquinas' third argument for the existence of God, like the first two, begins with an observation that everybody would agree is true. The observation is put in language that may be unfamiliar, but once explained, it seems evident enough. The observation is that contingent things exist. *The Third Argument: Contingency*

What does it mean to say that a thing is contingent? The opposite of contingency is necessity. What makes an object contingent or necessary?

You, I, the Washington Monument, the human race, the planet Earth, the solar system, and the Milky Way are all examples of contingent things. Although we all exist, we need not have existed. The world could have failed to include any of us. If the particular sperm and egg that produced you had not encountered each other, you would not have come into existence. Your parents would have had other kids or no children at all. Likewise for the human race; although the world obviously includes human beings, it need not have. So a contingent thing is something whose existence is not necessary. *Necessary and Congingent Beings*

I want to represent this idea of necessity and contingency by introducing a new idea. Consider the totality of things that have existed, now exist, or will exist at any place in the universe. This totality comprises a giant object that I will call "the actual world." The census of objects in the actual world we can imagine spread out on a very long time line on which the durations of various objects might be represented: *Possible Worlds*

```
/——w——/
      /——x——/            /——y——/          /——z——/
_____
Past                      Now                          Future
```

Notice that the life spans or durations of objects w and x overlap. Objects w and x existed in the past and now are no more. Object y came into existence in the past, exists now, and will continue to exist until some future date when it will cease to be. Object z has not come into being, but it will.

Of course, this is a dreadfully incomplete census of everything there was, is, or will be. Never mind. You get the idea that the actual world consists of everything that has existed, exists now, or will exist, anywhere in the universe.

We know that the world need not have had precisely the census it does. Some of the objects in this census might have failed to exist. Other objects, which don't actually exist, might have done so. Let us call each possible way the world might have been a "possible world." There are many of these.

We now may say that an object is contingent if it exists in some but not all possible worlds. And an object is necessary if it exists in all possible worlds. Suppose that the following are the censuses found in several possible worlds. As before, the horizontal line represents time within a possible world:

w	x	y	z	Actual World
a	b	y	z	Possible World 1
a	c	d	z	Possible World 2
Past		Now	Future	

Notice that w exists in the actual world, but not in the two alternative possible worlds represented. On the other hand, y exists in the actual world and in the first possible world, but not in the second.

Object z is different—it exists in all of the possible worlds mentioned. Of course, there are more than three possible worlds, since there are more than two alternative ways that the actual world might have been (the actual world is, of course, one of the possible worlds). Would z continue to exist if we listed not just a few possible worlds, but all of them? That's the question of whether z is a necessary being.

I cited some examples of contingent things—you, the Washington Monument, the planet Earth, and a few others. These examples might strike you as typical of everything that exists. That is, you might find plausible the following philosophical conjecture—that everything that exists is contingent. Familiar objects clearly have this property. But is *everything* contingent? Aquinas argues in the third proof of the existence of God that not everything is contingent. There is at least one necessary being, namely God.

Here is how his proof goes:

III (1) Contingent things exist.

    (2) Each contingent thing has a time at which it fails to exist ("contingent things are not omnipresent").

(3) So, if everything were contingent, there would be a time at which nothing exists (call this an "empty time").

(4) That empty time would have been in the past.

(5) If the world were empty at one time, it would be empty forever after (a conservation principle).

(6) So, if everything were contingent, nothing would exist now.

(7) But clearly, the world is not empty (see premiss 1).

(8) So there exists a being who is not contingent.

Hence, God exists.

Before I examine the details of this argument, I want to note one of its logical features. Aquinas tries to construct an argument that has a distinctive logical form; he aims to construct a *reductio ad absurdum* (a *reductio*, for short). When I talked about deductive validity in Lecture 2, I emphasized that the word "valid" in logic and philosophy does not mean what it means in everyday life. The same holds for the idea of reducing something to absurdity. In ordinary speech this means something like "making a mockery of an idea." However, in logic, *reductio* arguments are perfectly fine kinds of arguments—they are deductively valid.

Here's how a *reductio* argument works. You want to prove a proposition P. To do this, you argue that if P were false, some proposition A would have to be true. But you construct the argument so that A is obviously false (an "absurdity"). From this, you may validly conclude that P is true.

Reductio arguments, in other words, have the following valid logical form:

If P is false, then A is true.
A is false.

P is true.

Aquinas tries to establish the existence of a necessary being by *reductio*. He argues that if everything were contingent, then the world would have to be empty now. But it's obviously false that the world is now empty. Hence, not everything is contingent—there exists at least one necessary being.

I said before that Aquinas *aims* to provide a valid *reductio* argument. The question, though, is whether he succeeds. Is Aquinas' third argument for the existence of God a valid one? In addition, we want to determine if his premisses are plausible.

I'll begin be registering an objection to premiss (2). The fact that an object is contingent does not mean that there must be a time at which it fails to exist. I'll grant that familiar contingent objects are not omnipresent. You are an example. You might have failed to exist; in addition, there was a time before you were born and there will be a time after you die.

But this is just an example. We want to know whether *all* contingent beings must fail to be omnipresent. Notice first that the considerations affecting contingency differ from those affecting omnipresence. How can you tell whether an

Contingency and Omnipresence

object is contingent in a diagram like the one given before showing the actual world and two possible worlds? You look *down* the list of possible worlds, checking to see if the object in question is present in each one. In that diagram, we might say that contingency is represented "vertically." Omnipresence is different. To see whether an object present in a given possible world is omnipresent, you look *across* the representation of that possible world, checking to see if it exists at all times in that world. So omnipresence is represented "horizontally."

Could an object exist in only some possible worlds and still exist at all times in the actual world? That is, could an object be both contingent and omnipresent? Aquinas says no. Here is a consideration that suggests that he may be wrong.

The idea that material objects are made of very small indivisible particles has had a long history, going back at least to the ancient Greeks. Of course, we no longer think of atoms as indivisible particles — we have long since learned to talk about subatomic particles. But suppose for the moment that the word "atom" names such indivisible particles. These particles are the basic building blocks of all material things.

One idea that has been put forward in atomistic theories is that atoms (fundamental particles) cannot be created or detroyed. Large objects made of atoms can be created and destroyed by assembling and disassembling collections of atoms. But the basic particles themselves can't be destroyed, because you can't break them into pieces. Again, I'm not saying that this is true of the objects we now regard as the smallest material particles. I mention it only to describe a possible view of atoms.

Atoms, on the view I'm describing, are omnipresent. If a given atom exists now, it has always existed and it always will exist. Let us call one of the atoms that populates the actual world by the name "Charlie." Charlie is omnipresent.

Does it follow that Charlie is a necessary being — that the world could not have failed to include him? I would say not. The world could have included more atoms than it does, or fewer. Indeed, it does not seem impossible that the world might have been entirely empty of matter. So Charlie, like all the atoms that happen to actually exist, is a contingent being.

If this is right, then Aquinas' premiss (2) is mistaken. Charlie, I have claimed, is a contingent being, but he is omnipresent. So contingent things need not have a time at which they fail to exist.

The argument I have given against premiss (2) depends on a particular theory about the nature of atoms. If atoms really are indestructible, I can claim to have refuted Aquinas' premiss. But are they, in fact, indestructible? Again, remember that I'm discussing the smallest units of matter here. This is how I am using the word "atom."

Conservation Laws in Physics

Current physics does not support the view that atoms are indestructible. Before Einstein, physics upheld a principle that said that the quantity of mass in the universe is constant. But Einstein replaced this classical conservation law with another one. Mass is not conserved; rather, a quantity that Einstein called "mass-energy" is conserved. This principle says that mass can be destroyed; it may be converted into energy. Modern physics, therefore, does not seem to allow me to tell my story about Charlie the indestructible atom.

So matter *can* be destroyed, according to current theory. But this does not mean that every contingently existing particle WILL be destroyed, sooner or later. It is the latter claim that Aquinas advances in premiss (2). I don't know of any good reason to think that this is so.

My conclusion thus far is that premiss (2) is dubious; why must a contingent thing have a time at which it fails to exist?

Let's move on. The transition from premiss (2) to statement (3) involves a fallacy. Even if we grant that every contingent entity has a time at which it fails to exist, we cannot conclude that there is an empty time. The fallacy here is the same one discussed concerning Aquinas' first two arguments. Recall the point about birthdays; "everybody has a birthday" does not imply that there is a day that is everyone's birthday.

To make this point graphic, consider the following possible world in which no object is omnipresent, and yet there is no empty time:

$$\longleftarrow \quad \begin{array}{ccc} /\!\!-\!\!1\!\!-\!\!/ & /\!\!-\!\!3\!\!-\!\!/ & /\!\!-\!\!5\!\!-\!\!/ \\ /\!\!-\!\!2\!\!-\!\!/ & /\!\!-\!\!4\!\!-\!\!/ & /\!\!-\!\!6\!\!-\!\!/ \end{array} \quad \longrightarrow$$

$$\text{Past} \qquad \text{Now} \qquad \text{Future}$$

The arrows at the beginning and end indicate that the pattern should be repeated indefinitely into the past and into the future.

So the supposition that everything is contingent does not imply an empty time. But there is an additional unjustified step. Even if there did have to be an empty time, why must it have been in the past? I see no reason to assume this.

The assumption that Aquinas makes in premiss (5) I will not contest. I will grant him that you can't get something out of nothing, even though I mentioned previously that it is not beyond dispute that matter is conserved.

Necessary Beings Other Than God

I've noted some problems in Aquinas' attempted *reductio* proof that not everything is contingent. But suppose Aquinas were able to show that there is at least one necessary being. Could he conclude from this that God exists? I want to argue that this, too, does not follow. In discussing Aquinas' first two arguments, I claimed that the existence of God does not follow from the existence of a first cause. I now want to suggest that the existence of God does not follow from the existence of a necessary being.

To explain why this is so, I need to develop an idea from the philosophy of mathematics. Until now, I've described necessity and contingency as properties of entities. You and I are contingent beings, for example. But now I want to use the ideas of contingency and necessity as properties of propositions. Propositions, or statements, are true or false. They also have the properties of necessity and contingency.

Necessary and Contingent Propositions

Necessity and contingency as properties of propositions are definable in a way that parallels the way this distinction applies to entities. A proposition is necessarily true if it is true in all possible worlds. A proposition is necessarily false if it is false in all possible worlds. Contingent propositions are true in some possible worlds and false in others. A true statement is contingent if it is true in the actual world, though false in some possible world.

It is easy to cite examples of contingent propositions. Consider the fact that the United States is, in the twentieth century, a nation in North America. This is true, though only contingently so. Consider the following contingent falsehood: that the Rocky Mountains are no higher than 6000 feet above sea level. This is false, but there are possible worlds in which it is true.

Mathematical Truths

Are there any necessary truths? Many philosophers have held that mathematical truths are necessarily true. Consider the fact that $7 + 3 = 10$. It isn't just that this happens to be true in the actual world. There is no possible world in which it is false. The sum of 7 and 3 could not fail to equal 10.

To see why this is at least a plausible view of mathematical propositions, you've got to be clear on what the proposition says. The proposition does not say that if you put seven rabbits together with three others, there will be ten bunnies forever after. Rabbits reproduce, but this does not contradict any fact of arithmetic. Similarly, if you pour three cups of sugar into seven cups of water, you will not obtain ten cups of liquid. But, again, this does not contradict the fact that $7 + 3 = 10$. Arithmetic is unaffected by this result; it just so happens that liquids do not always combine additively.

Names Differ from the Things Named

Here's a somewhat more subtle point to notice. The proposition that $7 + 3 = 10$ does not say anything about the language we may use in expressing that fact to ourselves. It is a contingent fact that human beings use the numeral "7" to refer to the number 7. We might have called that number by another name—we might have used the numeral "2" to denote the number 7. Similarly, it is a contingent fact that we use the symbol " $=$ " to represent the relation of equality. So it is a contingent fact that the sentence "$7 + 3 = 10$" expresses what it does; and it is a contingent fact that that sentence expresses a true proposition rather than a false one.

But this does not show that $7 + 3$ might not have equalled 10. The fact could not have been otherwise, even though we might have used our notation differently.

The distinction I'm drawing here is very obvious in some contexts, though it's easy to lose sight of it in others. Few things are more different than a thing and its name. You are a person, but your name is not. Your name contains a certain number of letters, but you do not. Your name is a linguistic entity, but you are not.

We mark this difference by using quotation marks. If we want to talk about a thing, we use its name. If we want to talk about the name of a thing, we put the name in quotation marks. So if I want to talk about some mountains in western North America, I might say that the Rocky Mountains are tall. But if I want to talk about that mountain range's name, I'd say that the name "the Rocky Mountains" contains 17 letters.

Numbers Aren't Numerals

This is obvious, when you think about it. But when it comes to mathematics, we tend to confuse these ideas. Numerals are names of numbers. But the number and its name are different, just as the phrase "the Rocky Mountains" differs from the mountains themselves. I grant that it is a contingent matter that the sentence "7 + 3 = 10" expresses a truth. But I deny that 7 + 3 might have failed to equal 10. The idea is that the proposition is necessarily true, even though it is a contingent fact that the sentence expresses the proposition it does. Just as your name is a part of language, though you are not, so the sentence "2 + 3 = 10" is a part of language, though the proposition it expresses is not.

Sets

So what does the proposition that 7 + 3 = 10 actually mean? It does not by itself say anything about rabbit reproduction or about the way volumes combine when poured together. Nor does it say anything about the language we use. You can think of this statement as describing a basic property of mathematical objects called *sets*.

First I need a bit of terminology. The union of two sets is the set that includes all the members of the first and all the members of the second, and no others. A set is any collection of objects. The set (Groucho Marx, Napoleon, the Eiffel Tower) is a three-member set, and the set (Napoleon, the Rocky Mountains, the French Revolution) is also a three-member set. The items in a set need not have anything special in common with each other. There are sets of similar things, but also there are sets of dissimilar things. The union of the two sets just mentioned is this set: (Groucho Marx, Napoleon, the Eiffel Tower, the Rocky Mountains, the French Revolution).

The proposition that 7 + 3 = 10 can be understood to say the following: Consider any two sets such that the first contains exactly seven objects and the second contains exactly three. If these sets have no common members, then the union of these two sets will have precisely ten members.

Notice that the arithmetic proposition does not say that the Rocky Mountains exist or that there are at least seven material things in the universe. The arithmetic fact does not rule out the possibility that the world contains no material objects at all. It simply describes a basic property of the operation of set-theoretic union.

Necessity and Certainty Are Different

One final clarification of the thesis that mathematical truths are necessary. In saying that it is a necessary truth that 7 + 3 = 10, I am not saying that I know that the proposition is true with absolute certainty. Nor am I saying that I will never change my mind on the question of whether 7 + 3 equals 10.

This is a rather subtle point, because we sometimes express our lack of certainty about a proposition by saying that maybe the proposition isn't so. If I think there will be rain tomorrow, but entertain some small doubt that this will be so, I may express this by saying, "Possibly it won't rain tomorrow." But my certainty or uncertainty is a fact about me. It's a fact in the *subjective* realm. I want to distinguish this question from the question of whether a given proposition has the property of necessity or contingency. The later question does not have anything special to do with me. Necessity and contingency are *objective*.

Here's a nonmathematical example that may make this clearer. Could there be perpetual motion machines? A machine of this sort would not require any energy input to keep running, but it would provide a constant output of energy. Scientists for many hundreds of years tried to design such a machine. They always failed. Finally, in the nineteenth century, physicists working in the area called thermodynamics proved that perpetual motion machines are impossible.

Consider the proposition that there are or will be perpetual motion machines. This is, we now believe, a falsehood. Is it a necessary falsehood? I would say *yes*. It isn't just that no one will bother to build one; the point is that it is impossible to build one. This, at least, is what science tells us.

Now I'll ask an entirely separate question: Am I absolutely certain that no such machine will ever exist? I guess I am not absolutely certain. After all, science has been wrong before, so maybe it now is wrong when it says that such machines are impossible. Opinion has changed through history on the question of whether such machines could be built. Before the nineteenth century many serious scientists thought that such machines are possible. Later, opinion changed. Maybe it will change again.

So the certainty that a single scientist or a community of scientists may have about the issue may change. But there is something that does not change. Either it is possible for such things to exist or it is not. This should convince you that *certainty* and *necessity* are different. People may change their degree of certainty about a proposition; they may even think at one time that it is true, but later on think that it is false. But the proposition itself does not change from true to false. Nor does a proposition cease to be necessary just because people stop believing it.

Therefore, to say that arithmetic truths are necessary is not to say that people are certain about arithmetic, nor is it to say that people have never changed their minds about arithmetic propositions. Again, these are questions about our attitudes toward the propositions. But whether a proposition is necessary or not has nothing to do with our attitudes. In this respect necessity is like truth—both are objective issues, independent of what people happen to believe.

To sum up, I have described a prominent view in the philosophy of mathematics. It holds that arithmetic truths are necessary. I have not provided that view with a complete defense, but I hope you can see what it asserts. I also hope that it is at least somewhat plausible, if not entirely convincing.

What has this material about mathematics to do with the conclusion of Aquinas' third proof? Recall that Aquinas reasons that if there is a necessary being, then God must exist. Part of my point in talking about mathematical necessity here is that I want to describe a necessary being that no one would think is God.

Consider the fact that arithmetic includes various existence statements. Besides asserting that $7 + 3 = 10$, arithmetic also asserts that there is a whole number between 10 and 12. But if arithmetic truths are necessary, then it is a necessary truth that there exists a whole number between 10 and 12. To put it bluntly, the philosophy of mathematics I have described holds that the number 11 is a necessary being. It exists in all possible worlds. This follows from the thesis that arithmetic truths are necessary and from the fact that arithmetic contains existence claims.

Numbers Are Necessary Beings

The conclusion that there is a God does not follow from the assertion that not everything is contingent. A philosopher of mathematics might claim that the number 11 is a necessary being, but this would not entail that God exists. This is my last criticism of Aquinas' third argument.

I will not spend much time on Aquinas' fourth proof of the existence of God. It is rooted in an Aristotelian view of causality that seems radically implausible now. Here's the argument:

The Fourth Argument: Properties that Come in Degrees

(1) Objects have properties to greater or lesser extents.
(2) If an object has a property to a lesser extent, then there exists some other object that has that property to the maximum possible degree (call this a maximum exemplar of the property).
(3) So, there is an entity that has all properties to the maximum possible degree.

——————————

Hence, God exists.

The argument begins with an observation that is obviously true: Some things are more powerful and some less; some are more intelligent and others less, and so on. But the second premiss seems entirely implausible. The fact that Charlie Chaplin is less than maximally funny does not mean that there must exist a maximally funny comedian. And the fact that we are somewhat intelligent, though not perfectly so, does not seem to require that there exist a perfectly intelligent being.

The Aristotelian idea that Aquinas is using here is roughly as follows. Aristotle thought that fire is the maximally hot substance. When other objects are hot to some lesser degree, this is because fire is mixed in them to some extent. The property of heat can occur to a less than maximal degree in human beings, for example, only because there exists this substance, fire, which is hot to the maximum possible degree. Fire is the maximum exemplar of heat, from which lesser degrees of heat derive.

There are other problems with the argument. If each property has a maximum exemplar, it does not follow that there is an entity that is a maximum exemplar of all properties. Recall the Birthday Fallacy: The fact that everyone has a birthday does not imply that there is a single day on which everyone was born. So even if there is a maximum exemplar of intelligence and a maximum exemplar of power and a maximum exemplar of moral goodness, it does not follow that there is a single entity who is all-knowing, all-powerful, and all-good.

Finally, there is the problem of contradiction. If intelligence has a maximum exemplar, then presumably stupidity would have to have its maximum exemplar as well. By Aquinas' argument this leads us to say that there is a single being who is both maximally intelligent and maximally stupid. But this is impossible.

Criticizing an Argument versus Showing the Argument's Conclusion Is False

None of the four arguments I have discussed here is successful. Does this mean that there is no God? It means no such thing. There may be other arguments for the existence of God that are powerful and convincing. The fact that the four arguments discussed here don't work does not mean that no argument will work. Not one word has been said here that shows that atheism is true. All we have seen is that *some* arguments for theism are flawed. In the next lecture, I'll consider Aquinas' fifth argument for the existence of God. Maybe it will fare better.

Review Questions

1. What objections are there to the first cause argument?
2. What is "the Birthday Fallacy"? How does it figure in the discussion of Aquinas' arguments?
3. Explain what it means for an object to be necessary or contingent. What is a "possible world"?
4. How are necessity and omnipresence related? How does this bear on Aquinas' third argument?
5. What is a *reductio* argument? Give an example of one.
6. What is the difference between necessity and certainty? What is meant by saying that necessity is "objective"?
7. What would it mean for something to be a first cause without being God? What would it mean for something to necessarily exist without being God?

Problems for Further Thought

1. I said that Aquinas' arguments are abductive. Yet, in discussing the arguments I considered whether they are deductively valid. Recall from Lecture 3 that a deductively invalid argument can be abductively strong. Can any of Aquinas' arguments be reformulated so that it is abductively strong, even if it is not deductively valid?

2. The original text of Aquinas' arguments is reprinted in the Readings for this Part. Consult the original text and then reformulate one of Aquinas' arguments so that it avoids some of the objections I've made.

Lecture 5

The Design Argument

Aquinas' fifth argument for the existence of God has come to be called the Argument from Design. It has a variety of forms, some of which I'll describe. To start things off, here is a formulation that is close to the one Aquinas uses:

(1) Among objects that act for an end, some have minds whereas others do not.
(2) An object that acts for an end, but does not itself have a mind, must have been designed by a being that has a mind.
(3) So there exists a being with a mind who designed all mindless objects that act for an end.

   Hence, God exists.

Note as a preliminary point that the transition from (2) to (3) commits the Birthday Fallacy described in Lecture 4. If each mindless object that acts for an end has a designer, it does not follow that there is a *single* designer of all the mindless objects that act for an end. The fact that everybody has a birthday does not imply that there is a single day on which everybody was born.

What does Aquinas mean by "act for an end"? This phrase corresponds to the modern idea of a goal-directed system. Human beings act for an end because they have desires; these desires are the ends or purposes or goals to which behavior is directed.

Goal-Directed Systems

   Human beings are capable of goal-directed behavior because they have minds. But consider a different example: a guided missile. It is a goal-directed system. Its goal or function is to reach and destroy its target. If the target veers off to the side, the missile can adjust its behavior so that the missile will achieve its purpose.

   Guided missiles are goal-directed systems, but they do not have minds. How is this possible? The answer is consistent with what Aquinas says in premiss (2). Guided missiles are artifacts. They are devices built by creatures with minds — namely, human beings. This is how missiles obtained the machinery that allows them to engage in goal-directed behavior.

   Are there other examples of goal-directed systems besides human beings and artifacts? Nonhuman organisms provide a third category. Even bacteria, which evidently do not have beliefs and desires, seek out nutrients and avoid poisonous chemicals. It seems plausible to describe them as having the goal of surviving and reproducing. They are able to modify their behavior to achieve these ends.

   Does the list stop here — with human beings, artifacts, and nonhuman organisms? Aquinas followed Aristotle in thinking that even inanimate objects like rocks and comets have goals. This idea pretty much went out of fashion with the Scientific Revolution in the seventeenth century. It now seems implausible to describe a rock as being hard "in order to resist destruction." It also seems strange to say that rocks fall toward the center of the Earth when they are released "in order to attain the location that it is in their nature to seek." But this is how Aristotle thought about rocks; Aquinas agreed. Both thought that everything, whether it is living or not, should be thought of *teleologically*—that is, as a goal-directed system. (This point will be discussed further in Lecture 33.)

I won't take issue with this general teleological picture, except to note that it is far more encompassing than the one provided by modern science. Notice that the design argument can be formulated either by saying that *all* objects are goal-directed or by saying that *some* objects without minds are goal-directed. In both cases, Aquinas thought that the existence of God is the best explanation of the observations.

Two Kinds of Design Argument In what follows, I want to distinguish two kinds of design arguments. Aquinas would have been willing to endorse them both. David Hume (1711–1776), who examined various design arguments in his *Dialogues Concerning Natural Religion*, discusses both sorts. I'll call these two sorts of arguments *global* design arguments and *local* design arguments.

A global design argument cites some general feature of the whole universe and argues that this feature can only be explained by the hypothesis that it is the product of intelligent design. An example might be the argument that proposes to explain why the laws of nature are quite simple. Newton himself argued that the simplicity of natural laws is evidence that there exists an intelligent and perfect God who was their author.

A local design argument focuses on a more specific feature of the universe and claims that the hypothesis that God exists is the best or the only plausible explanation of that fact. The example that I will consider here concerns features of the organisms we observe on Earth. They are goal-directed systems; they are complex systems equipped with the ability to modify their behavior so that they can survive and reproduce.

In this lecture, I'll begin with the local argument just mentioned, in which it is special features of living things (including ourselves) that are said to require explanation. In Lecture 7, I'll return to design arguments that are global.

Paley's Watch In the eighteenth century and the early nineteenth century in Great Britain, design arguments were the rage. Numerous books were published arguing that the existence of God was required to explain this or that feature of the world. One of the most influential works of this sort was produced by William Paley (1743–1805). He wrote a volume in series of books called *The Bridgewater Treatises*. Paley tried to give the design argument its fullest and most powerful elaboration.

One of Paley's most striking arguments goes roughly like this: Suppose you were walking on a beach and found a watch lying on the sand (actually, Paley talks about a "heath"). Being a curious person, you ask yourself why this watch exists. Opening it up, you see that it is an intricate piece of machinery. You see that the machinery is complex; the parts work together to allow the hands to measure out equal intervals of time with considerable precision. What could explain the existence and characteristics of this object?

One hypothesis to consider I will call the Random Hypothesis. By the random action of the waves on the sand, a watch was accidentally produced. You may be willing to concede that this explanation is possible. But surely it is not very plausible. The idea that waves beating on sand could produce an object of such intricacy really doesn't make a lot of sense. It is about as plausible as suggesting that a monkey randomly pounding on a typewriter will write out the complete works of Shakespeare.

H_1: The Random Hypothesis

A far more acceptable explanation is the Design Hypothesis. The intricacy of the watch suggests that it is the product of intelligence. This hypothesis says that the watch exists because there was a watchmaker who produced it.

H_2: The Design Hypothesis

Why do we think that the Design Hypothesis is more plausible than the Random Hypothesis? If there were a designer at work, then it would not be surprising that an intricate watch should be found on the beach. However, if the only process at work were waves pounding on sand, then it would be enormously surprising that a watch should be found. The observed watch is possible, according to either hypothesis. But it is rather probable according to one, though vastly improbable according to the other. In preferring the Design Hypothesis, we prefer the hypothesis that strains our credulity less.

I hope you see that Paley's argument uses the Surprise Principle described in Lecture 3. You've made some observations (call them O) and are considering whether O strongly favors one hypothesis (H_1) over another (H_2). The Surprise Principle says that O strongly favors H_1 over H_2, if H_1 says that O is very probable while H_2 says that O is quite improbable. O would be unsurprising if H_1 were true, but O would be very surprising if H_2 were true.

Not only can we infer the existence of a watchmaker from the watch we found, we also can infer something about the watchmaker's characteristics. We can say that the designer must have been fairly intelligent to produce an object of such intricacy. Chimps are somewhat intelligent, but it is dubious that a chimp could have made the watch. Rather, what we naturally infer is that the watchmaker must have had an intelligence at least on the order of human intelligence, given the features of the watch we observe.

So far in this argument, Paley is simply describing what common sense would say about the watch on the beach. Paley then suggests an analogy. Look around at the living world. Notice that it is filled with organisms that are extremely intricate and adapted. In fact, organisms are far more complicated than watches. And as well suited as a watch is to the task of measuring time, an organism is even better suited to the task of surviving and reproducing.

The Analogy

How can we explain the fact that organisms are so amazingly intricate and adapted? One possibility is the Random Hypothesis — that by something akin to waves pounding on sand, kangeroos, chimps, and people came into existence. The other alternative is the Design Hypothesis — that an organism maker of considerable intelligence made the impressive pieces of machinery that we call living things.

Which explanation is more plausible? If the Random Hypothesis says that the existence of a watch is very improbable, then the Random Hypothesis also must say that the existence of intricate and adapted organisms is very improbable. So if inferring the existence of a watchmaker is plausible in the first case, then inferring the existence of a designer of all life is plausible in the second.

Finally, we may ask how intelligent this maker of organisms must be, given the intricacy and fineness of adaptation that organisms exhibit. From what watches are like, we can infer that watchmakers must be pretty smart. By the same reasoning, we infer that the maker of organisms must be *very very* intelligent — far more intelligent than human beings are. Paley's design argument concludes that the intricacy and adaptedness of organisms are best explained by postulating the existence of an extremely intelligent designer.

Abductions
Often
Postulate
Unobserved
Entities

A point that pertains to all Aquinas' arguments should be emphasized here. The design argument claims that there is something we observe — the complexity and adaptedness of living things — that is best explained by the hypothesis that there is a God. The conclusion of the argument concerns the existence of something that we have not directly observed. Although there may be defects in this argument, the fact that it reaches a conclusion about a being we have not observed is not one of them. Recall from Lecture 3 that abductive arguments frequently have this characteristic. It would cripple science to limit theorizing to a description of what scientists have actually observed.

So my construal of Paley's argument is that it is an abductive argument:

> Organisms are intricate and well suited to the tasks of survival and reproduction.
> ═══════════════
> Hence, organisms were created by intelligent design.

I've drawn a double line here to indicate that the argument does not aim at being deductively valid.

To show that this is a strong abductive argument, Paley argues that it is analogous to a second inference to the best explanation:

> The watch is intricate and well suited to the task of measuring time.
> ═══════════════
> Hence, the watch was created by intelligent design.

Paley claims that if you grant that the second abductive argument is convincing, you should grant that the first one is convincing as well.

Hume's *Dialogues on Natural Religion* contain numerous criticisms of the design argument. Sometimes he is talking about global design arguments—ones that argue that the entire universe must be the product of intelligent design. At other times, Hume discusses local arguments—ones that focus on the adaptedness and intricacy of organisms.

Hume's Criticisms of the Design Argument

I've claimed that design arguments are abductive. ~~Hume~~ paints a very different picture. ~~He represents the arguments as being~~ *inductive arguments* ~~or~~ *arguments from analogy*. This may not look like a very important difference, since all of these formulations involve a nondeductive inference. But you will see in what follows that two of Hume's criticisms of design arguments are not very convincing if we think of the design argument as an inference to the best explanation.

To see what Hume has in mind when he talks about arguments from analogy, consider the following example of an analogy argument:

Is the Design Argument a Weak Argument from Analogy?

> Human beings circulate their blood.
> ═══════════
> Dogs circulate their blood.

I've drawn a double line between the premiss and the conclusion, again to indicate that the argument is not deductively valid. In this argument let's call human beings the *analogs* and dogs the *targets*. I say that dogs are the "targets" here because they are the items about which the argument aims to reach a conclusion. Hume suggests, with some plausibility, that such arguments are stronger or weaker depending on how similar the analogs are to the targets.

To see what he means, compare the above argument with the following one:

> Human beings circulate their blood.
> ═══════════
> Plants circulate their blood.

This argument is quite weak because human beings and plants are not very similar.

We can formulate Hume's point by saying that an analogy argument has the following logical form:

> Object A has property P.
> Object A and object T are similar to degree n.
> $n[$═══════════
> T has property P.

A is the analog and T is the target. The number n measures the degree of similarity between A and T. It goes from a minimum value of 0 (meaning that A and T are not similar at all) to a maximum value of 1 (meaning that they share all their characteristics). This number also represents a probability—that's why n is next to the double line separating the premisses from the conclusion. A high value of n means that A and T are very similar and that the premisses make the conclusion very probable. This expresses Hume's idea that the more similar A and T are, the more probable it is that the target object T has the property found in the analog A.

Hume uses this idea about analogy arguments to criticize the design argument. He thinks that the design argument has the following form:

Watches are the products of intelligent design.

———————————————

The universe is the product of intelligent design.

This is a very weak argument, Hume says, since the analog is really not very similar to the target. Watches resemble the universe as a whole in some ways, but fail to do so in a great many others. So *n* has a low value.

Here Hume is criticizing what I have called a global design argument — an argument that focuses on some large-scale feature of the entire universe. But Hume's point also applies to local design arguments — to arguments that focus on organisms and their characteristics:

Watches are the products of intelligent design.

———————————————

Organisms are the product of intelligent design.

Hume's criticism is that organisms are really not very similar to watches. Watches are made of metal, but organisms are not. Kangeroos hop around, but watches do not. Organisms reproduce and obtain nutrition from their environment, but watches do not. And so on. Since analog and target are so dissimilar, the analogy argument is a very weak one; *n* is low here as well.

Hume's idea is that the strength or weakness of an analogy argument depends on the *overall similarity* of target and analog. You look at all the known characteristics of target and analog and try to say how similar they are overall. I grant that if you did this, you would conclude that watches and kangeroos are not very similar. And I will not contest Hume's thesis (though I do think it is debatable) that analogy arguments are weak when analog and target are overall very dissimilar.

However, my view is that this does not undermine the design argument when that argument is taken to be an abductive one. It is entirely irrelevant whether watches and kangeroos both have fur or whether both hop around or whether both reproduce. The design argument focuses on a *a single pair of features* of each of these and asks how it should be explained. A watch's intricacy, as well as its being well-suited to measuring time, requires that we think of it as the product of intelligent design. The suggestion is that an organism's intricacy, as well as its being well-suited to the tasks of survival and reproduction, ought to be explained in the same way. It does not matter that the one is made of metal while the other is not. *Overall* similarity is irrelevant here. I conclude that Hume is mistaken to criticize the design argument as a weak argument from analogy.

Is the Design Argument a Weak Induction? A second criticism that Hume levels at the design argument rests on thinking that the design argument must be inductive if it is to make sense at all. Recall from Lecture 2 that inductive arguments involve observing a sample and extrapolating from it to some claim about one or more objects not in the sample.

For example, suppose I call a large number of voters registered in a county and find that almost all of them are Democrats. This seems to license the inference that the next voter I call will probably be a Democrat. Hume observes, again with some plausibility, that the strength of an inductive inference is influenced by sample size. In particular, if my sample had included just one individual, I would be on rather shaky ground if I used this as my basis for predicting what the next voter called would be like. My inference would be on even shakier ground if I ventured a guess about the next telephone call, having never sampled even a single voter. A sample size of zero is just plain silly; an inductive argument cannot be weaker than that.

Hume claims that if we are to have a reason for thinking that the universe we inhabit is the product of intelligent design, we would have to base this conclusion on induction. What would this involve? We would have to examine a large number of other universes and see that most or all of them were the result of intelligent design. If our sample size were sufficiently large, that would justify a conclusion about the universe we inhabit.

But how big *is* our sample size? It is zero. The only universe we have ever experienced is the one we inhabit. And we cannot claim to have observed that this universe contains a designer of living things. So no inductive argument can be constructed here.

My view is that this is true, but irrelevant. Small sample size does weaken an inductive argument. However, the design argument is not an inductive argument. Hume assumed that the only sorts of inferences worth taking seriously are inductive and deductive. But this I deny. There is abduction as well. Mendel did not have to observe that lots of different organisms have genes before he could conclude that his pea plants have genes. Mendel never saw a single gene, but this did not prevent him from inferring their existence. His inference was abductive, not inductive.

I've reviewed two of Hume's criticisms of the design argument. They do not work. My view is that the hypothesis of intelligent design makes a great deal of sense as an explanation of the intricacy and adaptedness of organisms, if the only alternative hypothesis is that organisms are the result of purely random processes. But in the nineteenth century, a new hypothesis was elaborated that we now must take into account. Aquinas, Paley, and Hume did not have this alternative to consider, but we now do. It is Darwin's hypothesis of evolution by natural selection. In the next lecture, I will describe what this hypothesis asserts and discuss how it compares to the hypothesis of intelligent design.

Review Questions

1. What does it mean to say that the design argument is an abductive argument?
2. What is the difference between a global design argument and a local design argument?
3. How does Paley's argument about the watch use the Surprise Principle?

4. Hume formulated a principle that says how the strength of an analogy argument may be measured. What is it?

5. What two criticisms did Hume make of the design argument? Are these good criticisms if the argument is understood to be abductive in character?

Problems for Further Thought

1. I mentioned in passing that modern science no longer takes seriously the idea that *all* things are goal-directed systems. Consider the following pair of propositions. Can you think of a reason why the first of them might be true, whereas the second might be rejected?

    The function of the heart is to pump blood.
    The function of rain is to provide farm crops with water.

    What does it mean to attribute a "function" to something?

2. What is it about airplanes that allows them to fly? What is it about birds that allows them to fly? In both cases, the shape of the wing is relevant. Both direct airflow so that the air pressure below the wing is higher than the air pressure above it (the "Bernouilli effect"). Suppose we knew that this is the explanation for airplanes, but wondered whether it also applies to birds. Does the fact that birds and airplanes are dissimilar in many respects mean that we should not extend the explanation to cover birds? How does this problem bear on Hume's criticisms of the design argument?

Lecture 6

Evolution and Creationism

In this lecture, I want to describe some of the main lines of evidence that lead biologists to think that the hypothesis of evolution is correct. Whereas Aquinas, Paley, and others held that the intricacy and adaptedness of organisms could only be explained by viewing them as the product of intelligent design, the modern theory of evolution, stemming from Charles Darwin's (1809–1882) ideas, holds otherwise.

Because this is an introductory text, I will not be able to describe all of the interlocking arguments biologists now offer for evolutionary theory. Nor will I be able to give the details about even the ones I do touch on here. I also will not take much time to address all the criticisms of evolutionary theory that creationists have advanced.

Creationists (sometimes calling themselves "scientific creationists") are present-day defenders of the design argument. Their arguments against evolution are filled with mistakes and confusions. For example, creationists have argued that evolutionary theory is on shaky ground because hypotheses about the distant past cannot be proved with absolute certainty. They are right that evolutionary theory is not absolutely certain, but then nothing in science is absolutely certain. What one legitimately strives for in science is powerful evidence showing that one explanation is far more plausible than its competitors. Biologists now regard the hypothesis of evolution as about as certain as any hypothesis about the prehistoric past could be. Naturally, no scientist was on the scene some 4 billion years ago when life started to exist on Earth. But it is nonetheless possible to have strong evidence about matters that one cannot directly observe, as I hope my frequent mentions of abduction have made clear.

Another example of an error that creationists make is their discussion of the second law of thermodynamics. They claim that this law makes it impossible for order to arise from disorder by natural processes. Natural processes can lead an automobile to disintegrate into a junk heap, but creationists think the law says that no natural process can cause a pile of junk to assemble itself into a functioning car. Here creationists are arguing that a physical law is inconsistent with the claim that life evolved from nonlife.

What the second law actually says is that a *closed system* will (with high probability) move from states of greater order to states of lesser order. But if the system is not closed, the law says nothing about what will happen. So if the Earth were a closed system, its overall level of disorder would have to increase. But, of course, the Earth is no such thing—energy from the sun is a constant input.

If we think of the universe as a whole as a closed system, then thermodynamics does tell us that disorder will increase overall. But this overall trend does not prohibit "pockets" of order from arising and being maintained. The second law of thermodynamics offers no basis whatever for thinking that life could not have evolved from nonlife.

Another thing I will not do in this lecture is scrutinize the specific explanation that creationists have advanced. If you want to compare evolutionary theory and creationism, you can't just focus on whatever difficulties there may be in evolutionary ideas. You've also got to look carefully at what the alternative is. Doing this produces lots of difficulties for creationism. The reason is that creationists have not merely defended the hypothesis that life is the product of intelligent design. They also have advanced a very detailed story of just how this happened. For example, they claim that the Earth is very young—only 10,000 years old, or thereabouts.

This claim conflicts with a variety of very solid scientific findings. It isn't evolutionary theory that causes the problem here, but results from geology and physics. It isn't just evolutionary theory that you have to reject if you buy into the full creationist story, but a good deal of the rest of science as well.

Darwin's Two-Part Theory

Darwin put forward his theory of evolution in 1859 in his book *The Origin of Species*. Many of his ideas are still regarded as correct. Some have been refined or expanded. Others have been junked entirely. Although evolutionary theory has developed a long way since Darwin's day, I'll take his basic ideas as a point of departure.

Darwin's theory contains two main elements. First, there is the idea that all present-day life is related. The organisms we see did not come into existence independently by separate creation. Rather, organisms are related to each other by a family tree. You and I are related. If we go back far enough in time, we'll find a human being who is an ancestor of both of us. The same is true of you and a chimp, though, of course, one must go back even further in time to reach a common ancestor. And so it is for any two present-day organisms. Life evolved from nonlife, and then descent with modification gave rise to the diversity we now observe.

Notice that this first hypothesis says nothing about *why* new characteristics arose in the course of evolution. If all life is related, we may ask why it is that we find the variety of organisms we do. Why aren't all living things identical? Darwin's second main hypothesis is the idea of natural selection. This theory tries to explain why new characteristics appear and become common and why some old characteristics disappear.

It is very important to keep these two elements in Darwin's theory separate. The idea that present-day living things are related is not at all controversial now. The idea that natural selection is the principal cause of evolution is *somewhat* controversial, although it is still by far the majority view among biologists.

Part of the reason it is important to keep these ideas separate is that creationists have tried to score points by confusing them. Creationists sometimes suggest that the whole idea of evolution is something that even biologists regard with great doubt and suspicion. But the idea that all life is related is not at all controversial. What is controversial, at least to some degree, are ideas about natural selection.

I'll begin by describing the basic idea of natural selection. Then I'll say a little about what is still somewhat controversial about the idea. I'll then turn to the quite separate idea that all life is related and describe some of the lines of evidence that make biologists regard this idea as overwhelmingly plausible.

Natural Selection

Here's a simple example of how natural selection works. Imagine a population of zebras that all have the same top speed. They can't run faster than 38 mph. Now imagine that a novelty appears in the population. A mutation occurs—a change in the genes found in some zebra—which allow that newfangled zebra to run faster—at 42 mph. Suppose that running faster confers a fitness advantage; that is, a fast zebra is less likely to be caught and eaten by a predator than a slow one. An organism's fitness is just its ability to survive and reproduce.

If running speed is passed on from parent to offspring, what will happen?

What will occur (probably) is that the fast zebra will have more offspring than the average slow zebra. As a result, the percentage of fast zebras increases. In the next generation, fast zebras enjoy the same advantage, so the characteristic of being fast again will increase in frequency. After a number of generations, we expect all the zebras to have this new characteristic. Initially, all the zebras ran at 38 mph. After the selection process has run its course, all run at 42 mph.

So the process comes in two stages. First, a novel mutation is introduced, creating the variation upon which natural selection operates. Then, natural selection goes to work changing the composition of the population:

Start	Then	$\longrightarrow$ Finish
100% run at 38 mph.	A novel mutant runs at 42 mph; the rest run at 38 mph.	100% run at 42 mph.

We may summarize how this process works by saying that natural selection occurs in a population of organisms when there is *inherited variation in fitness*. Let's analyze what this means. The organisms must *vary*; if all the organisms are the same, then there will be no variants to select among. What is more, the variations must be passed down from parents to offspring. This is the requirement of *inheritance*. Lastly, it must be true that the varying characteristics in a population affect an organism's *fitness*—its chance of surviving and reproducing. If these three conditions are met, the population will evolve. By this, I mean that the frequency of characteristics will change.

The idea of natural selection is really quite simple. What Darwin did was to show how this simple idea has many implications and applications. Merely stating this simple idea would not have convinced anyone that natural selection is the right explanation of life's diversity. The power of the idea comes from the numerous detailed applications.

Notice that the introduction of novel characteristics into a population is a precondition for natural selection to occur. Darwin did not have a very accurate picture of how novel traits arise. He theorized about this, but did not come up with anything of lasting importance. Rather, it was later in the nineteenth century that Mendel started to fill in this detail. Genetic mutations, we now understand, are the source of the variation on which natural selection depends.

Notice that the little story I have told describes a rather modest change that occurs *within* a species of zebras. A single species of zebras goes from one running speed to another. Yet, Darwin's 1859 book was called *The Origin of Species*. How does change within a species help explain the coming into existence of new species—of speciation?

Speciation

Darwin's hypothesis was that small changes like the one I just described add up. Given enough little changes, the organisms will become very different. Modern evolutionists usually tell a story like the following one. Think of a single population of zebras. Imagine that a small number of zebras is separated from the

EVOLUTION AND
CREATIONISM

rest of the population for some reason; maybe they wander off or a river changes course and splits the old population in two. If the two resulting populations live in slightly different environments, selection will lead them to become increasingly different. Characteristics that are advantageous in one population will not be advantageous in the other. So after a long time the populations will have diverged. They will have become so different from each other that individuals from the one cannot breed with individuals from the other. Because of this, they will be two species, not two populations belonging to the same species.

Pretty much everybody in Darwin's day, including those who thought that God created the separate species, would have agreed that the little story about zebras evolving a greater speed could be true. The real resistance to Darwin's theory focused on his thesis that the mechanism responsible for small-scale changes *within* species also gives rise to large-scale changes, namely, to the origin of *new* species. This was a daring hypothesis, one that is now the mainstream view in evolutionary theory, though it is somewhat controversial.

In saying that it is somewhat controversial, I mean that there are evolutionists today who doubt that natural selection had the importance Darwin thought it did. They hold that other mechanisms play an important role in evolution. They grant that natural selection is part of the story, but deny that it is the whole story. Deciding how important natural selection has been is a subject of continuing investigation in evolutionary theory.

Another kind of open question exists about natural selection. Even biologists who hold that natural selection is the major cause of evolution can be puzzled about how it applies in particular cases. For example, it is now rather unclear why sexual reproduction evolved. Some creatures reproduce sexually, others asexually. Why is this? Even biologists who hold that the answer must be in terms of natural selection are puzzled.

So there are two sorts of open questions pertaining to natural selection. First, there is the issue of how important natural selection has been in the evolution of life. Second, there is the question of how the idea of natural selection should be applied to account for this or that characteristic. What I want to emphasize about both these questions is that they are not questions about whether we are related to chimps. This is not controversial. The questions I've mentioned so far have to do with the mechanism that accounts for *why* life evolved as it did, not *whether* it evolved.

The Tree of Life   I turn now to this uncontroversial idea. Why do biologist think it is so clear that living things are related to each other—that there is a family tree of terrestrial life just like there is a family tree of your family? Two kinds of evidence have seemed persuasive. I won't give the details here; rather, I want to describe the *kinds* of arguments that biologists deploy. As a philosopher I'm more interested that you grasp the logic of the arguments; for the biological details, you'll have to consult a biology book.

To illustrate how one of the lines of argument works, consider this simple problem. Suppose I assign a philosophy class the job of writing an essay on the meaning of life. As I read through the papers, I notice that your paper and one handed in by another student in the class are word-for-word identical. How should I explain this striking similarity?

One possibility, of course, is that the two of you worked independently and by coincidence arrived at exactly the same result. The independent origin of the two papers is not impossible. But I would regard this hypothesis as extremely implausible. Far more convincing is the idea that one of you copied from the other or that each of you copied from some common source—a paper in a fraternity file, perhaps. This hypothesis is a more plausible explanation of the observed similarity of the two papers.

I will call this idea the *Principle of the Common Cause*. This principle (formulated by Hans Reichenbach in *The Direction of Time*, University of California Press, 1956) says that if two objects display an intricate set of similarities, then it is more plausible to explain the similarity by the hypothesis of common cause than by the hypothesis of separate causes.

The Principle of the Common Cause

What makes the common cause hypothesis more plausible? Consider how probable the matching of the two papers is, according to the two hypotheses. If you and the other student copied from the same source, then it is rather probable that your papers should closely resemble each other. But if you and the other student worked independently, then it is enormously improbable that the two papers should be the same. The Principle of the Common Cause rests on the Surprise Principle described in Lecture 3: If one hypothesis says that the observations are very probable, whereas the other hypothesis says that the observations are very improbable, then the observations strongly favor the first hypothesis over the second.

Here's another example. Consider the fact that there are striking similarities between various human languages. For example, consider the names for the numbers 1–5 used in French, Italian, and Spanish:

	French	*Italian*	*Spanish*
1	un	uno	uno
2	deux	due	dos
3	trois	tre	tres
4	quatre	quattro	cuatro
5	cinq	cinque	cinco

Why do the three languages use such similar terminology?

It is possible, of course, that the three languages came into existence entirely independently of each other and by coincidence happened to exhibit these similarities. But it is far more plausible to see this similarity as indicating a common origin. Linguists think that various human languages are related to each other for just this reason. In reasoning this way, they make use of the Principle of the Common Cause.

The similarity just noted is evidence of common ancestry. But now consider a rather different characteristic exhibited by French, Italian, and Spanish. All three languages *contain names*. Is this fact strong evidence that these languages trace back to a common ancestor?

I would say not. I'd expect these three languages to contain names, even if they were historically unrelated. The Surprise Principle explains why this similarity does not strongly favor the hypothesis of common ancestry over the hypothesis of separate origination.

Two Kinds of Similarity

There are two kinds of similarities here, only one of which provides strong evidence for a common origin. When French and Italian give similar names to the numbers, this strongly suggests that they trace back to a common ancestor. But when two languages both have the property of containing names, this is not strong evidence that they have a common origin.

What is the difference? The idea, in a nutshell, is that which name a number receives is *arbitrary*. For example, there is no particular reason why the number one has to be called "un" or something like it. So when several languages name the numbers in the same or nearly the same way, that's evidence of a common origin.

The characteristic of containing names is a different matter. Maybe a language needs to use names if it is to perform its function of facilitating communication. If names are necessary, then it is not surprising that quite unrelated languages should all have them. Similarities that are *required for specific functional reasons* are not strong evidence of common origin. *Arbitrary* similarities provide far better evidence.

Arbitrary Similarities Among Organisms

I'll now apply this idea to the evolutionary case. One reason that biologists think all life is related is that all organisms (with some minor exceptions) use the same genetic code. To understand what this means, think of the genes in your body as a set of instructions for constructing more complex biological items—amino acids and then proteins, for example. The genes in our body and those in a frog's must be different, since you developed into one kind of organism whereas the frog developed into another. However, the striking fact is that the genes that code for a given amino acid in a frog code for that very same amino acid in people.

As far as we now know, there is no reason why the genes that code for a given amino acid had to code for that acid rather than some other. The code is arbitrary, just as it is an arbitrary matter that we call dogs by the word "dog" rather than by some other term.

Imperfect Adaptation

There is a second feature of life that lends plausibility to the hypothesis that life is related. It is the fact that organisms are *not* perfectly adapted to their environments. When I described Paley's design argument, I tried to convey the idea that Paley was very impressed by the perfection of nature. Paley thought that this exquisite fittingness of organisms to the environments they inhabit can only be explained by the hypothesis of intelligent design. But since Darwin's time, biologists have looked more closely at this idea. What biology tells us is that organisms are *not* perfectly suited to their environments. They are suited in a passable, often makeshift way. Adaptation is often imperfect; it is good enough so that species avoid extinction, at least in the short run.

Consider first an example that the biologist Stephen Jay Gould has used—the so-called panda's "thumb." Pandas are vegetarians—they eat bamboo shoots. A panda strips bamboo by running a branch between its paw and what seems to be a thumb. However, on closer examination it is clear that this thumb is not an opposable digit. Rather, the thumb is a spur of bone that sticks out from what might be called the panda's wrist.

This device for preparing the bamboo is really quite clumsy. It would be no great challenge for you or me or an engineer to design a better thumb for the panda to use. If God made organisms perfectly adapted to their ways of life, it really is quite puzzling why the panda is so ill equipped.

However, when we see that pandas are closely related to carnivorous bears, it is not so puzzling. There is a remarkable similarity between the paw structure of pandas and that of their nearest relatives. The panda's thumb is a modification of a structure that its ancestors possessed. So the panda's thumb is puzzling if you subscribe to the hypothesis that God made each organism perfectly adapted to its environment. On the other hand, the hypothesis that pandas are descended from carnivorous bears makes it unsurprising that they have thumbs of the sort they do. Again, the Surprise Principle says that the latter hypothesis is the more plausible one.

Biologists deploy a similar pattern of argument when they claim that *vestigial organs* are evidence of various species having a common ancestor. You may recall from high school biology that human embryos develop gill slits and then lose them. These gill slits have no apparent function; if each species were separately designed by a superintelligent designer, it would be very surprising to find gill slits in humans. However, if humans are descended from ancestors who had gills as adults, the characteristic found in human embryos is easier to understand. Natural selection modified the ancestral condition; human beings have gills only in the embryo stage, rather than in both the embryo and in the adult.

Another example, also pertaining to our species, is the human birth canal. Human birth is painful and dangerous. It would not require much by way of engineering to come up with a safer design. If God built human beings so that they are perfectly suited to their ways of life, it is puzzling why women have the birth canals they do. However, the hypothesis that human beings are descended from apes makes this fact about us much less surprising. The hip structures of human beings, of human-like fossils, and of apes show a telling similarity. Human beings evolved larger brains, which required larger heads, and these just barely manage to get born. The result is not perfect adaptation, but adaptation that gets by. Darwin's idea of natural selection says that the traits found in a

EVOLUTION AND
CREATIONISM

Humans from Nonhumans, Life from Nonlife

When people hear about the idea of evolution, sometimes there are two parts of that theory that strike them as puzzling. First, there is the idea that human beings are descended from ape-like ancestors. Second, there is the idea that life evolved from nonliving materials.

Scientists believe the first of these statements because there are so many striking similarites between apes and human beings. This is not to deny that there are differences. But the similarites (of which a few examples are given in this lecture) make sense if humans and apes have a common ancestor, whereas they do not make sense if each species was separately created by a superintelligent designer.

There is a big difference between having evidence that *humans are descended from ape-like ancestors* and having an explanation of precisely *why this happened*. The evidence for there being a common ancestor is overwhelming, but the details of why evolution proceeded in just the way it did are less certain. Students of human evolution continue to investigate why our species evolved as it did. In contrast, the claim that we did evolve is not a matter of scientific debate.

What about the second idea—that life arose from nonlife? Why not maintain that God created the first living thing and then let evolution by natural selection proceed to produce the diversity we now observe? Notice that this is a very different idea from what creationists maintain. They hold that each species is the result of separate creation by God. They deny that present-day species are united by common descent from earlier life forms.

One main sort of evidence for thinking that life evolved from nonlife on Earth about 4 billion years ago comes from laboratory experiments. Scientists have created laboratory conditions that are similar to the ones they believe were present shortly after the Earth came into existence about 4.5 billion years ago. They find that the nonliving ingredients present then can enter into chemical reactions, the products of which are simple organic materials.

For example, it is possible to run electricity (lightning) through a "soup" of inorganic molecules and produce amino acids. Why is this significant? Amino acids are an essential stage in the process whereby genes construct an organism. Similar experiments have generated a variety of promising results.

This subject in biology—prebiotic evolution–is very much open and incomplete. No one has yet been able to get inorganic materials to produce DNA. But the promising successes to date suggest that further work will further illuminate how life arose from nonlife.

Laboratory experiments do not aim to create a multicellular organism from inorganic materials. No one wants to make a chicken out of carbon, ammonia, and water. Evolution by natural selection proceeds by the accumulation of very small changes. So the transition from nonlife to life must involve the creation of a rather simple self-replicating molecule. Chickens came much later.

A self-replicating molecule is a molecule that makes copies of itself. A molecule of this sort is able to reproduce; with accurate replication, the offspring of a molecule will resemble its parent. Once a simple self-replicating molecule is in place, evolution by natural selection can begin.

It may sound strange to describe a simple self-replicating molecule as being "alive." Such a molecule will do few of the things that a chicken does. But from a biological point of view, reproduction and heredity (that is, similarity between parents and offspring) are of the essence.

population that are the best of the actually available alternatives will become common. The idea does not imply that the traits that evolve are the best of all the conceivable ones. *Imperfect* adaptations are predicted by Darwin's hypothesis; this is what we observe.

I've mentioned two lines of evidence that lead biologists to think that all life is related. There is the fact of arbitrary similarity and the fact of imperfect adaptation. Both are evidence favoring the hypothesis that life evolved; both count against the idea that organisms originated independently as the result of superintelligent design.

I have emphasized the importance of *imperfect* adaptation as evidence for evolution. More nearly *perfect* adaptation provides evidence that is much less telling. For example, consider the fact that sharks and whales both have a streamlined body shape. Is this strong evidence that they have a common ancestor? I would say not. There is an obvious functional reason why creatures that spend their life swimming through water should be shaped like this. If there is life on other galaxies and if some of that life is about as big as a whale or shark and also lives in water, we would probably expect it to have this sort of shape. Even if terrestrial life and life on other galaxies are not connected by descent, there are *some* similarities we would expect to find nonetheless. I conclude that the streamlined shape of whales and sharks is not strong evidence that they have a common ancestor, for reasons that the Surprise Principle makes clear.

Nearly Perfect Adaptation

My arguments have focused on comparing the following two hypotheses.

H_1: Life evolved by the process of natural selection.
H_2: Species arose independently of each other as the result of superintelligent design.

I think the observations favor the first over the second.

However, there are other hypotheses besides H_2 that might flesh out the idea that God is somehow involved in the explanation of the organisms we observe. Consider, for example, the following hypothesis:

H_3: God created each species separately, but endowed them with the very characteristics they would have had if they had evolved by natural selection.

H_3 is a wild card; although the observations I have mentioned strongly favor H_1 over H_2, they do not strongly favor H_1 over H_3.

Why is this? The reason is that H_1 and H_3 are *predictively equivalent*. If H_1 predicts that life will have a particular feature, so does H_3. Although arbitrary similarities and imperfect adaptations disconfirm H_2, they are perfectly consistent with H_3.

Does this mean that the evolution hypothesis, H_1, is not very well supported? I would say not. Consider the following pair of hypotheses:

J_1: You are now looking at a printed page.
J_2: You are now looking at a salami.

You have excellent evidence that J_1 is true and that J_2 is false. J_1 predicts that you are having particular sensory experiences. That hypothesis predicts certain visual, tactile, and gustatory sensations (take a bite of this page, if you like). J_2 makes quite different predictions about these matters. The sensory experiences you now are having strongly favor J_1 over J_2.

But now let's introduce a wild card. What evidence do you have that J_1 *as opposed to J_3* is true:

J_3: There is no printed page in front of you, but someone is now systematically misleading you into thinking that there is a printed page in front of you.

J_1 and J_3 are predictively equivalent. The experiences you now are having tell you that J_1 is more plausible than J_2, but they do not strongly favor J_1 over J_3.

In the section of this book on theory of knowledge that focuses on Descartes' *Meditations* (Lecture 13), the problem of choosing between J_1 and J_3 will be examined in detail. What I want you to see now is this: When you ask whether some hypothesis (H_1 or J_1, for example) is strongly supported by the evidence, you must ask yourself what the alternatives are against which the hypothesis is to be compared. If you compare H_1 (or J_1) to H_2 (or J_2), you'll conclude that H_1 (or J_1) is extremely well supported. The problem is quite different if you compare H_1 to H_3 (or J_1 to J_3).

If you asked me whether the hypothesis of evolution by natural selection is well supported, I would say *yes*. But this does not mean that I can cite observational evidence that favors H_1 over H_3. Similarly, if you asked me whether you now have evidence that there is a printed page in front of you, I would say *yes*. But this does not mean that you now have sensory evidence that favors J_1 over J_3.

Historically, the design hypothesis has been formulated roughly in the way that H_2 states. As such, it is disconfirmed by what we observe; H_1 is more plausible. But this is just one possible formulation of the idea that God is somehow responsible for the origin of life's diversity. H_3 is not ruled out by any observation I know of, but neither is J_3 ruled out as an alternative to J_1.

I conclude that there is no special defect in the theory of evolution. It is not absolutely certain, but nothing in science is absolutely certain. There is no evidence that supports it by ruling out a design hypothesis formulated so as to be predictively equivalent with the evolution hypothesis. But this is true for anything we believe: ~~The definition of predictive equivalence means that there can be no observation that discrimates between two predictively equivalent hypotheses.~~ If you think we have evidence for anything, I think you've got to concede that we have evidence that life evolved.

At the beginning of my discussion of the design argument, I contrasted *global* and *local* design arguments. ~~Local arguments focus on two characteristics of living things — their intricacy and adaptedness.~~ My thesis is that there is no need to bring the existence of God forward to explain these biological facts. We now have something that Aquinas, Paley, and Hume did not — a detailed and well-confirmed naturalistic explanation of life's diversity.

This does not address the question of whether global design arguments are successful. Maybe we do not need the existence of God to explain why living things exist and are adapted to their environments. But perhaps there are other features of the universe that we cannot explain except by the hypothesis that there is a God. It is to such global design arguments that I'll turn in the next lecture.

Review Questions

1. What are the two main elements of Darwin's theory?
2. Describe what the Principle of the Common Cause says. Why does this principle make sense?
3. There are two kinds of similarities: the shared characteristic may be "arbitrary" or it may have a functional explanation. Give examples of each for human languages and for biological species. Which kind of similarity strongly favors the hypothesis of common ancestry over the hypothesis of separate origination? Why?
4. The geneticist Francois Jacob recently said (in "Evolution and Tinkering," *Science*, Vol. 196, pp. 1161–1166, 1977) that "natural selection does not work as an engineer works. It works like a tinkerer — a tinkerer who does not know exactly what he is going to produce but uses whatever he finds around him." What does Jacob mean here? How is this point relevant to evaluating whether evolution or design is a more plausible explanation of the characteristics of living things?
5. What does it mean to say that two theories are "predictively equivalent"? Can the design hypothesis be formulated so that the fact of imperfect adaptation is not evidence against it?

Problems for Further Thought

1. Louis Pasteur (1822–1895) developed scientific evidence against the hypothesis of "spontaneous generation." For example, he argued that the maggots that develop on rotten meat are not the result of life springing spontaneously from nonliving materials; the maggots were hatched from eggs laid there by their

maggot parents. Does Pasteur's point mean that life could not have evolved from nonliving materials?

2. Suppose you are a crew member on the Star Ship Enterprise, bound for a new planet. You know that there is intelligent life there; the question you want to answer is whether these life forms have ever had any contact with Earth. Which sorts of observations would be relevant and which irrelevant to this question? Defend your interpretation. How is this problem related to the issues discussed in this lecture?

Lecture 7

Can Science Explain Everything?

In the previous lecture, I argued that the theory of evolution is about as well supported by evidence as any scientific hypothesis about the past can be. Astronomers make claims about the history of the Earth and the solar system; linguists develop theories about the origin and relationship of human languages. In each case, scientists do not directly observe the past events that their theories attempt to characterize. Of course, the same is true when Sherlock Holmes infers who the murderer was; Holmes did not directly observe the dirty deed. Rather, he makes an inference about the past based on the clues he observes in the present.

Before the development of evolutionary theory, I think it was somewhat plausible to take the design argument seriously. The intricacy and adaptedness of organisms once seemed to be a fact that required the existence of God to be explained. Now those facts seem to be explicable without bringing God into the picture. Science has replaced a theological explanation with a naturalistic one.

If you reject the design argument, do you have to be an atheist? The answer is *no*. Philosophers have constructed many arguments for theism; the fact that one of them does not work does not mean that none of them will. In addition, there are many religious traditions that have no problem with the idea of evolution. Fundamentalists insist on a literal reading of the Bible. They think that there are just two choices: Either God created each species separately or there is no God and life arose and diversified by purely natural processes. A nonliteral reading of *Genesis* might open up some further options.

The question I want to explore in this lecture is this: Should we expect that science will sooner or later do for every fact about the world what Darwin did for the intricacy and adaptedness of organisms? That is, will science sooner or later be able to explain everything and do this without postulating the existence of God?

"But How Do You Explain God?"

Sometimes people object to the suggestion that the existence of God is the explanation of a fact by asking: "But how do you explain the existence of God?" The implication behind this question is that it is not plausible to say that God explains something unless you are able to explain why God exists.

This criticism of abductive arguments for the existence of God is not a good one. Mendel was quite right to think that the existence of genes explains something. But Mendel had no idea how to explain the fact that genes exist. For hundreds of years before Newton's time, mariners had good evidence that the tides are correlated with the phases of the Moon, even though they had no very plausible explanation for why this should be so. And as noted in the previous lecture, evolutionists have excellent evidence that human beings are descended from ape-like ancestors, even though the explanation of this evolutionary event is now somewhat unclear.

So if abductive arguments for the existence of God are defective, this is not because no one knows how to explain why God exists.

Scientific Ignorance

It is easy to find facts about the world that science is not now able to explain. Every scientific discipline has its open questions. These are the things that keep scientists busy. Scientists don't spend their time repeating to each other things that everybody already knows; rather, they devote their energies to trying to puzzle out answers to heretofore unanswered questions.

Because there are plenty of facts about the world that science cannot now explain, it is easy to construct a particular kind of abductive argument for the existence of God. I mentioned in the previous lecture that evolutionary theory is currently unable to explain why some species reproduce sexually while others do not. Consider the following theological explanation for this puzzling fact: There is a God and God decided to make organisms reproduce in precisely the way they in fact do. Whereas evolutionists cannot (now) explain patterns of reproduction, a theologian can do this just by saying "it was God's will."

I doubt that any scientist would argue that patterns of reproduction will never be explained scientifically. To be sure, evolutionists can't *now* explain certain facts about sex. But science isn't over yet; it is reasonable to suspect that this example of scientific ignorance is only temporary.

The Only Game in Town Fallacy

What should we say *now*? Apparently, we can accept the theological explanation just sketched or have no explanation at all for why some species, but not others, reproduce sexually. I think it is clear that we are not obliged to accept the theological explanation. To think that we are required to accept the theological

CAN SCIENCE
EXPLAIN
EVERYTHING?

explanation, just because it is the only one on the table, is to commit the Only Game in Town Fallacy.

Recall the anecdote from Lecture 3. If you and I are sitting in a cabin and hear noises in the attic, it is easy to formulate an explanation of those noises. I suggest that the noises are due to gremlins bowling. This hypothesis has the property that if it were true, it would explain why we heard the noises. But this fact about the gremlin hypothesis does not mean that the hypothesis is plausible.

Instead of accepting a theological explanation of why organisms reproduce as they do, we should consider the option of simply admitting that we at present do not understand. If my prediction about the future of evolutionary theory is correct, we eventually will have a satisfactory scientific explanation. We just have to be patient.

I now want to consider a very different kind of scientific ignorance. Suppose there are facts about the world that science *in principle* cannot explain. It isn't a temporary gap, but a permanent one, I'm now considering. If there are such facts, then the choice will not be between a theological explanation and a naturalistic explanation that science will eventually produce; the choice will be between a theological explanation and no explanation at all—not now or in the future.

The Two Questions

There are two questions I want to raise: (1) Are there any facts about the world that science is inherently incapable of explaining? (2) If there are, can we plausibly argue that the best explanation of why those facts are true is that God exists?

To answer the first of these questions, I will sketch a picture of how scientific explanation works. I then will argue that this view of scientific explanation implies that there are certain facts about the world that science cannot explain. It isn't just that scientists have not worked out the explanation *yet*; the point is that the nature of scientific explanation precludes their ever doing so.

What Is a Scientific Explanation?

I want to focus on what scientists do when they explain why various events happen. There is another explanatory project that is important to science, which I will ignore. This is the task of explaining why various general laws are true. It is a scientific law that water at a certain amount of atmospheric pressure boils at 100° C. This generalization is about all past, present, and future water. The generalization is true and a chemist may attempt to explain why it is true. But let's be careful not to confuse events and generalizations. Generalizations are true or false; events are not true or false. Events happen or fail to happen. An event happens at a certain place and time; generalizations describe what is true of *all* places and times. I want to focus on the scientific project of explaining events—of explaining what happens.

My thesis is that science explains what happens by describing causes. I'll assume further (although this is not strictly necessary for what I want to conclude) that a cause has to precede its effects. So the causal explanation of an event E_1 that happens now is provided by citing one or more events in the past and showing how those events produced E_1.

Suppose we show that E_1 was caused by E_2. We then might be interested in explaining why E_2 occurred. This might lead us to describe a still earlier event, E_3. And so on. This project leads us to describe causal chains, which we trace back into the past.

Aquinas (Lecture 4) believed that causal chains extending back into the past can have only finitely many links. I will make no assumption about this.

So far I've described two relationships that can obtain between events: (1) some events precede others in time; (2) some events cause others. There is a third relationship. Some events are *parts* of other events. Consider the relationship between the storming of the Bastille and the French Revolution. The storming of the Bastille marked the beginning of the French Revolution. Both of these are events; the first is *part* of the second.

I want to focus on what science does when it tries to explain a spatiotemporal event. By "spatiotemporal," I simply mean that the event in question happened at some place and at some time. Of course, lots of events are "spread out." They don't occur in an instant, but take some length of time to occur. And they take place in a volume of space, not at a single spatial point. For example, the French Revolution lasted about 10 years and it took place in France.

My thesis is this: For science to be able to say why a spatiotemporal event E occurred, there must be events in space and time that are not included in E. I assume that no event explains itself. So if science is to explain E, there must be some event outside of E (but still inside of space and time) which can be cited as the explanation.

A Thesis About Explanation

It follows from this thesis that answerable why-questions about spatiotemporal events must focus on *part* of what happens in the history of the spatio-temporal universe. Why-questions cannot be answered if they ask why the *whole history* of the spatiotemporal universe was as it was.

Consider an exhaustive description of the past, present, and future of what happens in space and time:

$$\cdots \longrightarrow \quad E_3 \longrightarrow E_2 \longrightarrow E_1 \longrightarrow \quad \cdots$$

| past | present | future |

E_1 is explicable because there is something besides E_1 in the world that can be cited to do the explaining. And if E_1 is part of some bigger event (the way the storming of the Bastille is part of the French Revolution), then that more inclusive event will be explicable only if there is something outside of it that we can cite by way of explanation.

Such answerable why-questions about events I will call *local* why-questions. They focus on part of what has happened in the world's history. In contrast to them are *global* questions—questions that ask for an explanation of the totality of what has happened in the whole universe's history. I claim that science cannot answer global why-questions.

Why Is There Something Rather than Nothing?

Here's an example of a global why question: *Why is there something rather than nothing*? This question does not ask why there is something *now*. That, of course, is a local question, which can be answered by saying that the universe was nonempty in the past and then perhaps citing a conservation law (as Aquinas did—see Lecture 4) that says that if the world is nonempty at one time, it is nonempty forever after. What I have in mind here is the question of why the universe *ever* contained anything. That is, why wasn't the universe entirely devoid of material objects throughout its history?

The spatiotemporal universe is the totality of everything that was, is, or will be, anywhere. There is nothing impossible about a universe that contains no material objects. Obviously, the actual world is not this way. The actual world (the one we inhabit) corresponds to one total history. An empty universe corresponds to a different total history. Both of these totalities are possible, but only one is actual. The question of why there is something rather than nothing asks why the first of these possible worlds, rather than the second, is actual. My claim is that science cannot answer this question.

Can Physics Explain the Origin of the Universe?

Do not be misled by the fact that physicists talk about explaining the "origin of the universe." This phrase makes it sound like they are explaining why the universe is nonempty. My view is that they are doing no such thing. Rather, they are addressing a rather different question. The Big Bang theory does not show why the universe, in my sense of the word, came into existence. The universe, according to the way I am using the term, includes *everything* that there ever was, is, or will be. If the Big Bang produced the world we now inhabit, then the universe includes two stages: First there was a Big Bang and then there was the world we now inhabit. The Big Bang does not explain why the universe exists; the Big Bang is *part* of the universe. The scientific question addressed by physicists is local, not global.

So the question "Why this totality, rather than that one?" is not scientifically answerable; the reason is that the question is global. Can a theological answer be provided? Let us imagine that God is not a material object; he is outside the totality that I am calling "the universe." Can we explain why the material universe is nonempty by saying that God decided to make one totality actual rather than another?

Leibniz: God Chooses Which Possible World to Actualize

The seventeenth-century philosopher/scientist Gottfried Leibniz thought that this form of explanation is plausible. He said that God considered the set of all possible worlds and decided to make one of them actual. He did this by finding which world is best. This is why we live in the best of all possible worlds. If you think that the world we inhabit is morally imperfect, you may doubt Leibniz's story. In Lecture 11, I'll consider this issue when I take up the problem of evil. But Leibniz had another kind of perfection in mind besides moral perfection. Leibniz thought that this is the best of all possible worlds in the sense that this world has the maximum diversity of phenomena and the maximum simplicity of laws. Scientific laws are simple, but the kinds of events that happen in our world are enormously rich. This joint property of our world is what makes it perfect in this nonmoral sense.

I won't discuss the details of Leibniz's theory. My point is that he proposed a theological explanation for why there is something rather than nothing in the world of space and time. This fact about the world, being global, cannot be scientifically explained. The question I want to pose is this: If a fact can be explained by the hypothesis that there is a God, but cannot be explained scientifically, is this a good enough reason to conclude that there is a God?

The Only Game in Town Fallacy, Again

I think the answer to this question is *no*. Once again, the Only Game in Town Fallacy needs to be considered. There is a second option besides accepting the only explanation available. This is to admit that there are things about the universe we do not understand *and never will*. Why there is something rather than nothing may be inherently inexplicable.

I grant that *if* (1) there were an all-powerful God who exists outside of space and time and *if* (2) a God outside of the material world could, nonetheless, create a material world and *if* (3) God wanted to make the world nonempty, then this would explain why there is something rather than nothing in the spatiotemporal universe. These suppositions would explain the fact in question. But that does not show that this explanatory story is at all plausible.

Causality

To see what is problematic about this suggested explanation, consider the causal relationship that it says exists between God and the totality of the material universe. God is outside of space and time, but, nonetheless, manages to bring the whole material world into existence. This causal relationship is extremely hard to understand.

Think of the kinds of causal relationships we discuss in science and in everyday life. For example, we say that throwing the rock at the window caused the window to break. Here a causal relationship is said to obtain between two events, each of which occurred at a particular place and at a particular time. This is characteristic of well-understood claims about causality; *causation is a relationship that obtains between events that occur within space and time.* This is why it is so puzzling to say that a God outside of space and time causes the world of space and time to come into being.

I think it is misleading to use the statement "God did it" as a substitute for the statement "I really can't explain why this or that fact is true." The first statement advances an explanation, while the second admits to not having one. If the existence of God is to explain something, it must have more going for it than the fact that the observation under consideration is otherwise inexplicable.

I said before that evolutionary theory cannot now explain why some species reproduce sexually while others do not. This does not mean that evolutionists cannot make vague pronouncements such as "The pattern is due to natural selection." This vague remark is available to anyone who wants to make it. But no scientist would regard this single sentence as a satisfying explanation. The question—the main question—would be *how* natural selection managed to produce the results it did. What made sexual reproduction advantageous in some species and asexual reproduction advantageous in others? It is this more detailed question that, to date, has not been answered satisfactorily.

There is an analogy here with the theological case. The theologian can say "God did it." The evolutionist can say "natural selection did it." A scientist would regard the latter explanation as unsatisfying because it is too short on details. Why should the theological explanation of patterns of reproduction be taken any more seriously? Part of what is missing in the theological story is any indication of *how* or *why* God did what he did.

This may help explain why the theological explanation of patterns of reproduction should not be embraced. A theological explanation so short on details leaves too many questions unanswered to be convincing. In this circumstance, perhaps it is more plausible to admit that we do not understand than to pretend that the statement "God did it" gives us much of an explanation.

A similar diagnosis can be offered of why the theological explanation of why there is something rather than nothing is so unsatisfying. To say "God did it" is to leave too much unexplained. How is it possible for something outside of space and time to cause the entire spatiotemporal universe to come into being? Why should God have preferred to actualize this possible world rather than any of the others? To the degree that we do not understand these matters, we should conclude that the theological explanation is really not much of an explanation at all.

My conclusion is that science may not be able to explain everything. There are facts now known to be true for which science has not been able to account. And even if science progresses, as I expect it to do, I think there will remain facts that are intrinsically resistant to scientific treatment. Not only has science not explained them yet, it never will, because it can't. Of course, we should be open to the possibility that explanations from outside of science may have some plausibility. My point here is that bringing in the existence of God is often to trade one mystery for another, with no net gain in our understanding.

Review Questions

1. What is the difference between a global why-question and a local why-question?
2. Why think that science cannot answer global why-questions?
3. Is it possible to have evidence that something exists without having an explanation for why the thing exists?
4. Consider the following argument: "If science cannot explain some fact, but a theological story, if true, would explain that fact, then the fact is strong abductive evidence that the theological story is true." How is the Only Game in Town Fallacy relevant to assessing this argument?
5. What does it mean to say that causation is a relationship that obtains between

events in space and time? If this were a correct claim about causation, what implications would it have for the idea that God explains the sorts of global facts discussed in this lecture?

Problems for Further Thought

1. Philosophers sometimes use the term "brute fact" to describe a fact that is so simple and obvious that it cannot be justified or explained by appeal to any other fact. Consider the relationship between x and y described in the statement $x = y$. This is a relationship of *identity*. This is a relationship that everything bears to itself; "the Eiffel Tower = the Eiffel Tower" is true, but "the Eiffel Tower = the Statue of Liberty" is false.

   What explains the fact that everything is self-identical? Is this true because of the way we use the identity sign " $=$ "? Is it a brute fact?

2. In this lecture, I claimed that nothing explains itself. However, in everyday speech, we talk about something's being "self-explanatory." What does this mean? Is there a conflict between what I've said about explanation and the everyday idea?

   We also use the term "self-starter" to describe some people. Does this conflict with the idea that nothing causes itself?

Lecture 8

The Ontological Argument

The various arguments I have considered so far for the existence of God include premises that we know to be true by experience. By using our senses (of sight, hearing, touch, taste, and smell), we know that objects are in motion and that organisms are intricate and adapted. What is more, there is no other way to know these things; sensory experience is indispensable. Such propositions are called *a posteriori*. Notice the word "post," meaning *after*. An *a posteriori* truth is one that requires experience to be known (or justified). Accordingly, the arguments for the existence of God considered thus far are called *a posteriori* arguments.

Are all propositions *a posteriori*? Many philosophers have thought that there are propositions that can be known to be true by reason alone. These propositions are termed *a priori*. Note the word "prior"; such propositions are knowable prior to, or independently of, experience. Standard examples are mathematical truths and definitions. We can know that $7 + 3 = 10$ and that bachelors are unmarried merely by thinking about the concepts involved. You don't have to do experiments or conduct surveys to find out whether such statements are true. Reason suffices.

A Posteriori and A Priori

Let's be clear on what it means to claim that a given proposition is *a priori*. To say that we know *a priori* that bachelors are unmarried does not mean that we were born with the concepts of bachelorhood and marriage. For a proposition to be *a priori*, it is not essential that the concepts contained in the proposition be *innate*. Maybe none of us is born with the concept of a bachelor; maybe we must have various experiences to acquire that concept. But even if the concepts were acquired through experience, that wouldn't show that the proposition fails to be *a priori*. To say that a proposition is *a priori* true means that IF you understand the concepts involved, then reason will suffice for you to decide that the proposition is true. Do not forget the IF in this idea. The idea that there is *a priori* knowledge does not require that there be innate concepts.

The ontological argument for the existence of God is an *a priori* argument. It aims to establish the truth of theism without reliance on any *a posteriori* premiss. In particular, the idea is that we can prove that God must exist simply by examining the definition of the concept of God.

Definitions and Existence

This should strike you as a very surprising thing to try to do. Consider other definitions. For example, a bachelor is by definition an adult unmarried male. The thing to notice about this definition is that it does not imply that there are any bachelors. If you think about it, this seems to be true of most definitions. You can define what it is to be a unicorn or a golden mountain, but the definitions will not settle whether there are such things.

When we consider concepts such as *bachelor*, *unicorn*, or *golden mountain*, the definitions specify what it would take to be an individual of the kind in question; the definitions do not say whether there are zero, one, or many things of that kind. The ontological argument claims that the concept of God is different: From the definition of the concept of God, the existence of God is supposed to follow.

So the proposition that bachelors are unmarried is *a priori*, whereas the proposition that bachelors exist is *a posteriori*. The definition does not imply the existence claim. Are there any nontheistic examples of existence claims that can be known *a priori*? Perhaps existence claims in mathematics furnish examples. If mathematics is *a priori*, then mathematical existence claims are *a priori*. So it is an *a priori* truth that there exists a prime number between 12 and 14.

It is philosophically debatable whether there are any *a priori* truths at all. However, I will not discuss that issue here, but will go along with the idea that mathematical truths are *a priori*. This means that since mathematics contains existence claims, there are (I will assume) at least some existence statements that are *a priori* true. It follows that if there is a mistake in the ontological argument for the existence of God, it is not to be found in the fact that it says that some existence claims are *a priori* true.

Anselm's Argument

The ontological argument was formulated by Saint Anselm (1033–1109), who became Archbishop of Canterbury. Aquinas, who lived in the thirteenth century, rejected this argument and recommended in its stead the five *a posteriori* arguments we examined in Lectures 4 and 5. Philosophers down to the present have discussed the ontological argument and have constructed different versions of it. Here I'll consider a rather simplified formulation of the argument:

(O) (1) God is by definition the greatest being possible.
(2) A being who fails to exist in the actual world (while existing in other possible worlds) is less perfect than a being who exists in all possible worlds.

Hence, God exists, necessarily.

I label the argument "O" for future reference.

Premiss (1) is intended to capture what Anselm meant by saying that God is a being "than which none greater can be conceived." It isn't just that God is the most perfect being that happens to exist in the actual world. The actual world, after all, might contain only grossly imperfect beings, so that God's being the best of these wouldn't mean that he is *all*-powerful, *all*-knowing, and *all*-good. The idea is that God is a being who is the best possible being. There is no more perfect being in any possible world. (If you're a bit vague on the idea of a "possible world," go back to Lecture 4 and review.)

Although I gloss Anselm's talk of the best conceivable being by saying that God is the best possible being, I want to note an important difference between possibility and conceivability. What is possible is an objective question; it does not depend on what people know or believe. However, whether we can conceive of something is a fact about us as knowing subjects. Hence, conceivability is a subjective notion. (This should remind you of the point made in Lecture 4 that necessity and certainty are different.)

What can be conceived of may vary from individual to individual. We can conceive of things that dogs can't conceive of, and perhaps there are superintelligent beings elsewhere in the universe who can conceive of things that are beyond our grasp. In contrast, there is a sense of the term "possible," which I am using here, according to which what is possible does not vary from one thinker to another.

It is impossible, according to Einstein's special theory of relativity, for an object that has positive mass to go faster than the speed of light. This simply can't be done, no matter how powerful a rocket ship you build. Yet, this is something we can conceive of; we can describe what it would mean to go faster than the speed of light.

Newton thought that travel faster than the speed of light was possible. He not only could conceive of what this would be; he thought it was possible. But we now view Newton as mistaken. It is not possible to do this, and it never has been. For something to be possible, it isn't enough that you can conceive of its happening or that you can't see any reason why it couldn't happen.

If the human mind is limited in various ways, then maybe the most perfect being we can conceive of is still grossly imperfect in many ways. Maybe an ant can't conceive of a creature greater than an anteater, but that doesn't mean that

A Priori/A Posteriori and Necessity/Contingency

In Lecture 4, the ideas of necessity and contingency were introduced. A possible world, roughly, is a way the world might be. A necessary truth is a proposition that is true in all possible worlds; a contingent truth is a proposition true in the actual world, but not in all possible worlds.

In this lecture, the ideas of a priori and a posteriori were introduced. An a priori proposition can be known (or justified) independent of experience. How is the distinction between necessary and contingent propositions related to the distinction between a priori and a posteriori propositions?

This is a deep, controversial, and fundamental philosophical question. Some philosophers hold that the two distinctions divide up the propositions in exactly the same way. That is, they hold that all necessary propositions are a priori and that all contingent propositions are a posteriori. According to this theory, all the propositions that natural science discovers by observation are contingent.

Some of the discussion in previous lectures has assumed that this theory is false. I have suggested that empirical science (that is, science that relies on observation) is able to discover what is really possible. In Lecture 4, I mentioned some examples. I said that thermodynamics has discovered that perpetual motion machines are impossible (that is, it is a necessary truth that there are no perpetual motion machines); I also said that Einstein's theories of relativity tell us that no particle (with positive rest mass) can go faster than the speed of light (that is, objects with positive rest mass necessarily go slower than the speed of light).

In other words, I have suggested that some a posteriori propositions are necessary, even though other a posteriori propositions are contingent. What about a priori propositions? The examples discussed so far of a priori propositions (such as "bachelors are unmarried" and "2 + 3 = 5") are all cases of necessary truths. So the question remains: Are there any a priori propositions that are contingent?

The examples I'll give provide a preview of material that will be discussed in Lecture 13. Consider the proposition each of us formulates when we say to ourselves "I exist." You know this proposition to be true without using sight, hearing, taste, touch, or smell. Thought alone allows you to see that it is true. So it is a priori. The same seems to be true for the proposition you formulate by saying to yourself "I am thinking." Yet, it is not a necessary truth that you exist. You might have failed to do so. If this line of thinking is right, we may conclude that the proposition each of us considers when we say to ourselves "I exist" or "I am thinking" is a priori and contingent.

Fill in the following table with examples of the four types of propositions indicated:

	Necessary	Contingent
A priori		
A posteriori		

anteaters are the most perfect possible beings. Anselm, though he used the word "conceivable," really meant possible, I think. God isn't just the best being we mortals can conceptualize. God is supposed to be the best possible being.

Premiss (2) is intended to contrast the perfection that may attach to a contingent being with the perfection attaching to a necessary being. A contingent thing depends for its existence on other things. You and I are contingent things; we exist only because certain, other contingent beings acted as they did. But a truly perfect being would not depend for its existence on anything contingent. It would exist unconditionally. According to Anselm's second premiss, a necessary being is more perfect than a contingent one.

The ontological argument *looks* like it is deductively valid: If God is maximally perfect and if necessary existence is a perfection, then God exists necessarily. But from Anselm's time down to the present, there have been doubters. Many theists (and quite a few atheists) have thought that the ontological argument must involve a mistake.

Anselm describes a criticism formulated by his contemporary, Gaunilo. Gaunilo says the argument must be defective, since if it were not, you could prove the existence of a perfect island by a similar *a priori* argument. What did Gaunilo have in mind? *Gaunilo's Criticism*

Let's start with the concept of an island. The first point is that the concept of islandhood resembles the concept of bachelorhood. Its definition does not deductively imply that there are any objects of the kind defined. So any attempt to provide an *a priori* proof that islands exist must fail.

Now let's define a new concept: call it a *P*-island. A *P*-island is an island than which none greater can be conceived. *P*-islands are just like islands, except that they are, by definition, maximally perfect islands. Gaunilo thought that there can be no *a priori* demonstration that there are *P*-islands. Perhaps no such thing exists; and if there happen to be *P*-islands, this is not something that could be discovered by reason alone.

Consider the following argument, which mimics the structure of the ontological argument:

(I)   (1) A *P*-island is by definition the greatest possible island.
(2) An island that fails to exist in the actual world (while existing in other possible worlds) is less perfect than an island that exists in all possible worlds.

Hence, a *P*-island exists necessarily.

I label this argument "I" for future reference.

Gaunilo's conclusion was not that there are *P*-islands (as well as *P*-bagels, *P*-comedians, and so on). Rather, he thought that this argument about islands must be defective. It seems crazy to think that the existence of a perfect island could be proved *a priori*. Gaunilo concluded that Anselm's argument must have a mistake in it as well.

What sort of mistake did Gaunilo think these two arguments commit? He believed that the two premisses of the island argument are true. But Gaunilo holds that these premisses do not deductively imply the conclusion; the existence of a perfect island does not follow from these *a priori* premisses. Gaunilo concludes that the island argument (I) is invalid. He alleges that the same is true of the ontological argument (O).

Notice that Gaunilo's argument was obtained from Anselm's by substituting "*P*-island" for "God" and "island" for "being." We saw in Lecture 2 that the validity of an argument depends on its form, not on its subject matter. Gaunilo was suggesting that since his island argument is invalid, so too is Anselm's argument about God. Gaunilo thought that the island conclusion does not follow from the island premisses. By parity of reasoning, he claims that Anselm's conclusion does not follow from his premisses.

Guanilo is making an argument about these two arguments. In particular, he attempts to show that Anselm's argument is invalid by *reductio* (see Lecture 4 for this piece of terminology). Gaunilo argues as follows:

> If the ontological argument is deductively valid, then the island argument is deductively valid.
> The island argument is not deductively valid.
> _____
> The ontological argument is not deductively valid.

Anselm scornfully replies to this criticism. He says that his argument applies to God—the greatest possible being. It does not apply to a P-island—the greatest possible island.

Anselm's brief reply to Gaunilo is, to my mind, incomplete, at best. The same may be said of Gaunilo's criticism. Gaunilo's *reductio* argument, if it worked, would show that there has to be a mistake somewhere in Anselm's reasoning, but Gaunilo does not show exactly where the mistake occurs. As noted before, Anselm's argument *looks* valid; if it is not, we would like to see exactly where it goes wrong. In the same way, Anselm's reply does not show where Gaunilo has gone wrong; Anselm just says that the island argument is in some unspecified way not relevant.

Let's press Anselm for details. Could Anselm mean that his argument is deductively valid, even though Gaunilo's is not? This seems implausible, since deductive validity does not depend on an argument's subject matter, only on its form, and the two arguments seem to have the same logical form.

Another possibility would be that Anselm is claiming that the premisses of the island argument are implausible, though the premisses of the ontological argument are quite plausible. If Anselm were right about this, the arguments would be disanalogous. But the first premiss of the ontological argument and the first premiss of the island argument seem to be on a par. Anselm holds that his own definition of God is correct; it is hard to see how Gaunilo's definition of a *P*-island could be mistaken.

What about the second premiss of the two arguments? If necessary existence is a perfection of beings in general, why isn't it a perfection for islands in particular? I feel a little shaky about my ability to make such general judgments about "perfection," but I don't see why the second premiss of the ontological argument should be accepted and the second premiss of the island argument rejected. I conclude that the two arguments are fully parallel, contrary to what Anselm says in reply to Gaunilo. Gaunilo, I think, is on to something.

Centuries after the ontological argument was first presented, Immanuel Kant (1724–1804) suggested that the argument makes the mistake of assuming that existence is a property. Anselm defines God as a being with all possible perfections. This means that for any property P, if P is a perfection, then God has P. Anselm then treats existence (or necessary existence) as a property and proceeds to conclude that God has that property. So Kant is right to say that Anselm treats existence as a property of existing things. But why should this be a mistake?

Kant: "Existence Is Not a Property of Existing Things"

When we say that tigers are fierce, we are predicating a property of tigers, namely, the property of fierceness. But when we say that tigers exist, Kant thought we are not attributing the property of existence to those things. Rather, we are saying something about the concept of tigerhood. To say that tigers exist is to say that the concept of tigerhood is instantiated (that is, that the concept is exemplified by one or more things in the actual world). The proposition that tigers are fierce is about tigers, which are flesh-and-blood felines; but the proposition that tigers exist is about a concept; it is not about flesh-and-blood felines at all.

So Kant's claim is that Anselm made the mistake of treating existence as a "predicate" (that is, as a property of existing things). I find this criticism inconclusive. I don't see why existence is not a property of existing things. Granted, it may sound funny to talk about a property that everything under the sun possesses; most properties apply to some things but not to others. And maybe it is true that "tigers exist" can be paraphrased as "the concept of tigerhood is exemplified." However, these facts do not show that existence is not a property of existing things.

Anselm's argument (O) makes use of the idea that God is perfect. Gaunilo's parody of Anselm—Gaunilo's Island Argument (I)—also makes use of that concept. Gaunilo and Anselm shared a world view according to which everything in the universe occupies a particular position on the Great Chain of Being. At the top is God, next come the angels, then human beings, then animals, then plants. Anselm and Gaunilo believed that it was an entirely objective question how perfect a given thing is.

Dispensing with Perfection

I want to suggest that we can see a defect in the Ontological Argument by setting aside the concept of perfection. Let's not worry about inferring a being's existence from its perfection. Let's not worry about how perfect a particular thing is or about whether perfection is objective. Let's simply define a being as an existing thing and see what happens.

Unicorns do not exist. The concept of unicornhood is not exemplified in the actual world. But consider a new concept, which I call *E*-unicornhood. An *E*-unicorn is something that is an existing unicorn. Does it follow from the definition of an *E*-unicorn that there are *E*-unicorns? Not at all. The concept includes the property of existence, but that does not imply anything about the concept's being exemplified.

Let us define the concept of an *E*-God. An *E*-God is a being who is all-powerful, all-knowing, and all-good and who actually exists. Does it follow from the definition of an *E*-God that there is an *E*-God? Not at all. The existence of an *E*-God does not follow from the definition of *E*-Godhood any more than the existence of God follows from the definition of God as the being than which none greater can be conceived.

Concepts Are Defined, Not Things

In this lecture, I've talked about the "definition of God." But this is somewhat sloppy. In fact, what has been at issue is the definition of *the concept of God*. It is concepts that have definitions. We can define what it is to be a unicorn or a golden mountain, but that, of course, does not mean that there really are unicorns or golden mountains that we are defining. Defining unicorns differs in this way from catching unicorns.

When we talk about the definition of God, we are describing what a concept means. We are saying what would have to be true of an object if it were to fall under the concept. Anselm argued that our concept of God has built into it the idea that God necessarily exists. He thought this shows that God exists.

My criticism of the Ontological Argument comes to this: Let us grant that God is by definition the greatest possible being. And let us grant that necessary existence is a perfection. What follows from this is that necessary existence is part of the concept of God. Existence is built into the concept of God, just as omnipotence is. But the fact that existence is built into a concept does not imply that there are things to which the concept applies. An *E*-unicorn is by definition an existing unicorn, but this does not entail that there are any. And an *E*-God is by definition an existing God, but this does not entail that God exists.

Review Questions

1. What is the difference between an *a posteriori* proposition and an *a priori* proposition? What is the difference between saying that a proposition is *a priori* and saying that it is innate? Give an example of an *a posteriori* existence claim and an example of an *a priori* existence claim.
2. What is the difference between saying that a proposition is possible and saying that it is conceivable?
3. How does Gaunilo's point about islands bear on Anselm's argument about God? What is a *reductio* argument? In what way is Gaunilo employing this form of argumentation?

4. What did Kant mean by saying that "existence is not a predicate"? Does this provide a successful criticism of the ontological argument?

5. Suppose that God is, by definition, a being of a certain sort that exists in all possible worlds. Does it follow that God exists?

Problems for Further Thought

1. Consult the original text of Anselm's argument and Gaunilo's reply. Give a formulation of the argument that is more true to the text than the one presented in this lecture.

2. I have argued that building the idea of existence into a concept does not ensure that anything actually exemplifies the concept. That is the point of considering *E*-unicorns. But now consider the opposite problem. Is it possible to define a concept so that the definition ensures that *nothing* can exemplify it? Construct a definition that does this. How is it possible that definitions can have negative implications about existence, but not positive implications?

_____Lecture 9_____

Is the Existence of God Testable?

Up to this point, I have taken the question of whether God exists to be perfectly meaningful. It may be difficult to answer, but I have assumed that there *is* an answer. Theists, atheists, and agnostics agree on this. I've assumed that the sentence "God exists" says something; the question is whether what it says is true and whether we can know this.

Some philosophers—advocates of the position called *logical positivism*—have an altogether different view of this problem. They hold that the two-word sentence "God exists" is meaningless. It isn't true and it isn't false either. They hold that it is misguided to argue about whether God exists. Their idea is that we have been misled by a superficial grammatical similarity between the sentence "God exists" and "genes exist." The latter expresses a scientific statement that can be justified or rejected by appeal to evidence. In contrast, the former sentence expresses no proposition at all. Positivism maintains that we should not try to answer the question of whether God exists, but should reject it as meaningless.

Positivists advanced a theory that is supposed to justify this philosophical thesis.

Logical Positivism

This is the *testability theory of meaning*. It holds that for a sentence to be meaningful, it must be either *a priori* or *a posteriori*. The testability theory of meaning also includes specific proposals for how these two categories should be understood.

I've already explained that a truth is *a priori* if it can be justified without appeal to sense experience — it can be justified by reason alone. And a truth is *a posteriori* if it must rely on sense experience for its justifications.

This is what it means for a truth to be *a priori* or *a posteriori*. But falsehoods can fall into these categories as well. A mathematical truth such as "2 + 3 = 5" can be justified by reason alone; but the mathematical falsehood "2 + 4 = 7" can be *dis*proved by reason alone. And just as the statement "There is a book in front of you now" is an *a posteriori* truth, so the statement "There is no book in front of you now" is an *a posteriori* falsehood.

Some meaningful statements are true; others are false. In saying that each meaningful sentence is either *a priori* or *a posteriori*, positivists are saying that every meaningful sentence is *decidable in principle*. That is, they maintain that if *S* is a meaningful sentence, then it is possible to figure out whether *S* is true. If there is no way in principle to figure out whether *S* is true, positivists conclude that *S* is meaningless.

I now turn to the positivists' account of what makes a sentence *a priori* or *a posteriori*. Once each of these categories is clarified, they think the claim that God exists can be seen to fall into neither category. Positivists conclude that the claim is meaningless.

Analyticity

Positivists (and some other philosophers as well) hold that all *a priori* statements are *analytic*. An analytic truth (as opposed to a *synthetic* one) is a definition or a deductive consequence of a definition. The truth of "All bachelors are unmarried" follows from the definitions of the terms that occur in it. "Either it is raining or it is not raining" likewise follows from the definition of "or."

Symmetrically, positivism maintains that all *a posteriori* statements are *synthetic* — if a sentence depends on sense experience for its justification, its truth does not follow from definitions alone.

Where does the sentence "God exist" fit into this classification? Positivists reject the whole strategy behind the ontological argument. They hold that "God exists" is not decidable from definitions alone. So the sentence is not *a priori*. This means that if "God exists" is meaningful, it must be *a posteriori*. We now must examine the account that positivists give of what makes a sentence *a posteriori*. Positivists say that "God exists" is meaningless because they hold that there is no way to use observations to decide whether it is true. They claim that "God exists" is *untestable*.

Defenders of the testability theory of meaning say that sentences are to be tested by deducing predictions from them that can be checked by making observations. Mendel's theory was tested by deducing from it a prediction about the proportions of different characteristics that there should be in his pea plants. These predictions could then be checked observationally. Positivists argue that the sentence "God exists" makes no predictions whatever; so it is untestable.

Sometimes this idea is expressed by talking about falsification rather than testability. If a theory makes a prediction that can be checked observationally, the theory runs the risk of being refuted by observations. This is what the contemporary British philosopher Karl Popper (not a positivist himself) means by saying that a scientific theory should be falsifiable. This does not mean that a scientific theory should be false. *Falsifiable* does not mean *false*. What is crucial is that the theory should rule out at least some possible observations.

In science, confirmation and disconfirmation are intimately connected. An experiment has different possible outcomes. If some outcomes would be evidence *in favor of* the hypothesis, then other outcomes would be evidence *against* it. If you propose an experiment for testing a hypothesis and you think that every possible result would indicate that the hypothesis is true, there is no reason to run the experiment. The only way the experiment could offer you real evidence in favor of the hypothesis is if there were some possible result that would undermine the hypothesis. You then get evidence supporting the hypothesis if you run the experiment and find that those possible refuting outcomes do not come to pass. Getting evidence in favor of a hypothesis requires that the hypothesis rule out something.

What does the sentence "God exists" rule out? Is there anything we can imagine observing that would be evidence against theism? For example, if we observed that there is moral evil in the world, would that count against the hypothesis that there is a God? In Lecture 11, I'll discuss this question in some detail. For now, I'll merely note that theists have usually not taken the existence of evil to count against theism. They say that if the world had been morally perfect, that would be consistent with the existence of God, and if the world happens to contain moral evil, that too can be reconciled with theism. The fact of the matter seems to be that theists usually can reconcile their acceptance of the claim that God exists with just about anything.

Consider the doomsday pronouncements that pop up from time to time in different religions. Every so often, some religious group gets the idea that God is about to bring the world to an end. Such predictions have yet to come true. What has been the result of these failed predictions? A few end-of-the-worlders have had their faith shaken. But after some reflection, most theists have decided that the failed predictions of end-of-the-worlders do not count against the hypothesis that there is a God. If the world had come to an end, theists would have taken this to support their belief that there is a God. But when the world fails to come to an end, these same people continue to believe that God exists.

These remarks should give you an idea of what it means to ask whether the hypothesis that God exists is testable. I now want to be a little more precise about these ideas. I begin with two definitions:

> A hypothesis *H* is *strongly falsifiable* if *H* implies at least one observation statement *O*.
> An *observation statement* is a statement whose truth or falsehood can be determined by direct observation.

Falsifiability

Notice that strong falsifiability allows a hypothesis to be refuted by a valid deductive argument if the observational prediction it makes turns out to be false:

If *H*, then *O*.
Not *O*.
_____

Not *H*.

Auxiliary Assumptions Needed

I agree that the hypothesis that God exists is not strongly falsifiable. But the same is true of most of the hypotheses that science investigates. *Hypotheses rarely deductively imply predictions all by themselves.* Rather, you must conjoin auxiliary assumptions *A* to a hypothesis *H* to get *H* to deductively imply an observational prediction *O*. It isn't *H* that implies *O*, but the conjunction of *H* and *A* that does the trick.

I'll illustrate this idea with an example from outside science. Consider Sherlock Holmes again. Holmes wishes to test the hypothesis that Moriarty was the murderer. Does this hypothesis, all by itself, tell Holmes what he will observe at the scene of the crime? Not at all. Auxiliary assumptions are needed.

If Holmes knows that Moriarty wears a size 12 shoe, smokes El Supremo cigars, and fires a gun of type *X*, these auxiliary assumptions may lead him to expect to find certain clues. If he discovers a size 12 footprint, some El Supremo ash on the carpet next to the victim, and a bullet from a type *X* gun, his auxiliary assumptions may lead him to think that Moriarty is probably the murderer. On the other hand, if Holmes were to make *other* auxiliary assumptions, then the hypothesis that Moriarty was the murderer would lead Holmes to make quite different predictions. If Holmes thought that Moriarty does not smoke, that he has a size 8 shoe, and prefers to use a knife, then the hypothesis that Moriarty was the murderer would *not* predict the clues that Holmes found. The clues found at the scene of the crime don't say anything one way or the other about whether Moriarty was the murderer until auxiliary assumptions are added.

So most of the hypotheses we test do not, all by themselves, deductively imply observationally checkable statements. They do so only when supplemented with auxiliary assumptions. Where does this leave the thesis that the hypothesis that God exists is not testable?

The sentence "God exists" is not strongly falsifiable. But that is uninteresting, since most scientific hypotheses are not strongly falsifiable either. This brings us to the next question: Is the hypothesis that God exists testable when it is supplemented with auxiliary assumptions?

The answer is *yes*. Consider the following candidate auxiliary assumptions:

A_1: If there is a God, there will be living things in the world and they will be perfectly adapted to their environments.
A_2: If there is a God, there will be no living things.
A_3: If there is a God, there will be living things in the world, but they will not be perfectly adapted to their environments.

The hypothesis that there is a God, when conjoined with A_1, predicts something

Neptune and Vulcan

Most hypotheses in science do not entail predictions all by themselves; they have to be conjoined to auxiliary assumptions to do so. This means that if the prediction turns out to be false, scientists face a choice. They can reject the hypothesis or they can reject the auxiliary assumptions.

Two episodes in nineteenth-century astronomy illustrate these two options. Working separately, John Adams and Urbain Leverrier used Newtonian physics plus assumptions about the planets then known to exist to predict where the orbit of Uranus should be. These assumptions included the idea that Uranus is the planet farthest from the sun. The prediction obtained by conjoining Newton's theory with this assumption came out wrong. Adams and Leverrier therefore had to choose between rejecting Newtonian physics or rejecting one or more of the auxiliary assumptions. Because Newtonian theory was well supported by other observations, they were reluctant to reject it. They therefore suspected that the auxiliary assumptions were the culprit. They conjectured that Uranus is not the last planet. Two years later, astronomers were able to confirm this conjecture; they observed the planet we now call Neptune.

This same pattern of reasoning was subsequently applied to the planet Mercury. Newtonian physics plus auxiliary assumptions (including the assumption that there is no planet between Mercury and the Sun) predicted where Mercury's orbit should be. But the prediction turned out to be false. Scientists therefore faced a choice. Either Newton's theory is wrong or at least one auxiliary assumption is mistaken. Following the pattern of reasoning that worked so well for the case of Uranus, scientists conjectured that there is a planet lying between Mercury and the Sun. It was given the name "Vulcan."

As it turned out, this conjecture was mistaken. There is no such planet. It was not the auxiliary assumption (that there is no planet between Mercury and the Sun) that was responsible for the false prediction about Mercury's orbit; it was Newtonian physics itself that led to the error. Only when Newton's theories were replaced by Einstein's theories of relativity could the departure of Mercury's orbit from Newtonian values be explained.

In the reasoning about Uranus and the reasoning about Mercury, three sorts of statements play a role. There are theories (T), auxiliary assumptions (A), and predictions (P). Describe the logical form of the arguments that the scientists formulated in the two cases.

that I think we can check by making observations. The same would be true if we conjoined the theistic hypothesis with A_2 or with A_3.

So there is a twofold parallel between the hypothesis that God exists and a scientific hypothesis (or a detective's hypothesis): The hypothesis is not strongly falsifiable, but it is testable when conjoined with auxiliary assumptions. Does this mean that the hypothesis that God exists is no less testable than the hypotheses of science?

There does seem to be a difference between these cases, although it is not to be characterized in terms of the idea of strong falsifiability. In the case of Holmes's testing whether Moriarty was the murderer, I noted that different sets of auxiliary assumptions entail different predictions about what Holmes will find at the scene of the crime. If A_4 is true, we get one set of predictions; if A_5 is true, we get a quite different set:

A_4: Moriarty smokes El Supremo cigars, has a size 12 shoe, and uses a gun of kind X.

A_5: Moriarty does not smoke, has a size 8 shoe, and uses a knife as his preferred murder weapon.

If Holmes is to say whether the clues at the scene of the crime count for or against the hypothesis that Moriarty was the murderer, he must decide which of A_4 and A_5 is true.

Auxiliary Assumptions Must Be Independently Established In the scientific case as well as in the case of detective work, there is an important fact about auxiliary assumptions that goes beyond what I've said so far. Not only are auxiliary assumptions needed if the hypothesis is to make observational predictions, but in addition, *those auxiliary assumptions will be checkable independent of the hypothesis under test.* For example, Holmes can find out whether A_4 or A_5 is true without his having to already know if Moriarty was the murderer.

Can the same be done for the auxiliary hypotheses about God's nature, like A_1, A_2, or A_3? This is not so clear. In each era in which God's existence has been discussed, the picture of God's nature has been structured so that the idea that there is a God is consistent with what people believed about the world. Paley (Lecture 5) though that God would make organisms perfectly adapted to their environments. His auxiliary assumptions about God's nature turned out to lead to a false prediction. But we can always revise those auxiliary assumptions so that the hypothesis that God exists does not conflict with anything we have observed. We can even consider the possibility that God made the world so that there would be no evidence whatever that he exists.

In the detective case, Holmes would not endlessly revise his opinions about auxiliary assumptions just to preserve his faith that Moriarty must have been the murderer. To do so would be to fall prey to an obsession, not to do good detective work. Holmes would find out which of A_4 and A_5 is true and then use the independently confirmed auxiliary assumptions to test the hypothesis that Moriarty was the murderer. The result may be that Holmes has to conclude that Moriarty was probably innocent of the crime.

The problem with testing the hypothesis that God exists is that it is hard to determine which auxiliary assumptions to believe. The auxiliary assumptions can always be rejected if they, when conjoined with the theistic hypothesis, imply a prediction that has failed to come true. This means that the hypothesis itself never really stands a risk of being refuted.

How is what I'm saying different from what the testability theory of meaning maintains? To begin with, I am not using the idea of strong falsifiability to criticize the hypothesis that God exists. Furthermore, my remarks are directed mainly at the attitudes of many *theists*, not at the *hypothesis* that God exists. I am talking about people, not about statements. I am suggesting that the attitudes of theists often differ markedly from the attitudes of scientists to the hypotheses they try to test. Theists seem disposed to hold onto the belief that God exists no matter what they observe. Scientists often, if not always, are prepared to put their pet hypotheses at risk. Scientists generally think it is a bad strategy to endlessly revise their auxiliary assumptions just to keep their pet theory afloat. It isn't that scientists never do this in the short run. But to do so forever would bring science to a halt.

Defenders of the testability theory of meaning thought that the sentence "God exists" is different in kind from a sentence like "genes exist." My point is that the difference is not to be found in the sentences themselves, but in the way many theists treat the first sentence and the way many scientists treat the second. Imagine someone treating a scientific hypothesis exactly the way many theists treat the hypothesis that God exists. Think of someone insisting that the Earth is flat. Perhaps this once was a defensible position. But with time, adhering to this theory required more and more extreme views about other matters. But even at present, it is possible to be a Flat Earther if you are willing to abandon a large enough body of apparently well-confirmed findings. The point is that although it is *possible* to be a Flat Earther now, it is not *plausible* to take this position.

The hypothesis that the Earth is flat is testable and scientific. That is why science is in a position to say that there is considerable evidence against it. The fact that a Flat Earther can treat the hypothesis in an irrational way does not show that the hypothesis is unscientific. Rather, his behavior reflects on *him*, not on the *hypothesis*.

I think defenders of the testability theory of meaning made a mistake. They saw the way that some theists treat the hypothesis that God exists and concluded that the *hypothesis* is unscientific. They then invented the idea of strong falsifiability to show what is wrong with the hypothesis that God exists. However, the criterion of strong falsifiability is not appropriate. In addition, the behavior of some theists may simply reflect on *them*, not on the status of their pet *hypothesis*.

"God Exists" Is Meaningful

My view is that the hypothesis that there is a God is meaningful. It is possible to discuss whether there is evidence for or against it. Also, the hypothesis obviously has various logical properties; I noted before that it, in conjunction with various auxiliary statements, deductively implies various predictions. This is enough to show that the sentence "God exists" is not meaningless gibberish.

For all I've said, someone may someday come up with an independently defensible set of auxiliary assumptions that, together with the hypothesis that God exists, generates some observational predictions. It may even turn out that those predictions come true. Perhaps those successful predictions will provide strong evidence for the existence of God by satisfying the demands of the Surprise Principle. I do not say that this cannot happen. But I do not believe that this has happened yet.

Miracles   Various religious traditions have tried to provide such strong evidence. Consider the idea that the existence of *miracles* would be especially significant evidence that there is a God. Why is this? The Surprise Principle provides an answer. A miracle is supposed to be an event that would be very surprising if there were no God. If a theistic hypothesis could be developed that predicted the existence of a miracle, and if that miracle could be shown to have happened, then this occurrence would be important evidence that there is a God.

The trouble comes with showing that the miracle happened and with showing that the so-called miracle cannot have a purely naturalistic (nontheistic) explanation. Consider Jesus' rising from the dead or Joshua's making the Sun stop in the heavens. To see whether either of these is evidence that God exists, we must ask: (1) Did it really happen? (2) If it did happen, could we explain this event in a purely naturalistic way?

To answer question (1) affirmatively, we must examine whatever eyewitness testimony there is. Eyewitnesses are often unreliable, as courts of law have discovered. And when verbal reports are handed down through time, they can be distorted. For these two reasons, there can be room to wonder whether these events from long ago happened in just the way they are now described.

One problem with answering question (2) definitively is that science changes. What appears to be inexplicable by science at one time may look different later on. Science at one time might declare that the chemical elements are fixed and immutable; according to this position, there is no natural process for turning lead into gold. Imagine someone managing to do this and then declaring the transmutation a miracle. The science at the time would not be able to explain the transmutation, but that would not mean that the event really was a miracle. After all, our present science of radioactivity tells us that transmutation of elements is possible.

So miracles, if they occurred, would be strong evidence that there is a God. The Surprise Principle explains why. The problem comes with answering the two questions just listed.

Summary   I'll summarize my assessment of the testability theory of meaning as follows. I think that there are difficulties in testing the hypothesis that God exists. But this is not because I endorse the criterion of strong falsifiability; I do not. There are two reasons why it is difficult to obtain strong evidence that God exists: (1) It is difficult to decide which auxiliary assumptions to adopt; (2) even if the auxiliary assumptions we adopt allow the theistic hypothesis to make definite predictions, it is difficult to show that those predictions satisfy the Surprise Principle.

Review Questions

1. What does it mean to say that a hypothesis is "strongly falsifiable"? Does this mean that it is false? Is the hypothesis that organisms contain genes strongly falsifiable?
2. What is an "auxiliary assumption"? How does testing the hypothesis that God exists depend on a choice of auxiliary assumptions?
3. What does it mean to say that Holmes could "independently confirm" the auxiliary assumptions he needs concerning Moriarty? Independent of what?
4. How does the Surprise Principle explain why the existence of miracles would be strong evidence for the existence of God? What problems need to be addressed if one wishes to argue for theism in this way?

Problems for Further Thought

1. Consider the following passage from David Hume's (1748) "Essay on Miracles":

   > That no testimony is sufficient to establish a miracle unless the testimony be of such a kind, that its falsehood would be more miraculous than the fact which it endeavors to establish. . . . When any one tells me that he saw a dead man restored to life, I immediately consider with myself whether it be more probable that this person should either deceive or be deceived, or that the fact which he related should really have happened. I weigh the one miracle against the other, and according to the superiority which I discover, I pronounce my decision, and always reject the greater miracle. If the falsehood of his testimony would be more miraculous than the event which he relates, then, and only then, can he pretend to command my belief or opinion.

   What general point about eyewitness testimony is Hume making here? Does Hume's argument show that miracles never happen?

2. Can positivists say that a sentence is meaningful even though we will never actually find out whether it is true? Can they say that a sentence is meaningful if it is impossible for us to discover whether it is true? Does this mean that very detailed sentences about the prehistoric past are meaningless? Consider, for example, this sentence: "A dinosaur was standing exactly where the White House now is exactly 100,000,000 years before today."

3. The Readings for this part include a selection from A. J. Ayer's *Language, Truth, and Logic* (1936), which was a very influential defense of logical positivism. In this selection, Ayer says that there is no conflict between science and religion. He also says that positivism agrees with what many religious mystics maintain. Why does Ayer hold these views?

4. In the selection from Ayer's book, what criterion is used to determine if a sentence is meaningful? How is Ayer's criterion related to the falsifiability criterion?

Lecture 10

Pascal and Irrationality

Blaise Pascal (1623–1662), a French mystic and mathematician, was interested in the question of whether it could be rational to believe in God, even if you think that it is enormously improbable that God exists. Suppose that all the evidence is _against_ God's existence—you regard the idea that God exists as possible, though extremely implausible. Can it still make sense to be a theist?

Pascal was one of the founders of the modern mathematical theory of probability. His argument has come to be called "Pascal's wager" because Pascal argues that believing that God exists is a sensible wager, even if there is no evidence that God exists.

Prudential and Evidential Reasons for Belief

Before analyzing Pascal's argument, I want to describe two kinds of reasons someone might have for believing some proposition or for performing some action. Suppose one day we meet for lunch. I am carrying a machine gun and a briefcase. I open the briefcase and show you that it contains $1,000,000. I show you that the gun is loaded. Then, I make you an offer that I think you cannot refuse.

You probably do not believe that the President of the United States is juggling candy bars at this very moment. This proposition you regard as very improbable, though you grant that it is not entirely impossible. Here is my offer: If you can get yourself to believe that the President is juggling candy bars right now, I will give you $1,000,000. If you do not believe this proposition, I will shoot you with the machine gun. What is it reasonable for you to do, supposing that you think that I am entirely sincere in my threats and promises?

In one sense, it is rational to try to believe, even though you might think the proposition in question is very improbable. It would be prudent (that is, in your self-interest) to try to believe, supposing that you don't want to die and would like to have a million dollars. The kind of reason you have here I'll call a _prudential reason_.

However, in another sense, you do not have any reason to believe that the President of the United States is juggling candy bars right now. You have not one shred of evidence that the proposition is true. Let us describe this fact by saying that you do not have an _evidential reason_ for believing the proposition in question.

Pascal's wager is intended to provide you with a _prudential_ reason for believing that God exists even if you think that there is no _evidence_ that there is a God. Even if you think that all the evidence is against the existence of God, Pascal thinks he can give you a prudential reason for theism so long as you grant that the existence of God is at least possible.

Before stating Pascal's argument, I need to mention one other detail about gambling. Here is a fact about reasonable gambles: It can make sense to bet on improbable outcomes if the payoff is big enough. Suppose I offer you the following wager. If you pay me $1, you will be allowed to draw a single card from a standard deck of cards. If the card drawn turns out to be the ace of spades, I

The Expected Value of an Action

You have to decide between two actions: buying a lottery ticket and not buying one. If you buy the ticket, a card is drawn at random from a standard deck of cards. If the card is the ace of spades, you win $1,000,000. If not, you lose. The ticket costs $1. Should you buy the ticket if your only goal is to maximize your cash resources?

The expected value (expected utility) of an action is the average payoff you would receive if you performed the action again and again. If you buy the ticket, there is a 51 in 52 chance that the ace of spades will not appear; in this case, your resources will have dropped $1 (the cost of the ticket). On the other hand, if you buy the ticket, there is a 1 in 52 chance that you will win the million; in this case, your resources (taking account of the cost of the ticket) will have increased by $999,999. So the expected value of buying the ticket is

$$-(\$1)(51/52) + (\$999,999)(1/52) = \$19,230$$

What is the expected value of the alternative action—of not buying the ticket? That depends on what you would do with the $1 in question. Suppose you would simply put it in your pocket if you didn't buy into the lottery. In this case, you can be certain that your resources will neither increase nor decline. So the expected value of not buying a ticket is 0.

Notice that buying the ticket has a higher expected value than not buying. So the rule in decision theory—to maximize expected utility (or value)—tells you to by the ticket.

The expected value of buying the ticket is not the amount of money you can expect to get. If you enter the lottery, you'll either end up a dollar behind or $999,999 ahead. The expected value is what you would average if you bought into the lottery again and again. Most of the time, you'll lose; occasionally, you'll win. The average payoff per ticket over the long run is about $19,230.

The mathematical idea of an expectation applies to quantities other than value or utility. A probability theorist might say that the expected number of children for parents in the United States today is about 2.2. This does not mean that a couple can expect to have precisely this number of children. Rather, 2.2 is the expected number because it is the average. The same is true when life insurance companies describe the life expectancy of a person who is 19 years old.

will give you $1,000,000. If it turns out to be some other card, you receive nothing, and so you are out the dollar you paid for the chance. Question: Does it make sense to buy into this gamble, assuming that you can trust me to pay you if you win and that your goal is to maximize the amount of money you possess? The answer is *yes*. Although the probability of winning is only 1 in 52, the payoff if you win is so huge and the cost if you lose is so small that this is a great gamble to make. Bear this fact in mind as you consider Pascal's argument.

Pascal's
Argument

Pascal's wager can be represented as a solution to a problem in decision theory. This is a modern theory that describes how an agent should choose between different available *actions* by seeing what the *utilities* are of the different *outcomes*. Be sure to get clear on how each of these italicized terms figures in Pascal's argument.

You have to decide whether to believe that there is a God. These are the two possible actions. Quite independent of your decision here, there is the way the world is: Either there is a God or there is not. Hence, there are four possible outcomes — an outcome being composed of your performing an action when the world is a particular way.

The four outcomes are represented in the following two-by-two table:

		Ways the World Might Be	
		God exists	There is no God
Actions	Believe that God exists	$+\infty$	-10
	Do not believe that God exists	$-\infty$	$+10$

The upper-left entry represents the outcome in which you believe in God and there is a God. What is the result if this should come to pass? Pascal says that the payoff to you is an infinite reward — you go to heaven. Suppose, on the other hand, that you occupy the lower-left cell. This is the outcome in which you do not believe that there is a God, but there is a God. Here Pascal says you suffer an infinite punishment — you receive eternal damnation.

What about the other two entries? If you believe in God, but there is no God, perhaps you will have wasted your time with religious rituals and observances that you might have preferred to skip, had you only known that there was no God listening to your prayers. This isn't a horrible result, though it should be represented as a modest disutility — hence my entry of -10. On the other hand, if you don't believe in God and there is no God (the lower-right cell), you receive a modest benefit. Instead of engaging in religious practices that you may find boring at times, you can get involved in activities that are more fun or are otherwise rewarding. Pascal says that the entry in this cell should represent a modest benefit; my chosen value for the utility here is +10.

To summarize the structure of the problem: The agent must decide which action to perform. The possible outcomes are given by the possible pairings of the available actions with the different ways the world might be. And with each possible outcome, the agent associates a utility (a payoff), which represents how good or bad the outcome is for the agent.

How are the utilities of the different possible outcomes to be combined to reach a decision about which act is preferable? The *expected utility* of believing that there is a God needs to take account of two possibilities: There is the utility you receive if you believe and there is a God, and the quite different utility you receive if you believe and there is no God. Likewise the expected utility of not believing must take account of both outcome possibilities (represented in the bottom row).

Here is Pascal's solution. Even if you think that the existence of God is very improbable (say, you assign it a probability of only 1/1,000,000), the expected utility of believing is higher than the expected utility of not believing. The reason is that though the existence of God is very improbable, there is a huge benefit if you are a theist and God exists, but only a small cost if you are a theist and there is no God. It makes sense to bet on the existence of God, even if the existence of God is very improbable, for reasons that parallel the gamble I mentioned before. The gamble makes sense, even though it is improbable that there is a God.

Two criticisms have been made of this wager, only one of which is decisive. First, some philosophers have objected to treating belief as an action. Believing something is not something we have control over. In my story about the President, you may recognize that it is in your interest to believe that the President is now juggling candy bars. But seeing that this would be good for you doesn't mean that you can automatically make yourself believe the proposition. The objection is that you should not treat belief as a problem in decision theory, since decision theory is about choosing actions that you can perform if you want to.

First Criticism of Pascal's Argument

Pascal recognized this difficulty. After stating his wager, he comments that people who are convinced that the reasoning is sound may not be able to suddenly start being theists. He suggests to them that they go live among religious people. By doing this, habits of faith will gradually take hold. Pascal realized that you cannot simply decide to believe something. But he did see that you can choose to live your life in such a way that belief will come naturally, after a while.

This means that Pascal's wager can be reformulated so that the actions considered really are things under our control. Rather than treating belief and nonbelief as things we can choose to do directly, let us recognize that sincere belief can only occur in the right setting, where the right habits have been developed. So the immediate actions I might consider are going to live among religious people versus living among secular folks. I may choose the former, for reasons that Pascal sets forth—the former action will lead me to a sincere theism, and I recognize that theism is a very good gamble.

The second objection to Pascal's argument is more telling. In Lecture 9, I discussed the difficulty of establishing what God would be like if such a being existed. This is the problem of independently confirming auxiliary hypotheses, as I called them, about God's nature.

Pascal's wager makes very specific assumptions about what God would be like if there were such a being. The assumption is that God would send believers to heaven and nonbelievers to hell. But there are other conceptions: for example, that God would reward those who lead a good life and would punish those who are bad, independently of what those individuals' theological opinions may be. Or consider another possibility — that God sends everyone to heaven except those who are convinced by Pascal's wager.

The main problem with the wager is that it makes assumptions about God's nature that are part of one religious tradition but not part of many others. How can one tell which assumptions are true? In the absence of a convincing argument, I see no reason to think that Pascal's description of the payoffs is correct.

The Role of Reason Pascal argued that it can make sense to believe things that are totally unsupported by evidence. If you think that evidence is the hallmark of rational belief, then you'll interpret Pascal as giving a justification of irrationality. Of course, he did not abandon the standard of rationality altogether. He tried to provide a rational argument that shows that we should believe in God even if there is no evidence that God exists. Pascal aimed to provide a prudential reason, not an evidential reason.

Pascal rejected the idea that evidential reasoning should determine whether we believe in God. Other religious thinkers have done the same thing, but for reasons quite different from Pascal's. For example, it has been suggested that God is so different from other beings that techniques appropriate for discussing them are no longer appropriate when the question is a theological one. God is said to be an infinite being, one who may stand outside of space and time and yet be able to influence what happens in space and time. God is also supposed to be all-knowing, all-powerful, all-good. In all these respects, God is far different from the familiar objects about which we are accustomed to reasoning.

Let us grant that God is supposed to have these special features. Why do they show that reason is not an appropriate tool to use in trying to decide whether God exists? I noted in Lecture 2 and again in Lecture 9 that deductive validity depends on an argument's form, not on its subject matter. If this is right, then deductive reasoning should apply to the question of God's existence in the same way it applies to other questions.

Sometimes it is suggested that God is so shrouded in mystery that we cannot hope to understand God by rational inquiry. Maybe this is right — maybe the issues are so mysterious that you'll never be able to see that God exists if you adhere to rational standards of argument. But why does this mean that those standards should be abandoned? Why not take this to mean that we should not believe that God exists, precisely because no good argument can be produced for this conclusion?

I won't pursue these questions any further. Maybe it can be explained why usual standards of evidence and argument should be abandoned when the question is whether God exists. So far, I know of no reason to think this.

There is a curious fact here that really does require an explanation. If we were talking about virtually any topic from everyday or scientific life, no one would be very attracted by the advice that we should believe something on the basis of no evidence. Yet, when the question is whether God exists, people sometimes drop their critical standards. This is not true of everyone, of course. It was not true of Anselm, Aquinas, Hume, or Paley, for example. Still, the idea of switching from reason to faith has been attractive to many.

There is a psychological question I will pose, but not answer. Why are people sometimes inclined to believe without evidence when the question is whether God exists, but are much less willing to take this attitude when the question is a different one?

Note the difference between the philosophical and the psychological questions. Instead of asking why people *should* (or should not) believe in God, a psychologist might ask why many people, in fact, do. A philosopher might try to *justify* theism (or atheism); a psychologist might try to *explain* it.

In his essay, "The Future of an Illusion," Sigmund Freud (1856–1939), the founder of psychoanalysis, gave an answer that is worth pondering. Freud points out that the world is in many ways a frightening place. It is a relatively recent event in human history that people have come to exercise some mastery over nature. And even this recent mastery is enormously incomplete. Although we are not threatened every day by wild animals, lightning, drought, and flood, each of us has to face the inevitability of our own deaths. In this ultimate sense, we are as helpless as our ancient ancestors. With so much of nature out of our control, beyond our understanding, and threatening our survival, it is not surprising that human beings should invent myths that provide a quite different and more appealing picture of our place in the cosmos. Instead of viewing the universe as indifferent to us, impersonal, and incomprehensible, we are offered a comprehensible picture of forces more powerful than ourselves who take an interest in our fate. Freud's hypothesis was that belief in God persists in human history because of the psychological benefits it provides to believers.

Pascal aimed to provide a prudential argument for believing that God exists. Freud was an atheist, but aimed to provide an explanation for why many people believe that God exists. Pascal sought to justify theism; Freud did not seek to justify it, but to explain it.

In spite of these differences, we can use some of Freud's observations to formulate a prudential argument for theism that is stronger than the one that Pascal provided. The stumbling block for Pascal was the assumptions he made about what God would be like if he existed. However, we can avoid these difficult questions about God's nature and focus on something that is more familiar and closer to home — our own minds.

Suppose you are the sort of person who derives comfort and fulfillment from believing in God. Your belief in God provides your life with meaning. It gives you the courage to face adversity. Moreover, let us suppose that without believing in God, you would plunge into despair. You would become depressed, unable to live a productive life.

There are many people in the world who are not like this. First, there are cheerful agnostics and atheists—people who manage to make a meaningful life for themselves without needing a theological framework. Second, there are people who remain tormented by despair even after they become theists. In both these cases, I am talking about people whose general outlook is rather independent of the theological opinions they happen to have.

Nevertheless, let us suppose that there are some people for whom belief in God makes all the difference. Perhaps you are a person of this sort. If so, you can use these psychological facts to formulate a prudential argument for theism:

> If you believe in God, you will lead a happy and productive life
> If you do not believe in God, you will fall into depression and despair.
> _____
> The way to maximize expected utility in this case is for you to be a theist.

This argument resembles Pascal's in that it ignores whatever evidence there may be concerning whether God exists. But unlike Pascal's argument, this prudential argument does not make assumptions about what God would do to theists and atheists. This argument focuses on the psychological consequences of theism, not on speculations about heaven and hell.

This argument is more difficult to refute than Pascal's. The major issue it raises is a difficult one. Should we allow prudential reasons to influence what we believe or should we require that our beliefs be regulated by evidence alone?

Pragmatism

Pragmatism is a general philosophical position that has implications about this question. This philosophical idea was developed in the nineteenth and twentieth centuries principally by C. S. Peirce, William James, and John Dewey. In ordinary speech, "being pragmatic" means *being practical*. The philosophical position, however, is not fully captured by the everyday meaning of the word.

Pragmatists say that we should believe propositions that are useful to us. In everyday life, this usually means that we should be attentive to evidence. Suppose you are about to cross the street and want to know whether a bus is coming. The most useful thing to do here is to use your senses (sight, hearing, etc.). It would be silly to engage in wishful thinking—to refuse to consult any evidence and simply believe the proposition that you'd like to have be true.

In cases of this sort, the prudent thing to do is to attend to evidence. But there are cases in which prudential considerations can lead in one direction and evidential considerations in another. My story about the President juggling candy bars provides one example. A prudential argument for theism provides another.

In *The Will to Believe* (1897), William James says that a person is entitled to believe in God for purely prudential reasons (of the psychological sort previously described) if the belief provides a "vital benefit" and if no decision about theism can be made on the basis of the evidence available. But why shouldn't a pragmatist be more liberal? Even if there were *substantial* evidence against there being a God, why shouldn't sufficiently large prudential benefits outweigh the evidential considerations?

James's position does not provide a blanket justification of theism. As mentioned before, people who could lead happy, productive lives without being theists cannot claim they *need* to believe in God to avoid falling into despair. Yet, the spirit of pragmatism (if not the letter of James's formulation) seems to sanction believing in God if belief would be useful.

To do justice to the problems that pragmatism raises, we would need to consider a variety of cases. If it is a matter of life and death, is it reasonable for someone to be a theist on purely prudential grounds? In less extreme cases, is the comfort provided by theism reason enough to believe in God? This raises complex questions about the attitudes we should take to our lives. Some might reject pragmatic arguments for theism by saying that they prefer to look the universe square in the face without the benefit of comforting illusions. They might prefer a life of honest uncertainty and doubt over a life made comfortable by beliefs that have no evidential basis.

The pragmatist says that we should believe what it is useful to believe. An opponent of pragmatism might insist that prudential considerations are irrelevant; we should believe only those propositions that are well supported by evidence. Although Pascal's wager does not succeed in providing a prudential reason for theism, it is harder to refute the purely psychological argument just described.

Review Questions

1. What is the difference between a prudential reason and an evidential reason for believing something?
2. Can it ever make sense to bet on something that probably won't happen?
3. Given the payoffs that Pascal assigns to outcomes, what is the expected value of believing in God? Of not believing?
4. Do people believe what they do because they "decide to believe"? If not, does it follow that Pascal's argument is mistaken?
5. How does Pascal's argument depend on a set of auxiliary assumptions (in the sense of Lecture 9) about God's nature?
6. Describe a prudential argument for believing in God that avoids the problem that Pascal's argument confronts.

A Problem for Further Thought

In his essay "The Ethics of Belief" (1877), W. K. Clifford opposed the pragmatism described in the present lecture. He maintains that "it is wrong always, everywhere, and for any one, to believe anything upon insufficient evidence." Here is one of the arguments he gives:

... if I let myself believe anything on insufficient evidence, there may be no great harm done by the mere belief; it may be true after all, or I may never have occasion to exhibit it in outward acts. But I cannot help doing this great wrong towards Man, that I make myself credulous. The danger to society is not merely that it should believe wrong things, though that is great enough, but that it should become credulous and lose the habit of testing things and inquiring into them; for then it must sink back into savagery.

Is this a good argument against pragmatism?

Lecture 11

The Argument from Evil

So far, most of the arguments considered concerning the existence of God have had theistic conclusions. I now turn to an issue that many regard as providing an argument for atheism. It sometimes is thought that the fact that there is evil in the world proves that there is no God. An argument to this effect is called an argument from evil. I will consider three forms that this argument might take. I think that none of these successfully proves that there is no God. However, I will suggest that the third argument does show that if there is a God, then God must be different from what at least one religious tradition has said.

_First Version
of the
Argument_

The first form of the argument from evil is quite simple:

(1) If God were to exist, then that being would be all-powerful, all-knowing, and all-good (all-PKG, for short).
(2) If an all-PKG being existed, then there would be no evil.
(3) There is evil.

Hence, there is no God.

The argument is deductively valid; convince yourself of this by identifying the argument's logical form.

Sometimes it is said that the first premiss is a "definition" of what we mean by the concept of God. I'll say in a minute why I don't think that (1) is a "definition."

Premiss (2) is usually defended as follows. If God is all-good, he wants to prevent evil. If he is all-knowing, he knows the difference between right and wrong and knows what will prevent evils from coming into existence. And if he is all-powerful, he can prevent evil, should he wish to do so. So God, if he is all-PKG, has both the inclination and the ability to prevent evil from coming into existence.

What does evil mean in premiss (3)? Discussion of the argument from evil usually divides existing evils into two categories. There are the wrongs that are brought into existence by human actions. And there are the evils that exist because of natural events that are not under human control. In the first category fall the suffering that human beings inflict on each other; the second category includes the suffering that human beings (and other creatures) experience because of natural disasters, such as earthquakes and plagues.

As mentioned before, the argument is valid. Hence, if you wish to reject the conclusion, you must reject one or more of the premisses. What options are available?

One option is to deny the existence of evil (premiss 3). For example, you could take the view that there really is no difference between right and wrong. This is the idea that the universe is morally neutral; we human beings impose illusory moral categories upon it. This view about morality will be discussed in the fourth section of the book, especially in Lectures 28 and 29. For now I will ignore this option. I will assume that some of the murders, tortures, and other brutalities that have peppered human history really are ethically deplorable. I also will assume that the world would have been a better place if some of the suffering caused by natural disasters had not occurred. This assumption—that premiss (3) is correct—is shared by many, if not all, religious traditions.

Another option is to reject premiss (1). You could interpret the existence of evil as showing merely that if there is a God, then God is not all-PKG. This strategy grants premisses (2) and (3), but then concludes that if God exists, he cannot be exactly the way one religious tradition says he is.

The fact that this strategy is available shows, I think, that (1) is not "true by definition." If the first premiss really did define what the term "God" means, then the existence of evil could not be explained by rejecting this premiss. But this does seem to be a real option. What we need to recognize is that premiss (1) does not have the same status that the following sentence has: "A bachelor is an unmarried man." Suppose we found that a man we thought was a bachelor in fact is married. Would this lead us to consider the possibility that maybe bachelors could be married? I think not.

Premiss (1) embodies one theory about what God's nature is. It is one theory among many possible theories, none of which deserves to be viewed as "true by definition." The ancient Greeks denied that the gods are all-PKG. Zoroastrianism denies that God is all powerful. So rejecting premiss (1) is an option that we need to consider as a way of explaining why evil exists.

One other option remains—reject premiss (2). This is the strategy pursued by theists who think that premisses (1) and (3) are true. If you think that God is all-PKG and that evil is a reality, you need to show how God's being all-PKG does not imply that there would be no evil in the world. Traditional Christian theology uses the term *theodicy* to name the project of reconciling the existence of an all-PKG God with the fact that there is evil in the world.

I think that there is some plausibility in rejecting premiss (2). Notice that premiss (2) makes a very strong claim. It says that if an all-PKG God existed, there would be not even a tiny amount of evil in the world.

Soul-Building Evils Traditional theodicy has claimed that some evils have the property of being "soul-building." Soul-building evils are the ones that make us better people. Living through adversity strengthens our character; it makes us better people than we would have been if we had never suffered hardship.

I want to be careful about what I am conceding here. I grant that *some* evils are soul-building. But I think it is morally outrageous to say this of *all* the evils that human beings have experienced. Sometimes suffering does not make the victim stronger; sometimes suffering destroys people. And even when people survive brutal tortures, do we really think that they are always better people for it? Sometimes they survive as mere shells. Even when the torture victims in some sense are made stronger by their ordeals, do we still want to say that the experience was worth it? If it was worth it for *them,* would *you* choose to undergo it yourself? There are some strengths that are not worth having, because they cost too much to acquire.

Sometimes it is suggested that when people are destroyed by the sufferings they endure, the souls of other people are strengthened by watching this happen. I think that this is sometimes true. But it is often false. Sometimes the only effect on witnesses is that they are sickened by having to watch events they know full well to be horrible. Sometimes people who witness the suffering of others react with callousness and indifference. And some suffering occurs in private; in these cases, there is no audience whose souls can be made stronger by watching it happen.

Just as suffering often does not make the sufferer a better person, it is also true that one person's suffering often fails to make other people better. So in granting that *some* suffering is soul-building, I am granting something about a rather small portion of the huge mountain of agony the human race has experienced.

Is the fact that some evils are soul-building enough to refute premiss (2)? This is not so clear. If it is desirable that we be strong of heart, why couldn't God have made us this way without us having to experience evil? The point about soul-building is sometimes urged by an analogy concerning the way a benevolent parent treats a child. If you really care about your children, you will not shield them from all adversity. There are some experiences that involve pain and suffering that children need to have if they are to mature into morally sensitive and autonomous adults. If your child is being picked on by a bully at school, you may decide that she has to tough it out for herself. Intervening would save her a few scrapes and bruises *now*. But you might decide as a parent that this would not be in her long-term best interests.

You, as a parent, have the goal of seeing your children develop in a certain way. You choose not to prevent some bad things from happening to your child because you recognize that there is no other way for her to mature as you intend. But suppose you could have your child become a mature adult without her having to be kicked around by the bully. In this case, why would you allow the bully to continue to harass your child?

A parent might allow soul-building evils to befall a child when there is no other way to have the child's soul grow strong. But the limitations that might justify a parent's choice are not supposed to be present where God is concerned. If God is all-PKG, why couldn't he simply make us with strong souls?

Defenders of the soul-building idea reply that God wants us to be able to be proud of our own achievements. If we suffer through adversity, we get credit for the strong souls that result. But if God simply gave us strong souls *gratis*, we would deserve no credit. We couldn't be proud of ourselves; at best, we would simply be grateful to a benevolent deity.

To evaluate this suggestion, we would have to ask why it is so important that we be able to take credit for having strong characters. Why is it better to experience an evil and then get credit for having endured it rather than to not experience the evil but be a strong person because God makes us that way?

I raise this question, but will not attempt to answer it. I'll concede for now that an all-PKG God would allow at least some evils to exist. Some soul-building evils are of this sort. In other words, I'll concede that premiss (2) is false. Does this mean that there is no problem of evil—that the existence of evil poses no difficulty for the conception of God as an all-PKG being?

I think not. The soul-building evils that an all-PKG God would allow us to experience are a tiny portion of the evils that we need to explain. What needs to be explained is not why there is some evil *rather than none at all*. The deeper problem is to explain why there is so much evil *rather than one ounce less*.

So the second argument from evil is more difficult to refute. It takes the following form:

Second Version of the Argument

(4) If an all-PKG being existed, then the amount of evil would not exceed a soul-building minimum.
(5) The amount of evil does exceed a soul-building minimum.

Hence, if there is a God, that being is not all-PKG.

By "soul-building minimum," I mean the minimum amount of evil that suffices to make us have strength of character.

Notice that this argument, unlike the first argument from evil, does not conclude that there is no God. This second argument takes to heart the earlier idea that we should not regard premiss (1) as true by definition. The conclusion of this second argument is accordingly more modest: It does not say whether or not there is a God, but only that God, if he exists, cannot be the way some religious thinkers have pictured him.

To reject the conclusion of the present argument, one must find a reason that an all-PKG being might have for permitting evils to exist beyond the soul-building minimum. It sometimes is suggested that this reason is to be found in the area of *free will*. God made us free; this means it is up to us whether we do good or

Free Will

do evil. A consequence of this freedom is that there is more evil than would be strictly necessary for soul-building.

There is a question here that we will examine in detail in the part of this book on philosophy of mind. Why couldn't God have made us free agents who always freely choose to do what is right? Why assume that free people must sometimes produce evil? If a sinner can have free will, why can't a saint? I note this question only to postpone its detailed examination.

Let's assume, for the sake of argument, that human freedom requires that people sometimes produce evil and that this evil exceeds the minimum that would exist strictly from the point of view of soul-building. This means that premiss (4) in the second argument is mistaken. But again, I want to emphasize that this does not fully solve the problem of evil. The problem is to account for the vast quantity of evil that exists. Let us grant that some evil must exist for soul-building and some more evil will be a consequence of human freedom. Does this explain the quantity of evil that the world contains?

Examples Let's single out some horrendous evil that has befallen the human race. Think of all the suffering that Hitler caused. How could an all-PKG God have allowed this to happen? Is the answer that God made us free? I think this appeal to the importance of human freedom does not begin to address the difficulty.

Why didn't God intervene into human affairs on those rare occasions in which it would have made a dramatic difference? When the sperm and egg came together that produced Hitler, why didn't God prevent that fertilization event from coming to pass? To do so would still have allowed human beings to be free; in addition, that brief intervention would still have allowed there to be soul-building evils aplenty. Here I'm considering a minor foray into human affairs, not some major restructuring of human nature.

Suppose that if Hitler had never existed, many of the terrible things he did never would have happened. The world would have been a much better place. Most theists would agree with this. So why didn't God influence the course of human history for the better? What you must see here is that appeals to soul-building and to freedom do not provide an answer. Causing Hitler's parents to fail to conceive on that one occasion does not rob them of free will; the parents did not will that this particular sperm and this particular egg should achieve fertilization.

Another way to make this point is to consider horrendous evils that come into existence for reasons having nothing to do with human action. Consider the bubonic plague. If God had prevented that disease from existing, much suffering and death would have been avoided. To intervene into the lives of the relevant microorganisms does not rob them of free will, since these viruses don't have wills (minds) to begin with. Also, the amount of suffering that occurred because of the plague far exceeded what could be explained by the goal of soul-building. About a third of the European population died agonizing deaths from bubonic plague. Would our souls have been less strong if some smaller percentage had perished?

So the most powerful argument from evil is neither of the two versions I have enumerated. I grant that an all-PKG being would allow some evil to exist. Soul-building provides one reason; the importance of human freedom another. However, I cannot understand how an all-PKG being would allow the vast quantity of evil that the human race has experienced to have existed.

To this it may be replied that we have here a mystery that defies rational explanation. It is a paradox that an all-PKG God could have allowed Hitler and the bubonic plague to have existed. The suggestion is that we must have faith that an all-PKG God exists, even if we draw a blank when we try to rationally comprehend how this is possible.

I briefly discussed, in Lecture 10, the role reason plays in deciding whether God exists. Maybe it is true that we cannot understand how an all-PKG being could have allowed Hitler and the bubonic plague to have existed. But this does not solve the problem of evil. Indeed, our inability to reconcile these ideas is precisely what the following argument is pointing to:

Third Version of the Argument

    (6) If an all-PKG being existed, then there would be no more evil than the minimum required for soul-building and as a consequence of human freedom.
    (7) The quantity of evil found in human history exceeds the minimum required for soul-building and as a consequence of human freedom.

    Hence, if there is a God, that being is not all-PKG.

If the conclusion of this argument is to be rejected, one must provide a reason for thinking that premiss (6) or premiss (7) is false. Insisting that the mystery is too great is no reply to this third and final argument from evil.

Review Questions

1. One religious tradition holds that God is a being who is all-powerful, all-knowing, and all-good. Should we regard this proposition as a definition of what the word "God" means?
2. Does the existence of evil prove that God cannot exist?
3. What does it mean to say that some evils are "soul-building"?
4. Does the fact that some evils are soul-building while others are consequences of human freedom solve the problem of evil?

A Problem for Further Thought

Are there reasons beyond the goal of soul-building and the goal of giving us free will that an all-PKG God would have for allowing evil to exist? If so, would that solve the problem of evil?

·R·E·A·D·I·N·G·S·

Five Ways to Prove That God Exists

·SAINT THOMAS AQUINAS·

In this selection from Summa Theologica *(Part 1, Question 2, Article 3), Saint Thomas Aquinas provides five proofs of the existence of God. In each, an obvious and uncontroversial observation is the starting premiss.*

The existence of God can be proved in five ways.

The first and more manifest way is the argument from motion. It is certain, and evident to our senses, that in the world some things are in motion. Now whatever is moved is moved by another, for nothing can be moved except it is in potentiality to that towards which it is moved; whereas a thing moves inasmuch as it is in act. For motion is nothing else than the reduction of something from potentiality to actuality. But nothing can be reduced from potentiality to actuality, except by something in a state of actuality. Thus that which is actually hot, as fire, makes wood, which is potentially hot, to be actually hot, and thereby moves and changes it. Now it is not possible that the same thing should be at once in actuality and potentiality in the same respect, but only in different respects. For what is actually hot cannot simultaneously be potentially hot; but it is simultaneously potentially cold. It is therefore impossible that in the same respect and in the same way a thing should be both mover and moved, *i.e.*, that it should move itself. Therefore, whatever is moved must be moved by another. If that by which it is moved be itself moved, then this also must needs be moved by another, and that by another again. But this cannot go on to infinity, because then there would be no first mover, and, consequently, no other mover, seeing that subsequent movers move only inasmuch as they are moved by the first mover; as the staff moves only because it is moved by the hand. Therefore it is necessary to arrive at a first mover, moved by no other; and this everyone understands to be God.

The second way is from the nature of efficient cause. In the world of sensible things we find there is an order of efficient causes. There is no case known (neither is it, indeed, possible) in which a thing is found to be the efficient cause of itself; for so it would be prior to itself, which is impossible. Now in efficient causes it is not possible to go on to infinity, because in all efficient causes following in order, the first is the cause of the intermediate cause, and the intermediate is the cause of the ultimate cause, whether the intermediate cause be several, or one only. Now to take away the cause is to take away the effect. Therefore, if there be no first cause among efficient causes, there will be no ultimate, nor any intermediate, cause. But if in efficient causes it is possible to go on to infinity, there will be no first efficient cause, neither will there be an ultimate effect, nor any intermediate efficient causes; all of which is plainly false. Therefore it is necessary to admit a first efficient cause, to which everyone gives the name of God.

The third way is taken from possibility and necessity, and runs thus. We find in nature things that are possible to be and not to be, since they are found to be generated, and to be corrupted, and consequently, it is possible for them to be and not to be. But it is impossible for these always to exist, for that which can not-be at some time is not. Therefore, if everything can not-be, then at one time there was nothing in existence. Now if this were true, even now there would be nothing in existence, because that which does not exist begins to exist only through something already existing. Therefore, if at one time nothing was in existence, it would have been impossible for anything to have begun to exist; and thus even now nothing would be in existence — which is absurd. Therefore, not all beings are merely possible, but there must exist something the existence of which is necessary. But every necessary thing either has its necessity caused by another, or not. Now it is impossible to go on to infinity in necessary things which have their necessity caused by another, as has been already proved in regard to efficient causes. Therefore we cannot but admit the existence of some being having of itself its own necessity, and not receiving it from another, but rather causing in others their necessity. This all men speak of as God.

The fourth way is taken from the gradation to be found in things. Among beings there are some more and some less good, true, noble, and the like. But *more* and *less* are predicated of different things according as they resemble in their different ways something which is the maximum, as a thing is said to be hotter according as it more nearly resembles that which is hottest; so that there is something which is truest, something best, something noblest, and, consequently, something which is most being, for those things that are greatest in truth are greatest in being, as it is written in *Metaphysics* II [a work of Aristotle's]. Now the maximum in any genus is the cause of all in that genus, as fire, which is the maximum of heat, is the cause of all hot things, as is said in the same book. Therefore there must also be something which is to all beings the cause of their being, goodness, and every other perfection; and this we call God.

The fifth way is taken from the governance of the world. We see that things which lack knowledge, such as natural bodies, act for an end, and this is evident from their acting always, or nearly always, in the same way, so as to obtain the best result. Hence it is plain that they achieve their end, not fortuitously, but designedly. Now whatever lacks knowledge cannot move towards an end, unless it be directed by some being endowed with knowledge and intelligence; as the arrow is directed by the archer. Therefore some intelligent being exists by whom all natural things are directed to their end; and this being we call God.

The Design Argument

· WILLIAM PALEY ·

In this selection from his Natural Theology *(1805), William Paley elaborates an argument for the existence of God that traces back at least to the last of Aquinas' five ways. The term "natural theology" was used to label attempts to establish the existence and nature of God by rational means.*

I. State of the Argument

In crossing a heath, suppose I pitched my foot against a *stone*, and were asked how the stone came to be there, I might possibly answer, that for anything I knew to the contrary it had lain there forever; nor would it, perhaps, be very easy to show the absurdity of this answer. But suppose I had found a *watch* upon the ground, and it should be inquired how the watch happened to be in that place, I should hardly think of the answer which I had before given, that for anything I knew the watch might have always been there. Yet why should not this answer serve for the watch as well as for the stone; why is it not as admissible in the second case as in the first? For this reason, and for no other, namely, that when we come to inspect the watch, we perceive—what we could not discover in the stone—that its several parts are framed and put together for a purpose, *e.g.* that they are so formed and adjusted as to produce motion, and that motion so regulated as to point out the hour of the day; that if the different parts had been differently shaped from what they are, or placed after any other manner or in any other order than that in which they are placed, either no motion at all would have been carried on in the machine, or none which would have answered the use that is now served by it. To reckon up a few of the plainest of these parts and of their offices, all tending to one result: We see a cylindrical box containing a coiled elastic spring, which, by its endeavor, to relax itself, turns round the box. We next observe a flexible chain—artificially wrought for the sake of flexure—communicating the action of the spring from the box to the fusee. We then find a series of wheels, the teeth of which catch in and apply to each other, conducting the motion from the fusee to the balance and from the balance to the pointer, and at the same time, by the size and shape of those wheels, so regulating that motion as to terminate in causing an index, by an equable and measured progression, to pass over a given space in a given time. We take notice that the wheels are made of brass, in order to keep them from rust; the springs of steel, no other metal being so elastic; that over the face of the watch there is placed a glass, a material employed in no other part of the work, but in the room of which, if there had been any other than a transparent substance, the hour could not be seen without opening the case. This mechanism being observed — it requires indeed an examination of the instrument, and perhaps some previous knowledge of the subject, to perceive and understand it; but being once, as we have said, observed and understood, the inference we think is inevitable, that the watch must have had a maker — that there must have existed, at some time and at some place or other, an artificer or artificers who formed it for the purpose which we find it actually to answer, who comprehended its construction and designed its use. . . .

II. State of the Argument Continued

Suppose, in the next place, that the person who found the watch should after some time discover, that in addition to all the properties which he had hitherto observed in it, it possessed the unexpected property of producing in the course of its movement another watch like itself — the thing is conceivable; that it contained within it a mechanism, a system of parts — a mold, for instance, or a complex adjustment of lathes, files, and other tools — evidently and separately calculated for this purpose; let us inquire what effect ought such a discovery to have upon his former conclusion.

I. The first effect would be to increase his admiration of the contrivance, and his conviction of the consummate skill of the contriver. Whether he regarded the object of the contrivance, the distinct apparatus, the intricate, yet in many parts intelligible mechanism by which it was carried on, he would perceive in this new observation nothing but an additional reason for doing what he had already done — for referring the construction of the watch to design and to supreme art. If that construction *without* this property, or which is the same thing, before this property had been noticed, proved intention and art to have been employed about it, still more strong would the proof appear when he came to the knowledge of this further property, the crown and perfection of all the rest.

II. He would reflect, that though the watch before him were *in some sense* the maker of the watch which was fabricated in the course of its movements, yet it was in a very different sense from that in which a carpenter, for instance, is the maker of a chair — the author of its contrivance, the cause of the relation of its parts to their use. With respect to these, the first watch was no cause at all to the second; in no such sense as this was it the author of the constitution and order, either of the parts which the new watch contained, or of the parts by the aid and instrumentality of which it was produced. We might possibly say, but with great latitude of expression, that a stream of water ground corn; but no latitude of expression would allow us to say, no stretch of conjecture could lead us to think, that the stream of water built the mill, though it were too ancient for us to know who the builder was. What the stream of water does in the affair is neither more nor less than this: by the application of an unintelligent impulse to a mechanism previously arranged, arranged independently of it and arranged by intelligence, an effect is produced, namely, the corn is ground. But the effect results from the arrangement. The force of the stream cannot be said to be the cause or the author of the effect, still less of the arrangement. Understanding and plan in the formation of the mill were not the less necessary for any share which the water has in grinding the corn; yet is this share the same as that which the watch would have contributed to the production of the new watch, upon the supposition assumed in the last section. Therefore,

III. Though it be now no longer probable that the individual watch which our observer had found was made immediately by the hand of an artificer, yet doth not this alteration in anywise affect the inference, that an artificer had been originally employed and concerned in the production. The argument from design remains as it was. Marks of design and contrivance are no more accounted for now than they were before. In the same thing, we may ask for the cause of different properties. We may ask for the cause of the color of a body, of its hardness, of its heat; and these causes may be all different. We are now asking for the cause of that subserviency to a use, that relation to an end, which we have remarked in the watch before us. No answer is given to this question, by telling us that a preceding watch produced it. There cannot be design without a designer; contrivance, without a contriver; order, without choice; arrangement, without anything capable of arranging; subserviency and relation to a purpose, without that which could intend a purpose; means suitable to an end, and executing their office in accomplishing that end, without the end ever having been contemplated, or the means accommodated to it. Arrangement, disposition of parts, subserviency of means to an end, relation of instruments to a use, imply the presence of intelligence and mind. No one, therefore, can rationally believe that the insensible, inanimate watch, from which the watch before us issued, was the proper cause of the mechanism we so much admire in it — could be truly said to have constructed the instrument, disposed its parts, assigned their office, determined their order, action, and mutual dependency, combined their several motions into one result, and that also a result connected with the utilities of other beings. All these properties, therefore, are as much unaccounted for as they were before. . . .

The conclusion which the *first* examination of the watch, of its works, construction, and movement, suggested, was, that it must have had, for cause and author of that construction, an artificer who understood its mechanism and designed its use. This conclusion is invincible. A *second* examination presents us with a new discovery. The watch is found, in the course of its movement, to produce another watch similar to itself; and not only so, but we perceive in it a system or organization separately calculated for that purpose. What effect would this discovery have, or ought it to have, upon our former inference? What, as hath already been said, but to increase beyond measure our admiration of the skill which had been employed in the formation of such a machine? Or shall it, instead of this, all at once turn us round to an opposite conclusion, namely, that no art or skill whatever has been concerned in the business, although all other evidences of art and skill remain as they were, and this last and supreme piece of art be now added to the rest? Can this be maintained without absurdity? Yet this is atheism.

III. Application of the Argument

This is atheism; for every indication of contrivance, every manifestation of design which existed in the watch, exists in the works of nature, with the difference on the side of nature of being greater and more, and that in a degree which exceeds all computation. I mean, that the contrivances of nature surpass the contrivances of art, in the complexity, subtlety, and curiosity of the mechanism; and still more, if possible, do they go beyond them in number and variety; yet, in a multitude of cases, are not less evidently mechanical, not less evidently contrivances, not less evidently accommodated to their end or suited to their office, than are the most perfect productions of human ingenuity.

I know no better method of introducing so large a subject, than that of comparing a single thing with a single thing: an eye, for example, with a telescope. As far as the examination of the instrument goes, there is precisely the same proof that the eye was made for vision, as there is that the telescope was made for assisting it. They are made upon the same principles; both being adjusted to the laws by which the transmission and refraction of rays of light are regulated. I speak not of the origin of the laws themselves; but such laws being fixed, the construction in both cases is adapted to them. For instance, these laws require, in order to produce the same effect, that the rays of light, in passing from water into the eye, should be refracted by a more convex surface than when it passes out of air into the eye. Accordingly we find that the eye of a fish, in that part of it called the crystalline lens, is much rounder than the eye of terrestrial animals. What plainer manifestation of design can there be than this difference? What could a mathematical instrument maker have done more to show his knowledge of his principle, his application of that knowledge, his suiting of his means to his end—I will not say to display the compass or excellence of his skill and art, for in these all comparison is indecorous, but to testify counsel, choice, consideration, purpose?

Critique of the Design Argument

·DAVID HUME·

In this selection from his Dialogues Concerning Natural Religion *(1779),* Hume *describes a conversation between Cleanthes, Demea, and Philo. Hume did not publish this work during his lifetime, probably because he was apprehensive about what the public reaction would be.*

Not to lose any time in circumlocutions, said Cleanthes, addressing himself to Demea, much less in replying to the pious declamations of Philo, I shall briefly explain how I conceive this matter. Look round the world: Contemplate the whole and every part of it: You will find it to be nothing but one great machine, subdivided into an infinite number of lesser machines, which again admit of subdivisions to a degree beyond what human senses and faculties can trace and explain. All these various machines, and even their most minute parts, are adjusted to each other with an accuracy which ravishes into admiration all men who have ever contemplated them. The curious adapting of means to ends, throughout all nature, resembles exactly, though it much exceeds, the productions of human contrivance — of human design, thought, wisdom, and intelligence. Since therefore the effects resemble each other, we are led to infer, by all the rules of analogy, that the causes also resemble, and that the Author of Nature is somewhat similar to the mind of man, though possessed of much larger faculties, proportioned to the grandeur of the work which he has executed. By this argument *a posteriori*, and by this argument alone, do we prove at once the existence of a Deity and his similarity to human mind and intelligence.

I shall be so free, Cleanthes, said Demea, as to tell you that from the beginning I could not approve of your conclusion concerning the similarity of the Deity to men, still less can I approve of the mediums by which you endeavor to establish it. What! No demonstration of the Being of God! No abstract arguments! No proofs *a priori*! Are these which have hitherto been so much insisted on by philosophers all fallacy, all sophism? Can we reach no farther in this subject than experience and probability? I will say not that this is betraying the cause of a Deity; but surely, by this affected candor, you give advantages to atheists which they never could obtain by the mere dint of argument and reasoning.

What I chiefly scruple in this subject, said Philo, is not so much that all religious arguments are by Cleanthes reduced to experience, as that they appear not to be even the most certain and irrefragable of that inferior kind. That a stone will fall, that fire will burn, that the earth has solidity, we have observed a thousand and a thousand times; and when any new instance of this nature is presented, we draw without hesitation the accustomed inference. The exact similarity of the cases gives us a perfect assurance of a similar event, and a stronger evidence is never desired nor sought after. But wherever you depart, in the least, from the similarity of the cases, you diminish proportionably the evidence; and may at last bring it to a very weak *analogy*, which is confessedly liable to error and uncertainty. After having experienced the circulation of the blood in human creatures, we make no doubt that it takes place in Titius and Maevius; but from its circulation in frogs and fishes it is only a presumption, though a strong one, from analogy that it takes place in men and other animals. The analogical reasoning is much weaker when we infer the circulation of the sap in vegetables from our experience that the blood circulates in animals; and those who hastily followed that imperfect analogy are found, by more accurate experiments, to have been mistaken.

If we see a house, Cleanthes, we conclude, with the greatest certainty, that it had an architect or builder because this is precisely that species of effect which we have experienced to proceed from that species of cause. But surely you will not affirm that the universe bears such a resemblance to a house that we can with the same certainty infer a similar cause, or that the analogy is here entire and perfect. The dissimilitude is so striking that the utmost you can here pretend to is a guess, a conjecture, a presumption concerning a similar cause; and how that pretension will be received in the world, I leave you to consider.

It would surely be very ill received, replied Cleanthes; and I should be deservedly blamed and detested did I allow that the proofs of a Deity amounted to no more than a guess or conjecture. But is the whole adjustment of means to ends in a house and in the universe so slight a resemblance? the economy of final causes? the order, proportion, and arrangement of every part? Steps of a stair are plainly contrived that human legs may use them in mounting; and this inference is certain and infallible. Human legs are also contrived for walking and mounting; and this inference, I allow, is not altogether so certain because of the dissimilarity which you remark; but does it, therefore, deserve the name only of presumption or conjecture?

Good God! cried Demea, interrupting him, where are we? Zealous defenders of religion allow that the proofs of a Deity fall short of perfect evidence! And you, Philo, on whose assistance I depended in proving the adorable mysteriousness of the Divine Nature, do you assent to all these extravagant opinions of Cleanthes? For what other name can I give them? or, why spare my censure when such principles are advanced, supported by such an authority, before so young a man as Pamphilus?

You seem not to apprehend, replied Philo, that I argue with Cleanthes in his own way, and, by showing him the dangerous consequences of his tenets, hope at last to reduce him to our opinion. But what sticks most with you, I observe, is the representation which Cleanthes has made of the argument *a posteriori*; and, finding that that argument is likely to escape your hold and vanish into air, you think it so disguised that you can scarcely believe it to be set in its true light. Now, however much I may dissent, in other respects, from the dangerous principle of Cleanthes, I must allow that he has fairly represented that argument, and I shall endeavor so to state the matter to you that you will entertain no further scruples with regard to it.

Were a man to abstract from everything which he knows or has seen, he would be altogether incapable, merely from his own ideas, to determine what kind of scene the universe must be, or to give the preference to one state or situation of things above another. For as nothing which he clearly conceives could be esteemed impossible or implying a contradiction, every chimera of his fancy would be upon an equal footing; nor could he assign just reason why he adheres to one idea or system, and rejects the others which are equally possible.

Again, after he opens his eyes and contemplates the world as it really is, it would be impossible for him at first to assign the cause of any one event, much less the whole of things, or of the universe. He might set his fancy a rambling, and she might bring him in an infinite variety of reports and representations. These would all be possible; but, being all equally possible, he would never of himself give a satisfactory account for his preferring one of them to the rest. Experience alone can point out to him the true cause of any phenomenon.

CRITIQUE OF
THE DESIGN
ARGUMENT

Now, according to this method of reasoning, Demea, it follows (and is, indeed, tacitly allowed by Cleanthes himself) that order, arrangement, or the adjustment of final causes, is not of itself any proof of design, but only so far as it has been experienced to proceed from that principle. For aught we can know *a priori*, matter may contain the source or spring of order originally within itself, as well as mind does; and there is no more difficulty in conceiving that the several elements, from an internal unknown cause, may fall into the most exquisite arrangement, than to conceive that their ideas, in the great universal mind, from a like internal unknown cause, fall into that arrangement. The equal possibility of both these suppositions is allowed. But, by experience, we find (according to Cleanthes) that there is a difference between them. Throw several pieces of steel together, without shape or form they will never arrange themselves so as to compose a watch. Stone and mortar and wood, without an architect, never erect a house. But the ideas in a human mind, we see, by an unknown, inexplicable economy, arrange themselves so as to form the plan of a watch or house. Experience, therefore, proves that there is an original principle of order in mind, not in matter. From similar effects we infer similar causes. The adjustment of means to ends is alike in the universe, as in a machine of human contrivance. The causes, therefore, must be resembling.

I was from the beginning scandalized, I must own, with this resemblance which is asserted between the Deity and human creatures, and must conceive it to imply such a degradation of the Supreme Being as no sound theist could endure. With your assistance, therefore, Demea, I shall endeavor to defend what you justly call the adorable mysteriousness of the Divine nature, and shall refute this reasoning of Cleanthes, provided he allows that I have made a fair representation of it.

When Cleanthes had assented, Philo, after a short pause, proceeded in the following manner.

That all inferences, Cleanthes, concerning fact are founded on experience, and that all experimental reasonings are founded on the supposition that similar causes prove similar effects, and similar effects similar causes, I shall not at present much dispute with you. But observe, I entreat you, with what extreme caution all just reasoners proceed in the transferring of experiments to similar cases. Unless the cases be exactly similar, they repose no perfect confidence in applying their past observation to any particular phenomenon. Every alteration of circumstances occasions a doubt concerning the event; and it requires new experiments to prove certainly that the new circumstances are of no moment or importance. A change in bulk, situation, arrangement, age, disposition of the air, or surrounding bodies — any of these particulars may be attended with the most unexpected consequences. And unless the objects be quite familiar to us, it is the highest temerity to expect with assurance, after any of these changes, an event similar to that which before fell under our observation. The slow and deliberate steps of philosophers here, if anywhere, are distinguished from the precipitate march of the vulgar, who, hurried on by the smallest similitude, are incapable of all discernment or consideration.

But can you think, Cleanthes, that your usual phlegm and philosophy have been preserved in so wide a step as you have taken when you compared to the universe houses, ships, furniture, machines; and, from their similarity in some circumstances, inferred a similarity in their causes? Thought, design, intelligence, such as we discover in men and other animals, is no more than one of the springs and principles of the universe, as well as heat or cold, attraction or repulsion, and a hundred others which fall under daily observation. It is an active cause by which some particular parts of nature, we find, produce alterations on other parts. But can a conclusion, with any propriety, be transferred from parts to the whole? Does not the great disproportion bar all comparison and inference? From observing the growth of a hair, can we learn anything concerning the generation of a man? Would the manner of a leaf's blowing, even though perfectly known, afford us any instruction concerning the vegetation of a tree?

But allowing that we were to take the *operations* of one part of nature upon another for the foundation of our judgment concerning the *origin* of the whole (which never can be admitted), yet why select so minute, so weak, so bounded a principle as the reason and design of animals is found to be upon this planet? What peculiar privilege has this little agitation of the brain which we call *thought*, that we must thus make it the model of the whole universe? Our partiality in our own favor does indeed present it on all occasions, but sound philosophy ought carefully to guard against so natural an illusion.

So far from admitting, continued Philo, that the operations of a part can afford us any just conclusion concerning the origin of the whole, I will not allow any one part to form a rule for another part if the latter be very remote from the former. Is there any reasonable ground to conclude that the inhabitants of other planets possess thought, intelligence, reason, or anything similar to these faculties in men? When nature has so extremely diversified her manner of operation in this small globe, can we imagine that she incessantly copies herself throughout so immense a universe? And if thought, as we may well suppose, be confined merely to this narrow corner and has even there so limited a sphere of action, with what propriety can we assign it for the original cause of all things? The narrow views of a peasant who makes his domestic economy the rule for the government of kingdoms is in comparison a pardonable sophism.

But were we ever so much assured that a thought and reason resembling the human were to be found throughout the whole universe, and were its activity elsewhere vastly greater and more commanding than it appears in this globe; yet I cannot see why the operations of a world constituted, arranged, adjusted, can with any propriety be extended to a world which is in its embryo-state, and is advancing towards that constitution and arrangement. By observation we know somewhat of the economy, action, and nourishment of a finished animal; but we must transfer with great caution that observation to the growth of a foetus in the womb, and still more to the formation of an animalcule in the loins of its male parent. Nature, we find, even from our limited experience, possesses an infinite number of springs and principles which incessantly discover themselves on every change of her position and situation. And what new and unknown principles would actuate her in so new and unknown a situation as that of the formation of a universe, we cannot, without the utmost temerity, pretend to determine.

A very small part of this great system, during a very short time, is very imperfectly discovered to us; and do we thence pronounce decisively concerning the origin of the whole?

Admirable conclusion! Stone, wood, brick, iron, brass, have not, at this time, in this minute globe of earth, an order or arrangement without human art and contrivance; therefore, the universe could not originally attain its order and arrangement without something similar to human art. But is a part of nature a rule for another part very wide of the former? Is it a rule for the whole? Is a very small part a rule for the universe? Is nature in one situation a certain rule for nature in another situation vastly different from the former?

And can you blame me, Cleanthes, if I here imitate the prudent reserve of Simonides, who, according to the noted story, being asked by Hiero, *What God was?* desired a day to think of it, and then two days more; and after that manner continually prolonged the term, without ever bringing in his definition or description? Could you even blame me if I had answered, at first, *that I did not know*, and was sensible that this subject lay vastly beyond the reach of my faculties? You might cry out sceptic and railer, as much as you pleased; but, having found in so many other subjects much more familiar the imperfections and even contradictions of human reason, I never should expect any success from its feeble conjectures in a subject so sublime and so remote from the sphere of our observation. When two *species* of objects have always been observed to be conjoined together, I can *infer*, by custom, the existence of one wherever I *see* the existence of the other; and this I call an argument from experience. But how this argument can have place where the objects, as in the present case, are single, individual, without parallel or specific resemblance, may be difficult to explain. And will any man tell me with a serious countenance that an orderly universe must arise from some thought and art like the human because we have experience of it? To ascertain this reasoning it were requisite that we had experience of the origin of the worlds; and it is not sufficient, surely, that we have seen ships and cities arise from human art and contrivance. . . .

Philo was proceeding in this vehement manner, somewhat between jest and earnest, as it appeared to me, when he observed some signs of impatience in Cleanthes, and then immediately stopped short. What I had to suggest, said Cleanthes, is only that you would not abuse terms, or make use of popular expressions to subvert philosophical reasonings. You know that the vulgar often distinguish reason from experience, even where the question relates only to matter of fact and existence, though it is found, where that *reason* is properly analyzed, that it is nothing but a species of experience. To prove by experience the origin of the universe from mind is not more contrary to common speech than to prove the motion of the earth from the same principle. And a caviller might raise all the same objections to the Copernican system which you have urged against my reasonings. Have you other earths, might he say, which you have seen to move? Have . . .

Yes! cried Philo, interrupting him, we have other earths. Is not the moon another earth, which we see to turn round its center? Is not Venus another earth, where we observe the same phenomenon? Are not the revolutions of the sun also a confirmation, from analogy, of the same theory? All the planets, are they not earths which revolve about the sun? Are not the satellites moons which move round Jupiter and Saturn, and along with these primary planets round the sun? These analogies and resemblances, with others which I have not mentioned, are the sole proofs of the Copernican system; and to you it belongs to consider whether you have any analogies of the same kind to support your theory.

In reality, Cleanthes, continued he, the modern system of astronomy is now so much received by all inquirers, and has become so essential a part even of our earliest education, that we are not commonly very scrupulous in examining the reasons upon which it is founded. It is now become a matter of mere curiosity to study the first writers on that subject who had the full force of prejudice to encounter, and were obliged to turn their arguments on every side in order to render them popular and convincing. But if we peruse Galileo's famous *Dialogues* concerning the system of the world, we shall find that that great genius, one of the sublimest that ever existed, first bent all his endeavors to prove that there was no foundation for the distinction commonly made between elementary and celestial substances. The schools, proceeding from the illusions of sense, had carried this distinction very far; and had established the latter substances to be ingenerable, incorruptible, unalterable, impassible; and had assigned all the opposite qualities to the former. But Galileo, beginning with the moon, proved its similarity in every particular to the earth: its convex figure, its natural darkness when not illuminated, its density, its distinction into solid and liquid, the variations of its phases, the mutual illuminations of the earth and moon, their mutual eclipses, the inequalities of the lunar surface, etc. After many instances of this kind, with regard to all the planets, men plainly saw that these bodies became proper objects of experience, and that the similarity of their nature enabled us to extend the same arguments and phenomena from one to the other.

In this cautious proceeding of the astronomers you may read your own condemnation, Cleanthes; or rather may see that the subject in which you are engaged exceeds all human reason and inquiry. Can you pretend to show any such similarity between the fabric of a house and the generation of a universe? Have you ever seen nature in any such situation as resembles the first arrangement of the elements? Have worlds ever been formed under your eye, and have you had leisure to observe the whole progress of the phenomenon, from the first appearance of order to its final consummation? If you have, then cite your experience and deliver your theory.

The Ontological Argument

·SAINT ANSELM AND GAUNILO·

In this selection from the Proslogion, *Saint Anselm attempts to provide an* a priori *proof of the existence of God. Gaunilo, a contemporary of Anselm's, presents two criticisms of the argument. In one of them, he claims that if Anselm's argument establishes the existence of God, then the existence of a perfect island would be provable* a priori. *Anselm replies to each of Gaunilo's criticisms.*

Anselm

Chapter II. That God Truly Is

O Lord, you who give understanding to faith, so far as you know it to be beneficial, give me to understand that you are just as we believe, and that you are what we believe.

We certainly believe that you are something than which nothing greater can be conceived.

But is there any such nature, since "the fool has said in his heart: God is not"?

However, when this very same fool hears what I say, when he hears of "something than which nothing greater can be conceived," he certainly understands what he hears.

What he understands stands in relation to his understanding (*esse in intellectu*), even if he does not understand that it exists. For it is one thing for a thing to stand in relation to our understanding; it is another thing for us to understand that it really exists. For instance, when a painter imagines what he is about to paint, he has it in relation to his understanding. However, he does not yet understand that it exists, because he has not yet made it. After he paints it, then he both has it in relation to his understanding and understands that it exists. Therefore, even the fool is convinced that "something than which nothing greater can be conceived" at least stands in relation to his understanding, because when he hears of it he understands it, and whatever he understands stands in relation to his understanding.

And certainly that than which a greater cannot be conceived cannot stand only in relation to the understanding. For if it stands at least in relation to the understanding, it can be conceived to be also in reality, and this is something greater. Therefore, if "that than which a greater cannot be conceived" only stood in relation to the understanding, then "that than which a greater cannot be conceived" would be something than which a greater can be conceived. But this is certainly impossible.

Therefore, something than which a greater cannot be conceived undoubtedly both stands in relation to the understanding and exists in reality.

Chapter III. That It Is Impossible To Conceive That God Is Not

This so truly is that it is impossible to think of it as not existing.

It can be conceived to be something such that we cannot conceive of it as not existing.

This is greater than something which we can conceive of as not existing.

Therefore, if that than which a greater cannot be conceived could be conceived not to be, we would have an impossible contradiction: That than which a greater cannot be conceived would not be that than which a greater cannot be conceived.

Therefore, something than which a greater cannot be conceived so truly is, that it is impossible even to conceive of it as not existing.

This is you, O Lord our God. You so truly are that you cannot be thought not to be. And rightly so.

For if some mind could conceive of something better than you, the creature would rise above its Creator and would judge its Creator, which would be completely absurd.

Also, whatever else there is, except for you alone, can be conceived not to be.

Therefore, you alone, of all things exist in the truest and greatest way (*verissime et maxime esse*), for nothing else so truly exists and therefore everything else has less being.

Why, then, did the fool say in his heart: "God is not," since it is so obvious to the rational mind that you exist supremely above all things? Why, because he is stupid and foolish.

Chapter IV. How the Fool Said in His Heart
What Cannot Be Conceived

How was the fool able to "say in his heart" what he was unable to conceive? Or how was it that he could not conceive what he said in his heart? For to "say in one's heart" and to "conceive" are the same thing.

However, if—or rather because—he really did conceive of it (since he said it in his heart) and yet did not really say it in his heart (since he was unable to conceive of it), then there must be more than one way for something to be said in one's heart, or to be conceived.

Indeed, a thing is conceived of in one way when the word signifying it is thought; in another way when the very thing itself is understood.

Accordingly, God can be conceived not to be in the first way, but not at all in the second. Certainly no one who understands what God is can conceive that God is not. It is possible, however, for him to say this word in his heart, while giving it either no meaning at all or some alien meaning.

God is that than which a greater cannot be conceived. Whoever understands this correctly at least understands that he exists in such a way that even for thought he cannot not exist. Therefore, whoever understands that God is so cannot even conceive that he is not.

My thanksgiving to you, good Lord, my thanksgiving to you. For what I first believed through your giving I now so understand through your illumination that even if I did not want to believe that you are, I would be unable not to understand it.

Gaunilo

Consider this example: Certain people say that somewhere in the ocean there is an island, which they call the "Lost Island" because of the difficulty or, rather, the impossibility of finding what does not exist. They say that it is more abundantly filled with inestimable riches and delights than the Isles of the Blessed, and that although it has no owner or inhabitant, it excels all the lands that men inhabit taken together in the unceasing abundance of its fertility.

When someone tells me that there is such an island, I easily understand what is being said, for there is nothing difficult here. Suppose, however, as a consequence of this, that he then goes on to say: You cannot doubt that this island, more excellent than all lands, actually exists somewhere in reality, because it undoubtedly stands in relation to your understanding. Since it is more excellent, not simply to stand in relation to the understanding, but to be in reality as well, therefore this island must necessarily be in reality. Otherwise, any other land that exists in reality would be more excellent than this island, and this island, which you understand to be the most excellent of all lands would then not be the most excellent.

If, I repeat, someone should wish by this argument to demonstrate to me that this island truly exists and is no longer to be doubted, I would think he were joking; or, if I accepted the argument, I do not know whom I would regard as the greater fool, me for accepting it or him for supposing that he had proved the existence of this island with any kind of certainty. He should first show that this excellent island exists as a genuine and undeniable real thing, and not leave it standing in relation to my understanding as a false or uncertain something.

Anselm

My reasoning, you claim, is as if someone should say that there is an island in the ocean, which surpasses the whole earth in its fertility, but which is called a "Lost Island" because of the difficulty, or even impossibility, of finding something that does not exist; and as if he should then argue that no one can doubt that it actually does exist because the words describing it are easily understood.

I can confidently say that if anyone discovers for me something existing either in fact or at least in thought, other than "that than which a greater cannot be conceived," and is able to apply the logic of my argument to it, I shall find that "Lost Island" for him and shall give it to him as something which he will never lose again.

Gaunilo

When it is asserted to the fool [in *Proslogion* III] that this "greater than all things" is such that even to thought it cannot not be, and yet when this is proved to him on no other ground than that otherwise this "greater than all things" would not be greater than all things, he can give the same answer and reply: When did *I* ever say that such a being, one that is "greater than all things," exists in reality, so that from this you could prove to me that it exists so fully in reality that it cannot be conceived not to be? First of all, it should be proved by some most certain argument that some superior reality, that is, a nature which is greater and better than everything that is, actually exists. From this we can then prove all the other qualities which must not be lacking from that which is greater and better than all things.

Anselm

That which cannot possibly not be is obviously something that can be conceived and understood. He who conceives of this conceives of something greater than he who conceives of that which has the possibility of not being. Therefore, while he is conceiving of "that than which a greater cannot be conceived," if he conceives that it has the possibility of not being, he is obviously not conceiving of "that than which a greater cannot be conceived." However, the same thing cannot be both conceived and not conceived at the same time. Therefore, he who conceives of "that than which a greater cannot be conceived" is not conceiving of what can, but of what cannot possibly, not be. For that reason, what he is conceiving must necessarily exist, because whatever is able not to exist is not that of which he is conceiving.

The Meaninglessness of Religious Discourse

· ALFRED JULES AYER ·

In this selection from Language, Truth, and Logic *(1936), A. J. Ayer argues that the positivist theory of meaning shows that the claim that God exists is neither true nor false—it is meaningless.*

It is now generally admitted, at any rate by philosophers, that the existence of a being having the attributes which define the god of any non-animistic religion cannot be demonstratively proved. To see that this is so, we have only to ask ourselves what are the premises from which the existence of such a god could be deduced. If the conclusion that a god exists is to be demonstratively certain, then these premises must be certain; for, as the conclusion of a deductive argument is already contained in the premises, any uncertainty there may be about the truth of the premises is necessarily shared by it. But we know that no empirical proposition can ever be anything more than probable. It is only *a priori* propositions that are logically certain. But we cannot deduce the existence of a god from an *a priori* proposition. For we know that the reason *a priori* propositions are certain is that they are tautologies. And from a set of tautologies nothing but a further tautology can be validly deduced. It follows that there is no possibility of demonstrating the existence of a god.

What is not so generally recognised is that there can be no way of proving that the existence of a god, such as the God of Christianity, is even probable. Yet this also is easily shown. For if the existence of such a god were probable, then the proposition that he existed would be an empirical hypothesis. And in that case it would be possible to deduce from it, and other empirical hypotheses, certain experiential propositions which were not deducible from those other hypotheses alone. But in fact this is not possible. It is sometimes claimed, indeed, that the existence of a certain sort of regularity in nature constitutes sufficient evidence for the existence of a god. But if the sentence "God exists" entails no more than that certain types of phenomena occur in certain sequences, then to assert the existence of a god will be simply equivalent to asserting that there is the requisite regularity in nature; and no religious man would admit that this was all he intended to assert in asserting the existence of a god. He would say that in talking about God, he was talking about a transcendent being who might be known through certain empirical manifestations, but certainly could not be defined in terms of those manifestations. But in that case the term "god" is a metaphysical term. And if "god" is a metaphysical term, then it cannot be even probable that a god exists. For to say that "God exists" is to make a metaphysical utterance which cannot be either true or false. And by the same criterion, no sentence which purports to describe the nature of a transcendent god can possess any literal significance.

It is important not to confuse this view of religious assertions with the view that is adopted by atheists, or agnostics.[1] For it is characteristic of an agnostic to hold that the existence of a god is a possibility in which there is no good reason either to believe or disbelieve; and it is characteristic of an atheist to hold that it is at least probable that no god exists. And our view that all utterances about the nature of God are nonsensical, so far from being identical with, or even lending any support to, either of these familiar contentions, is actually incompatible with them. For if the assertion that there is a god is nonsensical, then the atheist's assertion that there is no god is equally nonsensical, since it is only a significant proposition that can be significantly contradicted. As for the agnostic, although he refrains from saying either that there is or that there is not a god, he does not deny that the question whether a transcendent god exists is a genuine

---

[1]This point was suggested to me by Professor H. H. Price.

question. He does not deny that the two sentences "There is a transcendent god" and "There is no transcendent god" express propositions one of which is actually true and the other false. All he says is that we have no means of telling which of them is true, and therefore ought not to commit ourselves to either. But we have seen that the sentences in question do not express propositions at all. And this means that agnosticism also is ruled out.

Thus we offer the theist the same comfort as we gave to the moralist. His assertions cannot possibly be valid, but they cannot be invalid either. As he says nothing at all about the world, he cannot justly be accused of saying anything false, or anything for which he has insufficient grounds. It is only when the theist claims that in asserting the existence of a trancendent god he is expressing a genuine proposition that we are entitled to disagree with him.

It is to be remarked that in cases where deities are identified with natural objects, assertions concerning them may be allowed to be significant. If, for example, a man tells me that the occurrence of thunder is alone both necessary and sufficient to establish the truth of the proposition that Jehovah is angry, I may conclude that, in his usage of words, the sentence "Jehovah is angry" is equivalent to "It is thundering." But in sophisticated religions, though they may be to some extent based on men's awe of natural process which they cannot sufficiently understand, the "person" who is supposed to control the empirical world is not himself located in it; he is held to be superior to the empirical world, and so outside it; and he is endowed with super-empirical attributes. But the notion of a person whose essential attributes are non-empirical is not an intelligible notion at all. We may have a word which is used as if it named this "person," but, unless the sentences in which it occurs express propositions which are empirically verifiable, it cannot be said to symbolize anything. And this is the case with regard to the word "god," in the usage in which it is intended to refer to a transcendent object. The mere existence of the noun is enough to foster the illusion that there is a real, or at any rate a possible entity corresponding to it. It is only when we enquire what God's attributes are that we discover that "God," in this usage, is not a genuine name.

It is common to find belief in a transcendent god conjoined with belief in an after-life. But, in the form which it usually takes, the content of this belief is not a genuine hypothesis. To say that men do not ever die, or that the state of death is merely a state of prolonged insensibility, is indeed to express a significant proposition, though all the available evidence goes to show that it is false. But to say there is something imperceptible inside a man, which is his soul or his real self, and that it goes on living after he is dead, is to make a metaphysical assertion which has no more factual content than the assertion that there is a transcendent god.

It is worth mentioning that, according to the account which we have given of religious assertions, there is no logical ground for antagonism between religion and natural science. As far as the question of truth or falsehood is concerned, there is no opposition between the natural scientist and the theist who believes in a transcendent god. For since the religious utterances of the theist are not genuine propositions at all, they cannot stand in any logical relation to the propositions of science. Such antagonism as there is between religion and science appears to consist in the fact that science takes away one of the motives which make men religious. For it is acknowledged that one of the ultimate sources of religious feeling lies in the inability of men to determine their own destiny; and science tends to destroy the feeling of awe with which men regard an alien world, by making them believe that they can understand and anticipate the course of natural phenomena, and even to some extent control it. The fact that it has recently become fashionable for physicists themselves to be sympathetic towards religion is a point in favour of this hypothesis. For this sympathy towards religion marks the physicists' own lack of confidence in the validity of their hypotheses, which is a reaction on their part from the anti-religious dogmatism of nineteenth-century scientists, and a natural outcome of the crisis through which physics has just passed.

It is not within the scope of this enquiry to enter more deeply into the causes of religious feeling, or to discuss the probability of the continuance of religious belief. We are concerned only to answer those questions which arise out of our discussion of the possibility of religious knowledge. The point which we wish to establish is that there cannot be any transcendent truths of religion. For the sentences which the theist uses to express such "truths" are not literally significant.

An interesting feature of this conclusion is that it accords with what many theists are accustomed to say themselves. For we are often told that the nature of God is a mystery which transcends the human understanding. But to say that something transcends the human understanding is to say that it is unintelligible. And what is unintelligible cannot significantly be described. Again, we are told that God is not an object of reason but an object of faith. This may be nothing more than an admission that the existence of God must be taken on trust, since it cannot be proved. But it may also be an assertion that God is the object of a purely mystical intuition, and cannot therefore be defined in terms which are intelligible to the reason. And I think there are many theists who would assert this. But if one allows that it is impossible to define God in intelligible terms, then one is allowing that it is impossible for a sentence both to be significant and to be about God. If a mystic admits that the object of his vision is something which cannot be described, then he must also admit that he is bound to talk nonsense when he describes it.

For his part, the mystic may protest that his intuition does reveal truths to him, even though he cannot explain to others what these truths are; and that we who do not possess this faculty of intuition can have no ground for denying that it is a cognitive faculty. For we can hardly maintain *a priori* that there are no ways of discovering true propositions except those which we ourselves employ. The answer is that we set no limit to the number of ways in which one may come to formulate a true proposition. We do not in any way deny that a synthetic truth may be discovered by purely intuitive methods as well as by the rational method of induction. But we do say that every synthetic proposition, however it may have been arrived at, must be subject to the test of actual experience. We do not deny *a priori* that the mystic is able to discover truths by his own special methods. We wait to hear what are the propositions which embody his discoveries, in order to see whether they are verified or confuted by our empirical observations. But the mystic, so far from producing propositions which are empirically verified, is unable to produce any intelligible propositions at all. And therefore we say that his intuition has not revealed to him any facts. It is no use his saying that he has apprehended facts but is unable to express them. For we know that if he really had acquired any information, he would be able to express it. He would be able to indicate in some way or other how the genuineness of his discovery might be empirically determined. The fact that he cannot reveal what he "knows," or even himself devise an empirical test to validate his "knowledge," shows that his state of mystical intuition is not a genuinely cognitive state. So that in describing his vision the mystic does not give us any information about the external world; he merely gives us indirect information about the condition of his own mind.

These considerations dispose of the argument from religious experience, which many philosophers still regard as a valid argument in favour of the existence of a god. They say that it is logically possible for men to be immediately acquainted with God, as they are immediately acquainted with a sense-content, and that there is no reason why one should be prepared to believe a man when he says that he is seeing a yellow patch, and refuse to believe him when he says that he is seeing God. The answer to this is that if the man who asserts that he is seeing God is merely asserting that he is experiencing a peculiar kind of sense-content, then we do not for a moment deny that his assertion may be true. But, ordinarily, the man who says that he is seeing God is saying not merely that he is experiencing a religious emotion, but also that there exists a transcendent being who is the object of this emotion; just as the man who says that he sees a yellow patch is ordinarily saying not merely that his visual sense-field contains a yellow sense-content, but also that there exists a yellow object to which the sense-content belongs. And it is not irrational to be prepared to believe a man when he asserts the existence of a yellow object, and to refuse to believe him when he asserts the existence of a transcendent god. For whereas the sentence "There exists here a yellow-coloured material thing" expresses a genuine synthetic proposition which could be empirically verified, the sentence "There exists a transcendent god" has, as we have seen, no literal significance.

We conclude, therefore, that the argument from religious experience is altogether fallacious. The fact that people have religious experiences is interesting from the psychological point of view, but it does not in any way imply that there is such a thing as religious knowledge, any more than our having moral experiences implies that there is such a thing as moral knowledge. The theist, like the moralist, may believe that his experiences are cognitive experiences, but, unless he can formulate his "knowledge" in propositions that are empirically verifiable, we may be sure that he is deceiving himself. It follows that those philosophers who fill their books with assertions that they intuitively "know" this or that moral or religious "truth" are merely providing material for the psychoanalyst.

For no act of intuition can be said to reveal a truth about any matter of fact unless it issues in verifiable propositions. And all such propositions are to be incorporated in the system of empirical propositions which constitutes science.

Defending Atheism

·ERNEST NAGEL·

In this excerpt from his essay "Philosophical Concepts of Atheism" (1959), Nagel reviews and criticizes some standard arguments for thinking that there is a God. Besides evaluating these criticisms, you should consider what positive argument Nagel develops for thinking that atheism is correct.

I

I must begin by stating what sense I am attaching to the word "atheism," and how I am construing the theme of this essay. I shall understand by "atheism" a critique and a denial of the major claims of all varieties of theism. And by theism I shall mean the view which holds, as one writer has expressed it, "that the heavens and the earth and all that they contain owe their existence and continuance in existence to the wisdom and will of a supreme, self-consistent, omnipotent, omniscient, righteous, and benevolent being, who is distinct from, and independent of, what he has created." Several things immediately follow from these definitions.

In the first place, atheism is not necessarily an irreligious concept, for theism is just one among many views concerning the nature and origin of the world. The denial of theism is logically compatible with a religious outlook upon life, and is in fact characteristic of some of the great historical religions. For as readers of this volume will know, early Buddhism is a religion which does not subscribe to any doctrine about a god; and there are pantheistic religions and philosophies which, because they deny that God is a being separate from and independent of the world, are not theistic in the sense of the word explained above.

The second point to note is that atheism is not to be identified with sheer unbelief, or with disbelief in some particular creed of a religious group. Thus, a child who has received no religious instruction and has never heard about God, is not an atheist—for he is not denying any theistic claims. Similarly, an adult who has withdrawn from the faith of his fathers without reflection or because of frank indifference to any theological issue is also not an atheist—for such an adult is not challenging theism and is not professing any views on the subject. . . .

One final word of preliminary explanation. I propose to examine some *philosophic* concepts of atheism, and I am not interested in the slightest in the many considerations atheists have advanced against the evidences for some particular religious and theological doctrine—for example, against the truth of the Christian story. What I mean by "philosophical" in the present context is that the views I shall consider are directed against any form of theism, and have their origin and basis in a logical analysis of the theistic position, and in a comprehensive account of the world believed to be wholly intelligible without the adoption of a theistic hypothesis. . . .

II

As I see it, atheistic philosophies fall into two major groups: (1) those which hold that the theistic doctrine is meaningful, but reject it either on the ground that (a) the positive evidence for it is insufficient or (b) the negative evidence is quite overwhelming; and (2) those who hold that the theistic thesis is not even meaningful, and reject it (a) as just nonsense or (b) as literally meaningless, but interpreting it as a symbolic rendering of human ideals, thus reading the theistic thesis in a sense that most believers in theism would disavow. It will not be possible in the limited space at my disposal to discuss the second category of atheistic critiques; and in any event, most of the traditional atheistic critiques of theism belong to the first group.

But before turning to the philosophical examination of the major classical arguments for theism, it is well to note that such philosophical critiques do not quite convey the passion with which atheists have often carried on their analyses of theistic views. For historically, atheism has been, and indeed continues to be, a form of social and political protest, directed as much against institutionalized religion as against theistic doctrine. Atheism has been, in effect, a moral revulsion against the undoubted abuses of the secular power exercised by religious leaders and religious institutions.

Religious authorities have opposed the correction of glaring injustices, and encouraged politically and socially reactionary policies. Religious institutions have been havens of obscurantist thought and centers for the dissemination of intolerance. Religious creeds have been used to set limits to free inquiry, to perpetuate inhumane treatment of the ill and the underprivileged, and to support moral doctrines insensitive to human suffering.

These indictments may not tell the whole story about the historical significance of religion; but they are at least an important part of the story. The refutation of theism has thus seemed to many an indispensable step not only toward liberating men's minds from superstition but also toward achieving a more equitable reordering of society. And no account of even the more philosophical aspects of atheistic thought is adequate which does not give proper recognition to the powerful social motives that actuate many atheistic arguments.

But however this may be, I want now to discuss three classical arguments for the existence of God, arguments which have constituted at least a partial basis for theistic commitments. As long as theism is defended simply as dogma, asserted as a matter of direct revelation or as the deliverance of authority, belief in the dogma is impregnable to rational argument. In fact, however, reasons are frequently advanced in support of the theistic creed, and these reasons have been the subject of acute philosophical critiques.

III

One of the oldest intellectual defenses of theism is the cosmological argument, also known as the argument from a first cause. Briefly put, the argument runs as follows. Every event must have a cause. Hence an event A must have as cause some event B, which in turn must have a cause C, and so on. But if there is no end to this backward progression of causes, the progression will be infinite; and in the opinion of those who use this argument, an infinite series of actual events is unintelligible and absurd. Hence there must be a first cause, and this first cause is God, the initiator of all change in the universe.

The argument is an ancient one . . . and it has impressed many generations of exceptionally keen minds. The argument is nonetheless a weak reed on which to rest the theistic thesis. Let us waive any question concerning the validity of the principle that every event has a cause, for though the question is important its discussion would lead us far afield. However, if the principle is assumed, it is surely incongruous to postulate a first cause as a way of escaping from the coils of an infinite series. For if everything must have a cause, why does not God require one for His own existence? The standard answer is that He does not need any, because He is self-caused. But if God can be self-caused, why cannot the world be self-caused? Why do we require a God transcending the world to bring the world into existence and to initiate changes in it? On the other hand, the supposed inconceivability and absurdity of an infinite series of regressive causes will be admitted by no one who has competent familiarity with the modern mathematical analysis of infinity. The cosmological argument does not stand up under scrutiny.

The second "proof" of God's existence is usually called the ontological argument. It too has a long history going back to early Christian days, though it acquired great prominence only in medieval times. The argument can be stated in several ways, one of which is the following. Since God is conceived to be omnipotent, he is a perfect being. A perfect being is defined as one whose essence or nature lacks no attributes (or properties) whatsoever, one whose nature is complete in every respect. But it is evident that we have an idea of a perfect being, for we have just defined the idea; and since this is so, the argument continues, God who is the perfect being must exist. Why must he? Because his existence follows from his defined nature. For if God lacked the attribute of existence, he would be lacking at least one attribute, and would therefore not be perfect. To sum up, since we have an idea of God as a perfect being, God must exist.

There are several ways of approaching this argumemt, but I shall consider only one. The argument was exploded by the 18th century philosopher Immanuel

Kant. The substance of Kant's criticism is that it is just a confusion to say that existence is an attribute, and that though the *word* "existence" may occur as the grammatical predicate in a sentence, no attribute is being predicated of a thing when we say that the thing exists or has existence. Thus, to use Kant's example, when we think of $100 we are thinking of the nature of this sum of money; but the nature of $100 remains the same whether we have $100 in our pockets or not. Accordingly, we are confounding grammar with logic if we suppose that some characteristic is being attributed to the nature of $100 when we say that a $100 bill exists in someone's pocket.

To make the point clearer, consider another example. When we say that a lion has a tawny color, we are predicating a certain attribute of the animal, and similarly when we say that the lion is fierce or is hungry. But when we say the lion exists, all that we are saying is that something is (or has the nature of) a lion; we are not specifying an attribute which belongs to the nature of anything that is a lion. In short, the word "existence" does not signify any attribute, and in consequence no attribute that belongs to the nature of anything. Accordingly, it does not follow from the assumption that we have an idea of a perfect being that such a being exists. For the idea of a perfect being does not involve the attribute of existence as a constituent of that idea, since there is no such attribute. The ontological argument thus has a serious leak and it can hold no water.

IV

The two arguments discussed thus far are purely dialectical, and attempt to establish God's existence without any appeal to empirical data. The next argument, called the argument from design, is different in character, for it is based on what purports to be empirical evidence. . . .

One variant of it calls attention to the remarkable way in which different things and processes in the world are integrated with each other, and concludes that this mutual "fitness" of things can be explained only by the assumption of a divine architect who planned the world and everything in it. For example, living organisms can maintain themselves in a variety of environments, and do so in virtue of their delicate mechanisms which adapt the organisms to all sorts of environmental changes. There is thus an intricate pattern of means and ends throughout the animate world. But the existence of this pattern is unintelligible, so the argument runs, except on the hypothesis that the pattern has been deliberately instituted by a Supreme Designer. If we find a watch in some deserted spot, we do not think it came into existence by chance, and we do not hesitate to conclude that an intelligent creature designed and made it. But the world and all its contents exhibit mechanisms and mutual adjustments that are far more complicated and subtle than are those of a watch. Must we not therefore conclude that these things too have a Creator?

The conclusion of this argument is based on an inference from analogy: The watch and the world are alike in possessing a congruence of parts and an adjustment of means to ends; the watch has a watch-maker; hence the world has a world-maker. But is the analogy a good one? Let us once more waive some important issues, in particular the issue of whether the universe is the unified system such as the watch admittedly is. And let us concentrate on the question of what is the ground for our assurance that watches do not come into existence except through the operations of intelligent manufacturers. The answer is plain. We have never run across a watch which has not been deliberately made by someone. But the situation is nothing like this in the case of the innumerable animate and inanimate systems with which we are familiar. Even in the case of living organisms, though they are generated by their parent organisms, the parents do not "make" their progeny in the same sense in which watchmakers make watches. And once this point is clear, the inference from the existence of living organisms to the existence of a supreme designer no longer appears credible.

Moreover, the argument loses all its force if the facts which the hypothesis of a divine designer is supposed to explain can be understood on the basis of a better supported assumption. And indeed, such an alternative explanation is one of the achievements of Darwinian biology. For Darwin showed that one can account for the variety of biological species, as well as for their adaptations to their environments, without invoking a divine creator and acts of special creation. The Darwinian theory explains the diversity of biological species in terms of chance variations in the structure of organisms, and of a mechanism of selection which retains those variation forms that possess some advantages for survival. The evidence for these assumptions is considerable; and developments subsequent to Darwin have only strengthened the case for a thoroughly naturalistic explanation of the facts of biological adaptation. In any event, this version of the argument from design has nothing to recommend it. . . .

V

The inconclusiveness of the three classical arguments for the existence of God was already made evident by Kant, in a manner substantially not different from the above discussion. There are, however, other types of arguments for theism that have been influential in the history of thought, two of which I wish to consider, even if only briefly.

Indeed, though Kant destroyed the classical intellectual foundations for theism, he himself invented a fresh argument for it. Kant's attempted proof is not intended to be a purely theoretical demonstration, and is based on the supposed facts of our moral nature. It has exerted an enormous influence on subsequent theological speculation. In barest outline, the argument is as follows. According to Kant, we are subject not only to physical laws like the rest of nature, but also to moral ones. These moral laws are categorical imperatives, which we must heed not because of their utilitarian consequences but simply because as autonomous moral agents it is our duty to accept them as binding. However, Kant was keenly aware that though virtue may be its reward, the virtuous man (that is, the man who acts out of a sense of duty and in conformity with the moral law) does not always receive his just desserts in this world; nor did he shut his eyes to the fact that evil men frequently enjoy the best things this world has to offer. In short, virtue does not always reap happiness. Nevertheless, the highest human good is the realization of happiness commensurate with one's virtue; and Kant believed that it is a practical postulate of the moral life to promote this good. But what can guarantee that the highest good is realizable? Such a guarantee can be found only in God, who must therefore exist if the highest good is not to be a fatuous ideal. The existence of an omnipotent, omniscient, and omnibenevolent God is thus postulated as a necessary condition for the possibility of a moral life.

Despite the prestige this argument has acquired, it is difficult to grant it any force. It is enough to postulate God's existence. But as Bertrand Russell observed in another connection, postulation has all the advantages of theft over honest toil. No postulation carries with it any assurance that what is postulated is actually the case. And though we may postulate God's existence as a means to guaranteeing the possibility of realizing happiness together with virtue, the postulation establishes neither the actual realizability of this ideal nor the fact of his existence. Moreover, the argument is not made more cogent when we recognize that it is based squarely on the highly dubious conception that considerations of utility and human happiness must not enter into the determination of what is morally obligatory. . . .

One further type of argument, pervasive in much Protestant theological literature, deserves brief mention. Arguments of this type take their point of departure from the psychology of religious and mystical experience. Those who have undergone such experiences often report that during the experience they feel themselves to be in the presence of the divine and holy, that they lose their sense of self-identity and become merged with some fundamental reality, or that they enjoy a feeling of total dependence upon some ultimate power. The overwhelming sense of transcending one's finitude, which characterizes such vivid periods of life, and of coalescing with some ultimate source of all existence, is then taken to be compelling evidence for the existence of a supreme being. In a variant form of this argument, other theologians have identified God as the object which satisfies the commonly experienced need for integrating one's scattered and conflicting impulses into a coherent unity, or as the subject which is of ultimate concern to us. In short, a proof of God's existence is found in the occurrence of certain distinctive experiences.

It would be flying in the face of well-attested facts were one to deny that such experiences frequently occur. But do these facts constitute evidence for the conclusion based on them? Does the fact, for example, that an individual experiences a profound sense of direct contact with an alleged transcendent ground of all reality, constitute competent evidence for the claim that there is such a ground and that it is the immediate cause of the experience? If well-established canons for evaluating evidence are accepted, the answer is surely negative. No one will dispute that many men do have vivid experiences in which such things as ghosts or pink elephants appear before them; but only the hopelessly credulous will without further ado count such experiences as establishing the existence of ghosts and pink elephants. To establish the existence of such things, evidence is required that is obtained under controlled conditions and that can be confirmed by independent inquirers. Again, though a man's report that he is suffering pain may be taken at face value, one cannot take at face value the claim, were he to make it, that it is the food he ate which is the cause (or a contributory cause) of his felt pain — not even if the man were to report a vivid feeling of abdominal disturbance. And similarly, an overwhelming feeling of being in the presence of the Divine is evidence enough for admitting the genuineness of such feeling; it is no evidence for the claim that a supreme being with a substantial existence independent of the experience is the cause of the experience.

VI

Thus far the discussion has been concerned with *noting inadequacies in various arguments widely used to support theism.* However, much atheistic criticism is also directed toward *exposing incoherencies in the very thesis of theism.* I want therefore to consider this aspect of the theistic critique, though I will restrict myself to the central difficulty in the theistic position, which arises from the simultaneous attribution of omnipotence, omniscience, and omnibenevolence to the Deity. The difficulty is that of reconciling these attributes with the occurrence of evil in the world. Accordingly, the question to which I now turn is whether, despite the existence of evil, it is possible to construct a theodicy which will justify the ways of an infinitely powerful and just God to man. . . .

I do not believe it is possible to reconcile the alleged omnipotence and omnibenevolence of God with the unvarnished facts of human existence. In point of fact, many theologians have concurred in this conclusion; for in order to escape from the difficulty which the traditional attributes of God present, they have assumed that God is not all-powerful, and that there are limits as to what he can do in his efforts to establish a righteous order in the universe. But whether such a modified theology is better off is doubtful; and in any event, the question still remains whether the facts of human life support the claim that an omnibenevolent Deity, though limited in power, is revealed in the ordering of human history. It is pertinent to note in this connection that though there have been many historians who have made the effort, no historian has yet succeeded in showing to the satisfaction of his professional colleagues that the hypothesis of a Divine Providence is capable of explaining anything which cannot be explained just as well without this hypothesis.

VII

This last remark naturally leads to the question whether, apart from their polemics against theism, philosophical atheists have not shared a common set of positive views, a common set of philosophical convictions which set them off from other groups of thinkers. In one very clear sense of this query the answer is indubitably negative. For there never has been what one might call a "school of atheism" in the way in which there has been a Platonic school or even a Kantian school. . . .

Nevertheless, despite the variety of philosophic positions to which atheists have subscribed at one time or another in the history of thought, it seems to me that atheism is not simply a negative standpoint. At any rate, there is a certain quality of intellectual temper that has characterized, and continues to characterize, many philosophical atheists. . . . I want therefore to conclude this discussion with a brief enumeration of some points of positive doctrine to which by and large philosophical atheists seem to me to subscribe. . . .

In the first place, philosophical atheists reject the assumption that there are disembodied spirits, or that incorporeal entities of any sort can exercise a causal agency. On the contrary, atheists are generally agreed that if we wish to achieve any understanding of what takes place in the universe, we must look to the operations of organized bodies. Accordingly, the various processes taking place in nature, whether animate or inanimate, are to be explained in terms of the properties and structures of identifiable and spatiotemporally located objects. Moreover, the present variety of systems and activities found in the universe is to be accounted for on the basis of the transformations things undergo when they enter into different relations with one another—transformations which often result in the emergence of novel kinds of objects. . . .

In the second place, atheists generally manifest a marked empirical temper, and often take as their ideal the intellectual methods employed in the contemporaneous empirical sciences. Philosophical atheists differ considerably on important points of detail in their account of how responsible claims to knowledge are to be established. But there is substantial agreement among them that controlled sensory observation is the court of final appeal in issues concerning matters of fact. It is indeed this commitment to the use of an empirical method which is the final basis of the atheistic critique of theism. For at bottom this critique seeks to show that we can understand whatever a theistic assumption is alleged to explain, through the use of the proved methods of the positive sciences and without the introduction of empirically unsupported *ad hoc* hypotheses about a Deity. It is pertinent in this connection to recall a familiar legend about the French mathematical physicist Laplace. According to the story, Laplace made a personal presentation of a copy of his now famous book on celestial mechanics to Napoleon. Napoleon glanced through the volume, and finding no reference to the Deity asked Laplace whether God's existence played any role in the analysis. "Sire, I have no need for that hypothesis," Laplace is reported to have replied. The dismissal of sterile hypotheses characterizes not only the work of Laplace; it is the uniform rule in scientific inquiry. The sterility of the theistic assumption is one of the main burdens of the literature of atheism both ancient and modern.

And finally, atheistic thinkers have generally accepted a utilitarian basis for judging moral issues, and they have exhibited a libertarian attitude toward human needs and impulses. The conceptions of the human good they have advocated are conceptions which are commensurate with the actual capacities of mortal men, so that it is the satisfaction of the complex needs of the human creature which is the final standard for evaluating the validity of moral ideal or moral prescription.

In consequence, the emphasis of atheistic moral reflection has been this-worldly rather than other-worldly, individualistic rather than authoritarian. The stress upon a good life that must be consummated in this world has made atheists vigorous opponents of moral codes which seek to repress human impulses in the name of some unrealizable other-worldly ideal. The individualism that is so pronounced a strain in many philosophical atheists has made them tolerant of human limitations and sensitive to the plurality of legitimate moral goals. On the other hand, this individualism has certainly not prevented many of them from recognizing the crucial role which institutional arrangements can play in achieving desirable patterns of human living. In consequence, atheists have made important contributions to the development of a climate of opinion favorable to pursuing the values of a liberal civilization, and they have played effective roles in attempts to rectify social injustices.

Atheists cannot build their moral outlook on foundations upon which so many men conduct their lives. In particular, atheism cannot offer the incentives to conduct and the consolations for misfortune which theistic religions supply to their adherents. It can offer no hope of personal immortality, no threats of Divine chastisement, no promise of eventual recompense for injustices suffered, no blueprints to sure salvation. For on its view of the place of man in nature, human excellence and human dignity must be achieved within a finite life-span, or not at all, so that the rewards of moral endeavor must come from the quality of civilized living, and not from some source of disbursement that dwells outside of time. Accordingly, atheistic moral reflection at its best does not culminate in a quiescent ideal of human perfection, but is a vigorous call to intelligent activity — activity for the sake of realizing human potentialities and for eliminating whatever stands in the way of such realization. . . .

Suggestions for Further Reading

On the Debate between Creationism and Evolutionary Theory

Douglas Futuyama, *Science on Trial: The Case for Evolution.* New York, Pantheon, 1982.
Dwayne Gish, *Evolution? The Fossils Say No!* San Diego, Creation-Life Publishers, 1979.
Philip Kitcher, *Abusing Science: The Case Against Creationism.* Cambridge, Massachusetts, MIT Press, 1982.
Henry Morris, *Scientific Creationism.* San Diego, Creation-Life Publishers, 1974.

On the Testability of Religious Claims

Essays by Anthony Flew, R. M. Hare, and Basil Mitchell, "Theology and Falsification," in Anthony Flew and Alisdair MacIntyre (eds.), *New Essays in Philosophical Theology.* New York, Macmillan, 1966.

Carl Hempel, "Empiricist Criteria of Cognitive Significance: Problems and Changes," in *Aspects of Scientific Explanation*, New York, Free Press, 1965.

On the Ontological Argument

John Hick and Arthur McGill (eds.), *The Many-Faced Argument: Recent Studies on the Ontological Argument for the Existence of God*. London, Macmillan, 1968.

Alvin Plantinga, *The Nature of Necessity*. Oxford, Oxford University Press, 1974.

On Pascal's Wager

James Cargile, "Pascal's Wager." *Philosophy*, vol. 41, pp. 229–236, 1966.

Blaise Pascal, *Penseé. Everyman's Library*. London, J. M. Dent & Sons, 1958.

On the Argument from Evil

Robert M. Adams, "Must God Create the Best?" *Philosophical Review*, vol. 81, pp. 317–332, 1972.

Richard Swinburne, "The Problem of Evil," in Stuart Brown (ed.), *Reason and Religion*. Ithaca, Cornell University Press, 1977.

PART III
Theory of Knowledge

·L·E·C·T·U·R·E·S·

Lecture 12

What Is Knowledge?

Epistemology   The concepts of knowledge and rational justification form the core of the area of philosophy called _epistemology_. This is sometimes defined as "the theory of knowledge," but I'll use the term more broadly to encompass ideas such as evidence and rational justification.

In everyday life, in science, and in philosophy as well, we talk of "knowing" things. We also say that some beliefs are "strongly supported by evidence"; we say that they are "justified" or "well-confirmed." We not only describe _ourselves_ with such terms; we also apply them to _others_.

Epistemology tries to evaluate the commonsense idea that we (often, if not always) have knowledge and that we are (often, if not always) rationally justified in the beliefs we have. Some philosophers have tried to defend these commonsense ideas with philosophical argumentation. Others have developed a philosophical position that involves denying these commonsense ideas. A philosopher who claims that we do not have knowledge, or that our beliefs are not rationally justified, is defending some version of _philosophical skepticism_.

In this lecture, I'll begin with some remarks about the problem of knowledge. In the next lecture, I'll examine the views of the seventeenth-century French philosopher René Descartes. Descartes tried to show that we really do possess knowledge of the world; Descartes tried to refute the skeptic. After evaluating Descartes' views about knowledge, I'll turn to an alternative way of thinking about knowledge, _the reliability theory of knowledge_ (Lecture 14).

In the second half of this part of the book, I'll examine the idea of rational justification. The eighteenth-century Scottish philosopher David Hume, whose views on the design argument we considered in Lecture 5, argued that the beliefs we have that are based on induction are not rationally justified. Hume was a skeptic about induction. We'll consider his argument for this philosophical position and also the attempts that some philosophers have made to show that Hume's startling view is mistaken.

So let's begin with the problem of knowledge. Before we can ask whether we know anything, we have to get clear on what knowledge is. To focus ideas, I want to distinguish three different ways we can talk about knowledge. Only one of these will be our concern in what follows.

Consider the difference between the following three statements, each concerning an individual, whom I'll call *S* (the subject):

> (1) *S* knows how to ride a bicycle.
> (2) *S* knows the President of the United States.
> (3) *S* knows that the Rockies are in North America.

Right now I'm not interested in saying which of these statements is true. The point is that they involve different kinds of knowledge.

The kind of knowledge described in (3) I'll call *propositional knowledge*. Notice that the object of the verb in (3) is a proposition—something that is either true or false. There is a proposition—that the Rockies are in North America—and (3) asserts that *S* knows that this proposition is true.

Statements (1) and (2) do not have this structure. The object of the verb in (2) is not a proposition, but a person. A similar kind of knowledge would be involved if I said that *S* knows Chicago. Statement (2) says that *S* is related to an object—a person, place, or thing—so I'll say that (2) describes an instance of *object knowledge*.

Is there a connection between object knowledge and propositional knowledge? Maybe to know the President of the United States, you must know some propositions that are about him. But which propositions? To know the President, do you have to know which state he comes from? This does not seem essential. And the same holds true for each other fact about the man: There does not seem to be any particular proposition that you've got to know for you to know him.

There is another aspect of the idea of object knowledge, one that is rather curious. Suppose I've read lots of books about the President. I know as many propositions about him as you might wish. Still, it won't be true that I know him, because I have never met him. Knowing people seems to require some sort of direct acquaintance. But it is hard to say exactly what is needed here. If I once was introduced to the President at some large party, that wouldn't be enough for me to say that I "know" him. It isn't just direct acquaintance, but something more. I won't try to describe this further. I'll merely conclude that propositional knowledge, no matter how voluminous, is not sufficient for object knowledge.

I turn next to the kind of knowledge described in statement (1). I'll call this *know-how* knowledge. What does it mean to know how to do something? I think that this idea has little connection with propositional knowledge. My son Aaron knew how to ride a bike when he was 5 years old. This means that he had certain abilities—he knew how to keep his balance, how to peddle, and so on. If you asked a physicist to describe what Aaron was doing that allowed him to ride the bike, the physicist could write out a set of propositions. There would be facts about gravity, forward momentum, and balancing of forces. But Aaron was not a physicist at age 5. He did not know the propositions that the physicist specifies. Aaron *obeyed* the physical principles that the physicist describes—his behavior conformed to what they say. But he did not do this by learning the

Necessary and Sufficient Conditions

Consider the following suggested definition of what a bachelor is:

> For any S, S is a bachelor if and only if
> (1) S is an adult.
> (2) S is male.
> (3) S is unmarried.

I'm not claiming that this definition precisely captures what "bachelor" means in ordinary English. Rather, I want to use it as an example of a proposed definition.

The definition is a generalization. It concerns any individual you care to consider. The definition makes two claims: The first is that IF the individual has characteristics (1), (2), and (3), then the individual is a bachelor. In other words, (1), (2), and (3) are together *sufficient* for being a bachelor. The second claim is that IF the individual is a bachelor, then the individual has all three characteristics. In other words, (1), (2), and (3) are each *necessary* for being a bachelor.

We can define what a necessary condition is and what a sufficient condition is as follows:

> "X is a necessary condition for Y" means that
> if Y is true, then X is true
> "X is a sufficient condition for Y" means that
> if X is true, then Y is true.

What does the expression "if and only if" mean in this proposed definition of bachelorhood? It means that the conditions listed are both necessary and sufficient. A good definition will specify necessary and sufficient conditions for the concept one wishes to define.

This means that there can be two sorts of defects in a proposed definition. A definition can provide conditions that are not sufficient. It can also provide conditions that are not necessary. And, of course, it can fall down on both counts. Which sort of defects are present in the following suggested definitions?

> S is a bachelor if and only if S is male.
> S is a bachelor if and only if S is an unmarried human
> adult male who is tall and lives in Detroit.

The first definition is said to be "too broad"; it admits too much. The second is "too narrow"; it admits too little.

propositions in question. Aaron had know-how knowledge, but little in the way of propositional knowledge.

Conversely, a physicist who has detailed knowledge of the physical principles that describe successful bike riding may yet not know how to ride a bike. The physicist may lack the ability to perform the behavior, but not because there is some proposition he or she fails to grasp.

I conclude that propositional knowledge is not necessary for knowing how to perform some task. And propositional knowledge is not sufficient for knowing how to perform some task.

The subject of this and the following two lectures will be *propositional knowledge*, not *object knowledge* or *know-how knowledge*. The goal is to understand what propositional knowledge is; that is, we want to answer the following questions: What must be true if an individual, *S*, knows that *p*, where *p* is some proposition, for example, the proposition that the Rockies are in North America? From now on, when I talk about "knowledge," it will be propositional knowledge that I'm discussing.

Two ideas that form part of the concept of knowledge should be noted at the outset. First, if *S* knows that *p*, then *S* must believe that *p*. Second, if *S* knows that *p*, then *p* must be true. Knowledge requires both *belief* and *truth*.

I won't try to argue for the first of these requirements, but will just assume that it is correct. The second does require some explanation, however. People sometimes say that they know things, which, in fact, turn out not to be true. But this is not a case of knowing things that are untrue, but of people *thinking* they know things, which happen to be untrue.

Knowledge has an objective and a subjective side. You should remember this pair of concepts from Lecture 1. A fact is objective if its truth does not depend on the way anyone's mind is. It's an objective fact that the Rocky Mountains are more than 10,000 feet above sea level. A fact is subjective, on the other hand, if it is not objective. The most obvious example of a subjective fact is a description of what's going on in someone's mind.

Whether someone believes that the Rockies are more than 10,000 feet above sea level is a subjective matter; but whether the Mountains really have that property is an objective matter. Knowledge requires both an objective and a subjective element. For *S* to know that *p*, *p* must be true and the subject, *S*, must believe that *p* is true.

I've just cited two necessary conditions for knowledge: Knowledge requires belief and knowledge requires truth. Is that it? That is, are these two conditions not just separately necessary, but also jointly sufficient? Is true belief enough for knowledge?

In the dialogue called *The Theaetetus*, the ancient Greek philosopher Plato (c. 430–345 B.C.), who was Aristotle's teacher, argues that the answer is *no*. Orators and lawyers sometimes trick people into believing things; sometimes those things happen to be true. People who have been duped in this way have true beliefs, but they do not have knowledge.

Two Requirements for Knowledge— Belief and Truth

Plato: True Belief Is Not Sufficient for Knowledge

WHAT IS
KNOWLEDGE?

Of course, the fact that orators and lawyers intend to deceive is not crucial for Plato's point. Think of an individual, Clyde, who believes that the story about Groundhog Day is true. Clyde thinks that if the groundhog sees its shadow, then spring will come early. Suppose Clyde puts this silly principle to work this year. He receives the news about the behavior of the Official Designated Groundhog, and so believes that spring will come early. Suppose Clyde turns out to be right about the early spring. If there is no real connection between the Groundhog's seeing its shadow and the coming of an early spring, then Clyde will have a true belief (that spring will come early), but he will not have knowledge.

What else is needed, besides true belief, for someone to have knowledge? A natural suggestion is that knowledge requires evidence, or a rational justification. The problem with Clyde is that he did not satisfy this further requirement (though perhaps he thought he did). Justification, notice, can't just mean that the subject *thinks* he has a reason.

What does it mean to say that an individual is "justified" in believing a proposition *p*? From Lectures 2 and 3, we know that there are several options open here. A justification might take the form of a deductive argument, an inductive argument, or an abductive argument. Perhaps there are options beyond these three. But no matter how we explain what we mean by "justification," it seems plausible to say that beliefs that are irrationally held are not cases of knowledge (even if they happen to be true). We mark this idea by saying that besides truth and belief, knowledge requires *justification*.

The JTB Theory Suppose that knowledge requires these three conditions. Is that it? That is, are these conditions not just separately necessary, but jointly sufficient? The theory of knowledge that asserts that this is so I'll call the JTB (justified true belief) theory. It says that knowledge is one and the same thing as justified true belief:

 (JTB) For any individual *S* and any proposition *p*,
 S knows that *p* if and only if
 (1) *S* believes that *p*.
 (2) *p* is true.
 (3) *S* is justified in believing that *p*.

The JTB theory states a generalization. It says what knowledge is for *any* person *S* and *any* proposition *p*. For example, let *S* be you and let *p* be "the moon is made of green cheese." The JTB theory says this: If the left-hand statement is true, then all three right-hand statements must be true as well. And if the left-hand statement is false, then at least one of the three right-hand statements must also be false. As in the previous definition of bachelorhood, the expression "if and only if" says that we are being given necessary and sufficient conditions for the defined concept.

In 1963, the U.S. philosopher Edmund Gettier published a pair of counterexamples to the JTB theory ("Is Justified True Belief Knowledge?" *Analysis*, vol. 23, pp. 121–123, 1963). What is a *counterexample?* It's an example that goes counter to what some general theory says. The JTB theory says that *all* cases of justified true belief are cases of knowledge. Gettier thought that his two examples show that an individual can have a justified true belief without having knowledge. If Gettier is right, then the three conditions given by the JTB theory are not sufficient.

Here is one of Gettier's examples: Smith works in an office. He knows that someone will soon be promoted. The boss, who is very reliable, tells Smith that Jones is going to get the promotion. Smith has just counted the coins in Jones's pocket and found ten coins there. Smith therefore has excellent evidence for the following proposition:

(a) Jones will get the promotion and Jones has ten coins in his pocket.

Smith then deduces from this statement the following:

(b) The man who will get the promotion has ten coins in his pocket.

Now suppose that, unknown to Smith, Jones will *not* get the promotion. Rather it is Smith himself who will be promoted. And suppose that Smith also happens to have ten coins in his pocket.

Smith believes (b), and (b) is true. Gettier also claims that Smith is justified in believing (b), since Smith deduced it from (a). Although (a) is false, Smith had excellent reason to think it is true. Gettier concludes that Smith has a justified true belief in (b), but Smith does not know that (b) is true.

Gettier's other example exhibits the same pattern. The subject validly deduces a true proposition from a proposition that is very well-supported by evidence even though it is, unbeknownst to the subject, false. I now want to describe a kind of counterexample to the JTB theory in which the subject reasons *non*deductively.

The British philosopher, mathematician, and social reformer Bertrand Russell (1872–1970) considers a very reliable clock that stands in a town square. This morning you walk by it and glance up to find out what time it is. As a result, you come to believe that the time is 9:55. You are justified in believing this, based on your correct assumption that the clock has been very reliable in the past. But suppose that, unbeknownst to you, the clock stopped exactly 24 hours ago. You now have a justified true belief that it is 9:55, but you do not know that this is the correct time.

Let me add a third example to Gettier's Smith/Jones story and to Russell's clock. You buy a ticket in a fair lottery. "Fair" means that one ticket will win and every ticket has the same chance. There are 1000 tickets and you get ticket number 452. You look at this ticket, think for a moment, and then believe the following proposition: Ticket number 452 will not win. Suppose that when the drawing occurs a week later, you are right. Your belief was true. And it seemed to be extremely well-justified; after all, its probability was extremely close to unity—there was only one chance in a thousand that you would be mistaken.

Yet, I think we want to say in this case that you did not *know* that the ticket would fail to win. Here is a third case of justified true belief that is not knowledge. Note that the reasoning here is nondeductive.

What the Counter-examples Have in Common

In all three of these cases, the subject has *highly reliable*, but not *infallible*, evidence for the proposition believed. The boss *usually* is right about who will be promoted; the clock *usually* is right as to what the time is; and it *usually* is true that a ticket drawn at random in a fair lottery does not win. But, of course, *usually* does not mean *always*. The sources of information that the subjects exploited in these three examples are *highly* reliable, but not *perfectly* reliable. All the sources of information were prone to error, to at least some degree.

Do these examples really refute the JTB theory? That depends on how we understand the idea of justification. If highly reliable evidence is enough to justify a belief, then the counterexamples do refute the JTB theory. But if justification requires something more like perfectly infallible evidence, then these examples do not undermine the JTB theory.

My view is that justifying evidence need not be infallible. I think we can have rational and well-supported beliefs even when we are not entitled to be absolutely certain that what we believe is true. From this, I conclude that JTB is not sufficient for knowledge.

An Argument for Skepticism

What more is required? The lottery example suggests the following idea. In this case, you *probably* will not be mistaken when you believe that ticket number 452 will lose. But high probability is not enough. To know that the ticket will lose, it must be *impossible* to be mistaken. You don't have knowledge in this example because there is a chance (small though it may be) that you will be wrong.

There is some plausibility to this suggestion about what knowledge requires. The problem is that this idea seems to lead immediately to skepticism—to the conclusion that we do not know anything. For it seems that virtually all the beliefs we have are based on evidence that is not infallible. Consider, just briefly, the beliefs we have that depend on the testimony of our senses. We use vision, hearing, touch, taste, and smell to gather evidence about the way the world is. Do such beliefs count as knowledge? The problem is that the senses are sometimes misleading.

Right now, you may believe that you are looking at a printed page. You believe this because of the visual experiences you are now having. Do you *know* that there is a printed page in front of you? According to the present suggestion, for you to know that there is a printed page in front of you, it must be the case that you could not possibly be mistaken in believing what you do. But the fact of the matter seems to be that you *could* be mistaken. You might be hallucinating, or dreaming, or your senses might be malfunctioning in some other way.

So here's where we are. The JTB theory is mistaken. Justified true belief does not suffice for knowledge. As an alternative to the JTB theory, we have this suggestion: Knowledge requires the impossibility of error. But this suggestion, plausible though it may be as a diagnosis of why you don't have knowledge in the lottery example, allows us to formulate the following argument for skepticism:

> If *S* knows that *p*, then it is not possible that *S* is mistaken in believing that *p*.
> It is possible that *S* is mistaken in believing that *p*.
> ────────────
> *S* does not know that *p*.

This form of argument can be used to argue that *a posteriori* knowledge is impossible. Recall from Lecture 9 that a proposition is *a posteriori* if it can be known only through the testimony of sense experience. The skeptic claims that beliefs based on sense experience are not totally immune from the possibility of error. People make perceptual mistakes—for example, in cases of illusion, hallucination, and dreaming. Since we can't absolutely rule out the possibility of error, the skeptic concludes that we must admit that the senses do not provide us with knowledge.

This argument for skepticism is deductively valid. (Identify its logical form.) The first premiss seems to describe a plausible requirement for knowing the proposition in question. The second premiss also seems plausible; it just says that the beliefs we have are not absolutely immune from the possibility of error. To refute skepticism, we have to reject one or both of these premisses. The problem is that both seem fairly plausible.

This is a problem, because the conclusion is rather outrageous. I think I know

---

Is Skepticism Self-Refuting?

Skeptics claim that people do not know anything. Can skeptics claim to know *that what they say is true? If not, does that show that their philosophical thesis is false?*

It is a contradiction to say that you know that no one (including you) knows anything. But a skeptic can assert *that people lack knowledge without claiming to know that this is so. In addition, a skeptic can claim to provide a good argument for skepticism. This is not contradictory.*

The thesis that no one knows anything, if true, cannot be known to be true. But that does not show that the position is false. If you think that all truths are knowable, you will say that this skeptical thesis cannot be true. But why think that all truths are knowable? Why not think, instead, that the universe may contain truths that we are incapable of knowing?

Another way for skeptics to avoid contradicting themselves is to be modest. Instead of claiming that no one knows anything, *they could limit themselves to the claim that no one ever knows anything through the testimony of the* senses. *If this more limited kind of skepticism could be supported by an* a priori *argument, the position would not be self-refuting.*

lots of things, and I believe that this is true of you as well. It is hard for me to accept the idea that I don't know that I have a hand. If you think that you now know that there is a printed page in front of you, you should balk at this argument.

The skeptical argument contradicts a fundamental part of our commonsense picture of the way we are related to the world around us. Common sense says that people have some knowledge of the world they inhabit; the skeptical argument says that common sense is mistaken in this respect. If there is a mistake in the argument, where is it?

Review Questions

1. Explain how object knowledge, know-how knowledge, and propositional knowledge differ.
2. What do the following pieces of terminology mean? (1) X is a necessary condition for Y; (2) X is a sufficient condition for Y; (3) X is true if and only if Y is true; (4) o is a counterexample to the statement "all emeralds are green."
3. Why think that true belief is not sufficient for knowledge? What is the JTB theory? What is the difference between highly reliable evidence and absolutely infallible evidence?
4. Describe the three counterexamples to the JTB theory (Gettier's, Russell's, and the lottery example). Do these counterexamples show that JTB is not necessary or that it is not sufficient for knowledge?
5. What is skepticism? Present the argument for skepticism given at the end of this lecture. Is the argument deductively valid?

Problems for Further Thought

1. People sometimes say, about a proposition that is difficult to take to heart, "I know it, but I don't believe it." Does this refute the claim that if S knows that p, then S believes that p?

2. I suggested that we lack knowledge in the lottery example because knowledge requires the impossibility of error. Can you think of some other explanation for why we lack knowledge in the other two examples that were used against the JTB theory?

Lecture 13

Descartes' Foundationalism

René Descartes (1596–1650) is sometimes described as the father of modern philosophy. The kind of epistemology he tried to develop is called foundationalism. Before launching into the details of Descartes' philosophy, I want to describe what kind of approach to the problem of knowledge foundationalism provides.

Foundation-alism

The word "foundationalism" should make you think of a building. What keeps a building from falling over? The answer has two parts. First, there is a solid foundation. Second, the rest of the building, which I will call the superstructure, is attached securely to that solid foundation. Descartes wanted to show that (many if not all of) the beliefs we have about the world are cases of genuine knowledge. To show this, he wanted to divide our beliefs into two categories. There are the foundational beliefs, which are perfectly solid. Second, there are superstructural beliefs, which count as knowledge because they rest securely on that solid foundation.

Besides the metaphor from architecture, there is another that should help you understand what Descartes' project was. You probably had a geometry course in high school. There you studied Euclid's development of the subject. Recall that Euclid divided the propositions of geometry into two categories. First, there are the axioms of geometry. These are supposed to be simple and totally obvious truths. Second, there are the theorems, which at first glance are somewhat less obvious. Euclid shows that the theorems are true by showing how they can be deduced from the axioms.

A foundationalist theory of knowledge could also be called a Euclidean theory of knowledge. To show that a given body of beliefs counts as knowledge, we use the following strategy. First, we identify the beliefs that will provide the foundations of knowledge (the axioms). These must be shown to have some special property, such as being absolutely certain. In a moment, I'll clarify what Descartes had in mind by this "special property." Second, we show that the rest of our beliefs count as knowledge because they bear some special relationship to the foundational items. In Euclid's geometry, the special relationship was deductive implication.

Euclid, of course, was interested only in the beliefs we have about geometry. Desacartes cast his net much wider. He was interested in the totality of what we believe. But whether the problem is to describe the foundations of geometry or the foundations of knowledge as a whole, there are two ideas that must be clarified. We need to identify what the foundational items are. And we need to describe the relationship that must obtain between foundational and superstructural items that qualifies the latter as knowledge.

*Euclid's
Parallel
Postulate*

One last comment on high school geometry: If your course was like mine, you spent most of your time seeing what theorems could be proved from the axioms. You spent little or no time seeing why the axioms should be regarded as true. You were told that they should be "obvious" or that they should just be accepted on faith. Maybe your teacher said that geometry is just a game and the axioms are the rules.

In fact, the question about the axioms is a serious one. One of Euclid's starting assumptions—his so-called fifth postulate—bothered geometers for about 2000 years. This postulate says the following: Through a point that is not on a given straight line, there is exactly one line that is parallel to the first. In other words, the parallel postulate says that if you extend all the lines passing through this point to infinity, exactly one of them will fail to intersect the initial line.

A number of subsequent geometers felt that this starting assumption of Euclid's was less obvious than the others he used. As a result, they tried to show that it could be proved from the other axioms. However, geometers failed to do this and eventually established that the parallel postulate could not be proved from Euclid's other assumptions; that is, they showed that the parallel postulate is *independent* of the other assumptions. This means that the denial of the parallel postulate is consistent with Euclid's other assumptions. It then transpired that non-Euclidean geometries could be developed, ones that retain Euclid's other assumptions, but reject his parallel postulate.

The details of this story don't matter here. However, the history of geometry does show that it sometimes is not so clear whether a given statement is "obviously true." Perhaps Euclid thought that the parallel postulate is obvious. If so, that would have been his justification for treating it as something that does not have to be proved; it would stand on its own as an axiom/postulate. But this does not mean that subsequent geometers had to regard Euclid's judgment as beyond question. What strikes one person as obvious may not be so obvious to someone else.

*Descartes'
Method
of Doubt*

Now let's consider Descartes' approach to the problem of knowledge. Descartes' goal is to refute skepticism. He wants to show that we really do have knowledge of the world we inhabit. His strategy for achieving this goal is foundationalist in character. This means that the first item on his agenda must be to identify the beliefs that are foundational.

At the beginning of his *Meditations on First Philosophy* (1641), Descartes proposes a method for determining which of the beliefs he has are foundational. He called this the *method of doubt*. You see whether it is possible to doubt a proposition. If it is possible to do this, you set the belief aside—it is not foundational. If it is not possible to do so (that is, if you find that the belief is indubitable), then you have identified a foundational item. Notice that failing the method of doubt test does not mean that the belief is *false*. It just means that the belief is not *absolutely certain*.

Descartes does not try to apply this method to beliefs one at a time. Think of all the beliefs you have—there are millions (at least). You believe that 1 is a number. You believe that 2 is a number. And so on. It would be time-consuming and also boring to try to consider each belief separately. Rather, what Descartes does is consider *kinds* of beliefs, considering whether all the beliefs in this or that category pass or fail the method of doubt test.

The first category Descartes considers is the set of beliefs that depend for their justification on sense experience. Many of our beliefs are based on sight, hearing, touch, taste, and smell. These propositions are *a posteriori* (Lecture 9). Is it possible to doubt these beliefs? Descartes says that the answer is *yes*. Your present belief that there is a printed page in front of you is based on vision. But vision can be misleading. Psychologists tell us about hallucinations and illusions. Maybe you've had such experiences yourself. If not, remember Macbeth, who was certain that a dagger was hovering in front of him. And besides hallucinations, there is the fact of dreaming. In a dream you may find yourself believing that there is a printed page in front of you. You may find yourself having visual experiences just like the ones you are having now. But in the dream, your belief is mistaken. Descartes takes this to show that the belief you have right now might be mistaken.

So beliefs that rest on the testimony of the senses fail the method of doubt test. Let's be clear on why Descartes thinks they do so. Descartes shows that such beliefs are dubitable by constructing a story of a particular kind. You now believe that there's a printed page in front of you on the basis of a set of visual experiences. Let's call the proposition you believe *B* and the experiences you now are having *E*. Your belief that *B* is true rests on your having experiences *E*. Descartes holds that *B* can be doubted because he can describe a situation in which you would have *E* and believe *B* even though *B* is false. Dreams and hallucinations show how this can happen. Descartes shows that a class of beliefs is dubitable by constructing a story of this sort.

In saying that a belief is dubitable, Descartes is not saying that we are able to take seriously the idea that it might be false. The proposition that there is a page in front of you is dubitable in Descartes' sense; this does not mean that you are now seriously in doubt as to whether it is true. A proposition is dubitable when a certain sort of story can be constructed; whether we think the story might well be true is not essential.

Descartes next turns his attention to propositions of mathematics. I believe that 2 + 3 = 5. I believe that squares have four sides. Descartes remarks that these are true "whether I'm awake or asleep." These propositions are *a priori* (recall this piece of vocabulary from Lecture 9). They do not depend for their justification on sensory experience. Do propositions justified by reason, independent of sense experience, pass the method of doubt test?

Descartes thinks that they fail. To show that they are not beyond doubt, Descartes asks us to imagine that our minds are deceived by an "evil demon." Imagine that the evil demon causes our faculty of reasoning to find propositions totally obvious that in fact are false. If this were so, we might believe that 2 + 3 = 5 even though the proposition is not true.

These conclusions — all reached in the first of the *Meditations* — are entirely negative. *A posteriori* beliefs about the character of the world outside the mind are

---

Indubitability

Very few propositions are made true just by your believing them. You can believe that there are unicorns, but that doesn't make such creatures pop into existence.

Consider the proposition "I am thinking." If you believe that this is true, then it must be true. Believing is a kind of thinking. Descartes thinks the same is true for propositions of the form "I seem to see that p." He also thinks this is true for propositions that say that you believe that p or want it to be true that q (where p and q are propositions). Believing them makes them true.

If a proposition is made true by your believing it, then it has this property: You cannot describe a situation in which you believe the proposition, but the proposition is false. Recall that Descartes determines whether a proposition is dubitable by seeing whether he can describe a situation of this kind. This means that a proposition is indubitable if the proposition is made true by the act of believing it.

Are there indubitable propositions that are not made true by your believing them? Some philosophers have held that simple logical truths such as "it is raining or it is not raining" are beyond doubt. Is it plausible to maintain that these are made true by your believing them?

---

dubitable. This we see by considering dreams and hallucinations. *A priori* propositions are also dubitable. This we see by considering the evil demon. If no belief in these two categories passes the method of doubt test, which beliefs could be the foundations of knowledge? What category of belief could possibly satisfy this very stringent requirement?

I Am Thinking, Therefore I Exist
In an earlier work, the *Discourse on the Method* (1637), Descartes identifies a pair of propositions that pass the test:

> I noticed that while I was trying to think everything false, it must be that I, who was thinking this, was something. And observing that this truth, *I am thinking, therefore I exist (Je pense, donc je suis; Cogito ergo sum* in Latin), was so solid and secure that the most extravagant suppositions of the sceptics could not overthrow it, I judged that I need not scruple to accept it as the first principle of the philosophy I was seeking.

In the *Second Meditation*, Descartes focuses on the belief "I am, I exist" as the first proposition that can be judged beyond doubt.

To understand what Descartes is driving at, you must think about yourself, formulating your thoughts in the first person. When Descartes considers the proposition "I am thinking," you are not supposed to consider the proposition

"Descartes is thinking." Rather, you should say to yourself precisely what Descartes says to himself.

Consider my belief that I am thinking. I cannot doubt this. I cannot construct a story in which I believe this proposition, though it is false. For if I *believe* the proposition, then I am thinking, so the proposition is true. So the attempt to doubt the proposition proves that it must be true. The proposition "I am thinking" passes the method of doubt test.

There are two important characteristics of the proposition "I am thinking" that you should note. First, it is important that the proposition is in the first person. When Descartes considers "I am thinking," he concludes that this proposition passes the method of doubt test. However, if he had considered "Descartes is thinking," the result would have been different. It *is* possible for Descartes to doubt that there is someone named "Descartes." He can invent a story in which there is no such person as Descartes; that such a story can be constructed shows that the proposition is dubitable.

The second feature of the proposition "I am thinking" is that it involves a psychological property. I cannot doubt that I am thinking, but I can doubt that I am now in North America. Both beliefs are first person. But only the former is psychological.

As noted, Descartes maintains that the proposition "I exist" also passes the method of doubt test. Take a few minutes and formulate an argument, similar to the one just described for "I am thinking," that shows that this is so.

So far, we have two propositions that Descartes thinks can serve as foundations for the rest of what we know. I cannot doubt that I am thinking, nor can I doubt that I exist. This is a meager foundation. Just as it would be hard to erect a big building on a foundation that is made of two bricks, so it would be hard to ground the whole of what we know about the world on this paltry foundation of two beliefs.

But there is more. Consider propositions solely about the contents of your own present sensory experiences. Such propositions describe the way things seem to you. You now seem to see a page in front of you. Descartes thinks that all such first-person descriptions of the way things seem are indubitable.

To understand Descartes' point, it is essential to recognize the difference between the following two propositions:

There is a page in front of me.
I seem to see a page in front of me.

It is fairly clear, as noted earlier, that the first of these can be doubted. That's the point about dreams and illusions. But Descartes maintains that the second proposition is different. He holds that it has this peculiar property: If you believe that the proposition is true, then you cannot be mistaken. If you believe that you seem to see a page in front of you, then you do seem to see a page in front of you. You can't be mistaken in your beliefs about the way things seem to be to you.

So the foundation of knowledge has just been augmented. "I am thinking" and "I exist" are indubitable, and so are the many first-person beliefs about the way things seem.

Thesis of the
Incorrigibility
of the Mental

Descartes went even further than this. He thought that people have infallible access to what they believe and desire. Introspection ("looking inward") is a method that the mind can use to accurately grasp its own contents. This is sometimes expressed by saying that Descartes believed in the thesis of the "incorrigibility of the mental." Although "there is a page in front of me" is not indubitable, Descartes thought "I believe that there is a page in front of me" is indubitable. If you believe that you have that belief, then it must be true that you have that belief. Ditto for desires. If you believe that you want some ice cream, then it must be true that you want some ice cream.

A great deal of work in psychology in the past one hundred years shows that this incorrigibility thesis is not plausible. Sigmund Freud, whose views on religion were discussed in Lecture 10, argued that we often misunderstand what we really believe and what we really want. At times our beliefs and desires would be very upsetting to us if we were conscious of them. So, as a defense mechanism, our minds repress them. The result is that we often have mistaken beliefs about what we really think and want.

An example of this is Freud's theory of the Oedipus complex. Freud held that little boys want to kill their fathers and marry their mothers. However, if you asked a little boy whether he wanted to do this, he probably would sincerely answer *no*.

You might well ask: What evidence can there be for this theory? If little boys deny having these desires, why think they have them? Freud's answer is that this theory is a reasonable explanation of what little boys *do*. It is their behavior that we must consider, not just what they say they believe and desire. Verbal reports about what we think and want are evidence as to what our beliefs and desires really are. But sincere reports do not settle the matter, since behavior may provide *other* evidence that is relevant.

Although this idea—that we often have a false picture of our own beliefs and desires—is very important in Freud's theories, it is not unique to them. A great many approaches in psychology deny Descartes' thesis of incorrigibility.

Descartes wants to include *all* first-person reports of his own beliefs and desires as foundations. Each, he thought, passes the method of doubt test. Freud and many other psychologists would disagree. I am on their side.

Where does this leave Descartes' foundations? It includes *I am thinking* and *I exist* and all first-person reports about the way the world seems to be to the agent. First-person reports about the contents of the agent's experience, which do not comment on the way the world is outside the agent's mind, Descartes took to be indubitable. Another example in this category (besides "I seem to see a page in front of me") is "I am in pain." Descartes' view was that if you believe that you are in pain, then you are in pain.

In Lecture 2, I pointed out that for a very large class of our beliefs, there is a huge difference between believing a proposition and that proposition's actually being true. To believe that the Rockies are over 10,000 feet is one thing; for the mountains to actually be that high is another. It is misguided wishful thinking to hold that believing the proposition guarantees that it is true.

This sensible separation of belief and truth, which seems right for a wide class of propositions, is called into question by the special examples Descartes thought pass the method of doubt test. According to Descartes, "I am in pain" must be true if I think it is. The same holds for "I am thinking" and "I seem to see a page in front of me." Wishful thinking seems to work *sometimes*, though not *always*.

These propositions, Descartes thought, are foundational. We cannot be mistaken in believing them. Some philosophers have argued with Descartes about this. They have maintained that it is possible to be mistaken in holding some of these beliefs. I'm not going to address that matter here. Instead I want to consider another problem.

Do First-Person Psychological Beliefs Provide a Sufficient Foundation?

Recall the architectural metaphor discussed at the beginning of this lecture. An adequate foundation for a building must have two properties. It must be (1) secure and (2) sufficient to support the house. The foundations of knowledge are subject to the same requirements. According to Descartes, they must be indubitable. In addition, it must be possible to rest everything else we know on them. Don't forget that the method of doubt is intended to identify the foundations; on that basis, the entire superstructure is supposed to rest.

Descartes, as I mentioned before, was not a skeptic. He thought that we know lots of things about the world outside our own minds. For example, you know that there is a page in front of you now. This belief about the external world is not indubitable; it did not pass the method of doubt test. But, nevertheless, it is (Descartes would agree) something that you know. How can Descartes show that this is true?

Recall the Euclidean analogy. We've just identified some axioms of the system of knowledge. Do these suffice to prove some theorems? We must show how you know that there's a page in front of you by showing how this proposition is connected with foundational ones. In Euclidean geometry, we justify theorems by deducing them from axioms. How can a superstructural belief be shown to be knowledge? We must show that it is connected with foundational pieces of knowledge in the right way. But what is this special connection supposed to be?

Can deduction do the trick? Euclid deduced theorems from axioms. Can Descartes deduce this proposition about the world outside the mind from beliefs that are all first-person psychological? To show that you know that there is a page in front of you, maybe we should try to deduce that proposition in the following way:

I seem to see a page in front of me.
_____

There is a page in front of me.

The premise of this argument is foundational. The problem is that it does not deductively imply the conclusion. The existence of a page in front of me does not deductively follow from the way things seem to me now. That's the point noted before about dreams and hallucinations.

The premiss given is not enough. And even if I augmented it with other reports about my present psychological state (for example, "I seem to feel a page," "I seem to taste a page"), that still would not be enough. Such premisses might be ones about which I am perfectly certain. But they do not provide a sufficient foundation for the beliefs I have about the world outside the mind. Such arguments are not deductively valid.

An Additional Foundational Item: God Exists and Is No Deceiver

Descartes saw quite clearly that the argument just represented needs an additional premiss, one that will bridge the gap between first-person psychological premisses and a conclusion that describes the world outside the mind. Descartes thought that he could provide such an additional premiss by proving that God exists.

How would the existence of God solve Descartes' problem? The answer is that Descartes thought that he could prove not only that God exists, but that God is no deceiver. Descartes had the following picture in mind: God created my mind and situated me in the world. What sort of mind did God give me? Obviously, he did not give me a mind that is infallible; my mind does not reach true conclusions about the world on each and every occasion. However, God would not have furnished me with a mind that leads me to false beliefs about the world, no matter how carefully I reason and no matter how much evidence I consult. If God had done this, he would have been a deceiver.

So the conclusion Descartes wants to establish is that God created us with minds that have the capacity to attain true beliefs about the world. We are neither infallible nor are we hopelessly trapped by falsehood. Rather, we are somewhere in the middle: We can reach true beliefs if we are careful about how we use the minds that God bestowed upon us.

Clarity and Distinctness Criterion

Descartes maintained that a *clear and distinct belief must be true*. The basic idea here is that if we examine our beliefs carefully and make sure that they are logically clear and unconfused, then we can be certain that they are true. The reason that clarity and distinctness ensure that the belief is true is that God is no deceiver. God furnished us with minds that are connected with the physical world in this special way. So God is responsible for the fact that we can use the clarity and distinctness of a belief as a criterion for its truth.

Descartes was not merely saying that the clarity and distinctness of a belief is *some evidence* that it is true. He went further: Clear and distinct ideas *must* be true, since God is no deceiver.

So far, the foundations of knowledge include only those propositions that report the current state of my mind. It is beyond doubt that I believe that there is a page in front of me. Descartes wants to augment this foundation. He believes that the proposition "God exists and is no deceiver" is foundational. It can be shown to pass the method of doubt test. If Descartes can demonstrate this, then he will be able to show that we really do have knowledge of the world outside our own minds.

At first glance, it may seem that Descartes is trying to do the impossible. He wants to show not just that God exists, but that this proposition is *indubitable*. Isn't the fact that some people are atheists or agnostics enough to refute him? If some people *actually* doubt that God exists, isn't that enough to show that it is *possible* to doubt that God exists?

Descartes believes that he has a proof of the existence of God whose premises are *indubitable*. In addition, the proof is so simple that once you attend carefully to it, you cannot doubt that there is a God. This is the proof that Descartes lays out in the ~~Third Meditation~~. Here it is, in outline:

(1) My idea of God is an idea of a perfect being.
(2) There must be at least as much perfection in the cause as there is in the effect.
   ────────
Hence, the cause of my idea is a perfect being — namely, God himself.

Premiss (1) of this argument Descartes thinks he can know by introspection. By looking inward at his mind's own contents, he can discern this fact about himself. Premiss (1), Descartes believes, is indubitable.

As to premiss (2), Descartes thinks that it is an indubitable principle about causality. It can be broken into two components. First, there is the idea that every event has a cause. Second, there is the idea that the cause must be at least as perfect as the effect.

It is not so clear why we should accept these principles about causality. Why couldn't some events occur for no reason at all? Descartes needs to show not only that this does not happen, but that it is inconceivable; remember, Descartes' claim is that these premises are indubitably true. This goes beyond the more modest thesis that they are true.

Premiss (2) needs to be clarified. Descartes distinguishes two kinds of perfection (or "reality") that an idea or representation might possess. To find out how *objectively* perfect a representation is, you must find out how perfect the thing is that the representation represents. Two photographs of a saint must have the same degree of objective perfection; two photographs of a trash can will have the same degree of objective perfection as well. And if saints are more perfect than trash cans, the first pair will have more objective perfection than the second.

This characterization of objective perfection requires a little fine-tuning. A picture of a unicorn has a certain degree of objective perfection, even though there are no unicorns. So, to determine how objectively perfect the picture is, you must ask yourself this question: If the picture represented something that actually existed, how perfect would that thing be?

I hope you can see from the definition of objective perfection why Descartes thinks that his concept of God has the maximum amount of objective perfection. This is something that Descartes can say just by examining the concept he has. Indeed, it is something that an atheist might agree to as well. If there were a God, then that being would have all the perfections; this means that my idea of God is objectively perfect.

The concept of objective perfection allows some representations to be ranked higher than others. My idea of God is at the top. Somewhere below that is my idea of a saint. And still farther down the list is my idea of a trash can. The second kind of perfection that Descartes discusses is different. This is what Descartes calls an idea's *formal perfection*. All mental contents have the same degree of formal perfection because they all are made of the same stuff.

To see what Descartes has in mind here, consider paintings. These may differ in their degree of objective perfection. But all are made of canvas and paint. In this sense, they have the same degree of formal perfection. Descartes thinks the same holds for all the ideas I may have.

In the argument for the existence of God that I just sketched, Descartes is talking about the *objective* perfection of his idea of God. Let's reformulate the argument to make this explicit:

(1) My idea of God is objectively perfect.
(2) If an idea is objectively perfect, then the cause of that idea must be a perfect being.

Hence, God exists.

Premiss (2) strikes me as implausible. Here is a way to see that it is false. I claim that people could form their concept of God (a perfect being) in the following way. They could look at *imperfect* things in the world and thereby form the idea of *limited* intelligence, *limited* goodness, and *limited* power. Then, by applying the concept of negation (the concept we express by the word "not") to these ideas, they would obtain the idea of a being who has *unlimited* intelligence, goodness, and power. This seems to be an entirely possible causal explanation for why we have the idea of a perfect being. If it is possible, then (2) is false.

In the *Third Meditation*, Descartes explicitly considers this suggestion. He rejects the idea that we might have acquired the concept of perfection by seeing imperfect things and then applying the concept of negation. You should consider Descartes' argument and decide whether you think it works. Descartes thinks that the only possible explanation for the fact that we have an idea of a perfect being is that a perfect being actually exists and caused us to have this idea.

Leaving this exercise to you, I'll conclude that Descartes' causal argument for the existence of God is defective. Descartes wanted to show that "God exists" is not just true, but indubitably true. It was to be a foundational element in the structure of our knowledge. The argument he gave falls short of this ambitious goal.

The Cartesian Circle Scholars have argued over whether Descartes' argument for the existence of God has an additional defect. Is the argument circular, given its place in Descartes' larger epistemological program? Recall that Descartes wants to prove that God exists and is no deceiver in order to be able to conclude that the clarity and distinctness of an idea is a criterion of its truth. The argument just surveyed, like all arguments, involves the use of reason. For us to recognize that the argument establishes the existence of God, we must use the faculty of reasoning we possess. Descartes' argument begins by examining his concept of God and determining that this is the idea of a perfect being. Descartes therefore seems to be using the clarity and distinctness criterion in arguing that God exists. Descartes vehemently denied that he was guilty of circular reasoning. This problem has come to be known as the problem of the Cartesian circle.

Here's how I see this issue: Descartes is using the method of doubt test to assemble foundations for knowledge. His goal is to assemble enough premisses by this procedure so that he can show that we have knowledge of the world outside our minds. The existence of a God who is no deceiver is supposed to be one of these premisses. Descartes thought that his causal argument for the existence of God is beyond doubt; he thought that as you reason your way through the argument, you must find it irresistible.

Why should we agree that the proposition "every event has a cause" is beyond doubt? Descartes' view seems to be that when we consider the proposition carefully, using the full resources of clarification and logic that we possess, we will be driven to conclude that the proposition must be true. This seems to mean that we are applying the clarity and distinctness criterion. If so, Descartes is reasoning in a circle.

In the *Fifth Meditation*, Descartes proposes another proof of the existence of God. This proof is a version of the ontological argument, which I discussed in Lecture 8. I won't repeat the objections to that argument that I have already developed. But it is worth emphasizing that Descartes sets himself a higher standard than do most philosophers who have argued that God exists. Most philosophers would be happy to be able to prove from plausible premisses that there is a God. Descartes wants to do more; he wants to show that the existence of God is *indubitable*. I do not think that the ontological argument can claim to do this.

Where does this leave the project of refuting skepticism? Descartes thought that first-person psychological beliefs are indubitable. He recognized that this, by itself, is not enough to show that the beliefs we have provide us with genuine knowledge of the world outside the mind. An extra premiss is needed. The following example argument shows how Descartes wanted to bridge the gap between the indubitable knowledge we have of our own mental states and the beliefs we have about the world outside our minds:

Conclusion

(1) I now believe that the object in front of me is a page.
(2) My present belief is clear and distinct.
(3) Clear and distinct ideas are true.

────────────

There is a page in front of me.

The argument is valid: If the premisses are true, the conclusion also must be true.

Premiss (1) I have already discussed; Descartes thought that it is indubitable. But what of the next two premisses? There is an unhappy tension between these two claims.

Suppose we grant Descartes that premiss (3) is right—that a clear and distinct idea cannot fail to be true. If we grant this, then it is not so obvious that my present belief about what is in front of me really is clear and distinct. I may *think* that it is, but this appearance may be deceiving. So if (3) is right, (2) cannot be beyond doubt.

Alternatively, suppose we assume that we are able to tell, by introspection, whether a belief is clear and distinct. That will be enough to underwrite the truth of (2). But in that case, there is no longer any absolute assurance that (3) is right.

The problem here concerns whether we should see "clarity and distinctness" as a purely subjective characteristic of a belief. If I can tell just by examining the contents of my own beliefs whether they are "clear and distinct," I see no reason to say that a clear and distinct belief must be true. On the other hand, if I treat "clarity and distinctness" as a characteristic that is necessarily connected with truth, I don't see how I can tell whether a belief is "clear and distinct" just by introspecting.

Descartes tried to refute the following skeptical argument, which I described at the end of the previous lecture:

> Knowledge requires the impossibility of error.
> It is now possible that I am mistaken in believing that there is a page in front of me.
> ————————
> Hence, I don't know that there is a page in front of me.

Descartes accepted the first premiss, but denied the second.

Descartes concedes that we often make mistakes. The senses sometimes play tricks on us, and so does our faculty of reasoning. But the fact that this *sometimes* happens does not show that it is happening *now*. If I am now reasoning in a careful and logically rigorous way, then I cannot now be mistaken in what I believe, or so Descartes maintained.

So Descartes' reply to the skeptic's argument can be put like this:

> If God exists and is no deceiver and I now have a clear and distinct belief that there is a page in front of me, then I can't be mistaken in thinking that there is a page in front of me.
> God exists and is no deceiver and I now have a clear and distinct belief that there is a page in front of me.
> ————————
> I can't be mistaken in thinking that there is a page in front of me.

The problem is that Descartes' argument for the second premiss of this last argument was not successful. He was not able to prove that we are embedded in the world in the special way described by the hypothesis that God exists and is no deceiver. In consequence, he was not able to refute the skeptic's argument.

Review Questions

1. What is foundationalism in epistemology? What does it have to do with Euclidean geometry? With building a house?
2. What is the method of doubt test? What does Descartes use this method to do? What fails the test? What passes?
3. What does it mean to say that there is a "gap" between our first-person psychological beliefs and the beliefs we have about the world outside the mind?
4. Descartes thought that proving that God exists would help show why we are able to have knowledge of the world around us. Why did he think this? Is the proposition that "God exists and is no deceiver" foundational, according to Descartes?
5. Analyze Descartes' causal argument for the existence of God. Suppose that one of Aquinas' arguments for the existence of God is valid and has true premises. Could Descartes have used it, instead of his causal argument, to prove that God exists?
6. What is the problem of the Cartesian circle?
7. In the previous lecture an argument for skepticism was presented. How would Descartes evaluate this argument?

Problems for Further Thought

1. Which of the following propositions pass the method of doubt test? How are they different from each other?

   I seem to remember seeing Joe fly.
   I remember seeming to see Joe fly.
   It seems to me that Joe once flew.

2. Can you think of how it might be possible for someone to think *I seem to see a coffee cup* and be mistaken? Is there any way to reject Descartes' claim that *I am thinking* is true each time I say it to myself?

3. I suggested that our idea of a perfect being might be obtained by observing imperfect things and then using the concept of negation. Descartes considers this suggestion in the *Third Meditation* and rejects it. What reasons does Descartes give for rejecting this explanation? Are his reasons plausible?

4. In his work *The Principles of Philosophy* (1644), Descartes defines clarity and distinctness as follows:

   I term that "clear" which is present and apparent to an attentive mind, in the same way that we see objects clearly when, being present to the regarding eye, they operate upon it with sufficient strength. But the "distinct" is that which is so precise and different from all other objects that it contains within itself nothing but what is clear. . . . Perceptions may be clear without being distinct, but cannot be distinct without also being clear.

   Given this definition, can a clear and distinct idea be false?

Lecture 14

The Reliability Theory of Knowledge

Descartes:
Knowledge Is
Internally
Certifiable According to Descartes, *knowledge is internally certifiable.* What does this mean? It means that if I know some proposition *p*, then there exists an argument that shows that *p* must be true, *whose premisses are either* a priori *true or knowable by introspection.* Recall how Descartes would explain why I now know that there is a page in front of me:

> I believe that there is a page in front of me.
> My belief that there is a page in front of me is clear and distinct.
> Clear and distinct ideas are true.
> _____
> There is a page in front of me.

The first two premisses I know by introspection—by gazing within my own mind and examining its contents. How do I know that the third premiss is true? I know by introspection that I have an idea of a perfect God; I (supposedly) know *a priori* that an idea of a perfect being must be caused by a perfect being. Putting these two thoughts together, I deduce that God—a perfect being—must exist. The third premiss is supposed to follow from this.

Notice that the word "knowledge" does not appear in the displayed argument. So what does this argument have to do with the issue of whether I *know* that there is a page in front of me? For Descartes, I know that the concluding proposition is true because I know the premisses are true. And how do I know the premisses? I know these by introspection and *a priori* reasoning.

I want to name the elements in this argument. There is a *subjective premiss*, an *objective conclusion*, and a *linking premiss*. The subjective premiss describes what is going on in the subject's mind ("I believe that there is a page in front of me"). The objective conclusion makes a claim about the world outside the subject's mind ("There is a page in front of me"). The linking premiss (or premisses) shows how the subjective premiss necessitates the objective conclusion ("If I have a particular belief and it is clear and distinct, then it is true").

This vocabulary can be used to say what is characteristic of Descartes' approach to the problem of knowledge. His idea—that knowledge is internally certifiable—comes to this: *If the subject knows that the objective conclusion is true, then the subject must know that the linking premiss is true and must know this independently of sense experience.* By introspection and *a priori* reasoning, I can establish the required connection between what is inside the mind and what is outside it.

The theory of knowledge I will discuss in this lecture involves a very different approach from that taken by Descartes. It agrees with Descartes that knowledge requires the existence of a connection between what is going on inside the mind and what is going on outside it. Knowledge requires that a particular linking premiss be true. But according to the *reliability theory of knowledge*, the linking premiss does not have to be knowable by introspection and *a priori* reasoning. In fact, this theory of knowledge maintains that the subject does not have to know that the linking premiss is true at all.

The reliability theory of knowledge claims that there is an important analogy between knowledge and a reliable measuring device. This analogy was first proposed by the Australian philosopher David Armstrong. If you know that there is a page in front of you now, then your belief is related to the world outside your mind in the same way that the reading of a reliable thermometer is related to the temperature.

What Makes a Thermometer Reliable?

Thermometers are devices that form representations of temperature. The height of the mercury column is the representation; the ambient temperature is the thing represented. Thermometer readings represent temperature, just as your beliefs represent the world outside your mind. Thermometer readings can be accurate or inaccurate, just as beliefs can be true or false.

To understand what knowledge is, we must grasp what it is for a measuring device (a thermometer, for example) to be reliable. Is a thermometer reliable simply because its readings are accurate?

To see why this will not do, consider a thermometer that was used once and then destroyed. The thermometer said "98°F." ("F" is for Fahrenheit.) The ambient temperature happened to be 98°F. The reading was accurate, but that does not mean that the thermometer was a reliable one. For all I've said, the thermometer may have been stuck. If so, it was not reliable, even though its one and only reading was accurate.

A reliable thermometer is one in which there is a *necessary connection* between readings and ambient temperatures. If the thermometer reads $n°F$, then the temperature *must be* $n°F$. If a thermometer is reliable, then its reading *must* be correct; it cannot be mistaken in what it says. A stuck thermometer is not reliable, even when its readings are correct. It is unreliable because its readings are correct only *by accident*.

Are there reliable thermometers? I think so. The mercury thermometers we use to check whether we have fevers are examples. In saying this, I am not denying two obvious facts. First, a thermometer can be reliable in one set of circumstances but not in another. A mercury thermometer wouldn't be very useful for measuring temperature if it were wrapped in insulation before being placed in the mouth. The second point is that in saying that a thermometer is reliable, I am not denying that it would be unreliable if it were broken. Hitting a reliable thermometer with a hammer will usually be enough to make it unreliable.

So there are two things that help make a thermometer reliable. First, it has to be used in the right environment (for example, it can't be wrapped in insulation).

Second, the internal makeup of the device has to be right (for example, the glass tube that holds the mercury can't be broken).

Notice that reliability is an objective feature of the relationship between the thermometer and its environment. The question is whether the thermometer and its environment make the following claim true: If the thermometer says that the temperature is $n°F$, then the temperature must be $n°F$. It is an entirely separate question whether you or I recognize this fact about the thermometer/environment relationship. Whether we notice this fact is a subjective question, but whether the relationship obtains is an objective question.

Let's imagine that you take a thermometer out of a child's mouth, see that it reads $n°F$, and then announce: "The thermometer is reliable, so the baby's temperature is $n°F$." Suppose a contentious philosopher (like me) comes along and tries to refute your claim. I say:

> Your thermometer is not reliable. It is unreliable because I can conceive of a circumstance in which its reading would be false. I can conceive of a situation in which the thermometer is wrapped in insulation. In that case, the thermometer reading would not be correct. I also can conceive of the thermometer's being broken. In that case as well, the thermometer reading would not be correct. It follows from the fact that I can conceive of these things that your thermometer is not reliable.

Should you be convinced by my argument? I think not. Whether the thermometer is reliable *here and now* has nothing to do with what I can conceive of. Granted, if the situations I described actually obtained, then the thermometer would not be reliable in *those* circumstances. But from this it does not follow that the thermometer is unreliable in the circumstances in which it actually was used.

How does this discussion of reliable thermometers bear on the problem of knowledge? The reliability theory of knowledge says that an individual knows a proposition if the individual is related to the proposition the way a reliable thermometer is related to the temperature it measures. A reliable thermometer would not read $n°F$ unless the temperature were $n°F$. An individual knows that there is a page in front of her precisely when the individual would not have believed that there is a page in front of her unless there were one there.

Another way to express this idea is by using the concept of *causality*. A thermometer is reliable in a given circumstance, if the only thing that could cause the thermometer to read $n°F$ is that the temperature really is $n°F$. Similarly, S knows that there is a page in front of her in a given circumstance, if the only thing that could cause S to believe this is that there really is a page in front of her.

I hope the connection between thermometers and knowledge is starting to become clear. Suppose S believes that there is a page in front of her. We want to know whether this belief is an instance of knowledge. The answer should depend on the *actual* relationship that obtains between S and her environment.

Suppose S's sensory system is functioning normally; she is not hallucinating, for example. In addition, suppose that there are no evil demons around who might choose to provide S with misleading evidence. If so, it may be true that S is a reliable indicator of the presence of a page. If you want to answer the question of whether S knows that there is a page present, it will be entirely irrelevant to point out that if S had taken a hallucinatory drug or if S were plagued by an evil demon, then S's belief would be (or might be) false. These *hypothetical* considerations do nothing to undermine the claim that S's sensory state is a reliable indicator of what is going on in her environment.

Here's how the reliability theory of knowledge (RTK) characterizes what knowledge is:

(RTK) S knows that p if and only if

> (1) S believes that p.
> (2) p is true.
> (3) in the circumstances that S occupies, if S believes that p, then p must be true.

The third condition can also be formulated in either of the following two ways:

> — in the circumstances that S occupies, S would not believe that p unless p were true.
> — in the circumstances that S occupies, it is impossible that S believe p and p be false.

Notice that the reliability theory of knowledge makes use of the concepts of *necessity* and *impossibility*. To understand this theory of knowledge, we need to look more carefully at what these concepts mean.

I want to discuss three kinds of impossibility. Consider the following three statements:

> (1) Joe can't be a married bachelor.
> (2) Joe can't go faster than the speed of light.
> (3) Joe can't tie his shoes.

Three Concepts of Impossibility

The word "can't" in each of these indicates that something is *im*possible. But different kinds of impossibility are involved.

The first statement is logically necessary. It has to be true, just by virtue of logic and the definitions of the terms involved. If definitions and their deductive consequences are *a priori* true (Lecture 8), then statement (1) expresses a necessary truth that is *a priori*.

In contrast, statement (2) is not *a priori*. We know that it is true because Einstein's theory of relativity—an *a posteriori* theory—says that it is so. Statement (2) is said to be "nomologically necessary" (from *nomos*, meaning *law*). It is necessary because of a law of nature, in this case an *a posteriori* law of physics.

What is meant by a "law of nature"? I won't try to give a full answer. However, one property of a law is worth noting. Laws are *a posteriori* generalizations that do not name any place, time, or individual. Newton's universal law of gravitation is an example. But "The Rockies are over 10,000 feet tall," though true, is not a law of nature.

Statement (3) differs from the first two examples. Its truth does not follow from logic and definitions, nor does its truth follow from any law of nature — physical, biological, or whatever. Rather, to see that statement (3) is true, you have to take into account particular facts about Joe. Joe can't tie his shoes (now) because he is carrying several bags of groceries. I'll call this third sort of necessity *circumstantial necessity*. By this I mean that the statement is necessarily true only because of facts about the circumstances described.

There is an additional fact about type (3) necessity that I should note. Whether we judge statement (3) true or false depends on how we interpret it; that is, (3) is ambiguous. If we interpret it to mean that Joe can't tie his shoes because he is otherwise occupied, (3) may be true. But suppose we take (3) to mean that even if Joe put down the bags, he still could not tie his shoes. If that is how we interpret (3), we may judge it false. This is an important feature of statements that are circumstantially necessary.

When I say that a thermometer is reliable, I mean that it and its environment are related in a special way. I am saying that its circumstances are such that its reading *must* be correct. In saying this, I am using the concept of *circumstantial necessity*.

Similarly, when I say that S knows that there is a page in front of her, I am saying that she is related to her environment in a special way. I am saying that she cannot be mistaken in believing what she does. Here again, I am using the concept of circumstantial necessity.

Suppose that a real printed page is the only thing that could get S to believe that a printed page is before her. Her senses are functioning normally. There are no evil demons lurking about who provide misleading evidence. If this is so and if S subsequently believes the proposition in question, then S will *know* that there is a printed page in front of her. This is what the reliability theory says. In this circumstance, her belief will be related to the world the way the reading of a reliable thermometer is related to the temperature.

To Have Knowledge, You Do Not Have to be Able to Construct a Philosophical Argument Refuting the Skeptic

It is important to notice that these claims about S are not refuted by the fact that S may not be able to defend her knowledge claim against clever philosophical interrogation. If I asked S how she knows that her impressions aren't caused by an evil demon, she may draw a blank. If I ask her how she knows that she is not dreaming, she may admit that she can't construct an argument proving that she is not dreaming. Such philosophical puzzles may even lead S to say "I guess I don't know that there is a printed page in front of me." But her comment does not show that she lacks knowledge. Rather, it shows only that S does not believe that she knows that there is a printed page in front of her.

If S is like a reliable thermometer, she has knowledge. But being like a reliable thermometer does not require that S have the ability to construct fancy philosophical arguments that show that she is like a thermometer. Thermometers can't construct philosophical arguments, yet they are sometimes reliable. *S* may be similar. She may be unable to refute the skeptic, but that does not show that she lacks knowledge.

S may even be a skeptic herself. She may believe that she lacks knowledge. But that does not mean that she really lacks it. Just as it is possible to mistakenly believe that a thermometer is unreliable, so it is possible to mistakenly believe

---

The KK Principle

The KK principle says that if you know that p, then you know that you know that p. The reliability theory rejects this principle. The following several paragraphs about this principle will be somewhat tough to grasp — so take a deep breath, read them slowly, and then read them again.

I have just argued that the following situation is possible: S knows that p, but S does not believe that she knows that p. This means that S might know that p even though she does not know that she knows that p. If I am right, the KK principle is false.

If the KK principle were true, S could prove that she lacked knowledge, just by becoming a philosophical skeptic. This would be very convenient — wouldn't it be nice to be able to prove some thesis just by believing it?

Suppose S believed, maybe for no reason at all, that she lacked knowledge. If so, the KK principle would imply that, indeed, she did lack knowledge. To see why, consider the following argument:

(1) If you do not believe that you have knowledge, then you don't know that you have knowledge.

(2) If you don't know that you have knowledge, then you don't have knowledge.

If you do not believe that you have knowledge, then you don't have knowledge.

This argument is deductively valid (what is its logical form?). Notice that premiss (1) is correct; it follows from the fact that knowing a proposition requires that you believe the proposition. Premiss (2) would be true if the KK principle were true.

Consequently, if the KK principle were true, then believing that skepticism is true would be enough to ensure that skepticisim is true. But if knowing is like being a reliable thermometer, then whether you have knowledge cannot depend on whether you think you have knowledge.

The reliability theory of knowledge holds that whether an agent knows something is settled by the objective relationship that obtains between the agent's belief and the environment. Whether the agent believes that this relationship obtains is irrelevant. Thus, the reliability theory rejects the KK principle.

that an individual lacks knowledge. In fact, it is possible to have false beliefs about our own situations: We can believe that we lack knowledge and yet be wrong.

In summary, the reliability theory of knowledge explains why S knows that there is a page in front of her by describing the following argument:

S believes that there is a page in front of her.
In the circumstances S occupies, she would not believe that there is a page in front of her unless there were a page in front of her.

———————

There is a page in front of S.

This argument does not use the word "know." So what does it have to do with knowledge? According to the reliability theory, S knows that the concluding proposition is true because the premisses are true. But S does not have to *know* that the premisses are true. Nor does S have to produce an argument independent of sense experience for the premisses. This shows why the reliability theory rejects Descartes' claim that knowledge is internally certifiable.

One virtue of the reliability theory is that it explains what is wrong with a standard skeptical argument. The skeptic claims that S does not know that there is a printed page in front of her on the grounds that it is possible to imagine that S is deluded in some way. You can imagine a situation in which S believes what she does, but is mistaken. The reliability theory shows why this act of imagination is irrelevant to the question of whether S has knowledge *in the real world situation she occupies.*

A Problem for the Reliability Theory

To conclude this discussion, I want to consider a problem that the reliability theory confronts. It involves a fact about circumstantial necessity that I mentioned before: Claims of circumstantial necessity often are *ambiguous*. I'll restate the point and then show how it is relevant to the reliability theory.

Consider the statement "Joe can't tie his shoes." Suppose I make this comment to you while we are looking at Joe, who is carrying two heavy bags of groceries. Is the quoted remark true? Here are two ways of interpreting it:

(1) If Joe tries to tie his shoes while holding the bags of groceries, he will fail.
(2) If Joe tries to tie his shoes after first putting down the groceries, he will fail.

If we interpreted "Joe can't tie his shoes" to mean (1), it might be true; if we interpreted it to mean (2), it might be false. Which reading you choose affects whether you will say that the quoted claim is true.

To see how this idea applies to the reliability theory of knowledge, let's switch examples—from knowing that there is a printed page in front of you, to knowing that there is a barn in the field next to the road on which you are driving. Suppose one day you go for a drive in Dane County, which is the county that contains Madison, Wisconsin. On your drive, you look at a field and say, "There is a barn in that field." Suppose that the proposition you've asserted is true. Is this belief of yours a case of knowledge?

The reliability theory says that we must ask whether, in the circumstances you occupy, there is anything besides a real barn that could have caused you to believe that a barn is present. The problem I want to focus on is that it is not entirely clear how to decide what is included and what is excluded by the expression "in the circumstances you occupy."

First, I'll define the idea of a "fool's barn." Fool's gold looks like gold, but is not gold at all. A fool's barn is something that looks like a barn but isn't one. Suppose that there are no fool's barns in Dane County. The only things that look like barns are real barns. This means that if I describe the circumstances you occupy by saying that you are in Dane County, then it will be true that the only thing that could have made you think that a barn is present is a real barn. Hence, your belief counts as a case of knowledge.

But now let us broaden our vision. In Hollywood, there are fool's barns. These are the facades used in movie sets. When viewed from one angle, they look like barns, but they are not buildings at all. So if you were driving around Hollywood and came to believe that a barn was present, your belief would not count as knowledge (even if your belief happened to be true). The reason is that the circumstances you then would occupy would make it false that the only thing that could cause you to have the belief is a real barn.

So if your circumstances are restricted to Dane County, you might know that a barn is present; if your circumstances are restricted to Hollywood, you would not. But now consider a puzzle.

I initially suggested that the circumstances you occupy are limited to the objects in Dane County. Given this array of objects, I argued that a real barn is the only thing (in the circumstances) that could cause you to think that a barn is present. But why describe your circumstances so narrowly? Why not describe your circumstances as including all the objects in the United States? If I take your circumstances in this way, it will be false that the only thing that could cause you to believe that a barn is present is a real barn.

Here's another form of the same problem. Suppose there are no fool's barns anywhere in the world. Assume that Hollywood has never constructed them, nor has anybody else. But suppose that Dane County farmers occasionally *talk* about putting one up, just to fool the tourists. The farmers have the lumber and nails at hand. It clearly is possible for them to construct a fool's barn if they choose to do so.

You are on your drive and think there is a barn in the field you are passing. Is this true belief of yours a case of knowledge? If we describe the circumstances you occupy as limited to the objects that actually exist, we'll conclude that the only thing that could cause you to think a barn is present is a real barn. On the other hand, if we think of your circumstances as including the possibility of fool's barns, we'll reach the opposite conclusion.

Here is the point: When we assert or deny that the only thing *in the circumstances* that could cause you to believe a barn is present is a real barn, we are making reference to the environment you occupy. The environment may be thought of as composed of a set of objects. If we describe that set narrowly, it may be true that the only thing in the set that could cause your belief is a real barn. If we enlarge the set, this assertion may no longer be true.

The problem for the reliability theory is that clause (3) requires elaboration. The theory must clarify what is encompassed by the phrase "in the circumstances that S occupies." If we tried to specify precisely what this means, two things might happen.

One possibility is that we would find that there is a single correct way to describe what the agent's environment includes. Maybe there is a set of principles that dictates whether your environment is limited to the things in Dane County, or to the things that actually exist in the United States, or to the things that exist or could be built. If there were a single correct solution to this puzzle, we would say that the reliability theory is true, though incomplete as characterized so far. It requires supplementation by further principles. Once these are provided, it will be true or false, in each case, whether the agent knows or fails to know the proposition in question.

Thesis of the Relativity of Knowledge

Alternatively, we might discover that there is no way to specify principles that define what an agent's circumstances are supposed to include. Perhaps it is arbitrary whether we take the environment in a narrower or more inclusive way. Perhaps there are a number of equally correct choices available. If so, we would conclude that *knowledge is relative*.

Let's be clear what this relativity thesis asserts. When you say that something is relative, you should be prepared to say *what* it is relative to. The thesis that knowledge is relative is the thesis that whether an agent knows a proposition depends on (is relative to) a specification of his or her circumstances. These circumstances can be specified in different equally correct ways, so there is no absolute answer to the question of whether the agent has knowledge.

Let's consider a down-to-earth example of relativity. Mary and Sue are walking down the street, side by side. Is Mary walking to the left of Sue? Well, that depends on the point of view. If you look at them from the front, you get one answer. If you look at them from the back, you get the other. The key thing to notice is that x's being to the left of y is not a relation between x and y alone. It involves some third item, z.

Does S know that p? The suggestion now being considered is that the question is incomplete. Whether S knows that p depends on a third item in addition to the agent S and the proposition p. It depends on a specification of S's environment. There are different true ways to describe S's environment. S is in Dane County. But it also is true that S is in the United States. Relative to one specification of the environment—call it E_1—it turns out that S knows that p. But relative to another equally true specification of the environment—call it E_2—it emerges that S does not know that p. The thesis that knowledge is relative is the thesis that there is no set of principles that tells you which true specification of the environment is the right one to consider when you're asking whether an agent knows something.

I've mentioned two possible reactions to the problem sketched. One is to say that the reliability theory of knowledge is true but incomplete; the theory requires supplementation by a set of principles that says what description of the environment ought to be considered in assessing claims about an agent's knowledge. The other possibility is that there is no such set of principles—that knowledge is an inherently relative phenomenon. Which of these is the correct reaction?

I will not try to say whether knowledge is relative. Rather, I want to describe an interesting consequence of the relativity thesis. Skepticism is the position that people do not have knowledge. Its opposite is the more commonsense idea that people often (if not always) know the propositions they believe. If the relativity thesis is true, then each of these theses is true in one sense, but false in another.

If the Relativity Thesis Is True, Is Skepticism True or False?

What's Relative About Einstein's Theory of Relativity?

Sometimes people say that Einstein proved that "everything is relative." This is not true. Neither is the more modest claim that Einstein proved that everything in physics is relative.

To say that a statement is relative is not to say that it is subjective or arbitrary. Rather, it is to say that the statement is incomplete in a particular way. Whether Sue is walking to the left of Mary is a relative matter. That means that there exists some third item, beyond the two people mentioned, that must be referred to if the statement is to be true or false. To say just that one is to the left of the other is to fail to express a complete thought.

It takes no enormous insight or creativity to see that whether one person is walking to the left of another is a relative, not an absolute, matter. In contrast, Einstein's idea that simultaneity is relative is anything but obvious. It was a brilliant theoretical conjecture, something that is not at all suggested by our commonsense talk about time and space.

Consider two events that occur at different places. Common sense suggests that either the events are simultaneous with each other or they are not. Einstein's theory says that this assertion is not true. Whether two events are simultaneous depends on the choice of some third item—a "rest frame." Relative to one rest frame, the events are simultaneous, but relative to another equally "correct" rest frame, they are not. Simultaneity is relative, not absolute.

Einstein did not say that everything in physics is relative. For example, in the special theory of relativity he defines a quantity called "the space–time interval." This quantity measures the amount of separation there is between events; it takes account of both spatial and temporal distances. The space–time interval between two events is not relative to the choice of a rest frame. Space–time interval is absolute, not relative.

THE RELIABILITY
THEORY
OF KNOWLEDGE

If the agent's environment is given a very broad specification, then skepticism is true. If the environment is given a narrower specification, then the opposite position will be correct. But notice that there is no conflict between the following two claims:

(1) S knows that p, relative to E_1.
(2) S does not know that p, relative to E_2.

These statements do not conflict with each other, any more than the following pair conflict with each other:

(3) Mary is walking to the left of Sue, when they are viewed from the front.
(4) Mary is not walking to the left of Sue, when they are viewed from the back.

So the dispute between skepticism and common sense seems to end in a stalemate, not in a victory for either side, if the relativity thesis is correct. Each position is correct in one sense, but incorrect in another.

Review Questions

1. At the beginning of this lecture, I said that Descartes held that knowledge is "internally certifiable." What does this mean? Does the reliability theory of knowledge agree?
2. What is the difference between logical necessity, nomological necessity, and circumstantial necessity?
3. What does it mean to say that claims about circumstantial necessity are "ambiguous"?
4. What does it mean to say that a thermometer is "reliable"? What analogy does the reliability theory of knowledge see between reliable thermometers and knowledge?
5. How does the reliability theory of knowledge assess the following skeptical argument: "I can imagine that my senses are now malfunctioning. Hence, I don't now know that there is a printed page in front of me."
6. What is the KK principle? Does the reliability theory accept it? Explain why the following claim is correct: "If the KK principle were true, then you could prove that skepticism is true just by believing that it is true."
7. What does it mean to say that knowledge is "relative"? Relative to what?
8. If the relativity thesis were true, would skepticism be true or false?

Problems for Further Thought

1. For any proposition p, we can construct the sentence "S knows that p." Since "S knows that lemons are yellow" is a sentence, we can construct the sentence "S knows that S knows that lemons are yellow." We can repeat this operation as many times as we please. The KK principle says that if S knows that p,

then *S* knows that *S* knows that *p*. Formulate similar principles for truth (the TT principle), belief (the BB principle), and surprise (the SS principle). Are any of these principles plausible? Defend your answers.

2. In this lecture, I posed the question of whether knowledge is relative. Do you think that it is? Why or why not?

3. Do you think that nonhuman organisms have knowledge? For example, do dogs? What is required for dogs to have knowledge, according to the reliability theory? How do these requirements differ from what would be demanded by the view that knowledge is internally certifiable?

Lecture 15

Justified Belief and Hume's Problem of Induction

In this lecture, I am going to shift gears; I'm going to present a new problem in epistemology. So far, I've discussed the concept of *knowledge,* and have examined Descartes' foundationalism (Lecture 13) and the reliability theory of knowledge (Lecture 14). The problem to be considered now concerns the idea of justified belief.

Before starting, let's be clear on how this problem differs from the previous one. What's the difference between knowledge and justified belief? Two differences should be clear. First, if *S* knows that *p*, then *p* must be true, whereas *S*'s having a justified belief that *p* does not require that *p* be true. Knowledge requires truth, but justified belief does not.

Knowledge versus Justified Belief

The second difference is that knowledge requires the impossibility of error; justified belief does not. Recall the lottery example discussed in Lecture 12. Suppose you believe, before the drawing, that ticket number 346 will not win in a fair lottery containing a thousand tickets. Suppose your belief turns out (after the drawing) to have been true. I claim that you didn't *know* that the ticket wouldn't win. Nevertheless, I concede that you had strong evidence for thinking that the ticket would lose. Your belief was reasonable or justified (I'll use these two terms interchangeably).

The lottery example also shows that justified belief does not require certainty or indubitability. Before the drawing, you're not absolutely certain that ticket number 346 will lose; nevertheless, it is reasonable to think that the ticket will lose. Often, we are justified in believing propositions that are not absolutely certain. Think of the beliefs we have about our immediate physical surroundings. Do our sensory experiences allow us to be absolutely certain about the way the world is outside the mind? Presumably not; maybe there is some small chance that we're mistaken. But this does not mean that our sensations don't provide us with excellent evidence about the way the world is. Perhaps certainty is impossible, but that does not mean that justified belief is impossible as well.

These comparisons of knowledge and justified belief are summarized in the following table:

	Is truth required?	Is the impossibility of error required?	Is certainty required?
Knowledge	Yes	Yes	No
Justified belief	No	No	No

Be sure you understand what this table means. You should see how some of the entries depend on thinking that the reliability theory of knowledge is correct.

We sometimes use the word "probability" to describe cases in which the evidence falls short of providing absolute certainty. We say that ticket number 346 *probably* will not win, to indicate that we are not absolutely sure that it will not. We might also say that our present experiences make the beliefs we have about the world outside the mind highly probable. Your present experiences don't make it absolutely certain that there is a printed page in front of you. But it seems plausible to say that your experiences make it very probable that your physical environment is as I just described it.

Skepticism About Justified Belief

Until now, I've talked about skepticism as if it were a single thesis. Now I want to distinguish skepticism about knowledge from a second kind of skepticism, which concerns the idea of justified belief.

The contrast between certainty and probability affects how we view the skeptical thesis that knowledge is something we simply do not have. We might be tempted to take the following stance to this sort of skeptical thesis:

> Perhaps we don't *know* the things we sometimes say we know. Maybe when we describe ourselves as knowing things, this is just sloppy talk. So maybe skepticism about knowledge is defensible. However, this does not mean that our beliefs about the world are groundless and arbitrary. Although skepticism about knowledge may be defensible, we still can insist that we have justified beliefs.

I'm not saying that we *should* make this concession to the knowledge-skeptic. All I'm saying is that even if we do, the integrity of our picture of the world is not terribly threatened. We can retain the beliefs we have about the physical world; we merely say that they are "reasonable" and "well-justified," even if they are not entitled to be labeled "knowledge." The point is that knowledge skepticism does not entail skepticism about rational belief.

The view just described involves agreeing with knowledge skepticism, but declining to be a skeptic about justified belief. It is this latter idea — that we really do have justified beliefs about the world — that David Hume challenged in his discussion of induction (recall Hume's discussion of the design argument from Lecture 5). Why should we think that the evidence we have really justifies us in believing what we do? Why isn't this just a prejudice we have about ourselves?

In Lecture 13, I emphasized that Descartes was not a skeptic; rather, his goal was to refute skepticism. I've just distinguished two sorts of skepticism — skepticism about knowledge and skepticism about justified belief. Descartes rejected both these skeptical theses.

I have discussed Descartes' efforts to show that we have knowledge about the world outside the mind, based on the contents of our own experience. Let's recast Descartes' problem as a problem about the concept of rational justification: How do the contents of my experience justify me in the beliefs I hold about my physical environment?

This problem might be expressed in the following way. I now seem to see a printed page in front of me. I also believe that there is a printed page in front of me. How does the former fact about me justify the latter belief about the world? Why is it reasonable to think that the world is the way one's senses say it is?

This Cartesian example concerns the connection between what is inside my mind here and now and the nature of the physical environment I inhabit here and now. But I have lots of beliefs that fall into neither category. For example, there are the beliefs I have about the future, the beliefs I have about the distant past, and the beliefs I have that are generalizations, which encompass past, present, and future together. In what way could this further category of beliefs — ones that extend beyond the here and now — be justified? At present, I have beliefs about tomorrow, but these are not based on my directly experiencing what tomorrow will bring. I believe that the sun will rise tomorrow. But my reason for this belief is not that I now am seeing tomorrow's sunrise. Rather, the basis I have for this belief is the observations I have made in the past and the ones I am making in the present.

Two Problems About Rational Justification

Descartes' problem involves the way in which my *present* experience justifies my belief about my *present* physical environment. Hume's problem of induction had to do with how the beliefs I have about my *present* and *past* physical environment justify my beliefs about the *future*.

So Descartes' problem (at least the one just described) and Hume's problem focus on two different links in the chain of justification that connects some of our beliefs with others. The contents of our memories and experiences justify some of the singular beliefs we have about the past and present. These latter beliefs justify the predictions we make about the future and the generalizations we believe to be true about past, present, and future. Descartes inquired into the first connection: Why do the contents of my perceptions and memories support the beliefs I have about the present and past? Hume inquired into the second:

Why do the beliefs I have about the present and past support the beliefs I have that are predictions and generalizations?

Consider an example that encompasses both problems. Suppose I get up early one morning and watch the sun rise. As I do so, two sorts of epistemological questions may come to mind. Why do I now think that the sun is rising? Presumably, this has to do with the content of my present experience. Why do I think that the sun has risen in the past? Presumably, this has to do with the memories I now possess of previous observations. These two questions concern what I am calling Descartes' problem. They address perception and memory; why should either be trusted?

Hume's problem arises when I ask why I should believe that the sun *will rise tomorrow*. Perhaps I am entitled to the perceptual beliefs and memories just mentioned. These involve beliefs about the present and the recent past. But what entitles me to form the expectations I do about the future?

This separation of Descartes' problem from Hume's problem can be depicted as follows:

Hume's problem	Prediction:	"The sun will rise tomorrow."
	↑	
	Present and past	"The sun is now rising."
Descartes' problem	observation:	"The sun has risen each day that I have made an observation."
	↑	
	Present mental contents:	"I now seem to see a sunrise." "I now seem to remember that the sun has risen on each day that I have made an observation."

The arrow between one level and another indicates the direction in which justification flows. Our present mental contents justify the beliefs we have about our present and past; these, in turn, justify the predictions we make about the future.

Descartes' problem asks whether we can justify the perceptual beliefs and memories we have, based on the level below them. Hume's problem about induction asks whether we can justify the predictions we now believe, based on our present perceptual beliefs and memories.

Founda-tionalism

The diagram just given depicts a variety of *foundationalism*. Lower items support (provide the foundations for) higher items. Descartes argued that the bottom items are indubitable (perfectly certain). Notice that I have not drawn arrows pointing to the opposite direction. It is the one-way flow of justification (bottom up, not top down) from base to superstructure that makes this picture foundational.

Although Descartes and Hume both considered skeptical problems, they reached very different conclusions about the problems they addressed. Descartes thought he could refute the skeptic. In contrast, Hume argues that the predictions and generalizations we believe are not rationally justifiable. Hume was a skeptic; Descartes was not.

I have stressed throughout this book that the main interest in philosophy lies in arguments. Anyone can announce an outrageous thesis. What is of interest is seeing whether a convincing argument can be offered in its defense. The reason that Hume is remembered as an important philosopher is not that he held bizarre opinions about various philosophical issues. The interest of Hume's philosophy lies in the arguments he provided to support them. What is important about Hume's skepticism about induction is his *argument* that skepticism is the right view to take. It is to this argument that I now turn.

We constantly form expectations about what the future will be like or about which generalizations (statements of the form "All *A*s are *B*) are true, based on evidence that is not deductively conclusive. Our beliefs about the future are based on perception and memory, but you can't deduce what the future will be like from premises that describe just the present and the recent past.

Hume's Skeptical Thesis About Induction

Let's focus on an example in order to get clear on this simple point. Suppose I have observed many emeralds and have found each of them to be green. I then formulate the prediction "the next emerald I observe will be green"; or maybe I formulate the generalization "all emeralds are green." Just so this can be an example of the kind I want, suppose that being green is not part of the meaning of the term "emerald." This means that the statement "all emeralds are green" is an empirical (*a posteriori*) one; if you want to know whether it is true or false, you have to make observations. Reflection on the meanings of the terms involved is not enough.

Common sense says that we are rational in believing the predictions and generalizations we do, if those beliefs are based on lots of evidence. Looking at lots of emeralds and finding that each is green seems to justify my expectation that the next emerald I examine will be green. Hume claims that this common-sense idea is mistaken. His thesis is that the predictions and generalizations we believe cannot be rationally justified.

It is important to see the radicalness of Hume's claim. It is obvious that we cannot *deduce* generalizations or predictions from our past observations. Hume is saying something more than this. He is saying that our past experience provides *no rational justification whatever* for the predictions and generalizations we believe.

It should be obvious that the premisses of the following arguments do not deductively imply their conclusions:

(GEN) I've observed numerous emeralds, and each has been green.
$$\overline{\qquad\qquad}$$
Hence, all emeralds are green.

(PRED) I've observed numerous emeralds, and each has been green.
$$\overline{\qquad\qquad}$$
Hence, the next emerald I observe will be green.

I've drawn a double line between premises and conclusions to indicate that these arguments are not deductively valid.

In both the generalization argument (GEN) and the prediction argument (PRED), we think that the conclusion reached is rationally grounded by the premises. We think that it isn't a mere prejudice to hold, in each case, that the premiss provides good evidence for the truth of the conclusion. Hume's thesis is that this conviction cannot be rationally defended.

So it is important to see that Hume's thesis goes far beyond the undisturbing claim that the (GEN) and (PRED) arguments just given are not deductively valid. That much is obvious. Rather, Hume is saying that the premises in those arguments do not rationally justify their conclusions. Hume's view is that there is absolutely no rational justification for the beliefs we have that are predictions or generalizations. That's quite an amazing claim.

Hume's view is that it is merely a habit we have that we regard such premises as providing good reason to believe such conclusions. This is a habit we can't abandon; it is part of human nature to expect the future to resemble the past. But it is a habit that we cannot rationally defend. When challenged by the skeptic to rationally justify this pattern in our thinking, we can only say that this is the way human beings in fact operate. We cannot produce a good argument to rationally justify this habit of mind.

Hume's Argument that Induction Cannot Be Rationally Justified

Why did Hume reach this startling conclusion about induction? Hume thought that the arguments previously stated (GEN and PRED) require an additional premiss. As they stand, the premiss does not support the conclusion. If the observation is to support the generalization or the prediction, then we must assume that the future will resemble the past. This assumption Hume calls the *Principle of the Uniformity of Nature* (PUN).

Hume thought that this principle plays an indispensable role in each and every inductive argument we make. The previous example concerns the color of emeralds. But consider the belief that the sun will rise tomorrow. This predictive belief is based on the premiss that the sun has risen on each of the days that we have bothered to make an observation. Why should these *past* observations support the prediction I make about *tomorrow*? Hume thought that I must be assuming that nature is uniform—that the future will resemble the past. Hume says that without this assumption, the past would be no guide to the future.

So each and every inductive argument presupposes PUN: We must assume PUN if the observational premiss is to support the prediction or generalization stated in the argument's conclusion. This means that if the conclusion we reach is rationally defensible, then a good argument must be found for thinking that PUN is true. If PUN cannot be defended, then anything we believe that depends on assuming that PUN is true must likewise be indefensible.

We now can state Hume's skeptical argument:

(1) Every inductive argument requires PUN as a premiss.
(2) If the conclusion of an inductive argument is rationally justified by

the premisses, then those premisses must themselves be rationally justifiable.

(3) So, if the conclusion of an inductive argument is justified, there must be a rational justification for PUN.

(4) If PUN is rationally justifiable, then there must be a good inductive argument or a good deductive argument for PUN.

(5) There is no good inductive argument for PUN, since any such argument will be circular.

(6) There cannot be a good deductive argument for PUN, since PUN is not *a priori* true, nor does PUN deductively follow from the observations we have made to date.

(7) So, PUN is not rationally justifiable.

Hence, there is no rational justification for the beliefs we have that take the form of predictions or generalizations.

In a nutshell, Hume's claim is that the beliefs we have about emerald color and tomorrow's sunrise (and lots of other beliefs as well) are not rationally justifiable because they rest on an assumption that can't be rationally justified.

Let's look more carefully at steps 4–6 in the argument. Consider what PUN asserts; it says that nature is uniform. More specifically, it says that the future will resemble the past — that past uniformities will continue to obtain in the future.

Is this something that we could know to be true on the basis of induction? If it were, the inductive argument would look like this:

Nature has been uniform in my past observations.

Nature in general is uniform.

Recall that Hume claims that *all* inductive arguments require that PUN be assumed as a premiss. But the argument just stated is inductive. Notice that if we insert PUN as a premiss, as Hume requires, the argument becomes circular — it assumes as a premiss the very proposition it tries to establish as a conclusion.

What about the other sort of justification? Can we give a deductive justification of PUN? Here again, Hume holds that the answer is *no*. The previous argument is not deductively valid; the general uniformity principle cannot be deduced from the observations I have made in the past.

Hume considers, and rejects, a second possible sort of deductive argument — could PUN be a definitional truth, deducible from the definitions of the terms it uses? If PUN were a definitional truth, it would have the same sort of *a priori* justification that "all bachelors are married" possesses.

Hume rejects this idea by saying that there is "no contradiction" in supposing that the universe should suddenly cease to be uniform. It is not a definitional truth that past regularities will continue into the future, Hume says.

It now should be clear how Hume's skeptical argument proceeds. First, there is a claim: Every inductive argument requires the premiss that nature is uniform. Second, Hume argues that no rational justification can be given for that premiss.

He defends this assertion by considering three options: (1) an inductive argument in favor of PUN; (2) a deduction of PUN from past observations; (3) a deduction of PUN from definitions. He asserts that none of these ways of defending PUN is going to work. This means that PUN cannot be justified. Hume concludes that the inductive inferences we make are not rationally justifiable.

Review Questions

1. What is the difference between knowledge and justified belief? Does skepticism about knowledge entail skepticism about rational justification? What does each of these skeptical theses assert?
2. What is the difference between Descartes' problem and Hume's problem?
3. Hume says that we cannot deduce what the future will be like from our present observations and memories. Does Hume's skeptical thesis say anything more than this?
4. What is the Principle of the Uniformity of Nature?
5. What is Hume's skeptical argument about induction?

Problems for Further Thought

1. Is the claim that nature is uniform falsifiable (Lecture 9)? That is, can you describe a possible observation that would count against this claim?

2. Can you identify a mistake in Hume's argument that induction is not rationally justifiable?

3. Is it possible that all of our beliefs could be rationally justified? Would this be possible if we had some finite number of beliefs? Would it be possible, if we had an infinite number of beliefs? What does it mean to say that a belief is rationally justified?

_____ *Lecture 16*_____

Can Hume's Skepticism Be Refuted?

In the previous lecture, I described Hume's skeptical argument about induction as focusing on the Principle of the Uniformity of Nature (PUN). This principle, recall, says that the future will resemble the past. In this lecture, I will criticize this version of Hume's argument. Then I'll formulate Hume's argument in another way. After that, I'll examine two suggestions that have been made for refuting Hume's very startling conclusion. Again, you want to be clear on what Hume's conclusion is. He didn't merely say that our predictions are uncertain; he said that they have *no rational justification whatever*. They are the product of a rationally indefensible habit that is deeply entrenched in human nature.

PUN says that the future will resemble the past. Recall that Hume held that every time we make an induction—inferring that the sun will rise tomorrow or that the next emerald we observe will be green—we are assuming that nature is uniform. So PUN is supposed to be an assumption that is required by each and every inductive argument.

What Does the Principle of the Uniformity of Nature Say?

But what, exactly, does PUN mean? Does it mean that nature is uniform *in each and every respect*? If so, it is fairly clear that we don't think that PUN is true. Summer leaves are green, but we do not expect autumn to resemble summer in this respect. So if we understand PUN in this way, the principle can't be something we must assume.

Let's try a second interpretation. Maybe PUN means that the future will resemble the past *in some respect*. This does seem to be something we believe. However, this claim about the future is so modest that it is hard to see how it will help very much in the task of inferring what the future will be like. If I want to know whether future emeralds will be green or blue based on my observation that so far they all have been green, this version of PUN is rather useless. It does not tell me whether it makes sense to expect emeralds to remain green or to expect a change.

These two attempts to clarify what PUN says illustrate a general problem. No one yet has been able to clarify the principle so that it has both of the following properties:

(1) PUN is plausible.
(2) PUN gives definite advice about what we should infer from present observations.

There is a third requirement that Hume's argument about induction says we should include. This is the requirement that the principle should play the role in inductive inference that Hume said it did:

(3) If we want to make inductive inferences about the world, PUN is something we must believe, no matter what else we believe.

This last condition expresses the idea that PUN is an assumption—a presupposition—that underlies the whole project of inductive inference.

If it is hard to formulate PUN so that it satisfies (1) and (2), it will be even harder to clarify the principle so that it satisfies (1), (2), and (3). I have not proved that it is impossible to do this. But no one has done so yet.

As a result, I suggest we drop the formulation of Hume's argument that involves

CAN HUME'S SKEPTICISM BE REFUTED?

PUN. Instead, I'll consider a different version of Hume's argument that induction cannot be rationally justified.

A New Concept — Degrees of Reliability

This new version of Hume's argument involves the idea that a method of inference possesses *some degree of reliability*. Induction is a method of inference. Like other methods of inference, it makes predictions and says what generalizations are true, based on a set of observations. We can say of a method of inference *how often* the predictions or generalizations it endorses have been true. A method that usually leads to truth is highly reliable. One that rarely does so is very unreliable.

This use of the concept of reliability departs somewhat from the one employed by the reliability theory of knowledge (Lecture 14). There I discussed reliability as an on/off concept; a thermometer is either reliable or it is not. Moreover, a reliable thermometer, in the sense employed there, *must* make true claims about the temperature.

Notice that the concept of *degrees of reliability* is not an on/off concept. In addition, a highly reliable method of inference can sometimes lead to falsehood. The point is that it does so *rarely*. A method of inference is highly reliable if the predictions it makes are *usually* true.

Induction is a rule that scientists use to evaluate hypotheses in the light of evidence. A scientist makes a finite number of observations — call them *O*. The goal is to say which hypothesis among a set of competing hypotheses is most plausible in the light of those observations. For example, suppose you've examined numerous emeralds and all have been green (call this *O*). The problem is to say which of the following hypotheses is better supported in the light of those observations:

H_1: All emeralds are green.
H_2: All emeralds are green until the year 2050; thereafter, they are blue.

Common sense suggests that H_1 is more plausible than H_2 in the light of the observations *O*. The philosophical question is to explain why this is so. Hume denied that this evaluation of the competing hypotheses can be rationally defended.

What Is a Rule of Inference?

Rules of inference provide *licenses*. A fishing licence permits you to fish. A rule of inference permits you to draw conclusions. In the previous example, induction permits you to conclude that H_1 is probably true, given *O*. That is, induction is a rule of inference that connects premiss to conclusion in the following argument:

I've examined lots of emeralds and all have been green.
I ═══════════
All emeralds are green.

I have drawn a double line to indicate that the argument is not deductively valid. I have written an "I" beside the double line to indicate that the rule of inference being used is induction. The problem of induction is to explain why we are entitled to use this inference rule.

Common sense may suggest that we are entitled to use induction now because induction has been reliable in the past. Induction has often been used to make predictions, and the predictions endorsed by inductive arguments usually, if not always, turned out to be correct. This is why we rightly take seriously what induction tells us.

Does the Past Reliability of Induction Provide an Answer?

Hume rejected this attempt to rationally justify induction. Let us examine it more carefully. Here is the argument we need to consider:

Induction has been highly reliable in the past.

I ═══════════

Induction will be highly reliable now and in the future.

The premiss of this argument is something we know by having observed the past track record of the inductive method. The conclusion makes a claim about what will be true now and in the future.

Every argument must use a rule of inference to license the transition from premiss to conclusion. What rule of inference is used here? Can the conclusion be validly deduced from the premiss? No; that is why I have drawn a double line. This is an *inductive* argument; induction (I) is the rule of inference that is being used.

Hume's point about this argument is that it is *circular* or *question-begging*. The philosophical question is whether induction can be rationally justified. This argument simply assumes that induction is legitimate. You can't justify using induction now by appeal to the fact that induction has been successful in the past.

So Hume's skeptical argument about induction can be formulated as follows:

Hume's Argument Reformulated

(1) To rationally justify induction, you must show that induction will be reliable.
(2) To show that induction will be reliable, you must construct an inductive argument or a deductively valid argument.
(3) You can't show that induction will be reliable by an inductive argument; that would be question-begging.
(4) You can't validly deduce that induction will be reliable from premisses describing the past reliability of induction (or from definitions).

————————

Hence, induction cannot be rationally justified.

This argument does not say anything about the Principle of the Uniformity of Nature (PUN). Can it be refuted?

Hume claimed that a rational justification for using induction must show that the method will probably be reliable. But the contemporary British philosopher Peter Strawson (in *Introduction to Logical Theory*, London, Methuen, 1952) has challenged this claim. Strawson rejects premiss (1) of Hume's argument.

Strawson: It's Analytic that Induction Is Rational.

Strawson's idea is a simple one. He thinks that the statement "induction is rational" is like the statement "bachelors are unmarried." Both are *a priori* truths. Both are deductive consequences of the definitions of the terms that occur in them. According to Strawson, induction is, by definition, a rational activity.

Strawson does not claim that "induction will be reliable" is an *a priori* truth. He agrees with Hume that this is not true by definition. But he thinks that you don't have to establish that an inference rule will be reliable if you want to show that using the rule is rational. Hume thought that rationality requires reliability. Strawson denies this.

According to Strawson, it is entirely rational to use inductive methods to formulate our beliefs about the future, even though we can offer no good reason for expecting that the method will probably lead to true beliefs. If it turns out later that we were entirely mistaken about what we thought the world would be like, no one can accuse us of having been irrational. We would have behaved perfectly reasonably, even though we ended up with false beliefs.

I find Strawson's argument unconvincing. Methods of inference are methods for doing things. Consider an analogy: Recipes also are methods for doing things. Suppose I told you that I have a great recipe for making a cake. To determine whether this is true, you would want to see if the method is reliable. The point of the recipe is to produce nice cakes. You evaluate the recipe by seeing if it is a reliable instrument. It would be puzzling if someone said that a particular recipe is excellent, even though he granted that there is no reason whatever to think that using the recipe would probably result in a nice cake.

But this is just what Strawson is saying about induction. The point of induction is to reach true beliefs about the world. That is the goal of inference. Whether it is reasonable to use induction or some other method depends on whether the method is a reliable instrument for attaining the specified goal. If it can't be shown that the instrument will attain the goal, it is hard to see how using the instrument is rationally justified. Strawson's mistake, I think, is to hold that the rationality of a method has nothing to do with its reliability.

Black: Induction Can Be Inductively Justified

I turn now to an attempt at providing an inductive justification of induction. The American philosopher Max Black ("Inductive Support of Inductive Rules," in *Problems of Analysis*, Ithaca, Cornell University Press, 1954) has argued that once you look carefully at what "circularity" means, you'll see that the inductive justification of induction is not circular at all; that is, Black holds that the following argument provides a perfectly good reason for accepting the conclusion:

> Induction has been highly reliable until now.
> I ═══════════
> Probably, induction will be highly reliable if we use it now and in the future.

Once again, I use the letter "I" to indicate that the rule of inference that licences passing from the premiss to the conclusion is the principle of induction.

What does Black think it means for an argument to be circular? His suggestion is roughly as follows: If an argument is circular, then the conclusion occurs as one of the premises. This isn't Black's exact formulation, but it captures the spirit of what he says. For Black, circularity involves a relationship between the conclusion and the premisses. It has nothing to do with what rule of inference is used to get from premises to conclusion.

I hope it is clear why, if you accept Black's definition of circularity, the previous inductive justification of induction is not circular. However, the point I want to make is that Black's definition is too narrow. There is a broader definition of circularity that shows that the previous argument is circular. It's this: An argument is circular if it couldn't possibly convince someone that the conclusion is true if they didn't believe the conclusion already. A circular argument can't change anybody's mind. If you have doubts about induction, the previous argument isn't going to lay them to rest.

Besides this, there is another problem confronting Black's suggestion. Consider a bizarre rule of inference that is the very mirror image of induction. It is called *counterinduction*. Induction tells you to expect past regularities to continue into the future. Counterinduction tells you to expect past regularities *not* to continue. For example, counterinduction licences the following inference:

I've examined lots of emeralds and all have been green.
CI ═══════════════
Future emeralds will *not* all be green.

Of course, induction would lead to a quite different conclusion. The problem of induction is, in part, to explain why we should use induction rather than counterinduction to formulate our predictions about the future.

What has this to do with Black's proposal? Black claims that the inductive justification of induction is not circular. If he is right, then neither is the following argument:

Counterinduction has been highly *un*reliable until now.
CI ═══════════════
Probably, counterinduction will be highly reliable if we use it now and in the future.

Here we have a counterinductive justification of counterinduction.

Counterinduction has had a poor track record in the past. How should we expect it to do in the future? That depends on what rule of inference we use. If we use induction, we will expect counterinduction's dismal past track record to continue into the future. But if we use counterinduction, we expect the pattern to reverse. Since the method has been *un*reliable in the past, we expect that counterinduction will be *reliable* in the future.

So we have two arguments to compare: the inductive justification of induction and the counterinductive justification of counterinduction. Which method of inference — induction or counterinduction — should we now use? The problem with Black's inductive justification of induction is that it gives us no reason to reject the counterinductive justification of counterinduction. This means that Black's favored inductive justification of induction, even if it is noncircular in Black's sense of the term, does not show why we should use induction rather than counterinduction. So Hume's problem has not been solved.

Is it possible to refute Hume's argument? We have examined two attempts to do so. I think that both fail. This does not mean that there is no way to prove Hume wrong. In the next lecture, I'll consider this problem from a different angle.

Review Questions

1. When we try to clarify exactly what the Principle of the Uniformity of Nature says, we run into a problem. What is the problem?
2. How can Hume's skeptical argument about induction be formulated without mentioning the Principle of the Uniformity of Nature?
3. What is Strawson's justification of induction? What objection to it was presented in this lecture?
4. What is Black's inductive justification of induction? What two objections to it were presented in this lecture?
5. What does it mean to say that a rule of inference is a "licence"? What is the difference between the licence provided by induction and the licence provided by counterinduction?

Problems for Further Thought

1. The problem of induction involves explaining why the observation of many emeralds, all of them green, supports H_1 better than H_2:

   H_1: All emeralds are green.
   H_2: All emeralds are green until the year 2050; thereafter, they are blue.

   Can the Surprise Principle (Lecture 3) be used to show that the observations strongly favor H_1 over H_2? Explain your answer.

2. Hume considers, and rejects, two kinds of arguments that might justify induction—deductive arguments and inductive arguments. Would considering abductive arguments change the sort of conclusion that Hume reaches about induction?

3. Consider the rules of inference that are used in arguments we think are deductively valid. How can these rules be justified? Formulate a skeptical problem about deduction that is similar to Hume's problem about induction. Can this problem be solved?

Lecture 17

Beyond Foundationalism

In the previous lecture, I briefly considered two attempts to refute Hume's skeptical argument about induction. I argued that neither is successful. However, from this we cannot be certain that no attempt to justify induction will succeed. So the question remains: Can Hume's skepticism be refuted?

In this lecture, I want to return to the similarity between Descartes' problem and Hume's problem, which I described in Lecture 15. I am going to argue that if we understand the idea of rational justification in the way Hume did, then he was right that induction cannot be rationally justified. Notice that the thesis I'll be arguing for has an *IF* in it. I will not claim that Hume's skepticism is correct. My conclusion will be more modest: Skepticism is correct *IF* the task of rational justification is understood in the way Hume understood it.

Hume's Problem and Descartes' Problem

Let's go back to the diagram I presented in the first lecture on Hume's problem (Lecture 15). Hume was a skeptic whereas Descartes was not. Even so, there is an important similarity between the problems they formulated. Descartes asked: How does my present mental state justify the beliefs I have about the world outside my mind? Hume asked: How do the observations I have made of my physical environment justify the beliefs I have about the future?

Both Descartes and Hume were foundationalists in the way they approached questions about knowledge and justification. By this I mean that each held that *IF* an item in the following diagram is justified or known, then it is justified or known solely on the basis of its relationship to things below it:

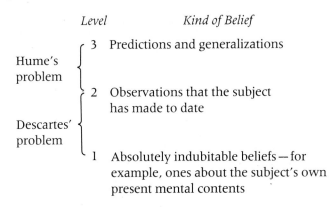

Foundationalism holds that justification flows from bottom to top, not in the other direction.

Hume reasoned that *IF* beliefs in category 3 were justified, they would have to be justified solely on the basis of items in category 2. Descartes reasoned that *IF* beliefs in category 2 were justified, they would have to be justified solely on the basis of items in category 1. Notice that both of these points are *IF* statements. They don't assert that the beliefs in question actually are justified; the point is that Descartes and Hume agreed about what would have to be true *IF* the items in question were justified. This is something on which a skeptic and a nonskeptic might agree.

I now want to advance a thesis about Descartes' problem and then extend that thesis so that it applies to Hume's problem as well.

Let's grant Descartes that each of us is absolutely certain about his or her own psychological state. My point is that these level 1 beliefs are not enough to justify the beliefs I have about the physical environment I inhabit (level 2). I need an additional assumption concerning the *relationship* between levels 1 and 2. This connecting principle might take the form of claiming that God exists and is no deceiver. Or it might take some other form. But the contents of my own experience are simply not enough, taken all by themselves.

The parallel thesis about Hume's problem is as follows: If my beliefs about my present and past environment (items at level 2) are to justify the predictions and generalizations I believe (items at level 3), then I have to assume something about the *relationship* between levels 2 and 3. Perhaps the Principle of the Uniformity of Nature ("the future will resemble the past") is an example of such a bridge principle. Or some other bridge principle might be proposed. But my present perceptions and memories are simply not enough, taken all by themselves.

Be clear on what I'm suggesting. First, let's note a trivial and obvious point: Level 1 statements do not deductively imply level 2 statements, and level 2 statements do not deductively imply level 3 statements. For example, statement (a) does not deductively imply statement (b), and statement (c) does not deductively imply statement (d):

- (a) I seem to see a printed page in front of me.
- (b) There is a printed page in front of me.
- (c) I've observed lots of emeralds and all have been green.
- (d) All emeralds are green.

My point is not this obvious fact about deductive relationships. I want to make a more ambitious claim. Not only do lower level statements fail to deductively imply higher level statements; I also want to claim that lower level statements, all by themselves, are not enough to provide a justification for higher level statements. Lower level statements, taken by themselves, do not even provide good evidence for higher level statements; that is, a strong nondeductive argument from (a) to (b) cannot be made unless additional assumptions are made about the relationship of level 1 to level 2; the same is true of an inference from (c) to (d).

This is a rather radical thesis, I admit. Do your present experiences provide evidence about the physical environment you occupy? That depends on what you assume about the *relationship* between your present experiences and the world outside your mind. Given one set of assumptions, statement (a) might be excellent evidence that statement (b) is true. But given a different set of assumptions, statement (a) would be good evidence that statement (b) is false. The point is that the assumptions you make, one way or the other, go beyond what is contained in level 1. Assumptions about the relationship of levels 1 and 2 are not, properly speaking, contained in level 1.

Whether X Is Evidence for Y Depends on Background Assumptions Z

I hope my discussion of Descartes makes plausible what I'm saying about the relationship of (a) and (b). If you assume that the environment is "normal" and that your senses are functioning properly, then (a) is evidence favoring (b). However, if you assume that your senses are misleading you, then (a) would be evidence against (b).

What would the parallel claim be about the relationship of (c) and (d)? We naturally take (c) to be evidence favoring (d). How could this be otherwise? Well, suppose you believed the following statement (the example is that of I. J. Good, "The White Shoe Is a Red Herring," *British Journal for the Philosophy of Science,* vol. 17, p. 322, 1967):

> Either there are lots of emeralds, of which 99% are green, or
> there are very few emeralds, and all of them are green.

If you believed this, then (c) would be evidence *against* (d). However, if you believed the following statement, then (c) would provide evidence *in favor of* (d):

> If you examine lots of emeralds and all have been found to be
> green, then probably all emeralds are green.

Notice that the two possible assumptions just listed are not strictly at level 2.

Whether (c) is evidence for or against (d) depends on what assumptions you make. If you make no assumptions about the relationship of level 2 and level 3, then the evidence described in (c) cannot be interpreted as either favorable or disfavorable to (d).

In a way, the present idea is something that has already been raised in this book. I have already pointed out that hypotheses are testable only when background assumptions are added to them (Lecture 9). Here's an elaboration of that idea: When you test a hypothesis H and obtain some observations O, it will usually be true that O is evidence for or against H only because of the background assumptions (A) you made.

We have here another example of a relativity thesis in philosophy. The idea of relativity, recall, was discussed in Lecture 14. Sue and Mary are walking side by side. Is Sue walking to the left of Mary? No answer can be given until a third term is specified: Viewed from the front, the answer is *yes*, but viewed from the

Another Relativity Thesis

back, the answer is *no*. We should not ask whether *x* is to the left of *y*, but whether *x* is to the left of *y*, relative to some third item, *z*, which we can specify.

Is statement (c) evidence for statement (d)? No answer can be given until a third term is specified. Relative to one set of assumptions the answer is *no*, but relative to another the answer is *yes*. We should not ask whether one statement is evidence for another, but whether one statement is evidence for another, relative to a set of background assumptions.

Foundational-ism Leads to Skepticism

I am stressing that the evidence relationship involves three things, not just two. Whether *O* is evidence for *H* depends on background assumptions (*A*). What impact does this point have on the problems that Hume and Descartes pursued about the concept of rational justification? My suggestion is that the problems they posed lead right to skepticism. If the challenge is to see if level 3 beliefs can be justified *strictly by level 2 beliefs*, we must conclude that this cannot be done. Likewise, if the problem is to see if level 2 beliefs can be justified *strictly by level 1 beliefs*, we are forced to reach a negative conclusion in this case as well.

Descartes was not a skeptic about the rational justifiability of level 2 beliefs. Hume was a skeptic about the rational justifiability of level 3 beliefs. My claim is that if we adopt a foundationalist understanding of what rational justification involves, then Descartes was wrong and Hume was right. In both Descartes' problem and Hume's problem, foundationalism leads to skepticism.

A Nonfounda-tionalist Approach to Justification

I do not think that this claim shows that our beliefs are totally lacking in rational justification. Rather, I believe that the foundationalist misunderstands what it takes to rationally justify a belief. We *can* justify a level 3 belief. We do this by appealing to other beliefs we have, some of which will themselves be at level 3. The same holds for the beliefs we have at level 2.

Think of how the task of justification works in everyday life and in science. If scientists make a prediction, or if we make one in our everyday lives, how are these predictions to be defended? If we say that the sun will rise tomorrow, we can support this prediction by appealing to other beliefs we have about the way the solar system has worked *and will continue to work*. In everyday life and science, we allow people to justify their beliefs at level 3 by appealing to other beliefs that also are at level 3. Often, predictions are justified by citing generalizations. In doing this, we are not playing by the rules that foundationalism lays down. We are not justifying a belief at one level strictly in terms of beliefs that are at lower levels.

What does this imply about whether our beliefs about the world are rationally justified? My point is to focus on what it means to ask for a rational justification. If we understand that idea in a foundationalist way, we will be led straight to skepticism—to the conclusion that the beliefs we have are not rationally justifiable. However, if we recognize that the idea of rational justification need not be understood in a foundationalist way, skepticism does not threaten. In everyday life and in science, we frequently say that our beliefs are justified. When we do this, we are not using a foundationalist understanding of the idea of rational justification. However, it seems to me that we often are perfectly correct in saying that some of our beliefs are well-justified. I think that people often use nonfoundationalist standards of justification in both science and in everyday life.

Our standards of rational justification often depend on the audience we have in mind. Suppose you believe some proposition that some other person does not. Your goal is to rationally persuade the other individual that you are right. In doing this, you will feel free to use as a premiss in your argument any belief that the two of you share. If you agree over lots of things, there will be many propositions that you can use as premises. But if your disagreement is more pervasive, you will be much more limited in the premises you can use. And if you somehow disagreed about *everything*, it would be impossible to construct a rational argument that shows this person that the proposition in question is correct.

What does it mean for one person to rationally justify a proposition p to another person who does not already believe p? This means that the first person constructs a good argument, based on premises that both parties would agree to, that p is correct. It is easier to rationally justify a proposition to someone who agrees with you about a lot than to someone who agrees with you about very little.

Rational Justification as an Activity

In everyday life, it is a familiar occurrence that one person rationally justifies some proposition to another. The same is true in science and in courts of law. But matters change when we ask someone to justify a proposition *to a skeptic*. A skeptic will not agree with you about many of the things you take for granted. If the skeptic differs with you on sufficiently many beliefs, perhaps it will be impossible to rationally convince the skeptic that the proposition is true.

Foundationalists say that when you try to provide a rational justification of some proposition p, you must construct an argument that would be compelling *to a skeptic who doubts all the propositions that are at the same level as p*. This is one sort of activity, but there are others. A more familiar problem of rational justification is to construct an argument that would convince someone who does not already believe p, but who has lots of other beliefs at the same level as p. Even if the foundationalist's problem is insoluble, this does not mean that more familiar problems of rational justification are also insoluble.

Review Questions

1. What is meant by saying that we have beliefs at level 1, level 2, and level 3? How does a foundationalist understand what it means for a belief at a level to be rationally justified? Are there any beliefs that are located at none of these three levels?
2. A relativity thesis is advanced in this lecture concerning the idea of inductive evidence. What is that thesis? How does it go beyond the "trivial and obvious" fact that level 2 beliefs do not deductively imply beliefs at level 3?
3. How could the observation of lots of green emeralds be evidence *against* the claim that all emeralds are green?

4. Foundationalists understand the problem of rational justification in one way, but people in ordinary life usually think of the problem in another. What's the difference?

Problems for Further Thought

1. Otto Neurath (1882–1945) thought that the following metaphor captures something important about how we go about rationally constructing and revising the beliefs we have: "We are like sailors who must rebuild their ship on the open sea, without being able to dismantle the ship in dry dock or being able to reconstruct it from the best components." What does this metaphor mean? What do you think Neurath's view was of foundationalism?

2. In Lecture 7, I argued that scientific explanation is possible only for *local* why-questions. In the present lecture, I argued that you can rationally justify a proposition to someone only if you agree with that person about something. What similarities are there between these two theses?

·R·E·A·D·I·N·G·S·

Knowledge Is Something More Than True Belief

·PLATO·

In this dialogue, The Theaetetus, *Plato (427–347 B.C.) describes a conversation between Socrates, who was his teacher, and Theaetetus. Theaetetus discovers, through Socrates' questioning, that he, Theaetetus, knows much less than he thought he did.*

Two main points emerge in these excerpts. First, knowledge is something more than true belief. The suggestion is made that knowledge requires true belief plus "an account." An account must involve some sort of justification. But what sort? If the propositions providing the account are not themselves known to be true, then it is hard to see how they can provide knowledge. However, it is circular and unhelpful to say that someone knows *a proposition* p *when the individual truly believes that* p *and knows some propositions that justify* p.

SOCRATES: To start all over again, then, what is one to say that knowledge is? For surely we are not going to give up yet.

THEAETETUS: Not unless you do so.

S: Then tell me, what definition can we give with the least risk of contradicting ourselves?

T: The one we tried before, Socrates. I have nothing else to suggest.

S: What was that?

T: That true belief is knowledge. Surely there can at least be no mistake in believing what is true and the consequences are always satisfactory.

S: Try, and you will see, Theaetetus, as the man said when he was asked if the river was too deep to ford. So here, if we go forward on our search, we may stumble upon something that will reveal the thing we are looking for. We shall make nothing out, if we stay where we are.

T: True. Let us go forward and see.

S: Well, we need not go far to see this much. You will find a whole profession to prove that true belief is not knowledge.

T: How so? What profession?

S: The profession of those paragons of intellect known as orators and lawyers. There you have men who use their skill to produce conviction, not by instruction, but by making people believe whatever they want them to believe. You can hardly imagine teachers so clever as to be able, in the short time allowed by the clock, to instruct their hearers thoroughly in the true facts of a case of robbery or other violence which those hearers had not witnessed.

T: No, I cannot imagine that, but they can convince them.

S: And by convincing you mean making them believe something.

T: Of course.

S: And when a jury is rightly convinced of facts which can be known only by an eyewitness, then, judging by hearsay and accepting a true belief, they are judging without knowledge, although, if they find the right verdict, their conviction is correct?

T: Certainly.

S: But if true belief and knowledge were the same thing, the best of jurymen could never have a correct belief without knowledge. It now appears that they must be different things.

T: Yes, Socrates, I have heard someone make the distinction. I had forgotten, but now it comes back to me. He said that true belief with the addition of an account (λόγος) was knowledge, while belief without an account was outside its range. Where no account could be given of a thing, it was not "knowable"—that was the word he used—where it could, it was knowable.

S: Well, then, what is this term "account" intended to convey to us? I think it must mean one of three things.

T: What are they?

S: The first will be giving overt expression to one's thought by means of vocal sound with names and verbs, casting an image of one's notion on the stream that flows through the lips, like a reflection in a mirror or in water. Do you agree that expression of that sort is an "account"?

T: I do. We certainly call that expressing ourselves in speech (λέγειν).

S: On the other hand, that is a thing that anyone can do more or less readily. If a man is not born deaf or dumb, he can signify what he thinks on any subject. So in this sense anyone whatever who has a correct notion evidently will have it "with an account," and there will be no place left anywhere for a correct notion apart from knowledge.

T: True.

S: Then we must not be too ready to charge the author of the definition of knowledge now before us with talking nonsense. Perhaps that is not what he meant. He may have meant being able to reply to the question, what any given thing is, by enumerating its elements.

T: For example, Socrates?

S: For example, Hesiod says about a wagon, "In a wagon are a hundred pieces of wood." I could not name them all; no more, I imagine, could you. If we were asked what a wagon is, we should be content if we could mention wheels, axle, body, rails, yoke.

T: Certainly.

S: But I dare say he would think us just as ridiculous as if we replied to the question about your own name by telling the syllables. We might think and express ourselves correctly, but we should be absurd if we fancied ourselves to be grammarians and able to give such an account of the name Theaetetus as a grammarian would offer. He would say it is impossible to give a scientific account of anything, short of adding to your true notion a complete catalogue of the elements, as, I think, was said earlier.

T: Yes, it was.

S: In the same way, he would say, we may have a correct notion of the wagon, but the man who can give a complete statement of its nature by going through those hundred parts has thereby added an account to his correct notion and, in place of mere belief, has arrived at a technical knowledge of the wagon's nature, by going through all the elements in the whole.

T: Don't you approve, Socrates?

S: Tell me if you approve, my friend, and whether you accept the view that the complete enumeration of elements is an account of any given thing, whereas description in terms of syllables or of any larger unit still leaves it unaccounted for. Then we can look into the matter further.

T: Well, I do accept that.

S: Do you think, then, that anyone has knowledge of whatever it may be, when he thinks that one and the same thing is a part sometimes of one thing, sometimes of a different thing, or again when he believes now one and now another thing to be part of one and the same thing?

T: Certainly not.

S: Have you forgotten, then, that when you first began learning to read and write, that was what you and your school-fellows did?

T: Do you mean, when we thought that now one letter and now another was part of the same syllable, and when we put the same letter sometimes into the proper syllable, sometimes into another?

S: That is what I mean.

T: Then I have certainly not forgotten, and I do not think that one has reached knowledge so long as one is in that condition.

S: Well then, if at that stage you are writing "Theaetetus" and you think you ought to write T and H and E and do so, and again when you are trying to write "Theodorus," you think you ought to write T and E and do so, can we say that you know the first syllable of your two names?

T: No, we have just agreed that one has no knowledge so long as one is in that condition.

S: And there is no reason why a person should not be in the same condition with respect to the second, third, and fourth syllables as well?

T: None whatever.

S: Can we, then, say that whenever in writing "Theaetetus" he puts down all the letters in order, then he is in possession of the complete catalogue of elements together with correct belief?

KNOWLEDGE IS
SOMETHING MORE
THAN TRUE BELIEF

T: Obviously.

S: Being still, as we agree, without knowledge, though his beliefs are correct?

T: Yes.

S: Although he possesses the "account" in addition to right belief. For when he wrote he was in possession of the catalogue of the elements, which we agreed was the "account."

T: True.

S: So, my friend, there is such a thing as right belief together with an account, which is not yet entitled to be called knowledge.

T: I am afraid so.

S: Then, apparently, our idea that we had found the perfectly true definition of knowledge was no better than a golden dream. Or shall we not condemn the theory yet? Perhaps the meaning to be given to "account" is not this, but the remaining one of the three, one of which we said must be intended by anyone who defines knowledge as correct belief together with an account.

T: A good reminder. There is still one meaning left. The first was what might be called the image of thought in spoken sound, and the one we have just discussed was going all through the elements to arrive at the whole. What is the third?

S: The meaning most people would give — being able to name some mark by which the thing one is asked about differs from everything else.

T: Could you give me an example of such an account of a thing?

S: Take the sun as an example. I dare say you will be satisfied with the account of it as the brightest of the heavenly bodies that go round the earth.

T: Certainly.

S: Let me explain the point of this example. It is to illustrate what we were just saying — that if you get hold of the difference distinguishing any given thing from all others, then, so some people say, you will have an "account" of it, whereas, so long as you fix upon something common to other things, your account will embrace all the things that share it.

T: I understand. I agree that what you describe may fairly be called an "account."

S: And if, besides a right notion about a thing, whatever it may be, you also grasp its difference from all other things, you will have arrived at knowledge of what, till then, you had only a notion of.

T: We do say that, certainly.

S: Really, Theaetetus, now I come to look at this statement at close quarters, it is like a scene painting. I cannot make it out at all, though, so long as I kept at a distance, there seemed to be some sense in it.

T: What do you mean? Why so?

S: I will explain, if I can. Suppose I have a correct notion about you; if I add to that the account of you, then, we are to understand, I know you. Otherwise I have only a notion.

T: Yes.

S: And "account" means putting your differentness into words.

T: Yes.

S: So, at the time when I had only a notion, my mind did not grasp any of the points in which you differ from others?

T: Apparently not.

S: Then I must have had before my mind one of those common things which belong to another person as much as to you.

T: That follows.

S: But look here! If that was so, how could I possibly be having a notion of you rather than of anyone else? Suppose I was thinking, Theaetetus is one who is a man and has a nose and eyes and a mouth and so forth, enumerating every part of the body. Will thinking in that way result in my thinking of Theaetetus rather than of Theodorus or, as they say, of the man in the street?

T: How should it?

S: Well, now suppose I think not merely of a man with a nose and eyes, but of one with a snub nose and prominent eyes. Once more shall I be having a notion of you any more than of myself or anyone else of that description?

T: No.

S: In fact, there will be no notion of Theaetetus in my mind, I suppose, until this particular snubness has stamped and registered within me a record distinct from all the other cases of snubness that I have seen, and so with every other part of you. Then, if I meet you tomorrow, that trait will revive my memory and give me a correct notion about you.

T: Quite true.

S: If that is so, the correct notion of anything must itself include the differentness of that thing.

T: Evidently.

S: Then what meaning is left for getting hold of an "account" in addition to the correct notion? If, on the one hand, it means adding the notion of how a thing differs from other things, such an injunction is simply absurd.

T: How so?

S: When we have a correct notion of the way in which certain things differ from other things, it tells us to add a correct notion of the way in which they differ from other things. On this showing, the most vicious of circles would be nothing to this injunction. It might better deserve to be called the sort of direction a blind man might give. To tell us to get hold of something we already have, in order to get to know something we are already thinking of, suggests a state of the most absolute darkness.

T: Whereas, if. . . ? The supposition you made just now implied that you would state some alternative. What was it?

S: If the direction to add an "account" means that we are to get to *know* the differentness, as opposed to merely having a notion of it, this most admirable of all definitions of knowledge will be a pretty business, because "getting to know" means acquiring knowledge, doesn't it?

T: Yes.

KNOWLEDGE IS
SOMETHING MORE
THAN TRUE BELIEF

s: So, apparently, to the question, "What is knowledge?" our definition will reply, "Correct belief together with knowledge of a differentness," for, according to it, "adding an account" will come to that.

t: So it seems.

s: Yes, and when we are inquiring after the nature of knowledge, nothing could be sillier than to say that it is correct belief together with a *knowledge* of differentness or of anything whatever.

So, Theaetetus, neither perception, nor true belief, nor the addition of an "account" to true belief can be knowledge.

t: Apparently not.

s: Are we in labor, then, with any further child, my friend, or have we brought to birth all we have to say about knowledge?

t: Indeed we have, and for my part I have already, thanks to you, given utterance to more than I had in me.

s: All of which our midwife's skill pronounces to be mere wind eggs and not worth the rearing?

t: Undoubtedly.

s: Then supposing you should ever henceforth try to conceive afresh, Theaetetus, if you succeed, your embryo thoughts will be the better as a consequence of today's scrutiny, and if you remain barren, you will be gentler and more agreeable to your companions, having the good sense not to fancy you know what you do not know. For that, and no more, is all that my art can effect; nor have I any of that knowledge possessed by all the great and admirable men of our own day or of the past. But this midwife's art is a gift from heaven; my mother had it for women, and I for young men of a generous spirit and for all in whom beauty dwells.

Meditations on First Philosophy

· RENÉ DESCARTES ·

In this work, René Descartes (1596–1650) tries to discover to what extent he has genuine knowledge of the world he inhabits. He pursues a foundationalist strategy. First, he attempts to discover which of his beliefs are beyond doubt. These will be the foundations for the rest of what he knows. Second, the task is to show how these foundational items support the rest of his knowledge.

Besides addressing the problem of knowledge, Descartes also considers the relationship that obtains between his mind and his body. In the Sixth Meditation *he argues that these are distinct objects. This position — dualism — will be discussed in the section of the text on philosophy of mind.*

Synopsis of the Following Six Meditations

In the First Meditation the reasons are given why we can doubt all things, especially material things, as long, of course, as we have no other foundations for the sciences than the ones which we have had up until now. Although it is not readily apparent that this doubt is useful, still it is the more so in that it frees us of all prejudices and paves an easy path for leading the mind away from the senses. Finally, it makes it impossible for us to doubt further those things that we shall discover to be true.

In the Second Meditation the mind, by using the freedom peculiar to it, supposes the nonexistence of all those things about whose existence it can have the least doubt, and judges that such a supposition is impossible unless the mind exists during that time. This is also of the greatest utility, since by this means it easily distinguishes what things pertain to it — that is, to an intellectual nature — and what things pertain to a body. But because perhaps many people expected to see proofs for the immortality of the soul here, they are to be put on notice that I believe that I have begun to write in this work only what I have carefully demonstrated. Therefore I was unable to follow any order but the one in use among geometricians, which is to state first everything on which the proposition in question depends, before concluding anything regarding that proposition. But what is required principally and primarily for knowing that the soul is immortal is that we formulate as clear a concept of the soul as possible, patently distinct from any concept of a body. This is what has been done here. Moreover, it is also required that we know that everything that we clearly and distinctly understand is true, in precisely the manner in which we understand them. This could not have been proven before the Fourth Meditation. Moreover, one must have a distinct concept of corporeal nature, which is formulated partly in the Second Meditation, and partly in the Fifth and Sixth. But from all this one ought to conclude that all things clearly and distinctly conceived as diverse substances — as, for example, mind and body are conceived — are indeed substances that are really distinct from one another. This is arrived at in the Sixth Meditation. The same thing is confirmed there from the fact that a body cannot be understood to be anything but divisible, whereas the mind cannot be understood to be anything but indivisible, for we cannot conceive of half a soul, as we can in the case of any body, however small. This is so much the case that the natures of mind and body are acknowledged to be not only diverse but even, in a manner of speaking, to be the contraries of one another. I have not written further on the matter in this treatise, both because these considerations suffice for showing that the annihilation of the mind does not follow from the corrupt state of the body — and therefore for giving mortal men hope in an afterlife — and also because the premises from which the immortality of the mind can be proven depend upon an account of the whole of physics: first, we must know that absolutely all substances, that is, everything that needs to be created by God in order to exist, are by their very nature incorruptible nor can they ever cease to be, unless by this very same God the denial of whose concurrence to them would reduce them to nothing.

Second, we must notice that a body, taken in a general sense, is a substance and that it therefore can never perish. But the human body, insofar as it differs from other bodies, is composed only of a certain configuration of members, together with other accidents of the same sort. But the human mind is not composed of any such accidents, but is a pure substance. For although all its accidents may undergo change—so that it understands some things, wills others, senses others, etc.—the mind does not for this reason become something else. But the human body does become something else by the mere fact that the shape of some of its parts changes. From these considerations it follows that a body can easily cease to be, whereas the mind by its nature is immortal.

In the Third Meditation I have explained at sufficient length, it seems to me, my principal argument for proving the existence of God. Be that as it may, I sought to use no comparisons drawn from corporeal things, in order to draw the souls of the readers as far as possible from the senses. Thus obscurities may perhaps have remained; but these, I hope, will later be easily removed in my Replies to the Objections. One such obscurity is this: how can the idea that is in us of a supremely perfect being have so much objective reality that it must be from a supremely perfect cause? This is illustrated in the Replies by a comparison with a very ingenious machine, the idea of which is in the mind of the artisan. For, just as the objective ingeniousness of this idea must have some cause (say, the knowledge possessed by the artisan or by someone else from whom he has received this knowledge), just so, the idea of God, which is in us, must have God himself for its cause.

In the Fourth Meditation I prove that all that we clearly and distinctly perceive is true; and, at the same time, I explain wherein the nature of falsity consists. These things necessarily ought to be known, as much for reinforcing what has just been said as for understanding what remains. But it should be borne in mind that in that Meditation I have not discussed sin—that is, an error committed in the pursuit of good and evil—but only that error which occurs in the discernment of the true and the false. Nor do I examine those matters pertaining to religious faith or to the conduct of life, but only those speculative truths that are known by the aid of the light of nature.

In the Fifth Meditation in addition to explaining corporeal nature in general, I also demonstrate the existence of God by means of a new proof. But again some difficulties arise. These are later resolved in my Replies to the Objections. Finally, I show how it is true that the certitude of geometrical demonstrations depends upon a knowledge of God.

Finally, in the Sixth Meditation I distinguish understanding from imagination; I describe the marks of this distinction. I prove that the mind is really distinct from the body (although I show that the mind is so closely joined to the body, that it forms one thing with the body). All the errors commonly arising from the senses are presented, along with all the ways in which these errors can be avoided. Finally, I append all the grounds on the basis of which the existence of material things can be inferred. Not that I believe these grounds to be very useful for proving what they prove—namely that there really is a world, that men have bodies, and other such things, concerning which no one of sound mind has ever seriously doubted — but because, by considering these grounds, I recognize that they are neither so firm nor so evident as are the grounds by means of which we arrive at a knowledge of our mind and of God, insofar as these latter grounds are, of all that can be known by the human mind, the most certain and the most evident. Proving this one thing was the goal of these Meditations. For this reason I pass over these other questions, which also will be given treatment in the Meditations at the appropriate occasion.

Meditations on First Philosophy in Which The Existence of God and the Distinction of the Soul from the Body Are Demonstrated

Meditation One: Concerning Those Things that Can Be Called into Doubt

Several years have now passed since I first realized how many were the false opinions that in my youth I took to be true, and thus how doubtful were all the things that I subsequently built upon these opinions. From the time I became aware of this, I realized that for once I had to raze everything in my life, down to the very bottom, so as to begin again from the first foundations, if I wanted to establish anything firm and lasting in the sciences. But the task seemed so enormous that I waited for a point in my life that was so ripe that no more suitable a time for laying hold of these disciplines would come to pass. For this reason, I have delayed so long that I would be at fault were I to waste on deliberation the time that is left for action. Therefore, now that I have freed my mind from all cares, and I have secured for myself some leisurely and carefree time, I withdraw in solitude. I will, in short, apply myself earnestly and openly to the general destruction of my former opinions.

Yet to this end it will not be necessary that I show that all my opinions are false, which perhaps I could never accomplish anyway. But because reason now persuades me that I should withhold my assent no less carefully from things which are not plainly certain and indubitable than I would to what is patently false, it will be sufficient justification for rejecting them all, if I find a reason for doubting even the least of them. Nor therefore need one survey each opinion one after the other, a task of endless proportion. Rather — because undermining the foundations will cause whatever has been built upon them to fall down of its own accord — I will at once attack those principles which supported everything that I once believed.

Whatever I had admitted until now as most true I took in either from the senses or through the senses; however, I noticed that they sometimes deceived me. And it is a mark of prudence never to trust wholly in those things which have once deceived us.

But perhaps, although the senses sometimes deceive us when it is a question of very small and distant things, still there are many other matters which one certainly cannot doubt, although they are derived from the very same senses: that I am sitting here before the fireplace wearing my dressing gown, that I feel this sheet of paper in my hands, and so on. But how could one deny that these hands and that my whole body exist? Unless perhaps I should compare myself to insane people whose brains are so impaired by a stubborn vapor from a black bile that they continually insist that they are kings when they are in utter poverty, or that they are wearing purple robes when they are naked, or that they have a head made of clay, or that they are gourds, or that they are made of glass. But they are all demented, and I would appear no less demented if I were to take their conduct as a model for myself.

All of this would be well and good, were I not a man who is accustomed to sleeping at night, and to undergoing in my sleep the very same things — or now and then even less likely ones — as do these insane people when they are awake. How often has my evening slumber persuaded me of such customary things as these: that I am here, clothed in my dressing gown, seated at the fireplace, when in fact I am lying undressed between the blankets! But right now I certainly am gazing upon this piece of paper with eyes wide awake. This head which I am moving is not heavy with sleep. I extend this hand consciously and deliberately and I feel it. These things would not be so distinct for one who is asleep. But this all seems as if I do not recall having been deceived by similar thoughts on other occasions in my dreams. As I consider these cases more intently, I see so plainly that there are no definite signs to distinguish being awake from being asleep that I am quite astonished, and this astonishment almost convinces me that I am sleeping.

Let us say, then, for the sake of argument, that we are sleeping and that such particulars as these are not true: that we open our eyes, move our heads, extend our hands. Perhaps we do not even have these hands, or any such body at all. Nevertheless, it really must be admitted that things seen in sleep are, as it were, like painted images, which could have been produced only in the likeness of true things. Therefore at least these general things (eyes, head, hands, the whole body) are not imaginary things, but are true and exist. For indeed when painters wish to represent sirens and satyrs by means of bizarre and unusual forms, they surely cannot ascribe utterly new natures to these creatures. Rather, they simply intermingle the members of various animals. And even if they concoct something so utterly novel that its likes have never been seen before (being utterly fictitious and false), certainly at the very minimum the colors from which the painters compose the thing ought to be true. And for the same reason, although even these general things (eyes, head, hands, and the like) can be imaginary, still one must necessarily admit that at least other things that are even more simple and universal are true, from which, as from true colors, all these things — be they true or false — which in our thought are images of things, are constructed.

To this class seems to belong corporeal nature in general, together with its extension; likewise the shape of extended things, their quantity or size, their number; as well as the place where they exist, the time of their duration, and other such things.

Hence perhaps we do not conclude improperly that physics, astronomy, medicine, and all the other disciplines that are dependent upon the consideration of composite things are all doubtful. But arithmetic, geometry, and other such disciplines — which treat of nothing but the simplest and most general things and which are indifferent as to whether these composite things do or do not exist — contain something certain and indubitable. For whether I be awake or asleep, two plus three makes five, and a square does not have more than four sides; nor does it seem possible that such obvious truths can fall under the suspicion of falsity.

All the same a certain opinion of long standing has been fixed in my mind, namely that there exists a God who is able to do anything and by whom I, such as I am, have been created. How do I know that he did not bring about that there be no earth at all, no heavens, no extended thing, no figure, no size, no place, and yet all these things should seem to me to exist precisely as they appear to do now? Moreover — as I judge that others sometimes make mistakes in matters that they believe they know most perfectly — how do I know that I am not deceived every time I add two and three or count the sides of a square or perform an even simpler operation, if such can be imagined? But perhaps God has not willed that I be thus deceived, for it is said that he is supremely good. Nonetheless, if it were repugnant to his goodness that he should have created me such that I be deceived all the time, it would seem, from this same consideration, to be foreign to him to permit me to be deceived occasionally. But we cannot make this last assertion.

Perhaps there are some who would rather deny such a powerful God, than believe that all other matters are uncertain. Let us not put these people off just yet; rather, let us grant that everything said here about God is fictitious. Now they suppose that I came to be what I am either by fate or by chance or by a continuous series of events or by some other way. But because being deceived and being mistaken seem to be imperfections, the less powerful they take the author of my being to be, the more probable it will be that I would be so imperfect as to be deceived perpetually. I have nothing to say in response to these arguments. At length I am forced to admit that there is nothing, among the things I once believed to be true, which it is not permissible to doubt — not for reasons of frivolity or a lack of forethought, but because of valid and considered arguments. Thus I must carefully withhold assent no less from these things than from the patently false, if I wish to find anything certain.

But it is not enough simply to have made a note of this; I must take care to keep it before my mind. For long-standing opinions keep coming back again and again, almost against my will; they seize upon my credulity, as if it were bound over to them by long use and the claims of intimacy. Nor will I get out of the habit of assenting to them and believing in them, so long as I take them to be exactly what they are, namely, in some respects doubtful as by now is obvious, but nevertheless highly probable, so that it is much more consonant with reason to believe them than to deny them. Hence, it seems to me, I would do well to turn my will in the opposite direction, to deceive myself and pretend for a considerable period that they are wholly false and imaginary, until finally, as if with equal weight of prejudice[1] on both sides, no bad habit should turn my judgment from the correct perception of things. For indeed I know that no danger or error will follow and that it is impossible for me to indulge in too much distrust, since I now am concentrating only on knowledge, not on action.

Thus I will suppose not a supremely good God, the source of truth, but rather an evil genius, as clever and deceitful as he is powerful, who has directed his entire effort to misleading me. I will regard the heavens, the air, the earth, colors, shapes, sounds, and all external things as nothing but the deceptive games of my dreams, with which he lays snares for my credulity. I will regard myself as having no hands, no eyes, no flesh, no blood, no senses, but as nevertheless falsely believing that I possess all these things. I will remain resolutely fixed in this meditation, and, even if it be out of my power to know anything true, certainly it is within my power to take care resolutely to withhold my assent to what is false, lest this deceiver, powerful and clever as he is, have an effect on me. But this undertaking is arduous, and laziness brings me back to my customary way of living. I am not unlike a prisoner who might enjoy an imaginary freedom in his sleep. When he later begins to suspect that he is sleeping, he fears being awakened and conspires slowly with these pleasant illusions. In just this way, I spontaneously fall back into my old beliefs, and dread being awakened, lest the toilsome wakefulness which follows upon a peaceful rest, have to be spent thenceforward not in light but among the inextricable shadows of the difficulties now brought forward.

Meditation Two: Concerning the Nature of the Human Mind: That the Mind Is More Known than the Body

Yesterday's meditation filled my mind with so many doubts that I can no longer forget about them—nor yet do I see how they are to be resolved. But, as if I had suddenly fallen into a deep whirlpool, I am so disturbed that I can neither touch my foot to the bottom, nor swim up to the top. Nevertheless I will work my way up, and I will follow the same path I took yesterday, putting aside everything which admits of the least doubt, as if I had discovered it to be absolutely false. I will go forward until I know something certain—or, if nothing else, until I at least know for certain that nothing is certain. Archimedes sought only a firm and immovable point in order to move the entire earth from one place to another. Surely great things are to be hoped for if I am lucky enough to find at least one thing that is certain and indubitable.

Therefore I will suppose that all I see is false. I will believe that none of those things that my deceitful memory brings before my eyes ever existed. I thus have no senses: body, shape, extension, movement, and place are all figments of my imagination. What then will count as true? Perhaps only this one thing: that nothing is certain.

[1]A "prejudice" is a judgment, that is, an adjudication of an issue without having first reviewed the appropriate evidence.

But on what grounds do I know that there is nothing over and above all those which I have just reviewed, concerning which there is not even the least cause for doubt? Is there not a God (or whatever name I might call him) who instills these thoughts in me? But why should I think that, since perhaps I myself could be the author of these things? Therefore am I not at least something? But I have already denied that I have any senses and any body. Still, I hesitate; for what follows from that? Am I so tied to the body and to the senses that I cannot exist without them? But I have persuaded myself that there is nothing at all in the world: no heaven, no earth, no minds, no bodies. Is it not then true that I do not exist? But certainly I should exist, if I were to persuade myself of something. But there is a deceiver (I know not who he is) powerful and sly in the highest degree, who is always purposely deceiving me. Then there is no doubt that I exist, if he deceives me. And deceive me as he will, he can never bring it about that I am nothing so long as I shall think that I am something. Thus it must be granted that, after weighing everything carefully and sufficiently, one must come to the considered judgment that the statement "I am, I exist" is necessarily true every time it is uttered by me or conceived in my mind.

But I do not yet understand well enough who I am — I, who now necessarily exist. And from this point on, I must take care lest I imprudently substitute something else in place of myself; and thus be mistaken even in that knowledge which I claim to be the most certain and evident of all. To this end, I shall meditate once more on what I once believed myself to be before having embarked upon these deliberations. For this reason, then, I will set aside whatever can be refuted even to a slight degree by the arguments brought forward, so that at length there shall remain precisely nothing but what is certain and unshaken.

What therefore did I formerly think I was? A man, of course. But what is a man? Might I not say a rational animal? No, because then one would have to inquire what an "animal" is and what "rational" means. And then from only one question we slide into many more difficult ones. Nor do I now have enough free time that I want to waste it on subtleties of this sort. But rather here I pay attention to what spontaneously and at nature's lead came into my thought beforehand whenever I pondered what I was. Namely, it occurred to me first that I have a face, hands, arms, and this entire mechanism of bodily members, the very same as are discerned in a corpse — which I referred to by the name "body." It also occurred to me that I eat, walk, feel and think; these actions I used to assign to the soul as their cause. But what this soul was I either did not think about or I imagined it was something terribly insubstantial — after the fashion of a wind, fire, or ether — which has been poured into my coarser parts. I truly was not in doubt regarding the body; rather I believed that I distinctly knew its nature, which, were I perhaps tempted to describe it such as I mentally conceived it, I would explain it thus: by "body," I understand all that is suitable for being bounded by some shape, for being enclosed in some place, and thus for filling up space, so that it excludes every other body from that space; for being perceived by touch, sight, hearing, taste, or smell; for being moved in several ways, not surely by itself, but by whatever else that touches it. For I judged that the power of self-motion, and likewise of sensing or of thinking, in no way pertains to the nature of the body. Nonetheless, I used to marvel especially that such faculties were found in certain bodies.

But now what am I, when I suppose that some deceiver— omnipotent and, if I may be allowed to say it, malicious—takes all the pains he can in order to deceive me? Can I not affirm that I possess at least a small measure of all those traits which I already have said pertain to the nature of the body? I pay attention, I think, I deliberate—but nothing happens. I am wearied of repeating this in vain. But which of these am I to ascribe to the soul? How about eating or walking? These are surely nothing but illusions, because I do not have a body. How about sensing? Again, this also does not happen without a body, and I judge that I really did not sense those many things I seemed to have sensed in my dreams. How about thinking? Here I discover that thought is an attribute that really does belong to me. This alone cannot be detached from me. I am; I exist; this is certain. But for how long? For as long as I think. Because perhaps it could also come to pass that if I should cease from all thinking I would then utterly cease to exist. I now admit nothing that is not necessarily true. I am therefore precisely only a thing that thinks; that is, a mind, or soul, or intellect, or reason—words the meaning of which I was ignorant before. Now, I am a true thing, and truly existing; but what kind of thing? I have said it already: a thing that thinks.

What then? I will set my imagination going to see if I am not something more. I am not that connection of members which is called the human body. Neither am I some subtle air infused into these members, not a wind, not a fire, not a vapor, not a breath—nothing that I imagine to myself, for I have supposed all these to be nothing. The assertion stands: the fact still remains that I am something. But perhaps is it the case that, nevertheless, these very things which I take to be nothing (because I am ignorant of them) in reality do not differ from that self which I know? This I do not know. I shall not quarrel about it right now; I can make a judgment only regarding things which are known to me. I know that I exist; I ask now who is this "I" whom I know. Most certainly the knowledge of this matter, thus precisely understood, does not depend upon things that I do not yet know to exist. Therefore, it is not dependent upon any of those things that I feign in my imagination. But this word "feign" warns me of my error. For I would be feigning if I should "imagine" that I am something, because imagining is merely the contemplation of the shape or image of a corporeal thing. But I know now with certainty that I am, and at the same time it could happen that all these images—and, generally, everything that pertains to the nature of the body—are nothing but dreams. When these things are taken into account, I would speak no less foolishly were I to say: "I will imagine so that I might recognize more distinctly who I am," than were I to say: "Now I surely am awake, and I see something true, but because I do not yet see it with sufficient evidence, I will take the trouble of going to sleep so that my dreams might show this to me more truly and more evidently." Thus I know that none of what I can comprehend by means of the imagination pertains to this understanding that

I have of myself. Moreover, I know that I must be most diligent about withdrawing my mind from these things so that it can perceive its nature as distinctly as possible.

But what then am I? A thing that thinks. What is that? A thing that doubts, understands, affirms, denies, wills, refuses, and which also imagines and senses.

It is truly no small matter if all of these things pertain to me. But why should they not pertain to me? Is it not I who now doubt almost everything, I who nevertheless understand something, I who affirm that this one thing is true, I who deny other things, I who desire to know more things, I who wish not to be deceived, I who imagine many things against my will, I who take note of many things as if coming from the senses? Is there anything in all of this which is not just as true as it is that I am, even if I am always dreaming or even if the one who created me tries as hard as possible to delude me? Are any of these attributes distinct from my thought? What can be said to be separate from myself? For it is so obvious that it is I who doubt, I who understand, I who will, that there is nothing through which it could be more evidently explicated. But indeed I am also the same one who imagines; for, although perhaps as I supposed before, no imagined thing would be wholly true, the very power of imagining does really exist, and constitutes a part of my thought. Finally, I am the same one who senses or who takes note of bodily things as if through the senses. For example, I now see a light, I hear a noise, I feel heat. These are false, since I am asleep. But I certainly seem to see, hear, and feel. This cannot be false: properly speaking, this is what is called "sensing" in me. But this is, to speak precisely, nothing other than thinking.

From these considerations I begin to know a little better who I am. But it still seems that I cannot hold back from believing that bodily things—whose images are formed by thought, and which the senses themselves examine—are much more distinctly known than this unknown aspect of myself which does not come under the imagination. And yet it would be quite strange if the very things which I consider to be doubtful, unknown, and foreign to me are comprehended by me more distinctly than what is true, what is known—than, in fine, myself. But I see what is happening: my mind loves to wander and does not allow itself to be restricted to the confines of truth. Let it be that way then: let us allow it the freest rein in every respect, so that, when we pull in the reins at the right time a little later, the mind may suffer itself to be ruled more easily.

Let us consider those things which are commonly believed to be the most distinctly comprehended of all: namely the bodies which we touch and see. But not bodies in general, for these generic perceptions are often somewhat more confused; rather let us consider one body in particular. Let us take, for instance, this piece of wax. It has very recently been taken from the honeycombs; it has not as yet lost all the flavor of its honey. It retains some of the smell of the flowers from which it was collected. Its color, shape, and size are obvious. It is hard and cold. It can easily be touched, and if you rap on it with a knuckle it makes a sound. In short, everything is present in it that appears to be needed in order that a body can be known as distinctly as possible. But notice that while

I am speaking, it is brought close to the fire; the remaining traces of the honey flavor are purged; the odor vanishes; the color is changed; the original shape disappears. Its magnitude increases, it becomes liquid and hot, and can hardly be touched; and now, when you knock on it, it does not emit any sound. Up to this point, does the same wax remain? One must confess that it does: no one denies it; no one thinks otherwise. What was there then in the wax that was so distinctly comprehended? Certainly none of the things that I reached by means of the senses. For whatever came under taste or smell or sight or touch or hearing by now has changed, yet the wax remains.

Perhaps the wax was what I now think it is: namely that it really never was the sweetness of the honey or the fragrance of the flowers, not this whiteness, not a figure, not a sound, but a body which a little earlier manifested itself to me in these ways, and now does so in other ways. But just what precisely is this thing which I imagine thus? Let us direct our attention to this and see what remains after we have removed everything which does not belong to the wax: only that it is something extended, flexible, and subject to change. What is this flexible and mutable thing? Is it not the fact that I imagine that this wax can change from a round to a square shape, or from the latter to a rectangular shape? Not at all: for I comprehend that the wax is capable of innumerable changes, yet I cannot survey these innumerable changes by imagining them. Therefore this comprehension is not accomplished by the faculty of imagination. What is this extended thing? Is this thing's extension also unknown? For it becomes larger in wax that is beginning to liquify, greater in boiling wax, and greater still as the heat is increased. And I would not judge rightly what the wax is if I did not believe that this wax can take on even more varieties of extension than I could ever have grasped by the imagination. It remains then for me to concede that I in no way imagine what this wax is, but perceive it by the mind only. I am speaking about this piece of wax in particular, for it is clearer in the case of wax in general. But what is this wax which is perceived only by the mind? It is the same that I see, touch, and imagine; in short it is the same as I took it to be from the very beginning. But we must take note of the fact that the perception of the wax is neither by sight, nor touch, nor imagination, nor was it ever so (although it seemed so before), but rather an inspection on the part of the mind alone. This inspection can be imperfect and confused, as it was before, or clear and distinct, as it is now, according to whether I pay greater or less attention to those things of which the wax consists.

But meanwhile I marvel at how prone my mind is to errors; for although I am considering these things within myself silently and without words, nevertheless I latch onto words themselves and I am very nearly deceived by the ways in which people speak. For we say that we see the wax itself, if it is present, and not that we judge it to be present from its color or shape. Whence I might conclude at once: the wax is therefore known by eyesight, and not by inspection on the part of the mind alone, unless I perhaps now might have looked out the window at the men crossing the street whom I say I am no less wont to see than the wax. But what do I see over and above the hats and clothing? Could not robots be concealed under these things? But I judge them to be men; thus what I believed I had seen with my eyes, I actually comprehend with nothing but the faculty of judgment which is in my mind.

But a person who seeks to know more than the common crowd should be ashamed of himself if he has come upon doubts as a result of an encounter with the forms of speech devised by the common crowd. Let us then go forward, paying attention to the following question: did I perceive more perfectly and evidently what the wax was when I first saw it and believed I had known it by the external sense—or at least by the common sense, as they say, that is, the imaginative power—than I know it now, after having examined more diligently both what the wax is and how it is known. Surely it is absurd to doubt this matter. For what was there in the first perception that was distinct? What was there that any animal could not have seemed capable of possessing? But when I distinguish the wax from its external forms, as if having taken off its clothes, as it were, I look at the naked wax, even though at this point there can be an error in my judgment; nevertheless I could not perceive it without a human mind.

But what am I to say about this mind, or about myself? For as yet I admit nothing else to be in me over and above my mind. What, I say, am I who seem to perceive this wax so distinctly? Do I not know myself not only much more truly and with more certainty, but also much more distinctly and evidently? For if I judge that the wax exists from the fact that I see it, certainly it follows much more evidently that I myself exist, from the fact that I see the wax. For it could happen that what I see is not truly wax. It could happen that I have no eyes with which to see anything. But it could not happen that, while I see or think I see (I do not now distinguish these two), I who think am not something. Likewise, if I judge that the wax exists from the fact that I touch it, the same thing will again follow: I exist. If from the fact that I imagine, or from whatever other cause, the same thing readily follows. But what I noted regarding the wax applies to all the other things that are external to me. Furthermore, if the perception of the wax seemed more distinct after it became known to me not only from sight or touch, but from many causes, how much more distinctly I must be known to myself; for there are no considerations that can aid in the perception of the wax or any other body without these considerations demonstrating even better the nature of my mind. But there are still so many other things in my mind from which one can draw a more distinct knowledge of the mind, so that those things which emanate from a body seem hardly worth enumerating.

But lo and behold, I have arrived on my own at the place I wanted. Since I know that bodies are not, properly speaking, perceived by the senses or by the faculty of imagination, but only by the intellect, and since, moreover, I know that they are not perceived by being touched or seen, but only insofar as they are .expressly understood, nothing can be more easily and more evidently perceived by me than my mind. But because an established habit of belief cannot be put aside so quickly, it is appropriate to stop here, so that by the length of my meditation this new knowledge may be more deeply impressed on my memory.

Meditation Three: Concerning God, that He Exists

Now I will shut my eyes, I will stop up my ears, I will divert all my senses, I will even blot out from my thoughts all images of corporeal things—or at least, since the latter can hardly be done, I will regard these images as nothing, empty and false as indeed they are. And as I converse only with myself and look more deeply into myself, I will attempt to render myself gradually better known and familiar to myself. I am a thing that thinks, that is to say, a thing that doubts, affirms, denies, knows a few things, is ignorant of many things, wills, rejects, and also imagines and senses. As I observed earlier, although these things that I sense or imagine may perhaps be nothing at all outside me, nevertheless I am certain that these modes of thinking—which I call sensations and imaginations—insofar as they are only modes of thinking, are within me.

In these few words I have summed up what I truly know, or at least what, so far, I have observed that I know. Now I will ponder more carefully to see whether perhaps there are other things pertaining to me that, up to this time, I have not yet noticed. I am certain that I am a thing that thinks. But do I not therefore also know what is required so that I may be certain of something? Surely in this first instance of knowing, there is nothing else than a certain clear and distinct perception of what I affirm. Yet this would hardly be sufficient to render me certain of the truth of a thing, if it could ever happen that something that I perceive so clearly and distinctly were false. And thus I now seem to be able to posit as a general rule that what I very clearly and distinctly perceive is true.

Nevertheless, I have previously admitted many things as wholly certain and evident that nevertheless I discovered afterward to be doubtful. What sort of things were these? Why, indeed, the earth, the heavens, the stars, and all the other things that I perceived by means of my senses. But what did I perceive clearly regarding these things? Certainly the ideas or thoughts of these things hovered before my mind. But I do not now deny that these ideas are in me. However, there was something else that I affirmed and that, because of my habit of believing it, I thought was something I clearly perceived, but that, in fact, I did not perceive—namely, that certain things as outside me, things from which those ideas proceed and things to which they were entirely similar. But on this point I was mistaken; or, if I judged truly, this judgment did not result from the force of my perception.

What then? When I considered something very simple and easy in the areas of arithmetic or geometry, for example that two plus three together make five, and the like, did I not intuit them at least clearly enough that I might affirm them to be true? To be sure, I did decide later on that I must doubt these things for no other reason than that it entered my mind that some God could have given me a nature such that I might be deceived—even about matters that seemed most evident. For every time this preconceived opinion about the supreme power of God occurs to me, I am constrained to admit that, if he wished, it is very easy for him to cause me to err, even in those matters that I think I have intuited as plainly as possible with the eyes of the mind. Yet every time I turn my attention to those very things that I think I perceive with such great clarity, I am so entirely persuaded by these things that I spontaneously burst out with these words: "let him who can deceive me; as long as I think that I am something, he will never bring it about that I am nothing, or one day make it true that I never existed, because it is true now that I am; nor will he ever bring it about that two plus three yield more or less than five, or that similar matters, in which I recognize an obvious contradiction, exist." And, certainly, because I have no occasion for thinking that there is a God who deceives, and because I am not certain whether there even is a God, the reason for doubting — depending as it does on the above hypothesis — is very tenuous and, so to speak, metaphysical. Moreover, in order to remove this doubt, I ought at the first opportunity to inquire if there is a God, and, if there is, whether or not he can be a deceiver. If I am ignorant of these matters, I do not think I can be certain of anything else.

Now, however, good order seems to demand that I first arrange all my thoughts into certain classifications, and inquire in which of these truth or falsity properly consists. Some of these thoughts are like images of things. To these alone does the word "idea" properly apply, for example, when I think of a man, a chimera, heaven, an angel, or God. Again there are other thoughts that take different forms: when I will, when I fear, when I affirm, when I deny, there is always something I grasp as the subject of my thought, yet I comprehend something that is more than the mere likeness of a thing. Some of these thoughts are called volitions or emotions, while others are called judgments.

Now as to what pertains to ideas, if they are considered alone and in their own right, without being referred to something else, they cannot then properly be considered false. For whether I imagine a she-goat or a chimera, it is no less true that I imagine the one than the other. Moreover, we need not fear that falsity exists in the will itself or in the emotions; although I can choose evil things or even things that nowhere exist, it does not follow it is untrue that I do choose these things. Thus there remain only judgments. I must take care not to be mistaken about these. Now the principal and most frequent error that can be found in judgments consists in the fact that I judge that the ideas, which are in me, are similar to, or in conformity with, certain things outside me. Indeed, if I consider these ideas only as certain modes of my thought, and do not refer them to something else, they can hardly give me any cause for error.

Among these ideas, some seem to me to be innate, some seem to be derived from an external source, and some seem to be produced by me. I understand what a thing is, what truth is, what thought is — I do not seem to have derived these from any source other than from my very own nature. But now I hear a noise, I see the sun, and I feel a fire; until this point I judged that these things proceeded from certain things existing outside me. Finally, I judged that sirens, hippogriffs, and the like have been formed by me. Or perhaps I could also suppose that all of these ideas are derived from an external source, or are innate, or are produced, for I have not yet ascertained clearly their true origin.

But in this meditation those ideas that I believe to be drawn from things existing outside me must especially be investigated. Just what reason is there that moves me so that I believe that these ideas are similar to those objects? Well, I seem to be taught that way by nature. Moreover, I know by experience that these ideas do not depend upon my will, nor consequently upon myself, for often I notice them against my will; as now—whether I will it or not—I feel heat, and therefore I believe that this feeling or idea of heat comes to me from something other than myself, namely from the fire I am near. Nothing is more obvious than the judgment that this object (rather than something else) grafts its likeness on to me.

I will now see whether these reasons are valid enough. When I say in this meditation that I have been taught so by nature, I understand only that I am driven by a spontaneous impulse to believing this position, and not that some light of nature shows me it is true. These two positions are at considerable odds with one another. For whatever this light of nature shows me—for example, that from the fact that I doubt, it follows that I am and so on—cannot in any way be doubtful, because there can be no other faculty in which I may trust as much as the light of nature that could teach which of these positions are not true. As for natural impulses, I have very often judged myself to have been driven by them to the poorer choice, when it was a question of choosing a good; I do not see why I should trust them any more in other matters.

Again, although these ideas do not depend upon my will, it does not therefore follow that they necessarily proceed from things existing outside me. Although these impulses I have discussed are in me, nevertheless they seem to be different from my will. Thus perhaps there is also in me some other faculty, one not yet sufficiently known to me, that produces these ideas, because it has always seemed that these ideas are formed in me when I sleep, without any aid from external things.

Again, even if these ideas do proceed from things other than myself, it does not therefore follow that they must be similar to these objects. Indeed it seems I have frequently noticed a vast difference in many respects. For example, I find within myself two distinct ideas of the sun. One idea derives, as it were, from the senses. Now it is this idea that, among those things I consider to be derived from outside me, is most in need of examination. By means of this idea the sun appears to me to be very small. Yet there is another idea, one derived from the computations of astronomy. This idea is elicited from certain notions innate in me (or is somehow made by me) through which the sun is shown to be several times larger than the earth. Both ideas surely cannot be similar to the same sun existing outside me, and reason convinces me that the one that seems to have emanated from it at such close proximity is the very one that is most dissimilar to the sun.

All of this demonstrates sufficiently that up to this point I have believed not by certain judgment, but only by a blind impulse that things exist outside me that send their ideas or images into me through the sense organs or by some other means.

But still another path occurs to me for inquiring whether there are some objects, from among those things of which there are ideas in me, that exist outside me.

Now, insofar as these ideas are merely modes of thought, I do not see any inequality among them; they all seem to proceed from me in the same way. But insofar as one idea represents one thing and another idea another thing, it is obvious they are very different from one another. There is no question that those ideas that exhibit substances to me are something more and, as I phrase it, contain more objective reality[1] in themselves than those which represent only modes or accidents. Again, the idea that enables me to understand a highest God, one who is eternal, infinite, omniscient, omnipotent, and creator of all things other than himself, has more objective reality in it than those ideas through which finite substances are exhibited.

But it is evident by the light of nature that at the very least there must be as much in the total efficient cause as there is in the effect of that same cause. For, I ask, where can an effect get its reality unless it be from its cause? And how can the cause give the reality to the effect, unless the cause also has that reality? Hence it follows that something cannot come into existence from nothing, nor even can what is more perfect, that is, that contains in itself more reality, come into existence from what contains less. But this is clearly true not merely for those effects whose reality is actual or formal, but also for ideas in which only objective reality is considered. This means, for example, that a stone, which did not exist before, can in no way begin to exist now, unless it be produced by something in which there is, either formally or eminently,[2] everything that is in the stone; nor can heat be introduced into a subject which was not hot before unless it is done by something that is of at least as perfect an order as heat—the same holds true for the rest. Moreover, in me there can be no idea of heat, or of a stone, unless it comes to me from some cause that has at least as much reality as I conceive to be in the heat or in the stone. Although this cause transmits none of its actual or formal reality into my idea, it is not to be thought that the idea must be less real. Rather, the very nature of this idea is such that it needs no formal reality other than itself—except what it borrows from my thought, of which it is a mode. That this idea contains this or that objective reality rather than some other one results from the fact that the idea gets its objective reality from a cause in which there is at least as much formal reality as there is objective reality contained in the idea. For if we posit that something is found in the idea that was not in its cause, then the idea would get it from nothing; but as imperfect a mode of being as this is, by which a thing exists in

[1]By "objective reality" Descartes means the content of an idea, or an object insofar as it is represented in an idea. By "formal reality" he means the object insofar as it actually exists in its own right, that is, independently of its being perceived.
[2]By a "formal cause" Descartes means a cause that contains exactly the same degree or amount of reality and perfection as its effect. For example, a human being in generating another human being is said to be the "formal cause" of the generated human being. Again, were an object, such as a tree stump, to cause in me a perception of a tree stump, then the object is said to be the "formal cause" of my perception. By an "eminent cause" Descartes means a cause that contains more reality and perfection than its effect. For example, God, in creating a human being, would be said to be the "eminent cause" of that human being because there is clearly a greater degree or amount of reality and perfection in God than in a human being. Again, were God to cause in me a perception of a tree stump, then God would be said to be the "eminent cause" of my perception of the tree stump.

the intellect objectively through an idea, it nevertheless is surely not nothing; hence it cannot get its existence from nothing.

Also, because the reality that I consider in my ideas is only objective, I should not suspect that there is no need for the same reality to be formally in the causes of these ideas, but that it suffices for it to be in them objectively. To the extent that the objective mode of being pertains to ideas by their very nature, so the formal mode of being belongs to the causes of ideas, at least to the first and preeminent ones, by their very nature. Although one idea can perhaps come into being from another, nevertheless there is no infinite regress here; at length some first idea must be reached whose cause is a sort of archetype that formally contains all the reality that is in the idea only objectively. Thus it is evident to me by the light of nature that my ideas are like images that can easily fail to match the perfection of the things from which they have been drawn, but my ideas cannot contain anything better or more perfect.

But the longer and more attentively I examine all these points, the more clearly and distinctly I know they are true. But what do I finally conclude? Why, if the objective reality is not formally or eminently in me, and that therefore I myself cannot be the cause of the idea, then it necessarily follows that I am not alone in the world, and that something else—the cause of this idea—also exists. If in fact no such idea is found in me, I shall plainly have no argument to make me certain of the existence of something other than myself. For I have looked at all of these arguments most diligently and so far I have been unable to find any other.

Among my ideas, in addition to the one that represents me to myself—about which there can be no difficulty at this point—there are some that represent God, others that represent inanimate, corporeal objects, others that represent angels, others that represent animals, and finally others that represent men like myself.

As to the ideas that represent other men, animals, or angels, I easily understand that they can be formed from the ideas I have of myself, of corporeal things, and of God—even if no men except myself, no animals, and no angels were to exist in the world.

As to the ideas of corporeal things, there is nothing in them which is such that is seems unable to have come from me. For if I investigate thoroughly and if I examine each one individually in the same way that I examined the idea of wax yesterday, I notice that there are only a very few properties that I perceive in them clearly and distinctly: namely, magnitude, or extension in length, breadth, and depth; shape, which arises from the limit of this extension; position, which the various shaped things possess in relation to one another; and motion, or the alteration of this position; to these can be added substance, duration, and number. The remaining properties, however—such as light and colors, sounds, odors, tastes, heat and cold and other tactile qualities—are thought by me only in a very confused and obscure manner, with the result that I do not know whether they are true or false, that is, whether the ideas that I have of these things are ideas of certain things or are not ideas of things. For although a short time ago I noted that falsity properly so called ("formal" falsity) can be found only in judgments, nevertheless there is another kind of falsity (called "material" falsity) in ideas; it occurs whenever judgments present a non-thing as if it were a thing. For example, the ideas I have of heat and cold fall so short of being clear and distinct that I cannot learn from them whether cold is only a privation of heat or whether heat is a privation of cold; whether both are real qualities or neither is. Because ideas can only be ideas of things, and if it is true that cold is nothing more than the privation of heat, then an idea such as this one, that represents something real and positive to me, will not inappropriately be called false — so too for the other ideas.

Assuredly it is not necessary for me to assign to these ideas an author distinct from me. For if they were false, that is, if they should represent no objects, I know by the light of nature that they proceed from nothing; that is, they are in me for no other reason than that something is lacking in my nature, that my nature is plainly not perfect. If, on the other hand, these ideas are true because they exhibit so little reality to me that I cannot distinguish them from a non-thing, then I see no reason why they cannot get their existence from myself.

As for those things that are the clear and distinct elements in the ideas of corporeal things, I seem able to have borrowed some from the idea of myself: namely, substance, duration, number, and whatever else there may be of this type. For when I think that a stone is a substance, that is to say, a thing that in its own right has an aptitude for existing, and that I too am a substance — although I conceive that I am a thing that thinks and not an extended thing, whereas a stone is an extended thing and not a thing that thinks — there is, accordingly, the greatest diversity between these two concepts, even though they seem to agree with one another when they are considered under the rubric of substance. Furthermore, when I perceive that I exist now and recall that I have previously existed for some time, and when I have several thoughts and know the number of these thoughts, I acquire the ideas of duration and number, which I then apply to everything else. However, all the other elements out of which the ideas of corporeal things are put together (namely extension, shape, positon, and motion) are not contained in me formally, because I am only a thing that thinks. But because they are only modes of a substance, and I too am a substance, they seem capable of being contained in me eminently.

Thus there remains only the idea of God. We must consider whether there is in this idea something which could not have originated from me. I understand by the word "God" an infinite and independent substance, intelligent and powerful in the highest degree, who created me along with everything else — if in fact there is anything else. Indeed all these qualities are such that, the more diligently I attend to them, the less they seem capable of having arisen from myself alone. Thus, from what has been said above, we must conclude that God necessarily exists.

For although the idea of substance is in me by virtue of the fact that I am a substance, nevertheless it would not for that reason be the idea of an infinite substance, unless it proceeded from some substance which is in fact infinite, because I am finite.

Nor should I think that I do not perceive the infinite by means of a true idea, but only through a negation of the finite, just as I perceive rest and shadows by means of a negation of motion and light. On the contrary, I clearly understand that there is more reality in an infinite substance than there is in a finite one. Thus the perception of the infinite somehow exists in me prior to the perception of the finite, that is, the perception of God exists prior to the perception of myself. Why would I know that I doubt and I desire, that is, that I lack something and that I am not wholly perfect, if there were no idea in me of a more perfect being by comparison with which I might acknowledge my defects?

Nor can it be said that this idea of God is perhaps materially false, and therefore can be from nothing, as I pointed out just now regarding the ideas of heat and cold and the like. On the contrary, because it is the most clear and distinct of all ideas and because it contains more objective reality than any other idea, no idea is truer in its own right, and there is no idea in which less suspicion of falsity is to be found. I maintain that this idea of a being most perfect and infinite is true in the highest degree. Although such a being can perhaps be imagined not to exist, it nevertheless cannot be imagined that this idea shows me nothing real, as was the case with the idea of cold that I referred to earlier. It is also an idea that is clear and distinct in the highest degree; for whatever I clearly and distinctly perceive that is real and true and that contains some perfection is wholly contained in that idea. It is not inconsistent to say that I do not comprehend the infinite or that there are countless other things in God that I can in no way either comprehend or perhaps even touch with thought. For the nature of the infinite is such that it is not comprehended by me, who am finite. And it is sufficient that I understand this very point and judge that all those things that I clearly perceive and that I know to contain some perfection — and perhaps even countless other things of which I am ignorant — are in God either formally or eminently. The result is that, of all those that are in me, the idea that I have of him is the most true, the most clear, and the most distinct.

But perhaps I am something greater than I take myself to be. Perhaps all these perfections that I attribute to God are somehow in me potentially, although they do not yet assert themselves and are not yet reduced to act. For I now observe that my knowledge is gradually being increased; I see nothing that stands in the way of my knowledge being increased more and more to infinity. I see no reason why, with my knowledge thus increased, I cannot acquire all the remaining perfections of God. And, finally, if the potential for producing these perfections is in me already, I see no reason why this potential does not suffice to produce the idea of these perfections.

Yet none of these things can be the case. First, while it is true that my knowledge is gradually increased and that in me there are many elements in potency which do not yet exist in act, nevertheless, none of these elements pertain to the idea of God, in which nothing whatever is potential; this gradual increase is itself a most certain argument for my imperfection. Moreover, although my knowledge might always increase more and more, nevertheless I understand that this knowledge will never by this means be infinite in act, because it will never reach a point where it is incapable of greater increase. On the contrary, I judge God to be infinite in act, with the result that nothing can be added to his perfection. Finally, I perceive that the objective being of an idea cannot be produced by a merely potential being (which, properly speaking, is nothing), but only by an actual or formal being.

Indeed there is nothing in all these matters that is not manifest by the light of nature to a person who is diligent and attentive. But when I am less attentive, and the images of sensible things blind my powers of discernment, I do not so easily recall why the idea of a being more perfect than me necessarily proceeds from a being that really is more perfect. This being the case, it is appropriate to ask further whether I myself who have this idea could exist, if such a being did not exist.

From what source, then, do I derive my existence? From myself, from my parents, or from whatever other things there are that are less perfect than God. Nothing more perfect than He, nothing even as perfect as He, can be thought or imagined.

But if I were derived from myself, I would not doubt, I would not hope, and I would not lack anything whatever. For I would have given myself all the perfections of which I have some idea; in so doing, I would be God! I must not believe that these things that I lack are perhaps more difficult to acquire than those which I now have. On the contrary, it is evident that it would have been much more difficult for me—that is, a thing or substance that thinks—to emerge from nothing than it would be to acquire the knowledge—something that is only an accident of this substance—of the many things about which I am ignorant. Certainly, if I received this greater quality from myself, I would not have denied myself at least those things that can be had more easily. Nor would I scarcely deny myself any of those other things that I perceive to be contained in the idea of God, because surely nothing seems to me more difficult to make. But if there were any of those other things that were more difficult to make, then they certainly would also seem more difficult to me, assuming, of course, that the remaining ones that I possess I have from myself, because I observe that with them my power is terminated.

Nor do I avoid the cogency of these arguments, if I suppose that perhaps I have always been as I am now, as if it then followed that no author of my existence need be sought. Because the entire period of one's life can be divided into countless parts, each of which in no way depends on the others, it does not follow from the fact that I existed a short while ago that I now ought to exist, unless some cause creates me once again, as it were, at this moment—that is to say, preserves me. For it is obvious to one who is cognizant of the nature of time that the same force and action is needed to preserve anything at all during the individual moments that it lasts as is needed to create that same thing anew—if it should happen not yet to exist. It is one of those things that is manifest by the light of nature that preservation differs from creation solely by virtue of a distinction of reason.

Therefore I ought now to ask myself whether I have some power through which I can bring it about that I myself, who now am, will also exist a little later? Because I am nothing but a thing that thinks—or at least because I am now dealing only with precisely that part of me that is a thing that thinks—if such a power were in me, then I would certainly be aware of it. But I observe that there is no such power; from this fact I know most evidently that I depend upon a being other than myself.

But perhaps this being is not God, and I have been produced either by my parents or by some other causes less perfect than God. Indeed, as I said before, it is evident that there ought to be at least as much in the cause as there is in the effect. Thus, because I am a thing that thinks and because I have within me an idea of God—whatever cause is at length assigned to me—it must be granted that it too is a thing that thinks and has an idea of all the perfections which I attribute to God. And one can again inquire whether it exists through itself or through another. For if it derived from itself, it is evident from what has been said that this thing is God, because, having the power of existing in its own right, it also unquestionably has the power of possessing in act all the perfections whose idea it has in itself—that is, all of those perfections that I conceive as being in God. However, if it is from another cause, one will then once again inquire in a similar fashion about this other thing—whether it is through itself or through another—until finally one arrives at the ultimate cause, which will be God.

For it is apparent enough that there can be no infinite regress, especially since I am dealing here not only with the cause that once produced me, but also and most especially with the cause that preserves me at the present time.

Nor can one imagine that perhaps several partial causes have concurred to bring me into being, and that from one cause I have taken the idea of one of the perfections I attribute to God and from another cause the idea of another perfection; so that all of these perfections are found somewhere in the universe, but not all joined together in one thing, which would be God. On the contrary, unity, simplicity, or the inseparability of those things which are in God is one of the principal perfections that I understand to be in him. Certainly the idea of the unity of all these perfections could not have been placed in me by a cause from which I do not also have the ideas of the other perfections; for it could not bring it about that I would instantaneously understand them to be joined to one another inseparably, unless it brought it about instantaneously that I recognize which ones these are.

Finally, as to my parents, even if everything that I ever believed about them were true, still they do not preserve me; nor did they bring me into being, insofar as I am a thing that thinks. Rather, they merely placed certain dispositions in the matter in which I judged that I—that is, a mind that is all that I now accept for myself—am contained. And thus there can be no difficulty here concerning these matters. Rather, one has no choice but to conclude that, from the simple fact that I exist and that an idea of a most perfect being, that is, God, is in me, it is most evidently demonstrated that God exists.

There remains only the question of how I received this idea of God. For I did not draw it from the senses, and it never came to me when I did not anticipate it, as the ideas of sensible things are wont to do when these things present themselves—or seem to present themselves—to the organs of the senses. Nor has it been produced by me, for I plainly cannot add or subtract anything from it. It thus remains that it is innate in me, just as the idea of myself is also innate in me.

To be sure it is not astonishing that in creating me, God endowed me with this idea, so that it would be like the sign of an artist impressed upon his work. Nor is it necessary that this sign be something distinct from the work itself. But from this one fact that God created me, it is highly believable that I have somehow been made in his image and likeness, and that I perceive this likeness (in which the idea of God is contained) by means of the same faculty through which I perceive myself. That is, when I turn my powers of discernment toward myself, I not only understand that I am something incomplete and dependent upon another, something aspiring indefinitely for greater and greater or better things, but instantaneously I also understand that the thing on which I depend has in himself all of these greater things—not merely indefinitely and potentially, but infinitely and actually. Thus it is God. The whole force of the argument rests on the fact that I recognize that it is impossible that I should exist, being of such a nature as I am—namely, having the idea of God in me—unless God in fact does exist. God, I say, that same being whose idea is in me: a being having all those perfections that I cannot comprehend, but in some way can touch with my thought, and a being subject to no defects. From these things it is sufficiently obvious that he cannot be a deceiver. For it is manifest by the light of nature that fraud and deception depend on some defect.

But before examining this idea more diligently and at the same time inquiring into the other truths that can be inferred from it, it is appropriate at this point to spend some time contemplating this God, to consider within myself his attributes and the beauty of this immense light, so far as the power of discernment in my darkened wit can carry me, to gaze, to admire, and to adore. For just as we believe by faith that the greatest felicity of the next life consists in nothing more than this contemplation of the divine majesty, so now, from the same— though much less perfect—contemplation we observe that the greatest pleasure of which we are capable in this life can be perceived.

Meditation Four: Concerning the True and the False

Thus have I lately become accustomed to withdrawing the mind from the senses. I have so carefully taken note of the fact that there are very few things that are truly perceived regarding corporeal things, and that a great many more things regarding the human mind—and yet still many more things regarding God—can be known, that with no difficulty do I direct my thinking away from things I can imagine to things that I can only understand, and that are separated from all matter. And I have a manifestly much more distinct idea of the human mind, insofar as it is a thinking thing—not extended in length, breadth or depth—receiving nothing else from a body except the idea of this or that body. And when I direct my attention to the fact that I am doubting, that is, that I am an incomplete and dependent thing, there comes to mind a clear and distinct idea of an independent and complete being, namely, God. And from the mere fact that this idea is in me, or that I who have this idea exist, I plainly conclude that God also exists, and that my existence depends entirely upon him at each and every moment. The result is that I am confident that nothing more evident, nothing more certain can be known by the human mind. From this contemplation of the true God, in whom are hidden all the treasures of knowledge and wisdom, I now seem to see a way by which I might attain knowledge of other matters.

To begin with, I acknowledge that it is impossible for him ever to deceive me, for in every trick or deception some imperfection is found. Although the ability to deceive seems to be an indication of cleverness or power, nevertheless, willful deception evinces maliciousness and weakness. Accordingly, deception is not compatible with God.

Next I observe that there is in me a certain faculty of judgment that I undoubtedly received from God, as is the case with all the other things that are in me. Since he has not wished to deceive me, he certainly has not given me a faculty such that, when I use it properly, I could ever make a mistake.

No doubt regarding this matter remains, except that then it seems to follow that I should never make a mistake, for if all that I have is from God—and he gave me no faculty of making a mistake—I seem incapable of ever erring. So, as long as I think about God alone and direct myself straightforwardly and directly at him, I discover no grounds for error or falsity. But, after I turn my attention back on myself, I nevertheless observe that I am subject to countless errors. Seeking a cause for these errors, I notice that not only a real and positive idea of God (that is, of a being supremely perfect), but also, so to speak, a certain negative idea of nothing (that is, of what is supremely lacking in every perfection) passes before me. I also notice that I have been so constituted as to be some kind of middle ground between God and nothing, or between supreme being and non-being, so that, insofar as I have been created by a supreme being, there is nothing in me by means of which I might be deceived or be led into error; but insofar as I am not the supreme being, I lack quite a few things—so much so that it is not surprising that I am deceived. Thus I certainly understand that error as such is not something real that depends upon God, but rather is only a defect. Nor for that reason is there a need to account for my errors by positing a faculty given to me by God. Rather, it happens that I make mistakes because the faculty of judging the truth, which I have from him, is not infinite in me.

Still, this is not yet altogether satisfactory; for error is not a pure negation, but a privation or a lack of some knowledge that somehow ought to be in me. It does not seem possible to one who attends to the nature of God that he could have placed in me a faculty that is not perfect within its class or that has been deprived of some perfection it ought to have. For if it is true that the more perfect the artisan, the more perfect the works he produces, then what can be made by that supreme creator of all things that is not perfect in all respects? No doubt God could have made me such that I never err; no doubt, again, God always wills what is best; is it not therefore better for me to be deceived than not to be?

While I mull over these things more carefully, it immediately dawns on me that there is no reason to marvel at the fact that God might make things the reasons for which I do not understand; his existence ought not therefore to be doubted, because I might happen to observe that there are other things that were made by him whose "why" and "how" I do not comprehend. Since I know now that my nature is very weak and limited, but that the nature of God is immense, incomprehensible, and infinite, therefore I also know with sufficient evidence that he can make innumerable things whose causes escape me. For this reason alone the whole class of causes, which people customarily derive from a things's "purpose," I judge to be useless in dealing with matters related to physics. It is not without rashness that I think myself competent to inquire into God's purposes.

It also occurs to me that whenever we ask whether the works of God are perfect, we should examine the whole universe together and not just one creature in isolation from the rest. Something, if all by itself, may rightfully appear very imperfect; but if it is seen in its role as a part in the universe, it is most perfect. However, from having wanted to doubt everything, I know with certainty only that I and God exist; nevertheless, from having taken note of the immense power of God, I am unable to deny that many other things have been made by him, or at least can be made by him, and, what is more, that I would take on the added significance of being a part in the universe of things.

Finally, focusing closer on myself and inquiring into the nature of my errors (the only things that argue for an imperfection in me), I note that these errors depend on the simultaneous concurrence of two causes: the faculty of knowing that is in me, and the faculty of choosing (in other words, the free choice of the will), that is, they depend on the intellect and will at the same time. Through the intellect alone I perceive only ideas concerning which I can make a judgment; no error, properly so-called, is to be found in the intellect thus precisely conceived. For although countless things about which I have no idea perhaps exist, nevertheless I must not be said, properly speaking, to be deprived of them. I am bereft of them only in a negative way, because I can give no argument by which to prove that God ought to have given me a greater faculty of knowing than he has. No matter how expert a craftsman I understand him to be, still I do not therefore believe he ought to have bestowed on each one of his works all the perfections that he can put into some. In fact, I cannot complain that I have received from God an insufficiently ample and imperfect will, or free choice, because I observe that it is limited by no boundaries. And it seems eminently worth noting that nothing else in me is so perfect or so great that I do not understand how they can be even more perfect or greater. If, for example, I consider the faculty of understanding, I immediately recognize that it is very small and quite finite in me, and at the same time I form an idea of another much greater faculty—in fact, the greatest and infinite; and from the fact that I can form an idea of this faculty, I perceive that it pertains to the nature of God. Similarly, if I examine the faculty of memory, imagination, or any other faculty, I manifestly find none, except what in me is feeble and limited, but what in God I understand to be immense. The sole exception is the will or free choice; I observe it to be so great in me that I grasp an idea of nothing greater, to the extent that the will is principally the basis for my understanding that I bear an image and likeness of God. Although it is incomparably greater in God than it is in me, both by virtue of the knowledge and power that are associated with it and that render it more resolute and efficacious—as well as by virtue of its object, for the divine will extends to more things; yet taken formally, will precisely as such, it does not seem greater, because willing is only a matter of being able to do or not do something (that is, of being able to affirm or deny, to pursue or to shun), or better still, the will consists solely in the fact that when something is proposed to us by our intellect either to affirm or deny, to pursue or to shun, we are moved by it in such a way that we sense that no external force could have imposed it on us. In order to be free it is unnecessary for me to be moved in [n]either direction; on the contrary, the more I am inclined toward one direction—either because I evidently grasp that there is in it an aspect of the good and the true, or because God has thus disposed the inner recesses of my thought—the more I choose that direction more freely. Nor indeed does divine grace or natural knowledge ever diminish one's liberty; rather it increases and strengthens it. However, the indifference that I observe when no reason moves me more in one direction than in another is the lowest level of freedom; it evinces no perfection in it, but rather a defect in my knowledge, or a certain negation. Were I always to see clearly what is true and good, I would never deliberate about what is to be judged or chosen. Thus, although I may be entirely free, I could never for that reason be indifferent.

But from these considerations I perceive that the power of willing, which is from God, is not—taken by itself—the cause of my errors, for in its own way it is most ample and perfect. The same goes for the power of understanding. Whatever I understand, because it is from God that I have the power of understanding, I doubtless understand rightly; it is impossible for anything to take place in the intellect that could cause me to be deceived. From what source, therefore, do my errors arise? Solely from the fact that, because the will extends further than the intellect, I do not contain the will within the same boundaries; rather, I even extend it to things I do not understand. Because my will is indifferent to these latter things, it easily turns away from the true and the good; in this way I am deceived and commit sin.

For example, during these last few days when I have been examining whether anything exists in the world, I have noticed that, from the very fact that I have made this examination, it evidently followed that I exist. I could not help judging that what I understood clearly is true; not that I was coerced into holding this judgment because of some external force, but because a great inclination of my will followed from a great light in the intellect—so much so that the more spontaneously and freely I believed it, the less I was indifferent to it. But now I not only know that I, insofar as I am a thing that thinks, exist, but I also know that, having observed some ideas of corporeal nature, I might question whether the thinking nature that is in me—or rather that I am—is something different from this corporeal nature, or whether both natures are the same thing. And I presume that no consideration has as yet occurred to my mind which convinces me of the one more than the other. Thus it certainly follows that I am indifferent about affirming or denying either one, or even about my making any judgment at all in the matter.

Moreover, this indifference extends not only to those things about which the intellect knows absolutely nothing, but generally to everything of which the intellect does not have a keen enough knowledge at the very time when the will is deliberating on them. Although probable guesses might lead me in one direction, all it takes to move me to assent to the very opposite is the knowledge that they are merely guesswork, not certain and indubitable proofs. These last few days I have ample experience of this point, since everything that I had once believed to be as true as it possibly could be, I have now presumed to be utterly false, for the sole reason that I noticed that I could one way or another raise doubts about it.

But if I hold off from making a judgment when I do not perceive with sufficient clarity and distinctness what is in fact true, I clearly would be acting properly and would not be deceived. But were I to make an assertion or a denial, then I would not be using my freedom properly. If I turn in the direction that happens to be false, I am plainly deceived. But if I should embrace either alternative, and in so doing happen upon the truth by accident, I would still not be without fault, for it is manifest by the light of nature that the intellect's perception must always precede the will's being determined. Inherent in this incorrect use of the free will is a privation that constitutes the very essence of error: a privation, I say, is inherent in this operation insofar as the operation proceeds from me, but not in the faculty that was given to me by God, nor even in the operation of the faculty insofar as it depends upon God.

Indeed, I have no cause for complaint on the grounds that God has not given me a greater power of understanding or a greater light of nature than he has given me, for it is of the very essence of a finite intellect not to understand many things, and it is of the very essence of a created intellect to be finite. Actually, rather than think that he has withheld from me or deprived me of those things that he has not given, I ought to thank him, who never owed me anything, for what he has given me.

Again, I have no cause for complaint on the grounds that God has bestowed upon me a will that is open to more things than my intellect; since the will consists of merely one thing, and, as it were, something indivisible, it does not seem that its nature could withstand anything being removed from it. Indeed, the more ample the will is, the more I ought to thank its giver.

Nor again should I complain because God concurs with me in eliciting those acts of the will, or those judgments, in which I am deceived. For those acts are absolutely true and good, insofar as they depend on God; and it is so to speak, a greater perfection in me in that I can elicit those acts than if I could not do so. But a privation, in which alone the meaning of falsehood and sin is to be found, in no way needs the concurrence of God, for a privation is not a thing; and it is not related to God as its cause; rather, it ought to be called only a negation. For it is no imperfection in God that he gave me the freedom to give or withhold my assent to things of which he has placed no clear and distinct perception in my intellect. But surely it is an imperfection in me that I not use my liberty well and that I make a judgment about what I do not rightly understand. Nevertheless, I see that God could easily have brought it about that, while remaining free and having finite knowledge, I still never err. This result could occur either had he given my intellect a clear and distinct perception of everything about which I would ever deliberate or had he only impressed firmly enough upon my memory — so that I could never forget it — that I should never judge anything that I do not clearly and distinctly understand. I readily understand that, insofar as I am something whole and complete in my own right, I would have been more perfect than I now am, were God to have made me that way. But I cannot therefore deny that it might be, so to speak, a greater perfection in the universe as a whole that some of its parts are not immune to error, while others are, than if they were all alike. And I have no right to complain that God wished to sustain me in the world as a person who is not the principal and most perfect of all.

Furthermore, even if I cannot abstain from errors in the first way, which depends upon the evident perception of everything concerning which one must deliberate, nevertheless I can do so by the second way, which depends solely on my remembering that whenever the truth of a given matter is not apparent, I must abstain from making judgments. Although I observe that there is in me this infirmity, namely that I am unable always to adhere fixedly to one and the same knowledge, nevertheless I can, by attentive and frequently repeated meditation, bring it to pass that I recall it every time the situation demands; thus, I would acquire a habit of not erring.

For this reason, since the greatest and chief perfection of man consists in investigating the cause of error and falsity, I think that today's meditation was quite profitable. Nor can this perfection be anything other than I have described; for whenever I restrain my will in making judgments, so that it extends only to those matters that are clearly and distinctly shown to it by the intellect, it can never happen that I err, because every clear and distinct perception is surely something. Hence it cannot derive its existence from nothing; rather, it necessarily has God for its author — that supremely perfect God, I say, to whom it is repugnant to be a deceiver — thus the perception is surely true. Nor today have I learned only what I must avoid so as not to be deceived; I have also simultaneously learned what I must do to search for the truth. I search for it indeed if only I attend enough to what I perfectly understand, and refrain from the rest that I apprehend more confusedly and more obscurely. I shall give this matter careful attention later.

Meditation Five: Concerning the Essence of Material Things, and Again Concerning God, that He Exists

Many matters still remain for me to examine concerning the attributes of God and of me, that is, concerning the nature of my mind. But perhaps I might take them up at some other time. For now, nothing seems more urgent — having noted what is to be avoided and what is to be done in order to attain the truth — than that I try to free myself from the doubts into which I have recently fallen, and that I see whether or not anything certain can be obtained concerning material things.

Before inquiring whether any such material things exist outside me, surely I ought to consider the ideas of those things, insofar as they are in my thought, and to see which ones are distinct and which ones are confused.

To be sure, I distinctly imagine that quantity, which philosophers commonly call "continuous": namely, the extension of its quantity, or rather the extension of the thing having quantitative dimensions of length, breadth, and depth. I enumerate the thing's various parts. I ascribe to these parts certain sizes, shapes, positions, and movements from place to place; to these movements I ascribe various durations.

Not only have I plainly known and examined those things, viewed thus in a general way, but also I perceive attentively the countless particular aspects of figures, number, movement, and so on. Their truth is open and suitable to my nature to such an extent that, when I first discover them, it is not so much that I seem to learn anything new but that I recall something I already knew. That is, I first notice things that were already in me, although I had not directed a mental gaze toward them.

This is what I believe most needs examination here: I find within me countless ideas of things, that, although perhaps not existing anywhere outside me, still cannot be said to be nothing. Although I somehow think them at will, nevertheless I have not put them together; rather, they have their own true and immutable natures. For example, when I imagine a triangle, although perhaps no such figure exists outside my thought anywhere in the world and never will, still its nature, essence, or form is completely determined, unchangeable, and eternal. I did not produce it and it does not depend on my mind. This point is evident from the fact that many properties can be demonstrated regarding this triangle — namely that its three angles are equal to two right angles, that its longest side is opposite the largest angle, and so on; whether I want to or not, I now clearly acknowledge them, although I had not previously thought of them at all when I imagined a triangle. For this reason, then, I have not produced them.

It is irrelevant to say that perhaps the idea of a triangle came to me from external things through the sense organs, on the grounds that on occasion I have seen triangular-shaped bodies. For I can think of many other figures, concerning which there can be no suspicion of their ever having entered me through the senses, and yet the various properties of these figures, no less than those of the triangle, can be demonstrated. All of these are patently true because they are clearly known by me; thus they are something and not merely nothing. For it is evident that everything that is true is something; I have already demonstrated at length that all that I know is clearly true. Had I not demonstrated this, certainly the nature of my mind is such that I nevertheless must assent to them, at least while I perceive them clearly; I remember that even before now, when I adhered very closely to the objects of the senses, I always took this type of truth to be the most certain of every truth that I evidently knew regarding figures, numbers, or other things pertaining to arithmetic, geometry, or, in general, to pure and abstract mathematics.

But if, from the mere fact that I can bring forth from my thought the idea of something, it follows that all that I clearly and distinctly perceive to pertain to something really does pertain to it, then is this not an argument by which to prove the existence of God? Certainly I discover within me an idea of God, that is, of a supremely perfect being, no less than the idea of some figure or number. And I understand clearly and distinctly that it pertains to his nature that he always exists, no less than whatever has been demonstrated about some figure or number also pertains to the nature of this figure or number. Thus, even if everything that I have meditated upon during these last few days were not true, I ought to be at least as certain of the existence of God as I have hitherto been about the truths of mathematics.

Nevertheless, this point is not wholly obvious at first glance, but has the appearance of a sophism. Since in all other matters I am accustomed to distinguishing existence from essence, I easily persuade myself that the essence of God can be separated off from his existence; thus God can be thought of as not existing. Be that as it may, it still becomes obvious to a very diligently attentive person that the existence of God can no more be separated from his essence than the essence of a triangle can be separated from the fact that its three internal angles equal two right angles, or the idea of a valley can be separated from the idea of a mountain. So it is no less repugnant to think of a God (that is, a supremely perfect being) lacking existence (that is, as lacking some perfection), than it is to think of a mountain lacking a valley.

But granted I could no more think of God as not existing than I can think of a mountain without a valley, still it does not follow that a mountain actually exists in the world. Thus, from the fact that I think of God as existing, it does not seem to follow that God exists; for my thought imposes no necessity on things. Just as one can imagine a winged horse, without there being a horse with wings, so in the same way perhaps I can attach existence to God, even though no such God exists.

But there is a sophism lurking here. From the fact that I am unable to think of a mountain except with a valley, it does not follow that a mountain and a valley cannot be separated from one another. But from the fact that I cannot think of God except as existing, it follows that existence is inseparable from God; for this reason he truly exists. Not because my thought brings this situation about, or imposes any necessity on anything; but because the necessity of this thing, namely of the existence of God, forces me to entertain this thought; for I am not free to think of God without existence (that is, the supremely perfect being apart from the supreme perfection), as I am free to imagine a horse with or without wings.

Further, it should not be said here that, having asserted that he has all perfections, I needed to assert that God exists — since existence is one of these perfections — but that my earlier assertion need not have been made. So, I need not believe that all four-sided figures are inscribed in a circle; but assuming that I do believe it, it would then be necessary for me to admit that a rhombus is inscribed in a circle — this is plainly false. Although it is not necessary that I happen upon any thought of God, nevertheless as often as I think of a being first and supreme — and bring forth the idea of God as if from the storehouse of my mind — I must of necessity ascribe all perfections to it, even though I do not at that time enumerate them all, nor take note of them one by one. This necessity plainly suffices so that afterwards, when I consider that existence is a perfection, I rightly conclude that a first and supreme being exists. In the same way, there is no necessity for me ever to imagine a triangle, but as often as I wish to consider a rectilinear figure having but three internal angles, I must ascribe to it those properties from which one rightly infers that the three internal angles of this figure are not greater than two right angles, even though I do not then take notice of this fact. But when I inquire which figures might be inscribed in a circle, there is absolutely no need whatever for my believing that all four-sided figures are of this sort; nor even, for that matter, can I possibly imagine it, as long as I wish to admit only what I clearly and distinctly understand. Consequently, there is a great difference between false beliefs of this sort and true ideas inborn in me, the first and principal of which is the idea of God. For I plainly understand in many ways that it is not an invention dependent upon my thought, but an image of a true and immutable nature. Firts, because I cannot think of anything but God himself to whose essence belongs existence; next, because I cannot understand two or more Gods of this kind; because, having asserted that one God now exists, I plainly see that it is necessarily the case that he has existed from eternity and will endure forever; finally, because I perceive many other things in God, none of which I can remove or change.

But, indeed, whatever proof I use, it always comes down to the fact that the only things that fully convince me are those that I clearly and distinctly perceive. Although some of those things that I thus perceive are obvious to everyone — while others are discovered only by those who look more closely and inquire more diligently — nevertheless, after they have been discovered, they are considered no less certain than the others. For example, although it is not so readily apparent in the case of a right triangle that the square of the hypotenuse is equal to the square of the other two sides as it is that the hypotenuse is opposite the largest angle; nonetheless, the former is no less believed — once it has been ascertained. However, I acknowledge nothing prior to, or easier than, what pertains to God, unless I am overwhelmed by prejudices or unless images of sensible things besiege my thought from all sides. For what in and of itself is more manifest than that a supreme being exists, or that God, to whose essence alone existence pertains, exists?

But, although I needed to pay close attention in order to perceive this point, nevertheless I not only am now as certain regarding this as I am regarding everything else that seems most certain, but also I observe that the certitude of other things so depends upon this point that without it I am unable ever to know anything perfectly.

Yet I am indeed of such a nature that, while I perceive something very clearly and distinctly, I cannot help but believe it to be true. And yet I am also of such a nature that I cannot keep the gaze of my mind always on the same thing in order to perceive it clearly; the memory of a judgment made earlier often comes to mind, when I no longer fully attend to the reasons for which I judged something. Thus, other reasons can be brought forward that, were I ignorant of God, would easily make me change my opinion; thus I would never have true and certain knowledge of anything, but I would have only vague and changeable opinions. Thus, for example, when I consider the nature of a triangle, it appears most evident to me—steeped as I am in the principles of geometry—that the three internal angles of the triangle are equal to two right angles; I must believe this to be true, as long as I attend to its demonstration. But as soon as I turn my power of discernment from the demonstration, even though I recall that I had looked at it most clearly, nevertheless, were I ignorant of God it can easily happen that I might doubt whether or not it is true. For I can convince myself that I have been so made by nature that I would occasionally be deceived about those things that I believe I quite evidently perceive, especially when I might recall that I have often taken many things to be true and certain, which later, upon bringing other considerations to bear, I have judged to be false.

But once I perceived that there is a God—because at the same time I also understood that all other things depend on him—and that he is no deceiver, I then concluded that everything that I clearly and distinctly perceive is necessarily true. Even if I no longer attend further to the reasons why I judged it to be true, provided that I remember that I did clearly and distinctly observe it, no contrary reason can be brought to bear which might force me to doubt it; rather, I have a true and certain knowledge of this matter. Not just this one either, but also everything else that I recall having once demonstrated, as in geometry, and so on. For what objections can now be raised to me? Have I been made such that I am often deceived? But now I know that I cannot be deceived in those matters that I clearly understand. On other occasions have I not taken many things to be true and certain, but that afterward I recognized as false? However, I did not clearly and distinctly perceive any of them, but—ignorant of this rule of truth—I believe them for other reasons, that I later discovered were less valid. What therefore will be said? Might I perhaps not be dreaming (as I recently objected to myself), or might everything about which I am now thinking be no more true than what passes before the mind of a person sleeping? Be that as it may, it changes nothing; for certainly, although I might be asleep, if something is evident to my intellect, it is wholly true.

And thus I plainly see that the certainty and truth of every science depends upon the knowledge of the true God, to such an extent that, before I had known him, I could not know anything perfectly about any other thing. But now it is possible for me to know certainly and fully countless things—both about God and other intellectual matters, as well as about all corporeal nature, which is the object of pure mathematics.

Meditation Six: Concerning the Existence of Material Things, and the Real Distinction of the Mind from the Body

It remains for me to examine whether material things exist. Indeed I now know that they can exist, at least insofar as they are the object of pure mathematics, because I clearly and distinctly perceive them. For no doubt God is capable of bringing about everything that I am thus capable of perceiving. And I have never judged that God was incapable of something, except when it was incompatible with being perceived by me distinctly. Moreover, from the faculty of imagination, which I observe that I use while I am engaged in dealing with these material things, it seems to follow that they exist; to someone paying very close attention to what imagination is, it appears to be nothing else but an application of the knowing faculty to a body intimately present to it—hence, a body that exists.

And to make this very clear, I first examine the difference between imagination and pure intellection. So, for example, when I imagine a triangle, I not only understand that it is a figure bounded by three lines, but at the same time I also intuit by my powers of discernment these three lines as present—this is what I call "imagining." But if I want to think about a chiliagon, I certainly understand just as well that it is a figure consisting of a thousand sides, and that a triangle is a figure consisting of three lines; but I do not imagine those thousand sides in the same way, that is, I do not intuit them as being present. Albeit that when I think of a chiliagon I may perchance represent to myself some figure confusedly—because whenever I think about something corporeal, I always, out of force of habit, imagine something—nevertheless it is evident that it is not a chiliagon. This is so because it is not really different from the figure I would represent to myself if I were to think of a myriagon or any other figure with a large number of sides. Nor is imagination of any help in knowing the properties that differentiate the chiliagon from other polygons. But if it is a question of a pentagon, I surely can understand its form, just as was the case with the chiliagon, without the help of my imagination. But I can also imagine it, that is, by applying the powers of discernment both to its five sides and, at the same time, to the area bounded by those sides; clearly I am aware at this point that I need a peculiar sort of effort on the part of the mind in order to imagine, one that I do not employ in order to understand. This new effort on the part of the mind clearly shows the difference between imagination and pure intellection.

Besides, I believe that this power of imagining that is in me, insofar as it differs from the power of understanding, is not a necessary element of my essence, that is, of the essence of my mind; for although I might lack this power, nonetheless I would undoubtedly remain the same person as I am now. Thus it seems to follow that the power of imagining depends upon something different from me. And I readily understand that were a body to exist to which a mind is so joined that it might direct itself to look at it anytime it wishes, it could happen that by means of this body I intuit corporeal things. The result would be that this mode of thinking differs from pure intellection only in the fact that the mind, when it understands, in a sense turns itself toward itself and gazes upon one of the ideas that are in it. But when it imagines, it turns itself toward the body, and intuits something in the body similar to an idea either understood by the mind or perceived by sense. I say I easily understand that the imagination can function in this way, provided a body does exist. But this is only a probability; although I may investigate everything carefully, nevertheless, I do not yet see how, from the distinct idea of corporeal nature that I find in my imagination, I can draw up an argument that necessarily concludes that some body exists.

But I am in the habit of imagining many other things—over and above the corporeal nature that is the object of pure mathematics—such as colors, sounds, tastes, pain, and so on, but not so distinctly. Inasmuch as I perceive these things better with those senses from which, with the aid of the memory, they seem to have come to the imagination, the same trouble should also be taken concerning the senses, so that I might deal with them more appropriately. It must be seen whether I can obtain any certain argument for the existence of corporeal things from those things that are perceived by the way of thinking that I call "sense."

First I will repeat to myself here what those things were that I believed to be true because I had perceived them by means of the senses and what the grounds were for so believing. Next I will assess the reasons why I called them into doubt. Finally, I will consider what I must now believe concerning these things.

So, first, I sensed that I have a head, hands, feet, and other members that composed this body; I viewed it as a part of me, or perhaps even as the whole of me. I sensed that this body is frequently amid many other bodies, and that these bodies can affect my body in pleasant and unpleasant ways; I gauged what was pleasant by a certain sense of pleasure, and what was unpleasant by a sense of pain. In addition to pain and pleasure, I also sensed in me hunger, thirst, and other such appetites, as well as certain corporeal tendencies to mirth, sadness, anger, and other such feelings. But, as for things external to me—besides the extension, shapes, and motions of bodies—I also sensed their roughness, heat, and other tactile qualities; I sensed, too, the light, colors, odors, tastes, and sounds from whose variety I distinguished the heavens, the earth, the seas, and the other bodies one from the other. Indeed, because of the ideas of all these qualities that presented themselves to my thought and that alone I properly and immediately sensed, it was not wholly without reason that I believed that I sensed things clearly different from my thought, namely, the bodies from which these ideas might proceed. For I knew by experience that they come upon me without my consent, to the extent that, wish as I may, I cannot sense any object unless it be present to the organ of sense, and I cannot fail to sense it when it is present. Since the ideas perceived by sense are much more vivid and clear-cut, and even, in their own way, more "distinct," than any of those that I willingly and knowingly formed by meditation or those that I found impressed on my memory, it seems impossible that they come from myself. Therefore, it remained that they came from other things. Since I had no knowledge of such things except from these ideas themselves, I could not help entertaining the view that these things were similar to those ideas. Also, because I recalled that I had used my senses earlier than my reason, and I saw that the ideas that I myself constructed were not as clear-cut as those that I perceived by means of the senses, I saw that these former ideas were for the most part composed of parts of these latter ideas; I easily convinced myself that I plainly have no idea in the intellect that I did not have beforehand in the sense. Not without reason did I judge that this body, which by a special right I called "mine," belongs more to me than to any other thing, for I could never be separated from it in the same way as I could be from the rest. I sensed all appetites and feelings in it and for it. Finally, I have noticed pain and pleasurable excitement in its parts, but not in other bodies external to it. But why a certain sadness of spirit arises from one feeling of pain or another, and why a certain elation arises from a feeling of excitement, or why some sort of twitching of the stomach, which I call hunger, should warn me to take in nourishment, or why dryness of throat should warn me to take something to drink, and so on—for all these I plainly had no explanation other than that I have been taught so by nature. For there is clearly no affinity, at least none I am aware of, between the twitching of the stomach and the will to take in nourishment, or between the sense of something that causes pain and the thought of the sadness arising from this sense. But nature seems to have taught me everything else that I judged concerning the objects of the senses, because I convinced myself—even before having spent time on any of the arguments that might prove it—that things were this way.

But afterwards many experiences gradually caused all faith that I had in the senses to totter; occasionally towers, which had seemed round from afar, appeared square at close quarters; very large statues, standing on their pinnacles, did not seem large to someone looking at them from ground level; in countless other such things I detected that judgments of the external senses deceived me—not just the external senses, but also the internal senses. What can be more intimate than pain? But I had once heard it said by people whose leg or arm had been amputated that it seems to them that they occasionally sense pain in the very limb that they lacked. Therefore, even in me, it did not seem to be clearly certain that some part of my body was causing me pain, although I did sense pain in it. To these causes of doubt I recently added two quite general ones: first, I believed I never sensed anything while I was awake that I could not believe I also sometimes perceive while asleep. Since I do not believe that what I seem to sense in my dreams comes to me from things external to me, I did not see any reason why I should have these beliefs about things that I seem to sense while I am awake. The second cause of doubt was that, since I was ignorant of the cause of my coming into being (or at least pretended that I was ignorant of it), I saw that nothing prevented my having been so constituted by nature that I should be deceived about even what appeared to me most true. As to the arguments by which I formerly convinced myself of the truth of sensible things, I found no difficulty in responding to them. Since I seemed driven by nature toward many things opposed to reason, I did not think what was taught by nature deserved much credence. Although the perceptions of the senses did not depend on my will, I did not think that we must therefore conclude that they came from things external to me, because perhaps there is in me some faculty, as yet unknown to me, that produces these perceptions.

However, now, after having begun to know better the cause of my coming to be, I believe that I must not rashly admit everything that I seem to derive from the senses. But, then, neither should I call everything into doubt.

First, because I know that all the things that I clearly and distinctly understand can be made by God exactly as I understand them, it is enough that I can clearly and distinctly understand one thing without the other in order for me to be certain that the one thing is different from the other, because at least God can establish them separately. The question of the power by which this takes place is not relevant to their being thought to be different. For this reason, from the fact that I know that I exist, and that meanwhile I judge that nothing else clearly belongs to my nature or essence except that I am a thing that thinks, I rightly conclude that my essence consists in this alone: that I am only a thing that thinks. Although perhaps (or rather, as I shall soon say, to be sure) I have a body that is very closely joined to me, nevertheless, because on the one hand I have a clear and distinct idea of myself — insofar as I am a thing that thinks and not an extended thing — and because on the other hand I have a distinct idea of a body — insofar as it is merely an extended thing, and not a thing that thinks — it is therefore certain that I am truly distinct from my body, and that I can exist without it.

Moreover, I find in myself faculties endowed with certain special modes of thinking — namely the faculties of imagining and sensing — without which I can clearly and distinctly understand myself in my entirety, but not vice versa: I cannot understand them clearly and distinctly without me, that is, without the knowing substance to which they are attached. For in their formal concept they include an act of understanding; thus I perceive that they are distinguished from me just as modes are to be distinguished from the thing of which they are modes. I also recognize certain other faculties — like those of moving from one place to another, of taking on various shapes, and so on — that surely no more can be understood without the substance to which they are attached than those preceding faculties; for that reason they cannot exist without the substance to which they are attached. But it is clear that these faculties, if in fact they exist, must be attached to corporeal or extended substances, but not to a knowing substance, because extension — but certainly not understanding — is contained in a clear and distinct concept of them. But now there surely is in me a passive faculty of sensing, that is, of receiving and knowing the ideas of sensible things; but I cannot use it unless there also exists, either in me or in something else, a certain active faculty of producing or bringing about these ideas. This faculty surely cannot be in me, since it clearly presupposes no intellection, and these ideas are produced without my cooperation and often against my will. Because this faculty is in a substance other than myself, in which ought to be contained — formally or eminently — all the reality that is objectively in the ideas produced by this faculty (as I have just now taken notice), it thus remains that either this substance is a body (or corporeal nature) in which is contained formally all that is contained in ideas objectively or it is God—or some other creature more noble than a body—in which it is all contained eminently. But, since God is not a deceiver, it is absolutely clear that he sends me these ideas neither directly and immediately—nor even through the mediation of any creature, in which the objective reality of these ideas is contained not formally but only eminently. Since he plainly gave me no faculty for making this discrimination—rather, he gave me a great inclination to believe that these ideas proceeded from things—I fail to see why God cannot be understood to be a deceiver, if they proceeded from a source other than corporeal things. For this reason, corporeal things exist. Be that as it may, perhaps not all bodies exist exactly as I grasp them by sense, because this grasp by the senses is in many cases very obscure and confused. But at least everything is in these bodies that I clearly and distinctly understand—that is, everything, considered in a general sense, that is encompassed in the object of pure mathematics.

But as to how this point relates to the other remaining matters that are either merely particular—as, for example, that the sun is of such and such a size or shape, and so on—or less clearly understood—as for example, light, sound, pain, and so on—although they are very doubtful and uncertain, still, because God is not a deceiver, and no falsity can be found in my opinions, unless there is also in me a faculty given me by God for the purpose of rectifying this falsity, these features provide me with a certain hope of reaching the truth in them. And plainly it cannot be doubted that whatever I am taught by nature has some truth to it; for by "nature," taken generally, I understand only God himself or the coordination, instituted by God, of created things. I understand nothing else by my nature in particular than the totality of all the things bestowed on me by God.

There is nothing that this nature teaches me in a more clear-cut way than that I have a body that is ill-disposed when I feel pain, that it needs food and drink when I suffer hunger or thirst, and so on. Therefore, I ought not to doubt that there is some truth in this.

By means of these feelings of pain, hunger, thirst and so on, nature also teaches that I am present to my body not merely in the way a seaman is present to his ship, but that I am tightly joined and, so to speak, mingled together with it, so much so that I make up one single thing with it. For otherwise, when the body is wounded, I, who am nothing but a thing that thinks, would not then sense the pain. Rather, I would perceive the wound by means of the pure intellect, just as a seaman perceives by means of sight whether anything in the ship is broken. When the body lacks food or drink, I would understand this in a clear-cut fashion; I would not have confused feelings of hunger and thirst. For certainly these feelings of thirst, hunger, pain, and so on are nothing but confused modes of thinking arising from the union and, as it were, the mingling of the mind with the body.

Moreover, I am also taught by nature that many other bodies exist around my body; some of them are to be pursued, and others are to be avoided. And to be sure, from the fact that I sense widely different colors, sounds, odors, tastes, heat, roughness, and so on, I rightly conclude that in the bodies from which these different perceptions of the senses proceed, there are differences corrresponding to the different perceptions — although perhaps the former are not similar to the latter. But from the fact that some of these perceptions are pleasant and others unpleasant, it is plainly certain that my body — or rather my whole self, insofar as I am composed of a body and a mind — can be affected by the various agreeable and disagreeable bodies in the vicinity.

But I have accepted many other things, and, although I seem to have been taught them by nature, still it was not really nature that taught them to me, but a certain habit of making unconsidered judgments. And thus it could easily happen that they are false, as, for example, the belief that any space where there is nothing that moves my senses is empty; or, for example, the belief that in a hot body there is something plainly similar to the idea of heat which is in me; or that in a white or green body there is the same whiteness or greenness that I sense; or in a bitter or sweet thing the same taste, and so on; or the belief that stars and towers, and any other distant bodies have only the same size and shape that they present to the senses — and other examples of the same sort. But lest I not perceive distinctly enough something about this matter, I ought to define more carefully what I properly understand when I say that I am "taught something by nature." For I am using "nature" here in a stricter sense than the totality of everything bestowed on me by God. For in this totality there are contained many things that pertain only to my mind, as, for example, that I perceive that what has been done cannot be undone, and everything else that is known by the light of nature. At the moment the discussion does not center on these matters. There are also many things that pertain only to the body, as, for example, that it tends downward, and so on. I am not dealing with these either, but only with what has been bestowed on me by God, insofar as I am composed of mind and body. Therefore it is nature, thus understood, that teaches me to flee what brings a sense of pain and to pursue what brings a sense of pleasure, and the like. But it does not appear that nature, so conceived, teaches that we conclude from these perceptions of the senses anything in addition to this regarding things external to us unless there previously be an inquiry by the intellect; for it pertains to the mind alone, and not to the composite, to know the truth in these matters. Thus, although a star affects my eye no more than the flame from a small torch, still there is no real or positive tendency in my eye toward believing that the star is any bigger than the flame; rather, ever since my youth, I have made this judgment without reason. Although I feel heat upon drawing closer to the fire, and I feel pain upon drawing even closer to it, there is indeed no argument that convinces me that there is something in the fire that is similar either to the heat or to the pain, but only that there is something in the fire that causes in us these feelings of heat or pain. Although there be nothing in a given space that moves the sense, it does not therefore follow that there is no body in it. I use the perceptions of the senses that properly have been given by nature only for the purpose of signifying to the mind what is agreeable and disagreeable to the composite, of which the mind is a part; within those limits these perceptions are sufficiently clear and distinct. However, I see that I have been in the habit of subverting the order of nature in these and many other matters, because I use the perceptions of the senses as certain rules for immediately discerning what the essence is of the bodies external to us; yet, in respect to this essence, these perceptions still show me nothing but obscurity and confusion.

I have already examined in sufficient detail how it could happen that my judgments are false, the goodness of God notwithstanding. But a new difficulty now comes on the scene concerning those very things that are shown to me by nature as things to be either sought or avoided, as well as concerning the internal senses in which I seem to have detected errors: for example, when a person, deluded by the pleasant taste of food, ingests a poison hidden inside it. But in this case he is impelled by nature only toward desiring the thing in which the pleasant taste is located, but not toward the poison, of which he obviously is unaware. Nothing else can be concluded here except that this nature is not all-knowing. This is not remarkable, since man is a limited being; thus only limited perfection is appropriate to man.

But we often err even in those things to which nature impels us; for example, when those who are ill desire food or drink that will soon be injurious to them. Perhaps it could have been said here that they erred because their nature was corrupt. But this does not remove our difficulty, because a sickly man is no less a creature of God than a healthy one; for that reason it does not seem any less repugnant that the sickly man got a deceiving nature from God. And just as a clock made of wheels and counter-weights follows all the laws of nature no less closely when it has been badly constructed and does not tell time accurately than when it satisfies on all scores the wishes of its maker, just so, if I should consider the body of a man—insofar as it is a kind of mechanism composed of and outfitted with bones, nerves, muscles, veins, blood and skin—even if no mind existed in it, the man's body would still have all the same motions that are in it now except for those motions that proceed either from a command of the will or, consequently, from the mind. I readily recognize that it would be natural for this body, were it, say, suffering from dropsy, to suffer dryness of the throat, which commonly brings a feeling of thirst to the mind, and thus too its nerves and other parts are so disposed by the mind to take a drink with the result that the sickness is increased. It would be no more natural for this body, when there is no such infirmity in it and it is moved by the same dryness, to drink something useful to it. And, from the point of view of the intended purpose of the watch, I could say that it turns away from its nature when it does not tell the right time. Similarly, considering the mechanism of the human body as equipped for the motions that typically occur in it, I might think that it too turns away from its nature, if its throat were dry, when taking a drink would not be beneficial to its continued existence. Nevertheless, I realize well enough that this latter usage of the term "nature" differs greatly from the former. For this latter "nature" is only an arbitrary denomination, extrinsic to the things on which it is predicated and dependent upon my thought, because it compares a man in poor health and a poorly constructed clock with the idea of a man in good health and a well-made clock. But by "nature" taken in the former sense, I understand something that really is in things, and thus it is not without some truth.

When it is said, in the case of the dropsical body, that its "nature" is corrupt — from the fact that this body has a parched throat, and yet does not need a drink — it certainly is only an extrinsic denomination of nature. But be that as it may, in the case of the composite, that is, of a mind joined to such a body, it is not a pure denomination, but a true error of nature that this body should thirst when a drink would be harmful to it. Therefore it remains here to inquire how the goodness of God does not stand in the way of "nature," thus considered, being deceptive.

Now, first, I realize at this point that there is a great difference between a mind and a body, because the body, by its very nature, is something divisible, whereas the mind is plainly indivisible. Obviously, when I consider the mind, that is, myself insofar as I am only a thing that thinks, I cannot distinguish any parts in me; rather, I take myself to be one complete thing. Although the whole mind seems to be united to the whole body, nevertheless, were a foot or an arm or any other bodily part amputated, I know that nothing would be taken away from the mind; nor can the faculties of willing, sensing, understanding, and so on be called its "parts," because it is one and the same mind that wills, senses, and understands. On the other hand, no corporeal or extended thing can be thought by me that I did not easily in thought divide into parts; in this way I know that it is divisible. If I did not yet know it from any other source, this consideration alone would suffice to teach me that the mind is wholly different from the body.

Next, I observe that my mind is not immediately affected by all the parts of the body, but merely by the brain, or perhaps even by just one small part of the brain — namely, by that part in which the "common sense" is said to be found. As often as it is disposed in the same manner, it presents the same thing to the mind, although the other parts of the body can meanwhile orient themselves now this way, now that way, as countless experiments show — none of which need to be reviewed here.

I also notice that the nature of the body is such that none of its parts can be moved by another part a short distance away, unless it is also moved in the same direction by any of the parts that stand between them, even though this more distant part does nothing. For example, in the cord ABCD, if the final part D is pulled, the first part A would be moved in exactly the same direction as it could be moved if one of the intermediate parts, B or C, were pulled and the last part D remained motionless. Just so, when I sense pain in the foot, physics teaches me that this feeling took place because of nerves scattered throughout the foot. These nerves, like cords, are extended from that point all the way to the brain; when they are pulled in the foot, they also pull on the inner parts of the brain to which they are stretched, and produce a certain motion in these parts of the brain. This motion has been constituted by nature so as to affect the mind with a feeling of pain, as if it existed in the foot. But because these nerves need to pass through the tibia, thigh, loins, back, and neck, with the result that they extend from the foot to the brain, it can happen that the part that is in the foot is not stretched; rather, one of the intermediate parts is thus stretched, and obviously the same movement will occur in the brain that happens when the foot was badly affected. The necessary result is that the mind feels the same pain. And we must believe the same regarding any other sense.

Finally, I observe that, since each of the motions occurring in that part of the brain that immediately affects the mind occasions only one sensation in it, there is no better way to think about this than that it occasions the sensation that, of all that could be occasioned by it, is most especially and most often conducive to the maintenance of a healthy man. Moreover, experience shows that such are all the senses bestowed on us by nature; therefore, clearly nothing is to be found in them that does not bear witness to God's power and goodness. Thus, for example, when the nerves in the foot are violently and unusually agitated, their motion, which extends through the marrow of the spine to the inner reaches of the brain, gives the mind at that point a sign to feel something—namely, the pain as if existing in the foot. This pain provokes it to do its utmost to move away from the cause, since it is harmful to the foot. But the nature of man could have been so constituted by God that this same motion in the brain might have displayed something else to the mind: either the motion itself as it is in the brain, or as it is in the foot, or in some place in between—or somewhere else entirely different. But nothing else serves so well the maintenance of the body. Similarly, when we need a drink, a certain dryness arises in the throat that moves its nerves, and, by means of them, the inner recesses of the brain. This motion affects the mind with a feeling of thirst, because in this situation nothing is more useful for us to know than that we need a drink to sustain our health; the same holds for the other matters.

From these considerations it is totally clear that, notwithstanding the immense goodness of God, the nature of man—insofar as it is composed of mind and body, cannot help but sometimes be deceived. For if some cause, not in the foot but in some other part through which the nerves are stretched from the foot to the brain—or perhaps even in the brain itself—were to produce the same motion that would normally be produced by a badly affected foot, then the pain will be felt as if it were in the foot, and the senses will naturally be deceived, because it is reasonable that the motion should always show the pain to the mind as something belonging to the foot rather than to some other part, since an identical motion in the brain can bring about only the identical effect and this motion more frequently is wont to arise from a cause that harms the foot than from something existing elsewhere. And if the dryness of the throat does not, as is the custom, arise from the fact that drink aids in the health of the body, but from a contrary cause—as happens in the case of the person with dropsy—then it is far better that it should deceive, than if, on the contrary, it were always deceptive when the body is well constituted. The same goes for the other cases.

This consideration is most helpful, not only for noticing all the errors to which my nature is liable, but also for easily being able to correct or avoid them. To be sure, I know that every sense more frequently indicates what is true than what is false regarding those things that concern the advantage of the body, and I can almost always use more than one sense in order to examine the same thing. Furthermore, I can use memory, which connects present things with preceding ones, plus the intellect, which now has examined all the causes of error. I should no longer fear lest those things that are daily shown me by the senses, are false; rather, the hyperbolic doubts of the last few days ought to be rejected as worthy of derision—especially the principal doubt regarding sleep, which I did not distinguish from being awake. For I now notice that a very great difference exists between these two; dreams are never joined with all the other actions of life by the memory, as is the case with those actions that occur when one is awake. For surely, if someone, while I am awake, suddenly appears to me, and then immediately disappears, as happens in dreams, so that I see neither where he came from or where he went, it is not without reason that I would judge him to be a ghost or a phantom conjured up in my brain, rather than a true man. But when these things happen, regarding which I notice distinctly where they come from, where they are now, and when they come to me, and I connect the perception of them without any interruption with the rest of my life, obviously I am certain that these perceptions have occurred not in sleep but in a waking state. Nor ought I to have even a little doubt regarding the truth of these things, if, having mustered all the senses, memory, and intellect in order to examine them, nothing is announced to me by one of these sources that conflicts with the others. For from the fact that God is no deceiver, it follows that I am in no way deceived in these matters. But because the need to get things done does not always give us the leisure time for such a careful inquiry, one must believe that the life of man is vulnerable to errors regarding particular things, and we must acknowledge the infirmity of our nature.

Induction Cannot Be Rationally Justified

·DAVID HUME·

In this excerpt from his Inquiry Concerning Human Understanding, *Hume (1711–1776) argues that there can be no rational justification of the inductions that people perform. The reason is that all such inductions depend on the Principle of the Uniformity of Nature, and this principle cannot be given a rational justification.*

Skeptical Doubts Concerning the Operations of the Understanding

Part I

All the objects of human reason or inquiry may naturally be divided into two kinds, to wit, "Relations of Ideas," and "Matters of Fact." Of the first kind are the sciences of Geometry, Algebra, and Arithmetic, and, in short, every affirmation which is either intuitively or demonstratively certain. *That the square of the hypotenuse is equal to the square of the two sides* is a proposition which expresses a relation between these figures. *That three times five is equal to the half of thirty* expresses a relation between these numbers. Propositions of this kind are discoverable by the mere operation of thought, without dependence on what is anywhere existent in the universe. Though there never were a circle or triangle in nature, the truths demonstrated by Euclid would forever retain their certainty and evidence.

Matters of fact, which are the second objects of human reason, are not ascertained in the same manner, nor is our evidence of their truth, however great, of a like nature with the foregoing. The contrary of every matter of fact is still possible, because it can never imply a contradiction and is conceived by the mind with the same facility and distinctness as if ever so conformable to reality. *That the sun will not rise tomorrow* is no less intelligible a proposition and implies no more contradiction than the affirmation *that it will rise.* We should in vain, therefore, attempt to demonstrate its falsehood. Were it demonstratively false, it would imply a contradiction and could never be distinctly conceived by the mind.

It may, therefore, be a subject worthy of curiosity to inquire what is the nature of that evidence which assures us of any real existence and matter of fact beyond the present testimony of our senses or the records of our memory. This part of philosophy, it is observable, had been little cultivated either by the ancients or moderns; and, therefore, our doubts and errors in the prosecution of so important an inquiry may be the more excusable while we march through such difficult paths without any guide or direction. They may even prove useful by exciting curiosity and destroying that implicit faith and security which is the bane of all reasoning and free inquiry. The discovery of defects in the common philosophy, if any such there be, will not, I presume, be a discouragement, but rather an incitement, as is usual, to attempt something more full and satisfactory than has yet been proposed to the public.

All reasoning concerning matter of fact seem to be founded on the relation of *cause* and *effect.* By means of that relation alone we can go beyond the evidence of our memory and senses. If you were to ask a man why he believes any matter of fact which is absent, for instance, that his friend is in the country or in France, he would give you a reason, and this reason would be some other fact: as a letter received from him or the knowledge of his former resolutions and promises. A man finding a watch or any other machine in a desert island would conclude that there had once been men in that island. All our reasonings concerning fact

INDUCTION CANNOT BE RATIONALLY JUSTIFIED

are of the same nature. And here it is constantly supposed that there is a connection between the present fact and that which is inferred from it. Were there nothing to bind them together, the inference would be entirely precarious. The hearing of an articulate voice and rational discourse in the dark assures us of the presence of some person. Why? Because these are the effects of the human make and fabric, and closely connected with it. If we anatomize all the other reasonings of this nature, we shall find that they are founded on the relation of cause and effect, and that this relation is either near or remote, direct or collateral. Heat and light are collateral effects of fire, and the one effect may justly be inferred from the other.

If we would satisfy ourselves, therefore, concerning the nature of that evidence which assures us of matters of fact, we must inquire how we arrive at the knowledge of cause and effect.

I shall venture to affirm, as a general proposition which admits of no exception, that the knowledge of this relation is not, in any instance, attained by reasonings *a priori*, but arises entirely from experience, when we find that any particular objects are constantly conjoined with each other. Let an object be presented to a man of ever so strong natural reason and abilities—if that object be entirely new to him, he will not be able, by the most accurate examination of its sensible qualities, to discover any of its causes or effects. Adam, though his rational faculties may be supposed, at the very first, entirely perfect, could not have inferred from the fluidity and transparency of water that it would suffocate him, or from the light and warmth of fire that it would consume him. No object ever discovers, by the qualities which appear to the senses, either the causes which produced it or the effects which will arise from it; nor can our reason, unassisted by experience, ever draw any inference concerning real existence and matter of fact.

This proposition, *that causes and effects are discoverable, not by reason, but by experience,* will readily be admitted with regard to such objects as we remember to have once been altogether unknown to us, since we must be conscious of the utter inability which we then lay under of foretelling what would arise from them. Present two smooth pieces of marble to a man who has no tincture of natural philosophy; he will never discover that they will adhere together in such a manner as to require great force to separate them in a direct line, while they make so small a resistance to a lateral pressure. Such events as bear little analogy to the common course of nature are also readily confessed to be known only by experience, nor does any man imagine that the explosion of gunpowder or the attraction of a loadstone could ever be discovered by arguments *a priori*. In like manner, when an effect is supposed to depend upon an intricate machinery or secret structure of parts, we make no difficulty in attributing all our knowledge of it to experience. Who will assert that he can give the ultimate reason why milk or bread is proper nourishment for a man, not for a lion or tiger?

But the same truth may not appear at first sight to have the same evidence with regard to events which have become familiar to us from our first appearance in the world, which bear a close analogy to the whole course of nature, and which are supposed to depend on the simple qualities of objects without any secret structure of parts. We are apt to imagine that we could discover these effects by the mere operation of our reason without experience. We fancy that, were we brought on a sudden into this world, we could at first have inferred that one billiard ball would communicate motion to another upon impulse, and that we needed not have waited for the event in order to pronounce with certainty concerning it. Such is the influence of custom that where it is strongest it not only covers our natural ignorance but even conceals itself, and seems not to take place, merely because it is found in the highest degree.

But to convince us that all the laws of nature and all the operations of bodies without exception are known only by experience, the following reflections may perhaps suffice. Were any object presented to us, and were we required to pronounce concerning the effect which will result from it without consulting past observation, after what manner, I beseech you, must the mind proceed in this operation? It must invent or imagine some event which it ascribes to the object as its effect; and it is plain that this invention must be entirely arbitrary. The mind can never possibly find the effect in the supposed cause by the most accurate scrutiny and examination. For the effect is totally different from the cause, and consequently can never be discovered in it. Motion in the second billiard ball is a quite distinct event from motion in the first, nor is there anything in the one to suggest the smallest hint of the other. A stone or piece of metal raised into the air and left without any support immediately falls. But to consider the matter *a priori,* is there anything we discover in this situation which can beget the idea of a downward rather than an upward or any other motion in the stone or metal?

And as the first imagination or invention of a particular effect in all natural operations is arbitrary where we consult not experience, so must we also esteem the supposed tie or connection between the cause and effect which binds them together and renders it impossible that any other effect could result from the operation of that cause. When I see, for instance, a billiard ball moving in a straight line toward another, even suppose motion in the second ball should by accident be suggested to me as the result of their contact or impulse, may I not conceive that a hundred different events might as well follow from that cause? May not both these balls remain at absolute rest? May not the first ball return in a straight line or leap off from the second in any line or direction? All these suppositions are consistent and conceivable. Why, then, should we give the preference to one which is no more consistent or conceivable than the rest? All our reasonings *a priori* will never be able to show us any foundation for this preference.

In a word, then, every effect is a distinct event from its cause. It could not, therefore, be discovered in the cause, and the first invention or conception of it, *a priori,* must be entirely arbitrary. And even after it is suggested, the conjunction of it with the cause must appear equally arbitrary, since there are always many other effects which, to reason, must seem fully as consistent and natural. In vain, therefore, should we pretend to determine any single event or infer any cause or effect without the assistance of observation and experience.

Hence we may discover the reason why no philosopher who is rational and

INDUCTION
CANNOT BE
RATIONALLY
JUSTIFIED

modest has ever pretended to assign the ultimate cause of any natural operation, or to show distinctly the action of that power which produces any single effect in the universe. It is confessed that the utmost effort of human reason is to reduce the principles productive of natural phenomena to a greater simplicity, and to resolve the many particular effects into a few general causes, by means of reasonings from analogy, experience, and observation. But as to the causes of these general causes, we should in vain attempt their discovery, nor shall we ever be able to satisfy ourselves by any particular explication of them. These ultimate springs and principles are totally shut up from human curiosity and inquiry. Elasticity, gravity, cohesion of parts, communication of motion by impulse — these are probably the ultimate causes and principles which we shall ever discover in nature; and we may esteem ourselves sufficiently happy if, by accurate inquiry and reasoning, we can trace up the particular phenomena to, or near to, these general principles. The most perfect philosophy of the natural kind only staves off our ignorance a little longer, as perhaps the most perfect philosophy of the moral or metaphysical kind serves only to discover larger portions of it. Thus the observation of human blindness and weakness is the result of all philosophy, and meets us, at every turn, in spite of our endeavors to elude or avoid it.

Nor is geometry, when taken into the assistance of natural philosophy, ever able to remedy this defect or lead us into the knowledge of ultimate causes by all that accuracy of reasoning for which it is so justly celebrated. Every part of mixed mathematics proceeds upon the supposition that certain laws are established by nature in her operations, and abstract reasonings are employed either to assist experience in the discovery of these laws or to determine their influence in particular instances where it depends upon any precise degree of distance and quantity. Thus it is a law of motion, discovered by experience, that the moment or force of any body in motion is in the compound ratio or proportion of its solid contents and its velocity, and, consequently, that a small force may remove the greatest obstacle or raise the greatest weight if by any contrivance or machinery we can increase the velocity of that force so as to make it an overmatch for its antagonist. Geometry assists us in the application of this law by giving us the just dimensions of all the parts and figures which can enter into any species of machine, but still the discovery of the law itself is owing merely to experience; and all the abstract reasonings in the world could never lead us one step toward the knowledge of it. When we reason *a priori* and consider merely any object or cause as it appears to the mind, independent of all observation, it never could suggest to us the notion of any distinct object, such as its effect, much less show us the inseparable and inviolable connection between them. A man must be very sagacious who could discover by reasoning that crystal is the effect of heat, and ice of cold, without being previously acquainted with the operation of these qualities.

Part II

But we have not yet attained any tolerable satisfaction with regard to the question first proposed. Each solution still gives rise to a new question as difficult as the foregoing and leads us on to further inquiries. When it is asked, *What is the nature of all our reasonings concerning matter of fact?* the proper answer seems to be, That they are founded on the relation of cause and effect. When again it is asked, *What is the foundation of all our reasonings and conclusions concerning that relation?* it may be replied in one word, *experience.* But if we still carry on our sifting humor and ask, *What is the foundation of all conclusions from experience?* this implies a new question which may be of more difficult solution and explication. Philosophers that give themselves airs of superior wisdom and sufficiency have a hard task when they encounter persons of inquisitive dispositions, who push them from every corner to which they retreat, and who are sure at last to bring them to some dangerous dilemma. The best expedient to prevent this confusion is to be modest in our pretensions and even to discover the difficulty ourselves before it is objected to us. By this means we may make a kind of merit of our very ignorance.

I shall content myself in this section with an easy task and shall pretend only to give a negative answer to the question here proposed. I say, then, that even after we have experience of the operations of cause and effect, our conclusions from that experience are *not* founded on reasoning or any process of the understanding. This answer we must endeavor both to explain and to defend.

It must certainly be allowed that nature has kept us at a great distance from all her secrets and has afforded us only the knowledge of a few superficial qualities of objects, while she conceals from us those powers and principles on which the influence of these objects entirely depends. Our senses inform us of the color, weight, and consistency of bread, but neither sense nor reason can ever inform us of those qualities which fit it for the nourishment and support of the human body. Sight or feeling conveys an idea of the actual motion of bodies, but as to that wonderful force or power which would carry on a moving body forever in a continued change of place, and which bodies never lose but by communicating it to others, of this we cannot form the most distant conception. But notwithstanding this ignorance of natural powers and principles, we always presume when we see like sensible qualities that they have like secret powers, and expect that effects similar to those which we have experienced will follow from them. If a body of like color and consistency with that bread which we have formerly eaten be presented to us, we make no scruple of repeating the experiment and foresee with certainty like nourishment and support. Now this is a process of the mind or thought of which I would willingly know the foundation. It is allowed on all hands that there is no known connection between the sensible qualities and the secret powers, and, consequently, that the mind is not led to form such a conclusion concerning their constant and regular conjunction by anything which it knows of their nature. As to past *experience*, it can be allowed to give *direct* and *certain* information of those precise objects only, and that precise period of time which fell under its cognizance: But why this experience should be extended to future times and to other objects which, for aught we know, may be only in appearance similar, this is the main question on which I would insist. The bread which I formerly ate nourished me; that is, a body of such sensible qualities was,

INDUCTION
CANNOT BE
RATIONALLY
JUSTIFIED

at that time, endued with such secret powers. But does it follow that other bread must also nourish me at another time, and that like sensible qualities must always be attended with like secret powers? The consequence seems nowise necessary. At least, it must be acknowledged that there is here a consequence drawn by the mind that there is a certain step taken, a process of thought, and an inference which wants to be explained. These two propositions are far from being the same: *I have found that such an object has always been attended with such an effect,* and *I foresee that other objects which are in appearance similar will be attended with similar effects.* I shall allow, if you please, that the one proposition may justly be inferred from the other: I know, in fact, that it always is inferred. But if you insist that the inference is made by a chain of reasoning, I desire you to produce that reasoning. The connection between these propositions is not intuitive. There is required a medium which may enable the mind to draw such an inference, if indeed it be drawn by reasoning and argument. What that medium is I must confess passes my comprehension; and it is incumbent on those to produce it who assert that it really exists and is the original of all our conclusions concerning matter of fact.

This negative argument must certainly, in process of time, become altogether convincing if many penetrating and able philosophers shall turn their inquiries this way, and no one be ever able to discover any connecting proposition or intermediate step which supports the understanding in this conclusion. But as the question is yet new, every reader may not trust so far to his own penetration as to conclude, because an argument escapes his inquiry, that therefore it does not really exist. For this reason it may be requisite to venture upon a more difficult task, and, enumerating all the branches of human knowledge, endeavor to show that none of them can afford such an argument.

All reasonings may be divided into two kinds, namely, demonstrative reasoning, or that concerning relations of ideas, and moral reasoning, or that concerning matter of fact and existence. That there are no demonstrative arguments in the case seems evident, since it implies no contradiction that the course of nature may change and that an object, seemingly like those which we have experienced, may be attended with different or contrary effects. May I not clearly and distinctly conceive that a body, falling from the clouds and which in all other respects resembles snow, has yet the taste of salt or feeling of fire? Is there any more intelligible proposition than to affirm that all the trees will flourish in December and January, and will decay in May and June? Now, whatever is intelligible and can be distinctly conceived implies no contradiction and can never be proved false by any demonstrative argument or abstract reasoning *a priori.*

If we be, therefore, engaged by arguments to put trust in past experience and make it the standard of our future judgment, these arguments must be probable only, or such as regard matter of fact and real existence, according to the division above mentioned. But that there is no argument of this kind must appear if our explication of that species of reasoning be admitted as solid and satisfactory. We have said that all arguments concerning existence are founded on the relation of cause and effect, that our knowledge of that relation is derived entirely from experience, and that all our experimental conclusions proceed upon the supposition that the future will be conformable to the past. To endeavor, therefore, the proof of this last supposition by probable arguments, or arguments regarding existence, must be evidently going in a circle and taking that for granted which is the very point in question.

In reality, all arguments from experience are founded on the similarity which we discover among natural objects, and by which we are induced to expect effects similar to those which we have found to follow from such objects. And though none but a fool or madman will ever pretend to dispute the authority of experience or to reject that great guide of human life, it may surely be allowed a philosopher to have so much curiosity at least as to examine the principle of human nature which gives this mighty authority to experience and makes us draw advantage from that similarity which nature has placed among different objects. From causes which appear similar, we expect similar effects. This is the sum of all our experimental conclusions. Now it seems evident that, if this conclusion were formed by reason, it would be as perfect at first, and upon one instance, as after ever so long a course of experience; but the case is far otherwise. Nothing so like as eggs, yet no one, on account of this appearing similarity, expects the same taste and relish in all of them. It is only after a long course of uniform experiments in any kind that we attain a firm reliance and security with regard to a particular event. Now, where is that process of reasoning which, from one instance, draws a conclusion so different from that which it infers from a hundred instances that are nowise different from that single one? This question I propose as much for the sake of information as with an intention of raising difficulties. I cannot find, I cannot imagine any such reasoning. But I keep my mind still open to instruction if anyone will vouchsafe to bestow it on me.

Should it be said that, from a number of uniform experiments, we *infer* a connection between the sensible qualities and the secret powers, this, I must confess, seems the same difficulty, couched in different terms. The question still occurs, On what process of argument is this *inference* founded? Where is the medium, the interposing ideas which join propositions so very wide of each other? It is confessed that the color, consistency, and other sensible qualities of bread appear not of themselves to have any connection with the secret powers of nourishment and support; for otherwise we could infer these secret powers from the first appearance of these sensible qualities without the aid of experience, contrary to the sentiment of all philosophers, and contrary to plain matter of fact. Here, then, is our natural state of ignorance with regard to the powers and influence of all objects. How is this remedied by experience? It only shows us a number of uniform effects resulting from certain objects, and teaches us that those particular objects, at that particular time, were endowed with such powers and forces. When a new object endowed with similar sensible qualities is produced, we expect similar powers and forces, and look for a like effect. From a body of like color and consistency with bread, we expect like nourishment and support. But this surely is a step or progress of the mind which wants to be explained. When a man says, *I have found, in all past instances, such sensible qualities, conjoined*

INDUCTION CANNOT BE RATIONALLY JUSTIFIED

with such secret powers, and when he says, *similar sensible qualities will always be conjoined with similar secret powers*, he is not guilty of tautology, nor are these propositions in any respect the same. You say that the one proposition is an inference from the other; but you must confess that the inference is not intuitive, neither is it demonstrative. Of what nature is it then? To say it is experimental is begging the question. For all inferences from experience suppose, as their foundation, that the future will resemble the past and that similar powers will be conjoined with similar sensible qualities. If there be any suspicion that the course of nature may change, and that the past may be no rule for the future, all experience becomes useless and can give rise to no inference or conclusion. It is impossible, therefore, that any arguments from experience can prove this resemblance of the past to the future, since all these arguments are founded on the supposition of that resemblance. Let the course of things be allowed hitherto ever so regular, that alone, without some new argument or inference, proves not that for the future it will continue so. In vain do you pretend to have learned the nature of bodies from your past experience. Their secret nature, and consequently all their effects and influence, may change without any change in their sensible qualities. This happens sometimes, and with regard to some objects. Why may it not happen always, and with regard to all objects? What logic, what process of argument secures you against this supposition? My practice, you say, refutes my doubts. But you mistake the purport of my question. As an agent, I am quite satisfied in the point; but as a philosopher who has some share of curiosity, I will not say skepticism, I want to learn the foundation of this inference. No reading, no inquiry has yet been able to remove my difficulty or give me satisfaction in a matter of such importance. Can I do better than propose the difficulty to the public, even though, perhaps, I have small hopes of obtaining a solution? We shall at least, by this means, be sensible of our ignorance, if we do not augment our knowledge.

I must confess that a man is guilty of unpardonable arrogance who concludes, because an argument has escaped his own investigation, that therefore it does not really exist. I must also confess that, though all the learned, for several ages, should have employed themselves in fruitless search upon any subject, it may still, perhaps, be rash to conclude positively that the subject must therefore pass all human comprehension. Even though we examine all the sources of our knowledge and conclude them unfit for such a subject, there may still remain a suspicion that the enumeration is not complete or the examination not accurate. But with regard to the present subject, there are some considerations which seem to remove all this accusation of arrogance or suspicion of mistake.

It is certain that the most ignorant and stupid peasants, nay infants, nay even brute beasts, improve by experience and learn the qualities of natural objects by observing the effects which result from them. When a child has felt the sensation of pain from touching the flame of a candle, he will be careful not to put his hand near any candle, but will expect a similar effect from a cause which is similar in its sensible qualities and appearance. If you assert, therefore, that the understanding of the child is led into this conclusion by any process of argument or ratiocination, I may justly require you to produce that argument, nor have you any pretense to refuse so equitable a demand. You cannot say that the argument is abstruse and may possibly escape your inquiry, since you confess that it is obvious to the capacity of a mere infant. If you hesitate, therefore, a moment or if, after reflection, you produce an intricate or profound argument, you, in a manner, give up the question and confess that it is not reasoning which engages us to suppose the past resembling the future, and to expect similar effects from causes which are to appearance similar. This is the proposition which I intended to enforce in the present section. If I be right, I pretend not to have made any mighty discovery. And if I be wrong, I must acknowledge myself to be indeed a very backward scholar, since I cannot now discover an argument which, it seems, was perfectly familiar to me long before I was out of my cradle.

Suggestions for Further Reading

On Descartes

Bernard Williams, *Descartes: The Project of Pure Inquiry*. London, Harvester Press, 1978.
Margaret Wilson, *Descartes*. London, Routledge and Kegan Paul, 1978.

On the Reliability Theory of Knowledge

David Armstrong, *Belief, Knowledge, and Truth*. London, Cambridge University Press, 1973.
Fred Dretske, *Knowledge and the Flow of Information*. Cambridge, Massachusetts, MIT Press, 1981.
Alvin Goldman, "A Causal Theory of Knowing," *Journal of Philosophy*, vol. 64, pp. 357–372, 1967.
Robert Nozick, *Philosophical Explanations*. Cambridge, Massachusetts, Harvard University Press, 1981.

On Hume

Barry Stroud, *Hume*. London, Routledge and Kegan Paul, 1977.

On Induction

Nelson Goodman, *Fact, Fiction, and Forecast*. Indianapolis, Bobbs Merrill, 1965.
Wesley Salmon, *Foundations of Scientific Inference*. Pittsburgh, Pennsylvania, University of Pittsburgh Press, 1968.
Brian Skyrms, *Choice and Chance*. Belmont, California, Wadsworth, 1986.

PART IV
Philosophy of Mind

·L·E·C·T·U·R·E·S·

Lecture 18

Dualism and the Mind/Body Problem

In this section of the book on philosophy of mind, I'll discuss three problems. The first is the mind/body problem (Lectures 18–22). The second is the problem of free will (Lectures 23–25). The last is the problem of psychological egoism (Lecture 26).

In different ways, the mind/body problem and the problem of free will address the issue of how the mind is related to the physical world of cause and effect. Is the mind quite separate from the body, or is the mind part of the physical world? If your beliefs and desires are caused by physical things outside of yourself, can it be true that you act the way you do of your own free will? The last problem—the problem of psychological egoism—concerns the motives that drive us to act the way we do. Are people genuinely moved by the welfare of others, or is all behavior, in reality, selfish?

These three problems concern different stages in the causal chain that leads from genes and environment, to the mind, to action:

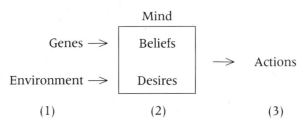

$$
\begin{array}{ccc}
 & \text{Mind} & \\
\text{Genes} \rightarrow & \boxed{\begin{array}{c}\text{Beliefs}\\[1em]\text{Desires}\end{array}} & \rightarrow \quad \text{Actions}\\
\text{Environment} \rightarrow & & \\
(1) & (2) & (3)
\end{array}
$$

The mind/body problem concerns the nature of the objects and events that exist at stage 2 in this diagram. What is a mind? What are beliefs and desires? The problem of free will concerns the relation of stage 1 to stage 2. If our beliefs and desires are caused by the genes we have and the environments we have inhabited, how can we possess free will? The problem of psychological egoism concerns the relationship of stages 2 and 3. If the actions we perform are caused by the desires we have, won't it be true that action is fundamentally selfish—aimed at satisfying the actor's own desires, not at satisfying the needs of others?

Of course, these are only preliminary statements of the philosophical problems. Each will be refined when the time comes.

The question posed by the mind/body problem is simple: What is the relationship between the mental and the physical? I have a mind, which contains various beliefs, desires, sensations, and emotions. I also have a brain; this physical thing is a structured piece of tissue containing an intricate web of neurons. Are the mind and the brain one and the same thing? Are my beliefs, desires, emotions, and sensations identical with physical things found in my brain? Or are the mind and the brain different objects?

What Is the Mind/Body Problem?

In the previous chapter, the discussion of Descartes focused on his epistemology. Descartes also advanced a solution to the mind/body problem. It is this view, now called Cartesian Dualism, that I'll discuss in this lecture. Dualism is the idea that there are two kinds of things in the world. There are physical objects on the one hand, and, on the other, there are mental objects (such as minds, pains, and beliefs).

Descartes' Dualism

Descartes did not deny that there is a causal interaction between the mental and the physical. Taking aspirin can cure headaches. The sound of trumpets can lift your spirits. In the other direction, it seems undeniable that beliefs and desires can cause the parts of your body to move in various ways (speaking, walking, and so on). But granting this two-way interaction did not drive Descartes to abandon dualism.

One alternative to dualism is provided by the mind/brain identity theory. This theory makes a claim about objects and also about the properties those objects possess. First, it says that your mind and your brain are one and the same object. Second, it claims that the mental properties you have (for example, believing that fire is hot, or wanting some ice cream, or being in pain) are physical properties; to be in pain is to have some physical event occur in your central nervous system.

The Mind/ Brain Identity Theory

The identity theory asserts that mental terminology and physical terminology describe the same items in the world. The following analogy may be instructive. People for a long time used the term "water" to denote various items in the world. This term was used in everyday life. At a certain point in the history of science, it was discovered that water is made of H_2O molecules. The discovery was that water and H_2O are one and the same thing.

There certainly is a difference between the two pieces of terminology: "water" and "H_2O." The first word has been used by ordinary people for a very long time. The second term was introduced much more recently as part of a scientific theory. Yet, it does not follow from this that the terms denote different things. Water is identical with H_2O, as chemistry has discovered.

Philosophers who defend the mind/brain identity theory say that the same point applies to the relationship of mental terms and neurophysiological terms. Common sense has for a very long time deployed terms such as "belief," "desire," "pain," and "mind." The identity theory suggests that what happened to water will happen to the mind. Eventually, neurophysiology will discover the nature of the mind, just as chemistry discovered the nature of water. Once various scientific theories have been developed, we will be able to say what it is to believe that snow is white, what it is to want some coffee, what it is to feel pain, what it is to have a mind. In each case, the answer will be given in the vocabulary provided by brain science. Right now, we have only a very partial picture of what these neurophysiological theories will be like. However, the identity theory predicts that science is headed in the direction of a purely materialistic account of the mind. The mind is a physical thing, even though we now have only an incomplete picture of what its physical nature is.

In addition to dualism and the mind/brain identity theory, there are other solutions to the mind/body problem that I'll discuss. These are logical behaviorism (Lecture 18) and functionalism (Lecture 22). Rather than describing them right now, I'll turn to the task of analyzing Cartesian Dualism.

Immortality of the Soul Before I present Descartes' arguments for dualism, I should note a connection between the mind/body problem and an issue in the philosophy of religion. If you believe the doctrine of the immortality of the soul but also hold that the body disintegrates at death, you may be attracted by dualism. The issue of whether the soul is immortal, of course, is not the same as the question (explored in Part II) of whether there is a God. After all, there are many religions that deny the immortality of the soul. And conceivably someone might hold that the soul survives the death of the body and yet deny that there is a God. But historically, it is worth remembering that what we might call "traditional" Christianity (this includes the Christianity of Descartes' time) espouses the doctrine of immortality. Dualism makes room for this possibility.

If the soul is part of the mind (even if it is not the entirety of the mind) and if the soul lives forever and the body does not, we have an argument for dualism. Descartes did not offer this as his argument for dualism, however. Perhaps the reason was as follows. Anyone who doubts dualism also will probably doubt that any part of the mind survives the death of the body. So you're not going to convince anyone that dualism is true by beginning with the premiss that the soul is immortal.

Leibniz's Law Note a structural feature of this argument for dualism. The argument proceeds by trying to find a property that the mind has but the brain lacks; the property in question is immortality. Quite apart from whether this argument works, we should note a perfectly sensible principle that it uses. The idea is that if a and b are identical, then they must have all the same properties. This principle is called Leibniz's Law, after the seventeenth-century philosopher/mathematician (who, incidentally, co-invented calculus with Newton). Leibniz was briefly discussed in Lecture 7; he believed that we live in the best of all possible worlds.

Leibniz's Law is sometimes called the *indiscernibility of identicals*. It states that if you can find even one property that a has and b lacks, then you will have shown that a and b are distinct entities. You'll see this principle at work in both the arguments that Descartes presents for dualism.

The following form of argument is deductively valid:

m has property *P*.

b does not have property *P*.

If *m* has property *P* and *b* lacks property *P*, then *m* ≠ *b*.

_____

m ≠ *b*

Be sure you see how the argument concerning immortality has this logical form. Since the argument is valid, if you reject the conclusion, you must reject at least one of the premisses. I suggest that the third premiss (Leibniz's Law) is true. This means that if you reject the conclusion, you must reject one of the first two premisses.

Now let's look at Descartes' first argument for dualism. In Lecture 13, I discussed how Descartes uses the method of doubt in his epistemology. He also uses the idea of doubt in his discussion of the mind/body problem.

Descartes' First Argument for Dualism

In the *Second Meditation*, Descartes claims that you cannot doubt that you have a mind. If you try to doubt that you have a mind, you will find yourself entertaining a thought, and so you must grant that you have a mind after all.

Descartes thought that the existence of the body has a quite different status. He thought that it *is* possible for you to doubt that you have a body. After all, you can entertain the thought that you are a disembodied spirit.

Descartes concludes that your mind has a property that your body lacks. You can doubt the existence of one, but not the other. Dualism follows, by Leibniz's Law.

Perhaps you are suspicious of what Descartes says about the body. Is it really possible for you to doubt that you have a body? Can you conceive of yourself being a disembodied spirit? You also should consider Descartes' other premiss. Is Descartes right that you cannot doubt that you have a mind?

I am not going to pursue these questions here. I'll grant Descartes that he *cannot* doubt that he has a mind and that he *can* doubt that he has a body. I want to consider whether dualism validly follows from these premisses. To see whether this follows, we must be very explicit about what the property is that the mind is supposed to have and the body is supposed to lack.

Descartes claims that his mind has the property of *indubitable existence* and that his body lacks that property. Let's look more closely at this property. For an object *X* to have this property means that the "owner" of *X* cannot doubt that *X* exists. I say "owner" since *my* mind does not have indubitable existence *for you*. I take it that *you* have no trouble entertaining the thought that *I* do not have a mind. It is the first person case that matters here — the subject can't doubt the existence of his or her own mind.

There is a subtle mistake in this argument. I won't be able to develop a complete account of why Descartes went wrong, however. The rough idea is that properties involving psychological concepts such as "doubts" and "wants" can be deceptive. They appear to be the kinds of properties that Leibniz's Law applies to, but in fact they may not be.

I'll illustrate this idea by an example — the Oedipus myth. This story of the ancient Greeks has it that the Fates decreed that Oedipus would kill his father and marry his mother. Oedipus, of course, did not want to do either of these things. In spite of this, Oedipus met a woman—Jocasta—whom he wanted to marry. Oedipus did not know that Jocasta was his mother—that is, until after they were married.

Consider Oedipus' situation before the marriage. If you had asked him if he wanted to marry Jocasta, he would have said *yes*. If you had asked him if he wanted to marry his mother, he would have said *no*. Does it follow from this (via Leibniz's Law) that Jocasta and Oedipus' mother are two different people? Not at all. The following argument is invalid:

> Oedipus wanted to marry Jocasta.
> Oedipus did not want to marry his mother.
> _____
> Jocasta and Oedipus' mother are different people.

On the surface, it looks as if this argument applies Leibniz's Law. It describes a property that Jocasta has and Oedipus' mother lacks and concludes that they are nonidentical. What you must see is that the argument does not describe any such property. Leibniz's Law, properly understood, does not license the conclusion of nonidentity.

Jocasta and Oedipus' mother had exactly the same properties. This is not contradicted by the fact that Oedipus wanted one of the following *propositions* to be true and the other to be false:

> Oedipus marries Jocasta.
> Oedipus marries his mother.

The fact that Oedipus desired one of these propositions to be true and the other to be false does not show that Jocasta and Oedipus' mother have different properties.

Likewise, Descartes says that I am able to doubt one, but not the other, of the following two *propositions*:

> I have a brain.
> I have a mind.

But from this it does not follow that my brain has a different property from my mind.

Propositional Attitudes and Aboutness The crucial distinction we have to note here is this: Doubting and desiring are attitudes we have to *propositions*; doubting, desiring, and believing are examples of *propositional attitudes*. Perhaps there are some propositions whose truth cannot be doubted, whereas other propositions we are able to doubt. And surely we desire that some propositions, but not others, should be true. But quite separate from this issue concerning propositions, there is the issue of what *objects* those propositions are about.

Here is the lesson I draw from the Oedipus example: *Even if one proposition is desired whereas another is not, it does not follow that what the first proposition is about differs from what the second proposition is about.* The same point holds when we consider other propositional attitudes, such as doubting.

What follows from these two statements?

> Oedipus wants it to be true that Oedipus marries Jocasta.
> Oedipus does not want it to be true that Oedipus marries his
>   mother.

What follows is that the proposition *Oedipus marries Jocasta* is a different proposition from the proposition *Oedipus marries his mother*. What does *not* follow is that the person the first proposition is about (Jocasta) differs from the person the second proposition is about (Oedipus' mother).

What follows from these two statements?

> I cannot doubt that I have a mind.
> I can doubt that I have a body.

What follows is that the proposition *I have a mind* is a different proposition from the proposition *I have a body*. What does *not* follow is that the object that the first proposition is about (my mind) differs from the object that the second proposition is about (my body).

With this diagnosis in hand, let's go back to the way that Descartes presents his argument. He says that his mind has the property of indubitable existence, whereas his body does not have that property. It *sounds* like Descartes is describing a property that the one thing has but the other thing lacks. But this, I claim, is deceptive. Indubitable existence is not a property of an object; rather, doubting is something we do or fail to do to propositions.

To say that my mind indubitably exists is just to say that I cannot doubt a particular proposition. To say that my body does not indubitably exist is just to say that I can doubt a particular proposition. But from this difference between propositions, nothing follows concerning whether those propositions are about the same or different things. This argument for dualism is invalid.

I turn now to Descartes' second argument for dualism. It's far simpler than the one just analyzed. In the *Sixth Meditation*, Descartes claims that physical things have spatial parts. For example, a surgeon could divide my brain into pieces. But my mind does not have spatial parts. From this, dualism follows, by Leibniz's Law.

Descartes' Second Argument for Dualism

Descartes also says that the body, but not the mind, has *extension*. By this he means that the body takes up physical space; it has spatial location. This also leads to dualism, by Leibniz's law.

I'll treat these two arguments togther: The body has the properties of divisibility and extension. The mind does not. I think that Descartes' argument here is valid. The question is whether his premises are true.

Sense and Reference

The philosopher/logician Gottlob Frege (1848–1925) wanted to explain a salient difference between these two statements:

The Evening Star is the Evening Star.
The Evening Star is the Morning Star.

The first of these is obviously true; it is a logical truth of the form "a = a." It is a priori; anyone who understands the meanings of the terms will be able to see that it is true, there being no need for astronomical observation.

The second statement is different. It describes a discovery that astronomers made; it is a posteriori. "The Evening Star" was a term used to refer to the first star to appear in the evening. "The Morning Star" was used to refer to the last star to disappear in the morning. It was discovered that these are one and the same object, namely, the planet Venus.

Notice that the terms occurring in the two statements refer to exactly the same thing. How, then, can the statements express different thoughts? Frege tried to explain this fact by saying that terms have sense (meaning) as well as reference. Although "the Morning Star" and "the Evening Star" are terms that refer to the same thing (the planet Venus), the two expressions are not synonymous; they have different meanings.

Frege thought that synonymous terms must refer to the same thing, but that coreferential terms need not be synonymous. The meaning of a term determines its reference, not conversely. He also believed that the "truth value" of a statement (that is, whether the statement is true or false) is settled just by the reference of the terms it contains.

Consider the statement "The inventor of bifocals is dead." This statement is true. If Frege were right to say that the truth value of a statement is determined by the reference of the terms it contains, then we should be able to remove any term we choose, replace it with a coreferring term, and have the resulting statement still be true. This we can do; "the inventor of bifocals" and "the first U.S. ambassador to France" are coreferential. Substituting one for the other, we obtain the following: "The first U.S. ambassdor to France is dead." This statement is true. In this case, a true statement remains true if one of its terms is replaced by another that is coreferring.

Statements describing propositional attitudes posed a problem for Frege. Even though "Jocasta" and "Oedipus' mother" refer to one and the same person, the first, but not the second, of these statements is true:

Oedipus wanted to marry Jocasta.
Oedipus wanted to marry his mother.

To account for this fact, Frege suggested that terms in such sentences do not

refer to the objects they normally refer to. Normally, "Jocasta" and "Oedipus'
mother" refer to a person. But in the above pair of sentences, Frege claimed that
a shift occurs; the first refers to the meaning of the term "Jocasta," while the
second refers to the meaning of the term "Oedipus' mother." Since these terms
have different meanings, it will not be true that the terms in the first sentence
refer to precisely the same things that the terms in the second sentence refer to.
This makes it possible for the first sentence to be true and the second false. In
this way, Frege was able to retain his principle that the truth value of a sentence
is determined by the reference of its constituent terms.

When you say "Oedipus married Jocasta," you are referring to Jocasta. When
you say "Oedipus wanted to marry Jocasta," you are not referring to Jocasta,
according to this proposal of Frege's. If you believe that you are referring to
Jocasta in both statements, then you will reject Frege's account of how propositional
attitude statements are to be understood.

I'll grant Descartes that it sounds odd to say that my mind has spatial parts
and that it is located between my ears. It also sounds strange to say that my
mind weighs about 3 pounds and has blood vessels running through it. How are
we to explain the fact that such claims sound funny to us? One explanation is
that they cannot be true. If this were right, dualism would follow, since we then
would have cited properties that my brain has, but which my mind does not.

However, there is another possible explanation for why it sounds odd to say
that my mind has spatial parts or weighs 3 pounds or has blood vessels running
through it. The explanation is that these ideas are extremely unfamiliar. The
assertions sound jarring because they radically depart from what we happen to
believe.

Consider the claim that water is H_2O. Before the advent of the atomic theory,
the claim that a liquid is made of numerous tiny particles may have sounded
rather strange to people. But this, of course, did not mean that water could not
be made of molecules of H_2O. For this reason, I claim that Descartes' second
argument for dualism is inconclusive. If the mind and the brain really are identical,
then many surprising facts may follow.

I conclude that Descartes' arguments for dualism do not work. The first argument (involving the idea of indubitable existence) is invalid. The second argument
(involving the ideas of divisibility and extension) is valid, but it begs the question.
There seems to be no reason to accept the premises (that the mind is indivisible and lacks extension) unless you already believe that the conclusion (dualism)
is true.

These negative verdicts do not show that dualism is false. All I've claimed so
far is that these two arguments don't work. I now turn to two criticisms that
have been made of dualism.

DUALISM AND THE
MIND/BODY
PROBLEM

One of the main stumbling blocks for dualism has been the idea, endorsed by Cartesian Dualism, that there can be causal interactions between physical and nonphysical things. Descartes thought that physical events in your body can cause sensations in your mind. These sensations, like all mental events, he thought lacked spatial location. But how can events that are located in space bring about events that lack spatial location? And how are causal relations in the opposite direction possible? In *The Passions of the Soul*, Descartes claimed that the pineal gland in the brain is the jumping off point for this interaction. Nerve impulses reach the pineal gland and then manage to affect the mind, even though the mind is not located anywhere at all. Conversely, your mind (which is no place at all) influences your body by making an impact on the pineal gland. This is very mysterious, and dualists since Descartes have not managed to make this process any less incomprehensible.

Causality is something we understand best when we consider two physical events that are linked by a physical signal. When we say that throwing the switch caused the light to go on, we are talking about two physical events, which occur at different times and at different places. These two events are connected by the flow of electricity. We not only know *that* throwing the switch caused the light to go on, we also know *how* throwing the switch managed to bring this about.

If we were unable to detect a physical signal passing from the switch to the light, we would be puzzled about how the first event was able to cause the second. Similarly, if I said that throwing the switch caused an event that is not located anywhere at all, you would be puzzled about how electricity or any other physical signal could reach an event that has no spatial location.

Some philosophers have suggested that dualism faces a second problem. Causal interactions among physical and nonphysical events seem to contradict well-confirmed physical principles. A car engine does not start without an input of energy. How can the body be set into motion without a physical input? To get the nonphysical to cause the physical looks like getting something from nothing; this seems to contradict the principle of the conservation of energy. Likewise, if physical energy could result in nonphysical effects, this would seem to involve the dissipation of energy. This too seems to violate conservation principles.

To avoid this problem, a dualist might propose that mind/body interactions always involve body/body interactions. Consider the following causal chain from a physical event (P_1) to a mental event (M) to a further physical event (P_2):

$$\longrightarrow P_1 \longrightarrow M \longrightarrow P_2 \longrightarrow$$

For example, P_1 might be the event of your taking some aspirin, M the event of your headache's disappearing, and P_2 some change in your brain state.

In this example, P_1 causes M, but there is no violation of conservation principles, since the physical energy that leaves P_1 eventually reaches P_2. It also is true that M causes P_2, but this does not involve getting something from nothing, since the energy reaching P_2 had P_1 as its source. Here we seem to have mind/body interactions without a violation of conservation principles.

Even if this avoids the problem posed by conservation principles, there is still the first problem of how "crossing over" from the physical to the mental and back again is possible. Wouldn't it be simpler to account for the causal interaction of the mind and the body by adopting the identity theory? If the mind and the brain are identical, it is not terribly puzzling how your beliefs and desires can cause you to behave in various ways. This does not prove that the mind/brain identity theory is correct; the point is just that what is hard for dualism to explain is not a special difficulty for the identity theory.

Review Questions

1. What does dualism assert? What is the mind/brain identity theory?
2. What is Leibniz's Law? How is it used in arguments against the mind/brain identity theory?
3. "I cannot doubt that I have a mind, but I can doubt that I have a body. Hence, my mind is not identical with my body." Is this argument valid?
4. "My brain is divisible into spatial parts, is located between my ears, weighs about 3 pounds, and has blood vessels running through it. My mind has none of these properties. Hence, my brain and my mind are nonidentical." Is this argument valid? If it is valid, must dualism be true?
5. Dualism has been thought to make it mysterious how the mind and the body can causally interact. What problems are involved here?

Problems for Further Thought

1. Descartes says that he can conceive of himself being a disembodied spirit (that is, having a mind but no body). What does conceiving of something mean? Does Descartes' claim entail that it is possible for him to be a disembodied spirit?

2. Is a statue identical with the stone it is made of? Is an organism identical with the collection of cells in its body? Can Leibniz's Law be used to show that either of these claims of identity is false?

3. In the *Sixth Meditation*, Descartes argues that he is *essentially* a thinking thing. An essential property of a thing is a property that the thing must have if it is to exist. Could Descartes be deprived of thought and still be Descartes? Could Descartes have been born without the capacity of thought and still be Descartes? If Descartes cannot doubt that he thinks, is that enough to show that Descartes is essentially a thinking thing?

Lecture 19

Logical Behaviorism

In 1949, Gilbert Ryle, a philosopher at Oxford University, published an influential book called _The Concept of Mind_. In it, he presented a solution to the mind/body problem that has come to be called logical behaviorism. His views have something in common with those expressed by Ludwig Wittgenstein in his posthumously published _Philosophical Investigations_ (1953). Later, an American philosopher who was deeply influenced by Wittgenstein, Norman Malcolm, elaborated this philosophical position in his book _Dreaming_ (1959).

Logical behaviorism is a thesis about the meaning of the mentalistic terms we use in ordinary speech. Logical behaviorism tries to describe what we mean when we talk of an individual's thoughts, beliefs, intentions, dreams, and sensations. This thesis about meaning is quite different from a doctrine called methodological behaviorism, which I'll discuss in the next lecture. Methodological behaviorism is a thesis about science. It does not offer a linguistic analysis of ordinary speech; rather, it gives advice about how a productive science of psychology should be developed.

Logical behaviorism advances both negative and positive claims. The negative part presents criticisms of other views of the mind. The positive part is an account of what mentalistic terminology means. I'll take these two components in this order.

The Attack on "the Ghost in the Machine"

Ryle thought that the commonsense view of the mind is deeply confused. According to Ryle, common sense is committed to the idea that mental states are inner causes of behavior. To see what he means, suppose we ask why Joe lifted the cup to his lips. A commonsense answer might be that he did this because he _wanted_ a drink and _believed_ that there was water in the cup. This commonsense explanation says that mental states are inner states that Joe occupies, ones that cause his outward behavior. According to common sense, we see the behavior (the drinking), but we do not see the beliefs and desires that cause it. The beliefs and desires are "inside"; they can't be directly observed, though their effects—behavior—can be. I will use the term "mentalism" to name this commonsense idea that mental states are inner causes of behavior. Ryle thought that this natural picture is deeply confused—mentalism is one half of what he called the myth of "the Ghost in the Machine."

Ryle also held that common sense embraces dualism. This is the other half of the myth of the Ghost in the Machine. Although Ryle lumped mentalism and dualism together, we need to keep them separate. Mentalism and dualism are different. Someone who thinks that the mind and the brain are identical—that mental states are states of the central nervous system—would reject dualism but would agree that mental states cause behavior. So mentalism does not imply dualism.

Why did Ryle reject mentalism—that minds exist and are quite different from the behaviors they cause? There are two main reasons. First, he thought that the view of minds as inner causes leads to what I'll call *third person skepticism*. Second, he thought that the claim that minds exist and are distinct from the behaviors they cause involves a *category mistake*. I'll examine these two arguments in turn.

Ryle's first argument is as follows. If mental states were inner, then the mental states of others would be hidden from us. Each of us would be able to observe the behavior of others, but not the beliefs and desires that others have. Because of this, we would not be able to know what others think or want. At best, the only facts we would know about the mind would come to us via *first person introspection*. I can tell by examining my own mind what I think, want, and feel. But if mental states were inner, I would have no way of knowing anything about what mental states you occupy. Ryle thought we clearly do have knowledge of the mental characteristics of others. He concluded that mental states cannot be inner causes of behavior.

Ryle's First Objection to Mentalism: It Leads to Skepticism

The deductively valid argument that Ryle advances goes like this:

(1) If mental states were inner causes of behavior, we would not have knowledge of the mental states of others.
(2) We do have knowledge of the mental states of others.

   ───────────────

   Hence, mental states are not inner causes of behavior.

Since the argument is valid, if you want to reject the conclusion, you must reject one or both of the premisses. My view is that premiss (2) is true. I also think that the conclusion is wrong. This means that I must reject premiss (1). To do this, I must explain how we can have knowledge of the inner mental states of others.

A traditional way of attempting to show how we could have third person knowledge of the mental is via an *argument by analogy*. In 1948, Bertrand Russell advanced this argument in his book *Human Knowledge: Its Scope and Limits*, but the argument has been put forward by many philosophers. It is offered as a solution to the so-called "problem of other minds."

Do We Know About the Mental States of Others by Analogy with Our Own Case?

By introspection I know that I have a mind. I also see by observing my own body that I behave in certain ways. I note that some of my behaviors tend to be associated with some of my mental states. For example, when I hurt my finger by stabbing it with a pin, I tend to say "Ouch!" For another example, I notice that when I drink something, this behavior usually occurs when I am thirsty. I then look at others and notice that they produce certain behaviors. They say "Ouch!" on some occasions and drink water on others. I reason, by analogy, that others probably have minds and occupy the mental states that I do when I produce the same behaviors.

LOGICAL
BEHAVIORISM

So the analogy argument goes like this:

In my own case, I notice that when I produce behavior
    B, I usually am in mental state M.
I observe that another individual (O) is now producing
    behavior B.

So, O is now in mental state M.

The double line indicates that the argument is not supposed to be deductively valid. Rather, the analogy argument says that the conclusion is probable if the premisses are true.

The analogy argument aims to show how we can have knowledge of the inner mental states of others. If the argument works, it refutes Ryle's claim that mentalism leads to third person skepticism. But is the analogy argument persuasive?

The usual criticism of this argument is that it is very weak because the evidence is limited to my own case. It's like arguing that since *I* have a green chair, probably *everyone* has one. I agree with this criticism: An induction from one's own case to a conclusion about *all* human beings is basing too ambitious a conclusion on too slender an evidential basis. The sample size is too small.

So the analogy argument does not refute premiss (1) in Ryle's argument. Nonetheless, I think this premiss is mistaken. We can see why by thinking about abduction, not induction.

Abduction Let's view the beliefs and desires we attribute to others as theoretical postulates. We do not directly observe what other individuals think and want; we observe their behavior. We then invent a "theory" whose adequacy is judged by its ability to explain and predict behavior. My suggestion is that there are many cases in which the ascription of mental states to others is well-confirmed by the behaviors we observe. (Of course, there are many cases in which our claims about what people think and want are undermined by what we subsequently observe them do, but that is not in dispute.)

What's the difference between this solution to the problem of other minds and the analogy argument? In the analogy argument we begin with observation of ourselves and then seek to extend that description to other individuals. In the abductive argument, I made no mention of introspection.

Mendel never observed a gene, but that is no objection to his theory. The fact that genes are inner causes of how tall a pea plant grows or of whether its peas will be wrinkled or smooth does not mean that we cannot know about genes. Likewise, the view that mental states are inner causes of behavior does not lead to third person skepticism.

There is a simple but important distinction I want to draw here. The following two questions are quite different; they need not have the same answers:

(1) Is proposition *P* about observable things and only observable things?

(2) Is proposition *P* testable by observation?

The Mendelian case as well as the case of claims about the mental states of others provide examples in which the answers are (1) *no* and (2) *yes*.

This discussion of the analogy argument and the problem of other minds should remind you of material covered in Lecture 5 concerning the role of analogy in the design argument for the existence of God. Hume criticized the design argument for being a very weak analogy argument. In both cases, I have tried to show how an argument that appears weak when taken to be an analogy argument may be quite strong if it is understood to be abductive.

In summary, I claim, contrary to Ryle's first argument, that we can think of beliefs and desires as inner causes of behavior without being driven to third person skepticism. The reason that skepticism does not follow is that abduction can give us evidence about things that we do not directly observe (such as genes and the mental states of others).

I turn now to Ryle's second argument for denying that mental states are inner causes of behavior. Ryle thinks that mentalism and dualism both involve "category mistakes." A category mistake is a misuse of language. According to Ryle, dualism and mentalism are not clearly formulated theories that happen to be false. They are disguised nonsense. To explain what he means by a "category mistake," I'll begin by presenting some of the examples he uses.

Ryle's Second Objection to Mentalism: It Involves a Category Mistake

Suppose I take a visitor to Oxford University on a tour. I show him the various colleges, libraries, and administrative buildings. He then asks me, "OK, I've seen all these, but where is the university?" This shows that he has misunderstood something. The university, Ryle says, is not something that exists over and above the colleges, libraries, and so on. His mistake was to think that the university belongs to the same category as these other items.

Ryle tells a parallel story about a man who sees a military parade. He notes the battalions, batteries, and squadrons as they pass, but then asks, "So where is the division?"

Another example is a bit different. A foreigner, Ryle says, watches a cricket match and is instructed as to the functions of the bowlers, batsmen, fielders, umpires, and scorers. He then inquires, "I see what function each of these individuals performs, but that means that there is no one left to perform the function of providing *team spirit*." In *The Concept of Mind*, Ryle describes the man's mistake like this:

> Team spirit is not another cricketing operation supplementary to all of the other special tasks. It is, roughly, the keenness with which each of the special tasks is performed, and performing a task keenly is not performing two tasks. Certainly exhibiting team spirit is not the same thing as bowling or catching, but nor is it a third thing such that we can say that the bowler first bowls *and* then exhibits team spirit or that a fielder is at a given moment *either* catching or displaying *esprit de corps*.

Displaying team spirit is not an activity on a par with bowling; rather they are in different "categories."

These examples perhaps convey a flavor of what Ryle has in mind; but still we must try to describe exactly what he means by a category ("logical type") and what it is for a statement to embody a category mistake.

Ryle thinks that these examples are parallel to an error committed by the commonsense view of the mind. Recall that dualism maintains that the mind and body are distinct items. Likewise, mentalism—the idea that mental states are inner causes of behavior—says that mind and behavior are distinct. Both these ideas, says Ryle, involve a confusion about the logic of the concepts involved.

What, then, is a category mistake? In *The Concept of Mind*, Ryle says:

> When two terms belong to the same category, it is proper to construct conjunctive propositions embodying them. Thus a purchaser may say that he bought a left-hand glove and a right-hand glove, but not that he bought a left-hand glove, a right-hand glove, and a pair of gloves. "She came home in a flood of tears and a sedan-chair" is a well-known joke based on the absurdity of conjoining terms of different types. . . . Now the dogma of the Ghost in the Machine does just this. It maintains that there exist both bodies and minds, that there occur both physical processes and mental processes. . . .

Some terminology: A conjunction is a compound statement (*X* and *Y*) whose components are joined by "and." The component parts (*X, Y*) are called the conjuncts.

Ryle's position is that certain conjunctions are absurd (that is, they violate rules of language), even though the component conjuncts are perfectly meaningful. It is all right to say that Descartes has a body. It is also permissible to say that he has a mind. What is not allowed is to say that he has a mind *and* a body. Conjunction creates a category mistake.

This is a neat way to refute dualism. You simply show that the doctrine violates a rule of English usage. You don't have to worry about indubitability arguments or about the nature of causality. You also don't have to look at empirical results from psychology or brain science. Linguistic analysis suffices.

The problem is that Ryle's doctrine about category mistakes proves too much. Not only does dualism end up being linguistically unacceptable; the same is true of the mind/brain identity theory. Both the following conjunctions are disallowed, according the Ryle's principle:

> Descartes has a mind and he has a brain, but these are distinct things.
> Descartes has a mind and he has a brain, and these are identical things.

In addition, Ryle's own doctrine seems to fall prey to his own principle, since the following statement is disallowed:

> It is true that people have minds and it's also true that they have bodies, but it is a mistake to think that the former is something that exists over and above the latter.

Consider the joke Ryle mentions: "She came home in a flood of tears and a sedan-chair." The joke involves a kind of double usage of the term "in." This conjunction results from putting together the following two sentences:

(1) She came home in a flood of tears.

(2) She came home in a sedan-chair.

In (1), "in" does not mean spatial containment; "in a flood of tears" simply means that she was crying a lot. In (2), "in" does tell you where she was located during her trip home. The joke is to make the term "in" convey two different meanings in the conjunction.

Does this mean that the conjunction violates a "rule of language"? I don't think so. It is not ungrammatical; it is not unintelligible gibberish.

Furthermore, even if Ryle were right in barring the conjunctions he thinks involve category mistakes, the mind/body problem would still remain. Remember, Ryle grants that each conjunct is quite intelligible. It violates no linguistic rule to say that Descartes has a mind. And it violates no rule to say that he has a body. Where you go wrong is combining these two separate sentences into a single conjunctive statement. But prohibiting conjunctions does not prevent me from posing the following question. What is the relationship between the facts described by the following two sentences?

(1) Descartes has a mind.

(2) Descartes has a body.

Dualism provides one answer; the mind/brain identity theory another. And, as we will see shortly, Ryle's own theory of logical behaviorism provides a third answer.

In summary, here are my objections to the category mistake argument. First, I do not believe that the conjunctions that Ryle says are "absurd" violate any rule of English usage. Maybe the sentences involved are unusual; maybe we would find it surprising and a little puzzling that someone might formulate them. But this does not show that they are ungrammatical or unintelligible gibberish. Second, even if such conjunctions were ruled out, that would not prevent mentalism and dualism (the two doctrines that Ryle finds objectionable) from being formulated.

Ryle's examples of category mistakes have something in common. Perhaps there is something to the idea that, in some sense, X is nothing over and above what Y is (university/colleges; the military division/the squadrons). But exactly what is the relationship? To say that X is in a different "category" from Y is not much of an answer. One partial answer might be this: If X is nothing over and above Y, then X would not exist if Y failed to exist. If you demolished the colleges, libraries, and other institutions that are part of Oxford University (without replacing them), I suppose that the university would no longer exist. Likewise for the military division and its squadrons.

The parallel claim about the mind/body relationship would be this: If I destroy your body, your mind will no longer exist. Those who believe in the immortality of the soul will disagree, but that is not my point here. Suppose you grant that the one depends for its existence on the other. This mutual dependence does not show that dualism is mistaken. After all, there are some dualists who believe that the mind and the body are mutually dependent. It also does not show that mentalism is mistaken. So the examples of so-called category mistakes that Ryle presents (the university, the squadron) do not support the idea that dualism and mentalism are mistaken. That is, even if you thought that Ryle was on to something with these analogies, it is unclear what lesson you should draw. Just as it makes sense to try to clarify the relationship of a university to its colleges, so it can make sense to try to clarify the relationship of the mind to the body.

Logical Behaviorism's Analysis of Mentalistic Vocabulary

So far, I have criticized Ryle's thesis that the idea of a category mistake somehow shows that dualism and mentalism are mistaken. I now want to consider the positive view that logical behaviorists advance. They don't simply say that belief is *not* an inner state; they also make a positive claim about what it *is* for an agent to believe something.

Logical behaviorism says that the meanings of mentalistic terms can be specified purely in terms of behavior. For example, we may ask what it means to say that someone is thirsty. The following proposal, though false, at least is consistent with the requirements that logical behaviorism imposes on the problem:

$$S \text{ is thirsty } =_{df} S \text{ drinks.}$$

The notation "$=_{df}$" means that the two statements are said to be equivalent by definition.

This proposal is false because thirsty people don't always drink, and people sometimes drink when they are not thirsty. But notice that the proposal obeys the rules that logical behaviorism lays down. The proposal analyzes the meaning of a mentalistic term ("thirsty") in purely behavioral language ("drinks").

Behaviorists usually admit that proposals like this one are too crude. They suggest, instead, that the meaning of mentalistic terminology is not to be given in terms of *actual* behavior, but in terms of *dispositions* to behave. A more satisfactory suggestion, logical behaviorists maintain, is the following:

$$S \text{ is thirsty } =_{df} S \text{ is disposed to drink.}$$

Although I concede that thirsty people are disposed to drink, it isn't true that a person who is disposed to drink must be thirsty. An actor in a play or an oafish beer drinker aiming to impress his pals may be disposed to drink without being thirsty. This sort of problem leads the logical behaviorist to say that the proposal is still too crude—we need to fine-tune the analysis still further.

Thirst is a sensation. Being thirsty and wanting to drink are not the same, as we see from considering the cases of the actor and the show-off. However, perhaps this kind of analysis would work if we used it to define the desire rather than the feeling of thirst. So let's consider this proposal:

$$S \text{ wants to drink some water } =_{df} S \text{ is disposed to drink water.}$$

Are there objections to this proposed analysis? Maybe a desire is just a disposition to behave in a certain way, as logical behaviorists maintain.

I have two criticisms of this proposal. First, it is incomplete. When the proposal is fleshed out, it is not consistent with the requirements of logical behaviorism. Second, I'll claim that even if the proposal were true, it would not establish what logical behaviorists hold, namely, that mental terminology does not describe inner causes of outward behavior.

I'll begin with the charge of incompleteness. Wanting water is supposed to be a disposition to drink water. Suppose Joe wants some water and we place a cup of it before him, but he does not drink. Why not? The answer presumably would be that he does not *believe* that the cup contains water. But this means that the proposal must be corrected as follows:

The Dispositional Analysis of Desire Is Incomplete

$$S \text{ wants to drink water } =_{df} S \text{ is disposed to drink}$$
$$\text{those things that } S \text{ believes are water.}$$

Notice that the proposal now is not consistent with behaviorist requirements. The present proposal analyzes a desire in terms of a disposition to behave *and* a belief. So we have not analyzed the mentalistic concept in *purely* behavorial terms.

I doubt that behaviorists can overcome this problem. Our commonsense mentalistic concepts seem to have the following property: Attributing a *single* mentalistic property to an agent does not, by itself, have implications for how the agent will behave. What has such implications are *batches* of mentalistic properties. If an agent wants, above all else, to drink water *and* believes that the cup before him contains water, perhaps this implies that he will reach for the cup and drink its contents. But the desire by itself has no such implication and neither does the belief.

My second objection to logical behaviorism's proposal for how mentalistic terms are to be analyzed is this: Even if mentalistic concepts could be analyzed in purely behavioral terms, that would not disprove the idea that mental states are inner causes of outward behavior.

A Dispositional Analysis Does Not Refute Mentalism

To see why, I want to describe an analogy that David Armstrong (whose views on the reliability theory of knowledge were discussed in Lecture 14) noticed between the supposed dispositional property of wanting a drink and other nonmental properties that clearly are dispositional in character. Dispositional properties are often named in English with "ible" or "able" suffixes. To say that a lump of sugar is soluable is to say that it is disposed to dissolve. Solubility is a dispositional property.

It is not hard to give a "behavioral analysis" of solubiltiy. To say that something is soluble is to say that it is disposed to behave in a certain way when placed in a certain situation:

$$X \text{ is soluble (in water) } =_{df}$$
$$\text{If } X \text{ were immersed (in water), then } X \text{ would dissolve.}$$

Dissolving is a behavior; to immerse something is to place it into a particular sort of environment. This definition of solubility seems to be suitably behavioristic, since it makes no mention of an inner state that soluble substances are said to occupy.

I have no objection to this behaviorist definition of solubility. The point I want to emphasize is that the adequacy of this definition does not imply that there is no inner state of lumps of sugar—a state that makes them dissolve when immersed.

It's a good thing that no such implication follows, since such inner states exist and chemistry has managed to tell us a great deal about them. Sugar lumps are soluble in virtue of having a particular physical structure.

We know two kinds of facts about solubility. First, there is the behavioral definition mentioned before. Second, we know that solubility has a *physical basis*— that for a lump of sugar to be water-soluble is for it to have a particular kind of physical structure, which chemistry has managed to elucidate. These two kinds of facts about solubility are not in conflict; they complement each other quite harmoniously. The fact that there is a "behaviorial analysis" of solubility does

---

Pain Without Pain Behavior?

Curare, the poison that some South American Indians have used on their darts, paralyzes its subject. In the 1930s and 1940s, scientists purified curare and studied its effects on the central nervous system. At first, some doctors thought that curare is a pain killer; they noticed that if you gave curare to your patient the patient would not move during surgery. After surgery, the patients complained that they experienced great pain, but for a time, physicians did not believe them (many of the patients were children). Eventually, a physician volunteered to undergo surgery with curare; he reported that the pain was vivid and excruciating. After that, doctors realized that curare is not a pain killer; it simply immobilizes.

Daniel Dennett ("Why You Can't Make a Computer that Feels Pain," in Brainstorms, Cambridge, Massachusetts, MIT Press, 1978) suggests the following puzzle. An amnesiac is a drug that makes you forget. Suppose you gave someone curare and an amnesiac before surgery. Would the individual feel pain?

The patient would not say "ouch" or writhe during surgery. And after surgery, the patient would not say, "That was horribly painful." Let us use the term "pain behavior" to name any behavior that usually accompanies pain. In Dennett's puzzle, there is no pain behavior, either during surgery or after it. The question is: Can there be pain without pain behavior?

Dennett's example suggests that the answer is yes. Would you be prepared to undergo surgery with curare and an amnesiac as the only drugs you get? If not, the reason is probably that you think that you would still feel pain.

What does this example show about the claim that mentalistic terms do not describe the inner causes of behavior, but only describe the behavior itself?

not mean that solubility is not an internal structural property of sugar, responsible for its behavior.

How is this relevant to the logical behaviorist's attempt to analyze mental states? Even if wanting a drink were a behavioral disposition — one that could be described without mentioning any inner state of the organism — this would not show that wants are not inner states. On the contrary, there is every reason to think that when something has a dispositional property, there is a physical basis of that disposition. When an organism is disposed to drink something, it is entirely appropriate to ask what it is about the organism's internal makeup that disposes it to act in this way.

This completes my criticism of logical behaviorism's positive thesis. I claim that the meaning of mentalistic terminology cannot be analyzed in purely behavioral language. In addition, I have argued that even if such an analysis could be provided (by describing mental states as "dispositions to behave"), it would not follow that mental states are not inner causes of behavior.

Review Questions

1. Ryle thought that the mental states of others would be unknowable if mental states were inner causes of behavior. Why did Ryle think this? What is the "problem of other minds"? Does the analogy argument from one's own case solve this problem? What difference does it make to think about abduction rather than analogy here?
2. Ryle thought that dualism involves a "category mistake." What is a category mistake? Does this idea show that dualism is mistaken? Does it show that mental states are not inner causes of behavior?
3. What is logical behaviorism? Can a logical behaviorist analysis be given of the statement "Jones believes that there is rat poison in the gravy"?
4. Suppose that a mentalistic concept (such as wanting a drink of water) could be analyzed as a disposition to behave. Would that show that wants are not inner causes of behavior?

Problems for Further Thought

1. I have suggested that an abductive argument can solve the problem of other minds. Construct such an argument, making clear how the Surprise Principle (Lecture 3) applies. Also, the abductive argument sketched in this lecture does not accord any role to the introspective knowledge we have of our own mental states. Can an abductive argument concerning the mental states of others be strengthed by bringing in introspection?

2. What does it mean to say that X is "nothing but" Y? It can't mean just that X would not exist if Y did not. We would not exist without oxygen. It does not follow that we are "nothing but" oxygen.

Lecture 20

Methodological Behaviorism

In the previous lecture, I emphasized that logical and methodological behaviorism are very different doctrines. The former says that the meanings of commonsense mentalistic concepts can be analyzed in purely behavioral terms. The latter is not a thesis about what such commonsense terms mean; rather, it is a recommendation for how the science of psychology ought to be pursued.

In a curious way, methodological and logical behaviorism take opposite views about the nature of commonsense mentalistic language. As noted earlier, logical behaviorism rejects the idea that beliefs and desires are inner states that cause behavior. Methodological behaviorism, by contrast, accepts the idea that our commonsense mentalistic vocabulary refers to inner states. Methodological behaviorism then argues that a scientific psychology should avoid talking about beliefs and desires precisely because they _are_ inner states.

In this lecture, I'll divide methodological behaviorism into a negative and positive thesis. (This is similar to my division of logical behaviorism into a negative and a positive thesis in the previous lecture.) First, I'll analyze the negative thesis; this is the claim that psychology should _not_ attempt to explain behavior in terms of people's beliefs and desires. Then I'll consider methodological behaviorism's positive thesis; this is the idea that people's behavior _can_ be explained solely in terms of their history of conditioning.

The Negative Thesis: Psychology Should Avoid Belief/Desire Explanations

Why should psychology avoid explaining the behavior of agents by attributing beliefs and desires to them? B. F. Skinner, one of the leading proponents of behaviorism, provides several answers to this question in his books _Science and Human Behavior_ (New York, Free Press, 1953), _Beyond Freedom and Dignity_ (New York, Knopf, 1971), and _About Behaviorism_ (New York, Random House, 1974).

Skinner's first objection to mentalistic explanation is that beliefs and desires are not observable. They are hidden. All we can directly observe is the behavior of others, not what goes on in their minds. By now, my view of this kind of argument should be clear. Science quite legitimately talks about things that are not or cannot be observed. The fact that beliefs and desires cannot be observed directly does not mean that claims about an individual's beliefs and desires cannot be tested by observing the individual's behavior. For example, suppose I claim that an individual wants a drink of water and believes that there is a cup of water before him. Suppose I further claim that the individual has no other desires that would override his desire to drink. These claims about the agent's mind predict that he will reach for the water and drink it. If that prediction fails, I have gained evidence against the description offered of the subject's mind. As in the Mendelian case, claims about what is not observed can be tested by seeing what they imply about what can be observed.

Another reason that Skinner gives for rejecting mentalistic theories is that they are "too easy." In the example just cited, I attributed to the subject a combination of beliefs and desires that predict something about his behavior. Suppose the individual does not reach for the water. What will I do? I will modify my claim about what he thinks and wants. I will not abandon my assumption that he has beliefs and desires and that these cause his behavior. So, apparently, the assumption of mentalism is not tested by observing behavior. Indeed, it appears that no matter what the individual does, I can always formulate a belief/desire story that is consistent with what I observe him do.

I want to clarify this point of Skinner's by distinguishing *specific belief/desire attributions* from what I'll call *the mentalistic thesis*, which is the claim that an individual's behaviors are caused by the beliefs and desires he or she possesses. The specific attributions are testable against the data of behavior; however, the mentalistic thesis does not seem to be. Skinner believes that the claims of science must be testable by observation; hence, he concludes, the mentalistic thesis does not deserve to be part of a scientific psychology.

Notice that even if the mentalistic thesis were untestable, this would not imply that science should not advance and test *specific belief/desire attributions*. Rather, the curious position is that psychologists may do this, but they are not allowed to say that mentalism is the framework within which they develop their explanations. So at the very most, Skinner's argument would prohibit science from stating what it is quite legitimate for science to do. This is a rather paradoxical claim.

In Lecture 9, I discussed the idea that scientific claims should be testable. I argued that the thesis of strong falsifiability is implausible. I now want to make a related point: *There are many perfectly respectable scientific statements that cannot be refuted by the result of a single experiment.* In the present case, we have an example of this kind of statement. Statements that describe the basic tenets of a *research program* are not strongly falsifiable.

Mentalism is such a thesis; it says that theories explaining behavior can be developed by extending and refining the ordinary concepts of belief and desire. Time will tell whether this thesis is a good idea for psychology or a dead end. The fact that a single theory within this framework fails does not show that the whole framework is bankrupt. One rotten apple need not show that the barrel is spoiled.

Curiously enough, precisely the same point applies to Skinner's own research program. Skinner rejects mentalism and espouses behaviorism. This is the thesis that behaviors can be explained by describing the stimuli people have received from their environments. Skinner says we do not need to describe the inner states—mental or physical—of individuals in order to explain their behavior.

This thesis states the framework of the Skinnerian research program. Suppose I follow its dictates and construct a detailed behaviorist explanation of why you are now reading this page. Suppose further that this explanation turns out to be inadequate. Does that refute behaviorism as a general research program? I would say not (and Skinner would probably agree).

METHODOLOGICAL
BEHAVIORISM

It is appropriate to demand that *specific explanations* be testable against the data of observations. It is not appropriate to demand that *theses about the framework of a research program* should be strongly falsifiable. Mentalism cannot be faulted on the ground that it is not testable. Specific mentalistic hypotheses can be tested. Time will tell whether the general thesis of mentalism will turn out to be correct. In this sense, the framework of mentalism, like the framework of behaviorism, *is* testable.

Methodological Behaviorism's Positive Thesis

I'll now consider methodological behaviorism's positive claim — that behavior can be explained without describing the inner states of the organism. I believe that there is a simple fact about people that shows that behaviorism cannot be successful — that the kind of explanations it demands cannot be had.

Recall that methodological behaviorism does not deny that we have inner mental states. It claims, rather, that psychology need not discuss them in its attempt to explain behavior. So behaviorism grants that the causal chain linking environmental stimuli to behavior has the following structure:

Environment $\longrightarrow$ Inner state of organism $\longrightarrow$ Behavior

The thesis is that present behavior can be explained in terms of (1) the past environments I have occupied and the behaviors I produced in them, and (2) my present environment.

Skinner's theory of stimulus conditioning describes how such explanations can be constructed. In his research, Skinner manipulated the behavior of chickens and other organisms by placing them into a totally controlled environment — a "Skinner box." Suppose you look at a chicken in a Skinner box and see that the chicken just pecked a key. You want to explain why it did so. Skinner says that you can explain this behavior by describing the chicken's past history of stimulus conditioning. When the chicken was first placed in the box, it pecked occasionally. The Skinner box contains a light that goes on and off. The box is so arranged that if the chicken pecks when the light is on, it receives a pellet of food. After some time, the chicken's pecking starts to happen pretty much only when the light goes on. In this stimulus/response experiment, the chicken has been conditioned to peck when the light is on. The conditioning works by rewarding the chicken in some circumstances, but not in others.

How are you to explain the chicken's pecking in the present case? A mentalistic explanation might say that the chicken is now pecking because it wants food and has learned that pecking produces pellets of food. This is an explanation in terms of beliefs and desires. Skinner believes that this mentalistic story is entirely unnecessary. You can give a behaviorist explanation of the present behavior by saying (1) in the past, the chicken was conditioned to peck when the light was on; (2) at the present time, the light is on.

After the chicken has been conditioned, there is a general pattern that holds true: If the light is on, then the chicken pecks. Notice that this if/then statement contains no mentalistic terms. We can use this stimulus/response statement to construct the following behaviorist explanation:

If the light is on, then the chicken pecks.
The light is on now.

Hence, the chicken now pecks.

You explain the present behavior by deducing it from the two facts listed as premisses.

Skinner thinks that what is true of the chicken's pecking in the experiment is true of all the chicken's behaviors, both those produced in the box and those that occur in less controlled environments (like the barnyard). In addition, Skinner believes that human beings are like the chicken in relevant respects. Each of our behaviors can be explained by describing our history of stimulus conditioning. This is the thesis on which the behaviorist research program rests. We don't need to talk about what human beings think and want in order to explain what human beings do.

Are we like the chicken in the Skinner box? Critics of behaviorism, like the linguist Noam Chomsky, have claimed that *novel behaviors* cannot be explained in the way the behaviorist demands. Let's look with some care at an example of Skinner's that illustrates this point.

First Objection to Behaviorism's Positive Thesis: Novel Behaviors

Suppose you are walking down the street one day and a robber jumps out of the shadows, sticks a gun in your face, and says "Your money or your life." You fumble nervously and then hand over your wallet. How should your behavior be explained? What makes the behavior novel is that you have never been robbed before. The only time anyone ever waved a gun in your face was when you were a child and the gun was a water gun. In that case, you didn't hand over your wallet; rather, you giggled and ran away. So why didn't you do the same thing this time?

The behaviorist needs to show that the present stimulus situation is similar to past ones in which you have behaved similarly. Skinner explains the chicken's present pecking by saying that the present situation is like previous ones in which the chicken pecked. The similarity is that the light is on in the Skinner box. The problem is that the present robbery is similar to many past situations you've been in. It's similar to your childhood play with water guns. It's also similar to the time your mother threatened to spank you if you didn't clean up your room. After all, the robbery involved a gun *and* a threat. Which of these past experiences is the right one to appeal to in explaining your present behavior?

Remember that you've never been robbed before. The only time anyone ever waved a gun in your face, the gun was a water gun and you giggled and ran away. And when your mom threatened to spank you, you apologized and cleaned up your room; you didn't hand her your wallet. What past episodes can a behaviorist say are similar to, and also explain, your current behavior?

The obvious answer is that you learned in the past that you should accommodate those who threatened you. Perhaps you were rewarded in the past for doing this and so the behavioral pattern became fixed. Although this sounds like the right sort of explanation to develop, it is not true to the demands of behaviorism.

In the chicken case, there was a physical property of the earlier stimulus situations that recurs in the present. In the past, *the light was on*. In the present case, *the light is on*. It is perfectly fine for a behaviorist to describe the history of conditioning in terms of such physical properties.

But what the behaviorist cannot say is that you are the sort of individual who behaves in ways you *believe* are accommodating when you *believe* that you are being threatened. This is a regularity about your stimulus history that involves inner mental states. These are just the items that the behaviorist says should *not* be included in the explanation.

I doubt that there is a physical similarity between past threats and the present one. In the past, your mom may have said, "If you don't clean up your room, I'll give you a spanking." The behavioral response on your part was not to hand

---

Minimal Explanation versus Deep Explanation

The behavior of a conditioned chicken in a Skinner box can be explained without describing the chicken's internal state. Why is the chicken now pecking the key? Skinner's answer is that the chicken pecks whenever the light is on, and the light is now on.

Since we have explained the behavior without mentioning the chicken's internal state, Skinner concludes that describing the internal state would be of no explanatory relevance. You don't need to describe what's going on inside, so why bother?

I grant that the purely behavioral account is an adequate explanation. However, I think there can be a deeper explanation of the chicken's behavior.

Consider an analogy. Why did this lump of sugar just dissolve? A behaviorist answer might be that sugar dissolves when immersed in water, and this lump was just immersed. This is an explanation. But it is possible to do better.

What is it about sugar that makes it dissolve when immersed? Here we request information about the internal structure of the sugar lump. Since sugar is water-soluble but wood is not, we expect that the one has some internal state that the other lacks. Once described, this internal state of the lump of sugar is relevant to explaining why it just dissolved.

The chicken pecks when the light is on. Surely we can ask what it is about the conditioned chicken that makes it peck when the light is on. A conditioned chicken has a disposition to behave that an unconditioned chicken does not have. It is legitimate to expect that the one has some internal state that the other lacks. Once described, this internal state of the conditioned chicken is relevant to explaining why it now is pecking.

Perhaps it is possible to explain the chicken's behavior in the way the methodological behaviorist demands. However, this does not mean that other explanations, which violate behaviorist principles, are irrelevant to understanding why the chicken pecks.

your wallet over, but to apologize and tidy things up. The only way to describe how this past event is similar to the present robbery is to describe your beliefs and desires.

If our behaviors always obeyed patterns that were describable in terms of a *physical similarity* between past and present stimulus conditions, behaviorism might work. But this seems to be radically untrue. What makes the past similar to the present is that we conceptualize past and present in similar ways. Take this mentalistic similarity away and behaviorism delivers radically mistaken predictions. In terms of purely physical similarities, I suppose that your participation in a water battle may be more similar to the present robbery than your being scolded by your mother. If you were to behave now in ways that are similar to the ways you behaved in previous *physically similar* past events, the prediction would be that you would giggle and run away.

The important fact about us is that small physical differences in a stimulus often make enormous differences in the response, and huge physical differences in the stimulus often make no differences in the response. If a robber walks into a bank and hands the teller a note that says "You give me the cash, "the teller produces one response. If the note had said "Me give you the cash," the response would have been different. The notes aren't that different physically, so why was the response so different? Likewise, receiving a few marks on paper can produce the same result as hearing a verbal command. But the marks on paper ("You give me the cash") and a verbal message ("Empty the cash drawers into this sack") are physically very different.

Behaviorism sounds plausible for two reasons. First, it is true that claims about the mental states of individuals should be tested against behavioral data. Second, what individuals do is importantly influenced by the environments they have lived through. But neither of these truisms shows what methodological behaviorism maintains — that it is possible to explain (and predict) behavior without mentioning mental states.

One final shortcoming of methodological behaviorism should be noted. Behaviorism is a radically environmentalist doctrine. That is, when it comes to the nature/nurture problem — the problem of saying how much a behavior is explained by genes and how much by environment — the behaviorist is entirely on the side of the environment. By saying that *inner states* need not be described in explaining behavior, the behaviorist is excluding genes as well as environmentally acquired mental states. My point is that environmentalism may be true in some cases, but not in others.

Second Objection to Behaviorism's Positive Thesis: It Assumes that Environmental Determinism Is True

Returning to the lowly chicken, it is interesting to note that there are some behaviors that you can't condition a chicken to perform. Speaking English is something that human beings learn to do when they are in the right kind of environment. A chicken in the same environment will not master this skill. Why not? Since the environments are the same, the answer cannot be environmental. Presumably, there is a genetic difference between chickens and human beings that explains this behavioral difference.

What is true about variation between species may also be true, in some cases, within species. There may be genetic differences between human beings that are relevant to explaining differences in behaviors. This area of investigation is now controversial. My point is that methodological behaviorism assumes in advance of any detailed analysis that environmental variables suffice to explain behavior. Such an assumption should not be made as a matter of doctrine, but should be empirically investigated on a case-by-case basis.

Scientists are considering the possibility that there may be a significant genetic component to diseases such as depression and schizophrenia; that is, in addition to environmental causes of these conditions, there also may be genetic ones. In contrast, a different characteristic may have a different causal explanation. No one now believes that there is a genetic component to explaining why some people speak one language while others speak another. In this case, variation in the behavior is entirely environmental in its explanation.

Environmental determinism is the view that genetic differences do not help explain *any* behavioral differences. Genetic determinism is the view that environmental differences do not help explain *any* behavioral differences. Both these views are too sweeping and extreme to be plausible. First, we must consider different behaviors separately. The kind of explanation we offer for schizophrenia may differ from the kind we want to give for speaking English. Second, we must recognize that there are nonextreme proposals that deserve a hearing; we want to consider the idea that a behavior has both environmental and genetic causes (and that one may be more important than the other).

The Two Objections Summarized

In conclusion, there are two kinds of questions, quite different from each other, that methodological behaviorism cannot address. The first is the kind of question typified by the robbery example. When I ask how your present behavior of handing over the money is explained by your previous experiences, it seems essential to describe your beliefs and desires. There is no purely physical similarity between the present holdup and your previous environments. Rather, the similarity exists only because you conceptualize the present situation in a way similar to the way you conceptualized previous (physically different) situations. Second, there is the idea of genetic (nonenvironmental) causes of behavior. If these exist, either between species or within them, then methodological behaviorism will be unable to explain why some organisms behave differently from others.

Methodological behaviorism began by rejecting mentalism; it claimed that mental states are irrelevant to explaining behavior. But, in fact, its thesis excludes brain science and genetics as well. The real thrust of behaviorism is to claim that explanations of behavior need not describe the *inner state* of the organism. Mentalism describes what goes on inside, but so do brain science and genetics.

By focusing on what happens in tightly controlled environments, behaviorism may seem to have established a general pattern for explaining all behavior. It is true that the pecking of the chicken in the Skinner box can be handled in the way that Skinner demands. However, it is a mistake to think that a successful explanation in this case can be generalized to all other behaviors. Take the chicken out of the Skinner box and perhaps it will produce novel behaviors, just as you did when the robber said "Your money or your life." And quite apart from the issue of novel behaviors, there is the nature/nurture issue, which methodological behaviorism addresses before looking at the relevant data.

Review Questions

1. What is the difference between methodological behaviorism and logical behaviorism?
2. What is mentalism? Is mentalism testable? How does the distinction between specific explanations and framework assumptions about a research program bear on this question?
3. Why do so-called "novel" behaviors pose a problem for methodological behaviorism? What does it mean to say that the present stimulus is "physically similar" to stimuli encountered in the past?
4. What does methodological behaviorism say about the relevance of genetics and brain science to the explanation of behavior? Why would innate differences in behavior be a problem for behaviorism?

Problems for Further Thought

1. Some psychotherapists call themselves "behaviorists." They treat patients with phobias (extreme fears) by helping them modify their behavior (such as increased heart rate, perspiration, and anxiety) rather than by helping them understand why they have the array of beliefs and desires that produce the reaction. Consider someone who is enormously afraid of being in closed areas (claustrophobia). Instead of trying to get the patient to understand why he has this fear, a behavioral therapist might concentrate on "desensitizing" the individual. The goal would be to modify the patient's behavior. Treatment might begin with very brief exposures to closed areas; gradually, as the patient gains confidence, longer exposures would be attempted. Here's the question: Do the criticisms I've made of methodological behaviorism imply that behavioral therapy won't be effective? Defend your answer.

2. *Saying that lemons are yellow* is a kind of event. Can it be defined by its physical characteristics? Is *saying the English sentence "Lemons are yellow"* definable by its physical characteristics? What is the difference between these two kinds of events?

Lecture 21

The Mind/Brain Identity Theory

So far, I have examined two theories about the nature of the mind and its relationship to the body. These were Cartesian dualism (Lecture 18) and logical behaviorism (Lecture 19). Methodological behaviorism (Lecture 20), recall, is not a thesis about the nature of the mind; since methodological behaviorism recommends that scientific explanations of behavior ignore the mind, it does not say much about what the mind is.

The Identity Theory Is A Posteriori

Cartesian dualism and logical behaviorism are very different positions. Yet, the arguments that each presents have something in common: Neither appeals to any result of science as evidence for what it maintains. Cartesian dualism says that we can recognize by introspection and philosophical reasoning that the mind has a property that the body lacks. Logical behaviorism says that we can see that mental states are not inner causes of behavior just by analyzing the meanings of commonsense mentalistic terms. Both theories are defended by arguments that are intended to be *a priori*.

The mind/brain identity theory is not only a different theory from those surveyed so far; it also is a different *kind* of theory. The identity theory argues for its solution to the mind/body problem by describing the progress that science has made so far and by predicting the progress that science will make in the future. The relationship of the mind and the body, says the identity theory, is something that science discovers by observation and experiment. It is not something that armchair philosophy—introspection and linguistic analysis—can hope to resolve. The identity theory is offered as an *a posteriori* proposition about the relationship of mind and body.

Materialism

The identity theory asserts that the history of science has been marked by success after success for a doctrine called *materialism* or *physicalism*. This is the view that every object in the world is a material (physical) object. If we go back in time, we find phenomena that were not well understood scientifically. For example, lightning was once profoundly perplexing. The ancient Greeks thought that lightning was Zeus' thunderbolt. But in the eighteenth and nineteenth centuries, the science of electricity established that lightning is an electrical discharge. Science was able to take a phenomenon that earlier had seemed to defy physicalistic description and show that it can be understood within the framework of the laws of physics.

Consider a statement that describes this scientific discovery:

Lightning is one and the same thing as a kind of electrical discharge.

This statement was not established by analyzing the meaning of the word "lightning." The statement is not an *a priori* truth, knowable by linguistic analysis; rather, it is an *a posteriori* truth that the science of electricity discovered. It could only be established by observation and experiment.

In the past century, there was a similar perplexity about the nature of life. What is the difference between living things and things that are not alive? A doctrine called *vitalism* held that living things contain a nonphysical substance that animates them with life — an *élan vital*. In this century, vitalism has been undermined by the discoveries of molecular biology. We now know that life is a physicochemical phenomenon. Organisms are made of the same basic elements (carbon, oxygen, and so on) as nonliving things. Life differs from nonlife because of how the basic physical constituents are organized. There is no extra nonphysical ingredient that magically makes organisms "alive."

Biology in the past one hundred years has discredited vitalism. The discovery of the molecular basis of life has been a triumph for materialism. By this I do not mean that each and every detail of the physical basis of life is well understood; if this were true, there would no longer be a need for research in molecular biology and biochemistry. Rather, what I mean is that the details are sufficiently well understood that there is no longer any real doubt that metabolism, reproduction, digestion, respiration, and so on are physical processes.

Cartesian dualism and vitalism are similar. Dualism says that an individual's mind is a nonmaterial substance. Thinking beings therefore are said to contain a nonphysical ingredient not found in beings that do not have minds. Vitalism says that living things contain a nonphysical substance — an *élan vital* — that is unique to them. Just as dualism opposes a materialistic solution to the mind/body problem, so vitalism opposes a materialistic answer to the question of how biological and physical processes are related to each other.

Dualism Resembles Vitalism

The mind/brain identity theory says that what has happened to the problem of life is in the process of happening to the problem of mind. We now have some knowledge of the physical basis — the neurophysiological basis — of the mind. If science progresses the way it has in other areas, this materialistic understanding will broaden and deepen. The identity theory predicts that science will fully vindicate the thesis that an individual's mind and brain are one and the same entity. Each mental charateristic (for example, believing that snow is white, wanting a drink, feeling pain) is identical with some physical characteristic. The identity theory is a version of materialism: *Mental objects are physical objects and mental characteristics are physical characteristics.*

During the 1950s and 1960s, identity theorists — for example, J. J. C. Smart, "Sensations and Brain Processes," and U. T. Place, "Is Consciousness a Brain Process" [both reprinted in V. Chappell (ed.), *The Philosophy of Mind*, Englewood Cliffs, Prentice Hall, 1962] — gave the following as an example of what they meant. Brain scientists at that time suggested that feeling pain is one and the same event as having the c-fibers in one's brain fire. This neurophysiological hypothesis about the physical basis of pain later turned out to be untrue. This did not deter identity theorists, who are quite happy to leave it to science to work out the details of the general hypothesis they formulate. The identity theorist claims that feeling pain is identical with being in *some physical state or other*; it is for science to tell us precisely what this physical state is.

Consider this example in more detail. How might a scientist investigate the connection between pain and c-fiber firing? The scientist would want to find out if people experience pain whenever their c-fibers fire and if people have their c-fibers fire whenever they experience pain. Here's a simple experiment that would help determine if these mental and physical events co-occur. A probe inserted into the subject's brain would indicate when the c-fibers fire. Perhaps the subject's own testimony, based on introspection, would indicate when he or she experiences pain. The experimenter occasionally hits the subject's thumb with a hammer. Ignoring complications, suppose that different human subjects, when placed in the same (morally questionable) experiment, generate the same data. Suppose that the data show a perfect correlation between experiences of pain and c-fiber firings.

Does this, by itself, show that the identity theory is true? No. Recall that dualism is quite consistent with there being a perfect correlation of mental events of a certain kind with physical events of a certain kind. Dualism claims that feeling pain and having your c-fibers fire are *two* distinct kinds of events. The identity theory, on the other hand, would say that feeling a pain and having one's c-fibers fire are perfectly correlated because they are one and the same kind of event.

How are we to choose between dualism and the identity theory? One consideration, mentioned in Lecture 18, is that dualism makes it difficult to understand how mind and body can causally interact. The identity theory, however, has no difficulty accommodating this fact.

Identity theorists offer a second reason for rejecting dualism. They claim that the identity theory is more parsimonious (simpler) than dualism. Their idea is that the scientific method says we should prefer simpler theories over more complex ones when both are consistent with the observations. It isn't just that more parsimonious ideas are easier to think about or are aesthetically more pleasing. Rather, their idea is that more parsimonious theories have a better claim to be regarded as *true*.

The identity theory is more parsimonious because it claims (if the experiment just described were to yield a perfect correlation) that feeling pain and having one's c-fibers fire are one and the same event. A dualist, however, says that these are two different events. The Principle of Parsimony, sometimes called "Ockham's razor" for the medieval philosopher William of Ockham, is an abductive principle. It says that we should prefer explanations that minimize the number of entities, processes, and events they postulate. Since one is less than two, the identity theory is more parsimonious. Identity theorists count this as a reason for thinking

---

Newton on Parsimony

The Principle of Parsimony has been used in many scientific debates. In his Principles of Natural Philosophy *(1690), Newton presents four "Rules of Reasoning in Philosophy." The first two concern abduction, the second two induction:*

1. We are to admit no more causes of natural things than such as are both true and sufficient to explain their appearances. *To this purpose the philosophers say that Nature does nothing in vain, and more is in vain when less will serve; for Nature is pleased with simplicity and affects not the pomp of superfluous causes.*

2. Therefore to the same natural effects we must, as far as possible, assign the same causes. *As to respiration in a man and in a beast, the descent of stones in Europe and in America, the light of our culinary fire and of the sun, the reflection of light in the earth and in the planets.*

3. The qualities of bodies, which admit neither intensification nor remission of degrees, and which are found to belong to all bodies within the reach of our experiments, are to be esteemed the universal qualities of all bodies whatsoever. *For since the qualities of bodies are only known to us by experiments, we are to hold for universal all such as universally agree with experiments, and such as are not liable to diminution can never be quite taken away. We are certainly not to relinquish evidence of experiments for the sake of dreams and vain fictions of our own devising; nor are we to recede from the analogy of Nature, which is wont to be simple and always consonant to itself. . . .*

4. In experimental philosophy we are to look upon propositions inferred by general induction from phenomena as accurately or very nearly true, notwithstanding any contrary hypotheses that may be imagined, till such time as other phenomena occur by which they may either be made more accurate or liable to exceptions. *This rule we must follow, that the argument of induction not be evaded by hypotheses.*

Rule 1 is pertinent to the debate between the identity theory and dualism. Rule 2 is similar to the Principle of the Common Cause discussed in connection with the design argument (Lecture 6). Rule 3 bears on the relevance of Descartes' method of doubt (Lecture 13) to the progress of science. Can you see how each of these rules applies to the philosophical ideas just mentioned?

that the identity theory is true and dualism is false, given that both are consistent with observed correlation of mental and physical states.

In the vitalism controversy, no biologist took seriously the idea that an *élan vital* exists, once the physical bases of life processes became reasonably clear.

THE MIND/BRAIN
IDENTITY THEOREY

Rather, the conclusion was that an organism's being alive is nothing above and beyond its having certain physical processes going on in its body. To say otherwise would be to admit a further entity—an *élan vital*—without necessity. This would contradict the Principle of Parsimony. Biologist took this principle to heart, once they obtained physical explanations of life processes. They realized that there was no reason to postulate the existence of an *élan vital*. For this reason, vitalism was rejected and materialism accepted.

If a perfect correlation could be found between mental characteristics and physical ones, what reason could there be to postulate the existence of an immaterial mind—one that just happens to exhibit psychological characteristics correlated with the physical characteristics of the brain? This seems entirely gratuitous—a violation of the Principle of Parsimony. For this reason, the identity theory suggests that dualism should be rejected and materialism accepted if science discovers perfect correlations between mental and physical characteristics.

Let us be clear on what the Principle of Parsimony recommends. In the problem of life, the principle leads one to deny the existence of an *élan vital*. It does not say that one should suspend judgment as to whether such an immaterial substance exists. Likewise, mind/brain identity theorists have argued that parsimony offers a reason to think that immaterial minds do not exist. Their recommendation was not to suspend judgment about dualism, but to conclude that dualism is false. In both cases, Ockham's razor leads one to conclude that *X* does not exist, not to conclude that one should suspend judgment as to whether *X* exists.

There is an interesting and difficult philosophical problem here, which I won't attempt to solve: Why should the greater simplicity or parsimoniousness of a theory be a reason to think that it is true? Does using the Principle of Parsimony in this way require us to assume that nature is simple? If so, what evidence do we have that nature is simple? I leave these questions to one side, since there is another objection to the identity theory that is independent of what one might think of the Principle of Parsimony. This objection will be the subject of the next lecture.

Review Questions

1. What is materialism? Is it the view that money is the most important thing?
2. What is vitalism? Is vitalism shown to be true by the fact that living things contain DNA while nonliving things do not?
3. In what way is vitalism (as a solution to the problem of life) similar to dualism (as a solution to the problem of mind)? What is meant by "the problem of life" and "the problem of mind"?
4. What is the Principle of Parsimony? Why is dualism said to be less parsimonious than the identity theory?
5. Does the Principle of Parsimony agree with the following claim: "Since dualism and the identity theory both predict that mental events will be correlated with physical events, there is no way to choose between the two theories"?

Problems for Further Thought

1. Suppose we observe a perfect correlation between some mental property (such as feeling pain) and some physical property (such as having one's c-fibers fire). Apply the Surprise Principle (Lecture 3) to see whether this observation strongly favors the identity theory over dualism.

2. In the passage from *Principia* quoted in this lecture, Newton defends the Principle of Parsimony by saying that "Nature does nothing in vain." Is this idea consistent with what we now know about natural selection (Lecture 6)?

Lecture 22

Functionalism

In the previous lecture, I described the mind/brain identity theory as applying to the mind/body problem the general thesis that *everything is material*. Minds are not made of an immaterial substance; rather, people have minds and mental characteristics in virtue of the fact that they have brains that possess various sorts of physical structures.

In the 1960s and 1970s, several philosophers—preeminently, Hilary Putnam ("The Nature of Mental States" in *Mind, Language, and Reality*, London, Cambridge University Press, 1975) and Jerry Fodor (*Psychological Explanation*, New York, Random House, 1968)—developed a criticism of the identity theory. They espoused a point of view that came to be called "functionalism." Although functionalism does not reject materialism, it does reject one important thesis of the identity theory.

Functionalism has two parts—one negative, the other positive. The negative part describes what psychological states are *not*. This is the functionalist critique of the identity theory. The positive part advances a proposal about what psychological states *are*. I'll take these two ideas in order.

To begin with, I need to draw a commonsense distinction. Suppose someone says to you, looking at your clothing, "We own the same shirt." What might this mean? There are two choices: One is that you and this person own the same *kind* of shirt. The other is that the very shirt on your back is jointly owned by the two of you.

Functionalism's Negative Thesis: What's Wrong with the Identity Theory?

Let's introduce some terminology to mark this distinction. Unique physical objects are called *tokens*. Kinds (or properties) are called *types*. The unique physical object that you are now wearing is a token of many types. It is a token of the type

The Type/ Token Distinction

shirt; it also is a token of the type *blue* and a token of the type *clothing*. To say that a single token is a token of many types is merely to say that a single object has many properties.

Conversely, a given type may have zero, one, or many tokens that fall under it. *Unicorn* is a type of animal that has no instances; there are no tokens of that type. *Golden mountain* is a type of geological object, one that happens to have no exemplars. You can see just from this pair of examples that two types (properties) may apply to exactly the same tokens and still be distinct types. Being a unicorn is not the same property as being a golden mountain, even though the set of unicorns has precisely the same members as the set of golden mountains. This example involves two types, each with no tokens falling under it. Can the same point be made with types that are exemplified? Can two types be different, even though they apply to the same (nonempty) set of objects? I leave it to you to find an example of this sort.

How does the type/token distinction apply to the mind/body problem? The identity theory is a claim about psychological tokens and also a claim about psychological types. The former category — of psychological tokens — includes the following: Descartes' mind, the pain I felt in my foot last Thursday, Jones' thinking to herself today that lemons are yellow. Each of these is a token, and the identity theory says that each is identical with some physical token.

In addition, there are psychological types (properties); the identity theory makes a claim about these as well. For example, there are the properties of having a mind, of feeling pain, and of believing that lemons are yellow. Note that each of these types has numerous tokens falling under it. Each type, therefore, describes something that various tokens have in common. The identity theory says that each of these psychological types (properties) is identical with some physical property or other.

Multiple Realizability

Functionalism rejects what the identity theory says about psychological types. Functionalists hold that psychological properties are not identical with physical properties. Instead, functionalists argue that psychological types have the property of *multiple realizability*. I'll explain this idea with an example.

Consider a type that is not psychological — the property of *being a mousetrap*. Each token mousetrap is a physical object. But think of all the different ways there are to build a mousetrap. Some are made of wood and wire and are loaded with cheese. Others are made of plastic and catch mice by injecting them with curare. Still others are made of a team of philosophers, who stalk around armed with inverted wastepaper baskets. There are many, perhaps endlessly many, ways to build a mousetrap.

Is there a single physical characteristic that all mousetraps have in common, and which non-mousetraps lack? This seems highly dubious. Each token mousetrap is a physical thing, but the property of being a mousetrap (the type) does not seem to be a physical property at all.

How does this analogy bear on the plausibility of the mind/brain identity theory? There is more than one (physical) way to build a mousetrap. The analogy is that there may be many physical ways to build a creature that has a mind and more than one way for a thinking being to have this or that psychological property.

Consider computers. It is not very plausible to regard very simple computers as having beliefs and desires. My desk calculator no more "knows" facts about simple arithmetic than my stove "knows" recipes for making soup. Rather, human beings can use these devices to do arithmetic or to make soup. A desk calculator, in this respect, is like paper and pencil. It facilitates *our* calculations, but does not itself engage in mental activity.

Could a Computer Have Psychological Characteristics?

Don't be misled by the fact that we sometimes use mentalistic terms to describe simple computers. For example, we talk about computer "memory." However, I don't think my home computer literally remembers anything. This is just a metaphor. If I write some thoughts on a piece of paper and those scribbles are not erased, it is true that the piece of paper has "retained" the inscriptions I placed there. But the piece of paper did not remember anything. In this respect, I think a simple computer is just like a piece of paper.

So I do not think that very simple machines have minds or mental states. But let us use our imaginations and think about what the future may bring. Could there be computers that have mental states? Could computers be built that can perceive—see and hear, for example? Could computers be built that can remember? Could a computer reason? Could a computer be built that has wants and needs and preferences?

Functionalists have generally regarded these as very real possibilities. Perhaps current computers can't do these things. And perhaps computer scientists at times exaggerate how close they are to making computers with these abilities. But take seriously for a moment the possibility that computers eventually will be built that have one or more of these abilities.

This possibility has serious implications for the identity theory. These computers, let us suppose, will not be made of DNA. Perhaps they will be made of silicon chips. There seems to be no reason to expect that these thinking machines must be physically very much like the brains we have. Just as there are many physical ways to build a mousetrap, so there seem to be many physical ways to have a mind and to have particular mental states.

We don't need to consider the future of computer science to see this idea. Organisms other than human beings have psychological states. Some can perceive and remember and feel pain, even if they are not capable of all the complex thoughts and emotions that human beings can have. Is it reasonable to suppose that these psychological states in other species must be based on precisely the same physical structures that are present in human beings? Even within the human species, there may be variation in the physical structures used to encode this or that mental state. Indeed, even within a single human being, there may be many ways that the brain can encode a single piece of information. Remem-

Multiple Realizability Within the Class of Living Things

bering that lemons are yellow may be something that your brain can do in various different physical ways.

This is the idea I mentioned before—of *multiple realizability*. A given mental type—believing that lemons are yellow, wanting a drink of water, feeling pain—is not identical with any single physical type. Functionalism claims that the mind/brain identity theory is false as a theory about psychological types. The reason the identity theory is false is that psychological types have multiple physical realizations.

This point might be formulated slightly sarcastically by saying that functionalism accuses the identity theory of being a "chauvinist" doctrine. [This quip is due to Ned Block, "Troubles with Functionalism," in W. Savage (ed.), *Perception and Cognition*, Minneapolis, University of Minnesota Press, 1978.] Identity theorists say that a computer or another species must be like us physically if it is to have a mind and mental characteristics. Functionalism regards this as implausibly restrictive.

This, then, is the negative thesis that functionalism advances. Mental properties are *not* identical with physical properties. Notice that this rejection of type identity is quite consistent with accepting token identity. Perhaps being a mousetrap is not a physical property, but each mousetrap is a physical thing. Perhaps believing that lemons are yellow is not a physical property, but my now believing that lemons are yellow might still be a state that my brain occupies. Functionalism rejects the identity theory's thesis of *type* identity, not its thesis of *token* identity.

The Birthday Fallacy, Again

The Birthday Fallacy, introduced in Lecture 4, is the mistake you make if you confuse the following two statements:

Everyone has a birthday.
There is a single day on which everyone was born.

The first is true, the second is false.

The same mistake is involved in confusing the following two statements:

Each mousetrap has physical properties that allow it to catch mice.
There is a single set of physical properties that all mousetraps have in common, which allows them to catch mice.

The first is true, the second false.

How can the Birthday Fallacy be used to describe functionalism's criticism of the identity theory?

The identity theory is a version of materialism. So is functionalism. The identity theory denies that minds are made of an immaterial substance; it denies that disembodied spirits exist. Functionalism agrees. The following chart shows how these two theories are related to each other, and also to dualism:

Are all mental _____s physical?

	Dualism	Functionalism	Identity Theory
Type	No	No	Yes
Token	No	Yes	Yes

In a sense, functionalism is an intermediate position; it is conceptually "in between" dualism and the identity theory.

So much for the negative thesis. What positive account does functionalism provide of what the mind and its properties are like? The name "functionalism" suggests what this positive account is. Let's return to the property of being a mousetrap. This property, I have argued, is not identical with any single physical property. What, then, makes something a mousetrap? What do the mousetraps have in common that makes them different from the non-mousetraps?

Functionalism's Positive Thesis

A vague, though suggestive, answer is that being a mousetrap is a functional property; a mousetrap is any device that functions to turn a free mouse into a caught one. Mousetraps are things that play a particular causal role. Any device that can produce certain effects in certain circumstances counts as a mousetrap, regardless of what physical materials it is made of or how it is physically constructed.

What does it mean, then, to claim that psychological properties are "functional" properties? Let's go back to the example of wanting a drink of water, discussed in Lecture 19. I noted there that beliefs plus desires lead to behavior in roughly the following way:

> If an agent *S* wants above all that proposition *W* be true and has a belief *B*, which says that action *A* is the best way to secure the truth of *W*, then the agent will perform action *A*.

There are some simplifications in this statement, but set them aside for the moment.

This principle says that the want (that *W* be true) and the belief (that *B* is true) jointly cause action *A*. Functionalism sees here a way of saying what it is to want some proposition *W* to be true. To want *W* to be true is to be in a state that is defined by its causal powers. To want *W* to be true is to be in a state such that believing *B* will lead you to perform action *A*. The proposal is that for an individual—whether it is a human being, a computer, or a Martian—to occupy a state that effects this causal connection between belief and action is for that individual to want that *W* be true. The point is that it isn't the physical realization of the state that matters, but its causal powers to connect other psychological states (such as beliefs) with behavior.

Perhaps this causal story about what a want is has some plausibility. Part of the problem for functionalism is to show how this kind of account generalizes. How can one use this pattern to say what it is to believe something? And there are other types of psychological states to consider as well.

Consider my belief that lemons are yellow. What functional role is played by this psychological state? I can mimic my account of wants, stated previously. I can say that if *S* believes a proposition *P*, then *S* is in a state with the following property: If you ask *S* whether *P* is true and *S* understands your question and wants to answer truthfully, then *S* will say *yes*. The idea is that beliefs are states that have the effect of producing behaviors of affirmation if the subject has the desire to answer sincerely and has the competence to do so.

Maybe this is a truth about what belief is. The problem is that there seems to be a great deal more to believing something than what I've just said. We base all kinds of actions on our beliefs. Answering yes-or-no questions is just the tip of the iceberg. In addition, beliefs have effects on other mental states; these are not described by the previous remark. So the problem with the proposal is not that it isn't true, but that it seems radically incomplete.

This kind of difficulty becomes especially graphic when we shift our attention from beliefs and desires to sensations. Consider what a functionalist says about the nature of pain, for example. When people are in pain, they are inclined to say "ouch!" They are inclined to withdraw their bodies from what they believe to be the painful stimulus. And being in pain diminishes a person's attention span and has other psychological effects as well.

Suppose I exhaustively described the causes and effects of being in pain. These would involve the relationship of being in pain to external stimuli, to behavior, and to other psychological states. Some of these I just mentioned. It is sometimes suggested that this functionalist account of pain leaves out the most important fact—that pain *hurts*. A state may play the functional role of pain and still not be a pain state, so this objection asserts. If this is right, then functionalism will fail as an account of the nature of pain.

I won't try to answer this question of whether functionalism is adequate. Perhaps there are some psychological phenomena that functionalism cannot explain. Maybe sensations (such as pain) are counterexamples. But even if this is true, there may be other psychological states for which functionalism is adequate; perhaps belief and desire can be understood along functionalist lines. This issue is now a controversial one in philosophy.

Summary So where are we? I've argued that dualism, logical behaviorism, and the mind/brain identity theory are each inadequate. I think there is nothing wrong with mentalism—the view that beliefs and desires are inner causes of outward behavior. Behavior *provides evidence* as to what an agent's mental states are; the behavior does not *define* what it is to be in a given mental state. To make sense of

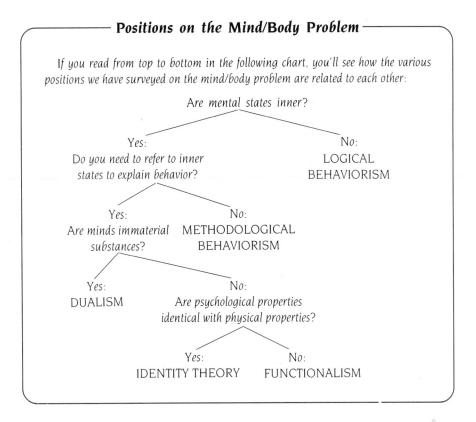

Positions on the Mind/Body Problem

If you read from top to bottom in the following chart, you'll see how the various positions we have surveyed on the mind/body problem are related to each other:

Are mental states inner?

Yes: — *No:*
Do you need to refer to inner   LOGICAL
states to explain behavior?   BEHAVIORISM

Yes: *No:*
Are minds immaterial   METHODOLOGICAL
substances?   BEHAVIORISM

Yes: *No:*
DUALISM   *Are psychological properties*
identical with physical properties?

Yes: *No:*
IDENTITY THEORY   FUNCTIONALISM

mentalism, we need not think that an agent's mind is made of some strange immaterial substance (as dualism maintains). Individuals have minds by virtue of the physical organization of their bodies. However, this does not require that all individuals who possess some psychological characteristic (such as feeling pain, or believing that lemons are yellow) have some single physical characteristic in common. My conclusion is that functionalism's negative thesis is correct. As to the positive thesis that functionalism advances, I take no stand on that issue here.

In the rest of this part of the book, I will explore two other philosophical problems about the mind. If human beings act as they do because of what they think and want, and if what they think and want is caused by things outside of themselves, how can human action be said to be free? This is the problem of free will, which I take up in Lectures 23–25. After that, I'll consider the problem of psychological egoism. If human beings act on the basis of what they think and want, doesn't it follow that people always act selfishly — that they try to satisfy their own wants and never act because other people would be benefited?

Review Questions

1. I return home from a furniture store and report to my family: "They're selling our sofa." I look at the plate of food in front of my son and say, "That's what I ate for lunch." How does the type/token distinction help disambiguate these two remarks?
2. What does it mean to say that a psychological property (a type) is "multiply realizable"?
3. Functionalists criticize the mind/brain identity theory for being "chauvinistic." What does this mean?
4. How is it possible to reject the identity theory without thinking that there are immaterial minds (disembodied spirits)?
5. Functionalists try to characterize what it is to have a psychological property (such as feeling pain or believing that Washington is the capital of the United States) by describing that property's "causal role." What does that mean?

Problems for Further Thought

1. In Lecture 6, I discussed the concept of fitness that is used in evolutionary theory. What would it mean to say that fitness is *multiply realizable?* Is it plausible to claim that fitness has this characteristic?

2. In the readings accompanying these lectures is an essay by Alan Turing on the question of whether a computer can think. Turing proposes a behavioral test for saying whether a machine is thinking. What is the test? How adequate is the test? To assess its adequacy, you should ask: Could the test falsely conclude that the subject is thinking, when it is not? And could the test falsely conclude that the subject is not thinking, when it is?

3. Here is *the inverted spectrum problem:* You have a particular characteristic sensation when you look at red things and a quite different sensation when you look at green things. Is it possible for someone to have precisely the reverse arrangement? This individual would have a red sensation when he looks at green things and a green sensation when he looks at red things. His behavior, including his use of language, would be precisely the same as yours. For example, he would apply the term "red" to fire engines and "green" to grasshoppers. If spectrum inversion is possible, what consequences does this have for functionalism's positive thesis about the nature of mental states?

Lecture 23

Freedom, Determinism, and Causality

In the previous lectures about the mind/body problem, there was a simple idea that no theory contested. Dualists, identity theorists, and functionalists all grant that the mind and the physical world causally interact. What you think and want together combine to cause your body to move in various ways. Behavior is a consequence of the agent's beliefs and desires. In addition, mental states themselves have causal antecedents in the physical world. What you now believe and the preferences you now have—indeed, your personality as a whole—can be traced back to experiences you have had. These experiences themselves are caused by items in your physical environment. In addition, modern science recognizes that some features of your mind may be influenced by the genetic endowment you received from your parents.

So just as the human mind has effects on the physical environment, so too does the physical world—both inside and outside our own bodies—affect our mental states. The following diagram represents these causal relationships:

Mind

Environment $\longrightarrow$

Genes $\longrightarrow$ | Beliefs + Desires | $\longrightarrow$ Behavior

The Problem of Freedom

The puzzle about the existence of human freedom can now be given a preliminary formulation. Your beliefs and desires, and hence your behavior, are caused by things outside your control. You didn't freely choose the genes you have or the sequence of environments in which you grew up. If you didn't freely choose them, how can it be said that your behavior is the result of a free choice on your part? How can you be responsible for actions that are caused by events (long ago) over which you exercised no control? It looks like you are no more free than a computer; a computer behaves as it does because it was programmed to do so.

Another way to see the problem is to attend to a different feature of the causal picture just presented. Suppose our behavior is the result of our beliefs and desires, just as a computer's behavior is the result of its programming. There is a feature of the computer's situation that seems also to characterize our own. Given the computer's program, it cannot act differently from the way it does. Suppose a computer is programmed to compute the sum of two numbers. This means that if you input 7 and 5, then the computer cannot fail to output 12. The computer cannot act other than the way it does.

Transitivity

Some objects stand in relation to others. Alice is taller than Ben. David loves Edward. The middle terms denote relationships. The names flanking the middle terms refer to objects that are said to be related to each other.

Some relations are transitive; others are not. If Alice is taller than Ben and Ben is taller than Cathy, then Alice is taller than Cathy. A relation R is said to be transitive precisely when it has this property: For any three objects a, b, and c, if a bears R to b and b bears R to c, then a must bear R to c. Being taller than is a transitive relation.

Loving is not a transitive relationship. The fact that David loves Edward and Edward loves Flo does not guarantee that David loves Flo.

Causality is a relation that obtains between events. Holmes' pulling.the trigger caused Moriarty to die. Moriarty's death caused alarm to spread in the London underworld. Does it follow that Holmes' pulling the trigger caused alarm to spread in the London underworld? That is, is causality a transitive relation? Does the distant causation argument discussed in this lecture assume that causality is transitive?

Are we like computers in this respect? Given the beliefs and desires we presently have, isn't it inevitable that we do precisely what we do? Our beliefs and desires leave open what we will do no more than a computer's program leaves open what the computer will do.

This fact about the computer, and about ourselves if we are like the computer, seems to rule out our being free. The reason is that if an action is performed freely, then it must have been possible for the agent to have done otherwise. If I freely lift a cup to my lips, then it must have been possible for me to refrain from lifting the cup to my lips. So the previous picture seems to imply that our actions are not free, since we cannot behave differently from the way our beliefs and desires lead us to act. Our actions are the inevitable consequences of our minds, just as a computer's output is the inevitable consequence of its program.

I've just pointed out two features of the previous causal picture, each of them suggesting its own argument for the thesis that no human action is free. The first argument I'll call the *Distant Causation Argument*; it focuses on the idea that our behaviors are caused by things that were beyond our control (our genes and environment). The second argument I'll call the *Could-Not-Have-Done-Otherwise Argument*; it focuses on the claim that we cannot act other than the way our beliefs and desires lead us to act. Both these arguments will be clarified later. For now it should be clear that if you think that we sometimes act freely, you must find a flaw in both these arguments.

It is important to see that both these arguments reach a conclusion of total generality; each concludes that *not one* of our actions is performed freely. This goes beyond the more modest and uncontroversial idea that *some* of our actions are not done freely.

Let's consider two sorts of behaviors that no one thinks are free. The first is behavior produced by *brainwashing*. Consider the case of Patti Hearst. Heiress to the Hearst newspaper fortune, Patti Hearst was kidnapped and abused mentally and physically by her captors for several months in 1974. She then participated with them in a bank robbery. Later, she was caught and brought to trial.

Examples of Unfree Acts

There was never any doubt that Patti Hearst helped rob the bank. The question was whether she did so of her own free will. The defense attorneys tried to establish that Hearst did not have free will at the time; they argued that her captors had so distorted her mental faculties that she was a mere pawn in their hands. Her actions were an expression of *their* wants, not of *hers,* or so they argued. The prosecution tried to show that Patti Hearst was a free agent; they argued that even though she had been abused, she eventually joined in with her captors willingly.

The prosecution won the case, and Patti Hearst went to jail. Quite apart from whether this was the right outcome, I want to draw your attention to an idea about which both the defense and the prosecution agreed: People who do what they do because of brainwashing are not acting of their own free will. Here, then, is one kind of behavior that I think we can safely regard as unfree.

The second category of unfree behavior is described by Freud. Freud describes a man who obsessively washes his hands. He is caught in the grip of a compulsion. Even after normal people would recognize that their hands are clean, the compulsive hand washer keeps scrubbing away. Sometimes the compulsion is so extreme that the person's flesh is eaten away, exposing the bone. "They can't help themselves," we may want to say.

Another example of this sort is kleptomania. A kleptomaniac is someone driven by the compulsion to steal. Even when they recognize that stealing is ruining their lives, kleptomaniacs find themselves powerless to change their behavior. Perhaps some people steal of their own free will; this does not seem to be true of kleptomaniacs.

Even philosophers who think that we sometimes act freely usually concede that brainwashing and compulsions rob us of our freedom. The question is whether there are *other* categories of behavior that are genuinely free. I've already described two arguments—the distant causation argument and the Could-Not-Have-Done-Otherwise Argument—that answer this question in the negative.

To decide whether we ever act freely, you will have to decide whether some of our behaviors differ significantly from the unfree behaviors just described. If brainwashing robs us of freedom, what should we say about the way a normal upbringing shapes us into the kinds of people we are? If indoctrination robs people of their freedom, what effect does education have on the possibility of free action? If a victim of brainwashing isn't responsible for what he or she does, how can we say that "normal" individuals are responsible for what they do?

Do All Behaviors Resemble Those Due to Brainwashing and Compulsions?

Shifting now to the examples of compulsive behavior, we can ask: If compulsive behavior is unfree, what should we say about normal cases of rational deliberation in which people act on the basis of the wants they have? Perhaps the only difference between someone said to have a compulsion and a "normal" person is that they have different wants. It is unusual to want to wash your hands two hundred times a day, but not so unusual to want to wash them after they get covered with dirt. If this is the only thing that distinguishes compulsive behavior from normal behavior, why say that the one is any less free than the other? To understand what freedom is, we will have to answer questions such as these.

A Clash of Plausible Conceptions   The problem of freedom of the will involves an apparent clash between two very fundamental ways we have of conceiving of ourselves. First, there is the idea that we are part of the causal network. Our actions do not spring out of nothing; rather, they trace back to the beliefs, desires, and other mental features we possess. And these mental characteristics themselves did not spring out of nothing; they too have their causal antecedents in our genes and environment. Second, there is the idea that (at least sometimes) we perform actions of our own free will. Is there a clash between these two ideas, or can they be reconciled?

The arguments considered previously concerned two different stages of the causal process represented in the figure. The distant causation argument concerns the relationship of your actions to your genes and environment. The could-not-have-done-otherwise argument concerns the relationship of your actions to your beliefs and desires. In spite of this difference, the two arguments have something in common. Both assert that your actions are caused. And both assert that some fact about how your actions are caused shows that those actions are not free. As noted before, if you think that some actions are performed freely, you must reject one or the other of these two premisses.

What Is Causality?   For the rest of this lecture, I want to focus on the second of these key concepts. What does it mean to say that some events "cause" others? Understanding causality has been a very deep philosophical problem, at least since David Hume's work in the eighteenth century. I won't attempt to get to the bottom of this cluster of problems. However, I will try to clarify what causality is—enough so that we can better understand the problem of seeing the relationship between causality and freedom.

What does it mean to say that striking a match caused the match to ignite? This does not mean that the striking was, all by itself, enough to get the match to light. After all, besides begin struck, the match had to be dry and there had to be oxygen in the air. So the first fact about causality is this: *A cause does not have to be a sufficient condition for its effect.*

The second fact about causality is that there usually are many ways to get a particular effect to occur. Striking the match caused it to light, but that does not mean that striking the match was the only way to have the match catch fire. Using a magnifying glass to focus sunlight on the match head would have done the trick. And putting the match into a heated frying pan also would have worked. So the second fact is this: *Causes often are not necessarily conditions for their effects.*

You might want to go back to Lecture 12 and review the definitions given there for the ideas of necessary and sufficient conditions.

I now want to note a difference between *a* cause of an event and what we may term *the whole cause* of that event. Striking the match is *a* cause. But it is only part of the whole complete set of causally relevant facts. Suppose I somehow were able to list all the causally relevant facts about the match at a given time. At that time, the match is struck in a certain way; there is oxygen present; the match is dry; and so on. Given all this information, what can we conclude as to what will happen next?

Can we say that the match *may* light? Yes. Can we say something more — namely, that the match *must* light, given this complete specification of all the causal facts? The idea that a complete description of the causal facts guarantees what will happen next is the thesis of *causal determinism*.

Causal Determinism

This thesis says that if you list all the causally relevant facts pertaining to the match and its environment at a given time, these facts uniquely determine what will happen next. The match's future is not left open by its present state. Given the match's present state, there is only one option as to what will happen next.

Sometimes we describe causally relevant facts about an object so that the description does leave open what will happen next. For example, suppose we say that a pair of dice is fair. If this is all I know, I'll conclude that the probability that the dice will land double-6 on the next roll is 1/36. The fact that the dice are fair and that I am now rolling them does not allow me to say what *must* happen. All I can say is that the dice may land double-6; but it also is true that they may fail to do so.

This does not mean that the pair of dice violates the thesis of causal determinism. That thesis says only that a *complete* description of the system determines what will happen next. So perhaps causal determinism is true and my description of the dice is incomplete.

This suggestion has some plausibility. For example, I didn't describe exactly how the dice would be rolled, what the surface is like on which they land, or what the wind conditions are that affect them as they leave my hand. Causal determinism says only that if *all* causally relevant facts are set out, these will leave open only one possible future for the pair of dice.

Is causal determinism true? Before I answer this question, let's be clear on what it would be for determinism to be false. If determinism is false, then the world is indeterministic. This means that a complete description of the causal facts at one time leaves open what will happen next. In such a universe, all one can say is that the present state of a system makes some futures more probable than others; the point is that even a complete description of the present will leave open more than one possible future.

Indeterminism

Until the twentieth century, causal determinism was a plausible and widely accepted thesis about the world. Newton's laws of motion, for example, are deterministic in character. You may recall from high school physics that those laws do not make use of the concept of probability. For example, "$F = ma$" says that if a billiard ball of mass m is acted on by a force of magnitude F, the ball will have an acceleration equal to F/m. It doesn't say that this will "probably" happen, as if there are other possibilities that could happen instead. Rather, the law says what will happen if the object is acted on in a certain way.

This Newtonian picture about how physical objects move provides a suggestive model for how *all* events in nature ultimately will be described. Living things are more complicated than billiard balls; creatures with minds are more complicated than many living things. But the idea I want to consider says that all things that are made of matter are ultimately governed by the laws of physics. So, since Newtonian theory is deterministic, the idea is that the behaviors of living things and of things with minds also must be deterministic in character. The idea involved in this generalized Newtonian thesis is that "determinism percolates up." If elementary particles are deterministic, so is everything that is made of elementary particles. If a person's mind is a material object, then his or her beliefs, desires, and subsequent behaviors are governed by deterministic laws. I am not saying that Newton was right about elementary particles, and I am not saying that the mind is a physical thing made of elementary particles. What I do want you to consider is a certain idea: *If* all matter is deterministic and *if* a person's mind is a material thing, then human behavior is physically determined.

One of the if's in what I've just described — the idea that matter is determinis-

---

Two Uses of Probability

We often use the concept of probability to describe our lack of knowledge. When we say that a coin has an equal chance of landing heads or tails on the next toss, we often mean that the coin is evenly balanced (fair) and that we do not know exactly how it will be tossed or what the wind conditions will be.

If determinism is true, then the only reason we need to talk about probabilities is that we lack a complete description of the coin's initial state. Recall that determinism says that a complete description of a system at one time uniquely determines what will happen next; the present cannot leave open different future possibilities that each have some chance of coming true; that is, if determinism is true, then the probability concept is needed only to describe something subjective, namely, the knowing subject's lack of information.

On the other hand, if determinism is false, then probability describes an objective fact about the world. Chance is a feature of the ways things are. In this case, probability talk is not simply a way to represent our ignorance.

In short, whether determinism is true affects how we can use the concept of probability.

tic—was not much questioned until the twentieth century. Quite apart from Einstein's theories of relativity, which replaced Newton's laws, our century saw the advent of the Quantum Theory. It is this theory that tells us that the behavior of particles is not deterministic. This theory has been tested numerous times and is now very well-confirmed. It says that even a complete description of a physical system leaves open what its future will be like. Some futures will be more probable than others, but the number of possibilities is always greater than one. In short, the present does not determine the future—chance is part of the way the world is.

Suppose we are made of matter. Suppose that our psychological characteristics are not due to the presence of some immaterial substance (a Cartesian ego), but are the consequences of how the matter we are made of is structured. If this is right, then I suggest that our behavior must be like the behaviors of physical particles in that both are affected by chance; that is, I am advancing the thesis that *in*determinism percolates up. Our beliefs and desires do not determine what our actions will be. Rather, those beliefs and desires makes some actions vastly more probable than others. Similarly, our genes plus the environments we inhabit do not determine what our thoughts and wants will be. Again, the relationship is probabilistic, not deterministic.

Most philosophers who have written about the issue of human freedom have not worried about the implications of the Quantum Theory. Usually, they have assumed that matter is deterministic and then have worried about what this implies about the question of whether we are free. This is entirely understandable for people like David Hume, who wrote about the issue of freedom long before Quantum Theory came on the scene; after all, Hume was writing in the heyday of the Newtonian world picture.

I said before that Quantum Theory, which is our current best theory relevant to the question of whether determinism is correct, says that determinism is false. If the Quantum Theory is disproved someday, then people may have to revise their view of whether determinism is true. But for *us*—for people *now*—the best guess about determinism (one supported by a lot of evidence) is that determinism is false.

Does Indeterminism Make Us Free?

If the world is indeterministic, how does that fact affect the issue of whether we are free? My suspicion is that the shift from determinism to indeterminism does not make much of a difference. The reason I say this is that if you suspect that determinism rules out freedom, you'll probably be inclined to think that we wouldn't be free if indeterminism were true instead.

Suppose you think we can't have free will on the grounds that our thoughts and wants are causally determined by factors outside our control We do not freely choose the genes we have or the environments we inhabited in early childhood. These are thrust upon us. They shape the kinds of people we are as well as the specific beliefs and desires we have. Given all this, how can our actions be regarded as free? This is the thought expressed in the distant causation argument.

Maybe you find the distant causation argument somewhat plausible. The question I want to ask is whether you would change your mind about freedom if chance were introduced into this story. That is, suppose that your beliefs and desires were due to genes, environments, *and chance*. If determinism robs you of freedom, chance seems to rob you of freedom as well.

The same point applies to the could-not-have-done-otherwise argument. Suppose you agree with this argument that our actions can't be free, since they are inevitable, given the beliefs and desires we have. Would introducing chance into this story make more room for freedom? I think not. If the fact that your beliefs and desires determine your action makes you unfree, I think you'd still be unfree if your actions were caused by your beliefs, desires, *and chance*.

To make this point graphic, consider a kind of brain surgery. Suppose you now are a deterministic system: Your beliefs and desires determine what you will do. I now offer you a brain implant, whereby a tiny roulette wheel is introduced into your deliberation processes. If you think you are unfree as a deterministic system, would the operation make you free? This seems implausible. Before the operation, you were a slave to your beliefs and desires. After the surgery, you are a slave to your beliefs, desires, and the roulette wheel. The shift from being a deterministic system to being an indeterministic system has not made a difference as far as the question of freedom is concerned.

Causality Is the Issue, Not Determinism

So my suggestion is that determinism *and* indeterminism both pose a problem for human freedom. The reason is that causality can exist in an indeterministic universe just as much as it can in a deterministic one. If your mental states are caused by factors outside your control, the puzzle is how you can be a free agent. Whether these causal factors *determine* your behavior is not essential.

It is not hard to visualize how some events can cause others in a deterministic universe. If striking the match causes the match to light, determinism tells us that the striking completed a set of causal conditions that determines that the match must light. But how could some events cause others if determinism were false?

The following example (due to Fred Dretske and Aaron Snyder, "Causal Irregularity," *Philosophy of Science*, vol. 39, pp. 69–71, 1972) shows, I think, that this is possible. Suppose a roulette wheel is connected to a gun, which is pointed at a cat. If I spin the roulette wheel and the ball were to land on 00, this would cause the gun to fire, which would then kill the cat. Suppose that the roulette wheel is an indeterministic system — spinning the wheel does not determine where the ball will drop. Now suppose I spin the wheel and the ball happens to fall on 00, thereby killing the cat. It seems to me that my spinning the wheel caused the cat to die, even though the process is not deterministic.

The death of the cat *traces back* to my spinning the wheel. For this to be true, it is not required that my spinning the wheel *made it inevitable* that the cat would die. This example show that it is possible to have causation without determinism.

So my hunch is that the real problem is not to see whether determinism and freedom can be reconciled. However, since the traditional positions about freedom all focus on deterministic causation, I'll do the same.

To fix ideas, let's be clear on how the thesis of determinism would apply to the diagram given earlier. This diagram represents the idea that genes and environment cause one's present mental state, and that this, in turn, causes one's behavior. What do these causal relations mean if causality is understood deterministically?

What Does Determinism Say About the Causation of Behavior?

Let's suppose for a moment that this diagram is *complete*; that is, suppose it represents *all* the factors that influence one's mental state and one's subsequent behavior. What does the thesis of determinism assert about this? It asserts this: Given one's genes and environment, one could not have had a set of beliefs and desires different from the set one, in fact, possesses. And given one's beliefs and desires, one could not have performed an action different from the action one, in fact, produced. Determinism, recall, is the thesis that the facts at one time uniquely determine what comes next.

Determinism is an entirely different doctrine from the idea termed *fatalism*. Fatalism is summed up in the saying, "Que sera sera" ("Whatever will be, will be"). It's easy to understand what fatalism is by seeing how it is used in the Greek story about Oedipus (I used this story to illustrate a quite different point in Lecture 18).

Determinism Differs from Fatalism

Oedipus was a victim of fate. The Fates decreed that he would kill his father and marry his mother. In the story, Oedipus does those things in spite of himself. The Fates somehow ensured that Oedipus would find himself in this sorry state of affairs no matter what choices he made and no matter what he did.

Determinism says that the present determines the future; it does *not* say that the future is cast in stone, unaffected by what is true of the present. Determinism is quite consistent with the idea that what is true at a later time *depends* on what is true earlier. Determinism does not rule out the idea that if the past had been different, the present would be different. Determinism does not rule out the idea that I can affect what the future will be like by now acting one way rather than another. Fatalism denies this; it says that the future is *independent* of what you do in the present.

Newton said that billiard balls are deterministic systems. If you hit the ball in a certain way (call it W_1), then the ball will move to a certain position (call it P_1) on the table. But Newtonian physics also says that if you hit the ball in some *other* way (W_2), the ball will move to a *different* position (P_2). Notice that in this theory, the present *makes a difference* to the future. The future is under the control of the present.

What would it be for Oedipus to be a deterministic system? Determinism does not require us to think that there are such things as the Fates. Oedipus would be a deterministic system if his actions were deterministically controlled by his beliefs and desires. If Oedipus has one set of beliefs and desires (call it S_1), then

Oedipus produces one action (call it A_1). But if he had had a different set of beliefs and desires (S_2), his action would have been entirely different (A_2).

Here is a picture of Oedipus according to which he is a deterministic system, but fatalism is false: Oedipus' beliefs and desires, plus the environment he was in, ensured that he would kill his father and marry his mother. But if he had had a different set of beliefs and desires, he would not have done this.

It is easy to confuse determinism and fatalism, even though they are very different ideas. In fact, they are almost opposite in what they say. Fatalism says that our beliefs and desires make no difference as far as what actions we perform and as far as what happens to us. In a sense, fatalism says that our beliefs and desires are impotent; they do not have the power to make a difference. But determinism, if modeled on the Newtonian idea, says that our beliefs and desires are not impotent; they determine — causally control — what we do and thereby powerfully influence what happens to us.

According to fatalism, there is no point in *trying* to do something. If it is fated that you will get an A in a course, you will get an A whether you try to get one or not; and if it is fated that you will get a D, you will whether you try to avoid this fate or not. On the other hand, to think that your efforts influence what happens to you — to think that trying makes a difference to the grade you receive — is to reject fatalism.

Greek mythology talked about the Fates. I'll assume that there are no such things. I'll assume that fatalism is false. This leaves open the quite separate question of whether determinism is true. Most previous writers on the free will problem have assumed that causality requires determinism. I hope you see why I reject this connection; I think that causality is a fact about the world we inhabit, even though the Quantum Theory tells us that determinism is false.

In the next lecture, I'll consider a variety of positions about the relationship of freedom and determinism. Even though I think that determinism is not the central problem — the real issue concerns the relationship of freedom and causality — the fact of the matter is that most writers have thought about freedom's connection with *determinism*. It is this traditional way of posing the problem that I'll investigate next.

Review Questions

1. What is the distant causation argument? What is the could-not-have-done-otherwise argument? What do these arguments have in common? How do they differ?
2. Two examples were given of unfree actions. What were they?
3. What does the thesis of determinism assert? What is indeterminism? How do these issues employ the concept of a "sufficient condition" and the concept of a "complete description"?
4. An unusual sort of brain surgery was described in this lecture. What was it and what relevance does it have to the problem of free will?
5. What is fatalism? How does it differ from determinism?

Problems for Further Thought

1. Suppose the Fates decided to get Oedipus to kill his father and marry his mother by controlling what Oedipus thinks and wants. For example, they make him fall in love with Jocasta. If this were so, how would determinism differ from fatalism?

2. Before the twentieth century, many philosophers (Immanuel Kant being a famous example) thought that determinism is an *a priori* truth. They held that if your theory tells you that chance plays a role in what happens, then your theory must be incomplete. In other words, these philosophers maintained that no observation could make it plausible to reject determinism. One amazing thing about quantum mechanics is that it has provided *a posteriori* arguments against determinism. Not only is determinism false (as far as we now know), but it is possible for us to find out experimentally that it is false. Episodes like this one in the history of science have made some philosophers (for example, W. Quine, "Two Dogmas of Empiricism," in *From a Logical Point of View*, Cambridge, Massachusetts, Harvard University Press, 1953) doubt that there are *a priori* truths. Can you see why?

Lecture 24

A Menu of Positions on Free Will

In this lecture, I'll present a menu of standard philosophical positions about the relationship of freedom and determinism. I then will make some critical remarks about some of the positions. This will set the stage for the positive proposal I will make in the next lecture about how the idea of freedom of the will should be understood.

Before proceeding, I need to define a piece of terminology from logic. To say that two propositions are *compatible* is to say that the truth of one would not rule out the truth of the other. Incompatibility means conflict; if one proposition were true, the other would have to be false.

"Compatibility" Defined

    Two propositions can be compatible, though neither is, in fact, true. And two propositions can be incompatible, even though both are false. Consider the following triplet of statements:

    (1) My shirt is green all over.

    (2) My shirt is red all over.

    (3) My shirt is torn.

Statements (1) and (2) are incompatible. Statements (1) and (3) are compatible. Do these two pieces of information tell you what color my shirt is? Do they tell you whether the shirt is torn? The answer to both questions is *no*.

Incompatibilism *Incompatibilism* is a thesis about the problem of free will. It does not claim that determinism is true. It also does not claim that we are unfree. It merely asserts an if/then statement: If determinism is true, then we are not free. So incompatibilism can lead to two sorts of positions. You can be an incompatibilist who holds that determinism is true; this will lead you to conclude that we are not free. This position has come to be called *hard determinism*. Alternatively, you can be an incompatibilist who holds that we are free; this will lead you to conclude that our actions are not causally determined. This position has come to be called *libertarianism*. So there are two varieties of incompatibilism.

Opposed to incompatibilism is the idea that determinism does not rule out the possibility that we are free. This view, not surprisingly, is called *compatibilism*. The basic idea in a compatibilist theory is that freedom does not require the absence of determinism, but rather requires that one's actions be caused in a particular way.

Notice that compatibilism does not say whether we're free or whether determinism is true. It simply says that the one issue does not settle the other. One form of compatibilism we'll consider holds that determinism is true and that we sometimes act freely. This is called *soft determinism*.

So the basic menu of positions is as follows:

I. Incompatibilism (if determinism is true, then we lack freedom).
    A. Hard Determinism: Incompatibilism and determinism are true, so we lack freedom.
    B. Libertarianism: Incompatibilism is true and we are free, so determinism is false.

II. Compatibilism (if determinism were true, that would not rule out the possibility that we are free).
    A. Soft Determinism: Compatibilism and determinism are true, and we are free.
    B,C,D.

Note that I have omitted mentioning some other possible forms of compatibilism (II- B,C,D) — ones that deny the conflict between free will and determinism, but do not assert that both are true (there are three such positions). My own view is located here. As mentioned in the previous lecture, I do not think that determinism is true. I also am a compatibilist. And I think that some of our actions are performed freely. The kind of compatibilist position I endorse will be described in the next lecture.

Soft determinism and libertarianism agree that we are free, whereas hard and soft determinism agree that determinism is true. To understand how these three positions are related, we can schematize each as endorsing an argument. Let F be the proposition that some of our actions are free and D be the proposition that determinism is true. Here is each position's characteristic argument:

Hard Determinism: If D, then not F.

D

_____

Not F.

Libertarianism: If D, then not F.

F

_____

Not D.

Soft Determinism: F

D

_____

It's false that (if D, then not F).

I'll begin by considering libertarianism; the philosopher C. A. Campbell (1897– 1974) is the libertarian on whom I'll focus. Before I describe how Campbell defends libertarianism, let me note that "libertarianism" with regard to the problem of free will is an entirely different doctrine from the idea that goes by that name in political philosophy. Libertarians in political philosophy argue that the state should not interfere in buying and selling or in other spheres of life. This is a *normative* view — a claim about the way things ought to be. On the other hand, Libertarianism with regard to the problem of free will is a *descriptive* claim, not a normative one. It asserts that we are free agents and that determinism is false. Libertarianism does not say whether this is good news or bad.

Libertarianism

Libertarians usually think they can tell by introspection that at least some of their actions are not determined by the beliefs, desires, and other psychological characteristics they have. For example, Campbell, in his book *Selfhood and Godhood* (London, Unwin Hyman, 1957), focuses on the fact that we sometimes perform actions that are "out of character." When we do this, he says, it is not true that our actions are determined by the characters we have.

I have two doubts about this line of thinking. First, as noted in Lecture 13, there is no reason to place such complete trust in introspection. The beliefs we form about ourselves by "gazing within" can be both incomplete and inaccurate. They can be incomplete because there may be facts about ourselves of which we are not conscious — facts that introspection fails to detect. In addition, introspection can be inaccurate because there are psychological mechanisms that systematically distort the way we appear to ourselves. Freud stressed both these ideas. In the latter category, he argued that some of the beliefs and desires we have would cause us great pain if we realized that we had them. As a "defense mechanism," introspection provides us with a false picture of what we really think and want. Although this view about introspection is characteristically Freudian, it is impor-

The Normative Problem of Freedom

Libertarianism, Soft Determinism, and Hard Determinism take different stances on the questions of whether we, in fact, are free. They do not advance claims as to whether it is a good thing or a bad thing to be free. In other words, these theories concern descriptive, not normative, issues.

There is a quite separate issue about freedom that arises in political philosophy. It involves the question of which freedoms people have a right to. Are people entitled to particular liberties, which may not be compromised by other individuals or by the state? This is a normative question about what people should and should not do. It is not the same as the question of whether people have free will.

Freedoms can come into conflict. Some defenders of capitalism hold that people should be free to engage in buying and selling without regulation by the state. However, this can result in "boom and bust" cycles that produce widespread suffering. If freedom from want is an entitlement that people have, then certain economic freedoms may have to be regulated or curtailed.

This and other normative questions about the freedoms that people are entitled to will be discussed in the section of the text on ethics.

tant to realize that many other approaches in psychology also endorse it. There is broad consensus that we should not take the testimony of introspection at face value.

There is an additional difficulty with Campbell's view. He says that when we act out of character, our actions are not determined by what our minds are like. I disagree. Consider a person who is usually cowardly but manages to act courageously on a given occasion. Is it plausible to think that the courageous act cannot be explained by what the person's mind was like? I find this highly dubious. I suspect that there are aspects of the person's mind that came into play. Perhaps a combination of unusual circumstances led the person to muster the courage in a way that earlier had not been possible. So I really don't see that the actions we call "acting out of character" pose a problem for determinism.

Campbell assumes that the phrase "acting out of character" means that the action is not caused by the agent's character. But this is to misunderstand what the phrase means. When people who usually have been cowardly manage to act courageously, we might say "evidently, they had it in them." This testifies to the fact that "acting out of character" is not something we think of as uncaused.

Campbell accepts incompatibilism, thinks that introspection shows that we sometimes produce free acts, and so concludes that determinism must be false. I have suggested that this introspective argument against determinism is very weak. If you think that free will and determinism are incompatible, I don't see how the introspective impression we have that we are free can be decisive. The behaviorist psychologist B. F. Skinner, whose views I discussed in Lecture 20, wrote a book called *Beyond Freedom and Dignity* (New York, Knopf, 1971). Skinner is an incompatibilist; in fact, he is a hard determinist. His view is that the introspective picture we have of ourselves as free agents is an illusion. It is a comforting idea — a fairy tale we tell ourselves. I do not agree with Skinner's hard determinism (remember, I'll eventually argue for compatibilism). However, my present point is that I think Skinner is right not to take introspection at face value.

If I thought that incompatibilism were true, I'd try to find out if human actions are determined. I would do this by seeing what science has to say about determinism and what psychology has to say about the causation of behavior. Campbell accepts incompatibilism, but argues in the opposite direction. He decides via introspection that some of our actions are free and concludes that our actions cannot be causally determined. This, I think, is the wrong order in which to address the questions.

Notice that Campbell's position, as I've presented it here, does not *argue* that incompatibilism is true. Rather, Campbell *assumes* that incompatibilism is true. He uses this as one of his premises to argue for the conclusion that our actions are not causally determined.

The same is true of the distant causation argument and the could-not-have-done-otherwise argument, discussed in the previous lecture. They do not provide arguments for incompatibilism. Rather, they conclude that we are unfree, based on premises that describe facts about how those actions are caused. So these arguments also *assume* that incompatibilism is true.

Is it possible to provide an argument for or against incompatibilism? The soft determinist theories I'll now describe try to do this. They seek to construct a plausible theory of freedom, one which shows how freedom is not ruled out by the idea that our actions are caused (or determined). I think the two compatibilist theories I'll now consider are defective. However, they provide lessons concerning how a more successful compatibilist theory might be constructed.

Two Soft Determinist Theories

The goal of a compatibilist theory is to show that an act is performed freely if it is caused in a particular sort of way; freedom does not require the absence of causality, but the right sort of causality. The goal is to make room for freedom in a world of causes.

I'll begin with the compatibilist account of freedom advanced by David Hume. His idea was that an action is performed freely when the agent could have done otherwise, had the agent wanted to. Suppose you accept an employer's offer of a summer job. Hume says you act freely if you could have declined the offer had you wanted to. By the same token, when you hand the robber your wallet after the robber says, "Your money or your life," you do so of your own free will, if the following were true: Had you wanted to die rather than stay alive, you could have refused to hand over your wallet. So Hume's theory is that free actions are ones that are under the causal control of the agent's beliefs and desires. When an action is under the agent's control in this way, it will be true

Hume

that if the agent had had a different set of wants, the agent would have selected and performed a different action.

Notice why this is a compatibilist theory. An action is said to be free when it is caused in a certain way. The idea of the action's being under the control of the agent's beliefs and desires describes a causal relationship between the agent's mind and the subsequent action. The idea is that freedom does not require the absence of causality, but the right sort of causality.

What would an *un*free action be like, according to Hume's theory? Suppose you want to leave the room but you can't because you are handcuffed to the floor. In this case, you do not remain in the room freely. You stay in the room *whether you want to or not.* What you do is not under the control of your beliefs and desires.

Here is another example of unfreedom. Suppose I performed a brain operation on you. I disconnected your beliefs and desires from the nerves that send impulses to the rest of your body. I then implant a radio transmitter, so that your body receives instructions from me. Now it is *my* beliefs and desires that dictate what *you* say and do. Your actions are no longer under the causal control of your own beliefs and desires.

In this bizarre arrangement, your body would become a robot— a slave to my will. It would do what *I* want because I want it. We might observe you drinking water, depositing money into my bank account, and so on. But you would not be doing these things of your own free will. Hume's theory explains why your actions are unfree in this case.

First Objection to Hume's Theory: Compulsive Behavior

I think the main objection to Hume's theory is to be found in cases of *compulsive behavior.* Think of the kleptomaniac discussed in the previous lecture. A kleptomaniac is a thief whose desire to steal is overpoweringly strong. A kleptomaniac wants to steal even though he may be quite convinced that he will be caught and punished. Even with full knowledge that stealing will hurt him rather than help, he continues to steal.

Kleptomaniacs are caught in the grip of an obsession. They are slaves to a desire that is not diminished by the realization that acting on the desire does them more harm than good. There are thieves who are not kleptomaniacs, of course. Such a thief may try to steal something, but his intention to do this would be affected by information about the chances of being caught and punished. None of this information makes any difference to a kleptomaniac. The kleptomaniac is stuck—his desire is not sensitive in the familiar way to considerations about self-interest.

I claim that the kleptomaniac does not steal of his own free will. Yet he satisfies Hume's requirements for what it takes to be free. Kleptomaniacs want, above all, to steal things. When a kleptomaniac steals, he does so because of the desires he has. If he had not wanted to steal, he would not have done so. The kleptomaniac's actions are under the control of his beliefs and desires. The problem is that there is something about the desires themselves and the way they work that make the kleptomaniac unfree.

The causal diagram from the previous lecture can be used to illustrate why Hume's account of freedom looks for freedom in the wrong place:

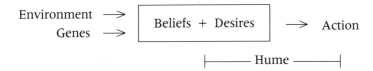

Hume's theory defines freedom in terms of a relation that obtains between beliefs and desires, on the one hand, and action, on the other. For Hume, free actions are ones that are controlled by the agent's desires. The case of compulsive behavior provides an objection to Hume's account. It is the nature of the kleptomaniac's desires that makes him unfree. This suggests that a compatibilist theory should not ignore the earlier links in the causal chain.

Second Objection to Hume's Theory: Locke's Locked Room

There is a second, more subtle problem with Hume's account. In his *Essay Concerning Human Understanding,* John Locke (1632–1704) describes a man who decides of his own free will to remain in a room in order to talk with a friend there. Unbeknownst to the man, the door of the room has been locked. The man remains in the room freely, although it is false that he could have done otherwise, had he chosen to do so.

To say that the man remains in the room of his own free will means that the action arose from a free decision that the man made. The man thought (erroneously) that he had a choice. He remains in his chair, talking with his friend, instead of getting up and approaching the door. He does this, Locke says, of his own free will.

If Locke is right in the way he describes this example, Hume's theory is mistaken. For you to have performed some action of your own free will, it isn't essential that you could have performed some other action if you had wanted to. According to Locke, you can perform some action freely, even though you are not free to act in any other way. The act was free because of *why it was performed,* and Hume's theory fails to pinpoint what the process lying behind free actions must be like.

Here's another example that illustrates Locke's point. Take any action that an agent performed of his or her own free will. For example, suppose that Joe attended a concert last night of his own free will. Now imagine that if he had not decided to go to the concert, he would have been kidnapped and taken there against his will. Joe did not know about this plot when he was deliberating about whether he would attend. The point of this example is that Joe attended the concert of his own free will, even though he could not have done otherwise.

One way to see what Locke is driving at is to contrast the man locked in the room (though he does not know he is) with the kleptomaniac. The kleptomaniac's thought processes have malfunctioned; there is something about his mind that makes his actions unfree. But there is nothing wrong with the mind of the man in Locke's example. His will is free, although he is not free to act in certain ways.

This contrast is important to bear in mind when you think about another important issue for the free will problem—coercion. Consider the robber who coerces you into handing over your cash by saying (convincingly) "Your money or your life." The robber has robbed you of your money. But has he also robbed you of your free will?

The robber presents you with an option—you can keep your money and die, or hand over your wallet and live. One option that he has taken away from you is for you to keep your money *and* your life as well. You are not free to do that. But has the robber robbed you of your free will?

This is a hard problem, but let me tentatively venture this answer: In many cases (if not in all), coerced actions do not rob their victims of free will. Of course, they can rob their victims of many things that are precious. And, of course, it often is wrong to place people in situations in which they have the choices (and only the choices) that the robber offers them.

But my point is that the robbery victim's calculation—that he is better off surrendering the wallet—is very different from the kleptomaniac's "decision" to steal. The robbery victim's mind is functioning quite well; it is the circumstances in which the victim finds himself that are objectionable. In contrast, something has gone seriously wrong with the kleptomaniac's mind— and it is this incapacity that makes him unfree.

I now want to consider a second compatibilist theory that is intended to meet the problem posed by compulsive behavior. Gerald Dworkin (in "Acting Freely," *Nous*, vol. pp. 367–83, 1970) has suggested that people in the grip of a compulsion are unfree because they act on the basis of desires that they would rather not have. Suppose you asked a kleptomaniac whether he would prefer to not have his overpowering desire to steal. The kleptomaniac might sadly reply that he would be glad to have this monkey off his back.

Dworkin's proposal requires us to distinguish first-order from second-order desires. A second-order desire is a desire about what one's desires should be like. "I'd like to be less selfish" is a second-order remark. It says that I would like to care more about the welfare of others. "I'd like to have an ice cream" or "I'd like Jones to get a raise" are first-order desires. They express desires about what should be true in the world outside the mind. So Dworkin's proposal is that people act freely when their second-order desires are related in a specific way to their first-order desires. To do an action *A* of one's own free will is to do *A* because one has desires *D*, where one does not mind having *D*. This last clause means that one does not have the second-order desire that *D* be dropped from one's list of first-order desires.

Although this proposal implies that many individuals in the grip of compulsions are unfree, it still is defective. Imagine a kleptomaniac who is so warped by his compulsion that he can't even recognize that it is harming him. Imagine a compulsive handwasher who has been brainwashed into thinking that hand washing is the greatest thing in the world. Such individuals may not mind having the desires they have. But that does not show they have free will; it shows only that they do not mind being unfree.

Dworkin's theory of freedom, like Hume's, fails to explain why some forms of compulsive behavior are unfree. This does not mean that no compatibilist theory will work, just that the two I've just examined are not satisfactory. In the next lecture, I'll outline a third compatibilist account.

Review Questions

1. What does it mean to say that X and Y are "compatible"? What does incompatibility mean? What do X and Y stand for?
2. Define compatibilism, incompatibilism, hard determinism, libertarianism, and soft determinism.
3. What argument have libertarians given for thinking that some actions are free? Assess this argument.
4. In the *Fourth Meditation*, Descartes argues that the will is infinite (that is, unlimited, and so absolutely free) as follows: "I know from experience that it [my will or freedom of choice] is not restricted in any way.... This is because the will simply consists in our ability to do or not do something (that is, to affirm or deny, to pursue or avoid); or rather, it consists simply in the fact that when the intellect puts something forward for affirmation or denial or for pursuit or avoidance, our inclinations are such that we do not feel we are determined by any external force." What is Descartes' argument? Evaluate its plausibility.
5. Explain Hume's theory of freedom. What makes it a compatibilist theory? Why does compulsive behavior provide a counterexample to this theory? Why does Locke's example of the man locked in the room provide a counterexample to Hume's theory? Are the following propositions equivalent in meaning? (1) S did A of his own free will; (2) S was free not to do A.
6. In Lecture 12 I explained that a definition can be defective because it fails to provide necessary conditions or because it fails to provide sufficient conditions. What sort of defect in Hume's definition of freedom is involved in (1) the example of compulsive behavior; (2) the example of the locked room?

Problems for Further Thought

1. In the selection from Campbell's *Selfhood and Godhood* reprinted at the end of this part of the book, Campbell argues that some actions occur neither by chance nor by necessity. These are examples of *creative activity* "in which . . . nothing determines the act save the agent's doing it." According to Campbell, these are the acts that are free. Define what "chance" and "necessity" mean, taking into account the definitions of determinism and indeterminism provided

in the previous lecture. Do your definitions allow that some actions may fall into neither category?

2. Political philosophers have often been interested in describing how much freedom of action a society allows its members. Would it be reasonable to measure this by determining how many of a person's desires are satisfiable in the society? There is an objection to this proposal similar to the objection I've formulated to Dworkin's definition of freedom. What is it?

Lecture 25

Compatibilism

In the previous lecture, I presented and criticized two compatibilist theories of freedom. Each sought to show that freedom does not require the absence of causality; both describe free actions as arising by a certain sort of causal process.

In this lecture, I'll present a third compatibilist theory, one inspired by the ideas of my colleague Dennis Stampe. After presenting a simplified version of this theory, I'll describe an objection to it. I won't propose a way of meeting this objection, but will leave the problem of freedom unsolved. However, I do hope to convince you that compatibilism is a plausible view, even though I do not claim that a completely plausible compatibilist theory has yet been articulated.

The Weather Vane Analogy   I'll begin with an analogy. Consider a weather vane. This is a device that farmers put on top of their barns to tell them the direction the wind is blowing. We talk about weather vanes being "stuck." We also talk about weather vanes being "free." What does this mean?

A free weather vane is one that responds to certain causal influences. If the wind is blowing north, a free weather vane will point north. The behavior of a free weather vane is not uncaused.

A stuck weather vane, on the other hand, does not respond to the wind's direction. When a weather vane is stuck pointing due north, there is a causal explanation for why it is pointing in that direction. However, the explanation has nothing to do with the direction the wind is blowing.

So the difference between a free weather vane and a stuck one is not that the position of the former is uncaused, whereas the position of the latter has a causal explanation. Both are caused to point in a certain direction by something or other. The difference is not in *whether* the behavior is caused, but in *what* causes it.

I have just described the ordinary meaning of "free" when it is applied to weather vanes. Notice that our commonsense understanding of this idea involves a compatibilist theory of what it is for a weather vane to be free. The idea is to use this as an analogy for constructing a compatibilist theory of what it is for the will to be free. Of course, weather vanes don't have minds, whereas the issue of freedom of the will has to do with a feature of the mind. But let us press on and see if the analogy can be developed.

Why do we say that the vane is free when it is causally responsive to the wind's direction? Why don't we describe a weather vane whose swivel is rusted solid as free, since in that case the direction it points is not influenced by the wind? A stuck weather vane, after all, is free from the wind's influences. I suggest that the answer is to be found in the fact that the weather vane has a *function*. When it performs its function, its behavior is caused by the wind's direction. When it is stuck, it cannot perform its function.

Function and Malfunction

How can this idea about function be applied to the human mind? If we think of different parts of the mind as having functions, then freedom of the will exists if the mind is functioning properly. A malfunction, however, may result in a "stuck" will — one which is unfree.

Consider the following diagram, which shows how beliefs and desires are formed and then lead, via deliberation, to intentions and thence to action:

Evidence $\longrightarrow$ BGD $\longrightarrow$ Beliefs $\Bigg\}$ $\longrightarrow$ Deliberation $\longrightarrow$ Intentions $\longrightarrow$ Actions

$?$ $\longrightarrow$ DGD $\longrightarrow$ Desires

The box labeled "BGD" is the belief generating device. It is the part of the mind that produces beliefs. Beliefs are its output. The belief generating device takes account of evidence (other beliefs and experiences); these are its inputs.

The BGD malfunctions when it is not sensitive to evidence — when it outputs beliefs in a way that ignores the evidence at hand. Perhaps paranoia — the irrational and unshakeable conviction that the whole world is conspiring against you — can be described as a malfunction of the BGD. In this situation, the person's beliefs are "stuck." The BGD has malfunctioned because it is not responsive to evidence.

The DGD is the desire generating device. It produces desires. Its inputs are the things that cause us to have the desires we do. I have put a question mark where the inputs to the DGD go; the inputs to this device are the things that the device is sensitive to when it is functioning properly. Later, I'll discuss what function the DGD might have.

The BGD and the DGD output beliefs and desires, which are fed into a deliberator. This device takes into account the agent's beliefs and desires and decides on the basis of them what the agent should do. This device completes its work when the agent forms the intention to perform some action.

By analogy with the weather vane, a person has free will when the various components involved in the process described in the diagram are functioning properly.

Before we can develop this idea much further, we must have some idea of what we mean by "function." In the case of the weather vane, we know what the function of the object is, because it was created by human beings for a certain purpose. If farmers put such objects on their barns for purely ornamental reasons, we might not regard them as malfunctioning when their swivels rust solid. But farmers want weather vanes to respond to the wind's direction; this is their intended function.

If the human mind were created by an Intelligent Designer and if we could find out why that Designer gave people the kinds of minds they have, we could say what functions the mind and its components subserve. However, if we want a naturalistic, not a theological, account of what it is for parts of the mind to have functions, we must set this idea about an Intelligent Designer (God) to one side.

Consider an analogous problem. We say that the function of the heart is to pump blood. What makes this true? After all, the heart does lots of things. It takes up space in your chest cavity. It also makes noise. But we do not say that a function of the heart is to take up space or to make noise. The problem is that the heart has many effects, but only some of these effects are what the heart is *for*—what it has as its function.

If the heart were created by an Intelligent Designer, that would solve our problem. The Designer's intentions would settle what the function of the heart is. But I will assume that we want a naturalistic, not a theological, account of heart function. We want to make sense of the idea of function without having to rely on the existence of an Intelligent Designer.

My proposal is that we understand the biological function of the heart in terms of the historical explanation of why people and other organisms have hearts. The reason hearts evolved is that they provided a benefit to the organisms possessing them. The benefit was that hearts pumped blood. As a side effect of the evolution of such blood pumps, it turned out that organisms had noisemakers in their chests. But the heart did not evolve because it made noise. Making noise provided no advantage for survival and reproduction.

Here, then, is a naturalistic account of what it is for an object (or characteristic) to have a function. We do not have to imagine that the object is present because of Intelligent Design. Natural selection (discussed in Lecture 6) is a perfectly satisfactory mechanism. My proposal is that "the function of o is to do F" means that o is present because o's do F. The function of the heart is to pump blood (rather than make noise), since individuals have hearts because hearts pump blood (not because they make noise).

Why do individuals have minds? More specifically, why do individuals have minds that are able to construct beliefs, desires, and intentions? Let us focus on desires and on the device that constructs them (the DGD). What use could this faculty have had in our evolutionary past?

The suggestion I want to consider is that the DGD has the function of representing what is good for the organism. Consider the case of thirst. When an organism gets dehydrated, it would be good for the organism to get some water. Organisms with minds seek out water when they are dehydrated because their DGD produces a desire for water. Like any device, the DGD might malfunction; if it fails to produce a desire for water when the organism is dehydrated, this could handicap the organism in its struggle to survive.

Bear in mind that there are other ways to get organisms to perform actions that satisfy their biological needs besides forming desires. Bacteria are capable of behavior that satisfies their needs, but they do not have minds (or desires) to help them do this. The suggestion, then, is that the DGD has the function of representing what would be good for the organism; it is not part of this suggestion that a DGD is the only way to get an organism to act so as to satisfy its needs.

Recall what this claim about the function of the DGD actually means. It means that we possess DGDs because, historically, such devices represented what was good for the organisms that possessed them; because of this, such organisms did better at surviving and reproducing than ones that lacked DGDs (or had DGDs that were differently constructed).

If this is right, we can understand why individuals who are in the grip of a compulsion are not free. Their DGD is stuck; it is malfunctioning because it no longer can represent what would be good for the agent. Kleptomaniacs want to steal, even though stealing is not good for them; indeed, kleptomaniacs sometimes want to steal even when they *know* that it is not good for them to have this want. Likewise, a compulsive hand washer has an overpowering desire to keep washing his hands even though there is ample evidence available that this is a harm, not a help.

A similar explanation can be given for why brainwashing is able to rob people of their freedom. When people are brainwashed, they are given beliefs and desires on which they subsequently act. These beliefs and desires are "implanted" by short-circuiting the normal function of the belief and desire generating devices. The process of brainwashing is intended to cause the BGD and the DGD to malfunction. This is why individuals who are brainwashed to perform some action do not perform that action of their own free will.

So my proposal about freedom is this: An agent freely performs an action if the agent's mind is functioning properly. This includes the idea that the agent's DGD is able to perform its function of representing what is good for the agent. In addition, the idea of well-functioning includes the requirement that the agent can rationally deliberate, given the beliefs and desires he or she has.

Although the present proposal and Hume's idea are both compatibilist theories, they are different. Hume thought that the crucial consideration was whether the agent's desires control the agent's behavior. The idea I've just described says that it is the entire psychological process—from belief and desire formation through the formation of an intention to act—that settles whether the agent's action is free.

I now want to consider what the present theory of freedom would say in reply to the arguments described in Lecture 23. Each of these arguments, recall, aimed to show that we can't be free because of some fact about how our beliefs, desires, and actions are caused.

I turn first to the Distant Causation Argument, which I represent as follows:

(1) If an agent freely performs an action, then the agent is responsible for the action.
(2) Agents are not responsible for actions that are caused by factors outside their control.
(3) Every action an agent performs is caused by factors (genes and early childhood environments) over which the agent had no control.

No action is performed freely.

The compatibilist theory of freedom advanced in this lecture (the "weather vane theory") must reject this argument. But how?

To reply to this argument, I need to examine the concept of responsibility. Consider what it means to say that a storm was responsible for some crop damage. Here "responsible for" simply means "causes."

The concept of moral responsibility is not so simple. If Patti Hearst was brainwashed by her kidnappers, we might say that she was not responsible for robbing the bank. However, this does not mean that she played no causal role in the robbery.

If the storm was not responsible for the crop damage, this means that the storm didn't cause the damage. But if Patti Hearst was not responsible for what she did, this does not mean that she did not do what she did. What, then, is the difference?

We sometimes say that we do not "hold" people responsible for some of the things they do. In contrast, it sounds funny to say that we do not hold the storm responsible for what it did. Holding X responsible and deciding not to hold X responsible seem to imply that X is a moral agent.

When we say that we don't hold Patti Hearst responsible for what she did, I think we mean that we do not *blame* her for her action. We do not think that she deserves moral criticism for the robbery if she did it while brainwashed. We might say the same thing if Patti Hearst had participated in the robbery because she had been threatened with death if she refused.

If an agent is morally responsible for an event (a bank robbery, say), this means (1) that the agent caused the event, and (2) that the occurrence of the event reflects on the agent's moral character. Moral responsibility differs from the simpler idea of causal responsibility; it is the latter concept that we apply to storms, there being no implication of moral praise and blame in such cases.

I think we are morally responsible for many (if not all) of the actions we perform, even though the beliefs and desires that cause those actions are themselves results of factors outside our control. The reason is that much of what we do shows what sorts of moral character we have.

To say that someone is morally responsible for doing something wrong does not automatically mean that he or she should be punished. Unfortuately, the law often seems to automaticaly connect these two issues. If members of the jury think that Patti Hearst should not be punished for the robbery, they must find that she was not responsible for her acts. But there is a question here that needs to be answered, which should not be allowed to slip by.

Suppose someone does something wrong and we take this to indicate a defect in his or her moral character. Perhaps the rather minor lies that people tell have this feature. But surely we don't want to pass laws that say that anyone who lies will go to jail or pay a fine. The reason might be that this legalistic apparatus would intrude into private life so much that society would be worse rather than better as a result. We hold people responsible when they do such things, but this doesn't mean that we think they should be punished.

The same can be said of some more serious breaches of law or morality. In 1974, the President of the United States, Richard Nixon, was suspected of having approved an illegal break-in at Democratic Party Headquarters at the Watergate Hotel in Washington. During the congressional hearings about the "Watergate affair," it was suggested that Richard Nixon should not be put on trial and sent to jail because this would cause too much agony to the U.S. electorate. "The nation has suffered enough," lots of people said. I am not agreeing or disagreeing with this opinion; my point is that considerations of this sort seem quite appropriate when we think about the legitimacy of punishment. I think that Nixon was morally responsible for what he did during the Watergate affair; but this does not automatically mean that he should have been tried and punished for whatever wrongs he committed.

What about the Distant Causation Argument? I think we are morally responsible for many of the things we do, even though those actions trace back to causal factors that existed before we were born. It is premiss (2) in this argument that I think is false. In just the same way, I think that the storm was causally responsible for the crop damage, even though the crop damage traces back to causes that existed before the storm came into being (think of the storm's causes). The Distant Causation Argument tries to make it look as if *we* have nothing to do with the actions we perform — as if it was Nixon's genes and environment that caused what Nixon did *rather than Nixon himself*. But this is absurd — *we* cause things to happen (which reflect on our characters), even though there are causal explanations for why we are the way we are.

I also have my doubts about premiss (1) — that we are morally responsible for all the actions we perform of our own free will. However, I'll postpone discussing this idea until I take up the topic of coercion.

The next argument from Lecture 23 is the Could-Not-Have-Done-Otherwise Argument. The argument can be represented as follows:

Reply to the Could-Not-Have-Done-Otherwise Argument

(1) If an agent freely performs some action *A*, then the agent could have done otherwise (that is, could have performed some action other than *A*).

(2) People can't perform actions other than the ones they do, in fact, perform.

_____

Agents never act freely.

Since I believe that the conclusion of this argument is false, I must reject one or both of the premisses.

Actually, I think that both are defective. Premiss (1) is mistaken for reasons that Locke clarified in his discussion of the man who decides of his own free will to remain in a room to talk to a friend; unbeknownst to him, the door has been locked. This was discussed in the previous lecture.

Premiss (2) also should be examined carefully. In Lecture 14, I formulated an idea that I called the thesis of the ambiguity of necessity. Statements about necessity and possibility often are ambiguous. The example I discussed there was the statement "Joe can't tie his shoes." Interpreted one way, the statement is true (Joe is holding two bags of groceries). Interpreted in another way, the statement is false (if he put down the groceries, he could do it).

I think that premiss (2) in the previous argument is ambiguous. It could mean either of the following:

(2a) Given the very beliefs and desires the agent had, and given that the agent rationally deliberated, he could not have performed a different action from the one he did.

(2b) Even if the agent had had a different set of beliefs and desires, the agent still could not have produced an action different from the one he did.

Proposition (2a) basically says that rational deliberation is a deterministic process: Beliefs and desires determine a unique choice of action if those beliefs and desires are rationally evaluated. Since I do not think that determinism is true, I doubt that proposition (2a) is correct. However, even if it were correct, I don't see why that would show that we are never free. Even if weather vanes were deterministic systems, that would not show that they are never free. I believe the same holds true of the human mind.

Proposition (2b) denies that the agent's beliefs and desires make a difference; (2b) says that the agent would have done the same thing even if the agent had had different beliefs and desires. I think that this statement is false — it is basically the doctrine of fatalism, which I discussed and set to one side in Lecture 23.

In summary, proposition (2) is ambiguous. If it is clarified to mean proposition (2a), then it fails to show that we are unfree. If it is clarified to mean proposition (2b), then it is false.

I conclude that the weather vane theory — the idea that actions are performed freely when the mind is well-functioning — has nothing to fear from the Distant Causation Argument and the Could-Not-Have-Done-Otherwise Argument. These arguments fail to show that freedom is an illusion. However, there is another issue we need to consider: What does the weather vane theory say about coercion?

It seems natural to say that coerced acts are not performed freely. However, when the robber coerces you into surrendering your wallet, it does not seem to be true that your mind has malfunctioned. You correctly realize that it is in your best interest to hand over your wallet, so that is what you do. Action under coercion is often no different from other, less dramatic actions produced by rational deliberation, at least as far as the inner workings of the mind are concerned. So if coerced actions are always unfree, the weather vane theory is in trouble, since the theory says that we act freely when our minds are functioning properly.

My reply is to claim that coercion does not rob an individual of free will. I think that when you hand you wallet to the robber because you want to stay alive, your will is functioning perfectly well. Your situation here is quite different

Are Coerced Actions Unfree?

What Is Coercion?

The gunman says, "Your money or your life." You would prefer to stay alive without forfeiting your money, but that option is not available. The choice is clear, so you hand over the money.

You are in a grocery store and want a loaf of bread. The grocer will let you have the loaf only if you pay $1.29. You would prefer to have the loaf without handing over the money, but that option is not available. The choice is clear, so you hand over the money.

The gunman has coerced you; the grocer has not. What is the difference?

There is a moral difference: What the gunman did was wrong, but the grocer did nothing wrong. However, this does not seem to define what coercion is. You can coerce people for morally impeccable reasons. Suppose you are using a life preserver for a pillow and I need the preserver to throw to someone who is drowning. If you refuse to hand it over willingly, I may have to coerce you. But in coercing you, I have done nothing wrong.

There is a difference in magnitude: In the case of the gunman, you want to stay alive far more than you want to hold onto your wallet. In the case of the grocer you would rather get the loaf than keep the $1.29, but the difference between these outcomes is far less momentous. Does this mean that coercion means putting people in situations in which it makes a great deal of difference to them what they do? Suppose I offer you $1000 if you smile. Have I coerced you into smiling? You would much rather have the money and smile than forgo the money and not smile. But that doesn't make my offer coercive.

Some years ago, there was a program for testing new drugs in prisons. Prisoners would receive time off their sentences if they agreed to run the risk of being guinea pigs. The program was discontinued, partly because the offer was thought to be coercive. Do you agree that this offer would be coercive?

Let's return to the original question: What distinguishes the grocer from the gunman? What, in short, is coercion?

---

from that of a kleptomaniac or compulsive hand washer, whose DGDs have malfunctioned.

There probably are *some* cases of coerced behavior that are unfree. Suppose that the robber's threat frightens you so much that you totally lose your capacity to think clearly. You are so overcome by fear that you hand over your wallet, but not for any good reason. In this case, perhaps the coerced action is unfree. However, I think that many (most) cases of coercion are not like this. People in such situations usually don't "lose their heads"; often they show a considerable degree of care and self-control (you gingerly hand over your wallet, all the while assuring the robber that you have no intention of resisting).

My conclusion is that a coerced action does not have to involve the will's being unfree. The weather vane theory correctly claims that some coerced actions are actions that the agent does freely.

I've assessed the Distant Causation Argument and Could-Not-Have-Not-Done-Otherwise Argument. I've claimed that each is mistaken in its conclusion that no actions are free. I've also discussed what the weather vane theory says about the case of coercion. I hope the analogy between human freedom and a free weather vane has convinced you that there is something to be said for compatibilism. In conclusion, I want to consider whether the details of the weather vane theory really are satisfactory.

An Objection to the Weather Vane Theory: Free, Rational Self-Sacrifice

I think there is a problem. I said that the function of the desire generating device (DGD) is to produce desires that represent what is good for the agent. We can see that this idea either is too vague or is mistaken if we consider the case of *rational self-sacrifice.* Consider people who calmly and rationally decide to sacrifice their own interests to help others (perhaps their family or friends or nation). A soldier, for example, decides to throw himself on a grenade in order to save the lives of his comrades. Is it possible for a soldier to do this of his own free will?

I would say *yes*, but what does the weather vane theory say? We have to ask whether the DGD is functioning properly here. Does the desire that it produces — the desire to sacrifice the agent's life to save the lives of his comrades — really represent what is good for the agent? Interpreted in one way, the answer seems to be *no*. The self-sacrifice would be good for the comrades, not good for the soldier himself. If the DGD has the function of representing what is good for the agent, then it seems to have malfunctioned in this instance.

The other alternative is to interpret the account given of the function of the DGD so that the soldier's DGD is not malfunctioning in this case. We might say that the soldier's DGD *is* representing what is good for him to do, since he believes a moral principle that says that this sort of self-sacrifice is morally required. But now "representing what is good for the agent" is being interpreted to mean "representing what the agent *thinks* is good." The problem with this way of understanding the function of the DGD is that the kleptomaniac who thinks that stealing is the best thing in the world also will be said to have a well-functioning DGD.

This suggests, I think, that the description I've been using of the DGD needs to be modified. I do not think that rational self-sacrifice indicates that the individual's will is unfree. According to the weather vane theory, free will requires that the individual's DGD not have malfunctioned. To be able to say this, we need to revise the description of what the function of the DGD is.

This is all I will say about the problem of freedom of the will. I hope you now understand what a compatibilist theory of freedom would be like. I hope that the weather vane idea is attractive enough (though I have not worked it out here in a completely satisfactory manner) for you to think that there may be some merit in the compatibilist position. There is a difference between people engaged in normal rational deliberation and people who are caught in the grip of a compulsion. The weather vane theory seeks to characterize what this difference is.

In the next lecture, I'll address a different problem in the philosophy of mind. I have repeatedly used the idea that in rational deliberation, agents take account of their beliefs and desires and decide what to do in the light of them. This suggests that rational agents are at bottom selfish—their actions always aim at the satisfaction of their own desires. This thesis—*psychological egoism*—is what I will investigate next.

Review Questions

1. In this lecture I sketched a commonsense picture of what it means to say that a weather vane is "free." What is this commonsense idea? Why say that it is "compatibilist" in character?
2. A weather vane has a function because it was designed by people to do something. What could it mean to say that the heart functions to pump blood if the heart is not the product of intelligent design?
3. What is the difference between saying that X is causally responsible for Y (as in "the storm was responsible for the crop damage") and saying that X is morally responsible for Y?
4. What is mistaken in the Distant Causation Argument and in the Could-Not-Have-Done-Otherwise Argument?
5. Are coerced actions performed freely? What consequence does the answer to this question have for the weather vane theory?
6. What problem does the existence of rational self-sacrifice pose for the weather vane theory?

Problems for Further Thought

1. In Lecture 5 on the design argument, I said that Aristotle's teleological conception of the universe has been rejected by modern science. People, tools, and nonhuman organisms are goal-directed systems; but it seems implausible to think of a mountain or the solar system in this way. In the present lecture, I presented an account of what it means to ascribe a function to something.

How does this account help explain why it is mistaken, for example, to say that the function of rain is to provide farm crops with water?

2. Can the weather vane theory of freedom be revised so that it avoids the counterexample presented here of free, rational self-sacrifice? How might this be done?

Lecture 26

Psychological Egoism

In earlier lectures, I have used a standard and commonsensical model of what rational deliberation is. This model was employed in the discussion of Pascal's wager (Lecture 10); in the three lectures (23–25) on the free will problem, I used it again. The idea is that rational deliberators decide what to do by taking account of their beliefs and desires. This commonsense idea has been made precise by the science called decision theory; rational agents are said to "maximize expected utility."

This idea seems to lead to the conclusion that rational people are fundamentally selfish: They act so as to achieve the goals they have — they act to get what they want. Not only is this true of a person we would ordinarily call selfish — for example, a business executive whose only goal is to make as much money as possible — the idea seems to apply to everybody. Even Mother Teresa, who has devoted her life to helping the needy in India, would count as selfish, according to this idea. It's true that Mother Teresa does not strive for wealth or material comfort. Her values place fundamental importance on seeing the conditions of the suffering improved. In devoting her life to this, she aimed at satisfying this goal. Mother Teresa gains satisfaction from her work, just as the businessman just mentioned gains satisfaction from his.

If Mother Teresa had done something else with her life, she would have felt guilty. Mother Teresa's payoff comes from reducing the suffering of others; she gains a feeling of satisfaction and also avoids the guilt feelings she would have experienced if she had done something else. The businessman also gains satisfaction; his comes in the currency of dollars and cents. The idea is that both are acting on the basis of their own wants; both do what they do in order to gain a feeling of satisfaction (and, possibly, to avoid such negative feelings as guilt).

The previous two paragraphs express in an imprecise way the idea I call _psychological egoism_ (PE, for short). In this lecture, I'll clarify what PE says and argue that in some important ways it is false. I won't reject the model of decision-making used so far — that rational agents act on the basis of the beliefs and desires they have. However, I'll argue that PE does not follow from this model. Even though the businessman and Mother Teresa both try to get what they want, there yet may be important differences between them; these I will try to clarify.

I want to formulate what PE says more precisely. First of all, the debate over whether PE is true is not settled by the following facts: *Two Truisms*

(1) Rational agents decide which action to perform by consulting their beliefs and desires.

(2) At times, rational agents are guided by desires that are other-directed.

Proposition (1) describes the model of rational deliberation I've been assuming. It says nothing about what the *content* is of people's desires; it does not say *what* people want. Proposition (1) just says that whatever it is that a rational agent wants, that agent's behavior will be aimed at achieving those goals. I assume that the debate over PE is not settled by (1); (1) is a "truism" to which defenders and critics of PE can agree.

Proposition (2) also is a truism. It says that people often have desires that concern the situations of others. A benevolent person may want others to suffer less. A sadist may want others to suffer more. Both of these individuals have what I will call "other-directed preferences." It makes a difference to them what the situations of other people are like.

I will use the term "other-directed preferences" to refer to preferences that people have about the situations of others, preferences that do not mention their own situation. If I prefer that *others suffer less rather than more*, this is an other-directed preference that I have; note that the italicized words, which specify the content of the preference, refer to others, but not to me.

Similarly, a self-directed preference is any preference that I have that refers to my own well-being, but does not say anything about the situation of others. If I prefer that *I have more money rather than less*, this is a self-directed preference that I have.

Some preferences are neither purely self-directed nor purely other-directed. They are mixed. If I want to be the best chess player in the world, this is a preference whose content refers both to me and to others.

Proposition (2) does not refute PE. I might genuinely desire that your back gets scratched; but I would be an egoist if my only reason for wanting this is that I see it as a way to have my back get scratched as well. Egoists don't have to deny the existence of other-directed preferences.

The philosopher/psychologist William James (1842–1910) discussed the issue of whether PE is true. In his *Principles of Psychology* (London, Henry Holt, 1890), he noted a fact about PE that we should consider. He pointed out (as had Aristotle) that an action may bring a feeling of satisfaction to an agent without the action's having been done in order to obtain the feeling. *Goals and Side Effects of an Act*

James thought that many altruistic acts are of this sort. We help people because we genuinely care about their situations. It happens that our helping others is accompanied by our receiving a glow of satisfaction. But, according to James, obtaining the glow was not the goal; it was an unintended side effect.

If James was right, PE would be false. But it seems to me that a defender of PE would deny part of what James is saying. A defender of PE might say that James has the story precisely backward. It's true that an action can produce an effect that is not the real goal of the action. But a psychological egoist might say that when we help others, what we really are after is the glow of satisfaction; the fact that others are benefited is merely a side effect of our trying to make ourselves feel good.

There is a point of agreement between James and this defender of PE. Although they disagree over which effect of the helping behavior is the goal and which is the mere side effect, they agree that there is a difference between the two. So let's identify a third proposition about which the two sides concur:

> (3) That an action has a particular effect does not necessarily mean that it was performed in order to produce that effect.

It is easy to see why proposition (3) is correct, quite apart from the issue of whether PE is true. Proposition (3) simply notes the difference between intended and unintended consequences of an action.

A Simple Example

In order to clarify what PE asserts, I want to focus on a simple example. You see an advertisement in a magazine. It asks you to send a check for $10 to help starving children. You are fairly well off. You could find enjoyable things to do with $10. But the picture in the ad is pathetic. You believe that a $10 contribution will make a real difference for the people involved (it won't solve the whole problem, of course). You think for a moment and then put a $10 check in the mail to the charity. In this case, were you an altruist or an egoist?

On the surface, it may appear that you were an altruist. After all, genuine concern for the welfare of the starving children seems to be what led you to contribute. But an advocate of PE would maintain that your real motives, of which perhaps you are not fully conscious, were selfish. You derived a glow of satisfaction—a nice feeling about yourself—from the donation. You also avoided feeling guilty. These psychological benefits were the real motives for your behavior, or so PE asserts.

To decide whether you were an altruist or an egoist in this situation, I want to describe four kinds of people. Two of them are altruists; two are egoists. After I've explained these four possibilities, I'll consider how we might go about discussing which of the categories you occupy.

Four Preference Structures

The first individual I'll call the Extreme Egoist. This individual cares nothing for the welfare of others; the only thing that matters to an Extreme Egoist is his or her own situation.

The following two-by-two table illustrates the preferences of Extreme Egoists. The table answers two questions about such individual's. What preferences do they have about whether they will receive a benefit? What preferences do they have about whether the children do better rather than worse? The first question has to do with their self-directed preference; the second concerns their other-directed preferences.

The Extreme Egoist

Other-Directed

		+	−
Self-Directed	+	4	4
	−	1	1

Extreme Egoists care only that they receive more (+) rather than less (−) of whatever the benefit is that is at issue. It is a matter of indifference to these individuals whether the children do better (+) or worse (−).

The numbers in this table represent the order of the agent's preferences. The absolute values have no meaning; I could just as easily have used "9" and "5" instead of "4" and "1."

It is a matter of indifference to Extreme Egoists whether the other person has more rather than less. The only thing that makes a difference to Extreme Egoists is their self-directed preference. These individuals are not benevolent; they also are not malevolent. They simply do not care one way or the other about others.

If you were an Extreme Egoist, would you give $10 to charity? The donation has two effects. You receive a glow of satisfaction, and the children are made better off. On the other hand, not donating the money also has two effects. You feel guilty about yourself, and the children are worse off. In this situation, there are two choices, which are represented in the table at the upper left (+ to self and + to other) and the lower right (− to self and − to other).

In this situation, Extreme Egoists will choose the first action. They therefore will choose an action that benefits others. However, this benefit to others is not the goal of their action, but is a mere side effect. If you were an Extreme Egoist, you would help the starving, but your real motive would be to make yourself feel good.

The second personality type is the mirror image of the Extreme Egoist. It is the Extreme Altruist:

The Extreme Altruist

Other-Directed

		+	−
Self-Directed	+	4	1
	−	4	1

Extreme Altruists care nothing about their own situation, but only want the other person to be better off.

What would Extreme Altruists do if they had to choose between the upper left and the lower right? They must either benefit both self and other or benefit neither. Notice that Extreme Altruists will choose the action that benefits both self and other.

If you were an Extreme Altruist, you would donate the money to charity. A consequence of doing this would be that you would feel good about yourself. However, in this case, the benefit to self would be a side effect of the act, not the act's real motive.

So in a choice between the upper left and the lower right, Extreme Altruists will do the same thing that Extreme Egoists will do. Their actions will be the same, but their motives will differ. Extreme Egoists act solely in order to benefit themselves; the benefit to the other person is just a side effect. Extreme Altruists act solely to benefit the other person; the benefit to self is just a side effect.

People Are Rarely Extreme Altruists or Extreme Egoists

Which of these preference structures describes real people? I think that in the vast majority of cases, the answer is *neither*. In most choice situations, most of us care about self *and* others. We don't like to feel guilty; we also enjoy the glow of satisfaction that comes from thinking well of ourselves. Most of us have preferences about having other goods (like money) as well. But besides these self-directed preferences, we also have other-directed preferences. We are almost always either benevolent (or malevolent) in how we feel about the situation of others.

Both the Extreme Egoist and the Extreme Altruist have only one kind of preference. Real people usually have both. So we must complicate our representation.

I now introduce a third character—the Moderate Egoist:

The Moderate Egoist

	Other-Directed	
	+	−
Self-Directed +	4	3
Self-Directed −	2	1

Moderate Egoists prefer that they be better off rather than worse off (since $4 > 2$ and $3 > 1$). They also prefer that other people be better off rather than worse off (since $4 > 3$ and $2 > 1$). So Moderate Egoists have both self-directed and other-directed preferences.

Why call such individuals egoists? Consider what they will do when their own interests *conflict* with those of others. Suppose the choice is between two actions. The first action provides a benefit to self while the other individual goes without; this is the outcome in the upper-right part of the box. The second action provides the other person with a benefit while the self goes without; this is the lower-left outcome. When self-interest and other-directed interests conflict, Moderate Egoists give priority to themselves ($3 > 2$). Egoists place themselves first.

What's the difference between Moderate Egoists and Extreme Egoists? Extreme Egoists do not care *at all* about the situation of others. Moderate Egoists do prefer that others be better off rather than worse. However, both place self before others when self-interest conflicts with the welfare of others.

The last character I want to describe is the Moderate Altruist:

The Moderate Altruist

Other-Directed

		+	−
Self-Directed	+	4	2
	−	3	1

Moderate Altruists differ from Extreme Altruists in that the former care about their own situation. Such individuals count as altruists because of what they do when self-interest and the interests of others conflict. If Moderate Altruists have to decide between the upper-right and lower-left choices, they will opt for the lower-left choice (3 > 2). They will sacrifice their own well-being so that the interests of the other person will be satisfied.

I noted before that when Extreme Altruists or Extreme Egoists face a choice between the upper left and the lower right, they behave in the same way—both choose the action that benefits both self and other. The same is true of the Moderate Altruist and the Moderate Egoist. The four characters behave identically when self-interest *coincides* with the welfare of others.

Let's return to your donation to charity. I hope it is clear that your behavior entirely fails to reveal whether you are an altruist or an egoist. You would have donated the money no matter which of these four preference structures you possessed. How, then, are we to tell whether you are an altruist or an egoist?

The Difference Between Altruism and Egoism

The difference between the egoist (whether moderate or extreme) and the altruist (whether moderate or extreme) shows up when there is a *conflict* between helping one's self and having others be better off. In a situation of this sort, the agent must choose between being in the upper-right part of the box (+ to self, − to other) and the lower-left part (− to self, + to other). In conflict situations, egoists put themselves first; altruists give priority to the interests of others. To find out whether you are an altruist or an egoist, we must put you in this sort of situation.

When you contemplated sending the $10, there was no conflict; what made you feel good also made the starving children better off. What would you have done if there had been a conflict? Would you have given the money to charity if there had been a conflict between your receiving a benefit and the starving children's being better off?

An Experimental Test

To visualize what such a conflict situation would be like, suppose I had made you the following promise as you sat at your desk deliberating whether to write a check to the charity:

> If you don't write the check, I'll give you a red pill which provides
> the glow of satisfaction and freedom from guilt. You can keep

the $10 for your own use. The pill will make you think that you generously wrote a check to charity.

On the other hand, if you do write the check, I'll give you a green pill, which will make you forget that you wrote the check. In this case, the starving children will be benefited, but you'll still feel guilty.

Suppose you trust me to do what I say I'll do. Will you write the check, or not?

In this hypothetical situation, self-interest and the welfare of others conflict. You can *either* feel good about yourself *or* help the starving children. You can't do both. What you choose shows what matters more to you.

My prediction is that you might well choose to write the check. If so, you are an altruist. On the other hand, if you decide not to write the check, this shows that you are an egoist.

When people send checks to charity, it may not be entirely clear why they do so. We can determine what their preference structures are if we consider what they would have done if self-interest and the interests of others had conflicted. The experiment described here is a way to think about that kind of situation. I believe that many people who give money to charity are altruists, in the sense defined here.

I think that psychological egoism is false as a generality. At least some of the time, people have preference structures that are altruistic. This does not mean that they don't care about themselves. It also does not mean that they don't value the glow of satisfaction and the freedom from guilt they receive from helping others. Altruists don't have to be Extreme Altruists. What it does mean is that altruists are disposed to sacrifice self-interest to advance the welfare of others if these come into conflict. In some choices that people face, people seem to be willing to do this.

In saying this, I'm not claiming that people are *always* altruistic. Few of us would die just to make another person smile. In some situations, we are altruistically motivated; in others, we are egoists. What I reject is the thesis that we are egoists *in every choice situation we face*. Once egoism is clarified in the way I've suggested, PE turns out to be false as a general theory of human motivation.

Review Questions

1. Give an example of an action that has two consequences, one of which was the goal of the action, the other of which was an unintended consequence.
2. What are self-directed and other-directed preferences? Give examples of each. Are there preferences that fall into neither category?
3. What is the difference between the Extreme Egoist and the Extreme Altruist? There is a kind of choice situation in which these two individuals will behave in the same way. Describe a case of this kind.

Apportioning Causal Responsibility

Events usually have more than one cause. A fatal car crash may be due to a slippery road surface, to the other driver's carelessness, to the condition of the car's tires, to the position of the concrete wall, and so on. It is a mistake to think that precisely one of these was the "real" cause; each factor played a causal role.

Once we recognize that an event has many causes, we may wish to say which was "more important." The following situation provides an example of how the issue of apportioning causal responsibility may be addressed.

Suppose you are a farmer who grows two fields of corn. The corn in the first field is shorter than the corn in the second. Upon investigation, you find that the corn in the first field has received less water and less fertilizer than the corn in the second. You suspect that the extra fertilizer going to the second field may have helped the corn there to grow taller; you also think that the additional water going to the second field may have helped as well. Your question is this: Did these factors really make a difference? And if so, which was more important, the extra fertilizer or the extra water?

This problem can be represented by a two-by-two table. The corn in the first field received one unit of fertilizer and one unit of water; the corn in the second field received two units of each. The table represents the average height of the corn in each field:

Water

		W^2	W^1
	F^2	4	
Fertilizer	F^1		1

What experiment would you perform to find out whether an increase in fertilizer makes a difference? How would you find out whether an increase in water makes a difference? What would it mean to say that each makes a difference, but that one makes more of a difference than the other?

How is this problem related to the issue of egoism and altruism discussed in this lecture?

---

4. What is the difference between the Moderate Altruist and the Extreme Altruist? What is the difference between the Moderate Egoist and the Extreme Egoist?
5. There is a kind of choice situation in which an altruist (whether extreme or moderate) will behave differently from an egoist (whether extreme or moderate). Describe a case of this kind.
6. When you help someone and this makes you feel good, how can you tell whether your motivation was altruistic or egoistic?

PSYCHOLOGICAL
EGOISM

Problems for Further Thought

1. In the experiment I described, there is a *time lag* between my describing the pill and your deciding what you will do . Suppose you end up sending the check to charity (and thereby taking a pill that makes you falsely believe that you did no such thing). I claimed that this behavior shows that you are an altruist. Could a defender of PE reply that you felt good about yourself in the time between my description and your decision, and that your behavior was therefore selfishly motivated?

2. Suppose adults with altruistic preference structures have them because when they were children, their parents rewarded them with love and approval for helping others. Would this show that altruists are really egoists — that what really motivates them is parental approval?

3. In this lecture, I have tried to clarify what it means to ask *whether* someone is an altruist. Two quantitative issues remain. How would you measure *how* altruistic someone is? And what would it mean to say that one person is *more altruistic* than another?

·R·E·A·D·I·N·G·S·

Other Minds Are Known by Analogy from One's Own Case

·BERTRAND RUSSELL·

In this excerpt from Human Knowledge: Its Scope and Limits *(1948), Russell argues that each of us knows about the mental characteristics of other people by analogy with our own case. You know by introspection which of your various mental states occurs when you behave in specific ways. Hence, the observation that others behave in similar ways makes it probable that they occupy similar mental states.*

In Lecture 19, I described Ryle's objection to this argument. It resembles an objection (discussed in Lecture 5) that Hume made to the Argument from Design.

The problem with which we are concerned is the following. We observe in ourselves such occurrences as remembering, reasoning, feeling pleasure, and feeling pain. We think that sticks and stones do not have these experiences, but that other people do. Most of us have no doubt that the higher animals feel pleasure and pain, though I was once assured by a fisherman that "Fish have no sense nor feeling." I failed to find out how he had acquired this knowledge. Most people would disagree with him, but would be doubtful about oysters and starfish. However this may be, common sense admits an increasing doubtfulness as we descend in the animal kingdom, but as regards human beings it admits no doubt.

It is clear that belief in the minds of others requires some postulate that is not required in physics, since physics can be content with a knowledge of structure. My present purpose is to suggest what this further postulate may be.

It is clear that we must appeal to something that may be vaguely called "analogy." The behavior of other people is in many ways analogous to our own, and we suppose that it must have analogous causes. What people say is what we should say if we had certain thoughts, and so we infer that they probably have these thoughts. They give us information which we can sometimes subsequently verify. They behave in ways in which we behave when we are pleased (or displeased) in circumstances in which we should be pleased (or displeased). We may talk over with a friend some incident which we have both experienced, and find that his reminiscences dovetail with our own; this is particularly convincing when he remembers something that we have forgotten but that he recalls to our thoughts. Or again: you set your boy a problem in arithmetic, and with luck he gets the right answer; this persuades you that he is capable of arithmetical reasoning. There are, in short, very many ways in which my responses to stimuli differ from those of "dead" matter, and in all these ways other people resemble me. As it is clear to me that the causal laws governing my behavior have to do with "thoughts," it is natural to infer that the same is true of the analogous behavior of my friends.

The inference with which we are at present concerned is not merely that which takes us beyond solipsism, by maintaining that sensations have causes about which *something* can be known. This kind of inference . . . suffices for physics. . . . We are concerned now with a much more specific kind of inference, the kind that is involved in our knowledge of the thoughts and feelings of others — assuming that we have such knowledge. It is of course obvious that such knowledge is more or less doubtful. There is not only the general argument that we may be dreaming; there is also the possibility of ingenious automata. There are calculating machines that do sums much better than our schoolboy sons; there are gramophone records that remember impeccably what So-and-so said on such-and-such an occasion; there are people in the cinema who, though copies of real people, are not themselves alive. There is no theoretical limit to what ingenuity could achieve in the way of producing the illusion of life where in fact life is absent.

But, you will say, in all such cases it was the thoughts of human beings that produced the ingenious mechanism. Yes, but how do you know this? And how do you know that the gramophone does *not* "think"?

There is, in the first place, a difference in the causal laws of observable behavior. If I say to a student, "Write me a paper on Descartes's reasons for believing in the existence of matter," I shall, if he is industrious, cause a certain response. A gramophone record might be so constructed as to respond to this stimulus, perhaps better than the student, but if so it would be incapable of telling me anything about any other philosopher, even if I threatened to refuse to give it a degree. One of the most notable peculiarities of human behavior is change of response to a given stimulus. An ingenious person could construct an automaton which would always laugh at his jokes, however often it heard them; but a human being, after laughing a few times, will yawn, and end by saying, "How I laughed the first time I heard that joke."

But the differences in observable behavior between living and dead matter do not suffice to prove that there are "thoughts" connected with living bodies other than my own. It is probably possible theoretically to account for the behavior of living bodies by purely physical causal laws, and it is probably impossible to refute materialism by external observation alone. If we are to believe that there are thoughts and feelings other than our own, that must be in virtue of some inference in which our own thoughts and feelings are relevant, and such an inference must go beyond what is needed in physics.

I am, of course, not discussing the history of how we come to believe in other minds. We find ourselves believing in them when we first begin to reflect; the thought that Mother may be angry or pleased is one which arises in early infancy. What I am discussing is the possibility of a postulate which shall establish a rational connection between this belief and data, e.g., between the belief "Mother is angry" and the hearing of a loud voice.

The abstract schema seems to be as follows. We know, from observation of ourselves, a causal law of the form "A causes B," where A is a "thought" and B a physical occurrence. We sometimes observe a B when we cannot observe any A; we then infer an unobserved A. For example: I know when I say, "I'm thirsty," I say so, usually, because I am thirsty, and therefore, when I hear the sentence "I'm thirsty" at a time when I am not thirsty, I assume that someone else is thirsty. I assume this more readily if I see before me a hot, drooping body which goes on to say, "I have walked twenty desert miles in this heat with never a drop to drink." It is evident that my confidence in the "inference" is increased by increased complexity in the datum and also by increased certainty of the causal law derived from subjective observation, provided the causal law is such as to account for the complexities of the datum.

It is clear that insofar as plurality of causes is to be suspected, the kind of inference we have been considering is not valid. We are supposed to know "A causes B," and also to know that B has occurred; if this is to justify us in inferring A, we must know that *only* A causes B. Or, if we are content to infer that A is probable, it will suffice if we can know that in most cases it is A that causes B. If you hear thunder without having seen lightning, you confidently infer that there was lightning, because you are convinced that the sort of noise you heard is seldom caused by anything except lightning. As this example shows, our principle is not only employed to establish the existence of other minds but is habitually assumed, though in a less concrete form, in physics. I say "a less concrete form" because unseen lightning is only abstractly similar to seen lightning, whereas we suppose the similarity of other minds to our own to be by no means purely abstract.

Complexity in the observed behavior of another person, when this can all be accounted for by a simple cause such as thirst, increases the probability of the inference by diminishing the probability of some other cause. I think that in ideally favorable circumstances the argument would be formally as follows:

From subjective observation I know that A, which is a thought or feeling, causes B, which is a bodily act, e.g., a statement. I know also that, whenever B is an act of my own body, A is its cause. I now observe an act of the kind B in a body not my own, and I am having no thought or feeling of the kind A. But I still believe, on the basis of self-observation, that only A can cause B; I therefore infer that there was an A which caused B, though it was not an A that I could observe. On this ground I infer that other people's bodies are associated with minds, which resemble mine in proportion as their bodily behavior resembles my own.

In practice, the exactness and certainty of the above statement must be softened. We cannot be sure that, in our subjective experience, A is the only cause of B. And even if A is the only cause of B in our experience, how can we know that this holds outside our experience? It is not necessary that we should know this with any certainty; it is enough if it is highly probable. It is the assumption of

OTHER MINDS ARE KNOWN BY ANALOGY FROM ONE'S OWN CASE

probability in such cases that is our postulate. The postulate may therefore be stated as follows:

> If, whenever we can observe whether A and B are present or absent, we find that every case of B has an A as a causal antecedent, then it is probable that most B's have A's as causal antecedents, even in cases where observation does not enable us to know whether A is present or not.

This postulate, if accepted, justifies the inference to other minds, as well as many other inferences that are made unreflectingly by common sense.

Mental Processes Are Physical

· J. J. C. SMART ·

In this excerpt from "Sensations and Brain Processes" (1959), Smart defends the mind/ brain identity theory against a number of objections.

... The suggestion I wish if possible to avoid is ... that [such a statement as] "I am in pain" is a genuine report, and that what it reports is an irreducibly psychical something. . . .

Why do I wish to avoid this suggestion? Mainly because of Occam's razor. It seems to me that science is increasingly giving us a viewpoint whereby organisms are able to be seen as physiochemical mechanisms; it seems that the behavior of man himself will one day be explicable in mechanistic terms. There does seem to be, so far as science is concerned, nothing in the world but increasingly complex arrangements of physical constituents. All except for one place: in consciousness. That is, for a full description of what is going on in a man you would have to describe not only the physical processes in his tissues, glands, nervous system, and so forth, but also his states of consciousness: his visual, auditory, and tactual sensations, his aches and pains. That these are *correlated* with brain processes does not help, for to say that they are *correlated* [with them] is to say that they are something "over and above" [them]. You cannot correlate something with itself. You correlate footprints with burglars, but not Bill Sykes the burglar with Bill Sykes the burglar. So sensations, states of consciousness, do seem to be the one sort of thing left outside the physicalist picture, and for various reasons I just cannot believe that this can be so. That everything should be explicable in terms of physics (together of course with descriptions of the ways in which parts are put together . . .) except the occurrence of sensations seems to me frankly unbelievable. . . . [I]t is the object of this paper to show that there are no philosophical arguments which compel us to be dualists. . . .

Why should not sensations just be brain processes of a certain sort? There are, of course, well known . . . philosophical objections to the view that reports of sensations are reports of brain processes, but I shall try to argue that these arguments are by no means as cogent as is commonly thought to be the case.

Let me first try to state more accurately the thesis that sensations are brain processes. It is not the thesis that, for example . . . "ache" means the same as "brain process of sort X" (where "X" is replaced by a description of a certain sort of brain process). It is that, in so far as "ache" [i.e., "so and so has an ache"] is the report of a process, it is a report of a process that *happens to be* a brain process. It follows that the thesis does not claim that sensations statements can be *translated* into statements about brain processes. Nor does it claim that the logic of a sensation statement is the same as that of a brain-process statement. All it claims is that in so far as a sensation statement is a report of something, that something is in fact a brain process. Sensations are nothing over and above brain processes. Nations are nothing "over and above" citizens, but this does not prevent the logic of nation statements from being very different from the logic of citizen statements, nor does it insure the translatability of nation statements into citizen statements.

When I say that a sensation is a brain process or that lightning is an electrical discharge, I am using "is" in the sense of strict identity. (Just as in the . . . proposition "7 is identical with the smallest prime number greater than 5".) When I say that a sensation is a brain process or that lightning is an electrical discharge I do not mean just that the sensation is somehow spatially or temporally continuous with the brain process or that the lightning is just spatially or temporally continuous with the discharge. . . .

I shall now discuss various possible objections to the view that the processes reported in sensation statements are in fact processes in the brain. Most of us have met some of these objections in our first year as philosophy students. All the more reason to take a good look at them. . . .

Objection 1. Any illiterate peasant can talk perfectly well about . . . how things look or feel to him, or about his aches and pains, and yet he may know nothing whatever about neurophysiology. A man may, like Aristotle, believe that the brain is an organ for cooling the body without any impairment of his ability to make true statements about his sensations. Hence the things we are talking about when we describe our sensations cannot be processes in the brain.

Reply. You might as well say that a nation of slugabeds, who never saw the Morning Star or knew of its existence, or who had never thought of the expression, "The Morning Star", but who used the expression "The Evening Star" perfectly well, would not use this expression to refer to the same entity as we refer to (and describe as) "the Morning Star". (Or consider the example of lightning). Modern physical science tells us that lightning is a certain kind of electrical discharge due to ionization of clouds of water vapor in the atmosphere. This, it is now believed, is what the true nature of lightning is. Note that there are not two things: a flash of lightning and an electrical discharge. There is one thing, a flash of lightning which is described scientifically as an electrical discharge to the earth from a cloud of ionized water molecules. The case is not at all like that of explaining a footprint by reference to a burglar. [In that case the footprints

MENTAL
PROCESSES ARE
PHYSICAL

were *caused by* the burglar, and of course the burglar is not the same thing as the footprints; but the lightning is not *caused by* an electrical discharge—it is one and the same thing as an electrical discharge.] We say what lightning really is, what its true nature as revealed by science is, is an electrical discharge. (It is not the true nature of a footprint to be a burglar.)

In short, the reply to Objection 1 is that there can be contingent statements of the form "A is identical with B", and a person may well know that something is an A without knowing that it is a B. An illiterate peasant might well be able to talk about his sensations without knowing about his brain processes, just as he can talk about lightning though he knows nothing of electricity.

Objection 2. It is only a contingent fact . . . that when we have a certain kind of sensation there is a certain kind of process in our brain. Indeed it is possible, though perhaps in the highest degree unlikely, that our present physiological theories will be as out of date as the ancient theory connecting mental processes with goings on in the heart. It follows that when we report a sensation we are not reporting brain processes.

Reply. The objection certainly proves that when we say "I have an [ache]" we cannot *mean* something of the form "I have such and such a brain process." But this does not show that what we report (having [an ache]) is not in *fact* a brain process. "I see lightning" does not *mean* "I see an electrical discharge". Indeed, it is logically possible (though highly unlikely) that the electrical discharge account of lightning might some day be given up. [But of course the fact that this is logically possible does not mean that that theory *is* incorrect, nor, therefore, that "lightning" reports are not in fact reports of electrical discharges.] . . .

. . . *Objection 4.* The [sensation] is not in physical space. The brain process is. So the [sensation] is not a brain process.

Reply. This is an *ignoratio elenchi* [i.e., an argument directed against something that is not being asserted]. I am not arguing that the [sensation] is a brain process, but that the experience of having [a sensation] is a brain process. It is the *experience* which is reported in the introspective report. [Consider an "afterimage", like the one you get after you look at the sun and then close your eyes.] Similarly, if it is objected that the afterimage is yellowy-orange [whereas the brain process is *not* yellowy-orange], my reply is that it is the experience of seeing yellowy-orange that is being described, and this experience is not a yellowy-orange something. So to say that a brain process cannot be yellowy-orange is not to say that a brain process can not be in fact the experience of having a yellowy-orange after-image. . . .

Objection 5. It would make sense to say of a molecular movement in the brain that it is swift or slow, straight or circular, but it makes no sense to say this of the experience of seeing something yellow. [Therefore, that experience cannot be *the same thing* as *e.g.* that molecular movement.]

Reply. So far we have not given sense to talk of experience as swift or slow, straight or circular. But I am not claiming that [the words] "experience" and "brain process" mean the same or even that they have the same logic. "Somebody" and "the doctor" do not have the same logic, but this does not lead us to suppose that talking about somebody telephoning is talking about someone over and above, say, the doctor. The ordinary man when he reports an experience is reporting that something is going on, but he leaves it open as to what sort of thing is going on, whether in a material solid medium or perhaps in some sort of gaseous medium, or even perhaps in some sort of nonspatial medium (if this makes sense). All that I am saying is that "experience" and "brain process" may in fact refer to the same thing, and if so we may easily adopt a convention . . . whereby it would make sense to talk of an experience in terms appropriate to physical processes.

Objection 6. Sensations are private, brain processes are *public.* If I sincerely say, "I see a yellowy-orange after-image", and I am not making a verbal mistake, then I cannot be wrong. But I can be wrong about a brain process. The scientist looking into my brain [and reporting upon what processes are apparently going on in there] might be having an illusion. Moreover, it makes sense to say that two or more people are observing the same brain process but not that two or more people are reporting the same inner experience.

Reply. This shows that the language of introspective reports has a different logic from the language of material processes. It is obvious that until the brain-process theory is much improved and widely accepted there will be no *criteria* for saying "Smith has an experience of such and such a sort" *except* Smith's introspective reports. So we have adopted a rule of language that (normally) what Smith says goes.

Objection 7. I can imagine myself turned to stone and yet having images, aches, pains, and so on. [So it could happen that there were *no* brain processes going on in me and yet I still had sensations; so sensations cannot *be* processes.]

Reply. I can imagine that the electrical theory of lightning is false, that lightning is some sort of purely optical phenomenon. I can imagine that lightning is not an electrical discharge . . . All the objection shows is that "experience" and "brain process" do not have the same meaning. It does not show that an experience is not in fact a brain process. . . .

I have now considered a number of objections to the brain-process thesis. I wish to conclude with some remarks on the logical status of the thesis itself. U.T. Place seems to hold that it is a straight-out scientific hypothesis. If so, he is partly right and partly wrong. If the issue is between (say) a brain-process thesis [i.e. sensations are brain processes] and a heart thesis [sensations are heart processes], or a liver thesis, then the issue is purely an empirical one, and the verdict is overwhelmingly in favor of the brain. The right sorts of things don't go on in the heart, liver, or kidney, nor do these organs possess the right sort of complexity of structure. On the other hand, if the issue is between a brain-or-liver-or-kidney thesis (that is, some form of materialism on the one hand and epiphenomenalism [a form of dualism] on the other hand, then the issue is not an empirical one. For there is no conceivable experiment which could decide between materialism and epiphenomenalism. The latter issue is not the average straight-out empirical issue in science, but like that between the 19th century English naturalist Philip Gosse and the orthodox geologists and paleontologists of his day. According to Gosse, the earth was created about 4000 B.C. exactly as described in *Genesis,* with twisted rock strata, "evidence" of erosion, and so forth, and all sorts of fossils, all in their appropriate strata, just as if the usual evolutionist story had been a true one. Let us ignore the theological setting in which Gosse's hypothesis had been placed, thus ruling out objections of a theological kind, such as "what a queer God who would go to such lengths to deceive us". Let us suppose that it is held that the universe [was not created by a God but] just *began* in 4004 B.C. with the initial conditions just everywhere as they were in 4004 B.C., and in particular that our own planet began with sediment in the rivers, eroded cliffs, fossils in the rocks, and so on. No scientist would ever entertain this as a serious hypothesis, consistent though it is with all possible evidence. The hypothesis offends against the principles of parsimony and simplicity. There would be far too many brute and inexplicable facts. Why are pterodactyl bones just as they are? No explanation in terms of the evolution of pterodactyls from earlier forms of life would any longer be possible. We would have millions of facts about the world as it was in 4004 B.C. that just have to be *accepted* [—i.e, facts that cannot be explained].

The issue between the brain process theory and epiphenomenalism seems to be of the above sort. . . . If it be agreed that there are no cogent philosophical arguments which force us into accepting dualism, and if the brain process theory and dualism are equally consistent with the facts, then the principles of parsimony and simplicity seem to me to decide overwhelmingly in favor of the brain process theory. As I pointed out earlier, dualism involves a large number of irreducible psycho-physical laws . . . of a queer sort, that just have to be taken on trust, and are just as difficult to swallow as the irreducible facts about the paleontology of the earth with which we are faced on Philip Gosse's theory.

Computing Machinery and Intelligence

· A. M. TURING ·

Alan Turing (1912–1954) was a founder of the mathematical theory of computation, on which all computer design rests. In his article "Computing Machinery and Intelligence" (1950), Turing does three things. He considers (and rejects) various reasons that might be offered for thinking that computers could never think. He describes the basic idea of a computer program. Finally, he proposes a behavioral test for determining whether a machine is thinking.

1. The Imitation Game

I propose to consider the question "Can machines think?" This should begin with definitions of the meaning of the terms "machine" and "think." The definitions might be framed so as to reflect so far as possible the normal use of the words, but this attitude is dangerous. If the meaning of the words "machine" and "think" are to be found by examining how they are commonly used it is difficult to escape the conclusion that the meaning and the answer to the question, "Can machines think?" is to be sought in a statistical survey such as a Gallup poll. But this is absurd. Instead of attempting such a definition I shall replace the question by another, which is closely related to it and is expressd in relatively unambiguous words.

The new form of the problem can be described in terms of a game which we call the "imitation game." It is played with three people, a man (A), a woman (B), and an interrogator (C) who may be of either sex. The interrogator stays in a room apart from the other two. The object of the game for the interrogator is to determine which of the other two is the man and which is the woman. He knows them by labels X and Y, and at the end of the game he says either "X is A and Y is B" or "X is B and Y is A." The interrogator is allowed to put questions to A and B thus:

C: Will X please tell me the length of his or her hair?

Now suppose X is actually A, then A must answer. It is A's object in the game to try to cause C to make the wrong identification. His answer might therefore be

"My hair is shingled, and the longest strands are about nine inches long."

In order that tones of voice may not help the interrogator the answers should be written, or better still, typewritten. The ideal arrangement is to have a tele-printer communicating between the two rooms. Alternatively the question and answers can be repeated by an intermediary. The object of the game for the third player (B) is to help the interrogator. The best strategy for her is probably to give truthful answers. She can add such things as "I am the woman, don't listen to him!" to her answers, but it will avail nothing as the man can make similar remarks.

We now ask the question, "What will happen when a machine takes the part of A in this game?" Will the interrogator decide wrongly as often when the game is played like this as he does when the game is played between a man and a woman? These questions replace our original, "Can machines think?"

2. Critique of the New Problem

As well as asking, "What is the answer to this new form of the question," one may ask, "Is this new question a worthy one to investigate?" This latter question we investigate without further ado, thereby cutting short an infinite regress.

The new problem has the advantage of drawing a fairly sharp line between the physical and the intellectual capacities of a man. No engineer or chemist claims to be able to produce a material which is indistinguishable from the human skin. It is possible that at some time this might be done, but even supposing this invention available we should feel there was little point in trying to make a "thinking machine" more human by dressing it up in such artificial flesh. The

COMPUTING MACHINERY AND INTELLIGENCE

form in which we have set the problem reflects this fact in the condition which prevents the interrogator from seeing or touching the other competitors, or hearing their voices. Some other advantages of the proposed criterion may be shown up by specimen questions and answers. Thus:

Q: Please write me a sonnet on the subject of the Forth Bridge.
A: Count me out on this one. I never could write poetry.
Q: Add 34957 to 70764.
A: (Pause about 30 seconds and then give as answer) 105621.
Q: Do you play chess?
A: Yes.
Q: I have K at my K1, and no other pieces. You have only K at K6 and R at R1. It is your move. What do you play?
A: (After a pause of 15 seconds) R-R8 mate.

The question and answer method seems to be suitable for introducing almost any one of the fields of human endeavor that we wish to include. We do not wish to penalize the machine for its inability to shine in beauty competitions, nor to penalize a man for losing in a race against an airplane. The conditions of our game make these disabilities irrelevant. The "witnesses" can brag, if they consider it advisable, as much as they please about their charms, strength or heroism, but the interrogator cannot demand practical demonstrations.

The game may perhaps be criticized on the ground that the odds are weighted too heavily against the machine. If the man were to try and pretend to be the machine he would clearly make a very poor showing. He would be given away at once by slowness and inaccuracy in arithmetic. May not machines carry out something which ought to be described as thinking but which is very different from what a man does? This objection is a very strong one, but at least we can say that if, nevertheless, a machine can be constructed to play the imitation game satisfactorily, we need not be troubled by this objection.

It might be urged that when playing the "imitation game" the best strategy for the machine may possibly be something other than imitation of the behavior of man. This may be, but I think it is unlikely that there is any great effect of this kind. In any case there is no intention to investigate here the theory of the game, and it will be assumed that the best strategy is to try to provide answers that would naturally be given by a man.

3. The Machines Concerned in the Game

The question which we put in §1 will not be quite definite until we have specified what we mean by the word "machine." It is natural that we should wish to permit every kind of engineering technique to be used in our machines. We also wish to allow the possibility that an engineer or team of engineers may construct a machine which works, but whose manner of operation cannot be satisfactorily described by its constructors because they have applied a method which is largely experimental. Finally, we wish to exclude from the machines men born in the usual manner. It is difficult to frame the definitions so as to satisfy these three conditions. One might for instance insist that the team of engineers should be all of one sex, but this would not really be satisfactory, for it is probably possible to rear a complete individual from a single cell of the skin (say) of a man. To do so would be a feat of biological technique deserving of the very highest praise, but we would not be inclined to regard it as a case of "constructing a thinking machine." This prompts us to abandon the requirement that every kind of technique should be permitted. We are the more ready to do so in view of the fact that the present interest in "thinking machines" has been aroused by a particular kind of machine usually called an "electronic computer" or "digital computer." Following this suggestion we only permit digital computers to take part in our game.

This restriction appears at first sight to be a very drastic one. I shall attempt to show that it is not so in reality. To do this necessitates a short account of the nature and properties of these computers.

It may also be said that this identification of machines with digital computers, like our criterion for "thinking," will only be unsatisfactory if (contrary to my belief), it turns out that digital computers are unable to give a good showing in the game.

There are already a number of digital computers in working order, and it may be asked, "Why not try the experiment straight away? It would be easy to satisfy the conditions of the game. A number of interrogators could be used, and statistics compiled to show how often the right identification was given." The short answer is that we are not asking whether all digital computers would do well in the game nor whether the computers at present available would do well, but whether there are imaginable computers which would do well. But this is only the short answer. We shall see this question in a different light later.

4. Digital Computers

The idea behind digital computers may be explained by saying that these machines are intended to carry out any operations which could be done by a human computer. The human computer is supposed to be following fixed rules; he has no authority to deviate from them in any detail. We may suppose that these rules are supplied in a book, which is altered whenever he is put on to a new job. He has also an unlimited supply of paper on which he does his calculations. He may also do his multiplications and additions on a "desk machine," but this is not important.

If we use the above explanation as a definition we shall be in danger of circularity of argument. We avoid this by giving an outline of the means by which the desired effect is achieved. A digital computer can usually be regarded as consisting of three parts:

(i) Store.

(ii) Executive unit.

(iii) Control.

The store is a store of information, and corresponds to the human computer's paper, whether this is the paper on which he does his calculations or that on which his book of rules is printed. Insofar as the human computer does calculations in his head a part of the store will correspond to his memory.

The executive unit is the part which carries out the various individual operations involved in a calculation. What these individual operations are will vary from machine to machine. Usually fairly lengthy operations can be done such as "Multiply 3540675445 by 7076345687" but in some machines only very simple ones such as "Write down 0" are possible.

We have mentioned that the "book of rules" supplied to the computer is replaced in the machine by a part of the store. It is then called the "table of instructions." It is the duty of the control to see that these instructions are obeyed correctly and in the right order. The control is so constructed that this necessarily happens.

The information in the store is usually broken up into packets of moderately small size. In one machine, for instance, a packet might consist of ten decimal digits. Numbers are assigned to the parts of the store in which the various packets of information are stored, in some systematic manner. A typical instuction might say —

"Add the number stored in position 6809 to that in 4302 and put the result back into the latter storage position."

Needless to say it would not occur in the machine expressed in English. It would more likely be coded in a form such as 6809430217. Here 17 says which of various possible operations is to be performed on the two numbers. In this case the operation is that described above, viz. "Add the number. . . ." It will be noticed that the instruction takes up 10 digits and so forms one packet of information, very conveniently. The control will normally take the instructions to be obeyed in the order of the positions in which they are stored, but occasionally an instruction such as

"Now obey the instruction stored in position 5606, and continue from there"

may be encountered, or again

"If position 4505 contains 0 obey next the instruction stored in 6707, otherwise continue straight on."

Instructions of these latter types are very important because they make it possible for a sequence of operations to be repeated over and over again until some condition is fulfilled, but in doing so to obey, not fresh instructions on each repetition, but the same ones over and over again. To take a domestic analogy. Suppose Mother wants Tommy to call at the cobbler's every morning on his way to school to see if her shoes are done; she can ask him afresh every morning. Alternatively she can stick up a notice once and for all in the hall which he will see when he leaves for school and which tells him to call for the shoes, and also to destroy the notice when he comes back if he has the shoes with him.

The reader must accept it as a fact that digital computers can be constructed, and indeed have been constructed, according to the principles we have described, and that they can in fact mimic the actions of a human computer very closely.

The book of rules which we have described our human computer as using is of course a convenient fiction. Actual human computers really remember what they have got to do. If one wants to make a machine mimic the behavior of the human computer in some complex operation one has to ask him how it is done, and then translate the answer into the form of an instruction table. Constructing instruction tables is usually described as "programming." To "program a machine to carry out the operation A" means to put the appropriate instruction table into the machine so that it will do A.

An interesting variant on the idea of a digital computer is a "digital computer with a random element." These have instructions involving the throwing of a die or some equivalent electronic process; one such instruction might for instance be, "Throw the die and put the resulting number into store 1000." Sometimes such a machine is described as having free will (though I would not use this phrase myself). It is not normally possible to determine from observing a machine whether it has a random element, for a similar effect can be produced by such devices as making the choices depend on the digits of the decimal for π.

Most actual digital computers have only a finite store. There is no theoretical difficulty in the idea of a computer with an unlimited store. Of course only a finite part can have been used at any one time. Likewise only a finite amount can have been constructed, but we can imagine more and more being added as required. Such computers have special theoretical interest and will be called infinite capacity computers.

The idea of a digital computer is an old one. Charles Babbage, Lucasian Professor of Mathematics at Cambridge from 1828 to 1839, planned such a machine, called the Analytical Engine, but it was never completed. Although Babbage had all the essential ideas, his machine was not at that time such a very attractive prospect. The speed which would have been available would be definitely faster than a human computer but something like 100 times slower than the Manchester machine, itself one of the slower of the modern machines. The storage was to be purely mechanical, using wheels and cards.

The fact that Babbage's Analytical Engine was to be entirely mechanical will help us to rid ourselves of a superstition. Importance is often attached to the fact that modern digital computers are electrical, and that the nervous system also is electrical. Since Babbage's machine was not electrical, and since all digital computers are in a sense equivalent, we see that this use of electricity cannot be of theoretical importance. Of course electricity usually comes in where fast signaling is concerned, so that it is not surprising that we find it in both these connections. In the nervous system chemical phenomena are at least as important as electrical.

In certain computers the storage system is mainly acoustic. The feature of using electricity is thus seen to be only a very superficial similarity. If we wish to find such similarities we should look rather for mathematical analogies of function.

5. Universality of Digital Computers

The digital computers considered in the last section may be classified among the "discrete state machines." These are the machines which move by sudden jumps or clicks from one quite definite state to another. These states are sufficiently different for the possibility of confusion between them to be ignored. Strictly speaking there are no such machines. Everything really moves continuously. But there are many kinds of machines which can profitably be *thought of* as being discrete state machines. For instance in considering the switches for a lighting system it is a convenient fiction that each switch must be definitely on or definitely off. There must be intermediate positions, but for most purposes we can forget about them. As an example of a discrete state machine we might consider a wheel which clicks round through 120° once a second, but may be stopped by a lever which can be operated from outside; in addition a lamp is to light in one of the positions of the wheel. This machine could be described abstractly as follows: The internal state of the machine (which is described by the position of the wheel) may be q_1, q_2 or q_3. There is an input signal i_0 or i_1 (position of lever). The internal state at any moment is determined by the last state and input signal according to the table

	Last State		
	q_1	q_2	q_3
i_0	q_2	q_3	q_1
Input			
i_1	q_1	q_2	q_3

The output signals, the only externally visible indication of the internal state (the light) are described by the table

State		
q_1	q_2	q_3
Output		
o_0	o_0	o_1

This example is typical of discrete state machines. They can be described by such tables provided they have only a finite number of possible states.

It will seem that given the initial state of the machine and the input signals it is always possible to predict all future states. This is reminiscent of Laplace's view that from the complete state of the universe at one moment of time, as described by the positions and velocities of all particles, it should be possible to predict all future states. The prediction which we are considering is, however, rather nearer to practicability than that considered by Laplace. The system of the "universe as a whole" is such that quite small errors in the initial conditions can have an overwhelming effect at a later time. The displacement of a single electron by a billionth of a centimeter at one moment might make the difference between a man being killed by an avalanche a year later, or escaping. It is an essential property of the mechanical systems which we have called "discrete state machines" that this phenomenon does not occur. Even when we consider the actual physical machines instead of the idealized machines, reasonably accurate knowledge of the state at one moment yields reasonably accurate knowledge any number of steps later.

As we have mentioned, digital computers fall within the class of discrete state machines. But the number of states of which such a machine is capable is usually enormously large. For instance, the number for the machine now working at Manchester is about $2^{165,000}$, i.e., about $10^{50,000}$. Compare this with our example of the clicking wheel described above, which had three states. It is not difficult to see why the number of states should be so immense. The computer includes a store corresponding to the paper used by a human computer. It must be possible to write into the store any one of the combinations of symbols which might have been written in the paper. For simplicity suppose that only digits from 0 to 9 are used as symbols. Variations in handwriting are ignored. Suppose the computer is allowed 100 sheets of paper each containing 50 lines each with room for 30 digits. Then the number of states is $10^{100 \times 50 \times 30}$, i.e., $10^{150,000}$. This is about the number of states of three Manchester machines put together. The logarithm to the base two of the number of states is usually called the "storage capacity" of the machine. Thus the Manchester machine has a storage capacity of about 165,000 and the wheel machine of our example about 1.6. If two machines are put together their capacities must be added to obtain the capacity of the resultant machine. This leads to the possibility of statements such as "The Manchester machine contains 64 magnetic tracks each with a capacity of 2560, eight electronic tubes with a capacity of 1280. Miscellaneous storage amounts to about 300 making a total of 174,380."

Given the table corresponding to a discrete state machine it is possible to predict what it will do. There is no reason why this calculation should not be carried out by means of a digital computer. Provided it could be carried out sufficiently quickly the digital computer could mimic the behavior of any discrete state machine. The imitation game could then be played with the machine in question (as B) and the mimicking digital computer (as A) and the interrogator would be unable to distinguish them. Of course the digital computer must have an adequate storage capacity as well as working sufficiently fast. Morover, it must be programed afresh for each new machine which it is desired to mimic.

This special property of digital computers, that they can mimic any discrete state machine, is described by saying that they are *universal* machines. The existence of machines with this property has the important consequence that, considerations of speed apart, it is unnecessary to design various new machines to do various computing processses. They can all be done with one digital computer, suitably programed for each case. It will be seen that as a consequence of this all digital computers are in a sense equivalent.

We may now consider again the point raised at the end of §3. It was suggested tentatively that the question, "Can machines think?" should be replaced by "Are there imaginable digital computers which would do well in the imitation game?" If we wish we can make this superficially more general and ask "Are there discrete state machines which would do well?" But in view of the universality property we see that either of these questions is equivalent to this, "Let us fix our attention on one particular digital computer C. Is it true that by modifying this computer to have an adequate storage, suitably increasing its speed of action, and providing it with an appropriate program, C can be made to play satisfactorily the part of A in the imitation game, the part of B being taken by a man?"

6. Contrary Views on the Main Question

We may now consider the ground to have been cleared and we are ready to proceed to the debate on our question, "Can machines think?" and the variant of it quoted at the end of the last section. We cannot altogether abandon the original form of the problem, for opinions will differ as to the appropriateness of the substitution and we must at least listen to what has to be said in this connection.

It will simplify matters for the reader if I explain first my own beliefs in the matter. Consider first the more accurate form of the question. I believe that in about fifty years' time it will be possible to program computers, with a storage capacity of about 10^9, to make them play the imitation game so well that an average interrogator will not have more than 70 per cent chance of making the right identification after five minutes of questioning. The original question, "Can machines think?" I believe to be too meaningless to deserve discussion. Nevertheless I believe that at the end of the century the use of words and general educated opinion will have altered so much that one will be able to speak of machines thinking without expecting to be contradicted. I believe further that no useful purpose is served by concealing these beliefs. The popular view that scientists proceed inexorably from well-established fact to well-established fact, never being influenced by any unproved conjecture, is quite mistaken. Provided it is made clear which are proved facts and which are conjectures, no harm can result. Conjectures are of great importance since they suggest useful lines of research.

I now proceed to consider opinions opposed to my own.

(1) The Theological Objection. Thinking is a function of man's immortal soul. God has given an immortal soul to every man and woman, but not to any other animal or to machines. Hence no animal or machine can think.[1]

I am unable to accept any part of this, but will attempt to reply in theological terms. I should find the argument more convincing if animals were classed with men, for there is a greater difference, to my mind, between the typical animate and the inanimate than there is between man and the other animals. The arbitrary character of the orthodox view becomes clearer if we consider how it might appear to a member of some other religious community. How do Christians regard the Moslem view that women have no souls? But let us leave this point aside and return to the main argument. It appears to me that the argument quoted above implies a serious restriction of the omnipotence of the Almighty. It is admitted that there are certain things that He cannot do such as making one equal to two, but should we not believe that He has freedom to confer a soul on an elephant if He sees fit? We might expect that He would only exercise this power in conjunction with a mutation which provided the elephant with an appropriately improved brain to minister to the needs of this soul. An argument of exactly similar form may be made for the case of machines. It may seem different because it is more difficult to "swallow." But this really only means that we think it would be less likely that He would consider the circumstances suitable for conferring a soul. The circumstances in question are discussed in the rest of this paper. In attempting to construct such machines we should not be irreverently usurping His power of creating souls, any more than we are in the procreation of children: rather we are, in either case, instruments of His will providing mansions for the souls that He creates.

However, this is mere speculation. I am not very impressed with theological arguments whatever they may be used to support. Such arguments have often been found unsatisfactory in the past. In the time of Galileo it was argued that the texts, "And the sun stood still . . . and hasted not to go down about a whole day" (Joshua x. 13) and "He laid the foundations of the earth, that it should not move at any time" (Psalm cv. 5) were an adequate refutation of the Copernican theory. With our present knowledge such an argument appears futile. When that knowledge was not available it made a quite different impression.

(2) The "Heads in the Sand" Objection. "The consequences of machines thinking would be too dreadful. Let us hope and believe that they cannot do so."

This argument is seldom expressed quite so openly as in the form above. But it affects most of us who think about it at all. We like to believe that Man is in some subtle way superior to the rest of creation. It is best if he can be shown to be *necessarily* superior, for then there is no danger of him losing his commanding position. The popularity of the theological argument is clearly connected with this feeling. It is likely to be quite strong in intellectual people, since they value the power of thinking more highly than others, and are more inclined to base their belief in the superiority of Man on this power.

I do not think that this argument is sufficiently substantial to require refutation. Consolation would be more appropriate; perhaps this should be sought in the transmigration of souls.

(3) The Mathematical Objection. There are a number of results of mathematical logic which can be used to show that there are limitations to the powers of discrete state machines. The best known of these results is known as Gödel's theorem, and shows that in any sufficiently powerful logical system statements can be formulated which can neither be proved nor disproved within the system, unless possibly the system itself is inconsistent. There are other, in some respects similar, results due to Church, Kleene, Rosser, and Turing. The latter result is the most convenient to consider, since it refers directly to machines, whereas the

COMPUTING
MACHINERY AND
INTELLIGENCE

others can only be used in a comparatively indirect argument: for instance if Gödel's theorem is to be used we need in addition to have some means of describing logical systems in terms of machines, and machines in terms of logical systems. The result in question refers to a type of machine which is essentially a digital computer with an infinite capacity. It states that there are certain things that such a machine cannot do. If it is rigged up to give answers to questions as in the imitation game, there will be some questions to which it will either give a wrong answer, or fail to give an answer at all however much time is allowed for a reply. There may, of course, be many such questions, and questions which cannot be answered by one machine may be satisfactorily answered by another. We are of course supposing for the present that the questions are of the kind to which an answer "Yes" or "No" is appropriate, rather than questions such as "What do you think of Picasso?" The questions that we know the machines must fail on are of this type, "Consider the machine specified as follows. ... Will this machine ever answer 'Yes' to any question?" The dots are to be replaced by a description of some machine in a standard form, which could be something like that used in §5. When the machine described bears a certain comparatively simple relation to the machine which is under interrogation, it can be shown that the answer is either wrong or not forthcoming. This is the mathematical result: it is argued that it proves a disability of machines to which the human intellect is not subject.

The short answer to this argument is that although it is established that there are limitations to the powers of any particular machine, it has only been stated, without any sort of proof, that no such limitations apply to the human intellect. But I do not think this view can be dismissed quite so lightly. Whenever one of these machines is asked the appropriate critical question, and gives a definite answer, we know that this answer must be wrong, and this gives us a certain feeling of superiority. Is this feeling illusory? It is no doubt quite genuine, but I do not think too much importance should be attached to it. We too often give wrong answers to questions ourselves to be justified in being very pleased at such evidence of fallibility on the part of the machines. Further, our superiority can only be felt on such an occasion in relation to the one machine over which we have scored our petty triumph. There would be no question of triumphing simultaneously over *all* machines. In short, then, there might be men cleverer than any given machine, but then again there might be other machines cleverer again, and so on.

Those who hold to the mathematical argument would, I think, mostly be willing to accept the imitation game as a basis for discussion. Those who believe in the two previous objections would probably not be interested in any criteria.

(4) The Argument from Consciousness. This argument is very well expressed in Professor Jefferson's Lister Oration for 1949, from which I quote. "Not until a machine can write a sonnet or compose a concerto because of thoughts and emotions felt, and not by the chance fall of symbols, could we agree that machine equals brain—that is, not only write it but know that it had written it. No mechanism could feel (and not merely artificially signal, an easy contrivance)

pleasure at its successes, grief when its valves fuse, be warmed by flattery, be made miserable by its mistakes, be charmed by sex, be angry or depressed when it cannot get what it wants."

This argument appears to be a denial of the validity of our test. According to the most extreme form of this view the only way by which one could be sure that a machine thinks is to *be* the machine and to feel oneself thinking. One could then describe these feelings to the world, but of course no one would be justified in taking any notice. Likewise according to this view the only way to know that a *man* thinks is to be that particular man. It is in fact the solipsist point of view. It may be the most logical view to hold but it makes communication of ideas difficult. A is liable to believe "A thinks but B does not" while B believes "B thinks but A does not." Instead of arguing continually over this point it is usual to have the polite convention that everyone thinks.

I am sure that Professor Jefferson does not wish to adopt the extreme and solipsist point of view. Probably he would be quite willing to accept the imitation game as a test. The game (with the player B omitted) is frequently used in practice under the name of *viva voce* to discover whether someone really understands something or has "learned it parrot fashion." Let us listen in to a part of such a *viva voce*:

INTERROGATOR: In the first line of your sonnet which reads "Shall I compare thee to a summer's day," would not a "a spring day" do as well or better?
WITNESS: It wouldn't scan.
I: How about "a winter's day." That would scan all right.
W: Yes, but nobody wants to be compared to a winter's day.
I: Would you say Mr. Pickwick reminded you of Christmas?
W: In a way.
I: Yet Christmas is a winter's day, and I do not think Mr. Pickwick would mind the comparison.
W: I don't think you're serious. By a winter's day one means a typical winter's day, rather than a special one like Christmas.

And so on. What would Professor Jefferson say if the sonnet-writing machine was able to answer like this in the *viva voce*? I do not know whether he would regard the machine as "merely artificially signaling" these answers, but if the answers were as satisfactory and sustained as in the above passage I do not think he would describe it as "an easy contrivance." This phrase is, I think, intended to cover such devices as the inclusion in the machine of a record of someone reading a sonnet, with appropriate switching to turn it on from time to time.

In short then, I think that most of those who support the argument from consciousness could be persuaded to abandon it rather than be forced into the solipsist position. They will then probably be willing to accept our test.

I do not wish to give the impression that I think there is no mystery about consciousness. There is, for instance, something of a paradox connected with any attempt to localize it. But I do not think these mysteries necessarily need to be

COMPUTING
MACHINERY AND
INTELLIGENCE

solved before we can answer the question with which we are concerned in this paper.

(5) Arguments from Various Disabilities. These arguments take the form, "I grant you that you can make machines do all the things you have mentioned but you will never be able to make one to do X." Numerous features X are suggested in this connection. I offer a selection:

> Be kind, resourceful, beautiful, friendly . . . have initiative, have a sense of humor, tell right from wrong, make mistakes . . . fall in love, enjoy strawberries and cream . . . , make someone fall in love with it, learn from experience . . . , use words properly, be the subject of its own thought . . . , have as much diversity of behavior as a man, do something really new . . . .

No support is usually offered for these statements. I believe they are mostly founded on the principle of scientific induction. A man has seen thousands of machines in his lifetime. From what he sees of them he draws a number of general conclusions. They are ugly, each is designed for a very limited purpose, when required for a minutely different purpose they are useless, the variety of behavior of any one of them is very small, etc., etc. Naturally he concludes that these are necessary properties of machines in general. Many of these limitations are associated with the very small storage capacity of most machines. (I am assuming that the idea of storage capacity is extended in some way to cover machines other than discrete state machines. The exact definition does not matter as no mathematical accuracy is claimed in the present discussion.) A few years ago, when very little had been heard of digital computers, it was possible to elicit much incredulity concerning them, if one mentioned their properties without describing their construction. That was presumably due to a similar application of the principle of scientific induction. These applications of the principle are of course largely unconscious. When a burned child fears the fire and shows that he fears it by avoiding it, I should say that he was applying scientific induction. (I could of course also describe his behavior in many other ways.) The works of customs of mankind do not seem to be very suitable material to which to apply scientific induction. A very large part of space-time must be investigated if reliable results are to be obtained. Otherwise we may (as most English children do) decide that everybody speaks English, and that it is silly to learn French.

There are, however, special remarks to be made about many of the disabilities that have been mentioned. The inability to enjoy strawberries and cream may [strike] the reader as frivolous. Possibly a machine might be made to enjoy this delicious dish, but any attempt to make one do so would be idiotic. What is important about this disability is that it contributes to some of the other disabilites, e.g., to the difficulty of the same kind of friendliness occurring between man and machine as between white man and white man, or between black man and black man.

The claim that "machines cannot make mistakes" seems a curious one. One is tempted to retort, "Are they any worse for that?" But let us adopt a more sympathetic attitude, and try to see what is really meant. I think this criticism can be explained in terms of the imitation game. It is claimed that the interrogator could distinguish the machine from the man simply by setting them a number of problems in arithmetic. The machine would be unmasked because of its deadly accuracy. The reply to this is simple. The machine (programed for playing the game) would not attempt to give the *right* answers to the arithmetic problems. It would deliberately introduce mistakes in a manner calculated to confuse the interrogator. A mechanical fault would probably show itself through an unsuitable decision as to what sort of mistake to make in the arithmetic. Even this interpretation of the criticism is not sufficiently sympathetic. But we cannot afford the space to go into it much further. It seems to me that this criticism depends on a confusion between two kinds of mistakes. We may call them "errors of functioning" and "errors of conclusion." Errors of functioning are due to some mechanical or electrical fault which causes the machine to behave otherwise than it was designed to do. In philosophical discussions one likes to ignore the possibility of such errors; one is therefore discussing "abstract machines." These abstract machines are mathematical fictions rather than physical objects. By definition they are incapable of errors of functioning. In this sense we can truly say that "machines can never make mistakes." Errors of conclusion can only arise when some meaning is attached to the output signals from the machine. The machine might, for instance, type out mathematical equations, or sentences in English. When a false proposition is typed we say that the machine has committed an error of conclusion. There is clearly no reason at all for saying that a machine cannot make this kind of mistake. It might do nothing but type out repeatedly "$0 = 1$." To take a less perverse example, it might have some method for drawing conclusions by scientific induction. We must expect such a method to lead occasionally to erroneous results.

The claim that a machine cannot be the subject of its own thought can of course only be answered if it can be shown that the machine has *some* thought with *some* matter. Nevertheless, "the subject matter of a machine's operations" does seem to mean something, at least to the people who deal with it. If, for instance, the machine was trying to find a solution to the equation $x^2 - 40x - 11 = 0$ one would be tempted to describe this equation as part of the machine's subject matter at that moment. In this sort of sense a machine undoubtedly can be its own subject matter. It may be used to help in making up its own programs, or to predict the effect of alterations in its own structure. By observing the results of its own behavior it can modify its own programs so as to achieve some purpose more effectively. These are possibilities of the near future, rather than Utopian dreams.

The criticism that a machine cannot have much diversity of behavior is just a way of saying that it cannot have much storage capacity. Until fairly recently a storage capacity of even a thousand digits was very rare.

The criticisms that we are considering here are often disguised forms of the argument from consciousness. Usually if one maintains that a machine *can* do one of these things, and describes the kind of method that the machine could use, one will not make much of an impression. It is thought that the method (whatever it may be, for it must be mechanical) is really rather base. Compare the parenthesis of Jefferson's statement quoted above.

(6) Lady Lovelace's Objection. Our most detailed information of Babbage's Analytical Engine comes from a memoir by Lady Lovelace. In it she states, "The Analytical Engine has no pretensions to *originate* anything. It can do *whatever we know how to order it* to perform" (her italics). This statement is quoted by Hartree who adds: "This does not imply that it may not be possible to construct electronic equipment which will 'think for itself,' or in which, in biological terms, one could set up a conditioned reflex, which would serve as a basis for 'learning.' Whether this is possible in principle or not is a stimulating and exciting question, suggested by some of these recent developments. But it did not seem that the machines constructed or projected at the time had this property."

I am in thorough agreement with Hartree over this. It will be noticed that he does not assert that the machines in question had not got the property, but rather that the evidence available to Lady Lovelace did not encourage her to believe that they had it. It is quite possible that the machines in question had in a sense got this property. For suppose that some discrete state machine has the property. The Analytical Engine was a universal digital computer, so that, if its storage capacity and speed were adequate, it could by suitable programing be made to mimic the machine in question. Probably this argument did not occur to the Countess or to Babbage. In any case there was no obligation on them to claim all that could be claimed.

This whole question will be considered again under the heading of learning machines.

A variant of Lady Lovelace's objection states that a machine can "never do anything really new." This may be parried for a moment with the saw, "There is nothing new under the sun." Who can be certain that "original work" that he has done was not simply the growth of the seed planted in him by teaching, or the effect of following well-known general principles. A better variant of the objection says that a machine can never "take us by surprise." This statement is a more direct challenge and can be met directly. Machines take me by surprise with great frequency. This is largely because I do not do sufficient calculation to decide what to expect them to do, or rather because, although I do a calculation, I do it in a hurried, slipshod fashion, taking risks. Perhaps I say to myself, "I suppose the voltage here ought to be the same as there: anyway let's assume it is." Naturally I am often wrong, and the result is a surprise for me, for by the time the experiment is done these assumptions have been forgotten. These admissions lay me open to lectures on the subject of my vicious ways, but do not throw any doubt on my credibility when I testify to the surprises I experience.

I do not expect this reply to silence my critic. He will probably say that such surprises are due to some creative mental act on my part, and reflect no credit on the machine. This leads us back to the argument from consciousness, and far from the idea of surprise. It is a line of argument we must consider closed, but it is perhaps worth remarking that the appreciation of something as surprising requires as much of a "creative mental act" whether the surprising event originates from a man, a book, a machine or anything else.

The view that machines cannot give rise to surprises is due, I believe, to a fallacy to which philosophers and mathematicians are particularly subject. This is the assumption that as soon as a fact is presented to a mind all consequences of that fact spring into the mind simultaneously with it. It is a very useful assumption under many circumstances, but one too easily forgets that it is false. A natural consequence of doing so is that one then assumes that there is no virtue in the mere working out of consequences from data and general principles.

(7) Argument from Continuity in the Nervous System. The nervous system is certainly not a discrete state machine. A small error in the information about the size of a nervous impulse impinging on a neuron, may make a large difference to the size of the outgoing impulse. It may be argued that, this being so, one cannot expect to be able to mimic the behavior of the nervous system with a discrete state system.

It is true that a discrete state machine must be different from a continuous machine. But if we adhere to the conditions of the imitation game, the interrogator will not be able to take any advantage of this difference. The situation can be made clearer if we consider some other simpler continuous machine. A differential analyzer will do very well. (A differential analyzer is a certain kind of machine not of the discrete state type used for some kinds of calculation.) Some of these provide their answers in a typed form, and so are suitable for taking part in the game. It would not be possible for a digital computer to predict exactly what answers the differential analyzer would give to a problem, but it would be quite capable of giving the right sort of answer. For instance, if asked to give the value of π (actually about 3·1416) it would be reasonable to choose at random between the values 3·12, 3·13, 3·14, 3·15, 3·16 with the probabilities of 0·05, 0·15, 0·55, 0·19, 0·06 (say). Under the circumstances it would be very difficult for the interrogator to distinguish the differential analyzer from the digital computer.

(8) The Argument from Informality of Behavior. It is not possible to produce a set of rules purporting to describe what a man should do in every conceivable set of circumstances. One might for instance have a rule that one is to stop when one sees a red traffic light, and to go if one sees a green one, but what if by some fault both appear together? One may perhaps decide that it is safest to stop. But some further difficulty may well arise from this decision later. To attempt to provide rules of conduct to cover every eventuality, even those arising from traffic lights, appears to be impossible. With all this I agree.

From this it is argued that we cannot be machines. I shall try to reproduce the argument, but I fear I shall hardly do it justice. It seems to run something like this. "If each man had a definite set of rules of conduct by which he regulated his life he would be no better than a machine. But there are no such rules, so men cannot be machines." The undistributed middle is glaring. I do not think the argument is ever put quite like this, but I believe this is the argument used nevertheless. There may however be a certain confusion between "rules of conduct" and "laws of behavior" to cloud the issue. By "rules of conduct" I mean precepts such as "Stop if you see red lights," on which one can act, and of which one can be conscious. By "laws of behavior" I mean laws of nature as applied to a man's body such as "if you pinch him he will squeak." If we substitute "laws of behavior which regulate his life" for "laws of conduct by which he regulates his life" in the argument quoted the undistributed middle is no longer insuperable. For we believe that it is not only true that being regulated by laws of behavior implies being some sort of machine (though not necessarily a discrete state machine), but that conversely being such a machine implies being regulated by such laws. However, we cannot so easily convince ourselves of the absence of complete laws of behavior as of complete rules of conduct. The only way we know of for finding such laws is scientific observation, and we certainly know of no circumstances under which we could say, "We have searched enough. There are no such laws."

We can demonstrate more forcibly that any such statement would be unjustified. For suppose we could be sure of finding such laws if they existed. Then given a discrete state machine it should certainly be possible to discover by observation sufficient about it to predict its future behavior, and this within a reasonable time, say a thousand years. But this does not seem to be the case. I have set up on the Manchester computer a small program using only 1000 units of storage, whereby the machine supplied with one sixteen-figure number replies with another within two seconds. I would defy anyone to learn from these replies sufficient about the program to be able to predict any replies to untried values.

(9) The Argument from Extra-Sensory Perception. I assume that the reader is familiar with the idea of extra-sensory perception, and the meaning of the four items of it, viz., telepathy, clairvoyance, precognition and psychokinesis. These disturbing phenomena seem to deny all our usual scientific ideas. How we would like to discredit them! Unfortunately, the statistical evidence, at least for telepathy, is overwhelming. It is very difficult to rearrange one's ideas so as to fit these new facts in. Once one has accepted them it does not seem a very big step to believe in ghosts and bogies. The idea that our bodies move simply according to the known laws of physics, together with some others not yet discovered but somewhat similar, would be one of the first to go.

This argument is to my mind quite a strong one. One can say in reply that many scientific theories seem to remain workable in practice, in spite of clashing with E.S.P.; that in fact one can get along very nicely if one forgets about it. This is rather cold comfort, and one fears that thinking is just the kind of phenomenon where E.S.P. may be especially relevant.

A more specific argument based on E.S.P. might run as follows: "Let us play the imitation game, using as witnesses a man who is good as a telepathic receiver, and a digital computer. The interrogator can ask such questions as 'What suit does the card in my right hand belong to?' The man by telepathy or clairvoyance gives the right answer 130 times out of 400 cards. The machine can only guess at random, and perhaps gets 104 right, so the interrogator makes the right identification." There is an interesting possibility which opens here. Suppose the digital computer contains a random number generator. Then it will be natural to use this to decide what answer to give. But then the random number generator will be subject to the psychokinetic powers of the interrogators. Perhaps this psychokinesis might cause the machine to guess right more often than would be expected on a probability calculation, so that the interrogator might still be unable to make the right identification. On the other hand, he might be able to guess right without any questioning, by clairvoyance. With E.S.P. anything may happen.

If telepathy is admitted it will be necessary to tighten our test. The situation could be regarded as analogous to that which would occur if the interrogator were talking to himself and one of the competitors was listening with his ear to the wall. To put the competitors into a "telepathy-proof room" would satisfy all requirements.

7. Learning Machines

The reader will have anticipated that I have no very convincing arguments of a positive nature to support my views. If I had I should not have taken such pains to point out the fallacies in contrary views. Such evidence as I have I shall now give.

Let us return for a moment to Lady Lovelace's objection, which stated that the machine can only do what we tell it to do. One could say that a man can "inject" an idea into the machine, and that it will respond to a certain extent and then drop into quiescence, like a piano string struck by a hammer. Another simile would be an atomic pile of less than critical size: an injected idea is to correspond to a neutron entering the pile from without. Each such neutron will cause a certain disturbance which eventually dies away. If, however, the size of the pile is sufficiently increased, the disturbance caused by such an incoming neutron will very likely go on and on increasing until the whole pile is destroyed. Is there a corresponding phenomenon for minds, and is there one for machines? There does seem to be one for the human mind. The majority of them seem to be "subcritical," i.e., to correspond in this analogy to piles of subcritical size. An idea presented to such a mind will on an average give rise to less than one idea in reply. A smallish proportion are supercritical. An idea presented to such a mind may give rise to a whole "theory" consisting of secondary, tertiary and more remote ideas. Animals' minds seem to be very definitely subcritical. Adhering to this analogy we ask, "Can a machine be made to be supercritical?"

The "skin of an onion" analogy is also helpful. In considering the functions of the mind or the brain we find certain operations which we can explain in purely mechanical terms. This we say does not correspond to the real mind: it is a sort of skin which we must strip off if we are to find the real mind. But then in what remains we find a further skin to be stripped off, and so on. Proceeding in this way do we ever come to the "real" mind, or do we eventually come to the skin which has nothing in it? In the latter case the whole mind is mechanical. (It would not be a discrete state machine however. We have discussed this.)

These last two paragraphs do not claim to be convincing arguments. They should rather be described as "recitations tending to produce belief."

The only really satisfactory support that can be given for the view expressed at the beginning of §6, . . . will be that provided by waiting for the end of the century and then doing the experiment described. But what can we say in the meantime? What steps should be taken now if the experiment is to be successful?

As I have explained, the problem is mainly one of programing. Advances in engineering will have to be made too, but it seems unlikely that these will not be adequate for the requirements. Estimates of the storage capacity of the brain vary from 10^{10} to 10^{15} binary digits. I incline to the lower values and believe that only a very small fraction is used for the higher types of thinking. Most of it is probably used for the retention of visual impressions. I should be surprised if more then 10^9 was required for satisfactory playing of the imitation game, at any rate against a blind man. (Note: The capacity of the *Encyclopedia Britannica,* eleventh edition, is 2×10^9.) A storage capacity of 10^7 would be a very practicable possiblity even by present techniques. It is probably not necessary to increase the speed of operations of the machines at all. Parts of modern machines which can be regarded as analogues of nerve cells work about a thousand times faster than the latter. This should provide a "margin of safety" which could cover losses of speed arising in many ways. Our problem then is to find out how to program these machines to play the game. At my present rate of working I produce about a thousand digits of program a day, so that about sixty workers, working steadily through the fifty years might accomplish the job, if nothing went into the waste-paper basket. Some more expeditious method seems desirable.

In the process of trying to imitate an adult human mind we are bound to think a good deal about the process which has brought it to the state that it is in. We may notice three components,

(a) The initial state of the mind, say at birth,
(b) The education to which it has been subjected,
(c) Other experience, not to be described as education, to which it has been subjected.

Instead of trying to produce a program to simulate the adult mind, why not rather try to produce one which simulates the child's? If this were then subjected to an appropriate course of education one would obtain the adult brain. Presumably the child-brain is something like a notebook as one buys it from the stationers. Rather little mechanism, and lots of blank sheets. (Mechanism and writing are from our point of view almost synonymous.) Our hope is that there is so little mechanism in the child-brain that something like it can be easily programed. The amount of work in the education we can assume, as a first approximation, to be much the same as for the human child.

We have thus divided our problem into two parts—the child-program and the education process. These two remain very closely connected. We cannot expect to find a good child-machine at the first attempt. One must experiment with teaching one such machine and see how well it learns. One can then try another and see if it is better or worse. There is an obvious connection between this process and evolution, by the identifications

Structure of the child-machine	=	Hereditary material
Changes of the child-machine	=	Mutations
Natural selection	=	Judgment of the experimenter

One may hope, however, that this process will be more expeditious than evolution. The survival of the fittest is a slow method for measuring advantages. The experimenter, by the exercise of intelligence, should be able to speed it up. Equally important is the fact that he is not restricted to random mutations. If he can trace a cause for some weakness he can probably think of the kind of mutation which will improve it.

It will not be possible to apply exactly the same teaching process to the machine as to a normal child. It will not, for instance, be provided with legs, so that it could not be asked to go out and fill the coal scuttle. Possibly it might not have eyes. But however well these deficiencies might be overcome by clever engineering, one could not send the creature to school without the other children making excessive fun of it. It must be given some tuition. We need not be too concerned about the legs, eyes, etc. The example of Miss Helen Keller shows that education can take place provided that communication in both directions between teacher and pupil can take place by some means or other.

We normally associate punishments and rewards with the teaching process. Some simple child-machines can be constructed or programed on this sort of principle. The machine has to be so constructed that events which shortly preceded the occurrence of a punishment-signal are unlikely to be repeated, whereas a reward-signal increases the probability of repetition of the events which led up to it. These definitions do not presuppose any feelings on the part of the machine. I have done some experiments with one such child-machine, and succeeded in teaching it a few things, but the teaching method was too unorthodox for the experiment to be considered really successful.

The use of punishments and rewards can at best be a part of the teaching process. Roughly speaking, if the teacher has no other means of communicating to the pupil, the amount of information which can reach him does not exceed the total number of rewards and punishments applied. By the time a child has learned to repeat "Casablanca" he would probably feel very sore indeed, if the text could only be discovered by a "Twenty Questions" technique, every "NO" taking the form of a blow. It is necessary therefore to have some other "unemotional" channels of communication. If these are available it is possible to teach a machine by punishments and rewards to obey orders given in some language, e.g., a symbolic language. These orders are to be transmitted through the "unemotional" channels. The use of this language will diminish greatly the number of punishments and rewards required.

Opinions may vary as to the complexity which is suitable in the child-machine.

One might try to make it as simple as possible consistently with the general principles. Alternatively one might have a complete system of logical inference "built in."[2] In the latter case the store would be largely occupied with definitions and propositions. The propositions would have various kinds of status, e.g., well-established facts, conjectures, mathematically proved theorems, statements given by an authority, expressions having the logical form of proposition but not belief-value. Certain propositions may be described as "imperatives." The machine should be so constructed that as soon as an imperative is classed as "well-established" the appropriate action automatically takes place. To illustrate this, suppose the teacher says to the machine, "Do your homework now." This may cause "Teacher says 'Do your homework now'" to be included among the well-established facts. Another such fact might be, "Everything that teacher says is true." Combining these may eventually lead to the imperative, "Do your homework now," being included among the well-established facts, and this, by the construction of the machine, will mean that the homework actually gets started, but the effect is very unsatisfactory. The processes of inference used by the machine need not be such as would satisfy the most exacting logicians. There might for instance be no hierarchy of types. But this need not mean that type fallacies will occur, any more than we are bound to fall over unfenced cliffs. Suitable imperatives (expressed *within* the systems, not forming part of the rules *of* the system) such as "Do not use a class unless it is a subclass of one which has been mentioned by teacher" can have a similar effect to "Do not go too near the edge."

The imperatives that can be obeyed by a machine that has no limbs are bound to be of a rather intellectual character, as in the example (doing homework) given above. Important among such imperatives will be ones which regulate the order in which the rules of the logical system concerned are to be applied. For at each stage when one is using a logical system, there is a very large number of alternative steps, any of which one is permitted to apply, so far as obedience to the rules of the logical system is concerned. These choices make the difference between a brilliant and a footling reasoner, not the difference between a sound and a fallacious one. Propositions leading to imperatives of this kind might be "When Socrates is mentioned, use the syllogism in Barbara" or "If one method has been proved to be quicker than another, do not use the slower method." Some of these may be "given by authority," but others may be produced by the machine itself, e.g., by scientific induction.

The idea of a learning machine may appear paradoxical to some readers. How can the rules of operation of the machine change? They should describe completely how the machine will react whatever its history might be, whatever changes it might undergo. The rules are thus quite time-invariant. This is quite true. The explanation of the paradox is that the rules which get changed in the learning process are of a rather less pretentious kind, claiming only an ephemeral validity. The reader may draw a parallel with the Constitution of the United States.

An important feature of a learning machine is that its teacher will often be very largely ignorant of quite what is going on inside, although he may still be able to some extent to predict his pupil's behavior. This should apply most strongly to the later education of a machine arising from a child-machine of well-tried design (or program). This is in clear contrast with normal procedure when using a machine to do computations: one's object is then to have a clear mental picture of the state of the machine at each moment in the computation. This object can only be achieved with a struggle. The view that "the machine can only do what we know how to order it do do,"[3] appears strange in face of this. Most of the programs which we can put into the machine will result in its doing something that we cannot make sense of at all, or which we regard as completely random behavior. Intelligent behavior presumably consists in a departure from the completely disciplined behavior involved in computation, but a rather slight one, which does not give rise to random behavior, or to pointless repetitive loops. Another important result of preparing our machine for its part in the imitation game by a process of teaching and learning is that "human fallibility" is likely to be omitted in a rather natural way, i.e., without special "coaching." . . . Processes that are learned do not produce a hundred per cent certainty of result; if they did they could not be unlearned.

It is probably wise to include a random element in a learning machine. . . . A random element is rather useful when we are searching for a solution of some problem. Suppose for instance we wanted to find a number between 50 and 200 which was equal to the square of the sum of its digits, we might start at 51 then try 52 and go on until we got a number that worked. Alternatively we might choose numbers at random until we got a good one. This method has the advantage that it is unnecessary to keep track of the values that have been tried, but the disadvantage that one may try the same one twice, but this is not very important if there are several solutions. The systematic method has the disadvantage that there may be an enormous block without any solutions in the region which has to be investigated first. Now the learning process may be regarded as a search for a form of behavior which will satisfy the teacher (or some other criterion). Since there is probably a very large number of satisfactory solutions the random method seems to be better than the systematic. It should be noticed that it is used in the analogous process of evolution. But there the systematic method is not possible. How could one keep track of the different genetical combinations that had been tried, so as to avoid trying them again?

We may hope that machines will eventually compete with men in all purely intellectual fields. But which are the best ones to start with? Even this is a difficult decision. Many people think that a very abstract activity, like the playing of chess, would be best. It can also be maintained that it is best to provide the machine with the best sense organs that money can buy, and then teach it to understand and speak English. This process could follow the normal teaching of a child. Things would be pointed out and named, etc. Again I do not know what the right answer is, but I think both approaches should be tried.

We can only see a short distance ahead, but we can see plenty there that needs to be done.

COMPUTING
MACHINERY AND
INTELLIGENCE

Notes

1. Possibly this view is heretical. Saint Thomas Aquinas (*Summa Theologica*, quoted by Bertrand Russell, *A History of Western Philosophy* [New York; Simon & Schuster, 1945], p. 458) states that God cannot make a man to have no soul. But this may not be a real restriction on His powers, but only a result of the fact that men's souls are immortal, and therefore indestructible.
2. Or rather "programed in" for our child-machine will be programed in a digital computer. But the logical system will not have to be learned.
3. Compare Lady Lovelace's statement, . . . which does not contain the word "only."

Of Liberty and Necessity

·DAVID HUME·

In this passage from Enquiries Concerning Human Understanding *(1748), Hume defends what has come to be called a "soft determinist" solution to the problem of free will. He maintains that actions are both free and causally determined. A free action, for Hume, is one in which the agent could have done otherwise had the agent wished to do so.*

Part I

It might reasonably be expected in questions which have been canvassed and disputed with great eagerness, since the first origin of science and philosophy, that the meaning of all the terms, at least, should have been agreed upon among the disputants; and our enquiries, in the course of two thousand years, been able to pass from words to the true and real subject of the controversy. For how easy may it seem to give exact definitions of the terms employed in reasoning, and make these definitions, not the mere sound of words, the object of future scrutiny and examination? But if we consider the matter more narrowly, we shall be apt to draw a quite opposite conclusion. From this circumstance alone, that a controversy has been long kept on foot, and remains still undecided, we may presume that there is some ambiguity in the expression, and that the disputants affix different ideas to the terms employed in the controversy. For as the faculties of the mind are supposed to be naturally alike in every individual; otherwise nothing could be more fruitless than to reason or dispute together; it were impossible, if men affix the same ideas to their terms, that they could so long form different opinions of the same subject; especially when they communicate their views, and each party turn themselves on all sides, in search of arguments which may give them the victory over their antagonists. It is true, if men attempt the discussion of questions which lie entirely beyond the reach of human capacity, such as those concerning the origin of worlds, or the economy of the intellectual system or region of spirits, they may long beat the air in their fruitless contests, and never arrive at any determinate conclusion. But if the question regard any subject of common life and experience, nothing, one would think, could preserve the dispute so long undecided but some ambiguous expressions, which keep the antagonists still at a distance, and hinder them from grappling with each other.

This has been the case in the long disputed question concerning liberty and necessity; and to so remarkable a degree that, if I be not much mistaken, we shall find, that all mankind, both learned and ignorant, have always been of the same opinion with regard to this subject, and that a few intelligible definitions would immediately have put an end to the whole controversy. I own that this dispute has been so much canvassed on all hands, and has led philosophers into such a labyrinth of obscure sophistry, that it is no wonder, if a sensible reader indulge his ease so far as to turn a deaf ear to the proposal of such a question, from which he can expect neither instruction or entertainment. But the state of the argument here proposed may, perhaps, serve to renew his attention; as it has more novelty, promises at least some decision of the controversy, and will not much disturb his ease by any intricate or obscure reasoning.

I hope, therefore, to make it appear that all men have ever agreed in the doctrine both of necessity and of liberty, according to any reasonable sense, which can be put on these terms; and that the whole controversy has hitherto turned merely upon words. We shall begin with examining the doctrine of necessity.

It is universally allowed that matter, in all its operations, is actuated by a necessary force, and that every natural effect is so precisely determined by the energy of its cause that no other effect, in such particular circumstances, could possibly have resulted from it. The degree and direction of every motion is, by the laws of nature, prescribed with such exactness that a living creature may as soon arise from the shock of two bodies as motion in any other degree or direction than what is actually produced by it. Would we, therefore, form a just and precise idea of *necessity*, we must consider whence that idea arises when we apply it to the question of bodies.

It seems evident that, if all the scenes of nature were continually shifted in such a manner that no two events bore any resemblance to each other, but every object was entirely new, without any similitude to whatever had been seen before, we should never, in that case, have attained the least idea of necessity, or of a connexion among these objects. We might say, upon such a supposition, that one object or event has followed another; not that one was produced by the other. The relation of cause and effect must be utterly unknown to mankind. Inference and reasoning concerning the operations of nature would, from that moment, be at an end; and the memory and senses remain the only canals, by which the knowledge of any real existence could possibly have access to the mind. Our idea, therefore, of necessity and causation arises entirely from the uniformity observable in the operations of nature, where similar objects are constantly conjoined together, and the mind is determined by custom to infer the one from the appearance of the other. These two circumstances form the whole of that necessity, which we ascribe to matter. Beyond the constant *conjunction* of similar objects, and the consequent *inference* from one to the other, we have no notion of any necessity or connexion.

If it appear, therefore, that all mankind have ever allowed, without any doubt or hesitation, that these two circumstances take place in the voluntary actions of men, and in the operations of mind; it must follow, that all mankind have ever agreed in the doctrine of necessity, and that they have hitherto disputed, merely for not understanding each other.

As to the first circumstance, the constant and regular conjunction of similar events, we may possibly satisfy ourselves by the following considerations. It is universally acknowledged that there is a great uniformity among the actions of men, in all nations and ages, and that human nature remains still the same, in its principles and operations. The same motives always produce the same actions. The same events follow from the same causes. Ambition, avarice, self-love, vanity, friendship, generosity, public spirit: these passions, mixed in various degrees, and distributed through society, have been, from the beginning of the world, and still are, the source of all the actions and enterprises, which have ever been observed among mankind. Would you know the sentiments, inclinations, and course of life of the Greeks and Romans? Study well the temper and actions of the French and English: You cannot be much mistaken in transferring to the former *most* of the observations which you have made with regard to the latter. Mankind are so much the same, in all times and places, that history informs us of nothing new or strange in this particular. Its chief use is only to discover the constant and universal principles of human nature, by showing men in all varieties of circumstances and situations, and furnishing us with materials from which we may form our observations and become acquainted with the regular springs of human action and behaviour. These records of wars, intrigues, factions, and revolutions, are so many collections of experiments, by which the politician or moral philosopher fixes the principles of his science, in the same manner as the physician or natural philosopher becomes acquainted with the nature of plants, minerals, and other external objects, by the experiments which he forms concerning them. Nor are the earth, water, and other elements, examined by Aristotle, and Hippocrates, more like to those which at present lie under our observation than the men described by Polybius and Tacitus are to those who now govern the world.

Should a traveller, returning from a far country, bring us an account of men, wholly different from any with whom we were ever acquainted; men, who were entirely divested of avarice, ambition, or revenge; who knew no pleasure but friendship, generosity, and public spirit; we should immediately, from these circumstances, detect the falsehood, and prove him a liar, with the same certainty as if he had stuffed his narration with stories of centaurs and dragons, miracles and prodigies. And if we would explode any forgery in history, we cannot make use of a more convincing argument, than to prove, that the actions ascribed to any person are directly contrary to the course of nature, and that no human motives, in such circumstances, could ever induce him to such a conduct. The veracity of Quintus Curtius is as much to be suspected, when he describes the supernatural courage of Alexander, by which he was hurried on singly to attack multitudes, as when he describes his supernatural force and activity, by which he was able to resist them. So readily and universally do we acknowledge a uniformity in human motives and actions as well as in the operations of body.

Hence likewise the benefit of that experience, acquired by long life and a variety of business and company, in order to instruct us in the principles of human nature, and regulate our future conduct, as well as speculation. By means of this guide, we mount up to the knowledge of men's inclinations and motives, from their actions, expressions, and even gestures; and again descend to the interpretation of their actions from our knowledge of their motives and inclinations. The general observations treasured up by a course of experience, give us the clue of human nature, and teach us to unravel all its intricacies. Pretexts and appearances no longer deceive us. Public declarations pass for the specious colouring of a cause. And though virtue and honour be allowed their proper weight and authority, that perfect disinterestedness, so often pretended to, is never expected in multitudes and parties; seldom in their leaders; and scarcely even in individuals of any rank or station. But were there no uniformity in human actions, and were every experiment which we could form of this kind irregular and anomalous, it were impossible to collect any general observations concerning mankind; and no experience, however accurately digested by reflection, would ever serve to any purpose. Why is the aged husbandman more skilful in his calling than the young beginner but because there is a certain uniformity in the operation of the sun, rain, and earth towards the production of vegetables; and experience teaches the old practitioner the rules by which this operation is governed and directed.

We must not, however, expect that this uniformity of human actions should be carried to such a length as that all men, in the same circumstances, will always act precisely in the same manner, without making any allowance for the diversity of characters, prejudices, and opinions. Such a uniformity in every particular, is found in no part of nature. On the contrary, from observing the variety of conduct in different men, we are enabled to form a greater variety of maxims, which still suppose a degree of uniformity and regularity.

Are the manners of men different in different ages and countries? We learn thence the great force of custom and education, which mould the human mind from its infancy and form it into a fixed and established character. Is the behaviour and conduct of the one sex very unlike that of the other? Is it thence we become acquainted with the different characters which nature has impressed upon the sexes, and which she preserves with constancy and regularity? Are the actions of the same person much diversified in the different periods of his life, from infancy to old age? This affords room for many general observations concerning the gradual change of our sentiments and inclinations, and the different maxims which prevail in the different ages of human creatures. Even the characters, which are peculiar to each individual, have a uniformity in their influence; otherwise our acquaintance with the persons and our observation of their conduct could never teach us their dispositions, or serve to direct our behaviour with regard to them.

I grant it possible to find some actions, which seem to have no regular connexion with any known motives, and are exceptions to all the measures of conduct which have ever been established for the government of men. But if we would willingly know what judgement should be formed of such irregular and extraordinary actions, we may consider the sentiments commonly entertained with regard to those irregular events which appear in the course of nature, and the operations of external objects. All causes are not conjoined to their usual effects with like uniformity. An artificer, who handles only dead matter, may be disappointed of his aim, as well as the politician, who directs the conduct of sensible and intelligent agents.

The vulgar, who take things according to their first appearance, attribute the uncertainty of events to such an uncertainty in the causes as makes the latter often fail of their usual influence; though they meet with no impediment in their operation. But philosophers, observing that, almost in every part of nature, there is contained a vast variety of springs and principles, which are hid, by reason of their minuteness or remoteness, find, that it is at least possible the contrariety of events may not proceed from any contingency in the cause, but from the secret operation of contrary causes. This possibility is converted into certainty by farther observation, when they remark that, upon an exact scrutiny, a contrariety of effects always betrays a contrariety of causes, and proceeds from their mutual opposition. A peasant can give no better reason for the stopping of any clock or watch than to say that it does not commonly go right: But an artist easily perceives that the same force in the spring or pendulum has always the same influence on the wheels; but fails of its usual effect, perhaps by reason of a grain of dust, which puts a stop to the whole movement. From the observation of several parallel instances, philosophers form a maxim that the connexion between all causes and effects is equally necessary, and that its seeming uncertainty in some instances proceeds from the secret opposition of contrary causes.

Thus, for instance, in the human body, when the usual symptoms of health or sickness disappoint our expectation; when medicines operate not with their wonted powers; when irregular events follow from any particular cause; the philosopher and physician are not surprised at the matter, nor are even tempted to deny, in general, the necessity and uniformity of those principles by which the animal economy is conducted. They know that a human body is a mighty complicated machine: That many secret powers lurk in it, which are altogether beyond our comprehension: That to us it must often appear very uncertain in its operations: And that therefore the irregular events, which outwardly discover themselves, can be no proof that the laws of nature are not observed with the greatest regularity in its internal operations and government.

The philosopher, if he be consistent, must apply the same reasoning to the actions and volitions of intelligent agents. The most irregular and unexpected resolutions of men may frequently be accounted for by those who know every particular circumstance of their character and situation. A person of an obliging disposition gives a peevish answer: But he has the toothache, or has not dined. A stupid fellow discovers an uncommon alacrity in his carriage: But he has met with a sudden piece of good fortune. Or even when an action, as sometimes happens, cannot be particularly accounted for, either by the person himself or by others; we know, in general, that the characters of men are, to a certain degree, inconstant and irregular. This is, in a manner, the constant character of human nature; though it be applicable, in a more particular manner, to some persons who have no fixed rule for their conduct, but proceed in a continued course of caprice and inconstancy. The internal principles and motives may operate in a uniform manner, notwithstanding these seeming irregularities; in the same manner as the winds, rain, clouds, and other variations of the weather are supposed to be governed by steady principles; though not easily discoverable by human sagacity and enquiry.

Thus it appears, not only that the conjunction between motives and voluntary actions is as regular and uniform as that between the cause and effect in any part of nature; but also that this regular conjunction has been universally acknowledged among mankind, and has never been the subject of dispute, either in philosophy or common life. Now, as it is from past experience that we draw all inferences concerning the future, and as we conclude that objects will always be conjoined together which we find to have always been conjoined; it may seem superfluous to prove that this experienced uniformity in human actions is a source whence we draw *inferences* concerning them. But in order to throw the argument into a greater variety of lights we shall also insist, though briefly, on this latter topic.

The mutual dependence of men is so great in all societies that scarce any human action is entirely complete in itself, or is performed without some reference to the actions of others, which are requisite to make it answer fully the intention of the agent. The poorest artificer, who labours alone, expects at least the protection of the magistrate, to ensure him the enjoyment of the fruits of his labour. He also expects that, when he carries his goods to market, and offers them at a reasonable price, he shall find purchasers, and shall be able, by the money he acquires, to engage others to supply him with those commodities which are requisite for his subsistence. In proportion as men extend their dealings, and render their intercourse with others more complicated, they always comprehend, in their schemes of life, a greater variety of voluntary actions, which they expect, from the proper motives, to co-operate with their own. In all these conclusions they take their measures from past experience, in the same manner as in their reasonings concerning external objects; and firmly believe that men, as well as all the elements, are to continue, in their operations, the same that they have ever found them. A manufacturer reckons upon the labour of his servants for the execution of any work as much as upon the tools which he employs, and would be equally surprised were his expectations disappointed. In short, this experimental inference and reasoning concerning the actions of others enters so much into human life that no man, while awake, is ever a moment without employing it. Have we not reason, therefore, to affirm that all mankind have always agreed in the doctrine of necessity according to the foregoing definition and explication of it?

Nor have philosophers ever entertained a different opinion from the people in this particular. For, not to mention that almost every action of their life supposes that opinion, there are even few of the speculative parts of learning to which it is not essential. What would become of *history,* had we not a dependence on the veracity of the historian according to the experience which we have had of mankind? How could *politics* be a science, if laws and forms of government had not a uniform influence upon society? Where would be the foundation of *morals,* if particular characters had no certain or determinate power to produce particular sentiments, and if these sentiments had no constant operation on actions? And with what pretence could we employ our *criticism* upon any poet or polite author, if we could not pronounce the conduct and sentiments of his actors either natural or unnatural to such characters, and in such circumstances? It seems almost impossible, therefore, to engage either in science or action of any kind without acknowledging the doctrine of necessity, and this *inference* from motive to voluntary actions, from characters to conduct.

And indeed, when we consider how aptly *natural* and *moral* evidence link together, and form only one chain of argument, we shall make no scruple to allow that they are of the same nature, and derived from the same principles. A prisoner who has neither money nor interest, discovers the impossibility of his escape, as well when he considers the obstinacy of the gaoler, as the walls and bars with which he is surrounded; and, in all attempts for his freedom, chooses rather to work upon the stone and iron of the one, than upon the inflexible nature of the other. The same prisoner, when conducted to the scaffold, foresees his death as certainly from the constancy and fidelity of his guards, as from the operation of the axe or wheel. His mind runs along a certain train of ideas: The refusal of the soldiers to consent to his escape; the action of the executioner; the separation of the head and body; bleeding, convulsive motions, and death. Here is a connected chain of natural causes and voluntary actions; but the mind feels no difference between them in passing from one link to another: Nor is less certain of the future event than if it were connected with the objects present to the memory or senses, by a train of causes, cemented together by what we are pleased to call a *physical* necessity. The same experienced union has the same effect on the mind, whether the united objects be motives, volition, and actions; or figure and motion. We may change the name of things; but their nature and their operation on the understanding never change.

Were a man, whom I know to be honest and opulent, and with whom I live in intimate friendship, to come into my house, where I am surrounded with my servants, I rest assured that he is not to stab me before he leaves it in order to rob me of my silver standish; and I no more suspect this event than the falling of the house itself, which is new, and solidly built and founded—*But he may have been seized with a sudden and unknown frenzy.*—So may a sudden earthquake arise, and shake and tumble my house about my ears. I shall therefore change the suppositions. I shall say that I know with certainty that he is not to put his hand into the fire and hold it there till it be consumed: And this event, I think I can foretell with the same assurance, as that, if he throw himself out at the window. and meet with no obstruction, he will not remain a moment suspended in the air. No suspicion of an unknown frenzy can give the least possibility to the former event, which is so contrary to all the known principles of human nature. A man who at noon leaves his purse full of gold on the pavement at Charing-Cross, may as well expect that it will fly away like a feather, as that he will find it untouched an hour after. Above one half of human reasonings contain inferences of a similar nature, attended with more or less degrees of certainty proportioned to our experience of the usual conduct of mankind in such particular situations.

I have frequently considered, what could possibly be the reason why all mankind, though they have ever, without hesitation, acknowledged the doctrine of necessity in their whole practice and reasoning, have yet discovered such a reluctance to acknowledge it in words, and have rather shown a propensity, in all ages, to profess the contrary opinion. The matter, I think, may be accounted for after the following manner. If we examine the operations of body, and the production of effects from their causes, we shall find that all our faculties can never carry us farther in our knowledge of this relation than barely to observe that particular objects are *constantly conjoined* together, and that the mind is carried, by a *customary transition,* from the appearance of one to the belief of the other. But though this conclusion concerning human ignorance be the result of the strictest scrutiny of this subject, men still entertain a strong propensity to believe that they penetrate farther into the powers of nature, and perceive something like a necessary connexion between the cause and the effect. When again they turn their reflections towards the operations of their own minds, and *feel* no such connexion of the motive and the action; they are thence apt to suppose, that there is a difference between the effects which result from material force, and those which arise from thought and intelligence. But being once convinced that we know nothing farther of causation of any kind than merely the *constant conjunction* of objects, and the consequent *inference* of the mind from one to another, and finding that these two circumstances are universally allowed to have place in voluntary actions; we may be more easily led to own the same necessity common to all causes. And though this reasoning may contradict the systems of many philosophers, in ascribing necessity to the determinations of the will, we shall find, upon reflection, that they dissent from it in words only, not in their real sentiment. Necessity, according to the sense in which it is here taken, has never yet been rejected, nor can ever, I think, be rejected by any philosopher. It may only, perhaps, be pretended that the mind can perceive, in the operations of matter, some farther connexion between the cause and effect; and connexion that has not place in voluntary actions of intelligent beings. Now whether it be so or not, can only appear upon examination; and it is incumbent on these philosophers to make good their assertion, by defining or describing that necessity, and pointing it out to us in the operations of material causes.

It would seem, indeed, that men begin at the wrong end of this question concerning liberty and necessity, when they enter upon it by examining the faculties of the soul, the influence of the understanding, and the operations of the will. Let them first discuss a more simple question, namely, the operations of body and of brute unintelligent matter; and try whether they can there form any idea of causation and necessity, except that of a constant conjunction of objects, and subsequent inference of the mind from one to another. If these circumstances form, in reality, the whole of that necessity, which we conceive in matter, and if these circumstances be also universally acknowledged to take place in the operations of the mind, the dispute is at an end; at least, must be owned to be thenceforth merely verbal. But as long as we will rashly suppose, that we have some farther idea of necessity and causation in the operations of external objects; at the same time, that we can find nothing farther in the voluntary actions of the mind; there is no possibility of bringing the question to any determinate issue, while we proceed upon so erroneous a supposition. The only method of undeceiving us is to mount up higher; to examine the narrow extent of science when applied to material causes; and to convince ourselves that all we know of them is the constant conjunction and inference above mentioned. We may, perhaps, find that it is with difficulty we are induced to fix such narrow limits to human understanding: But we can afterwards find no difficulty when we come to apply this doctrine to the actions of the will. For as it is evident that these have a regular conjunction with motives and circumstances and characters, and as we always draw inferences from one to the other, we must be obliged to acknowledge in words that necessity, which we have already avowed, in every deliberation of our lives, and in every step of our conduct and behaviour.[1]

But to proceed in this reconciling project with regard to the question of liberty and necessity; the most contentious question of metaphysics, the most contentious science; it will not require many words to prove, that all mankind have ever agreed in the doctrine of liberty as well as in that of necessity, and that the whole dispute, in this respect also, has been hitherto merely verbal. For what is meant by liberty, when applied to voluntary actions? We cannot surely mean that actions have so little connexion with motives, inclinations, and circumstances, that one does not follow with a certain degree of uniformity from the other, and that one affords no inference by which we can conclude the existence of the other. For these are plain and acknowledged matters of fact. By liberty, then, we can only mean *a power of acting or not acting, according to the determinations of the will;* that is, if we choose to remain at rest, we may; if we choose to move, we also may. Now this hypothetical liberty is universally allowed to belong to every one who is not a prisoner and in chains. Here, then, is no subject of dispute.

Whatever definition we may give of liberty, we should be careful to observe two requisite circumstances; *first,* that it be consistent with plain matter of fact; *second,* that it be consistent with itself. If we observe these circumstances, and render our definition intelligible, I am persuaded that all mankind will be found of one opinion with regard to it.

It is universally allowed that nothing exists without a cause of its existence, and that chance, when strictly examined, is a mere negative word, and means not any real power which has anywhere a being in nature. But it is pretended that some causes are necessary, some not necessary. Here then is the advantage of definitions. Let any one *define* a cause, without comprehending, as a part of the definition, a *necessary connexion* with its effect; and let him show distinctly the origin of the idea, expressed by the definition; and I shall readily give up the whole controversy. But if the foregoing explication of the matter be received, this must be absolutely impracticable. Had not objects a regular conjunction with each other, we should never have entertained any notion of cause and effect; and this regular conjunction produces that inference of the understanding, which is the only connexion, that we can have any comprehension of. Whoever attempts a definition of cause, exclusive of these circumstances, will be obliged either to employ unintelligible terms or such as are synonymous to the term which he endeavours to define.[2] And if the definition above mentioned be admitted; liberty, when opposed to necessity, not to constraint, is the same thing with chance; which is universally allowed to have no existence.

Part II

There is no method of reasoning more common, and yet none more blameable, than, in philosophical disputes, to endeavour the refutation of any hypothesis, by a pretence of its dangerous consequences to religion and morality. When any opinion leads to absurdities, it is certainly false; but it is not certain that an opinion is false, because it is of dangerous consequence. Such topics, therefore, ought entirely to be forborne; as serving nothing to the discovery of truth, but only to make the person of an antagonist odious. This I observe in general, without pretending to draw any advantage from it. I frankly submit to an examination of this kind, and shall venture to affirm that the doctrines, both of necessity and of liberty, as above explained, are not only consistent with morality, but are absolutely essential to its support.

Necessity may be defined two ways, conformably to the two definitions of *cause*, of which it makes an essential part. It consists either in the constant conjunction of like objects, or in the inference of the understanding from one object to another. Now necessity, in both these senses, (which, indeed, are at bottom the same) has universally, though tacitly, in the schools, in the pulpit, and in common life, been allowed to belong to the will of man; and no one has ever pretended to deny that we can draw inferences concerning human actions, and that those inferences are founded on the experienced union of like actions, with like motives, inclinations, and circumstances. The only particular in which any one can differ, is, that either, perhaps, he will refuse to give the name of necessity to this property of human actions: But as long as the meaning is understood, I hope the word can do no harm: Or that he will maintain it possible to discover something farther in the operations of matter. But this, it must be acknowledged, can be of no consequence to morality or religion, whatever it may be to natural philosophy or metaphysics. We may here be mistaken in asserting that there is no idea of any other necessity of connexion in the actions of the mind, but what everyone does, and must readily allow of. We change no circumstance in the received orthodox system with regard to the will, but only in that with regard to material objects and causes. Nothing, therefore, can be more innocent, at least, than this doctrine.

All laws being founded on rewards and punishments, it is supposed as a fundamental principle, that these motives have a regular and uniform influence on the mind, and both produce the food and prevent the evil actions. We may give to this influence what name we please; but, as it is usually conjoined with the action, it must be esteemed a *cause,* and be looked upon as an instance of that necessity, which we would here establish.

The only proper object of hatred or vengeance is a person or creature, endowed with thought and consciousness; and when any criminal or injurious actions excite that passion, it is only by their relation to the person, or connexion with him. Actions are, by their very nature, temporary and perishing; and where they proceed not from some *cause* in the character and disposition of the person who performed them, they can neither redound to his honour, if good; nor infamy, if evil. The actions themselves may be blameable; they may be contrary to all the rules of morality and religion: But the person is not answerable for them; and as they proceed from nothing in him that is durable and constant, and leave nothing of that nature behind them, it is impossible he can, upon their account, become the object of punishment or vengeance. According to the principle, therefore, which denies necessity, and consequently causes, a man is as pure and untainted, after having committed the most horrid crime, as at the first moment of his birth, nor is his character anywise concerned in his actions, since they are not derived from it, and the wickedness of the one can never be used as a proof of the depravity of the other.

Men are not blamed for such actions as they perform ignorantly and casually, whatever may be the consequences. Why? but because the principles of these actions are only momentary, and terminate in them alone. Men are less blamed for such actions as they perform hastily and unpremeditatedly than for such as proceed from deliberation. For what reason? but because a hasty temper, though a constant cause or principle in the mind, operates only by intervals, and infects not the whole character. Again, repentance wipes off every crime, if attended with a reformation of life and manners. How is this to be accounted for? but by asserting that actions render a person criminal merely as they are proofs of criminal principles in the mind; and when, by an alteration of these principles, they cease to be just proofs, they likewise cease to be criminal. But, except upon the doctrine of necessity, they never were just proofs, and consequently never were criminal.

It will be equally easy to prove, and from the same arguments, that *liberty,* according to that definition above mentioned, in which all men agree, is also essential to morality, and that no human actions, where it is wanting, are susceptible of any moral qualities, or can be the objects either of approbation or dislike. For as actions are objects of our moral sentiment, so far only as they are indications of the internal character, passions, and affections; it is impossible that they can give rise either to praise or blame, where they proceed not from these principles, but are derived altogether from external violence.

I pretend not to have obviated or removed all objections to this theory, with regard to necessity and liberty. I can foresee other objections, derived from topics which have not here been treated of. It may be said, for instance, that, if voluntary actions be subjected to the same laws of necessity with the operations of matter, there is a continued chain of necessary causes, pre-ordained and pre-determined, reaching from the original cause of all to every single volition of every human creature. No contingency anywhere in the universe; no indifference; no liberty. While we act, we are, at the same time, acted upon. The ultimate Author of all our volitions is the Creator of the world, who first bestowed motion on this immense machine, and placed all beings in that particular position, whence every subsequent event, by an inevitable necessity, must result. Human actions, there-fore, either can have no moral turpitude at all, as proceeding from so good a cause; or if they have any turpitude, they must involve our Creator in the same guilt, while he is acknowledged to be their ultimate cause and author. For as a man, who fired a mine, is answerable for all the consequences whether the train he employed be long or short; so wherever a continued chain of necessary causes is fixed, that Being, either finite or infinite, who produces the first, is likewise the author of all the rest, and must both bear the blame and acquire the praise which belong to them. Our clear and unalterable ideas of morality establish this rule, upon unquestionable reasons, when we examine the consequences of any human action; and these reasons must still have greater force when applied to the volitions and intentions of a Being infinitely wise and powerful. Ignorance or impotence may be pleaded for so limited a creature as man; but those imper-fections have no place in our Creator. He foresaw, he ordained, he intended all those actions of men, which we so rashly pronounce criminal. And we must therefore conclude, either that they are not criminal, or that the Deity, not man, is accountable for them. But as either of these positions is absurd and impious, it follows, that the doctrine from which they are deduced cannot possibly be true, as being liable to all the same objections. An absurd consequence, if neces-sary, proves the original doctrine to be absurd; in the same manner as criminal actions render criminal the original cause, if the connexion between them be necessary and evitable.

This objection consists of two parts, which we shall examine separately; *First,* that, if human actions can be traced up, by a necessary chain, to the Deity, they can never be criminal; on account of the infinite perfection of that Being from whom they are derived, and who can intend nothing but what is altogether good and laudable. Or, *Secondly,* if they be criminal, we must retract the attribute of perfection, which we ascribe to the Deity, and must acknowledge him to be the ultimate author of guilt and moral turpitude in all his creatures.

The answer to the first objection seems obvious and convincing. There are many philosophers who, after an exact scrutiny of all the phenomena of nature, conclude, that the WHOLE, considered as one system, is, in every period of its existence, ordered with perfect benevolence; and that the utmost possible happi-ness will, in the end, result to all created beings, without any mixture of positive or absolute ill or misery. Every physical ill, say they, makes an essential part of this benevolent system, and could not possibly be removed, even by the Deity himself, considered as a wise agent, without giving entrance to greater ill, or excluding greater good, which will result from it. From this theory, some philosophers, and the ancient *Stoics* among the rest, derived a topic of consolation under all afflictions, while they taught their pupils that those ills under which they laboured were, in reality, goods to the universe; and that to an enlarged view, which could comprehend the whole system of nature, every event became an object of joy and exultation. But though this topic be specious and sublime, it was soon found in practice weak and ineffectual. You would surely more irritate than appease a man lying under the racking pains of the gout by preaching up to him the rectitude of those general laws, which produced the malignant humours in his body, and led them through the proper canals, to the sinews and nerves, where they now excite such acute torments. These enlarged views may, for a moment, please the imagination of a speculative man, who is placed in ease and security; but neither can they dwell with constancy on his mind, even though undisturbed by the emotions of pain or passion; much less can they maintain their ground when attacked by such powerful antagonists. The affections take a narrower and more natural survey of their object; and by an economy, more suitable to the infirmity of human minds, regard alone the beings around us, and are actuated by such events as appear good or ill to the private system.

The case is the same with *moral* as with *physical* ill. It cannot reasonably be supposed, that those remote considerations, which are found of so little efficacy with regard to one, will have a more powerful influence with regard to the other. The mind of man is so formed by nature that, upon the appearance of certain characters, dispositions, and actions, it immediately feels the sentiment of approbation or blame; nor are there any emotions more essential to its frame and constitution. The characters which engage our approbation are chiefly such as contribute to the peace and security of human society; as the characters which excite blame are chiefly such as tend to public detriment and disturbance: Whence it may reasonably be presumed, that the moral sentiments arise, either mediately or immediately, from a reflection of these opposite interests. What though philosophical meditations establish a different opinion or conjecture; that everything is right with regard to the WHOLE, and that the qualities, which disturb society, are, in the main, as beneficial, and are as suitable to the primary intention of nature as those which more directly promote its happiness and welfare? Are such remote and uncertain speculations able to counterbalance the sentiments which arise from the natural and immediate view of the objects? A man who is robbed of a considerable sum; does he find his vexation for the loss anywise diminished by these sublime reflections? Why then should his moral resentment against the crime be supposed incompatible with them? Or why should not the acknowledgment of a real distinction between vice and virtue be reconcilable to all speculative systems of philosophy, as well as that of a real distinction between personal beauty and deformity? Both these distinctions are founded in the natural sentiments of the human mind: And these sentiments are not to be controlled or altered by any philosophical theory or speculation whatsoever.

The *second* objection admits not of so easy and satisfactory an answer; nor is it possible to explain distinctly, how the Deity can be the mediate cause of all the actions of men, without being the author of sin and moral turpitude. These are mysteries, which mere natural and unassisted reason is very unfit to handle; and whatever system she embraces, she must find herself involved in inextricable difficulties, and even contradictions, at every step which she takes with regard to such subjects. To reconcile the indifference and contingency of human actions with prescience; or to defend absolute decrees, and yet free the Deity from being the author of sin, has been found hitherto to exceed all the power of philosophy. Happy, if she be thence sensible of her temerity, when she pries into these sublime mysteries; and leaving a scene so full of obscurities and perplexities, return, with suitable modesty, to her true and proper province, the examination of common life; where she will find difficulties enough to employ her enquiries, without launching into so boundless an ocean of doubt, uncertainty, and contradiction!

Notes

1. The prevalence of the doctrine of liberty may be accounted for, from another cause, viz, a false sensation or seeming experience which we have, or may have, of liberty or indifference, in many of our actions. The necessity of any action, whether of matter or of mind, is not, properly speaking, a quality in the agent, but in any thinking or intelligent being, who may consider the action; and it consists chiefly in the determination of his thoughts to infer the existence of that action from some preceding objects; as liberty, when opposed to necessity, is nothing but the want of that determination, and a certain looseness or indifference, which we feel, in passing, or not passing, from the idea of one object to that of any succeeding one. Now we may observe, that, though, in *reflecting* on human actions, we seldom feel such a looseness, or indifference, but are commonly able to infer them with considerable certainty from their motives, and from the dispositions of the agent; yet it frequently happens, that, in *performing* the actions themselves, we are sensible of something like it: And as all resembling objects are readily taken for each other, this has been employed as a demonstrative and even intuitive proof of human liberty. We feel, that our actions are subject to our will, on most occasions; and imagine we feel, that the will itself is subject to nothing, because, when by a denial of it we are provoked to try, we feel, that it moves easily every way, and produces an image of itself (or a *Velleïty*, as it is called in the schools) even on that side, on which it did not settle. This image, or faint motion, we persuade ourselves, could, at that time, have been completed into the thing itself; because, should that be denied, we find, upon a second trial, that, at present, it can. We consider not, that the fantastical desire of showing liberty, is here the motive of our actions. And it seems certain, that, however we may imagine we feel a liberty within ourselves, a spectator can commonly infer our actions from our motives and character; and even where he cannot, he concludes in general, that he might, were he perfectly acquainted with every circumstance of our situation and temper, and the most secret springs of our complexion and disposition. Now this is the very essence of necessity, according to the foregoing doctrine.
2. Thus, if a cause be defined, *that which produces any thing;* it is easy to observe, that *producing* is synonymous to *causing.* In like manner, if a cause be defined, *that by which any thing exists;* this is liable to the same objection. For what is meant by these words, *by which?* Had it been said, that a cause is *that* after which *any thing constantly exists;* we should have understood the terms. For this is, indeed, all we know of the matter. And this constancy forms the very essence of necessity, nor have we any other idea of it.

Has the Self "Free Will"?

· C. A. CAMPBELL ·

In this excerpt from his book On Selfhood and Godhood (1957), *Campbell defends a libertarian solution to the problem of free will. He argues that we know by introspection that some of our actions are free. Campbell claims that these actions, therefore, cannot possess causal explanations.*

1. . . . . It is something of a truism that in philosophic enquiry the exact formulation of a problem often takes one a long way on the road to its solution. In the case of the Free Will problem I think there is a rather special need of careful formulation. For there are many sorts of human freedom; and it can easily happen that one wastes a great deal of labour in proving or disproving a freedom which has almost nothing to do with the freedom which is at issue in the traditional problem of Free Will. The abortiveness of so much of the argument for and against Free Will in contemporary philosophical literature seems to me due in the main to insufficient pains being taken over the preliminary definition of the problem. . . .

Fortunately we can at least make a beginning with a certain amount of confidence. It is not seriously disputable that the kind of freedom in question is the freedom which is commonly recognised to be in some sense a precondition of moral responsibility. Clearly, it is on account of this integral connection with moral responsibility that such exceptional importance has always been felt to attach to the Free Will problem. But in what precise sense is free will a precondition of moral responsibility, and thus a postulate of the moral life in general? This is an exceedingly troublesome question; but until we have satisfied ourselves about the answer to it, we are not in a position to state, let alone decide, the question whether "Free Will" in its traditional, ethical, significance is a reality.

Our first business, then, is to ask, exactly what kind of freedom is it which is required for moral responsibility? And as to method of procedure in this inquiry, there seems to me to be no real choice. I know of only one method that carries with it any hope of success; viz. the critical comparison of those acts for which, on due reflection, we deem it proper to attribute moral praise or blame to the agents, with those acts for which, on due reflection, we deem such judgments to be improper. The ultimate touchstone, as I see it, can only be our moral consciousness as it manifests itself in our more critical and considered moral judgments. . . .

2. The first point to note is that the freedom at issue (as indeed the very name "Free *Will* Problem" indicates) pertains primarily not to overt acts but to inner acts. The nature of things has decreed that, save in the case of one's self, it is only overt acts which one can directly observe. But a very little reflection serves to show that in our moral judgments upon others their overt acts are regarded as significant only in so far as they are the expression of inner acts. We do not consider the acts of a robot to be morally responsible acts; nor do we consider

the acts of a man to be so save insofar as they are distinguishable from those of a robot by reflecting an inner life of choice. Similarly, from the other side, if we are satisfied (as we may on occasion be, at least in the case of ourselves) that a person has definitely elected to follow a course which he believes to be wrong, but has been prevented by external circumstances from translating his inner choice into an overt act, we still regard him as morally blameworthy. Moral freedom, then, pertains to *inner* acts.

The next point seems at first sight equally obvious and controversial; but, as we shall see, it has awkward implications if we are in real earnest with it (as almost nobody is). It is the simple point that the act must be one of which the person judged can be regarded as the *sole* author. It seems plain enough that if there are any *other* determinants of the act, external to the self, to that extent the act is not an act which the *self* determines, and to that extent not an act for which the self can be held morally responsible. The self is only part-author of the act, and his moral responsibility can logically extend only to those elements within the act (assuming for the moment that these can be isolated) of which he is the *sole* author.

The awkward implications of this apparent truism will be readily appreciated. For, if we are mindful of the influences exerted by heredity and environment, we may well feel some doubt whether there is any act of will at all of which one can truly say that the self is sole author, sole determinant. No man has a voice in determining the raw material of impulses and capacities that constitute his hereditary endowment, and no man has more than a very partial control of the material and social environment in which he is destined to live his life. Yet it would be manifestly absurd to deny that these two factors do constantly and profoundly affect the nature of a man's choices. That this is so we all of us recognise in our moral judgments when we "make allowances," as we say, for a bad heredity or a vicious environment, and acknowledge in the victim of them a diminished moral responsibility for evil courses. Evidently we do *try*, in our moral judgments, however crudely, to praise or blame a man only in respect of that of which we can regard him as *wholly* the author. And evidently we do recognise that, for a man to be the author of an act in the full sense required for moral responsibility, it is enough merely that he "wills" or "chooses" the act: since even the most unfortunate victim of heredity or environment does, as a rule, "will" what he does. It is significant, however, that the ordinary man, though well enough aware of the influence upon choices of heredity and environment, does not feel obliged thereby to give up his assumption that moral predicates *are* somehow applicable. Plainly he still believes that there is *something* for which a man is morally responsible, something of which we can fairly say that he is the sole author. *What is this something?* To that question common sense is not ready with an explicit answer—though an answer is, I think, implicit in the line which its moral judgments take. I shall do what I can to give an explicit answer later in this lecture. Meantime it must suffice to observe that, if we are to be true to the deliverances of our moral consciousness, it is very difficult to deny that *sole* authorship is a necessary condition of the morally responsible act.

Thirdly we come to a point over which much recent controversy has raged. We may approach it by raising the following question. Granted an act of which the agent is sole author, does this "sole authorship" suffice to make the act a morally free act? We may be inclined to think that it does, until we contemplate the possibility that an act of which the agent is sole author might conceivably occur as a necessary expression of the agent's nature; the way in which, e.g. some philosophers have supposed the Divine act of creation to occur. This consideration excites a legitimate doubt, for it is far from easy to see how a person can be regarded as a proper subject for moral praise or blame in respect of an act which he *cannot help* performing—even if it be his own "nature" which necessitates it. Must we not recognise it as a condition of the morally free act that the agent "could have acted otherwise" than he in fact did? It is true, indeed, that we sometimes praise or blame a man for an act about which we are prepared to say, in the light of our knowledge of his established character, that he "could do no other." But I think that a little reflection shows that in such cases we are not praising or blaming the man strictly for what he does *now* (or at any rate we ought not to be), but rather for those past acts of his which have generated the firm habit of mind from which his *present* act follows "necessarily." In other words, our praise and blame, so far as justified, are really retrospective, being directed not at the agent *qua* performing *this* act, but to the agent *qua* performing those past acts which have built up his present character, and in respect to which we presume that he *could* have acted otherwise, that there really *were* open possibilities before him. These cases, therefore, seem to me to constitute no valid exception to what I must take to be the rule, viz. that a man can be morally praised or blamed for an act only if he could have acted otherwise.

Now philosophers today are fairly well agreed that it is a postulate of the morally responsible act that the agent "could have acted otherwise" in *some* sense of that phrase. But sharp differences of opinion have arisen over the way in which the phrase ought to be interpreted. There is a strong disposition to water down its apparent meaning by insisting that it is not (as a postulate of moral responsibility) to be understood as a straightforward categorical proposition, but rather as a disguised hypothetical proposition. All that we really require to be assured of, in order to justify our holding X morally responsible for an act, is, we are told, that X could have acted otherwise *if* he had *chosen* otherwise (Moore, Stevenson); or perhaps that X could have acted otherwise *if* he had had a different character, of *if* he had been placed in different circumstances.

I think it is easy to understand, and even, in a measure, to sympathise with, the motives which induce philosophers to offer these counter-interpretations. It is not just the fact that "X could have acted otherwise," as a bald categorical statement, is incompatible with the universal sway of causal law—though this is, to some philosophers, a serious stone of stumbling. The more widespread objection is that it at least looks as though it were incompatible with that causal continuity of an agent's character with his conduct which is implied when we believe (surely with justice) that we can often tell the sort of thing a man will do from our knowledge of the sort of man he is.

We shall have to make our accounts with that particular difficulty later. At this stage I wish merely to show that neither of the hypothetical propositions suggested—and I think the same could be shown for *any* hypothetical alternative—is an acceptable substitute for the categorical proposition "X could have acted otherwise" as the presupposition of moral responsibility.

Let us look first at the earlier suggestion—"X could have acted otherwise *if* he had chosen otherwise." Now clearly there are a great many acts with regard to which we are entirely satisfied that the agent is thus situated. We are often perfectly sure that—for this is all it amounts to—if X had chosen otherwise, the circumstances presented no external obstacle to the translation of that choice into action. For example, we often have no doubt at all that X, who in point of fact told a lie, could have told the truth *if* he had so chosen. But does our confidence on this score allay all legitimate doubts about whether X is really blameworthy? Does it entail that X is free in the sense required for moral responsibility? Surely not. The obvious question immediately arises: "But *could* X have *chosen* otherwise than he did?" It is doubt about the true answer to *that* question which leads most people to doubt the reality of moral responsibility. Yet on this crucial question the hypothetical proposition which is offered as a sufficient statement of the condition justifying the ascription of moral responsibility gives us no information whatsoever.

Indeed this hypothetical substitute for the categorical "X could have acted otherwise" seems to me to lack all plausibility unless one contrives to forget why it is, after all, that we ever come to feel fundamental doubts about man's moral responsibility. Such doubts are born, surely, when one becomes aware of certain reputable world-views in religion or philosophy, or of certain reputable scientific beliefs, which in their several ways imply that man's actions are necessitated, and thus could not be otherwise than they in fact are. But clearly a doubt so based is not even touched by the recognition that a man could very often act otherwise *if* he so chose. That proposition is entirely compatible with the necessitarian theories which generate our doubt: indeed it is this very compatibility that has recommended it to some philosophers, who are reluctant to give up either moral responsibility or Determinism. The proposition which we *must* be able to affirm if moral praise or blame of X is to be justified is the categorical proposition that X could have acted otherwise because—not if—he could have chosen otherwise; or, since it is essentially the inner side of the act that matters, the proposition simply that X could have chosen otherwise.

For the second of the alternative formulae suggested we cannot spare more than a few moments. But its inability to meet the demands it is required to meet is almost transparent. "X could have acted otherwise," as a statement of a precondition of X's moral responsibility, really means (we are told) "X could have acted otherwise *if* he were differently constituted, of *if* he had been placed in different circumstances." It seems a sufficient reply to this to point out that the person whose moral responsibility is at issue is *X*; a specific individual, in a specific set of circumstances. It is totally irrelevant to *X*'s moral responsibility that we should be able to say that some person differently constituted from X, or X in a different set of circumstance, could have done something different from what X did.

3. Let me, then, briefly sum up the answer at which we have arrived to our question about the kind of freedom required to justify moral responsibility. It is that a man can be said to exercise free will in a morally significant sense only insofar as his chosen act is one of which he is the sole cause or author, and only if — in the straightforward, categorical sense of the phrase — he "could have chosen otherwise".

I confess that this answer is in some ways a disconcerting one. Disconcerting, because most of us, however objective we are in the actual conduct of our thinking, would *like* to be able to believe that moral responsibility is real: whereas the freedom required for moral responsibility, on the analysis we have given, is certainly far more difficult to establish than the freedom required on the analyses we found ourselves obliged to reject. If, e.g. moral freedom entails only that I could have acted otherwise *if* I had chosen otherwise, there is no real "problem" about it at all. I am "free" in the normal case where there is no external obstacle to prevent my translating the alternative choice into action, and not free in other cases. Still less is there a problem if all that moral freedom entails is that I could have acted otherwise *if* I had been a differently constituted person, or been in different circumstances. Clearly I am *always* free in *this* sense of freedom. But, as I have argued, these so-called "freedoms" fail to give us the pre-conditions of moral responsibility, and hence leave the freedom of the traditional free-will problem, the freedom that people are really concerned about, precisely where it was. . . .

5. That brings me to the second, and more constructive, part of this lecture. From now on I shall be considering whether it is reasonable to believe that man does in fact possess a free will of the kind specified in the first part of the lecture. If so, just how and where within the complex fabric of the volitional life are we to locate it? — for although free will must presumably belong (if anywhere) to the volitional side of human experience, it is pretty clear from the way in which we have been forced to define it that it does not pertain simply to volition as such; not even to all volitions that are commonly dignified with the name of "choices." It has been, I think, one of the more serious impediments to profitable discussion of the Free Will problem that Libertarians and Determinists alike have so often failed to appreciate the comparatively narrow area within which the free will that is necessary to "save" morality is required to operate. It goes without saying that this failure has been gravely prejudicial to the case for Libertarianism. I attach a good deal of importance, therefore, to the problem of locating free will correctly within the volitional orbit. Its solution forestalls and annuls, I believe, some of the more tiresome clichés of Determinist criticism.

We saw earlier that Common Sense's practice of "making allowances" in its moral judgments for the influence of heredity and environment indicates Common Sense's conviction, both that a just moral judgment must discount determinants of choice over which the agent has no control, and also (since it still accepts moral judgments as legitimate) that *something* of moral relevance survives which can be regarded as genuinely self-originated. We are now to try to discover what this "something" is. And I think we may still usefully take Common Sense as our guide. Suppose one asks the ordinary intelligent citizen *why* he deems it proper to make allowances for X, whose heredity and/or environment are unfortunate. He will tend to reply, I think, in some such terms as these: that X has more and stronger temptations to deviate from what is right than Y or Z, who are normally circumstanced, so that he must put forth a *stronger moral effort* if he is to achieve the same level of external conduct. The intended implication seems to be that X is just as morally praiseworthy as Y or Z *if* he exerts an equivalent moral effort, even though he may not thereby achieve an equal success in conforming his will to the "concrete" demands of duty. And this implies, again, Common Sense's belief that *in moral effort* we have something for which a man is responsible *without qualification,* something that is *not* affected by heredity and environment but depends *solely* upon the self itself.

Now in my opinion Common Sense has here, in principle, hit upon the one and only defensible answer. Here, and here alone, so far as I can see, in the act of deciding whether to put forth or withhold the moral effort required to resist temptation and rise to duty, is to be found an act which is free in the sense required for moral responsiblity; an act of which the self is sole author, and of which it is true to say that "it could be" (or, after the event, "could have been") "otherwise." Such is the thesis which we shall now try to establish.

6. The species of argument appropriate to the establishment of a thesis of this sort should fall, I think, into two phases. First, there should be a consideration of the evidence of the moral agent's own inner experience. What *is* the act of moral decision, and what does it imply, from the standpoint of the actual participant? Since there is no way of knowing the act of moral decision — or for that matter any other form of activity — except by actual participation in it, the evidence of the subject, or agent, is on an issue of this kind of primary importance. It can hardly, however, be taken as in itself conclusive. For even if that evidence should be overwhelmingly to the effect that moral decision does have the characteristics required by moral freedom, the question is bound to be raised — and in view of considerations from other quarters pointing in a contrary direction is *rightly* raised — Can we *trust* the evidence in inner experience? That brings us to what will be the second phase of the argument. We shall have to go on to show, if we are to make good our case, that the extraneous considerations so often supposed to be fatal to the belief in moral freedom are in fact innocuous to it.

In the light of what was said [previously] about the self's experience of moral decision as a *creative* activity, we may perhaps be absolved from developing the first phase of the argument at any great length. The appeal is throughout to one's own experience in the actual taking of the moral decision in the situation of moral temptation. "Is it possible," we must ask, "for anyone so circumstanced to *dis*believe that he could be deciding otherwise?" The answer is surely not in doubt. When we decide to exert moral effort to resist a temptation, we feel quite certain that we *could* withhold the effort; just as, if we decide to withhold the effort and yield to our desires, we feel quite certain that we *could* exert it — otherwise we should not blame ourselves afterwards for having succumbed. It may be, indeed, that this conviction is mere self-delusion. But that is not at the moment our concern. It is enough at present to establish that the act of deciding to exert or to withhold moral effort, as we know it from the inside in actual moral living, belongs to the category of acts which "could have been otherwise."

Mutatis mutandis, the same reply is forthcoming if we ask, "Is it possible for the moral agent in the taking of his decision to *dis*believe that he is the *sole* author of that decision?" Clearly he cannot disbelieve that it is *he* who takes the decision. That, however, is not in itself sufficient to enable him, on reflection, to regard himself as *solely* responsible for the act. For his "character" as so far formed might conceivably be a factor in determining it, and no one can suppose that the constitution of his "character" is uninfluenced by circumstances of heredity and environment with which *he* has nothing to do. But as we pointed out . . . , the very essence of the moral decision as it is experienced is that it is a decision whether or not to *oppose* our character. I think we are entitled to say, therefore, that the act of moral decision is one in which the self is for itself not merely "author" but "sole author."

7. We may pass on, then, to the second phase of our constructive argument; and this will demand more elaborate treatment. Even if a moral agent *qua* making a moral decision in the situation of "temptation" cannot help believing that he has free will in the sense at issue — a moral freedom between real alternatives, between genuinely open possibilities — are there, nevertheless, objections to a freedom of this kind so cogent that we are bound to distrust the evidence of "inner experience"?

I begin by drawing attention to a simple point whose significance tends, I think, to be underestimated. If the phenomenological analysis we have offered is substantially correct, no one while functioning as a moral agent can help believing that he enjoys free will. Theoretically he may be completely convinced by Determinist arguments, but when actually confronted with a personal situation of conflict between duty and desire he is quite certain that it lies with him here and now whether or not he will rise to duty. It follows that if Determinists could produce convincing theoretical arguments against a free will of this kind, the awkward predicament would ensue that man has to deny as a theoretical being what he had to assert as a practical being. Now I think the Determinist ought to be a good deal more worried about this than he usually is. He seems to imagine that a strong case on general theoretical grounds is enough to prove that the "practical" belief in free will, even if inescapable for us as practical beings, is mere illusion. But in fact it proves nothing of the sort. There is no reason whatever why a belief that we find ourselves obliged to hold *qua* practical beings should be required to give way before a belief which we find ourselves obliged to hold *qua* theoretical beings; or, for that matter, vice versa. All that the theoretical arguments of Determinism can prove, unless they are reinforced by a refutation of the phenomenological analysis that support Libertarianism, is that there is a radical conflict between the theoretical and the practical sides of man's nature, an antinomy at the very heart of the self. And this is a state of affairs with which no one can easily rest satisfied. I think therefore that the Determinist ought to concern himself a great deal more than he does with phenomenological analysis, in order to show, if he can, that the assurance of free will is not really an inexpungable element in man's practical consciousness. There is just as much obligation upon him, convinced though he may be of the soundness of his theoretical arguments, to expose the errors of the Libertarian's phenomenological analysis, as there is upon us, convinced though we may be of the soundness of the Libertarian's phenomenological analysis, to expose the errors of the Determinist's theoretical arguments.

8. However, we must at once begin the discharge of our own obligation. The rest of this lecture will be devoted to trying to show that the arguments which seem to carry most weight with Determinists are, to say the least of it, very far from compulsive.

Fortunately a good many of the arguments which at an earlier time in the history of philosophy would have been strongly urged against us make almost no appeal to the bulk of philosophers today, and we may here pass them by. That applies to any criticism of "open possibilities" based on a metaphysical theory about the nature of the universe as a whole. Nobody today *has* a metaphysical theory about the nature of the universe as a whole! It applies also, with almost equal force, to criticisms based upon the universality of causal law as a supposed postulate of science. There have always been, in my opinion, sound philosophic reasons for doubting the validity, as distinct from the convenience, of the causal postulate in its universal form, but at the present time, when scientists themselves are deeply divided about the need for postulating causality even within their own special field, we shall do better to concentrate our attention upon criticisms which are more confidently advanced. I propose to ignore also, on different grounds, the type of criticism of free will that is sometimes advanced from the side of religion, based upon religious postulates of Divine Omnipotence and Omniscience. So far as I can see, a postulate of human freedom is every bit as necessary to meet certain religious demands (e.g. to make sense of the "conviction of sin"), as postulates of Divine Omniscience and Omnipotence are to meet certain other religious demands. If so, then it can hardly be argued that religious experience as such tells more strongly against than for the position we are defending; and we may be satisfied, in the present context, to leave the matter there. It will be more profitable to discuss certain arguments which contemporary philosophers do think important, and which recur with a somewhat monotonous regularity in the literature of anti-Libertarianism.

These arguments can, I think, be reduced in principle to no more than two; first, the argument from "predictability"; second, the argument from the alleged meaninglessness of an act supposed to be the self's act and yet not an expression of the self's character. Contemporary criticism of free will seems to me to consist almost exclusively of variations on these two themes. I shall deal with each in turn.

9. On the first we touched in passing at an earlier stage. Surely it is beyond question (the critic urges) that when we know a person intimately we can foretell with a high degree of accuracy how he will respond to at least a large number

of practical situations. One feels safe in predicting that one's dog-loving friend will not use his boot to repel the little mongrel that comes yapping at his heels; or again that one's wife will not pass with incurious eyes (or indeed pass at all) the new hat-shop in the city. So to behave would not be (as we say) "in character." But, so the criticism runs, you with your doctrine of "genuinely open possibilities," of a free will by which the self can diverge from its own character, remove all rational basis from such prediction. You require us to make the absurd supposition that the success of countless predictions of the sort in the past has been mere matter of chance. If you *really* believed in your theory, you would not be surprised if tomorrow your friend with the notorious horror of strong drink should suddenly exhibit a passion for whisky and soda, or if your friend whose taste for reading has hitherto been satisfied with the sporting columns of the newspapers should be discovered on a fine Saturday afternoon poring over the works of Hegel. But of course you *would* be surprised. Social life would be sheer chaos if there were not well-grounded social expectations; and social life is not sheer chaos. Your theory is hopelessly wrecked upon obvious facts.

Now whether or not this criticism holds good against some versions of Libertarian theory I need not here discuss. It is sufficient if I can make it clear that against the version advanced in this lecture according to which free will is localised in a relatively narrow field of operation, the criticism has no relevance whatsoever.

Let us remind ourselves briefly of the setting within which, on our view, free will functions. There is X, the course which we believe we ought to follow, and Y, the course towards which we feel our desire is strongest. The freedom which we ascribe to the agent is the freedom to put forth or refrain from putting forth the moral effort required to resist the pressure of desire and do what he thinks he ought to do.

But then there is surely an immense range of practical situations — covering by far the greater part of life — in which there is no question of a conflict within the self between what he most desires to do and what he thinks he ought to do? Indeed such conflict is a comparatively rare phenomenon for the majority of men. Yet over that whole vast range there is nothing whatever in our version of Libertarianism to prevent our agreeing that character determines conduct. In the absence, real or supposed, of any "moral" issue, what a man chooses will be simply that course which, after such reflection as seems called for, he deems most likely to bring him what he most strongly desires; and that is the same as to say the course to which his present character inclines him.

Over by far the greatest area of human choices, then, our theory offers no more barrier to successful prediction on the basis of character than any other theory. For where there is no clash of strongest desire with duty, the free will we are defending has no business. There is just nothing for it to do.

But what about the situations — rare enough though they may be — in which there *is* this clash and in which free will does therefore operate? Does our theory entail that there at any rate, as the critic seems to suppose, "anything may happen"?

Not by any manner of means. In the first place, and by the very nature of the case, the range of the agent's possible choices is bounded by what he thinks he ought to do on the one hand, and what he most strongly desires on the other. The freedom claimed for him is a freedom of decision to make or withhold the effort required to do what he thinks he ought to do. There is no question of a freedom to act in some "wild" fashion, out of all relation to his characteristic beliefs and desires. This so-called "freedom of caprice," so often charged against the Libertarian, is, to put it bluntly, a sheer figment of the critic's imagination, with no *habitat* in serious Libertarian theory. Even in situations where free will does come into play it is perfectly possible, on a view like ours, given the appropriate knowledge of a man's character, to predict within certain limits how he will respond.

But "probable" prediction in such situations can, I think, go further than this. It is obvious that where desire and duty are at odds, the felt "gap" (as it were) between the two may vary enormously in breadth in different cases. The moderate drinker and the chronic tippler may each want another glass, and each deem it his duty to abstain, but the felt gap between desire and duty in the case of the former is trivial beside the great gulf which is felt to separate them in the case of the latter. Hence it will take a far harder moral effort for the tippler than for the moderate drinker to achieve the same external result of absention. So much is matter of common agreement. And we are entitled, I think, to take it into account in prediction, on the simple principle that the harder the moral effort required to resist desire the less likely it is to occur. Thus in the example taken, most people would predict that the tippler will very probably succumb to his desires, whereas there is a reasonable likelihood that the moderate drinker will make the comparatively slight effort needed to resist them. So long as the prediction does not pretend to more than a measure of probability, there is nothing in our theory which would disallow it.

I claim, therefore, that the view of free will I have been putting forward is consistent with predictability of conduct on the basis of character over a very wide field indeed. And I make the further claim that the field will cover all the situations of life concerning which there is any empirical evidence that successful prediction is possible.

10. Let us pass on to consider the second main line of criticism. This is, I think, much the more illuminating of the two, if only because it compels the Libertarian to make explicit certain concepts which are indispensable to him, but which, being desperately hard to state clearly, are apt not to be stated at all. The critic's fundamental point might be stated somewhat as follows:

"Free will as you describe it is completely unintelligible. On your own showing no *reason* can be given, because there just *is* no reason, why a man decides to exert rather than to withhold moral effort, or vice versa. But such an act—or more properly, such an 'occurrence'—it is nonsense to speak of as an act of a *self*. If there is nothing in the self's character to which it is, even in principle, in any way traceable, the self has nothing to do with it. Your so-called 'freedom,' therefore, so far from supporting the self's moral responsibility, destroys it as surely as the crudest Determinism could do."

If we are to discuss this criticism usefully, it is important, I think, to begin by getting clear about two different senses of the word "intelligible."

If, in the first place, we mean by an "intelligible" act one whose occurrence is in principle capable of being inferred, since it follows necessarily from something (though we may not know in fact from what), then it is certainly true that the Libertarian's free will is unintelligible. But that is only saying, is it not, that the Libertarian's "free" act is not an act which follows necessarily from something! This can hardly rank as a *criticism* of Libertarianism. It is just a description of it. That there can be nothing unintelligible in *this* sense is precisely what the Determinist has got to *prove*.

Yet it is surprising how often the critic of Libertarianism involves himself in this circular mode of argument. Repeatedly it is urged against the Libertarian, with a great air of triumph, that on his view he can't say *why* I now decide to rise to duty, or now decide to follow my strongest desire in defiance of duty. Of course he can't. If he could he wouldn't *be* a Libertarian. To "account for" a "free" act is a contradiction in terms. A free will is *ex hypothesi* the sort of thing of which the request for an *explanation* is absurd. The assumption that an explanation must be in principle possible for the act of moral decision deserves to rank as a classic example of the ancient fallacy of "begging the question."

But the critic usually has in mind another sense of the word "unintelligible." He is apt to take it for granted that an act which is unintelligible in the *above* sense (as the morally free act of the Libertarian undoubtedly is) is unintelligible in the *further* sense that we can attach no meaning to it. And this is an altogether more serious matter. If it could really be shown that the Libertarian's "free will" were unintelligible in this sense of being meaningless, that, for myself at any rate, would be the end of the affair. Libertarianism would have been conclusively refuted.

But it seems to me manifest that this can *not* be shown. The critic has allowed himself, I submit, to become the victim of a widely accepted but fundamentally vicious assumption. He has assumed that whatever is meaningful must exhibit its meaningfulness to those who view it from the standpoint of external observation. Now if one chooses thus to limit one's self to the role of external observer, it is, I think, perfectly true that one can attach no meaning to an act which is the act of something we call a "self" and yet follows from nothing in that self's character. But then *why should we* so limit ourselves, when what is under consideration is a subjective activity? For the apprehension of subjective acts there is *another* standpoint available, that of *inner experience,* of the practical consciousness in its actual functioning. If our free will should turn out to be something to which we can attach a meaning from *this* standpoint, no more is required. And no more ought to be expected. For I must repeat that only from the inner standpoint of living experience *could* anything of the nature of "activity" be directly grasped. Observation from without is in the nature of the case impotent to apprehend the active *qua* active. We can from without observe sequences of states. If into these we read activity (as we sometimes do), this can only be on the basis of what we discern in ourselves from the inner standpoint. It follows that if anyone insists upon taking his criterion of the meaningful simply from the standpoint of external observation, he is really deciding in advance of the evidence that the notion of activity, and *a fortiori* the notion of a free will, is "meaningless." He looks for the free act through a medium which is in the nature of the case incapable of revealing it, and then, because inevitably he doesn't find it, he declares that it doesn't exist!

But if, as we surely ought in this context, we adopt the inner standpoint, then (I am suggesting) things appear in a totally different light. From the inner standpoint, it seems to me plain, there is no difficulty whatever in attaching meaning to an act which is the self's act and which nevertheless does not follow from the self's character. So much I claim has been established by the phenomenological analysis . . . of the act of moral decision in face of moral temptation. It is thrown into particularly clear relief where the moral decision is to make the moral effort required to rise to duty. For the very function of moral effort, as it appears to the agent engaged in the act, is to enable the self to act against the line of resistance, against the line to which his character as so far formed most strongly inclines him. But if the self is thus conscious here of *combating* his formed character, he surely cannot possibly suppose that the act, although his own act, *issues from* his formed character? I submit, therefore, that the self knows very well indeed—from the inner standpoint—what is meant by an act which is the *self's* act and which nevertheless does not follow from the self's *character*.

What this implies—and it seems to me to be an implication of cardinal importance for any theory of the self that aims at being more than superficial—is that the nature of the self is for itself something more than just its character as so far formed. The "nature" of the self and what we commonly call the "character" of the self are by no means the same thing, and it is utterly vital that they should not be confused. The "nature" of the self comprehends, but is not without remainder reducible to, its "character"; it must, if we are to be true to the testimony of our experience of it, be taken as including *also* the authentic creative power of fashioning and re-fashioning "character."

The misguided, and as a rule quite uncritical, belittlement, of the evidence offered by inner experience has, I am convinced, been responsible for more bad argument by the opponents of Free Will than has any other single factor. How often, for example, do we find the Determinist critic saying, in effect, "*Either* the act follows necessarily upon precedent states, *or* it is a mere matter of chance and accordingly of no moral significance." The disjunction is invalid, for it does not exhaust the possible alternatives. It seems to the critic to do so only because he *will* limit himself to the standpoint which is proper, and indeed alone possible, in dealing with the physical world, the standpoint of the external observer. If only he would allow himself to assume the standpoint which is not merely proper for, but necessary to, the apprehension of subjective activity, the inner standpoint of the practical consciousness in its actual functioning, he would find himself obliged to recognise the falsity of his disjunction. Reflection upon the act of moral decision as apprehended from the inner standpoint would force him to recognise a *third* possibility, as remote from chance as from necessity, that, namely, of *creative activity*, in which (as I have ventured to express it) nothing determines the act save the agent's doing of it.

11. There we must leave the matter. But as this lecture has been, I know, somewhat densely packed, it may be helpful if I conclude by reminding you, in bald summary, of the main things I have been trying to say. Let me set them out in so many successive theses.

1. The freedom which is at issue in the traditional Free Will problem is the freedom which is presupposed in moral responsibility.

2. Critical reflection upon carefully considered attributions of moral responsibility reveals that the only freedom that will do is a freedom which permits to inner acts of choice, and that these acts must be acts (*a*) of which the self is *sole* author, and (*b*) which the self could have performed otherwise.

3. From phenomenological analysis of the situation of moral temptation we find that the self as engaged in this situation is inescapably convinced that it possesses a freedom of precisely the specified kind, located in the decision to exert or withhold the moral effort needed to rise to duty where the pressure of its desiring nature is felt to urge it in a contrary direction.

4. Of the two types of Determinist criticism which seem to have most influence today, that based on the predictability of much human behaviour fails to touch a Libertarianism which confines the area of free will as above indicated. Libertarianism so understood is compatible with all the predictability that the empirical facts warrant. And:

5. The second main type of criticism, which alleges the "meaninglessness" of an act which is the self's act and which is yet not determined by the self's character, is based on a failure to appreciate that the standpoint of inner experience is not only legitimate but indispensable where what is at issue is the reality and nature of a subjective activity. The creative act of moral decision is inevitably meaningless to the mere external observer, but from the inner standpoint it is as real, and as significant, as anything in human experience.

Suggestions for Further Readings

On the Mind/Body Problem

Ned Block (ed.), *Readings in the Philosophy of Psychology*, 2 vols. Cambridge, Massachusetts, MIT Press, 1981.

Daniel Dennett, *Brainstorms*. Cambridge, Massachusetts, MIT Press, 1978.

Jerry Fodor, *Psychological Explanation*. New York, Random House, 1968.

John Haugland, *Mind Design*. Cambridge, Massachusetts, MIT Press, 1981.

David Rosenthal (ed.), *Materialism and the Mind-Body Problem*. Englewood Cliffs, Prentice-Hall, 1971.

John Searle, "Minds, Brains, and Programs," in *Behavior and Brain Sciences*, vol. 3, pp. 417–457, 1980.

On Freedom of the Will

Daniel Dennett, *Elbow Room*. Cambridge, Massachusetts, MIT Press, 1985.

Gerald Dworkin (ed.), *Determinism, Free Will, and Moral Responsibility*. Englewood Cliffs, Prentice-Hall, 1970.

Gary Watson (ed.), *Free Will*. New York, Oxford University Press, 1982.

On Egoism and Altruism

Robert Axelrod, *The Evolution of Cooperation*. New York, Basic Books, 1985.

Joel Feinberg, "Psychological Egoism," in J. Feinberg (ed.), *Reason and Responsibility*. Belmont, California, Wadsworth, 1981.

PART V
Ethics

·L·E·C·T·U·R·E·S·

Lecture 27

Ethics — Normative and Meta

The philosophical study of ethics (morality) concerns the nature of good and bad, right and wrong, justice and injustice. In the section of this course on the theory of knowledge, I addressed the question of what a person should _believe_. Ethics focuses on the question of _action_ — what actions should a person undertake to perform? Ethics deals with what may be the most fundamental personal question of all — how should you lead your life?

Ethics and Religion

People often think that ethical questions are inseparable from religious ones. During childhood, many of us had our moral training and our religious training mixed together. We were taught basic ethical principles (such as the Golden Rule) by being told how God wants us to act. In adulthood, disagreements about some ethical questions (for example, the permissibility of contraception or abortion) sometimes reflect differences over some religious doctrine.

If you think that ethics and religion are tightly bound together, it must puzzle you how an atheist or an agnostic could have strong moral convictions. Maybe you suspect that such people are being a little inconsistent: Perhaps you think that if someone does not believe that God exists, then he or she really should deny that there is a difference between right and wrong. A character in Fyodor Dostoyevsky's novel _The Brothers Karamazov_ expresses this idea when he says, "If God is dead, then everything is permitted."

If you tend to connect God and morality in this way, it may surprise you that a very central tradition in Western philosophy has sought to separate questions of ethics from questions about what God wants us to do. This tradition goes all the way back to Plato in fourth-century B.C. Greece. The philosophers in this tradition usually were not atheists. They believed in God (or in the gods, in Plato's case), but thought that ethical questions should be addressed independently of assumptions about whether there is a God and what God commands. I'll discuss this idea in Lecture 30.

Metaethics and Normative Ethics

The study of ethics divides into two large areas. These are _mataethics_ and _normative ethics_. The prefix "meta" suggests the idea of "aboutness." For example, metamathematics involves theories that are about mathematical theories; metalinguistic statements are statements about language. In metaethics, we consider general questions about the nature of morality and about the meaning of moral concepts. In metaethics we don't ask whether murder is wrong rather than right. Rather, we might inquire as to whether there really is a difference between right and wrong, or try to clarify what it means to classify an action as "wrong" or "right."

In normative ethics, on the other hand, we assume that there is a difference between right and wrong and ask: Which actions fall into the one category and which into the other? For example, utilitarians say that whether an action should be performed depends on whether it promotes the greatest happiness for the greatest number of people. An alternative position is that actions should not be performed if they are unjust, where the dictates of justice may not always coincide with what makes people happy. This dispute assumes that there is a correct answer to the question of what principles people should use to guide their actions. The problem in normative ethics is to determine what those principles are.

Truth and Opinion

Back in Lectures 1 and 2, I drew a distinction between truth and opinion. It's one thing to say that

> The Rockies are over 10,000 feet tall.

It's something else to say that

> Many people believe that the Rockies are over 10,000 feet tall.

The first of these propositions is true independently of anyone's believing it or saying that it is so. The second, obviously, depends for its truth on what people believe. There are objective facts about geology over and above the subjective opinions that people may happen to have.

Does this distinction apply to the case of ethics? There is variation in ethical opinions—people sometimes disagree about whether a given action is right or wrong, for example. But is there, in addition, a fact of the matter as to whether the action really *is* right or wrong? That is, are there objective facts in ethics, which exist above and beyond the subjective opinions that people have? This is the primary question I will consider in metaethics.

After surveying a range of possible answers to this question, I will move on to normative ethics in Lecture 31. When I do this, I will simply assume that there is a real difference between right and wrong. Given this assumption, I will ask what makes some actions have the one property and other actions have the other.

Alternative Metaethical Positions

To get started on the metaethical question of whether there are objective facts in ethics, I'm going to provide a road map to the different positions I'll consider. These positions divide up according to how they answer the following two questions:

(1) Are there any ethical truths?

(2) If so, what makes the ethical truths true?

Subjectivism   What would it mean to answer "no" to the first question? The idea here is that there are various ethical *opinions* that people have about right and wrong. But no statement that says that an action *is* right (or wrong) is, in fact, *true*. Opinions occupy what I have called *the subjective realm*. So the theory that says that there is opinion but no truth in ethics I'll call *ethical subjectivism*.

One way to describe this position is to use a distinction that David Hume made famous. It is the distinction between *is* and *ought*. Science aims to discover what *is* the case; ethics tries to describe the way things *ought* to be. A negative answer to question (1) might be understood to mean that all true propositions are *is*-propositions; there are no true *ought*-propositions. I'll consider in the next two lectures several arguments that have been suggested for saying "no" to question (1).

Realism   Consider next what the options are if you answer "yes" to question (1); that is, suppose that some ethical statements are true. Question (2) then becomes relevant: What makes those statements true? One possibility is that they are true independently of anyone's say-so. Ethical truths are true whether or not anyone thinks they are. This position I will call *ethical realism*.

Realism here does not mean what it means in politics — as when we say that someone is a political realist. We sometimes call people "political realists" when they are "practical" — they do not try too hard to do the right thing, because they think that the right thing is unattainable anyway. Humphrey Bogart is a realist of this sort at the beginning of the movie *Casablanca*, though he changes at the end.

Rather, ethical realism is the view that there are objective ethical facts that exist independently of anyone's say-so. If murder is wrong, this is not because you, I, or anyone says (or thinks) it is wrong. Hamlet says that nothing is right or wrong, unless thinking makes it so. This bit of poetry rejects ethical realism.

Conventionalism   The remaining option asserts that there are ethical truths, but maintains that these truths are true because of someone's say-so. I call this point of view *conventionalism*. Conventionalists differ from subjectivists in the way they answer question (1); they differ from realists in the way they answer question (2).

In the United States, people drive on the right side of the road. In England, they drive on the left. There is nothing inherently better about one procedure (suppose). They are equally workable as long as everybody in a country does the same thing. The key idea about conventions is that they embody *arbitrary decisions*. The reason you should drive on the right in the United States is simply that the people there have agreed that that is the rule to follow. In this case, a fact is brought into being by people's saying that things shall be one way rather than the other.

In Lecture 2, I made a general remark about how we should avoid "wishful thinking." For the vast majority of propositions we could consider, thinking (or saying) that they are true does not, all by itself, make them true. Saying or thinking that the Rocky Mountains are over 10,000 feet high does not make them so. Descartes (Lecture 13) thought he had found an exception to this pattern: He thought that the proposition "I am thinking" is made true by my thinking that it is true.

Conventionalism in ethics holds that the same goes for right and wrong. Someone's saying (or believing) that murder is wrong makes murder wrong. But conventionalists disagree among themselves as to whose say-so does the job.

The first conventionalist theory I'll consider is called *the Divine Command Theory*. It says that an act is right or wrong because and only because God says that it is. It isn't that murder (or whatever) is inherently bad. Rather, murder has the moral status it does only because God commanded that we behave in a certain way.

The second conventionalist theory is called *ethical relativism*. This view says that what is right or wrong is determined by the society you inhabit. If your society adopts norms that prohibit murder, then it is wrong for you to murder. If some other society adopts different standards, then it may be quite permissible for someone in that society to murder. Ethical truths are relative, not absolute. Murder isn't wrong absolutely; it is wrong relative to the norms of one society, but may be right relative to the norms of another. According to ethical relativism, it isn't God's say-so that makes the ethical truths true, but society's.

The third and last conventionalist theory I'll consider asserts that each individual constructs his or her own morality. It isn't just that each of us must decide for ourselves how we should live. Rather, the idea is that we make our actions right or wrong by deciding what standards to adopt. This idea is part of one version of the philosophy called *existentialism*.

In his book *Existentialism*, the French philosopher Jean-Paul Sartre (1905–1980) describes a young Frenchman during World War II who must decide between joining the Resistance to fight the Nazis or staying home to care for his ailing mother. Sartre says that there is no standard of conduct that determines what the young man should do. *He* must choose whether he wants to be one sort of person or another. Once this choice is made, his subsequent action thereby counts as good or bad. For Sartre's existentialism, it is the individual's say-so that makes his actions right or wrong.

This menu of options in metaethics is summarized on the next page. At the bottom of the flow chart are the names of the positions described above them.

In the next two lectures, I'll consider various arguments that have been made for subjectivism. After that, I'll discuss various conventionalist theories in metaethics, beginning with the Divine Command Theory and Plato's famous criticism of it. The position I'll reach by the end of my discussion of metaethics is that there is no good argument against ethical realism. I don't claim that I can prove that realism is true, but I do think that the attempts to refute it by conventionalists and subjectivists have not worked.

Review Questions

1. What is subjectivism? What does it mean to distinguish objective fact from subjective opinion in science? In ethics?

ETHICS —
NORMATIVE AND
META

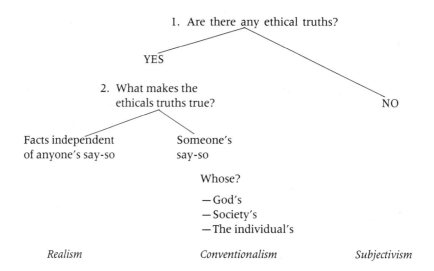

1. Are there any ethical truths?

YES

2. What makes the
   ethicals truths true?

NO

Facts independent
of anyone's say-so

Someone's
say-so

Whose?

— God's
— Society's
— The individual's

Realism   *Conventionalism*   *Subjectivism*

2. What does it mean to say that ethical truths are "conventional"?
3. What does it mean to say that ethical truths are "relative," as ethical relativism asserts? Relative to what?
4. What is ethical realism? How is it similar to conventionalism? How is it different?

A Problem for Further Thought

The study of ethics often involves discussion of principles that tell people that they should have acted in a way different from the way they did act; sometimes these principles require people to be less selfish and more altruistic. In Part IV, I argued that people have free will and that the thesis of psychological egoism is false. If either of these claims were false, would there still be a point to discussing ethical principles? Defend your answer.

Lecture 28

The Naturalistic Fallacy and the Is/Ought Gap

From the previous lecture, you should have a preliminary grasp of what ethical subjectivism is and of how it differs from ethical realism and ethical conventionalism. In this lecture and the next, I will consider several arguments for thinking that subjectivism is true. I'll suggest that none of these arguments is convincing.

In the previous lecture, I said that subjectivism is the view that no ethical statement is true. Often the view is given a slightly different formulation: Subjectivism says that ethical statements are *neither true nor false*. I think this representation of the doctrine is less apt to mislead, so I'll use it from now on. This is a small change, since if a statement is neither true nor false, then it is not true.

Subjectivism says that ethical statements have a particular characteristic. But what is an ethical statement? Examples include any statement of the form "*X* is morally wrong," or "*X* is morally permissible," or "*X* is unfair," or "*X* is unjust." The *X* may be filled in by a description of an action. So *both* the following statements are ethical statements:

(1) Murder is always morally wrong.

(2) Murder is sometimes morally permissible.

Ethical subjectivism claims that the first of these statements is not true. According to subjectivism, it isn't true that murder is always wrong. But the reason this isn't true is not that it is sometimes morally permissible to murder. Remember,

Subjectivism: Ethical Statements Are Neither True Nor False

Emotivism

Subjectivism says that there are no ethical facts. If subjectivism is true, why do we have ethical sentences in our language? What function do they perform, if there are no ethical facts for them to describe? The emotive theory of ethics ("emotivism") attempts to provide an answer.

"Ouch!" I exclaim when I hit my thumb with a hammer. "Whoppee!" I exclaim when a birthday cake is placed before me. In both cases, I have used language, but not to make an assertion. It would be a mistake to ask whether my utterances were true or false. They were neither.

"Ouch!" and "Whoppee!" express how I feel. Emotivism claims that ethical sentences allow speakers to express their feelings and attitudes. To say "murder is wrong" is not to make an assertion that is either true or false; it is to express a certain sort of attitude toward murder.

There is no doubt that ethical language is sometimes used in this expressive way. The question is whether there is anything more to ethical discourse than this.

When someone says,"You are an ignorant pig," the sentence is used to express the speaker's attitudes or feelings. However, that does not show that the sentence is neither true nor false. Besides having an expressive function, the sentence makes an assertion that is either true or false, depending on the characteristics of the person whom the speaker is addressing.

(1) and (2) are both ethical statements, and subjectivism claims that no ethical statement is true.

At first glance, it might seem that statements (1) and (2) have the following characteristic: Either one of them is true or the other is. Ethical subjectivism denies this, because it holds that there do not exist any ethical facts about murder. The formulation of ethical subjectivism that I am using—that ethical statements are *neither true nor false*—should alert you to the fact that subjectivism says that statements (1) and (2) are *both* untrue.

Does the Existence of Ethical Disagreement Show that Subjectivism Is True?

What arguments might be presented to support this view? Sometimes it is suggested that there can't be any ethical facts on the grounds that people disagree over what is right and what is wrong. In our own society, there are moral controversies. Some people hold that abortion is sometimes permissible, others that it is not. And even when you find actions about which there is broad consensus in our society, you can find other times and places at which there was no such consensus. For example, most people in our society would now agree that slavery is wrong, but if you go back 150 years (or even less), there was no such broad consensus.

Is the fact that ethical opinions vary (in space and time) a reason to accept subjectivism? I do not think so. Science also contains controversies. And what is now accepted often was controversial in the past. To use an example discussed in Lectures 5 and 6, scientists now accept the idea that life has evolved. But this scientific consensus did not always exist. And even now, there are people—creationists—who deny that evolution is a fact.

Even though there is and has been variation in opinion about whether evolution has occurred, all parties in this dispute believe that there is a fact of the matter about whether life has evolved. No one denies that there are facts about the history of life on earth. So lack of consensus about a question does not show that there is no objective answer to the question.

It is important to remember that ethical subjectivism is *not* the view that some ethical statements are controversial or are hard to prove or disprove. It says that each and every ethical statement is untrue. This includes "slavery is wrong" and "torturing babies for fun is wrong," just as much as it includes presently controversial claims about the moral status of abortion or capital punishment. If you are prepared to say that even one moral statement is true, you are rejecting subjectivism.

The Genetic Fallacy

Another argument for subjectivism says that the explanation of why we hold the ethical beliefs we do shows that there can't be any ethical facts. Most people would agree that it is wrong to totally neglect one's children. What might account for why we think this? Two kinds of explanation come to mind. First, society teaches us to think this way. Second, evolution may have led us to think this way; people who totally neglected their children would have been less reproductively successful than people who did not, and so the less fit trait of total child neglect would gradually have disappeared from the population. (For the basics on how a selection process is supposed to work, see Lecture 6.)

Suppose that there is a social or evolutionary explanation for why people think it is wrong to totally neglect their children. Does it follow that the ethical statement — "It is wrong to totally neglect your children" — is untrue? I do not think so. A belief is not shown to be untrue by the mere fact that you can explain why people hold the belief. Consider arithmetic. How do you explain the fact that most of us think that $2 + 3 = 5$? Society has taught us to think as much, and I suppose that evolution has somehow contributed to our capacity to have opinions about mathematics. But this does not show that there is no fact of the matter about whether $2 + 3 = 5$.

Philosophers call the mistake I'm discussing here "the genetic fallacy." The word "genetic" means *cause* (as in the "genesis" of a belief); the word has nothing much to do with chromosomes. The mistake is to think that a fact about how you come to believe something by itself settles whether the belief is true. In the next lecture, I'll consider a slightly different and more subtle version of this argument. For now the point is that you don't establish subjectivism just by pointing out that there is an explanation for why we have the ethical beliefs we do.

So much for these two arguments for subjectivism. I now turn to two others. The first involves the idea of a "naturalistic fallacy"; the second focuses on Hume's distinction between is-statements and ought-statements.

The idea of a "naturalistic fallacy" is due to the English philosopher G. E. Moore (1873–1958). In his book *Principia Ethica* (1903), Moore criticized the idea that the ethical properties of an action — for example, its rightness or wrongness — might be identical with some "natural" property of that action. An example of such a naturalistic theory is provided by one form of utilitarianism, which I'll call hedonistic utilitarianism. This theory says that for an action to be ethically right is for it to maximize pleasure and minimize pain for those affected by it.

The Naturalistic Fallacy

I'm not suggesting that this theory is correct. My point is that it is an example of a moral theory that identifies an ethical property with a natural property. In particular, the theory says that the rightness or wrongness of an action is one and the same property as a certain set of the action's psychological consequences. A natural scientist — a psychologist — could inquire whether one action produces more pleasure and less pain than another. According to hedonistic utilitarianism, this scientist would be investigating whether the first action is ethically preferable to the second.

So utilitarianism proposes an "identity thesis," which bears a logical similarity to the mind/brain identity thesis discussed in Lecture 21. An ethical property is said to be identical with a natural property. By "natural property," I mean a property that the natural sciences (including psychology) might investigate.

Moore thought that the theory just described makes a mistake, which he called the naturalistic fallacy. He thought it is always a mistake to say that an ethical property of an action is the same property as one of its natural properties. Why is it a fallacy to do this? According to Moore, we can see this by considering the meanings of the terms involved. The term "morally right" does not mean the same thing as the term "maximizes pleasure and minimizes pain." From this, Moore thought it followed that hedonistic utilitarianism is mistaken.

So Moore's argument goes like this:

(NFA)

> The expression "x is morally preferable to y" does not mean the same thing as the expression "x produces more pleasure and less pain than y."
> _____
> Hence, the property named by the first expression is not identical with the property named by the second.

Moore thought that any ethical theory that equates an ethical property with a natural property could be refuted by this type of argument. Any such theory, he said, commits the naturalistic fallacy. Let us call this argument of Moore's the naturalistic fallacy argument (NFA).

I claim that Moore is mistaken. For two terms to refer to the same property, it isn't essential that they mean the same thing (be synonymous). Chemistry tells us that the temperature of a gas is one and the same property as the mean molecular kinetic energy of the gas. This claim is not refuted by the fact that "temperature" and "mean kinetic energy" are not synonymous expressions. Consider the following argument:

> The expression "temperature" does not mean the same thing as the expression "mean kinetic energy."
> _____
> Hence, the property named by the first expression is not identical with the property named by the second.

This argument is a fallacy. So is Moore's. In other words, I think that Moore's argument concerning the naturalistic fallacy is itself a fallacy. He commits what I will call (following John Searle) the naturalistic fallacy fallacy.

Moore failed to establish the thesis that ethical properties are not identical with naturalistic properties. Call this "Moore's thesis." I now want to consider a quite separate question. Suppose, just for the sake of argument, that Moore's thesis is correct. Would subjectivism follow from this?

Moore did not think so. Moore was no subjectivist. He believed that there are ethical facts and that these ethical facts exist quite apart from the naturalistic facts investigated by science. For Moore, there are two kinds of truths—ethical truths and naturalistic ones.

Others have gone in the opposite direction; they have thought that Moore's thesis leads to ethical subjectivism; they have claimed that if ethics fails to reduce to naturalistic facts, then there are no ethical facts at all.

Moore's thesis does not, all by itself, imply subjectivism. Rather, Moore's thesis, combined with a second idea, leads to subjectivism. Here's the argument we need to consider:

(S1): An Argument for Subjectivism with Moore's Thesis as a Premiss

> Ethical properties are not identical with naturalistic properties (Moore's thesis).
>
> (S1) If ethical properties are not identical with naturalistic properties, then ethical statements are neither true nor false (reductionist thesis).
> _____
> Hence, ethical statements are neither true nor false.

I'll call this argument (S1) ("S" for subjectivism).

I have suggested that Moore's argument for the first premiss in (S1) does not work. What I want you to see now is that the first premiss, even if it were true, would not be enough to establish subjectivism. To reach the conclusion that subjectivism is true, (S1) requires the reductionist thesis as well as Moore's thesis. I call the second premiss "reductionist" because it says that a property must reduce to (be identical with) a naturalistic (scientific) property if there are to be any ethical facts.

Moore accepted the first premiss of (S1), but rejected the second. I have not said how I view the second premiss. But I have claimed that Moore's defense of the first premiss does not work. I'll return to the second premiss in a moment.

I said before that two ideas are sometimes confused when people discuss "the naturalistic fallacy." The first is Moore's; the second is Hume's. Although I claimed that Moore failed to establish his thesis, I think Hume was right in what he claimed. However, once again, I'm going to argue that what Hume was right about does not entail subjectivism.

Hume: The Is/Ought Gap

Hume claimed that an ethical statement (describing what *ought* to be the case) cannot be validly deduced from a set of premisses that describes only what *is* the case. Consider the following argument:

> Torturing babies for fun causes great suffering.
> _____
> Hence, torturing babies for fun is wrong.

The single premiss of this argument describes what is the case, not what ought to be the case. The conclusion concerns what ought to be the case. Hume said you can't deduce an ought-conclusion from exclusively is-premisses. The argument just given, he claimed, is not deductively valid.

Of course, this argument can be turned into a deductively valid argument by adding another premiss. The following argument *is* deductively valid:

> Torturing babies for fun causes great suffering.
> Causing great suffering is wrong.
> _____
> Hence, torturing babies for fun is wrong.

Remember what it means to say that an argument is deductively valid (Lecture 2). In a deductively valid argument, IF the premisses are true, then the conclusion cannot fail to be true. In saying that an argument is valid, I am not saying that the premisses are true (remember the IF!).

The argument just displayed does not deduce an ought-conclusion from exclusively is-premisses. The second premiss is an ethical statement. So Hume's point might be put like this: If a deductively valid argument has an ethical conclusion, at least one of the premisses must be ethical in character as well.

Hume's point is sometimes characterized by saying that you can't infer an ethical conclusion from purely nonethical premisses. This is an acceptable rendition of Hume's thesis if "infer" is taken to mean *validly deduce*. However, if nondeductive inference (Lecture 3) is involved, I don't accept the formulation just given. It seems to me that the fact that torturing babies causes great suffering is an excellent reason for thinking that the action is wrong. *X* can be a reason for *Y* even though *Y* does not deductively follow from *X*.

(S2): An Argument for Subjectivism With Hume's Thesis as a Premiss

Hume's thesis concerns a fact about deductive implication. Does this thesis lead to subjectivism? Again, I think the answer is *no*. To see why, consider the following argument for subjectivism:

> You can't validly deduce an ethical statement from purely is-premisses (Hume's thesis).
> _____
>
> Hence, ethical statements are neither true nor false.

This argument is not deductively valid. However, a premiss can be added so that the resulting argument is valid:

> You can't deduce an ethical statement from purely is-premisses (Hume's thesis).
>
> (S2) If ethical statements are not deducible from purely is-premisses, then ethical statements are neither true nor false (reductionist premiss).
> _____
>
> Hence, ethical statements are neither true nor false.

(S2) is a valid argument for subjectivism. However, I find the second premiss highly dubious. Why not adopt an antireductionist view of the status of ethical statements? That is, why not hold that some ethical statements are true even though they are not reducible to (deducible from) purely is-statements?

Here's an analogy. It's fairly clear that astronomy and anthropology describe different sorts of facts. Astronomers are interested in planets, stars, and other heavenly objects. Anthropologists, on the other hand, study similarities and differences among human cultures.

What does it mean to say that these are different subjects? One implication is that you can't deduce anthropological statements from purely astronomical ones. Describing the orbits and masses of the planets in the solar system does not allow you to deduce which customs are followed in which human cultures.

Would it be plausible to conclude that there are no anthropological facts simply because anthropological statements cannot be deduced from astronomical statements? Presumably not. That is, the following statement is not deductively valid:

> You can't deduce anthropological statements from purely astronomical premisses.
> _____
> Hence, anthropological statements are neither true nor false.

This next argument, though deductively valid, has a dubious reductionist second premiss:

> You can't deduce anthropological statements from purely astronomical premisses.
> If a statement is not deducible from purely astronomical premisses, then the statement is neither true nor false (reductionist premiss).
> _____
> Hence, anthropological statements are neither true nor false.

We should reject this argument. A perfectly sensible position is that there are facts in anthropology and facts in astronomy, even though neither reduces to (is deducible from) the other. The facts coexist as separate aspects of reality.

Hume correctly noted that you can't deduce an ought-conclusion from purely is-premisses. But subjectivism does not follow just from this point. Rather, to get subjectivism from Hume's insight, you've got to make a reductionist assumption. I see no compelling reason to be a reductionist about ethical statements. Even if ethical statements can't be deduced from purely is-premisses, that does not show that ethical statements are neither true nor false. I conclude that Hume's insight does not lead to subjectivism. So I reject argument (S2).

Moore correctly claimed that ethical expressions are not synonymous with naturalistic expressions. However, Moore went on to claim that ethical properties are not identical with naturalistic properties. This thesis of Moore's does not follow. And even if Moore were right that ethical properties are irreducibly different from natural properties, subjectivism would not follow from that. So I reject argument (S1).

Although (S1) and (S2) are different arguments for subjectivism, they have something in common. Both assume that if there are ethical truths, these truths must be connected in an especially intimate way with naturalistic truths; ethical statements must "boil down to" the facts described by is-propositions if ethical statements are to be true. Can this assumption that the two arguments share be defended or refuted?

Review Questions

1. How do subjectivists view the statement, "Lying is always wrong"? Do subjectivists reject this statement because they think that lying is sometimes morally legitimate?

2. Does the fact that people disagree about ethical issues show that subjectivism is true?

3. Suppose that there is a social or a biological explanation for why people have the ethical beliefs they do. Does this show that those beliefs are untrue?

4. What does Moore mean by the "naturalistic fallacy"? If Moore were right about the naturalistic fallacy, would subjectivism follow?

5. Hume saw that there is a "gap" between *is* and *ought*. What does this mean? Does Hume's insight show that subjectivism is true?

Problems for Further Thought

1. In Lecture 18, I explained Frege's distinction between *sense* and *reference*. Explain how that distinction can be used to clarify the mistake Moore makes in his naturalistic fallacy argument (NFA).

2. In discussing the genetic fallacy, I argued that you don't prove that a sentence is untrue just by showing that there is a causal explanation for why people believe the sentence. Can you construct an example in which the explanation for why people believe a sentence makes it highly improbable that the sentence is true? If such an example can be constructed, does this show that the so-called genetic fallacy is not a fallacy at all?

3. To say that someone is *cruel* is to describe the person's mind. In addition, the description seems to imply that there is something bad about the person. So a descriptive statement seems to imply a normative one. Does this refute Hume's thesis about the gap between is-statements and ought-statements?

_____ *Lecture 29* _____

Observation and Explanation in Ethics

Some people find ethical subjectivism an attractive philosphical position because they think that ethics and science are fundamentally different. To them, it is reasonable to talk about scientific facts. But it strikes them that ethics is very different — different enough that it is a mistake to think that there are ethical facts. The problem for subjectivism is to make precise the gut feeling that there is a difference here: Can it be stated in such a way that a convincing case for ethical subjectivism emerges?

All too often, the idea that there is an important difference between science and ethics rests on a misconception of one, the other, or both. One such misconception is the idea that reasoning can play no role in ethics—that ethics is nothing more than the irrational outpouring of feelings about what we think and do.

It is not to be denied that people often are strongly moved by feelings when they talk about right and wrong. But people sometimes care passionately about scientific matters and about nonethical matters that arise in everyday life.

In addition, it is important to see that reasoning *can* play a role in ethics—that ethical statements can be subjected to rational criticism. An example of how this can occur is provided by Gilbert Harman (in his book *The Nature of Morality*, New York, Oxford University Press, 1977). He asks us to consider the following principle: "If you have a choice between five people alive and one dead or one alive and five dead, you should always choose the first option over the second."

This principle is a generalization. Should we accept it? One way to tell is to see what it implies about specific examples—about concrete situations that people might find themselves in. Harman asks us to consider the following example, which is one test case for the principle:

> You are a doctor in a hospital's emergency room when six accident victims are brought in. All six are in danger of dying but one is much worse off than the others. You can just barely save that person if you devote all your resources to him and let the others die. Alternatively you can save the other five if you are willing to ignore the most seriously injured person.

Harman says that in this case, the doctor should save the five and let the sixth person die. This is Harman's moral judgment about the example problem. I agree with Harman about this, and I'll assume that you do too. So in this case, what we are prepared to say about the example is consistent with the dictates of the principle. Harman concludes that this example is *evidence in favor* of this principle.

Harman next considers a quite different situation that a doctor might face:

> You have five patients in the hospital who are dying, each in need of a separate organ. One needs a kidney, another a lung, a third a heart, and so forth. You can save all five if you take a single healthy person and remove his heart, lungs, kidneys, and so forth, to distribute to these five patients. Just such a healthy person is in Room 306. He is in the hospital for routine tests. Having seen his test results, you know that he is perfectly healthy and of the right tissue compatibility. If you do nothing, he will survive without incident; the other patients will die, however. The other five patients can be saved only if the person in Room 306 is cut up and his organs distributed. In that case, there would be one dead but five saved.

Harman's judgment about this case, with which I also agree, is that it would be wrong for the doctor to save the five by taking the organs of the sixth. This example, then, is evidence that the general principle stated before is false.

OBSERVATION
AND
EXPLANATION IN
ETHICS

Testing General Principles by Applying Them to Specific Examples

In this kind of discussion, we reason about the correctness of a general principle by seeing what it implies about concrete cases. We reject the principle because of an ethical judgment we are prepared to make about a concrete case (the second one just mentioned). Or, if we disagree with Harman about his judgment on this second case, we might conclude that the general principle is plausible after all. The point is that we can run a *consistency check* on the various ethical opinions we have, making sure that our general principles do not contradict what we believe about specific cases.

This kind of procedure is very important in ethics. Philosophers frequently evaluate a general moral theory by seeing what it implies about specific examples. For this procedure to be possible, we must be prepared to make ethical judgments about the cases considered. This is what Harman did when he used his moral judgment about the second example to argue that the general principle is false.

Let's compare this specimen of ethical reasoning to what scientists do when they want to test a theory. Scientists test a general theory by seeing what it implies about particular cases. For example, a general theory about electrons might predict that a laboratory instrument in a certain experiment will read "7.6" at a certain time. The scientist then can look at the instrument and see if it reads what the theory predicts. If the reading differs from what is predicted, this may count against the theory.

Thought Experiments Versus Real Experiments

In science, one sees what a theory implies about what can be observed; then, one goes ahead and makes the required observations. However, in the ethical case just discussed, no observation was required. We figured out what the general principle implies about the hypothetical case of the doctor contemplating the transplant operations, decided that this implication is unacceptable, and thereby rejected the general principle. The ethics case involved what is sometimes called a "thought experiment."

Thought experiments differ from real experiments in that thought experiments do not involve actually making observations. So we now face this question: Does ethics differ from science in that science involves observation, whereas ethics does not? Harman poses the question as follows:

> You can observe someone do something, but can you ever perceive the rightness or wrongness of what he does? If you round a corner and see a group of young hoodlums pour gasoline on a cat and ignite it, you do not need to *conclude* that what they are doing is wrong; you do not need to figure anything out; you can *see* that it is wrong. But is your reaction due to the actual wrongness of what you see or is it simply a reflection of your moral "sense," a "sense" that you have acquired perhaps as a result of your moral upbringing?

Observations Are "Theory Laden"

Harman then argues that there are no "pure" observations, that all observation is "theory laden." What does this mean? For you to see *that the children have poured gasoline on a cat and have ignited it*, you have to understand the concepts involved. If you don't know what a child is, or what a cat is, or what gasoline is, then you will not see that this is what is going on.

To make this more precise, let's distinguish two aspects of the process we call *seeing*. We talk of seeing objects ("*S* sees the cat"). And we talk of seeing that this or that proposition is true ("*S* sees that the cat is on fire"). I'll call these *objectual seeing* and *propositional seeing*. Notice that the expression following the verb in objectual seeing names an object ("the cat"), whereas the expression following the verb in propositional seeing expresses a proposition ("that the cat is on fire"). The distinction between these two kinds of seeing is somewhat similar to that drawn in Lecture 12 between objectual and propositional knowledge.

Can you see a cat without knowing what a cat is? I would say *yes*. Young children can see a nuclear power plant without knowing that that is what they are looking at. But propositional seeing is different. To see that it is a cat that's on fire, you must understand the concepts that are found in the proposition. So propositional seeing is "theory laden" — you have to have information of various sorts to be able to see that a particular proposition is true.

Now let's go back to the comparison between ethics and science. When you round the corner and see what the children are doing, do you see *that they are doing something wrong*? I agree with Harman that the answer is *yes*. You make use of your background information — in this case, information about right and wrong. In just the same way, when you round the corner, you are able to see *that the children are setting a cat on fire* by making use of your background information (concerning what a cat looks like, and so on).

So Harman concludes (and I agree) that we make ethical observations every day, just as we make observations that concern nonethical matters. We are able to do this by using the background information we have to interpret the visual, auditory, and other sensory signals we receive.

Of course, a person who had no beliefs at all about right and wrong would not be able to see that what the children are doing is wrong. But it also is true that the child who has no information about what a nuclear power plant is would be unable to see that there is a nuclear power plant on the hill. The child's incapacity does not show that there are no objective facts about whether the hill has a nuclear power plant on it. I claim that we should say the same thing about the moral ignoramus. This person is unable to see that what the children are doing is wrong, but that does not refute the idea that what the children are doing *is* objectively wrong. You don't prove that subjectivism is true just by describing the incapacities of a moral ignoramus.

Observation Does Not Imply Objectivity

Saying that people make ethical observations does not imply that ethical facts exist. Consider aesthetic judgments — judgments about the beauty of a painting, for example. Suppose you are looking at a painting by Monet and judge that it is a beautiful example of French Impressionism. You would not be able to do this without a certain fund of background information. In addition, you needed to use your visual system to make this judgment. So perhaps it is true that you see that the painting has the characteristic just mentioned. We may conclude that observations occur in aesthetics. But this is not enough to show that there are "aesthetic facts" — that it is an objective question whether a given painting is beautiful. Someone might concede that people make aesthetic observations and still insist that beauty is in the eye of the beholder.

So far I've criticized two ideas — that ethics does not involve reasoning and that there is no such thing as observation in ethics. Both may seem to mark a difference between ethics and science, but neither really does. At the same time, the fact that ethics involves both reasoning and observation does not prove that there are ethical facts.

Insoluble
Disagreements

I'll now consider a third possible difference between science and ethics. It sometimes seems that there is not much possibility of rational persuasion in ethics. Two people may quite sincerely hold the views they do, and no matter how much they discuss their differences, neither will budge. In science, disagreements are common, but often they can be solved by bringing in new evidence that neither party initially had available. In ethics, it seems that people sometimes will stick to their convictions no matter how much new information is imparted. If so, we have *insoluble* disagreements in ethics. Perhaps this marks a difference between ethics and science.

I won't argue that there is no difference here (even though we should not forget that people can be pigheaded about nonethical matters as well). However, I do want to claim that the alleged difference is not enough to establish ethical subjectivism.

Think of a slave owner and an abolitionist in the United States in the 1850s arguing at length over the morality of slavery. Suppose the slave owner has shut his eyes to the humanity of slaves and to the suffering they endured. Imagine that the slave owner was made to take these facts to heart. Maybe some slave owners would have changed their minds if they had had to confront the full implications of slavery. But probably there were some slave owners whose hearts were sufficiently hardened (at least partly from economic self-interest) that even full information would not have made a difference to them. Let us imagine that the slave owner and the abolitionist are caught in an insoluble disagreement of this kind. Does it follow that there are no ethical facts?

Ethical facts, if they exist, often will be very hard for people to grasp. The reason is that our apprehension of them often will be clouded over by self-interest and self-deception. As difficult as scientific questions about atoms and molecules sometimes are, ethics is in this respect even harder. Perhaps ethics will be the last frontier of human knowledge; even after we have unlocked the secrets of the atom and of life itself, the problem of discovering the truths of ethics may remain unsolved.

So *IF* ethical facts were to exist, it would not be surprising that there are ethical disagreements, even insoluble ones. And of course, *IF* subjectivism were true, it likewise would not be surprising that there are ethical disagreements. So both hypotheses — that there are ethical facts and that there are not — can account for the observation that insoluble ethical disputes sometimes occur.

Values in Science

Hume's distinction between is-statements and ought-statements often leads people to think that science is value free. This seems to follow from the idea that science aims to establish what is the case and takes no stand on any ethical issue.

It is important not to confuse a distinction between different kinds of statements with a distinction between different sorts of activities. Hume's distinction concerned the former; it does not follow from Hume's distinction that science is an activity that is value free.

In fact, the practice of science is saturated with values. Some of these are more or less internal to the practice of research; others have to do with how science affects the rest of society.

A scientist's decision to pursue one research problem rather than another is a decision about what is of value. Sometimes a problem is worth pursuing because it promises to yield practical benefits. Research in medicine and engineering provides obvious examples. At other times, a scientist will pursue a problem because it is thought to be theoretically important. This too is a judgment of value; in sciences that are more theoretical than practical (more "pure" than "applied"), a problem may be judged important because scientists believe that its solution would advance our understanding of the world.

Judging the value of pursuing a research problem, whether practical or theoretical, becomes especially important when the research would impose significant costs. Research is often expensive, and the expense is often supported by government money. Another cost arises when the research is done on living things that may suffer and die in the course of the investigation. Responsible science requires that these considerations be taken into account.

After the scientist chooses a problem, value issues continue to be important. When scientists judge that the available evidence counts strongly against some theory, they will conclude that they ought not to believe it. Judgments about plausibility and evidence are normative; they concern what we should and should not believe.

Once the scientist has reached some judgment about what the solution is to the problem under investigation, another value issue arises. Should the results be published? If so, in what forum should they be aired? It is sometimes suggested that scientists should keep their results to themselves if publishing would be harmful. Others hold that society is better off in the long run if even the most unpleasant scientific results are made public. Notice that both these opposing positions take a stand on an issue of value: When should a scientist make the carefully tested results of inquiry public?

OBSERVATION
AND
EXPLANATION IN
ETHICS

We face two competing hypotheses: subjectivism, which denies that there are ethical truths, and realism, which asserts that there are ethical truths that are true independently of anyone's say-so. Is there any way to choose between these two hypotheses? Perhaps subjectivism has the advantage of being more *parsimonious* (an idea discussed in Lecture 21 on the mind/brain identity theory). If subjectivism can explain everything we observe just as well as the hypothesis that says there are ethical facts, then perhaps we should prefer the former hypothesis.

Harman advances an argument of this sort. He thinks that in spite of the similarities between science and ethics just described, there is, nevertheless, one big difference. It concerns the problem of explanation. In abductive arguments (Lecture 3), you obtain a reason for thinking that something exists if you can show that the existence of the thing is needed to explain an observation. Recall that Mendel never saw a gene, but he had a good abductive reason to think that genes exist.

Harman argues that we do not need to postulate the existence of ethical facts to explain any observations. Adding to this a principle of parsimony (which tells you that you should assume that something does not exist if it is not needed to explain anything), Harman concludes that subjectivism is correct.

Harman describes a physicist who is looking at the screen of a cloud chamber (a device for observing particle interactions). He sees a vapor trail on the screen and says, "There goes a proton." How should we explain why the scientist believes that a proton is present? The answer, according to Harman, involves a fact about what is going on inside the cloud chamber, namely, that there really is a proton in there. The proton produces the vapor trail; the scientist sees the vapor trail and comes to believe that a proton is present in the chamber. Part of the explanation of why the scientist has the belief is that what he believes, in fact, is true. The causal chain that explains the scientist's belief goes like this:

There is a proton in the cloud chamber.	$\longrightarrow$	A vapor trail is displayed on the screen.	$\longrightarrow$	The scientist believes that there is a proton in the chamber.

Notice that the causal chain traces something in the subjective realm (a belief) back to something in the objective realm (a proton).

Our commonsense beliefs often have a similar explanation. Suppose you want to explain why Jane believes that there is a tiger in the cage. You might do this by citing the fact that her visual system is in good working order, that she knows what a tiger looks like, and that, indeed, there *is* a tiger in the cage. We explain a person's perceptual beliefs (apart from illusions and hallucinations) by describing the ways things are outside the mind. In this case, the causal chain looks like this:

There is a tiger in the cage.	$\longrightarrow$	Light passes from the cage to Jane.	$\longrightarrow$	Jane believes that there is a tiger in the cage.

Part of the explanation of why Jane believes the proposition is that the proposition, in fact, is true.

Let's compare Harman's example from science and the similar example about Jane to the moral judgment we made when we saw the young hoodlums set fire to the cat. How are we to explain the fact that we hold this ethical belief? Harman says that we do not need to postulate the existence of an ethical fact to explain this. All we need to do is show how our moral beliefs were shaped by our upbringing—by the society in which we live (and perhaps by the genes we possess).

So according to Harman, there is a striking difference between ethics and science. Scientific facts *are* needed to explain why people have the scientific beliefs they do. But ethical facts are *not* needed to explain why people have the ethical beliefs they do. According to Harman, this is why we have a good abductive reason to think that there are protons, genes, and so on, but no good abductive reason to think that there are ethical facts.

Harman concedes that moral priniciples may help explain why it is wrong for the children to have acted as they did. If asked why the children were wrong to have set the cat on fire, we might appeal to some general ethical principle—for example, that it's wrong to impose gratuitous suffering. But Harman's point is that you don't need to postulate ethical facts to explain why we *believe* the children were wrong in what they did. Ethical facts are not needed to explain why people have *beliefs* about right and wrong (though scientific facts *are* needed to explain why scientists have some of the scientific beliefs they do).

Harman's picture of the explanatory relationships is as follows:

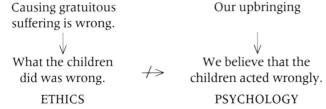

I'm not going to contest Harman's claim that this diagram is correct. What I do want to argue is that subjectivism does not follow.

Does Subjectivism Follow?

The principle of parsimony says that we should not postulate the existence of something if the something is not needed to explain *anything*. If postulating the existence of ethical facts served no explanatory purpose whatever, the principle of parsimony would conclude that there are no ethical facts. But Harman has not shown that ethical facts are not needed to explain anything. Rather, he has shown something more modest—simply, that you don't need to postulate ethical facts to explain why people have the ethical beliefs they do. Ethical facts aren't needed to explain this fact about our psychology.

Harman grants that we sometimes make ethical observations. We look at the children and say, "What they are doing is wrong." Harman also grants that the ethical properties of specific actions may be explained by general ethical principles. As already noted a general principle might help explain why what the children did was wrong. Putting these two points together, we may conclude that *general ethical principles can help explain the ethical properties of specific actions.*

The point I want to make here is quite similar to what I said about Hume's distinction between is-statements and ought-statements in the previous lecture. The argument for subjectivism I called (S2) says that since ought-statements are not deducible from is-statements, there are no ethical facts. I pointed out that this argument requires a reductionist premiss. To reach the subjectivist conclusion, you need to assume that if ethical facts exist, they must be deducible from is-statements.

Harman's argument concerns abduction, not deduction. I grant that ethical facts are not needed to explain why we have the beliefs we do. Nevertheless, for subjectivism to follow from this, an additional assumption is needed. Harman needs to assume that we should not postulate the existence of ethical facts if they are not needed to explain why we have the beliefs we do. I find this assumption implausible. Why should the reality of ethical facts stand or fall on their role in psychological explanation?

An Explanatory Role for Ethical Principles

The diagram just given *does* accord an explanatory role to some ethical facts. If what the children did was wrong, then there is at least one ethical truth that requires explanation. General ethical theories may be evaluated by their ability to explain this and other specific ethical facts about example situations. If one theory does a better job of explaining such ethical facts than another, it is plausible to hold that the former is more likely to be true.

Thus, if you concede that there are at least some ethical facts, then postulating other ethical facts can be justified on abductive grounds. However, if you demand that ethical facts be judged by their ability to explain facts in psychology, you'll end up with subjectivism.

I conclude that Harman's argument does not justify subjectivism. He has not shown that there are no ethical facts, nor has he shown that postulating ethical facts is not needed to explain *anything*. Rather, the more modest point he has established (I grant) is that postulating ethical facts is not needed to explain certain facts about psychology (that is, about why we believe what we do).

Review Questions

1. Why does Harman think that reasoning from general principles to claims about specific cases occurs in both science and ethics? Why does he think that observation is something we do in both science and ethics?
2. Does the occurrence of reasoning and observation in ethics show that there are ethical facts?
3. Suppose there is someone who cannot be convinced that slavery is wrong. Does this show that subjectivism is true?
4. What does the principle of parsimony have to do with the question of whether there are ethical facts?
5. Harman says that an abductive argument can be found for thinking that protons exist, but none for thinking that ethical facts exist. Why does he think this? Is his argument correct?

Problems for Further Thought

1. If parsimony is a good reason to prefer a materialistic theory such as the mind/brain identity theory or functionalism over dualism, why isn't it also a good reason to favor ethical subjectivism over ethical realism?

2. Consider the following passage from Hume's *Treatise of Human Nature* (1739; III,1,1):

> Morality [does not consist] in any matter of fact, which can be discover'd by the understanding. . . . Take any action allow'd to be vicious: Wilful murder, for instance. Examine it in all lights, and see if you can find that matter of fact, or real existence, which you call vice. In whichever way you take it, you find only certain passions, motives, volitions, and thoughts. There is no other matter of fact in the case. The vice entirely escapes you, as long as you consider the object. You never can find it, till you turn your reflexion into your own breast, and find a sentiment of disapprobation, which arises in you, toward this action. It lies in yourself, not in the object. So that *when you pronounce any action or character to be vicious, you mean nothing but that from the constitution of your nature you have a feeling or sentiment of blame from the contemplation of it.* Vice or virtue, therefore, may be compar'd to sounds, colours, heat and cold, which according to modern philosophy, are not qualities in objects, but perceptions in the mind: And this discovery in morals, like that other in physics, is to be regarded as a considerable advancement of the speculative sciences; tho', like that too, it has little or no influence on practice. Nothing can be more real, or concern us more, than our own sentiments of pleasure or uneasiness; and if these be favourable to virtue, and unfavourable to vice, no more can be requisite to the regulation of our conduct and behavior.

What analogy is Hume drawing between moral properties and colors? Is Hume right to think they are similar? Does Hume's analogy justify ethical subjectivism?

Lecture 30

Conventionalist Theories

It isn't very standard to lump together under one heading the three theories I'll discuss in this lecture; nor is it especially standard to label any of these theories "conventionalist." So let me explain why I am lumping and labeling in this way.

The divine command theory holds that an action is right or wrong because God says that it is; ethical relativism maintains that an action is made right or wrong in a society by the norms the society adopts; and the existentialism of

Jean-Paul Sartre says that individuals freely create the ethical standards that determine whether their lives are good ones or bad ones.

Existentialist writers often begin with the idea that there is no God, and argue that people therefore must create their own ethical facts. This is obviously quite different from the framework of the divine command theory, which sees ethical truth as flowing from God. Both these positions differ from ethical relativism, which views ethics as neither divinely given nor individually chosen, but as socially constructed.

What Makes
a View
Conventionalist?

In spite of these differences, the three views have two things in common. First, they agree that there are ethical truths. Second, they agree that those truths are made true by someone's say-so. All three theories reject subjectivism, on the one hand, and realism, on the other. The disagreement among them arises when these theories are asked to specify *whose* say-so does the trick — are ethical propositions made true by God's, society's or the individual's decision?

Why say that these theories are forms of "conventionalism"? Each claims that there is nothing inherent in an action (torture, for example) that makes it right or wrong. The action, considered all by itself, could just as easily be right or wrong. Rather, something outside of the action (extrinsic to it) makes the action right or wrong. It is God, society, or an individual who makes a pronouncement on the action and thereby endows it with one ethical property rather than the other.

In Lecture 27, I gave an example of something that I think really is conventional. It is a conventional matter which side of the road people drive their cars on. The essential ingredients in a convention are *arbitrariness* and *decision*. Let me give another example that illustrates what this means.

Trivial
Semantic
Conventionalism

Consider the fact that we use the word "dog" to refer to dogs. Things didn't have to be this way. Many other words would have worked just fine. We could have called dogs by the name "cat" and cats by the name "dog." So how did dogs come to have the one name rather than the other? Dogs have the name they do because of a *decision*. *We* make it true that dogs are called "dogs." The rules of our language are something we control; they are not forced on us from the outside.

This kind of conventionalism I'll call *trivial semantic conventionalism*. I call it trivial because it describes a fairly boring and unimportant fact. I call it *semantic* because it describes how pieces of language come to refer to things in the world.

A philosophically interesting conventionalist theory must say something beyond what trivial semantic conventionalism says. The ethical views I'll consider here don't make the trivial point that the words "right" and "good" might have been used to mean something different from what they mean in present-day English. If we used the word "right" to mean *morally wrong*, then some of us would treat the sentence "Torturing babies for fun is right" as expressing a truth. But this is trivial.

To see how a substantive form of conventionalism (SC) differs from trivial semantic conventionalism (TSC), we need to distinguish a proposition from the sentence
that expresses it (a distinction drawn in Lecture 4). The first of the following
claims is true, whereas the second is false:

*Substantive
Versus Trivial
Conventionalism*

(TSC) If we used language differently, the word "dog" might not name
a four-legged animal.

(SC) If we used language differently, dogs might not be four-legged
animals.

The sentence "Dogs are four-legged animals" would not express a truth if we used
the word "dog" to refer to a fish. But changing the way we talk would not affect
the proposition that the sentence expresses; talking differently would not turn dogs
into fish!

Conventionalism in ethics is not a thesis about language. It doesn't assert that
ethical *language* is under the control of someone's say-so. It says that ethical
propositions are made true or false by someone's decision. Ethical conventionalism
asserts a substantive thesis, not to be confused with trivial semantic conventionalism.

Ethical conventionalism holds that ethical propositions are very different from
most of the propositions we might consider. Consider the fact that the Rocky
Mountains are over 10,000 feet high. This proposition is not made true by someone's believing it or saying it; rather, it is true *independent* of anyone's say-so.
Conventionalism in ethics rejects the idea that ethical propositions have the same
status as geographical propositions like this one.

One of the earliest discussions of the divine command theory is in Plato's dialogue
The Euthyphro. This is a dialogue between Plato's teacher, Socrates, and Euthyphro. They meet in a law court where Euthyphro is bringing a charge of murder
against his own father. A servant of his father had killed a slave. Euthyphro's
father had the servant chained up and thrown in a ditch while someone went
to the priest to ask what should be done. In the meantime, the servant died.
Euthyphro is confident that indicting his father is the pious thing to do, even
though Euthyphro's relatives are angry at him for prosecuting his father for
murdering a murderer. Socrates and Euthyphro discuss what piety is. Euthyphro
claims to have a clear view of this, but Socrates shows that Euthyphro is very
confused.

*Plato's
Critique of the
Divine
Command
Theory*

The divine command theory comes up when Socrates asks: Is an action pious
because it is loved by the gods, or is it loved by the gods because it is pious?
We might substitute any moral term we wish (such as "obligatory" or "right"
or "good" or "just") for piety. And also, if we wish, we may substitute monotheism
for the polytheism of the ancient Greeks. With these substitutions, we can reformulate Socrates' question as follows: Is an action morally obligatory because God
commands us to do it, or does God command us to do it because it is morally

obligatory? Socrates' question has to do with which item is the cause and which the effect in the following diagram:

The divine command theory says that the arrow goes from left to right. Ethical realism, on the other hand, holds that an action is right or wrong independent of anyone's say-so (even God's). So if you are a realist and think that God exists and makes true pronouncements on ethical matters, you'll think that the arrow goes from right to left. Your view will be that God knows a fact that exists independently of him and correctly describes what that fact is.

Notice that both the options in the diagram assume there is a God. So rejecting the divine command theory is not the same as embracing atheism. A whole series of philosophers, beginning with Plato himself, were theists and ethical realists at the same time.

Since the problem that Socrates poses assumes that the gods exist (in our reformulation, that there is a God), I'll go along with this assumption. We now want to ask what determines what in the diagram.

One point that Socrates emphasizes is that the gods disagree. (In many of the Greek myths, one god approves of an action, while another disapproves.) This allows Socrates to convict the divine command theory of being contradictory. Socrates does this by supposing that the divine command theory says that an action is right (or wrong) if at least one god says that it is. So if the gods disagree about an action, the theory entails that the action is both right and wrong at the same time.

Socrates sees that it is easy to reformulate the theory so that it avoids this problem. Suppose the theory says that an action is right (or wrong) if *all* the gods say it is. The theory then says nothing about those actions on which the gods disagree. Plato thinks that this theory is still not satisfactory, but I won't go into his reasons for saying this.

If the theism we assume is monotheistic, what happens to this problem? We won't be able to discuss what the theory says when the gods disagree, since the assumption is that there is just one God. But two further kinds of problems confront monotheistic versions of the divine command theory.

Problems for the Divine Command Theory

The first problem has to do with knowledge. Consider the fact that there are many *religions*. If different religions disagree about what God commands, how are we to tell what God wants us to do? And even if all religions agree about how God regards some action, there is still the question of whether they correctly report what God commands.

The second difficulty is quite different from these problems about knowledge. To pinpoint this further problem, let's suppose not just that there is a God, but that we know what God wants us to do. For example, let's suppose that God wants us to follow the Ten Commandments. We now can ask Socrates' question:

Does God say that we should not murder (for example) because it is wrong to murder, or is it wrong to murder because God says so?

If the divine command theory were true, then *anything at all* would be right (even torturing babies for fun) if God said that it were. Likewise *anything at all* would be wrong (even reducing the suffering of sick children) if God said that it were.

The idea that God might order us to torture babies for fun probably strikes you as quite horrible. "Surely God would not order us to do this," you'll say, "since God is good." Let us analyze this reaction more carefully.

My point about the divine command theory is not that God would order us to do horrible things. My point is that the theory says that *if* God said that an action is right, then the action would have to be right.

In addition, the reaction just noted ("that God would not order these things, because God is good") is actually inconsistent with the divine command theory. For this reaction to make sense, there would have to be such a thing as goodness, which exists independently of God's say-so. To say that "God would not do X, since X is wrong" is to say that the arrow points from right to left, not from left to right, in the diagram.

Remember, the divine command theory says that there is nothing inherent in an action that makes it good or bad; the action has the moral standing it does simply because God chooses to label it good or bad.

I'm not doubting here that God has the power to make us the kind of creatures we are. Let's assume that God has given us bodies that make us capable of feeling pain. It follows that God is partially responsible for why the following ethical truth is true:

> Stabbing someone for fun is wrong.

God helps make this proposition true because God is responsible for the fact that stabbing people causes them pain (if he had made our bodies otherwise, that might not be so). But the divine command theory says much more than this. It claims that the following ethical proposition is true only because God says it is:

> Inflicting pain for fun is wrong.

This last proposition strikes me as true independent of anyone's say-so, even God's.

I now want to consider ethical relativism. This theory holds that the rightness or wrongness of an action is settled by the say-so of the society in which the action occurs. In traditional Eskimo culture, it was customary for people to put their aging ailing parents outside to die in winter; according to ethical relativism, an Eskimo who did this would have been doing the right thing. In contemporary U.S. society, this is not the social norm; so relativism asserts that in our society, it would be wrong to act in this way. Ethical relativism says that what it is right or wrong to do depends on (is relative to) the society in which you live.

*Ethical
Relativism*

CONVENTIONALIST
THEORIES

I want to make this theory more precise. First, we need to be clear that ethical relativism is a normative thesis, not a descriptive one. It makes a claim about how people *should* act. There is a quite separate descriptive thesis, which says that customs and norms *in fact* vary from society to society. Having already absorbed Hume's point about the is/ought gap (Lecture 28), you should be able to see that descriptive relativism (an is-proposition) does not deductively imply normative relativism (an ought-proposition).

A comment on the descriptive claim: It is fairly obvious that societies do vary in their customs and values. But it is less obvious that they do so with respect to the values that are most fundamental. For example, someone might grant that traditional Eskimos practiced euthanasia ("mercy killing") in contexts that we do not, but still maintain that deep down Eskimo culture and our own have the same fundamental values. Perhaps both societies adopt norms that aim to promote general welfare; but because of different conditions of life, we and they end up arranging the details of life in different ways. I do not maintain that there are such "fundamental universals." I merely point out that descriptive relativism might be granted for some "superficial" customs, but denied for some more "fundamental" ones. Anthropology is the subject that can assess whether this conjecture is correct.

The second point of clarification is that there is an obvious sense in which what we ought to do depends on (is relative to) the situation we are in. I think that in most situations, it is wrong to steal. But suppose your family is starving and you have no money to buy food for them. Suppose you have the opportunity to steal a loaf of bread from a prosperous baker (this is the situation that Jean Valjean faced in Victor Hugo's novel *Les Miserables*). In this case, I think you would be doing the right thing to steal the loaf.

People in different societies often live in different circumstances. People in one society may face situations in which it is wrong for them to steal. People in another may face situations in which stealing is the right thing to do. Ethical relativism, however, says more than this. It goes beyond the unsurprising fact that what you ought to do depends on the situation you are in.

To see what this extra ingredient is, we must remind ourselves that normative ethical relativism is a conventionalist theory. It doesn't just say that what someone should do varies from society to society. It says that an action is right or wrong *because* of society's say-so. An ethical realist can grant that people in one society should not steal whereas those in another should do so; a realist, however, will reject the relativist's explanation of why this is so.

So far, I've presented two clarifications of ethical relativism. First, it's a normative theory, not a descriptive one. Second, it's a conventionalist theory. Having said this, let's see whether there is any reason to think that it is true.

Ethical relativism has enjoyed a fair amount of popularity in the social sciences (in anthropology, especially) during this century. As Western social scientists improved their understanding of other cultures, they often came to feel considerable respect for those cultures. The idea took hold that it is wrong for Western nations to impose their own standards on other cultures. From the sixteenth century to the present, many Western nations have created and extended empires by conquest and commercial domination. Often this was said to be justified in the name of bringing Christianity to the conquered peoples; Europeans sometimes talked of a "white man's burden" — of a responsibility to bring Western civilization to the rest of the world.

Maybe you'll find ethical relativism an attractive moral theory if this sort of imperialism strikes you as wrong. If you think that the idea of a "white man's burden" was simply a rationalization for exploitation, what better way to express this than by saying that each society determines its own ethical values? Europe does not get to decide what is right and wrong for the rest of the world. Rather, each society must decide this matter for itself. Partly for this reason, ethical relativism became popular among those who defended a kind of noninterventionism (this is the idea that one society should not meddle in the affairs of another).

Let's assume that there have been many cases in history in which one society was wrong to impose its will on another. Does this view make ethical relativism plausible? I think not.

Are we prepared to say that a society can do anything it pleases to the individuals in it as long as most of the people in the society believe that this is the right thing to do? It could become "customary" in a society that a certain group of people is oppressed (such as the Untouchables in India), even systematically murdered (such as Jews and Gypsies in Nazi Germany). Would this be made right if most people in the society thought it was right? I find this highly dubious.

Don't confuse the question of rightness with the question of whether some other country should intervene militarily to put a stop to the objectionable practice. These are separate issues. There might be cases in which foreign intervention would be wrong, even though some practices going on inside the country are wrong. For a practice to be wrong is one thing; what steps should be taken to end the wrong is quite a separate matter.

In addition, you should see that ethical relativism does not prohibit the kind of interventions that its supporters tend to condemn. Should members of my society engage in colonial conquest? According to ethical relativism, I should answer this question by seeing whether the norms of my society permit people to engage in colonial conquest. Far from condemning interventionism, this consideration will have the consequence of justifying it. If you asked in nineteenth-century Britain whether it was "customary" for individuals to help extend and maintain the British Empire, the answer would have been *yes*. Paradoxically, ethical relativism does not imply that societies ought to respect each other.

Finally, it is important to see that the kinds of objections I made against the divine command theory also apply to ethical relativism. A conventionalist view of this kind says that an action is made right in a society simply because it is the norm. But this view has such bizarre consequences as the following:

> If our society considered it ethically permissible to torture babies
> for fun, then it would be ethically permissible for us to do this.

Ethical relativism does not say that our society will ever be like this. However, it does endorse the if/then statement just given.

My view is that this if/then statement is false. If our society were to adopt this norm, then our society would have become morally abhorrent. To say this is to talk like an ethical realist. What is morally right and wrong is not settled by society's say-so.

Sartre's
Existentialism

I now turn to the third conventionalist theory—existentialism. There is a lot more to existentialism than I will be able to discuss here. And it is important to realize that existentialist writers differ a great deal among themselves. Here I am focusing on a single strand in the thinking of some important existentialists; this is the idea (expressed by Sartre and by Søren Kierkegaard, a nineteenth-century Danish philosopher and religious thinker) that individual human beings must freely create their own moral values.

Sartre held that the scope of human freedom is far wider than most of us suspect. People often believe that only a small range of options is open to them—that the large-scale features of their lives are forced upon them from the outside. Sartre thinks that this is an illusion; people stumble without reflection into stereotypes and conventional ways of life without realizing that they, in fact, are making a choice. Freedom is a frightening burden that we must shoulder without kidding ourselves. Sartre goes so far as to say that we are responsible for every feature of the lives we live.

Although I think that this last idea is a piece of rhetorical overstatement, Sartre's general stress on the responsibility of individuals to shape their own lives is important. There is a lot to be said for really reflecting about what you think and do—for regarding options critically and not falling into a pattern out of unreflective habit. But Sartre says something more than this; this something more is the conventionalist element in his existentialism that I want to identify and criticize.

You'll remember from Lecture 27 that Sartre (in his book *Existentialism*) describes a young Frenchman during World War II as having to decide whether to join the Resistance or stay home to care for his ailing mother. Let us distinguish two claims that might be made about this young man.

(1) He should think the choice over carefully and not do what he does out of unreflective habit.

(2) There is no moral fact of the matter about what he should do until he makes a decision. If he decides that he wants above all to be a good son, he should stay home; if he decides that he wants above all to be a good Frenchman, he should join the Resistance. But there is no standard that exists independently of his choice that determines what he should want most of all.

Sartre claimed that both (1) *and* (2) are true. He thought that this story about the young Frenchman exhibits a quite general pattern. In *every* choice we make, we have to create moral facts. It is claim (2) that embodies the conventionalist element in Sartre's existentialism.

Sartre chose this example because he thought it poses a difficult moral problem. But even if the problem were one that we would see as clear-cut, Sartre would view it as calling for an arbitrary decision. Consider a third option that the young man has: He could leave home and volunteer to torture prisoners for the Gestapo. The young man has to decide whether he wants to be a good son, a good Frenchman, or a good Nazi. Sartre's position is that there is no fact of the matter about what the young man should do until he makes a decision about what he wants most.

Just like the other conventionalist theories discussed in this lecture, Sartre's existentialism implies the following if/then statement:

> If the young man decides that he wants above all to be a good
> X, then it is morally permissible for him to do what it takes to
> be a good X.

I've already noted why I find this claim implausible.

Sartre thinks that this conventionalist thesis follows from the fact that there is no God: If there is no God to lay down the moral law, then each of us must lay down the law for ourselves. An ethical realist would disagree. Why can't moral facts exist independently of anyone's (God's, society's, or the individual's) say-so? Sartre has no very good argument against this realist alternative.

In this and the previous lectures, I have not provided any strong argument in favor of ethical realism. Rather, I have criticized the subjectivist and conventionalist alternatives to realism. In what follows, I'll assume that there are ethical truths that are true independently of anyone's say-so. The goal will be to consider some theories about what those truths are.

Review Questions

1. What is the difference between trivial semantic conventionalism and substantive conventionalism?
2. Consider this statement: "We should do what God says we should do." Can an ethical realist and a defender of the divine command theory agree on this? If so, what do they disagree about?
3. Consider this statement: "What may be right for a person in one culture to do may not be right for a person in another culture to do." Can an ethical realist and a defender of ethical relativism agree on this? If so, what do they disagree about?
4. Does ethical relativism entail that people in one culture should respect the standards of conduct obeyed in another culture?
5. Consider this statement: "People have to figure out for themselves what they should do." Can an ethical realist and a defender of Sartre's existentialism agree on this? If so, what do they *disagree* about?

Problems for Further Thought

1. Is there a third coherent option for the theist, which rejects both the divine command theory and ethical realism? Defend your answer.

2. Do facts about evolution suggest that there may be fundamental ethical values that all cultures share, even though there is enormous variation among human cultures with respect to their ethical values?

3. There is a Yiddish story about the wise men of Chelm. The town council met to discuss what could be done about the shortage in sour cream. They decided to solve the problem by calling water "sour cream." The problem of what they would do about the resulting water shortage they put aside for future deliberation. How does this story illustrate the difference between Trivial Semantic Conventionalism and Substantive Conventionalism?

Lecture 31

Utilitarianism

Utilitarianism is an ethical theory that says (roughly) that an ethically correct action is one that promotes the greatest happiness of all those affected by it. I say "roughly" since I'll want to fine-tune this idea and discuss some of the various forms that utilitarianism might take.

Utilitarianism is a philosophical idea that has exercised considerable influence on the world of practical affairs. Jeremy Bentham (1748–1832) and John Stuart Mill (1806–1873) were deeply involved in the political controversies of their age. Both defended utilitarianism in publications that the educated classes in Britain read with great attention. Utilitarianism wasn't an abstract "ivory tower" theory that only professors found worth discussing. It stirred the interest of great numbers of people who cared about the institutions of their society.

Bentham and Mill thought that many of these institutions needed reform because they failed to promote human welfare. A central political agenda at this time was extending the vote to men who did not own property. Mill also wrote in favor of women's suffrage, although women did not receive the vote until much later. The abolition of slavery was another political struggle in which utilitarians participated. In these and other cases, utilitarians argued that institutions had to be changed because they advanced the interests of the few to the detriment of the many. Utilitarians attacked the idea that the rich and powerful had some special "right" to arrange society as they saw fit. On the contrary, the point of utilitarianism is that each individual must be taken into account, because each individual is capable of experiencing happiness.

In this lecture, I'll discuss the general ethical theory, not the specific political issues that at one time were the focus of utilitarian concern. By now (nearing the end of this book) it should be abundantly clear that the following is not a valid deduction:

> If utilitarianism is true, then slavery is morally wrong.
> Slavery is morally wrong.
> _____
> Utilitarianism is true.

I don't doubt the premisses, but I'll try to show that there is plenty of room to doubt the conclusion.

Mill's Defense of the Greatest Happiness Principle

Before describing in more detail what utilitarianism says, I want to discuss how someone might assess whether the basic idea of utilitarianism is true. Mill calls this basic idea the Greatest Happiness Principle. It says that the action we ought to perform in a given situation is the one that promotes the greatest happiness.

In his essay "Utilitarianism" (1861), Mill attempted to prove that the Greatest Happiness Principle is correct. The argument begins with an analogy between desirability and visibility. He says that just as the only proof that something is visible is that someone sees it, so the only proof that something is desirable is that someone desires it. He then claims that what people ultimately want is their own happiness. Mill concludes from this that the most desirable action is the one that produces the most happiness.

I'll reconstruct Mill's argument as follows:

(1) Seeing something proves that it is visible.
(2) Hence, desiring something proves that it is desirable.
(3) The only thing that each person ultimately desires is his or her own happiness.
(4) The only thing that is ultimately desirable for a person is his or her own happiness.
_____
> Hence, each person should perform those actions that promote the greatest happiness.

There are several problems with this reasoning. First, premiss (1) does not provide much of a reason for accepting premiss (2). Visibility and desirability are different. If something is visible, this means that it is possible to see it. However, if something is desirable, this does not mean that it is *possible* to desire it, but that it *should* be desired. Visibility is a descriptive concept, while desirablity is a normative one. So although "*x* is visible" does follow from "*x* is seen," "*x* is desirable" does not follow from "*x* is desired."

What does the word "ultimately" mean in premiss (3)? It means that everything else that people want they want only as a means to the end of securing their own happiness. If I desire that the starving receive food, Mill is saying that I want this only as a way to make myself happy. I argued against this thesis in Lecture 26; it simply asserts a form of psychological egoism. Three of the four preference structures discussed there (all except Extreme Egoism) involve thinking that the welfare of others has an importance quite separate from the importance the agent attaches to his or her own happiness. Since, as a matter of fact, many of us are often like this, I think that premiss (3) is false.

Does premiss (4) follow from premiss (3)? No, for the same reason that (2) does not follow from (1). It is not automatic that the most desirable thing for a person is to have his or her desires satisfied. That would depend on the nature of the desires in question. For people with truly horrible desires, perhaps the best thing for them would be to change what they want, not for them to get what they want.

Finally, even if premiss (4) were true, the conclusion of the argument would not follow. The fact that your own happiness is the most desirable thing *for you* does not imply that you should maximize *everyone's* happiness. The conclusion of this argument sometimes requires you to act unselfishly — to sacrifice your own happiness if doing so brings with it a more than compensating increase in the happiness of others. This does not follow from premiss (4).

Reciprocal For a utilitarian, the Greatest Happiness Principle is the ultimate moral principle.
Illumination If you want to know how you should act or how the laws of a society should be arranged, you should (if you're a utilitarian) consult this principle. But if this principle is an ultimate one, how is it possible to justify the principle in terms of other ideas? If these other ideas were to provide a justification, wouldn't they have to be even more ultimate? The suspicion this raises is that Mill was trying to do the impossible — if the principle is ultimate, then it cannot be deduced from anything that is more ultimate still.

Mill had another idea about how utilitarianism should be defended. Instead of trying to deduce the Greatest Happiness Principle from premises that would be plausible even to a nonutilitarian, we can try to justify the principle by seeing how it accords with the moral judgments we are prepared to make about concrete cases. This was the method I described in Lecture 29. A general principle has implications about what it is wrong or right to do in specific cases. If we are prepared to make ethical judgments about the cases, we can use these judgments to evaluate the general theories (recall Harman's example about the transplant operation). If a theory implies that an action is right in a given situation and we believe that the action would be quite wrong, we might take this as evidence that the theory is false.

So judgments about specific cases can lead us to reject a general theory. The reverse can happen as well. If we think that a theory is quite plausible and then find that it implies that a given action is wrong (or right), we might decide to allow the theory to guide us — to lead us to revise our opinions about the ethical problem posed by the particular case.

So there is a two-way interaction here — a process of reciprocal illumination — by which our judgments about specific cases can influence how we regard a theory, and our views about a theory can affect our judgments about specific cases. A utilitarian who does not think that slavery was wrong might come to see that one or the other of these ideas must be abandoned. Which idea should be abandoned depends on which is overall more plausible (the general theory or the judgment about the specific institution), given the other beliefs he or she has.

Mill offers this sort of defense of utilitarianism. He thought that if we ask what it is about the actions that we think wrong that distinguishes them from the actions we think right, we will be led to the Greatest Happiness Principle. I now want to use this technique of evaluation to fine-tune utilitarianism and then to suggest that it faces some very serious difficulties.

I'll begin by focusing on the idea of happiness. What is happiness? I'm not asking *What Is* what activities cause happiness. Rather, I want to know what happiness itself is. *Happiness?* Compare: If I ask you what bankruptcy is, I'm not asking you what activities cause bankruptcy. Bankruptcy is not the same as reckless investment; neither is happiness one and the same thing as a warm puppy.

A partial answer might be that happiness is a feeling. This is only partial, of course, because there are many other feelings besides happiness. But if happiness is something in the mind (something subjective), we can formulate a problem that utilitarianism must address.

In Lecture 13, I discussed how Descartes grappled with the problem of refuting the hypothesis that he was systematically misled by an evil demon. Contemporary philosophers sometimes give Descartes' problem a modern twist by asking how we know that we are not brains in vats. The challenge here is for you to show how you know that you are not merely a brain hooked up to a giant computer that provides you with a variety of electrical impulses. These impulses generate the illusion that you have a body and that you are having sensory contact (sight, smell, hearing, and so on) with the external world. According to this strange hypothesis, your brain rests in a vat filled with a liquid that keeps it alive. The computer furnishes you with a rich stream of experiences. Your brain provides you with memories. But according to the brain-in-the-vat hypothesis, almost everything you believe about your present and past is false. You don't really have a face; you're not really looking at a philosophy book right now. And so on.

The brain-in-the-vat problem is a problem about knowledge. I want to reformulate it so that it becomes a problem in ethics.

Consider an experience machine. If you plug yourself into this machine, you will *The Problem* receive experiences that produce great happiness. If being a concert violinist *of the* would give you pleasure, plugging into the machine will give you a rich, complex *Experience* sequence of experiences of this sort. If you would be happiest being a political *Machine* leader loved and admired by millions of people, the experience machine can furnish the feelings that would derive from being loved and admired by millions. The experience machine does not make you into a real concert violinist or political leader. Rather, the machine gives you the precise set of experiences you would get from having those sorts of lives.

If utilitarianism were true, it would be preferable for people to plug into experience machines rather than lead real lives that provide a lesser degree of happiness. But contrary to what utilitarianism says about this kind of choice, I for one (and I bet you feel the same way) put considerable value on leading a real life. If you're plugged into the experience machine, virtually all your beliefs are false. You are proud of yourself because you think you are a great violinist and you take pleasure in your skill. If the machine leads you to think that you are a great political leader, you may think you have ended the arms race and so you feel good about doing so. But in both cases, your pride and your pleasure rest on an illusion.

Most of us value something beyond the feeling of happiness that comes from doing certain things. We also value the reality of the doing. This is contrary to the form of utilitarianism we're considering.

A number of science fiction novels and movies make this same point. Aldous Huxley's *Brave New World* and Woody Allen's *Sleeper* are examples. These works of fiction describe a future in which people are drugged by their governments into being docile, happy citizens. People are contented, but the novel or movie usually takes the point of view that there is something deeply wrong with such a society. Usually, what is wrong is that people lack autonomy. Their own beliefs and desires have been distorted or altogether destroyed; what they do and feel is the result of the drugs they take. If you agree that there is something wrong with a society of this sort, you may have to say that there is something over and above "happiness" (a state of mind) that is ethically important.

Mill on "Higher" and "Lower" Pleasures

Mill himself grappled with a problem of this kind. He asked why it is better to be "'Socrates dissatisfied" rather than a satisfied fool. Socrates was acutely aware of the imperfections of the world around him; he could hardly take pleasure in many of his daily experiences. In contrast, a satisfied fool, Mill says, is tickled by every detail of life. If the latter individual is happier, utilitarianism seems to recommend that we becomer more like the fool and less like Socrates.

Mill denied that utilitariansim has this implication. He thought that Socrates was capable of enjoying "higher" pleasures, whereas the fool, he says, could only experience "lower" pleasures. Mill claimed that higher pleasures provide more happiness than lower ones. To see that this is true, he said that you must ask individuals who have experienced both sorts of pleasures which they enjoyed more. Mill was confident that these "competent judges" would say that the higher pleasures bring more happiness than the lower ones.

There are some higher and lower pleasures for which Mill's prediction might be true. For example, someone who does nothing but drink beer and watch television might find that "higher" pleasures are better, once he or she is exposed to them. But there are other cases in which Mill's prediction seems mistaken. Imagine someone who has been leading a real life and then is plugged into an experience machine. Once he is unplugged, we could ask him which life made him happier. I think most people would have to admit that their life while plugged in provided a greater quantity of happiness than the real life they led before. This does not mean that people *prefer* to live plugged into the experience machine; it just means that life in the experience machine provides a greater quantity of happiness.

The same may be true of the people in the science fiction works previously described. Perhaps the drugs provide these people with more happiness than they would receive if they were autonomous. Again, this doesn't mean that they *prefer* being drugged by their governments, but that they receive a greater quantity of happiness in that state.

To move closer to real life, consider a drug such as heroin. Suppose someone could live a life as a heroin addict without facing such dangers as AIDS and being killed by drug dealers. Perhaps in that case the drug would be so intensely pleasurable that people who had experienced life with it and life without it would have to concede that life is happier with it. This does not mean that they would *prefer* to have such a life. Rather, what it shows is that our preferences are influenced by factors other than the quantity of happiness we receive.

My conclusion is that Mill's argument about higher and lower pleasures does not work. Mill believed that Socrates dissatisfied had a better life than a satisfied fool, but I don't see that Mill has a way of explaining why this is so. So we have here an objection to the first form of utilitarianism I want to distinguish. It is *hedonistic utilitarianism,* which says that the right action is the one that maximizes pleasure and minimizes pain (not just for the agent, but for all individuals who are affected).

Objection to Hedonistic Utilitarianism

However, there is another form of utilitarianism, which is not undermined by these problems. I call it *preference utilitarianism*. The idea of this kind of utilitarianism is not to maximize pleasure, but to maximize the degree to which people get their preferences satisfied. If people generally prefer to lead real lives rather than to plug into experience machines, then a preference utilitarian will have no problem explaining why it would be wrong to plug people into experience machines. If people prefer to live their lives drug-free, then it will be no problem for preference utilitarianism to explain why it would be wrong for the government or anyone else to surreptitiously give people a diet of pleasure-producing drugs. And contrary to Mill, if people genuinely prefer drinking beer and watching television to doing philosophy and discussing politics, then a preference utilitarian will claim that the former activities should be favored over the latter.

Preference Utilitarianism

So preference utilitarianism avoids a problem that is fatal to hedonistic utilitarianism. But preference utilitarianism has problems of its own. The first of these becomes clear when we try to apply the view to specific cases.

The problem is that it often is difficult to know how to compare one person's preferences with those of another. This is something that a preference utilitarian must do if those preferences conflict. Consider a state government that has to

The Apples and Oranges Problem

decide whether a tract of land should be opened to commercial use or reserved for recreational use. There are the profits and jobs that some people will receive, on the one hand, and the enjoyment from camping and swimming that other people will receive, on the other. How are these two interests to be compared?

Sometimes people decide what they think about an issue like this by deciding which sort of activity is more important in the light of the ethical principles they have adopted. This strategy does not address the question in a strictly utilitarian way. Utilitarians must focus on how intensely each person prefers one option over the other. Then they have to sum over this totality of individual preferences to decide which action maximizes the satisfaction of preferences collectively. If the economic losses from not going the commercial route were small, whereas the recreational (and aesthetic) losses from going the commercial route were large, this would settle the question. My point, though, is that it often is quite obscure what "small" and "large" could mean in such cases. Let's call this the *apples and oranges problem*: How can you compare the intensity of one person's gain with the intensity of another person's loss?

Sometimes this kind of question is settled by using money as a mode of comparison. How much do the developers want to develop the land commercially? See how much they are prepared to pay to do so. How much do people want to preserve the land for recreational use? See how much they are prepared to pay to do so. Then see how much money stacks up on the one side and how much on the other.

The problem with this procedure is that how much money people are willing to spend often is influenced by factors other than the intensity of their desires. A rich person may be prepared to pay more for a loaf of bread than a poor one, but that does not mean that the rich person wants it more.

Sometimes this problem is settled by taking a vote among the individuals affected. A utilitarian might say that a referendum should be held, with each person having a single vote. The problem with using voting as a way of solving the apples and oranges problem is that voting does not represent the intensities of people's desires. If I mildly prefer the commercial option to the recreational one, I'll vote for the commercial option; if you strongly prefer the recreational use to the commercial one, you will vote for the recreational use. Your vote and mine count equally, but this fails to represent something that is important to the calculation a preference utilitarian must make.

In practical politics, voting is often a reasonable procedure (whether it *always* is reasonable will come up in what follows). However, I'm not talking about choosing a workable (if imperfect) procedure. I'm talking about the problem of making sense of what preference utilitarianism actually says. The problem is that it often is unclear what it means to say that a given action has higher utility for one person than the opposite action has for another person.

In what follows, I'm going to assume that the apples and oranges problem can be solved. I won't doubt that the intensity of people's preferences can be compared. What I will do is review some arguments that try to show that preference utilitarianism is sometimes mistaken in its claims about what we ought to do.

I'll begin with a problem that can be illustrated by an example — the Case of the Lonesome Stranger. A gruesome murder has occurred in a town. The sheriff has discovered that the murderer himself is dead; however, the sheriff knows that no one will believe him if he says this and lays out all the evidence he has. Meanwhile, the townspeople are becoming more and more agitated. The sheriff realizes that if a suspect is not put on trial very soon, there will be a riot and it is quite probable that many innocent people will be injured and a few killed. As the sheriff is mulling this over in his office, in strolls a lonesome stranger. This fellow tells the sheriff that he has no friends or relations in the world and that he has wandered into town for no reason in particular. The sheriff then gets an idea: Why not frame the lonesome stranger? There is capital punishment in this locale, so the sheriff can arrange for the stranger to be tried, convicted, and executed. Suppose the sheriff can arrange it that the framing will always remain a secret. Should the sheriff frame the stranger?

What would a utilitarian say here? For a hedonistic utilitarian, the answer is easy. If you frame the stranger (and keep the facts secret), one person dies, but the peace of mind of the townspeople is restored; if you do not frame him, a bloody riot will ensue and more than one person will die. The way to maximize happiness is for the sheriff to frame the stranger and keep this to himself.

For a preference utilitarian, the question is more complicated. If the people in the town have strong preferences that innocent people should not be punished, then the sheriff should not frame the stranger. But suppose the people don't care about this; let's suppose that they care only about their own safety and peace of mind. In this case, preference utilitarianism will tell the sheriff that he ought to frame the stanger and keep the truth to himself.

The problem here is that utilitarian considerations seem to conflict with considerations of *justice*. It is unjust to punish people for crimes they did not commit. If you think this moral requirement overrides considerations that reflect the social utility of punishing the lonesome stranger, then you will interpret this example as an objection to utilitarianism.

Before considering how a utilitarian might reply to this objection, I want to say a little more about punishment. A utilitarian will evaluate the idea of punishment by asking whether punishment does any good. If punishment does not deter people from similar wrongdoing and does not reform the character of the person punished, then a utilitarian may say that there is no point in punishing people who are guilty of awful crimes. For a utilitarian, the distinction between guilt and innocence does not have to coincide with the distinction between those who should be punished and those who should not be.

A nonutilitarian view of punishment (there is more than one) will see things differently. The principle of an eye for an eye — of retribution for wrongdoing — is not a utilitarian idea. Retributionists want the punishment to fit the crime; utilitarians want the punishment to be chosen for the benefits it can be expected to produce.

In any case, my judgment is that the lonesome stranger example provides an

Utilitarianism and Justice: The Case of the Lonesome Stranger

Punishment

objection to utilitarianism (whether of the hedonistic or the preference variety). It illustrates how considerations of justice can conflict with utilitarianism. Recall that for me to be able to say this, I must be prepared to make a moral judgment about the example situation. Without this, there is no way to use specific cases to evaluate the general principle.

A Utilitarian Reply: Distinguish Rule and Act Utilitarianism

There is a standard reply that utilitarians often make to this and similar objections. Their strategy is to distinguish two kinds of utilitarian theory and to claim that one of them is perfectly consistent with the idea that the lonesome stranger should not be framed.

I described utilitarianism as saying that an action should be performed only if it promotes the greatest happiness or the greatest preference satisfaction. But there is an ambiguity here. Are we evaluating *kinds* of actions, or individual actions, one by one? Here I am drawing the type/token distinction discussed in Lecture 22 and applying it to the question of how utilitarianism should be formulated.

That is, utilitarianism (regardless of whether it says to maximize happiness or preference satisfaction) can take the form of *rule utilitarianism* or *act utilitarianism*. How does this choice affect the way we understand the lonesome stranger example? According to the rule utilitarian, the sheriff's task has two parts. First, he must decide what general rule should govern everyone's conduct. Second, he must determine how that general rule applies to the concrete case he confronts.

The first problem involves deciding which of the following two alternatives has the best long-term consequences:

(R_1) Punish the innocent when it is convenient.

(R_2) Never punish the innocent.

A rule utilitarian will argue that (R_2) has better consequences for people's welfare in the long run, so it is (R_2) that the sheriff should use. Note that once (R_2) is applied to the specific situation, the sheriff will decide *not* to frame the stranger.

Why think that (R_2) is better than (R_1) in the long run? Part of the reason is that rules that are used again and again become generally known. If people generally believe that (R_1) is the policy the government follows, then following (R_1) will produce a great deal of unhappiness.

An act utilitarian, on the other hand, will not focus on general rules, but will focus on the specific choice at hand. The act utilitarians's procedure has one step, not two. So the suggestion is that the example of the lonesome stranger constitutes an objection to act utilitarianism, not to rule utilitarianism. The idea is that rule utilitarianism recommends that the sheriff not frame the stranger, and this recommendation coincides with what we find plausible.

I don't believe that adopting a rule utilitarian formulation saves utilitarianism. I agree that (R_2) has better consequences as a general policy than (R_1) does. But it seems to me that a utilitarian must concede that (R_2) is inferior to the following rule:

(R_3) Don't punish the innocent, unless doing so will maximize utility.

I think a utilitarian must agree that (R_3) is preferable on utilitarian grounds to (R_2). And the sheriff, acting on (R_3), will frame the lonesome stranger. I conclude that the objection to utilitarianism embodied in this example is not avoided by rule utilitarianism any more than it is by act utilitarianism.

I'll now consider another objection to utilitarianism. An important fact about preference utilitarianism is that it does not allow you to morally evaluate people's preferences. People's preferences, whether we approve of them or not, must be taken into account when we decide what laws our society should adopt or what actions each of us should perform. The problem is that we sometimes want to *ignore* people's preferences because we think they are morally objectionable. If it is ever morally legitimate to do this, preference utilitarianism is in trouble.

Utilitarianism and Tolerance: The Problem of the Fanatical Majority

Consider what happens to nonconformists in a society of fanatics. Here we might be talking about people in a minority religion who live in a society in which the majority is made of religious fanatics. Or consider a society in which a minority of people are homosexual and the heterosexual majority is very intolerant. Another case concerns political nonconformity—a minority with one set of political beliefs living with a majority that not only disagrees with them, but is extremely hostile toward them. How would a utilitarian view the idea that people should be free to live as they see fit?

A utilitarian will decide this question by calculating how policies of repression or toleration would satisfy people's preferences. The point I want to make is that if the intolerant majority is fanatical enough, the utilitarian scales may tip in favor of prohibiting nonconformity. If a fanatical majority gets upset enough at the presence of nonconformists, then there will be a utilitarian justification for banning nonconformity. Of course, this sort of policy will not be what the nonconformists prefer. But since they are in the minority, their strong preferences may be outweighed by the strong preferences of the fanatical majority.

Many of us would want to say that people have certain rights—to freely pursue the religion of their choice (or no religion at all), to engage in the sexual practices they prefer (or none at all), to discuss and promulgate their favored political opinions—as long as doing so does not endanger the life and property of others. The fact that these practices might antagonize an intolerant majority, many of us would want to say, simply does not count against people's being entitled to do what they want. To think this way is not to think like a utilitarian.

We have here an objection to utilitarianism. I will call it the *problem of the fanatical majority.*

Mill considered this issue in his famous essay "On Liberty" (1859). Mill was a liberal in the nineteenth-century sense of that word. Liberals believed in liberty. An imprecise slogan embodying liberalism is that "people should be free to do what they want, as long as doing so does not hurt others." One reason this is imprecise is that fanatics might claim to be "hurt" (offended, distressed, outraged, and so on) simply by knowing that there are people who live their lives differently from the way they do.

Liberalism and Conservatism

Mill believed that the right to personal nonconformity flowed from utilitarian considerations. He also thought that economic activity was public and therefore might have to be limited for utilitarian reasons. A corporation's activities (even a single person's buying and selling) affect others. A regulated economy (as opposed to an absolutely free market) therefore is preferable, Mill thought, on utilitarian grounds.

Mill was a liberal in the nineteenth-century meaning of that term. Liberals believed in liberty—that each person should have the maximum amount of freedom, consistent with not compromising the freedom of others.

The terms "liberal" and "conservative" have different meanings today. To understand what each involves, let's distinguish two "markets" in which each of us participates—the marketplace of ideas and the economic marketplace (of goods and services that we buy and sell). Liberals in the United States now often oppose censorship and think that the government should not promote religion (or promote one religion over any other). They believe that the government should not interfere in the marketplace of ideas. Yet, they tend to believe, on utilitarian grounds, that the government should regulate the economy.

So-called "conservatives," on the other hand, tend to take the opposite view. They often favor censorship and want the government to promote religion (by encouraging prayer in the public schools, for example). Yet, when it comes to the economic marketplace, they tend to favor more freedom and less regulation.

Although both political positions are influenced by utilitarian considerations, each makes use of nonutilitarian ideas as well. Liberals often talk about "rights" of free speech, which people are said to have even if some forms of free speech make lots of people very unhappy. And conservatives sometimes argue that pornography should be censored on religious grounds or on other grounds that are not utilitarian.

Liberalism and conservatism are not the only political options available. In the United States, both hold that capitalism is a workable form of economic organization. And both have favored military interventions of various kinds (in Korea and Vietnam, for example). Some critics on the left—socialists and communists, for example—doubt the viability of capitalism and have opposed military interventions like the ones mentioned. Critics on the right—libertarians, for example—reject the government's entitlement to intervene in people's lives without their consent—for example, to collect taxes, to censor pornography, and to regulate the economy.

Mill defended a totally free (laissez-faire) marketplace of ideas. He described ideas as being in competition. Everyone benefits from unrestrained competition, Mill said, because competition tends to select the best ideas. Ideas compete in the same way organisms do in the process of Darwinian natural selection (Lecture 6).

Defenders of a free economic marketplace have often put forward a similar argument. In The Wealth of Nations, the eighteenth-century economist Adam

Smith argued that when everyone freely pursues his or her selfish economic interests, everyone benefits. The nation as a whole becomes richer, and so prosperity "trickles down" to even the worst off in the society.

Liberals have criticized this trickle down defense of a perfectly free market economy. They claim that an unregulated economy produces catastrophic swings ("boom and bust cycles," like the one that produced the Crash of 1929 and the ensuing Depression). An unfettered market, they argue, can make everyone worse off than they would be if the market were regulated. This liberal argument against a perfectly free market is utilitarian in character.

Mill was a utilitarian who believed in the kinds of personal liberties I just mentioned. How can utilitarianism and the idea that people have a right to certain freedoms be reconciled? Mill distinguished between public and private actions. A public action affects individuals in addition to the actor; a private action, on the other hand, does not affect others. Mill argues that people are entitled to live lives of nonconformity, if they wish, since the activities involved are private, not public.

Does this argument secure the kinds of freedoms I have been discussing? Not entirely. In a society in which large numbers of people are intolerant fanatics, the most that a nonconforming minority can hope for is the right to be *secret* nonconformists. It is only when such practices are performed in secret that they can count as private in Mill's sense. However, I think most of us believe in liberties that are more extensive than this. Whether it be in the religious, sexual, or political arenas, most of us think that there are practices that affect others (because they are not kept secret), which a minority is entitled to engage in, even if this distresses fanatics.

Utilitarianism and Personal Integrity: the Problem of Dirty Hands

The next objection to utilitarianism I want to discuss I'll call the *dirty hands objection*. Consider an individual contemplating a choice between an action that is clearly right and one that is clearly wrong. However, the morally wrong action has this characteristic: If the individual does not perform this bad action himself or herself, someone else will.

An example of this kind of situation is provided by a case I discussed in Lecture 30 in connection with Sartre's existentialism. Imagine someone who is considering whether he should become a torturer for the Nazis. Suppose that if he does not do it, someone else will.

Examples that are less horrible than this are common in everyday life. Suppose you are an engineer. You receive a job offer to work on developing a weapon system. You feel that it is wrong to have this system developed — that it heats up the arms race and doesn't make our country or any other more secure. Of course, your participation is not necessary for the weapon to get developed. If you don't do the job, someone else will.

What will a utilitarian say about such cases? If you decline the job offer, the bad consequences (the torturing, the development of the weapon system) occur nonetheless, but without your participation. If you accept, the same bad consequences occur, this time with your participation. A utilitarian will have to conclude that it makes no difference, morally speaking, whether you accept the job offer or decline it. The net consequences are the same.

I think that in many cases like this, it *does* make a moral difference what you decide to do. It is a bad thing to be a torturer for the Nazis, for example. If you become a torturer, you have done something wrong; if you do not become a torturer, you have avoided doing something evil. There is a moral difference here that should guide your conduct. This moral issue is not something that utilitarianism takes into account. According to utilitarianism, what you should do in such cases is look at the net consequences that would occur under different circumstances; this is different from considering what kind of a person you ought to be.

Sometimes utilitarians reply to this objection in the same way I described them replying to the lonesome stranger example. They propose a distinction between rule and act utilitarianism and claim that rule utilitarianism has the plausible consequence that it *does* make a moral difference whether you become a torturer or not.

They reason as follows. To decide what you ought to do in this specific choice situation, you first must decide which general rule should be followed by you and others. The two rules you might consider here are as follows:

(S_1) If the government offers someone a job as a torturer, the offer should be accepted.

(S_2) If the government offers someone a job as a torturer, the offer should be rejected.

The rule utilitarian then points out that the consequences would be better if everyone adopted (S_2) than if everyone adopted (S_1). The conclusion about this pair of rules is then applied to the specific choice situation you confront. You should apply (S_2) to decide what to do; hence, you should decline the offer from the Nazis.

I hope you see how this pattern of argument parallels what rule utilitarians say in reply to the objection based on the lonesome stranger example. In this case, just as in that one, I don't think that the reply really works.

I grant that (S_2) has better consequences than (S_1). But it seems to me that a utilitarian cannot explain why (S_2) is superior to the following rule:

(S_3) If the government offers someone a job as a torturer, the offer should be rejected, unless it makes no difference to the collective utility whether it is accepted or rejected.

A utilitarian cannot explain why (S_2) is a better rule than (S_3). For this reason, the dirty hands problem is, I think, a telling objection to utilitarianism.

The last kind of problem I want to consider concerns the role that personal loyalties play in our judgments about morality. Imagine that a boating accident occurs and you have to choose which of two people you are going to save from drowning. One of them is your own daughter. The other is another child. What should you do?

Utilitarianism and Personal Loyalties

If you think that it makes a moral difference what you should do, how can this be explained? It may be true that the consequences for the collective welfare are the same, whether your child lives and the other child dies, or yours dies and the other lives. If so, utilitarianism cannot explain the special obligations we have to our own family.

By now, the rule utilitarian reply to this objection should be something you can anticipate. Compare the general consequences of following the first general rule and those of following the second:

(T_1) People should not make an effort to preserve the lives of their own children.

(T_2) People should make an effort to preserve the lives of their own children.

Of course, general adherence to (T_2) has better consequences than general adherence to (T_1). But that isn't enough to get utilitarianism out of trouble, since it is hard to see how a utilitarian can argue that (T_2) is superior to (T_3):

(T_3) People should make an effort to preserve the lives of their own children, except when no additional utility comes from doing so.

There is a different sort of reply that utilitarians sometimes make to examples like this one. They say that in a situation of crisis, people don't have time to calculate what they ought to do. They merely act on impulse. What they do in such cases is more a consequence of the habits of character they have developed than of reasoning from general principles.

A Psychological Objection to My Criticisms of Utilitarianism

I grant these psychological points, but they seem to me to be irrelevant. Utilitarianism makes a claim about which actions are right and which are wrong. It does not demand that people take the time and energy to reason dispassionately about what the Greatest Happiness Principle implies. Nor does utilitarianism say that people, in fact, engage in dispassionate calculation in situations of crisis. My criticisms of utilitarianism have to do with what the theory says people *ought* to do; in each of the cases I have surveyed, I have argued that the theory errs in its moral recommendations.

I have raised several objections to utilitarianism. The lonesome stranger objection is supposed to show how utilitarianism can sometimes conflict with the value of justice. The problem of the fanatical majority shows how utilitarianism can sometimes conflict with the value of liberty. The problem of dirty hands shows how utilitarian considerations can be insensitive to the importance of personal integrity. Finally, the problem of loyalty shows that utilitarianism contradicts the idea that

Summary

we have special obligations to people because of certain special relationships we have with them.

In each of these cases, utilitarianism was judged by seeing what it implies about a concrete example situation. The arguments all proceeded by advancing a moral judgment about the examples, and then showing that this judgment conflicts with the dictates of utilitarianism. I grant that someone who is not prepared to endorse the moral claims I have made about the examples will not find this discussion a conclusive refutation of utilitarianism. But agreeing with what I have said about one or more of these examples should be enough to make you doubt that utilitarianism is correct.

Review Questions

1. Mill attempts to prove the Greatest Happiness Principle. He also says that the principle can be defended by what I have called "reciprocal illumination." Explain what Mill's proof is and what reciprocal illumination is.
2. What is the difference between hedonistic utilitarianism and preference utilitarianism? How does the example of the experience machine bear on each of these theories?
3. What is the apples-and-oranges problem?
4. How does the case of the lonesome stranger pose a problem for utilitarianism?
5. How does the fanatical majority problem present a difficulty for utilitarianism?
6. How does the dirty hands problem present a difficulty for utilitarianism?
7. How might a utilitarian use the distinction between act utilitarianism and rule utilitarianism to reply to the objections involved in questions 4–6?

Problems for Further Thought

1. Hedonistic utilitarianism says that the pleasure and pain of *all beings* affected by an act must be taken into account in deciding whether that act should be performed. Preference utilitarianism says that the preferences of *all beings* affected by an act must be taken into account in deciding whether that act should be performed. Utilitarians (for example, Peter Singer in *Animal Liberation*, New York, Random House, 1975) have often concluded that human treatment of animals is morally outrageous. They argue that the pleasure and nutrition we obtain from eating meat does not outweigh the suffering and death of the animals we eat. Is there any way to avoid this conclusion while still remaining true to utilitarian principles?

2. If utilitarianism requires us to maximize the amount of happiness there is in the world, won't it require us to have as many children as possible? Even if overpopulation lowers the *average* (per person) quality of life, won't this be outweighed by the total number of individuals who obtain some amount of happiness from the lives they live?

Lecture 32

Kant's Moral Theory

To understand the basic approach that Immanuel Kant (1724–1804) developed in his moral theory, it is useful to begin with a somewhat commonsensical idea—an idea that Kant rejects. This is the idea that reason can play only an "instrumental" role in guiding people's actions. Reason does not tell you what your goals should be; rather, it tells you what you should do, given the goals you have. To say that reason is purely instrumental is to say that it is merely a tool that helps you achieve your goals, your goals having been determined by something other than reason.

This simple idea can be elaborated by viewing actions as the joint products of belief and desires. Reason can tell you what to believe, given the evidence at hand. But reason cannot tell you what to want. Desires must have some other source:

$$\boxed{\text{Reason}} \begin{array}{c} \longrightarrow \\ \not\longrightarrow \end{array} \left. \begin{array}{l} \text{Beliefs} \\ \text{Desires} \end{array} \right\} \longrightarrow \text{Action}$$

David Hume articulated this idea about the contribution of reason to the actions we perform. In *A Treatise of Human Nature* (1738), he says that "reason is and ought to be the slave of the passions." Hume expresses the same idea in the following passage:

Hume on Reason's Role

> 'Tis not contrary to reason to prefer the destruction of the whole world to the scratching of my finger. . . . 'Tis as little contrary to reason to prefer even my own acknowledg'd lesser good to my greater, and have a more ardent affection for the former than the latter.

The main point about Hume's idea is that *actions never derive from reason alone; they must always have a nonrational source.*

A fundamental part of Kant's theory of morality rejects this Humean doctrine. According to Kant, it is only sometimes true that actions are produced by the agent's beliefs and (nonrationally generated) desires. When we act out of "inclination," this is what happens. However, when we act out of duty—when our actions are guided by moral considerations rather than by our inclinations—matters are entirely different.

Kant Rejects the Idea that Reason Is Purely Instrumental

When we act, there is a goal we have in mind—an end in view—and also a means we use to try to achieve that goal. Hume thought that reason determines the means, not the end. Kant agreed that this is correct when we act out of inclination. But when morality drives our actions, reason determines the end as well as the means.

Kant thought that morality derives its authority from reason alone. Reason alone determines whether an action is right or wrong, regardless of what the desires are that people may happen to have. According to Kant, when we act morally, our actions are guided by reason in a way that Hume's theory rules out.

Kant; Moral
Rules Are
Categorical
Imperatives

It is clear, as Hume said, that reason can show us which means to use, given the ends we have. If I want to be healthy, reason may tell me that I should stop smoking. Here reason delivers an imperative that is *hypothetical* in form: It says that I should stop smoking *if* I want to protect my health. Hume thought that reason can do no more than this. Kant, however, held that moral rules are *categorical*, not hypothetical, in form. An act that is wrong, is wrong — period. Moral rules say "Don't do X." They don't say "Don't do X if your goal is G." Kant tried to show that these moral rules — categorical imperatives — are derived from reason just as surely as hypothetical imperatives are.

Moral rules, which take the form of categorical imperatives, describe what we must do whether we want to or not. They have an authority quite separate from the inclinations we have. So when we act morally, Kant thought, we are guided by reason, not inclination. In this case, reason plays something more than a purely instrumental role.

The Moral
Law

Another important ingredient in Kant's moral philosophy is his idea that moral laws and scientific laws have something deep in common. A scientific law is a generalization that says what *must* be true in a specified kind of situation. Newton's universal law of gravitation says that the gravitational force (F_g) between two objects is proportional to the products of their masses (m_1 and m_2) and inversely proportional to the square of the distance (r) between them:

$$F_g = G(m_1 m_1)/r^2.$$

That is, the law says that if the masses are m_1 and m_2 and if the distance is r, then the gravitational force *must* take the value $G(m_1 m_2)/r^2$, where G is the gravitational constant.

There is clearly a difference between scientific laws and moral rules (such as "Don't cause gratuitous suffering!"). Newton's law does not say what the planets ought to do; it says what they do, of necessity. If a scientific law is true, then nothing in the universe disobeys it. On the other hand, people sometimes violate moral laws. Moral laws say how people ought to behave; they do not say what people, in fact, will do. To use vocabulary introduced earlier, moral laws are normative, while scientific laws are descriptive.

In spite of this difference, Kant thought there is a deeper similarity between them. Scientific laws are *universal* — they involve *all* phenomena of a specific kind. They are not limited to certain places or certain times. Furthermore, a proposition that states a law does not mention any particular person, place, or thing. "All of Napoleon's friends spoke French" may be a true generalization, but it can't be a law, since it mentions a specific individual—Napoleon. I'll mark this feature of scientific laws by saying that they are "impersonal."

Moral laws, Kant thought, also must be universal and impersonal. If it is right for me to do something, then it is right for anyone in similar circumstances to do the same thing. It isn't possible that Napoleon should have the right to do something simply because he is Napoleon. Moral laws, like scientific laws, do not mention specific people.

One more element in Kant's moral philosophy must be mentioned before I can describe how Kant thought that reason alone dictates what our moral principles should be. Recall from the previous lecture that utilitarianism claims that the moral characteristics of an action are to be determined by the consequences the action would have for people's happiness or preference satisfaction. Kant did not think of morality as focusing on the maximizing of happiness. In particular, Kant did not think of the consequences of an action as the true test of its moral features. Rather, what Kant thought of as central is the "maxim that the action embodies."

Each action can be described as an action of a certain kind. If you help someone, you may think of this as an act of charity. In this case, you may be acting on the maxim that you should help others. Alternatively, when you provide the help, you perhaps are thinking of this as a way of making the recipient feel indebted to you. Here the maxim of your action might be that you should place others in your debt. To see what moral value your action has, look at the maxim you had in mind that led you to do what you did.

Kant: The Moral Value of an Act Derives from Its Maxim, Not from Its Consequences

The reason we need to look at the agent's motives, and not at the action's consequences, is not hard to grasp. Kant describes a shopkeeper who never cheats his customers. The reason is that he is afraid that if he cheats them, they will stop patronizing his store. Kant says that the shopkeeper does the right thing, but not for the right reason. He acts in *accordance with* morality, but not *from* morality. To discover the moral value of an action, Kant says we must see *why* the actor performs it; the consequences of the action do not reveal this.

If the shopkeeper acts by applying the maxim "Always be honest," his action has moral value. However, if his action is a result of the maxim "Don't cheat people if it is likely to harm you financially," his action is merely prudential, not moral. Moral value comes from motives, and the motives are given by the maxim that the agent applies in deciding what to do.

Kant is undoubtedly correct in saying that knowing an individual's motives is important in assessing *some* moral properties of an action. If we wish to evaluate an agent's moral character, knowing the motives is important; the consequences the action has may be an imperfect guide. After all, a good person can unintentionally cause harm to others, and a malevolent person can unintentionally provide others with a benefit. However, it is important to see that this point does not imply that an action's consequences are irrelevant to deciding whether to do it. Kant held this further thesis: What makes an action right or wrong is not

Kant Rejected Consequentialism

whether the consequences are harmful or beneficial. Kant rejects *consequentialism* in ethics.

I now can describe Kant's idea that reason (not desire) determines what it is right and wrong to do. Recall that a moral law (like a scientific law) must be universal. This means that a moral action must embody a maxim that is *universalizable*. To decide whether it would be right to perform a particular action, Kant says you should ask whether you can will (intend) that the maxim of your act should be a universal law. Universalizability is the basis of all categorical imperatives—that is, of all unconditional moral injunctions. Moral acts can be universalized; immoral acts cannot.

It is important to grasp what this test is supposed to involve. It is a mistake to think that Kant is saying that you should ask whether it would be a good thing or a bad thing if everyone did the act you are contemplating. The point about immoral actions is not that it would be *bad* for everyone to do them; rather, the point is that it is *impossible* for everyone to do them (or it is *impossible* for you to will that everyone do them). As Kant's examples will illustrate, there is, so to speak, a logical test for whether an action is moral.

In his book *The Groundwork of the Metaphysics of Morals* (1785), Kant applies this idea to four examples. He first describes a man who is tired of life and is contemplating suicide. Kant says that the maxim the man is considering is to end one's life if continuing to live would produce more pain than pleasure. Kant says that it is

> questionable whether this principle of self-love could become a universal law of nature. One immediately sees a contradiction in a system of nature whose law would be to destroy life by the feeling whose special office is to impel the improvement of life. In this case it would not exist as nature; hence that maxim cannot obtain as a law of nature, and thus it wholly contradicts the supreme principle of all duty.

Kant is suggesting that it is impossible for there to exist a world in which all living things decide to commit suicide when their lives promise more pain than pleasure. Since there could be no such world, it is wrong for the individual in Kant's example to commit suicide. The act is wrong because it cannot be universalized.

Kant's second example concerns promise-keeping. You need money and are deciding whether to borrow. The question is whether it would be permissible for you to promise to pay back the money, even though you have no intention of doing so. Kant argues that morality requires you to keep your promise (and so not borrow the money under false pretenses):

> For the universality of a law which says that anyone who believes himself to be in need could promise what he pleased with the

intention of not fulfilling it would make the promise itself and the end to be accomplished by it impossible; no one would believe what was promised to him but would only laugh at any such assertion as vain pretense.

Kant is saying that promise-keeping could not exist as an institution if everyone who made promises did so with the intention of not keeping them. That is, the institution can exist only because people are usually trustworthy. Again, the reason we are obliged to keep our promises is that it is impossible to have a world in which everyone made promises with the intention of breaking them. Universalizability is the acid test.

Kant's third example is intended to show that each of us has an obligation to develop our talents. Why should we work hard at "broadening and improving our natural gifts"? Why not, instead, choose a life of "idleness, indulgence, and propagation"? Each person must choose the former, Kant says, "for, as a rational being, he necessarily wills that all his faculties should be developed, inasmuch as they are given to him for all sorts of possible purposes."

The fourth example concerns a man whose life is going well, but who sees that others live lives of great hardship. Is he obliged to help others? Kant grants that the human race could exist in a state in which some do well while others suffer. But he claims that no rational agent could intend (will) that the world be that way:

Now although it is possible that a universal law of nature according to that maxim could exist, it is nevertheless impossible to will that such a principle should hold everywhere as a law of nature. For a will which resolved this would conflict with itself, since instances can often arise in which he would need the love and sympathy of others, and in which he would have robbed himself, by such a law of nature springing from his own will, of all hope of the aid he desires.

Kant's point is not that the pattern cannot be universal, but that no rational agent could will that it be universal.

Of these examples, the first is perhaps the weakest. It is not impossible for there to be a world in which all terminally ill people who are the victims of great suffering commit suicide. Nor does there seem to be any reason why a rational agent could not will that all people spare themselves a pointlessly agonizing death. *Evaluation of Kant's Examples*

The second example is more plausible. The institution of promise-keeping does seem to rely on the fact that people usually believe the promises made to them. If people never intended to keep their promises, could the institution persist? Kant says no. However, perhaps tricky circumstances can be contrived in which this conclusion is evaded. I leave this an exercise for the reader.

Perhaps there also is something to be said for Kant's argument about our duty to help others. Each of us needs some sort of help at some time in our lives.

Each of us therefore would wish to avoid a situation in which no one would give us the help we need. We therefore cannot will that no one should ever give help. This means that it would be wrong for us to lead a life in which we totally refuse to help others. Again, the reason it would be wrong is that we cannot will that the pattern be universal.

What is Kant's argument, in his fourth example, concerning the duty we have to develop our talents? Perhaps the thought is similar to the one Kant deploys in his discussion of the duty to help others. I want others to develop talents that would be beneficial to me; for example, I want physicians to perfect their skills, since one day I will need them. But this means that I cannot will that all people should neglect to develop their talents. It is supposed to follow that I have a duty to develop my own talents.

There is a difference between the duty of not lying and the duties we have to help others and to develop our talents. The latter two leave open whom we should help and which talents we should develop. The first one is more clear-cut: You are obliged to not lie to anyone. There is no choice here about which of the people you deal with should be treated honestly. Philosophers call relatively indeterminate duties "imperfect" and more clear-cut ones "perfect."

I emphasized earlier that the universalizability criterion does not ask whether it would be a good thing if everyone performed the action the agent is contemplating. Kant's question is whether it would be *possible* for everyone to do so or whether it would be *possible to will* that everyone should do so.

If we keep this clearly in mind, it is doubtful whether Kant can reach the conclusions he wants concerning his last two examples without taking consequences into account. Clearly, it *is* possible that the world be a place in which no one helps others and no one develops their talents. This is a sorry state of affairs, not an impossible one. What about Kant's second option—could a rational agent *will* that no one help others and that no one develop their talents?

That depends on what one means by "rational." If rational means instrumentally rational, then there seems to be no impossibility here. As Hume says, I might be perfectly clear in my means/end reasoning (and so be instrumentally rational) and still have the most bizarre desires you can imagine. On the other hand, there is a sense of "rational" according to which a rational agent would not want the world to be a place in which people do not help others or develop their talents. A rational agent would not want this *because of the consequences such behaviors would have*. There would be a great deal of suffering, alienation, and despair; life would be bleak.

I conclude that it is unclear how Kant can analyze his last two examples as he does without considering the consequences that would follow from making the actions universal.

A Problem for the Universaliz-ability Criterion A general problem pertains to all of Kant's examples—indeed, to the whole idea of the universalizability criterion. Recall a simple point from the lecture on functionalism (Lecture 22): *A token exemplifies many types.* This means that a given (token) action can be described as embodying many different properties. Kant seems to assume that there is just one maxim that each action embodies, so we can test the morality of the act by looking at the universalizability of this maxim. But there are many maxims that might lead to a given action; some of these may universalize while others do not.

Let's return to Kant's example of promise-keeping to see this problem. A man has to decide whether to borrow money by promising to repay it, though he has no intention of keeping his promise. What would it mean for everyone to behave like this? One way to describe this action is to say that it flows from the maxim "Make a promise even though you intend to break it." Kant claims that universalizing this is impossible because the following proposition is a contradiction:

> Everyone makes promises, even though no one intends to keep the promises they make.

However, we can also describe the man's action as flowing from a rather different maxim: "Don't make a promise unless you intend to keep it, except when you are in a life and death situation and your intention to break your promise would not be evident to others." Universalizing this maxim does not lead to contradiction, since the following is a perfectly possible way the world might be:

> Everyone makes promises, and people generally expect to keep their promises. The exception arises when there is an enormous personal advantage to making a promise without the intention to keep it, and the intention to break the promise is not evident to others.

Far from being impossible, this generalization seems to describe fairly accurately the world we inhabit.

You should notice a similarity between the problem that Kant faces and a problem that rule utilitarianism confronted in the previous lecture. "What would happen if everyone did it?" is a question that the rule utilitarian thinks is important in assessing the moral properties of an action. Kant's question is a different one; he asks "Could everyone do it?" or "Could I will that everyone do it?" Though the questions differ, similar problems derive from the fact that there are multiple ways of describing any action.

The universalizability criterion may seem plausible if one takes seriously the analogy between moral laws and scientific laws. Both must be universal and impartial. But another comparison of these two ideas may diminish the plausibility that anything like Kant's universalizability criterion can be made to work. Scientific laws must be universal, but no one thinks that the true explanation of a specific phenomenon can be derived *a priori*. Reason alone cannot tell me why the earth moves in an elliptical orbit around the sun, even if I assume that the explanation of this fact must hold true for all similar planetary systems. On the other hand, Kant held that what it is right to do in a specific situation is dictated by the rational requirement of universalizability.

Evidently, it is an important fact about morality that if it is right for me to do a particular action, then it is right for anyone similarly situated to do it as well. This is the idea that moral laws — the general principles that dictate what it is right to do — are universal and impersonal. The problem is that this requirement is not sufficient to reveal which moral generalizations are true. If so, the analogy between scientific laws and moral laws has implications different from the ones that Kant tried to develop.

Kant: People Are Ends in Themselves

Kant believed that an important consequence of his universalizability test is that we should treat people as ends in themselves and not as mere means. By this Kant meant that we should not treat people as means to ends to which they could not rationally consent. Kant believed that slavery is prohibited by this principle. The same may be true for punishing someone for a crime he or she did not commit, even if doing so would placate a dangerous mob. Kantian theory seems to provide firmer grounds than utilitarianism does for the idea that individuals have rights that cannot be overridden by considerations of utility. It is not the maximization of happiness that matters in Kant's theory. Reason alone is supposed to dictate principles of fairness, impartiality, and justice.

Even though Kant predates the utilitarians, his theory seems designed to correct the defects present in utilitarianism. The idea of rights is a plausible corrective to the idea that every aspect of an individual's life has to pass the test of maximizing the happiness of all. Yet, there are major logical difficulties in Kant's theory. And the absoluteness of some of his pronouncements seems to be wildly at odds with strongly held commonsense moral convictions. Is it at all plausible to think that promises must *always* be kept — that we must *never* tell a lie — no matter what the consequences are? Besides noting the defects in the arguments intended to justify such injunctions, we also should note that these moral requirements should not receive an unconditional justification in the first place.

Iı the universalizability criterion fails to provide a procedure for deciding which actions are right, and if Kant's moral judgments about promise-keeping, suicide, and other actions are implausible, what is of value in his ethical theory? Many philosophers find Kant's description of *the moral point of view* to be one of his enduring and preeminent contributions. Desires and preferences can move us to action, and these actions can produce different mixtures of pleasure and pain. But this sequence of events could occur among creatures — cows and dogs, perhaps — who by no stretch of the imagination have a morality. What, then, distinguishes action motivated by morality from action driven by inclination, whether benevolent or malevolent?

Kant's answer was that moral action is driven by principles that have a special sort of rational warrant. Ordinary language is perhaps a little misleading here, since we can talk about the desire to act morally as if it were on the same footing as the desire to please or to profit. But Kant did not think of the determination to do one's duty as one inclination among many. He saw morality and inclination as existing in entirely different realms from each other. To identify the moral thing to do, one must *set aside* one's inclinations. By fixing our attention on universal and impersonal laws, we can hope to diminish the way self-interest tends to distort our judgment of what we ought to do.

Review Questions

1. Why did Hume maintain that every action has a cause that is "nonrational"? Why did Kant reject this?
2. Kant believed that there are important similarities between scientific laws and moral laws. What are these?
3. What is meant by saying that utilitarianism is a consequentialist theory, whereas Kant's theory is not?
4. What does Kant's universalizability criterion assert? Does it say that you should not do an action if the world would be a worse place if everyone did the same?
5. How does Kant try to show that the obligation of promise-keeping follows from the universalizability criterion? Is he successful?
6. You are in a boat that is tipping dangerously to one side because all the passengers are on the right. You are considering whether it would be a good idea to move to the left. You ask yourself, "What would happen if everyone did this?" This question has an ambiguity in it. What is it? How is this ambiguity relevant to assessing Kant's universalizability criterion?

Problems for Further Thought

1. Kant believes that the duty to treat others as ends in themselves, not as means, follows from the universalizability criterion. Try to construct an argument that shows how this might be true. Is Kant correct in thinking that these two principles are closely related?

2. Kant thought of the moral law as constraining what one's life should be like, but not as determining each and every detail of it. That is, for Kant, one is free to pursue one's private goals and projects as long as these do not violate any categorical imperative. These particular projects are morally permissible, not morally obligatory.

   Utilitarianism, by contrast, sees morality as determining each and every aspect of one's life. Each action one performs must be evaluated in terms of the Greatest Happiness Principle. A private project is permissible only if it promotes the greatest good for the greatest number of people. Such acts are not just permissible, but obligatory.

   Construct a concrete example in which these features of the two theories lead them to make opposite judgments about whether an act is morally permissible. Which theory strikes you as more plausible in what it says about your example?

KANT'S MORAL
THEORY

3. Kant's ethics has had a powerful influence on the political philosophy of John Rawls. In *A Theory of Justice* (Cambridge, Massachusetts, Harvard University Press, 1971), Rawls argues that the correct rules of justice for a society are ones that all persons would choose if (1) they were self-interested, and (2) they did not know various details about themselves (such as their talents, sex, race, and conception of what projects they wish to pursue). The only facts that people know in this hypothetical situation are general facts about human psychology and human life. Rawl's idea is partially an attempt to capture Kant's idea that personal inclinations must be set to one side if one wants to see what one's obligations are. What principles of conduct do you think people would choose in this hypothetical situation?

Lecture 33

Aristotle on the Good Life

How Far Do Obligations Extend? Some ethical theories hold that every aspect of a person's life is to be decided by ethical principles that describe obligations. Utilitarianism, for example, says that it is wrong to do some action if an alternative action could be performed that would better promote people's happiness or preference satisfaction.

Other ethical theories hold that considerations of obligation do not answer every question about how people should lead their lives. Kant's ethical theory is often thought to be of this type. According to Kant, you must treat others with justice and accord them dignity and respect. But this seems to leave open a large number of issues concerning what sort of life you ought to pursue.

The same would be true of an ethical theory that held that all obligations flow from the principle that people have the right to structure their own lives as long as doing so does not infringe on the rights of others. If you accepted an ethics like this, the question would still remain of how you should live your life.

The reason this question is still left open is that the ethical principle just mentioned is largely *negative* in its implications. It mainly tells you what you should *not* do. In consequence, questions like the following are left unanswered: What sort of work should you take up? Should you get married? Should you have children? What sorts of friendships should you try to nurture? Should you try to develop talents you have other than those that figure in the work you do? Should you participate in the political affairs of your community? Nation? the Earth? What importance should you assign to these various activities? The ethical principle that says "Do no harm" provides little or no guidance on these matters.

Philosophers sometimes distinguish the *theory of the right* from the *theory of the good*. In doing so, they are indicating that principles of obligation and prohibition fail to address questions such as the ones listed in the previous paragraph. The theory of the good attempts to describe what the good life would be like.

According to this distinction, living a good life is not limited to fulfilling your obligations. It's easy to miss this point, since "Be good" may sound like the same advice as "Do the right thing." One way to see that there is a difference here is to imagine someone who breaks no moral prohibitions, but still fails to lead a good life. An example might be someone who breaks no laws, but shuns all human contact, has a dull and repetitive job, and spends all time outside work reading comic books. This person may do no harm, but it would be implausible to say of him, "He really led a good life."

The Theory of the Right and the Theory of the Good

It seems plausible that the theory of the right will include principles of some generality. "Do not murder" is a rule that covers you, me, and everyone else. Are there comparable principles to be found in the theory of the good? That is, are there principles that describe what a good life would be like that cover all human beings? Or is the issue of the good life a more personal and individualistic one? Perhaps we are subject to the same obligations and prohibitions (described in the theory of the right), but there is nothing interesting in common between what would be a good life for you and a good life for me.

In his ethical theory (as developed primarily in *The Nicomachean Ethics*), Aristotle (384–322 B.C.) attempts to describe what a good life would be like. In fact, his goal is to describe what *the* good life for human beings amounts to. As I'll explain soon, he maintains that since we are all members of the same biological species, some general principles can be described that specify what a good life would be for any human being. For Aristotle, the good life is to be understood by way of the idea of human nature.

Are There General Principles About the Good Life?

A good person lives a good life. But what makes a person good? Aristotle proposes to understand the idea of a *good human being* by first considering what it means to say that something is good. What is a good hammer? Here we are not talking about ethical issues, of course. A hammer is a tool. A hammer is a good hammer when it is able to perform the tasks that are specific to hammers. Hammers have the function of banging nails into wood. A good hammer optimally performs that function.

Consider another example, this one having to do with the roles that human beings play. What is a good father? To answer this question we have to ask what the function of a father is. Plausibly, a father's function is to help his children grow into loving, responsible, and independent adults. If so, then a good father is one who optimally performs that function.

Human beings perform other functions. What is a good nurse? Nurses train to help the sick. Plausibly, the function of a nurse is to help the patient return to full health as much as possible. If this is right, we can tell from the function of a nurse what a good nurse would be.

What Is a Good X?

Good Versus Green

A green apple and a green shirt must have something in common. But according to Aristotle, a good hammer and a good violinist need have nothing in common. What is the difference between greenness and goodness that accounts for this?

To be a green apple is to be green and an apple. To be a green shirt is to be green and a shirt. Being a green apple is a conjunctive property ("conjunction" means and). Being a green apple involves having two properties; the same is true of being a green shirt. This explains why there is something that green apples and green shirts have in common; there is a property—greenness—that they share.

To be a good hammer is not the same as being good and a hammer. To be a good violinist is not the same as being good and a violinist. Neither is a conjunctive property. To be a good violinist is to have a single complex property, not to possess two separate properties at once. This is why good hammers and good violinists need have nothing in common.

Consider other adjectives. We use terms such as "big," "soft," and "old." Are these more like "green" or more like "good"?

These examples—the hammer, the father, the nurse—tell us something about the concept of goodness. First, we decide what it is to be a good *X* by seeing what the function is of *X*s. The concept of goodness is intimately connected with concepts of goal, function, and purpose. The second lesson is that what it takes to be a good *X* depends on the choice of *X*. For example, the character traits required for being a good father may be quite different from the ones required for being a good harpist or a good baseball player. Aristotle emphasizes both these points about the concept of goodness.

It is no mystery what a good hammer is. And it is not that difficult to say what it means to be a good father or a good nurse. Perhaps the same strategy will work when we ask what a good person is. Aristotle thought that once we say what the function is of human life, we will know what a good human being is. This, in turn, will tell us what the good life amounts to.

Human Beings Are Goal-Directed Systems

In Lecture 5, I briefly explained how Aristotle's biology and physics are *teleological* in character. He thought that living things as well as inanimate objects are goal-directed systems. The goal of a living thing is to grow and reproduce. The goal of a rock is to reach the place where the center of the earth now is. Of course, not all living things grow and reproduce. And not all rocks find their way to the earth's center. But each has a *natural tendency* to do those things. *Interfering forces* may prevent an object from reaching its natural state.

We human beings are goal-directed systems. What is the end state that we seek? Aristotle's answer is that human beings seek *happiness*. A good life is a life of happiness—a life in which the goal of human life has been achieved.

Before saying how Aristotle understood happiness, it is important to note a difference between human beings and other goal-directed systems. Human beings seek happiness; trees aim to grow and reproduce. The difference between us and other living things comes from *how* we pursue the goals we have. Other living things pursue the goals of growth and reproduction *innately*. A tree does not have to be taught to send its roots deep into the soil or to send its leaves where they can absorb sunlight. Trees do these things *by nature*.

In contrast, we human beings are better or worse at seeking happiness according to the upbringing we receive. Some people seek their happiness in wealth or fame or power. Others seek it in love. *How* we seek our happiness is not determined by our nature, but by our upbringing. For Aristotle, a good upbringing is one that helps us develop habits and character traits that are conducive to the good life.

In Lecture 20, on methodological behaviorism, I briefly discussed the nature/nurture controversy. We now understand that dispute in terms of the task of explaining variation in some characteristic (such as height or intelligence). Human beings have various heights. How much of that variation is explained by genetic differences, and how much by differences in environment (such as nutrition)?

Aristotle also drew the nature/nurture distinction, but in a rather different way. First, he did not have the idea of genes. Second, the fact of variation within a species was much less important to him than it is in present-day biology. What is biologically significant about human beings is that human beings have something in common; this is what *human nature* is. When Aristotle thought about "nature" (as opposed to nurture), he thought about characteristics that all members of a species share; current biology thinks about "nature" (as opposed to nurture) in terms of genetic *differences* among members of the same species.

For Aristotle, human beings have a common nature that sets them apart from the rest of the living world. It is part of human nature to seek happiness. How human beings go about doing this varies from person to person. The explanation for this variation, Aristotle held, is environmental. It is differences in nurture—in our upbringing—that explain why human beings live their lives in different ways.

The Capacity to Reason

The function of a hammer is something that distinguishes hammers from other tools. A hammer that is able to perform that function well counts as a good hammer. By the same line of thinking, we can approach the question of what function human beings have by asking what distinguishes human beings from other beings. A human being who is able to perform that function well will count as a good human being.

Human beings are organisms, so survival, growth, and reproduction are goals that human beings aim at. But in addition, there is a characteristic that distinguishes human beings from other organisms. This is the development of rationality—the capacity for abstract thinking.

The basic contours of Aristotle's theory of happiness can now be stated. Human beings, unique among living things, possess the capacity of rationality. The good life for human beings is one in which rational capacities are developed and exercised to a high degree. In doing this, human beings find the best sort of happiness that is possible for them.

Aristotle draws a distinction between theoretical and practical reasoning. Practical reasoning involves the kind of means/ends reasoning so familiar in everyday life. The conclusion you draw in practical reasoning is the determination to do something. For example, you want an article of clothing that will keep you warm in winter. You realize that a cloak will perform this task. So you decide to buy a cloak. Note that this bit of reasoning concludes with the intention to buy a new cloak, not with a prediction that you will do so.

In contrast, the conclusion you draw in theoretical reasoning is that some proposition is true. Theoretical reasoning is reasoning given over to the disinterested search for knowledge. It is "pure" inquiry not "applied." In theoretical inquiry you seek understanding for its own sake. The life of contemplation is devoted to the sort of intellectual activity that occurs in science, philosophy, and the arts. The best life, for Aristotle, is the life of theoretical reason.

Aristotle: Happiness Is Not a Subjective State

When Aristotle asked what happiness is, he wanted to know what sorts of activities comprise the happy life. The word "activity" is important here; a happy life is a life of *doing*. The good life is one in which those traits that are specifically human are brought to a high level of cultivation. The happy life is one of flourishing — of doing well.

Happiness, for Aristotle, is emphatically not the same as pleasure. The sensation of pleasure is possible for a brain in a vat; but a brain in a vat is not a flourishing human being, even if it has the illusion of leading an ideal life.

Real happiness, then, is not a sensation (compare this with the discussion of happiness in Lecture 31). People can believe themselves to be happy and still not be. Whether you are flourishing is not settled by the mere fact that you think you are.

Although pleasure is not the goal of human life, pleasure naturally accompanies the good life. The good life crucially involves exercising the faculty of reason. It is natural for people to take pleasure in exercising this ability, just as people take pleasure in the well-functioning of a healthy body, as in athletics.

Aristotle thought that human beings have god-like as well as animal characteristics. Our nature as animals decrees that we must eat, grow, breathe, and reproduce. In addition, we are social beings by nature, and so the good life includes participation in politics. But the divine spark is also present, and this means that we are directed toward the divine activity of contemplation. When Aristotle says that the good life consists of contemplation (intellectual activity), he is not denying that activities we share with animals are important to us; nor did he mean that involvement in practical political affairs is unimportant. But the life of contemplation was for him a life that emphasized what was best (= highest) in us. It is an expression of what we have in common with the gods.

I have already mentioned Aristotle's main reason for thinking that the human goal of happiness is best achieved by the life of rational activity; the capacity to be rational is unique to us in the living world. But Aristotle had two other ways of reaching this conclusion.

The first is more specifically tied to his conception of how the human mind works. Aristotle thought that activities that call for fine and multifaceted discriminations make people happier than activities that call for fewer and more one-dimensional discriminations. Chess is superior to checkers, and checkers is superior to tic-tac-toe. Sports that require a variety of skills are better than ones that require fewer; and sports that require fine discriminations are better than sports that require only coarse discriminations.

Aristotle saw this as a basic feature of the human mind. Its highest happiness is to be found in activities of these sorts. Aristotle thought that theoretical reasoning—the kind that artists, scholars, scientists, and philosophers pursue—involves mental activities in which the finest and most multifaceted discriminations are drawn.

A further consideration led Aristotle to this conclusion. In choosing a life for ourselves, we must decide which of our capacities we wish to develop. This might involve trying to become a great athlete or a great politician, to name two possibilities. Aristotle thinks it is highly significant that succeeding in these sorts of aims depends on a number of factors that are outside the individual's control. Athletes of great talent can suffer injuries. Politicians can be deprived of power if others oppose them.

In contrast, the life of rational activity is much less dependent on factors outside the agent's control. Contemplation can last a lifetime. It does not require a youthful body, wealth, power, or the admiration of others. Of course, it is not wholly independent of external circumstances. But given the perils that can subvert other plans for life, the life of contemplation makes the most sense, according to Aristotle.

Although Aristotle holds that the good life is devoted to theoretical reasoning, he has a great deal to say about the character traits that good people will display in dealing with other human beings. For example, Aristotle discusses friendship, justice, liberality, and courage. These virtues, he believes, can be understood within a single theoretical framework, provided by his Doctrine of the Mean.

The Doctrine of the Mean

This doctrine says that many (if not all) virtues are located on a continuum, their perfection consisting in the fact that they avoid both excess and deficiency. For example, courage is a virtue; Aristotle claims that it is in between foolhardiness and cowardice. Similarly, liberality is a virtue; people who are liberal with their money are neither misers nor spendthrifts.

Aristotle did not think that the mean had to be an arithmetic average. If 10 units of food is too much and 2 units is too little, the correct amount is somewhere in between; it need not be 6. Furthermore, Aristotle emphasized that the right amount for one person might not be the right amount for another. The wrestler

Milo requires more food than do other people. The mean for him would not be the mean for others.

Although the Doctrine of the Mean is sometimes represented by the slogan "moderation in all things," this is a rather misleading summary of Aristotle's idea. Aristotle says that spitefulness and envy are bad, as are adultery, theft, and murder. They are wrong in themselves; virtue does not consist in doing them a little but not too much.

Once these points are noted, it is unclear how much of a theory the Doctrine of the Mean actually provides. To apply it in a given case, we first must decide what the continuum is on which the activity or virtue is located. Generosity is fairly easy; the scale on which it is located is the amount of money you give away. But what is the scale on which justice is located? And if abstaining from murder is a mean, what is the scale on which it is to be represented?

A second problem arises after one has identified the scale on which the activity or character trait is to be represented. Let us grant that being liberal with money is a mean between being a miser and being a spendthrift. The question is why the intermediacy of the trait should be what makes it a virtue. Does the reason it is better to be courageous than to be cowardly or foolish have much to do with the fact that courage falls between cowardice and foolhardiness? Aristotle thought that it did, but it is by no means clear that he was correct.

In the remainder of the lecture, I want to develop two other criticisms of Aristotle's theory. The first concerns the connection he draws between being a good human being and leading a life that is a good one for human beings to lead. The second has to do with the reasons Aristotle gives for thinking that the life of contemplation is the highest form of happiness.

Defining What a Good X Is Differs from Saying What Is Good for Xs

Let's recall the overall strategy of Aristotle's argument. He begins by asking what the good life for human beings is. This question, he believes, would be answered if we knew what a good human being is. He then proposes to say what a good human being is by inquiring what function human beings have.

It is the first step in this reasoning that I want to question. Aristotle assumes that if a good human being is rational, then rationality is good for human beings. The general principle Aristotle uses here is this:

If a good X is R, then R is good for Xs.

To say that someone is a good X is often just to say that they are good at X-ing. A good teacher is good at teaching. A good parent is good at parenting. A good butcher is good at butchering. A good torturer is good at torturing.

As this last example suggests, to say that you are a good X is not to say that it is a good thing for you to be an X. You might be a good torturer, even though torturing is bad for you. The same may be true for other, less gruesome, activities at which you excel. This is why I reject the principle just displayed.

A good human being, Aristotle holds, is someone who is good at characteristically human activities. Aristotle singles out the use of reason as the characteristic activity and concludes that good human beings devote themselves to lives of contemplation, developing their rational faculties to the utmost.

My criticism suggests that it is not always correct to think about the concepts of a good *X* in the functional way Aristotle proposes. It is plausible to think of a good hammer and a good harpist in the way Aristotle suggests. Perhaps the concept of a good human being requires a different treatment.

Why Single Out Contemplation as the Best Life?

My last criticism has to do with Aristotle's exclusive focus on rationality. He notes that human beings share with other animals the tendency to grow and reproduce. He then asks which characteristic is uniquely human and comes up with rationality as his answer. But surely there are many behaviors and capacities that are unique to human beings. Collecting money for charity is one of them; engaging in genocide is another. If the good life consists in developing those capacities that are uniquely human, why should contemplation be *the* good life? There are many ways to be uniquely human.

Aristotle provides a second reason for singling out the life of theoretical reason as best. Human beings find happiness in drawing fine discriminations and in mastering complex tasks. The life of contemplation provides the greatest opportunity to do these things.

Even if we accept this as basic fact about the human mind, it is unclear why this shows that the life of contemplation is best. Human beings find happiness in other activities as well. Why think of mastering complexity as *the best* activity? Aristotle's answer seems to be the one just discussed: What is best for human beings is the development of traits that are uniquely human. I have already noted the problem with this answer.

Aristotle gives a third reason for thinking that the life of contemplation is best. This life is least dependent on others. But here again, it is hard to see that this characteristic is unique to the life devoted to theoretical reason. It also is hard to see why this characteristic should make that life the one most worth living.

Aristotle thinks that loving others, including your children, is part of the good life. He goes so far as to say that you cannot be happy—lead a good life—if your children suffer or hate you. Notice that in saying this, Aristotle is granting that the good life involves dependency on others. Given this, it is hard to see why the life of contemplation is best *because* it is relatively independent of others.

In summary, Aristotle offers three arguments for thinking that the life of theoretical reason provides the best form of happiness. The first and most important argument appeals to the fact that the capacity to reason is uniquely human. The second claims that human beings find happiness in drawing fine discriminations and in mastering complex tasks. The third sees the contemplative life as supremely good because it is most independent of others. I have suggested that none of these arguments is very persuasive.

In each of them, Aristotle attempts to show why the contemplative life is the best one for human beings without assuming a fully developed theory of value. For example, in the first argument, it is a fact about human biology that justifies his conclusion. In suggesting these arguments, Aristotle is following the analogy with other goal-directed systems. We can say what a good hammer is, or a good father, or a good nurse, without assuming anything about whether it is a good thing or a bad thing to be a hammer, a father, or a nurse.

Perhaps the reason that Aristotle's various arguments run into trouble is that there is a disanalogy between these cases and the problem of describing what the good life is. The good life must be a life that is worth living. A good life must be a life that would be good to have. You can approach questions about what a good teacher is (or a good general, or a good nurse) with a certain detachment. You can say what this role requires without committing yourself to taking it up for yourself. But the problem of the good life admits no such detachment. If you grant that the life of contemplation is the good life for human beings, you commit yourself to the desirability of living such a life.

This may help explain why Aristotle's strategy for solving this important problem was unsuccessful. Another reason may be that Aristotle thought in terms of a single form of life being *the* best one for everyone. His arguments pay scant attention to the differences that distinguish each of us from other human beings. As noted before, the good life for human beings is to be discovered by investigating human nature, and human nature is what all human beings have in common.

Aristotle had the idea that the good life involves actualizing the best capacities we possess. We must find what is best in ourselves and build a whole life on that foundation. Perhaps we should accept this idea, even if we reject Aristotle's suggestion that the good life for every human being consists in actualizing the characteristic that is uniquely human. Perhaps there is no such thing as *the* good life for human beings; rather, there may be many good lives, each uniquely fitted to the unique constellation of traits that each of us possesses.

Review Questions

1. What is the difference between the theory of the right and the theory of the good?
2. What do a good pizza and a good dancer have in common? What does "good" mean?
3. Why did Aristotle think that the good life for human beings would be a life of contemplation?
4. What is the Doctrine of the Mean? Does it say that we should pursue each activity a little but not too much?
5. What connection did Aristotle see between the concept of *a good human being* and the idea that certain activities would be *good for human beings*? Was he right in connecting these ideas in the way he did?

Problems for Further Thought

1. Aristotle says that the function of human beings is to reason well. This is what human beings are *for*. In Lecture 25, on the weather vane of freedom, I defined what it means to say that *the function of the heart is to pump blood.*

The definition I offered involves the modern idea of natural selection; the theory of natural selection, of course, was unknown to Aristotle. Apply this definition of function to the statement *the function of human beings is to be rational*. Is what Aristotle says plausible if his claim about function is understood in this modern way? Explain your answer.

2. There is an interpretation of what Aristotle thinks the good life is that differs from the one I have offered. Instead of seeing the good life as given over to contemplation, this interpretation has Aristotle saying that a good life is one in which reason suffuses all human activities, both theoretical and practical. This interpretation relies on the fact that human beings are *not* the only things capable of rationality—there are the gods as well. What is unique to human beings is the *mixture* of animal nature and the capacity to reason. Gods can engage in pure contemplation; human beings must lead less monolithic lives.

So good human beings judiciously apply reason to the activities that they take up. If Aristotle is interpreted in this way, two problems remain for his view. The first is that we need to provide a list of the activities that comprise the good life. The second is that some principle needs to be provided that says how these various activities are to be integrated and balanced against each other. For example, if the good life includes a family, participation in politics, and contemplation, how are the demands that each activity places on your time and energy to be judged?

Without answering these questions, the advice to use reason in all your activities seems to be fairly empty. Do the passages from Aristotle's *Nicomachean Ethics*, reprinted at the end of this part of the book help provide any answers?

·R·E·A·D·I·N·G·S·

Critique of the Divine Command Theory

·PLATO·

In this excerpt from The Euthyphro, *Plato (427–347 B.C.) presents a dialogue in which the principal subject is the relationship between what piety is and what the gods command. The point at issue is not restricted to the question of what piety is, but pertains to any ethical category: Is an act morally obligatory because God commands it, or does God command it because the act is obligatory?*

EUTHYPHRO: What's new, Socrates, to make you leave your usual haunts in the Lyceum and spend your time here by the king-archon's court? Surely you are not prosecuting any one before the king archon as I am?

SOCRATES: The Athenians do not call this a prosecution but an indictment, Euthyphro.

E: What is this you say? Someone must have indicted you, for you are not going to tell me that you have indicted someone else.

S: No indeed.

E: But someone else has indicted you?

S: Quite so.

E: Who is he?

S: I do not really know him myself, Euthyphro. He is apparently young and unknown. They call him Meletus, I believe. He belongs to the Pitthean deme, if you know anyone from that deme called Meletus, with long hair, not much of a beard, and a rather aquiline nose.

E: I don't know him, Socrates. What charge does he bring against you?

S: What charge? A not ignoble one I think, for it is no small thing for a young man to have knowledge of such an important subject. He says he knows how our young men are corrupted and who corrupts them. He is likely to be wise, and when he sees my ignorance corrupting his contemporaries, he proceeds to accuse me to the city as to their mother. I think he is the only one of our public men to start out the right way, for it is right to care first that the young should be as good as possible, just as a good farmer is likely to take care of the young plants first, and of the others later. So, too, Meletus first gets rid of us who corrupt the growth of the young, as he says, and then afterwards he will obviously take care of the older and become a source of great blessings for the city, as seems likely to happen to one who started out this way.

E: I could wish this were true, Socrates, but I fear the opposite may happen. He seems to me to start out by harming the very heart of the city by attempting to wrong you. Tell me, what does he say you do to corrupt the young?

S: Strange things, to hear him tell it, for he says that I am a maker of gods, that I create new gods while not believing in the old gods, and he has indicted me for this very reason, as he puts it.

E: I understand, Socrates. This is because you say that the divine sign keeps coming to you. So he has written this indictment against you as one who makes innovations in religious matters, and he comes to court to slander you, knowing that such things are easily misrepresented to the crowd. The same is true in my case. Whenever I speak of divine matters in the assembly and foretell the future, they laugh me down as if I were crazy; and yet I have foretold nothing that did not happen. Nevertheless, they envy all of us who do this. One need not give them any thought, but carry on just the same.

S: My dear Euthyphro, to be laughed at does not matter perhaps, for the Athenians do not mind anyone they think clever, as long as he does not teach his own wisdom, but if they think that he makes others to be like himself they get angry, whether through envy, as you say, or for some other reason.

E: I have certainly no desire to test their feelings toward me in this matter.

S: Perhaps you seem to make yourself but rarely available, and not to be willing to teach your own wisdom, but my liking for people makes them think that I pour out to anybody anything I have to say, not only without charging a fee but appearing glad to reward anyone who is willing to listen. If then they were intending to laugh at me, as you say they laugh at you, there would be nothing unpleasant in their spending their time in court laughing and jesting, but if they are going to be serious, the outcome is not clear except to you prophets.

E: Perhaps it will come to nothing, Socrates, and you will fight your case as you think best, as I think I will mine.

S: What is your case, Euthyphro? Are you the defendant or the prosecutor?

E: The prosecutor.

S: Whom do you prosecute?

E: One whom I am thought crazy to prosecute.

S: Are you pursuing someone who will easily escape you?

E: Far from it, for he is quite old.

S: Who is it?

E: My father.

S: My dear sir! Your own father?

E: Certainly.

S: What is the charge? What is the case about?

E: Murder, Socrates.

CRITIQUE OF
THE DIVINE
COMMAND THEORY

S: Good heavens! Certainly, Euthyphro, most men would not know how they could do this and be right. It is not the part of anyone to do this, but of one who is far advanced in wisdom.

E: Yes by Zeus, Socrates, that is so.

S: Is then the man your father killed one of your relatives? Or is that obvious, for you would not prosecute your father for the murder of a stranger.

E: It is ridiculous, Socrates, for you to think that it makes any difference whether the victim is a stranger or a relative. One should only watch whether the killer acted justly or not; if he acted justly, let him go, but if not, one should prosecute, even if the killer shares your hearth and table. The pollution is the same if you knowingly keep company with such a man and do not cleanse yourself and him by bringing him to justice. The victim was a dependent of mine, and when we were farming in Naxos he was a servant of ours. He killed one of our household slaves in drunken anger, so my father bound him hand and foot and threw him in a ditch, then sent a man here to enquire from the priest what should be done. During that time he gave no thought or care to the bound man, as being a killer, and it was no matter if he died, which he did. Hunger and cold and his bonds caused his death before the messenger came back from the seer. Both my father and my other relatives are angry that I am prosecuting my father for murder on behalf of a murderer, as he did not even kill him. They say that such a victim does not deserve a thought and that it is impious for a son to prosecute his father for murder. But their ideas of the divine attitude to piety and impiety are wrong, Socrates.

S: Whereas, by Zeus, Euthyphro, you think that your knowledge of the divine, and of piety and impiety, is so accurate that, when those things happened as you say, you have no fear of having acted impiously in bringing your father to trial?

E: I should be of no use, Socrates, and Euthyphro would not be superior to the majority of men, if I did not have accurate knowledge of all such things.

S: It is indeed most important, my admirable Euthyphro, that I should become your pupil, and as regards this indictment challenge Meletus about these very things and say to him: that in the past too I considered knowledge about the divine to be most important, and that now he says that I improvise and innovate about the gods I have become your pupil. I would say to him: "If, Meletus, you agree that Euthyphro is wise in these matters, consider me, too, to have the right beliefs and do not bring me to trial. If you do not think so, then prosecute that teacher of mine for corrupting the older men, me and his own father, by teaching me and by exhorting and punishing him. If he is not convinced, does not discharge me, or indicts you instead of me, I shall repeat the same challenge in court.

E: Yes by Zeus, Socrates, and, if he should try to indict me, I think I would find his weak spots and the talk in court would be about him rather than about me.

S: It is because I realize this that I am eager to become your pupil, my dear friend. I know that other people as well as this Meletus do not even seem to notice you, whereas he sees me so sharply and clearly that he indicts me for ungodliness. So tell me now, by Zeus, what you just now maintained you clearly knew: what kind of thing do you say that godliness and ungodliness are, both as regards murder and other things; or is the pious not the same and alike in every action, and the impious the opposite of all that is pious and like itself, and everything that is to be impious presents us with one form or appearance in so far as it is impious.

E: Most certainly, Socrates.

S: Tell me then, what is the pious, and what the impious, do you say?

E: I say that the pious is to do what I am doing now, to prosecute the wrongdoer, be it about murder or temple robbery or anything else, whether the wrongdoer is your father or your mother or anyone else; not to prosecute is impious. And observe, Socrates, that I can quote the law as a great proof that this is so. I have already said to others that such actions are right, not to favour the ungodly, whoever they are. These people themselves believe that Zeus is the best and most just of the gods, yet they agree that he bound his father because he unjustly swallowed his sons, and that he in turn castrated his father for similar reasons. But they are angry with me because I am prosecuting my father for his wrongdoing. They contradict themselves in what they say about the gods and about me.

S: Indeed, Euthyphro, this is the reason why I am a defendant in the case, because I find it hard to accept things like that being said about the gods, and it is likely to be the reason why I shall be told I do wrong. Now, however, if you, who have full knowledge of such things, share their opinions, then we must agree with them too, it would seem. For what are we to say, we who agree that we ourselves have no knowledge? Tell me, by the god of friendship, do you really believe these things are true?

E: Yes, Socrates, and so are even more surprising things, of which the majority has no knowledge.

S: And do you believe that there really is war among the gods, and terrible enmities and battles, and other such things as are told by the poets, and other sacred stories such as are embroidered by good writers and by representations of which the robe of the goddess is adorned when it is carried up to the Acropolis. Are we to say these things are true, Euthyphro?

E: Not only these, Socrates, but, as I was saying just now, I will, if you wish, relate many other things about the gods which I know will amaze you.

S: I should not be surprised, but you will tell me these at leisure some other time. For now, try to tell me more clearly what I was asking just now, for, my friend, you did not teach me adequately when I asked you what the pious was, but you told me that what you are doing now, to prosecute your father for murder, is pious.

E: And I told the truth, Socrates.

S: Perhaps. You agree, however, that there are many other pious actions.

E: There are.

CRITIQUE OF
THE DIVINE
COMMAND THEORY

s: Bear in mind then that I did not bid you tell me one or two of the many pious actions but that form itself that makes all pious actions pious, for you agreed that all impious actions are impious and all pious actions pious through one form, or don't you remember?

E: I do.

s: Tell me then what the form itself is, so that I may look upon it, and using it as a model, say that any action of yours or another's that is of that kind is pious, and if it is not that it is not.

E: If that is how you want it, Socrates, that is how I will tell you.

s: That is what I want.

E: Well then, what is dear to the gods is pious, what is not is impious.

s: Splendid, Euthyphro! You have now answered in the way I wanted. Whether your answer is true I do not know yet, but you will obviously show me that what you say is true.

E: Certainly.

s: Come then, let us examine what we mean. An action or a man dear to the gods is pious, but an action or a man hated by the gods is impious. They are not the same, but opposites, the pious and the impious. Is that not so?

E: It is indeed.

s: And that seems to be a good statement?

E: I think so, Socrates.

s: We have also stated that the gods are in a state of discord, that they are at odds with each other, Euthyphro, and that they are at enmity with each other. That too has been said.

E: It has.

s: What are the subjects of difference that cause hatred and anger? Let us look at it this way. If you and I were to differ about numbers as to which is the greater, would this difference make us enemies and angry with each other, or would we proceed to count and soon resolve our difference about this?

E: We would certainly do so.

s: Again, if we differed about the larger and the smaller, we would turn to measurement and soon cease to differ.

E: That is so.

s: And about the heavier and the lighter, we would resort to weighing and be reconciled.

E: Of course.

s: What subject of difference would make us angry and hostile to each other if we were unable to come to a decision? Perhaps you do not have an answer ready, but examine as I tell you whether these subjects are the just and the unjust, the beautiful and the ugly, the good and the bad. Are these not the subjects of difference about which, when we are unable to come to a satisfactory decision, you and I and other men become hostile to each other whenever we do.

E: That is the difference, Socrates, about those subjects.

s: What about the gods, Euthyphro? If indeed they have differences, will it not be about these same subjects?

E: It certainly must be so.

s: Then according to your argument, my good Euthyphro, different gods consider different things to be just, beautiful, ugly, good and bad, for they would not be at odds with one another unless they differed about these subjects, would they?

E: You are right.

s: And they like what each of them considers beautiful, good, and just, and hate the opposites of these?

E: Certainly.

s: But you say that the same things are considered just by some gods and unjust by others, and as they dispute about these things they are at odds and at war with each other. Is that not so?

E: It is.

s: The same things then are loved by the gods and hated by the gods, both god-loved and god-hated.

E: It seems likely.

s: And the same things would be both pious and impious, according to this argument.

E: I'm afraid so.

s: So you did not answer my question, you surprising man. I did not ask you what same thing is both pious and impious, and it appears that what is loved by the gods is also hated by them. So it is in no way surprising if your present action, namely punishing your father, may be pleasing to Zeus but displeasing to Kronos and Ouranos, pleasing to Hephaestus but displeasing to Hera, and so with any other gods who differ from each other on this subject.

E: I think, Socrates, that on this subject no gods would differ from one another, that whoever has killed anyone unjustly should pay the penalty.

s: Well now, Euthyphro, have you ever heard any man maintaining that one who has killed or done anything else unjustly should not pay the penalty?

E: They never cease to dispute on this subject, both elsewhere and in the courts, for when they have committed many wrongs they do and say anything to avoid the penalty.

s: Do they agree they have done wrong, Euthyphro, and in spite of so agreeing do they nevertheless say they should not be punished?

E: No, they do not agree on that point.

s: So they do not say or do anything. For they do not venture to say this, or dispute that they must not pay the penalty if they have done wrong, but I think they deny doing wrong. Is that not so?

E: That is true.

s: Then they do not dispute that the wrongdoer must be punished, but they may disagree as to who the wrongdoer is, what he did and when.

E: You are right.

CRITIQUE OF
THE DIVINE
COMMAND THEORY

S: Do not the gods have the same experience, if indeed they are at odds with each other about the just and the unjust, as your argument maintains? Some assert that they wrong one another, while others deny it, but no one among gods or men ventures to say that the wrongdoer must not be punished.

E: Yes, that is true, Socrates, as to the main point.

S: And those who disagree, whether men or gods, dispute about each action, if indeed the gods disagree. Some say it is done justly, others unjustly. Is that not so?

E: Yes, indeed.

S: Come now, my dear Euthyphro, tell me, too, that I may become wiser, what proof you have that all the gods consider that man to have been killed unjustly who became a murderer while in your service, was bound by the master of his victim, and died in his bonds before the one who bound him found out from the seers what was to be done with him, and that it is right for a son to denounce and to prosecute his father on behalf of such a man. Come, try to show me a clear sign that all the gods definitely believe this action to be right. If you can give me adequate proof of this, I shall never cease to extol your wisdom.

E: This is perhaps no light task, Socrates, though I could show you very clearly.

S: I understand that you think me more dull-witted than the jury, as you will obviously show them that these actions were unjust and that all the gods hate such actions.

E: I will show it to them clearly, Socrates, if only they will listen to me.

S: They will listen if they think you show them well. But this thought came to me as I was speaking, and I am examining it, saying to myself: "If Euthyphro shows me conclusively that all the gods consider such a death unjust, to what greater extent have I learned from him the nature of piety and impiety? This action would then, it seems, be hated by the gods, but the pious and the impious were not thereby now defined, for what is hated by the gods has also been shown to be loved by them." So I will not insist on this point; let us assume, if you wish, that all the gods consider this unjust and that they all hate it. However, is this the correction we are making in our discussion, that what all the gods hate is impious, and what they all love is pious, and that what some gods love and others hate is neither or both? Is that how you now wish us to define piety and impiety?

E: What prevents us from doing so, Socrates?

S: For my part nothing, Euthyphro, but you look whether on your part this proposal will enable you to teach me most easily what you promised.

E: I would certainly say that the pious is what all the gods love, and the opposite, which all the gods hate, is the impious.

S: Then let us again examine whether that is a sound statement, or do we let it pass, and if one of us, or someone else, merely says that this is so, do we accept that it is so? Or should we examine what the speaker means?

E: We must examine it, but I certainly think that this is now a fine statement.

S: We shall soon know better whether it is. Consider this: Is the pious loved by the gods because it is pious, or is it pious because it is loved by the gods?

E: I don't know what you mean, Socrates.

S: I shall try to explain more clearly; we speak of something being carried and something carrying, of something being led and something leading, of something being seen and something seeing, and you understand that these things are all different from one another and how they differ?

E: I think I do.

S: So there is something being loved and something loving, and the loving is a different thing.

E: Of course.

S: Tell me then whether that which is (said to be) being carried is being carried because someone carries it or for some other reason.

E: No, that is the reason.

S: And that which is being led is so because someone leads it, and that which is being seen because someone sees it?

E: Certainly.

S: It is not seen by someone because it is being seen but on the contrary it is being seen because someone sees it; nor is it because it is being led that someone leads it but because someone leads it that it is being led; it is not because it is being seen that someone sees it, but it is being seen because someone sees it; nor does someone carry an object because it is being carried, but it is being carried because someone carries it. Is what I want to say clear, Euthyphro? I want to say this, namely, that if anything comes to be, or is affected, it does not come to be because it is coming to be, but it is coming to be because it comes to be; nor is it affected because it is being affected but because something affects it. Or do you not agree?

E: I do.

S: What is being loved is either something that comes to be or something that is affected by something?

E: Certainly.

S: So it is in the same case as the things just mentioned; it is not loved by those who love it because it is being loved, but it is being loved because they love it?

E: Necessarily.

S: What then do we say about the pious, Euthyphro? Surely that it is loved by all the gods, according to what you say?

E: Yes.

S: Is it loved because it is pious, or for some other reason?

E: For no other reason.

S: It is loved then because it is pious, but it is not pious because it is loved?

E: Apparently.

S: And because it is loved by the gods it is being loved and is dear to the gods?

E: Of course.

S: The god-beloved is then not the same as the pious, Euthyphro, nor the pious the same as the god-beloved, as you say it is, but one differs from the other.

E: How so, Socrates?

S: Because we agree that the pious is beloved for the reason that it is pious, but it is not pious because it is loved. Is that not so?

E: Yes.

S: And that the god-beloved, on the other hand, is so because it is loved by the gods, by the very fact of being loved, but it is not loved because it is god-beloved.

E: True.

S: But if the god-beloved and the pious were the same, my dear Euthyphro, and the pious were loved because it was pious, then the god-beloved would be loved because it was god-beloved, and if the god-beloved was god-beloved because it was loved by the gods, then the pious would also be pious because it was loved by the gods; but now you see that they are in opposite cases as being altogether different from each other: the one is of a nature to be loved because it is loved, the other is loved because it is of a nature to be loved. I'm afraid, Euthyphro, that when you were asked what piety is, you did not wish to make its nature clear to me, but you told me an affect or quality of it, that the pious has the quality of being loved by all the gods, but you have not yet told me what the pious is. Now, if you will, do not hide things from me but tell me again from the beginning what piety is, whether loved by the gods or having some other quality—we shall not quarrel about that—but be keen to tell me what the pious and the impious are.

E: But Socrates, I have no way of telling you what I have in mind, for whatever proposition we put forward goes around and refuses to stay put where we establish it.

S: Your statements, Euthyphro, seem to belong to my ancestor, Daedalus. If I were stating them and putting them forward, you would perhaps be making fun of me and say that because of my kinship with him my conclusions in discussion run away and will not stay where one puts them. As these propositions are yours, however, we need some other jest, for they will not stay put for you, as you say yourself.

E: I think the same jest will do for our discussion, Socrates, for I am not the one who makes them go round and not remain in the same place; it is you who are the Daedalus; for as far as I am concerned they would remain as they were.

S: It looks as if I was cleverer than Daedalus in using my skill, my friend, in so far as he could only cause to move the things he made himself, but I can make other people's move as well as my own. And the smartest part of my skill is that I am clever without wanting to be, for I would rather have my arguments remain unmoved than possess the wealth of Tantalus as well as the cleverness of Daedalus. But enough of this. Since I think you are making unnecessary difficulties, I am eager as you are to find a way to teach me about piety, and do not give up before you do. See whether you think all that is pious is of necessity just.

E: I think so.

S: And is then all that is just pious? Or is all that is pious just, but not all that is just pious, but some of it is and some is not?

E: I do not follow what you are saying, Socrates.

S: Yet you are younger than I by as much as you are wiser. As I say, you are making difficulties because of your wealth of wisdom. Pull yourself together, my dear sir, what I am saying is not difficult to grasp. I am saying the opposite of what the poet said who wrote: "You do not wish to name Zeus, who had done it, and who made all things grow, for where there is fear there is also shame." I disagree with the poet. Shall I tell you why?

E: Please do.

S: I do not think that "where there is fear there is also shame," for I think that many people who fear disease and poverty and many other such things feel fear, but are not ashamed of the things they fear. Do you not think so?

E: I do indeed.

S: But where there is shame there is also fear. Does anyone feel shame at something who is not also afraid at the same time of a reputation for wickedness?

E: He is certainly afraid.

S: It is then not right to say "where there is fear there is also shame," but that where there is shame there is also fear, for fear covers a larger area than shame. Shame is a part of fear just as odd is a part of number, with the result that it is not true that where there is number there is also oddness, but that where there is oddness there is also number. Do you follow me?

E: Surely.

S: This is the kind of thing I was asking before, whether where there is piety there is also justice, but where there is justice there is not always piety, for the pious is a part of justice. Shall we say that, or do you think otherwise?

E: No, but like that, for what you say appears to be right.

S: See what comes next; if the pious is a part of the just, we must, it seems, find out what part of the just it is. Now if you asked me something of what we mentioned just now, such as what part of number is the even, and what number that is, I would say it is the number that is divisible into two equal, not unequal, parts. Or do you not think so?

E: I do.

S: Try in this way to tell me what part of the just the pious is, in order to tell Meletus not to wrong us any more and not to indict me for ungodliness, since I have learned from you sufficiently what is godly and pious and what is not.

CRITIQUE OF
THE DIVINE
COMMAND THEORY

E: I think, Socrates, that the godly and pious is the part of the just that is concerned with the care of the gods, while that concerned with the care of men is the remaining part of justice.

S: You seem to me to put that very well, but I still need a bit of information. I do not know yet what you mean by care, for you do not mean it in the sense as the care of other things, as, for example, not everyone knows how to care for horses, but the horse breeder does.

E: Yes, I do mean it that way.

S: So horse breeding is the care of horses.

E: Yes.

S: Nor does everyone know how to care for dogs, but the hunter does.

E: That is so.

S: So hunting is the care of dogs.

E: Yes.

S: And cattle raising is the care of cattle.

E: Quite so.

S: While piety and godliness is the care of the gods, Euthyphro. Is that what you mean?

E: It is.

S: Now care in each case has the same effect; it aims at the good and the benefit of the object cared for, as you can see that horses cared for by horse breeders are benefited and become better. Or do you not think so?

E: I do.

S: So dogs are benefited by dog breeding, cattle by cattle raising, and so with all the others. Or do you think that care aims to harm the object of its care?

E: By Zeus, no.

S: It aims to benefit the object of its care.

E: Of course.

S: Is piety then, which is the care of the gods, also to benefit the gods and make them better? Would you agree that when you do something pious you make some one of the gods better?

E: By Zeus, no.

S: Nor do I think that this is what you mean—far from it—but that is why I asked you what you meant by the care of gods, because I did not believe you meant this kind of care.

E: Quite right, Socrates, that is not the kind of care I mean.

S: Very well, but what kind of care of the gods would piety be?

E: The kind of care, Socrates, that slaves take of their masters.

S: I understand. It is likely to be the service of the gods.

E: Quite so.

S: Could you tell me to the achievement of what goal service to doctors tends? Is it not, do you think to achieving health?

E: I think so.

S: What about service to shipbuilders? To what achievement is it directed?

E: Clearly, Socrates, to the building of a ship.

S: And service to housebuilders to the building of a house?

E: Yes.

S: Tell me then, my good sir, to the achievement of what aim does service to the gods tend? You obviously know since you say that you, of all men, have the best knowledge of the divine.

E: And I am telling the truth, Socrates.

S: Tell me then, by Zeus, what is that excellent aim that the gods achieve, using us as their servants?

E: Many fine things, Socrates.

S: So do generals, my friend. Nevertheless you could tell me their main concern, which is to achieve victory in war, is it not?

E: Of course.

S: The farmers too, I think, achieve many fine things, but the main point of their efforts is to produce food from the earth.

E: Quite so.

S: Well then, how would you sum up the many fine things that the gods achieve?

E: I told you a short while ago, Socrates, that it is a considerable task to acquire any precise knowledge of these things, but, to put it simply, I say that if a man knows how to say and do what is pleasing to the gods at prayer and sacrifice, those are pious actions such as preserve both private houses and public affairs of state. The opposite of these pleasing actions are impious and overturn and destroy everything.

S: You could tell me in far fewer words, if you were willing, the sum of what I asked, Euthyphro, but you are not keen to teach me, that is clear. You were on the point of doing so, but you turned away. If you had given that answer, I should now have acquired from you sufficient knowledge of the nature of piety. As it is, the lover of inquiry must follow it wherever it may lead him. Once more then, what do you say that piety and the pious are, and also impiety? Are they a knowledge of how to sacrifice and pray?

E: They are.

S: To sacrifice is to make a gift to the gods, whereas to pray is to beg from the gods?

E: Definitely, Socrates.

S: It would follow from this statement that piety would be a knowledge of how to give to, and beg from, the gods.

E: You understood what I said very well, Socrates.

S: That is because I am so desirous of your wisdom, and I concentrate my mind on it, so that no word of yours may fall to the ground. But tell me, what is this service to the gods? You say it is to beg from them and to give to them?

E: I do.

S: And to beg correctly would be to ask from them things that we need?

CRITIQUE OF
THE DIVINE
COMMAND THEORY

E: What else?

S: And to give correctly is to give them what they need from us, for it would not be skillful to bring gifts to anyone that are in no way needed.

E: True, Socrates.

S: Piety would then be a sort of trading skill between gods and men?

E: Trading yes, if you prefer to call it that.

S: I prefer nothing, unless it is true. But tell me, what benefit do the gods derive from the gifts they receive from us? What they give us is obvious to all. There is for us no good that we do not receive from them, but how are they benefited by what they receive from us? Or do we have such an advantage over them in the trade that we receive all our blessings from them and they receive nothing from us?

E: Do you suppose, Socrates, that the gods are benefited by what they receive from us?

S: What could those gifts from us to the gods be, Euthyphro?

E: What else, you think, than honour, reverence, and what I mentioned before, gratitude.

S: The pious is then, Euthyphro, pleasing to the gods, but not beneficial or dear to them?

E: I think it is of all things most dear to them.

S: So the pious is once again what is dear to the gods.

E: Most certainly.

S: When you say this, will you be surprised if your arguments seem to move about instead of staying put? And will you accuse me of being Daedalus who makes them move, though you are yourself much more skillful than Daedalus and make them go round in a circle? Or do you not realize that our argument has moved around and come again to the same place? You surely remember that earlier the pious and the god-beloved were shown not to be the same but different from each other. Or do you not remember?

E: I do.

S: Do you then not realize that when you say now that what is dear to the gods is the pious? Is this not the same as the god-beloved? Or is it not?

E: It certainly is.

S: Either we were wrong when we agreed before, or, if we were right then, we are wrong now.

E: That seems to be so.

S: So we must investigate again from the beginning what piety is, as I shall not willingly give up before I learn this. Do not think me unworthy, but concentrate your attention and tell the truth. For you know it, if any man does, and I must not let you go, like Proteus, before you tell me. If you had no clear knowledge of piety and impiety you would never have ventured to prosecute your old father for murder on behalf of a servant. For fear of the gods you would have been afraid to take the risk lest you should not be acting rightly, and would have been ashamed before me, but now I know well that you believe you have clear knowledge of piety and impiety. So tell me, my good Euthyphro, and do not hide what you believe.

E: Some other time, Socrates, for I am in a hurry now, and it is time for me to go.

S: What a thing to do, my friend! By going you have cast me down from a great hope I had, that I would learn from you the nature of the pious and the impious and so escape Meletus' indictment by showing that I had acquired wisdom· in divine matters from Euthyphro, and my ignorance would not longer cause me to be careless and inventive about such things, and that I would be better for the rest of my life.

Existentialism

·JEAN-PAUL SARTRE·

In this section of his essay "Existentialism and Humanism," Sartre explains the fundamental ideas in his version of this philosophy. Human beings must realize that there is no God who dictates what is morally required of them. Instead, morality is a free creation that each individual must fashion for him or herself.

What is meant by the term *existentialism?* Can it be that what really scares [people] in the doctrine I shall try to present here is that it leaves to man a possibility of choice? To answer this question, we must re-examine it on a strictly philosophical plane.

Actually, it is the least scandalous, the most austere of doctrines. It is intended strictly for specialists and philosophers. Yet it can be easily defined. What complicates matters is that there are two kinds of existentialist; first, those who are Christian, among whom I would include Jaspers and Gabriel Marcel, both Catholic; and on ·the other hand the atheistic existentialists, among whom I class Heidegger, and then the French existentialists and myself. What they have in common is that they think that existence precedes essence, or, if you prefer, that subjectivity must be the starting point.

Just what does that mean? Let us consider some object that is manufactured, for example, a book or a paper-cutter: here is an object which has been made by an artisan whose inspiration came from a concept. He referred to the concept of what a paper-cutter is and likewise to a known method of production, which is part of the concept, something which is, by and large, a routine. Thus, the paper-cutter is at once an object produced in a certain way and, on the other hand, one having a specific use; and one can not postulate a man who produces a paper-cutter but does not know what it is used for. Therefore, let us say that, for the paper-cutter, essence—that is, the ensemble of both the production routines and the properties which enable it to be both produced and defined—precedes existence. Thus, the presence of the paper-cutter or book in front of me is determined. Therefore, we have here a technical view of the world whereby it can be said that production precedes existence.

When we conceive God as the Creator, He is generally thought of as a superior sort of artisan. Whatever doctrine we may be considering, whether one like that of Descartes or that of Leibnitz, we always grant that will more or less follows understanding or, at the very least, accompanies it, and that when God creates He knows exactly what He is creating. Thus, the concept of man in the mind of God is comparable to the concept of paper-cutter in the mind of the manufacturer, and, following certain techniques and a conception, God produces man, just as the artisan, following a definition and a technique, makes a paper-cutter. Thus, the individual man is the realization of a certain concept in the divine intelligence.

In the eighteenth century, the atheism of the *philosophes* discarded the idea of God, but not so much for the notion that essence precedes existence. To a certain extent, this idea is found everywhere; we find it in Diderot, in Voltaire, and even in Kant. Man has a human nature; this human nature, which is the concept of the human, is found in all men, which means that each man is a particular example of a universal concept, man. In Kant, the result of this universality is that the wild-man, the natural man, as well as the bourgeois, are circumscribed by the same definition and have the same basic qualities. Thus, here too the essence of man precedes the historical existence that we find in nature.

Atheistic existentialism, which I represent, is more coherent. It states that if God does not exist, there is at least one being in whom existence precedes essence, a being who exists before he can be defined by any concept, and that this being is man, or, as Heidegger says, human reality. What is meant here by saying that existence precedes essence? It means that, first of all, man exists, turns up, appears on the scene, and, only afterwards, defines himself. If man, as the existentialist conceives him, is indefinable, it is because at first he is nothing. Only afterward will he be something, and he himself will have made what he will be. Thus, there is no human nature, since there is no God to conceive it. Not only is man what he conceives himself to be, but he is also only what he wills himself to be after this thrust toward existence.

Man is nothing else but what he makes of himself. Such is the first principle of existentialism. It is also what is called subjectivity, the name we are labeled with when charges are brought against us. But what do we mean by this, if not that man has a greater dignity than a stone or table? For we mean that man first exists, that is, that man first of all is the being who hurls himself toward a future and who is conscious of imagining himself as being in the future. Man is at the start a plan which is aware of itself, rather than a patch of moss, a piece of garbage, or a cauliflower; nothing exists prior to this plan; there is nothing in heaven; man will be what he will have planned to be. Not what he will want to be. Because by the word "will" we generally mean a conscious decision, which is subsequent to what we have already made of ourselves. I may want to belong to a political party, write a book, get married; but all that is only a manifestation of an earlier, more spontaneous choice that is called "will." But if existence really does precede essence, man is responsible for what he is. Thus existentialism's first move is to make every man aware of what he is and to make the full responsibility of his existence rest on him. And when we say that a man is responsible for himself, we do not only mean that he is responsible for his own individuality, but that he is responsible for all men.

The word subjectivism has two meanings, and our opponents play on the two. Subjectivism means, on the one hand, that an individual chooses and makes himself; and, on the other, that it is impossible for man to transcend human subjectivity. The second of these is the essential meaning of existentialism. When we say that man chooses his own self, we mean that every one of us does likewise; but we also mean by that that in making this choice he also chooses all men. In fact, in creating the man that we want to be, there is not a single one of our acts which does not at the same time create an image of man as we think he ought to be. To choose to be this or that is to affirm at the same time the value of what we choose, because we can never choose evil. We always choose the good, and nothing can be good for us without being good for all.

If, on the other hand, existence precedes essence, and if we grant that we exist and fashion our image at one and the same time, the image is valid for everybody and for our whole age. Thus, our responsibility is much greater than we might have supposed, because it involves all mankind. If I am a workingman and choose to join a Christian trade-union rather than be a communist, and if by being a member I want to show that the best thing for man is resignation, that the kingdom of man is not of this world, I am not only involving my own case — I want to be resigned for everyone. As a result, my action has involved all humanity. To take a more individual matter, if I want to marry, to have children; even if this marriage depends solely on my circumstances or passion or wish, I am involving all humanity in monogamy and not merely myself. Therefore, I am responsible for myself and for everyone else. I am creating a certain image of man of my own choosing. In choosing myself, I choose man.

This helps us understand what the actual content is of such rather grandiloquent words as anguish, forlornness, despair. As you will see, it's all quite simple.

First, what is meant by anguish? The existentialists say at once that man is anguish. What that means is this: the man who involves himself and who realizes that he is not only the person he chooses to be, but also a lawmaker who is, at the same time, choosing all mankind as well as himself, can not help escape the feeling of his total and deep responsibility. Of course, there are many people who are not anxious; but we claim that they are hiding their anxiety, that they are fleeing from it. Certainly, many people believe that when they do something, they themselves are the only ones involved, and when someone says to them, "What if everyone acted that way?" they shrug their shoulders and answer, "Everyone doesn't act that way." But really, one should always ask himself, "What would happen if everybody looked at things that way?" There is no escaping this disturbing thought except by a kind of double-dealing. A man who lies and makes excuses for himself by saying "not everybody does that," is someone with an uneasy conscience, because the act of lying implies that a universal value is conferred upon the lie.

Anguish is evident even when it conceals itself. This is the anguish that Kierkegaard called the anguish of Abraham. You know the story: an angel has ordered Abraham to sacrifice his son; if it really were an angel who has come and said, "You are Abraham, you shall sacrifice your son," everything would be all right. But everyone might first wonder, "Is it really an angel, and am I really Abraham? What proof do I have?"

There was a madwoman who had hallucinations; someone used to speak to her on the telephone and give her orders. Her doctor asked her, "Who is it who talks to you?" She answered, "He says it's God." What proof did she really have that it was God? If an angel comes to me, what proof is there that it's an angel? And if I hear voices, what proof is there that they come from heaven and not from hell, or from the subconscious, or a pathological condition? What proves that they are addressed to me? What proof is there that I have been appointed to impose my choice and my conception of man on humanity? I'll never find any proof or sign to convince me of that. If a voice addresses me, it is always for me to decide that this is the angel's voice; if I consider that such an act is a good one, it is I who will choose to say that it is good rather than bad.

Now, I'm not being singled out as an Abraham, and yet at every moment I'm obliged to perform exemplary acts. For every man, everything happens as if all mankind had its eyes fixed on him and were guiding itself by what he does. And every man ought to say to himself, "Am I really the kind of man who has the right to act in such a way that humanity might guide itself by my actions?" And if he does not say that to himself, he is masking his anguish.

There is no question here of the kind of anguish which would lead to quietism, to inaction. It is a matter of a simple sort of anguish that anybody who has had responsibilities is familiar with. For example, when a military officer takes the responsibility for an attack and sends a certain number of men to death, he chooses to do so, and in the main he alone makes the choice. Doubtless, orders come from above, but they are too broad; he interprets them, and on this interpretation depend the lives of ten or fourteen or twenty men. In making a decision he can not help having a certain anguish. All leaders know this anguish. That doesn't keep them from acting; on the contrary, it is the very condition of their action. For it implies that they envisage a number of possibilities, and when they choose one, they realize that it has value only because it is chosen. We shall see that this kind of anguish, which is the kind that existentialism describes, is explained, in addition, by a direct responsibility to the other men whom it involves. It is not a curtain separating us from action, but is part of action itself.

When we speak of forlornness, a term Heidegger was fond of, we mean only that God does not exist and that we have to face all the consequences of this. The existentialist is strongly opposed to a certain kind of secular ethics which would like to abolish God with the least possible expense. About 1880, some French teachers tried to set up a secular ethics which went something like this: God is a useless and costly hypothesis; we are discarding it; but, meanwhile, in order for there to be an ethics, a society, a civilization, it is essential that certain values be taken seriously and that they be considered as having an *a priori* existence. It must be obligatory, *a priori,* to be honest, not to lie, not to beat your wife, to have children, etc., etc. So we're going to try a little device which will make it possible to show that values exist all the same, inscribed in a heaven of ideas, though otherwise God does not exist. In other words — and this, I believe, is the tendency of everything called reformism in France — nothing will be changed if God does not exist. We shall find ourselves with the same norms of honesty, progress, and humanism, and we shall have made of God an outdated hypothesis which will peacefully die off by itself.

The existentialist, on the contrary, thinks it very distressing that God does not exist, because all possibility of finding values in a heaven of ideas disappears along with Him; there can no longer be an *a priori* Good, since there is no infinite and perfect consciousness to think it. Nowhere is it written that the Good exists, that we must be honest, that we must not lie; because the fact is we are on a plane where there are only men. Dostoevsky said, "If God didn't exist, everything would be possible." That is the very starting point of existentialism. Indeed, everything is permissible if God does not exist, and as a result man is forlorn, because neither within him nor without does he find anything to cling to. He can't start making excuses for himself.

If existence really does precede essence, there is no explaining things away by reference to a fixed and given human nature. In other words, there is no determinism, man is free, man is freedom. On the other hand, if God does not exist, we find no values or commands to turn to which legitimize our conduct. So, in the bright realm of values, we have no excuses behind us, nor justification before us. We are alone, with no excuses.

That is the idea I shall try to convey when I say that man is condemned to be free. Condemned, because he did not create himself, yet, in other respects is free; because, once thrown into the world, he is responsible for everything he does. The existentialist does not believe in the power of passion. He will never agree that a sweeping passion is a ravaging torrent which fatally leads a man to certain acts and is therefore an excuse. He thinks that man is responsible for his passion.

The existentialist does not think that man is going to help himself by finding in the world some omen by which to orient himself. Because he thinks that man will interpret the omen to suit himself. Therefore, he thinks that man, with no support and no aid, is condemned every moment to invent man. Ponge, in a very fine article, has said, "Man is the future of man." That's exactly it. But if it is taken to mean that this future is recorded in heaven, that God sees it, then it is false, because it would really no longer be a future. If it is taken to mean that, whatever a man may be, there is a future to be forged, a virgin future before him, then this remark is sound. But then we are forlorn.

To give you an example which will enable you to understand forlornness better, I shall cite the case of one of my students who came to see me under the following circumstances: his father was on bad terms with his mother, and, moreover, was inclined to be a collaborationist; his older brother had been killed in the German offensive of 1940, and the young man, with somewhat immature but generous feelings, wanted to avenge him. His mother lived alone with him, very much upset by the half-treason of her husband and the death of her older son; the boy was her only consolation.

The boy was faced with the choice of leaving for England and joining the Free French Forces—that is, leaving his mother behind—or remaining with his mother and helping her to carry on. He was fully aware that the woman lived only for him and that his going-off—and perhaps his death—would plunge her into despair. He was also aware that every act that he did for his mother's sake was a sure thing, in the sense that it was helping her to carry on, whereas every effort he made toward going off and fighting was an uncertain move which might run aground and prove completely useless; for example, on his way to England he might, while passing through Spain, be detained indefinitely in a Spanish camp; he might reach England or Algiers and be stuck in an office at a desk job. As a result, he was faced with two very different kinds of action: one, concrete, immediate, but concerning only one individual; the other concerned an incomparably vaster group, a national collectivity, but for that very reason was dubious, and might be interrupted en route. And, at the same time, he was wavering between two kinds of ethics. On the one hand, an ethics of sympathy, of personal devotion; on the other, a broader ethics, but one whose efficacy was more dubious. He had to choose between the two.

Who could help him choose? Christian doctrine? No. Christian doctrine says, "Be charitable, love your neighbor, take the more rugged path, etc., etc." But which is the more rugged path? Whom should he love as a brother? The fighting man or his mother? Which does the greater good, the vague act of fighting in a group, or the concrete one of helping a particular human being to go on living? Who can decide *a priori*? Nobody. No book of ethics can tell him. The Kantian ethics says, "Never treat any person as a means, but as an end." Very well, if I stay with my mother, I'll treat her as an end and not as a means; but by virtue of this very fact, I'm running the risk of treating the people around me who are fighting, as means; and, conversely, if I go to join those who are fighting, I'll be treating them as an end, and, by doing that, I run the risk of treating my mother as a means.

If values are vague, and if they are always too broad for the concrete and specific case that we are considering, the only thing left for us is to trust our instincts. That's what this young man tried to do; and when I saw him, he said, "In the end, feeling is what counts. I ought to choose whichever pushes me in one direction. If I feel that I love my mother enough to sacrifice everything else for her—my desire for vengeance, for action, for adventure—then I'll stay with her. If, on the contrary, I feel that my love for my mother isn't enough, I'll leave."

But how is the value of a feeling determined? What gives his feeling for his mother value? Precisely the fact that he remained with her. I may say that I like so-and-so well enough to sacrifice a certain amount of money for him, but I may say so only if I've done it. I may say "I love my mother well enough to remain with her" if I have remained with her. The only way to determine the value of this affection is, precisely, to perform an act which confirms and defines it. But, since I require this affection to justify my act, I find myself caught in a vicious circle.

On the other hand, Gide has well said that a mock feeling and a true feeling are almost indistinguishable; to decide that I love my mother and will remain with her, or to remain with her by putting on an act, amount somewhat to the same thing. In other words, the feeling is formed by the acts one performs; so, I can not refer to it in order to act upon it. Which means that I can neither seek within myself the true condition which will impel me to act, nor apply to a system of ethics for concepts which will permit me to act. You will say, "At least, he did go to a teacher for advice." But if you seek advice from a priest, for example, you have chosen this priest; you already knew, more or less, just about what advice he was going to give you. In other words, choosing your adviser is involving yourself. The proof of this is that if you are a Christian, you will say, "Consult a priest." But some priests are collaborating, some are just marking time, some are resisting. Which to choose? If the young man chooses a priest who is resisting or collaborating, he has already decided on the kind of advice he's going to get. Therefore, in coming to see me he knew the answer I was going to give him, and I had only one answer to give: "You're free, choose, that is, invent." No general ethics can show you what is to be done; there are no omens in the world. The Catholics will reply, "But there are." Granted—but, in any case, I myself choose the meaning they have.

When I was a prisoner, I knew a rather remarkable young man who was a Jesuit. He had entered the Jesuit order in the following way: he had had a number of very bad breaks; in childhood, his father died, leaving him in poverty, and he was a scholarship student at a religious institution where he was constantly made to feel that he was being kept out of charity; then, he failed to get any of the honors and distinctions that children like; later on, at about eighteen, he bungled a love affair; finally at twenty-two, he failed in military training, a childish enough matter, but it was the last straw.

This young fellow might well have felt that he had botched everything. It was a sign of something, but of what? He might have taken refuge in bitterness or despair. But he very wisely looked upon all this as a sign that he was not made for secular triumphs, and that only the triumphs of religion, holiness, and faith were open to him. He saw the hand of God in all this, and so he entered the order. Who can help seeing that he alone decided what the sign meant?

Some other interpretation might have been drawn from this series of setbacks; for example, that he might have done better to turn carpenter or revolutionist. Therefore, he is fully responsible for the interpretation. Forlornness implies that we ourselves choose our being. Forlornness and anguish go together.

As for despair, the term has a very simple meaning. It means that we shall confine ourselves to reckoning only with what depends upon our will, or on the ensemble of probabilities which make our action possible. When we want something, we always have to reckon with probabilities. I may be counting on the arrival of a friend. The friend is coming by rail or street-car; this supposes that the train will arrive on schedule, or that the street-car will not jump the track. I am left in the realm of possibility; but possibilities are to be reckoned with only to the point where my action comports with the ensemble on these possibilities, and no further. The moment the possibilities I am considering are not rigorously involved by my action, I ought to disengage myself from them, because no God, no scheme, can adapt the world and its possibilities to my will. When Descartes said, "Conquer yourself rather than the world," he meant essentially the same thing. . . .

Actually, things will be as man will have decided they are to be. Does that mean that I should abandon myself to quietism? No. First, I should involve myself; then, act on the old saw, "Nothing ventured, nothing gained." Nor does it mean that I shouldn't belong to a party, but rather that I shall have no illusions and shall do what I can. For example, suppose I ask myself, "Will socialization, as such, ever come about?" I know nothing about it. All I know is that I'm going to do everything in my power to bring it about. Beyond that, I can't count on anything. Quietism is the attitude of people who say, "Let others do what I can't do." The doctrine I am presenting is the very opposite of quietism, since it declares, "There is no reality except in action." Moreover, it goes further, since it adds, "Man is nothing else than his plan; he exists only to the extent that he fulfills himself; he is therefore nothing else than the ensemble of his acts, nothing else than his life."

According to this, we can understand why our doctrine horrifies certain people. Because often the only way they can bear their wretchedness is to think, "Circumstances have been against me. What I've been and done doesn't show my true worth. To be sure, I've had no great love, no great friendship, but that's because I haven't met a man or woman who was worthy. The books I've written haven't been very good because I haven't had the proper leisure. I haven't had children to devote myself to because I didn't find a man with whom I could have spent my life. So there remains within me, unused and quite viable, a host of propensities, inclinations, possibilities, that one wouldn't guess from the mere series of things I've done."

Now, for the existentialist there is really no love other than one which manifests itself in a person's being in love. There is no genius other than one which is expressed in works of art; the genius of Proust is the sum of Proust's works; the genius of Racine is his series of tragedies. Outside of that, there is nothing. Why say that Racine could have written another tragedy, when he didn't write it? A man is involved in life, leaves his impress on it, and outside of that there is nothing. To be sure, this may seem a harsh thought to someone whose life hasn't been a success. But, on the other hand, it prompts people to understand that reality alone is what counts, that dreams, expectations, and hopes warrant no more than to define a man as a disappointed dream, as miscarried hopes, as vain expectations. In other words, to define him negatively and not positively. However, when we say, "You are nothing else than your life," that does not imply that the artist will be judged solely on the basis of his works of art; a thousand other things will contribute toward summing him up. What we mean is that a man is nothing else than a series of undertakings, that he is the sum, the organization, the ensemble of the relationships which make up these undertakings.

Defence of Utilitarianism
·JOHN STUART MILL·

This selection is divided into two main sections. In the first, from his book Utilitarianism, *Mill (1806–1873) explains some of the basic principles of his theory. He states and defends the Greatest Happiness Principle, and explains why he thinks that higher pleasures are better on utilitarian grounds than lower ones. In the second section, from* On Liberty, *Mill tries to show why extensive personal liberties are protected by the utilitarian philosophy.*

A. From Utilitarianism
Chapter I General Remarks

There are few circumstances among those which make up the present condition of human knowledge, more unlike what might have been expected, or more significant of the backward state in which speculation on the most important subjects still lingers, than the little progress which has been made in the decision of the controversy respecting the criterion of right and wrong. From the dawn of philosophy, the question concerning the *summum bonum*, or, what is the same thing, concerning the foundation of morality, has been accounted the main problem in speculative thought, has occupied the most gifted intellects, and divided them into sects and schools, carrying on a vigorous warfare against one another. And after more than two thousand years the same discussions continue, philosophers are still ranged under the same contending banners, and neither thinkers nor mankind at large seem nearer to being unanimous on the subject, than when the youth Socrates listened to the old Protagoras, and asserted (if Plato's dialogue be grounded on a real conversation) the theory of utilitarianism against the popular morality of the so-called sophist.

· · · · · · · ·

On the present occasion, I shall, without further discussion of the other theories, attempt to contribute something towards the understanding and appreciation of the Utilitarian or Happiness theory, and toward such proof as it is susceptible of. It is evident that this cannot be proof in the ordinary and popular meaning of the term. Questions of ultimate ends are not amenable to direct proof. Whatever can be proved to be good, must be so by being shown to be a means to something admitted to be good without proof. The medical art is proved to be good by its conducing to health; but how is it possible to prove that health is good? The art of music is good, for the reason, among others, that it produces pleasure; but what proof is it possible to give that pleasure is good? If, then, it is asserted that there is a comprehensive formula, including all things which are in themselves good, and that whatever else is good, is not so as an end, but as a means, the formula may be accepted or rejected, but is not a subject of what is commonly understood by proof. We are not, however, to infer that its acceptance or rejection must depend on blind impulse, or arbitrary choice. There is a larger meaning of the word proof, in which this question is as amenable to it as any other of the disputed questions of philosophy. The subject is within the cognisance of the rational faculty; and neither does that faculty deal with it solely in the way of intuition. Considerations may be presented capable of determining the intellect either to give or withhold its assent to the doctrine; and this is equivalent to proof.

We shall examine presently of what nature are these considerations; in what manner they apply to the case, and what rational grounds, therefore, can be given for accepting or rejecting the utilitarian formula. But it is a preliminary condition of rational acceptance or rejection, that the formula should be correctly understood. I believe that the very imperfect notion ordinarily formed of its meaning, is the chief obstacle which impedes its reception; and that could it be cleared, even from only the grosser misconceptions, the question would be greatly simplified, and a large proportion of its difficulties removed. Before, therefore, I attempt to enter into the philosophical grounds which can be given for assenting to the utilitarian standard, I shall offer some illustrations of the doctrine itself; with the view of showing more clearly what it is, distinguishing it from what it is not, and disposing of such of the practical objections to it as either originate in, or are closely connected with, mistaken interpretations of its meaning. Having thus prepared the ground, I shall afterwards endeavor to throw such light as I can upon the question, considered as one of philosophical theory.

Chapter II What Utilitarianism Is

. . . The creed which accepts as the foundation of morals, Utility, or the Greatest Happiness Principle, holds that actions are right in proportion as they tend to promote happiness, wrong as they tend to produce the reverse of happiness. By happiness is intended pleasure, and the absence of pain; by unhappiness, pain, and the privation of pleasure. To give a clear view of the moral standard set up by the theory, much more requires to be said; in particular, what things it includes in the ideas of pain and pleasure; and to what extent this is left an open question. But these supplementary explanations do not affect the theory of life on which this theory of morality is grounded—namely, that pleasure, and freedom from pain, are the only things desirable as ends; and that all desirable things (which are as numerous in the utilitarian as in any other scheme) are desirable either for the pleasure inherent in themselves, or as means to the promotion of pleasure and the prevention of pain.

Now, such a theory of life excites in many minds, and among them in some of the most estimable in feeling and purpose, inveterate dislike. To suppose that life has (as they express it) no higher end than pleasure—no better and nobler object of desire and pursuit—they designate as utterly mean and grovelling; as a doctrine worthy only of swine, to whom the followers of Epicurus were, at a very early period, contemptuously likened; and modern holders of the doctrine are occasionally made the subject of equally polite comparisons by its German, French, and English assailants.

When thus attacked, the Epicureans have always answered, that it is not they, but their accusers, who represent human nature in a degrading light; since the accusation supposes human beings to be capable of no pleasures except those of which swine are capable. If this supposition were true, the charge could not be gainsaid, but would then be no longer an imputation; for if the sources of pleasure were precisely the same to human beings and to swine, the rule of life which is good enough for the one would be good enough for the other. The comparison of the Epicurean life to that of beasts is felt as degrading, precisely because a beast's pleasures do not satisfy a human being's conceptions of happiness. Human beings have faculties more elevated than the animal appetites, and when once made conscious of them, do not regard anything as happiness which does not include their gratification. I do not, indeed, consider the Epicureans to have been by any means faultless in drawing out their scheme of consequences from the utilitarian principle. To do this in any sufficient manner, many Stoic, as well as Christian elements require to be included. But there is no known Epicurean theory of life which does not assign to the pleasures of the intellect, of the feelings and imagination, and of the moral sentiments, a much higher value as pleasures than to those of mere sensation. It must be admitted, however, that utilitarian writers in general have placed the superiority of mental over bodily pleasures chiefly in the greater permanency, safety, uncostliness, etc., of the former—that is, in their circumstantial advantages rather than in their intrinsic nature. And on all these points utilitarians have fully proved their case; but they might have taken the other, and, as it may be called, higher ground, with entire consistency. It is quite compatible with the principle of utility to recognise the fact, that some *kinds* of pleasure are more desirable and more valuable than others. It would be absurd that while, in estimating all other things, quality is considered as well as quantity, the estimation of pleasures should be supposed to depend on quantity alone.

If I am asked, what I mean by difference of quality in pleasures, or what makes one pleasure more valuable than another, merely as a pleasure, except its being greater in amount, there is but one possible answer. Of two pleasures, if there be one to which all or almost all who have experience of both give a decided preference, irrespective of any feeling of moral obligation to prefer it, that is the more desirable pleasure. If one of the two is, by those who are competently acquainted with both, placed so far above the other that they prefer it, even though knowing it to be attended with a greater amount of discontent, and would not resign it for any quantity of the other pleasure which their nature is capable of, we are justified in ascribing to the preferred enjoyment a superiority in quality, so far outweighing quantity as to render it, in comparison, of small account.

Now it is an unquestionable fact that those who are equally acquainted with, and equally capable of appreciating and enjoying, both, do give a most marked preference to the manner of existence which employs their higher faculties. Few human creatures would consent to be changed into any of the lower animals, for a promise of the fullest allowance of a beast's pleasures; no intelligent human being would consent to be a fool, no instructed person would be an ignoramus, no person of feeling and conscience would be selfish and base, even though they should be persuaded that the fool, the dunce, or the rascal is better satisfied with his lot than they are with theirs. They would not resign what they possess more than he for the most complete satisfaction of all the desires which they have in common with him. If they ever fancy they would, it is only in cases of unhappiness so extreme, that to escape from it they would exchange their lot for almost any other, however undesirable in their own eyes. A being of higher faculties requires more to make him happy, is capable of more acute suffering, and certainly accessible to it at more points, than one of an inferior type; but in spite of these liabilities, he can never really wish to sink into what he feels to be a lower grade of existence. We may give what explanation we please of this unwillingness; we may attribute it to pride, a name which is given indiscriminately to some of the most and to some of the least estimable feelings of which mankind are capable: we may refer it to the love of liberty and personal independence, an appeal to which was with the Stoics one of the most effective means for the inculcation of it; to the love of power, or to the love of excitement, both of which do really enter into and contribute to it: but its most appropriate appellation is a sense of dignity, which all human beings possess in one form or other, and in some, though by no means in exact, proportion to their higher faculties, and which is so essential a part of the happiness of those in whom it is strong, that nothing which conflicts with it could be, otherwise than momentarily, an object of desire to them. Whoever supposes that this preference takes place at a sacrifice of happiness—that the superior being, in anything like equal circumstances, is not happier than the inferior—confounds the two very different ideas, of happiness, and content. It is indisputable that the being whose capacities of enjoyment are low, has the greatest chance of having them fully satisfied; and a highly endowed being will always feel that any happiness which he can look for, as the world is constituted, is imperfect. But he can learn to bear its imperfections, if they are at all bearable; and they will not make him envy the being who is indeed unconscious of the imperfections, but only because he feels not at all the good which those imperfections qualify. It is better to be a human being dissatisfied than a pig satisfied; better to be Socrates dissatisfied than a fool satisfied. And if the fool, or the pig, are of a different opinion, it is because they only know their own side of the question. The other party to the comparison knows both sides.

It may be objected, that many who are capable of the higher pleasures, occasionally, under the influence of temptation, postpone them to the lower. But this is quite compatible with a full appreciation of the intrinsic superiority of the higher. Men often, from infirmity of character, make their election for the nearer good, though they know it to be the less valuable; and this no less when the choice is between two bodily pleasures, than when it is between bodily and mental. They pursue sensual indulgences to the injury of health, though perfectly aware that health is the greater good. It may be further objected, that many who begin with youthful enthusiasm for everything noble, as they advance in years sink into indolence and selfishness. But I do not believe that those who undergo this very common change, voluntarily choose the lower description of pleasures in preference to the higher. I believe that before they devote themselves exclusively to the one, they have already become incapable of the other. Capacity for the nobler feelings is in most natures a very tender plant, easily killed, not only by hostile influences, but by mere want of sustenance; and in the majority of young persons it speedily dies away if the occupations to which their position in life has devoted them, and the society into which it has thrown them, are not favourable to keeping that higher capacity in exercise. Men lose their higher aspirations as they lose their intellectual tastes, because they have not time or opportunity for indulging them; and they addict themselves to inferior pleasures, not because they deliberately prefer them, but because they are either the only ones to which they have access, or the only ones which they are any longer capable of enjoying. It may be questioned whether any one who has remained equally susceptible to both classes of pleasures, ever knowingly and calmly preferred the lower; though many, in all ages, have broken down in an ineffectual attempt to combine both.

From this verdict of the only competent judges, I apprehend there can be no appeal. On a question which is the best worth having of two pleasures, or which of two modes of existence is the most grateful to the feelings, apart from its moral attributes and from its consequences, the judgment of those who are qualified by knowledge of both, or, if they differ, that of the majority among them, must be admitted as final. And there needs be the less hesitation to accept this judgment respecting the quality of pleasures, since there is no other tribunal to be referred to even on the question of quantity. What means are there of determining which is the acutest of two pains, or the intensest of two pleasurable sensations, except the general suffrage of those who are familiar with both? Neither pains nor pleasures are homogeneous, and pain is always heterogeneous with pleasure. What is there to decide whether a particular pleasure is worth purchasing at the cost of a particular pain, except the feelings and judgment of the experienced? When, therefore, those feelings and judgment declare the pleasures derived from the higher faculties to be preferable *in kind*, apart from the question of intensity, to those of which the animal nature, disjoined from the higher faculties, is susceptible, they are entitled on this subject to the same regard.

I have dwelt on this point, as being a necessary part of a perfectly just conception of Utility or Happiness, considered as the directive rule of human conduct. But it is by no means an indispensable condition to the acceptance of the utilitarian standard; for that standard is not the agent's own greatest happiness, but the greatest amount of happiness altogether; and if it may possibly be doubted whether a noble character is always the happier for its nobleness, there can be no doubt that it makes other people happier, and that the world in general is immensely a gainer by it. Utilitarianism, therefore, could only attain its end by the general cultivation of nobleness of character, even if each individual were only benefited by the nobleness of others, and his own, so far as happiness is concerned, were a sheer deduction from the benefit. But the bare enunciation of such an absurdity as this last, renders refutation superfluous.

According to the Greatest Happiness Principle, as above explained, the ultimate end, with reference to and for the sake of which all other things are desirable (whether we are considering our own good or that of other people), is an existence exempt as far as possible from pain, and as rich as possible in enjoyments, both in point of quantity and quality; the test of quality, and the rule for measuring it against quantity, being the preference felt by those who in their opportunities of experience, to which must be added their habits of self-consciousness and self-observation, are best furnished with the means of comparison. This, being, according to the utilitarian opinion, the end of human action, is necessarily also the standard of morality; which may accordingly be defined, the rules and precepts for human conduct, by the observance of which an existence such as has been described might be, to the greatest extent possible, secured to all mankind; and not to them only, but, so far as the nature of things admits, to the whole sentient creation.

. . . .

I must again repeat, what the assailants of utilitarianism seldom have the justice to acknowledge, that the happiness which forms the utilitarian standard of what is right in conduct, is not the agent's own happiness, but that of all concerned. As between his own happiness and that of others, utilitarianism requires him to be as strictly impartial as a disinterested and benevolent spectator. In the golden rule of Jesus of Nazareth, we read the complete spirit of the ethics of utility. To do as you would be done by, and to love your neighbour as yourself, constitute the ideal perfection of utilitarian morality. As the means of making the nearest approach to this ideal, utility would enjoin, first, that laws and social arrangements should place the happiness, or (as speaking practically it may be called) the interest, of every individual, as nearly as possible in harmony with the interest of the whole; and secondly, that education and opinion, which have so vast a power over human character, should so use that power as to establish in the mind of every individual an indissoluble association between his own happiness and the good of the whole; especially between his own happiness and the practice of such modes of conduct, negative and positive, as regard for the universal happiness prescribes; so that not only he may be unable to conceive the possibility of happiness to himself, consistently with conduct opposed to the general good, but also that a direct impulse to promote the general good may be in every individual one of the habitual motives of action, and the sentiments connected therewith may fill a large and prominent place in every human being's sentient existence. If the impugners of the utilitarian morality represented it to their own minds in this its true character, I know not what recommendation possessed by any other morality they could possibly affirm to be wanting to it; what more beautiful or more exalted developments of human nature any other ethical system can be supposed to foster, or what springs of action, not accessible to the utilitarian, such systems rely on for giving effect to their mandates.

The objectors to utilitarianism cannot always be charged with representing it in a discreditable light. On the contrary, those among them who entertain anything like a just idea of its disinterested character, sometimes find fault with its standard as being too high for humanity. They say it is exacting too much to require that people shall always act from the inducement of promoting the general interests of society. But this is to mistake the very meaning of a standard of morals, and confound the rule of action with the motive of it. It is the business of ethics to tell us what are our duties, or by what test we may know them; but no system of ethics requires that the sole motive of all we do shall be a feeling of duty; on the contrary, ninety-nine hundredths of all our actions are done from other motives, and rightly so done, if the rule of duty does not condemn them. It is the most unjust to utilitarianism that this particular misapprehension should be made a ground of objection to it, inasmuch as utilitarian moralists have gone beyond almost all others in affirming that the motive has nothing to do with the morality of the action, though much with the worth of the agent. He who saves a fellow creature from drowning does what is morally right, whether his motive be duty, or the hope of being paid for his trouble; he who betrays the friend that trusts him, is guilty of a crime, even if his object be to serve another friend to whom he is under greater obligations. But to speak only of actions done from the motive of duty, and in direct obedience to principle: it is a misapprehension of the utilitarian mode of thought, to conceive it as implying that people should fix their minds upon so wide a generality as the world, or society at large. The great majority of good actions are intended not for the benefit of the world, but for that of individuals, of which the good of the world is made up; and the thoughts of the most virtuous man need not on these occasions travel beyond the particular persons concerned, except so far as is necessary to assure himself that in benefiting them he is not violating the rights, that is, the legitimate and authorized expectations, of any one else. The multiplication of happiness is, according to the utilitarian ethics, the object of virtue: the occasions on which any person (except one in a thousand) has it in his power to do this on an extended scale, in other words to be a public benefactor, are but exceptional; and on these occasions alone is he called on to consider public utility; in every other case, private utility, the interest or happiness of some few persons, is all he has to attend to. Those alone the influence of whose actions extends to society in general, need concern themselves habitually about so large an object. In the case of abstinences indeed — of things which people forbear to do from moral considerations, though the consequences in the particular case might be beneficial — it would be unworthy of an intelligent agent not to be consciously aware that the action is of a class which, if practised generally, would be generally injurious, and that this is the ground of the obligation to abstain from it. The amount of regard for the public interest implied in this recognition, is no greater than is demanded by every system of morals, for they all enjoin to abstain from whatever is manifestly pernicious to society

The same considerations dispose of another reproach against the doctrine of utility, founded on a still grosser misconception of the purpose of a standard of morality, and of the very meaning of the words right and wrong. It is often affirmed that utilitarianism renders men cold and unsympathising; that it chills their moral feelings towards individuals; that it makes them regard only the dry and hard consideration of the consequences of actions, not taking into their moral estimate the qualities from which those actions emanate. If the assertion means that they do not allow their judgment respecting the rightness or wrongness of an action to be influenced by their opinion of the qualities of the person who does it, this is a complaint not against utilitarianism, but against having any standard of morality at all; for certainly no known ethical standard decides an action to be good or bad because it is done by a good or bad man, still less because done by an amiable, a brave, or a benevolent man, or the contrary. These considerations are relevant, not to the estimation of actions, but of persons; and there is nothing in the utilitarian theory inconsistent with the fact that there are other things which interest us in persons besides the rightness and wrongness of their actions. The Stoics, indeed, with the paradoxical misuse of language which was part of their system, and by which they strove to raise themselves above all concern about anything but virtue, were fond of saying, that he who has that has everything; that he, and only he, is rich, is beautiful, is a king. But no claim of this description is made for the virtuous man by the utilitarian doctrine. Utilitarians are quite aware that there are other desirable possessions and qualities besides virtue, and are perfectly willing to allow to all of them their full worth. They are also aware that a right action does not necessarily indicate a virtuous character, and that actions which are blamable, often proceed from qualities entitled to praise. When this is apparent in any particular case, it modifies their estimation, not certainly of the act, but of the agent. I grant that they are, notwithstanding, of opinion, that in the long run the best proof of a good character is good actions; and resolutely refuse to consider any mental disposition as good, of which the predominant tendency is to produce bad conduct. This makes them unpopular with many people; but it is an unpopularity which they must share with every one who regards the distinction between right and wrong in a serious light; and the reproach is not one which a conscientious utilitarian need be anxious to repel.

If no more be meant by the objection than that many utilitarians look on the morality of actions, as measured by the utilitarian standard, with too exclusive a regard, and do not lay sufficient stress upon the other beauties of character which go towards making a human being lovable or admirable, this may be admitted. Utilitarians who have cultivated their moral feelings, but not their sympathies nor their artistic perceptions, do fall into this mistake; and so do all other moralists under the same conditions. What can be said in excuse for other moralists is equally available for them, namely, that, if there is to be any error, it is better that it should be on that side. As a matter of fact, we may affirm that among utilitarians as among adherents of other systems, there is every imaginable degree of rigidity and of laxity in the application of their standard: some are even puritanically rigorous, while others are as indulgent as can possibly be desired by sinner or by sentimentalist. But on the whole, a doctrine which brings prominently foward the interest that mankind have in the repression and prevention of conduct which violates the moral law, is likely to be inferior to no other in turning the sanctions of opinion against such violations. It is true, the question,

What does violate the moral law? is one on which those who recognize different standards of morality are likely now and then to differ. But difference of opinion on moral questions was not first introduced into the world by utilitarianism, while that doctrine does supply, if not always an easy, at all events a tangible and intelligible mode of deciding such differences.

It may not be superfluous to notice a few more of the common misapprehensions of utilitarian ethics, even those which are so obvious and gross that it might appear impossible for any person of candour and intelligence to fall into them; since persons, even of considerable mental endowments, often give themselves so little trouble to understand the bearings of any opinion against which they entertain a prejudice, and men are in general so little conscious of this voluntary ignorance as a defect, that the vulgarest misunderstandings of ethical doctrines are continually met with in the deliberate writings of persons of the greatest pretensions both to high principle and to philosophy. We not uncommonly hear the doctrine of utility inveighed against as a *godless* doctrine. If it be necessary to say anything at all against so mere an assumption, we may say that the question depends upon what idea we have formed of the moral character of the Deity. If it be a true belief that God desires, above all things, the happiness of his creatures, and that this was his purpose in their creation, utility is not only not a godless doctrine, but more profoundly religious than any other. If it be meant that utilitarianism does not recognise the revealed will of God as the supreme law of morals, I answer, that a utilitarian who believes in the perfect goodness and wisdom of God, necessarily believes that whatever God has thought fit to reveal on the subject of morals, must fulfil the requirements of utility in a supreme degree. But others besides utilitarians have been of opinion that the Christian revelation was intended, and is fitted, to inform the hearts and minds of mankind with a spirit which should enable them to find for themselves what is right, and incline them to do it when found, rather than to tell them, except in a very general way, what it is; and that we need a doctrine of ethics, carefully followed out, to *interpret* to us the will of God. Whether this opinion is correct or not, it is superfluous here to discuss; since whatever aid religion, either natural or revealed, can afford to ethical investigation, is as open to the utilitarian moralist as to any other. He can use it as the testimony of God to the usefulness or hurtfulness of any given course of action, by as good a right as others can use it for the indication of a transcendental law, having no connexion with usefulness or with happiness.

Again, Utility is often summarily stigmatised as an immoral doctrine by giving it the name of Expediency, and taking advantage of the popular use of that term to contrast it with Principle. But the Expedient, in the sense in which it is opposed to the Right, generally means that which is expedient for the particular interest of the agent himself; as when a minister sacrifices the interests of his country to keep himself in place. When it means anything better than this, it means that which is expedient for some immediate object, some temporary purpose, but which violates a rule whose observance is expedient in a much higher degree.

The Expedient, in this sense, instead of being the same thing with the useful, is a branch of the hurtful. Thus, it would often be expedient, for the purpose of getting over some momentary embarrassment, or attaining some object immediately useful to ourselves or others, to tell a lie. But inasmuch as the cultivation in ourselves of a sensitive feeling on the subject of veracity, is one of the most useful, and the enfeeblement of that feeling one of the most hurtful, things to which our conduct can be instrumental; and inasmuch as any, even unintentional, deviation from truth, does that much towards weakening the trustworthiness of human assertion, which is not only the principal support of all present social well-being, but the insufficiency of which does more than any one thing that can be named to keep back civilisation, virtue, everything on which human happiness on the largest scale depends; we feel that the violation, for a present advantage, of a rule of such transcendent expediency, is not expedient, and that he who, for the sake of a convenience to himself or to some other individual, does what depends on him to deprive mankind of the good, and inflict upon them the evil, involved in the greater or less reliance which they can place in each other's word, acts the part of one of their worst enemies. Yet that even this rule, sacred as it is, admits of possible exceptions, is acknowledged by all moralists; the chief of which is when the withholding of some fact (as of information from a malefactor, or of bad news from a person dangerously ill) would save an individual (especially an individual other than oneself) from great and unmerited evil, and when the withholding can only be effected by denial. But in order that the exception may not extend itself beyond the need, and may have the least possible effect in weakening reliance on veracity, it ought to be recognised, and, if possible, its limits defined; and if the principle of utility is good for anything, it must be good for weighing these conflicting utilities against one another, and marking out the region within which one or the other preponderates.

Again, defenders of utility often find themselves called upon to reply to such objections as this—that there is not time, previous to action, for calculating and weighing the effects of any line of conduct on the general happiness. This is exactly as if any one were to say that it is impossible to guide our conduct by Christianity, because there is not time, on every occasion on which anything has to be done, to read through the Old and New Testaments. The answer to the objection is, that there has been ample time, namely, the whole past duration of the human species. During all that time, mankind have been learning by experience the tendencies of actions; on which experience all the prudence, as well as all the morality of life, are dependent. People talk as if the commencement of this course of experience had hitherto been put off, and as if, at the moment when some man feels tempted to meddle with the property or life of another, he had to begin considering for the first time whether murder and theft are injurious to human happiness. Even then I do not think that he would find the question very puzzling; but, at all events, the matter is now done to his hand. It is truly a whimsical supposition that, if mankind were agreed in considering utility to be the test of morality, they would remain without any agreement as to what *is* useful, and would take no measures for having their notions on the subject taught to the young, and enforced by law and opinion. There is no difficulty in proving any ethical standard whatever to work ill, if we suppose universal idiocy to be conjoined with it; but on any hypothesis short of that, mankind must by this time have acquired positive beliefs as to the effects of some actions on their happiness; and the beliefs which have thus come down are the rules of morality for the multitude, and for the philosopher until he has succeeded in finding better. That philosophers might easily do this, even now, on many subjects; that the received code of ethics is by no means of divine right; and that mankind have still much to learn as to the effects of actions on the general happiness, I admit, or rather, earnestly maintain. The corollaries from the principle of utility, like the precepts of every practical art, admit of indefinite improvement, and, in a progressive state of the human mind, their improvement is perpetually going on. But to consider the rules of morality as improvable, is one thing; to pass over the intermediate generalisations entirely, and endeavour to test each individual action directly by the first principle, is another. It is a strange notion that the acknowledgment of a first principle is inconsistent with the admission of secondary ones. To inform a traveller respecting the place of his ultimate destination, is not to forbid the use of landmarks and direction-posts on the way. The proposition that happiness is the end and aim of morality does not mean that no road ought to be laid down to that goal, or that persons going thither should not be advised to take one direction rather than another. Men really ought to leave off talking a kind of nonsense on this subject, which they would neither talk nor listen to on other matters of practical concernment. Nobody argues that the art of navigation is not founded on astronomy, because sailors cannot wait to calculate the Nautical Almanack. Being rational creatures, they go to sea with it ready calculated; and all rational creatures go out upon the sea of life with their minds made up on the common questions of right and wrong, as well as on many of the far more difficult questions of wise and foolish. And this, as long as foresight is a human quality, it is to be presumed they will continue to do. Whatever we adopt as the fundamental principle of morality, we require subordinate principles to apply it by; the impossibility of doing without them, being common to all systems, can afford no argument against any one in particular; but gravely to argue as if no such secondary principles could be had, and as if mankind had remained till now, and always must remain, without drawing any general conclusions from the experience of human life, is as high a pitch, I think, as absurdity has ever reached in philosophical controversy.

The remainder of the stock arguments against utilitarianism mostly consist in laying to its charge the common infirmities of human nature, and the general difficulties which embarrass conscientious persons in shaping their course through life. We are told that a utilitarian will be apt to make his own particular case an exception to moral rules, and, when under temptation, will see a utility in the breach of a rule, greater than he will see in its observance. But is utility the only creed which is able to furnish us with excuses for evil doing, and means of cheating our own conscience? They are afforded in abundance by all doctrines which recognise as a fact in morals the existence of conflicting considerations;

which all doctrines do, that have been believed by sane persons. It is not the fault of any creed, but of the complicated nature of human affairs, that rules of conduct cannot be so framed as to require no exceptions, and that hardly any kind of action can safely be laid down as either always obligatory or always condemnable. There is no ethical creed which does not temper the rigidity of its laws, by giving a certain latitude, under the moral responsibility of the agent, for accommodation to peculiarities of circumstances; and under every creed, at the opening thus made, self-deception and dishonest casuistry get in. There exists no moral system under which there do not arise unequivocal cases of conflicting obligations. These are the real difficulties, the knotty points both in the theory of ethics, and in the conscientious guidance of personal conduct. They are overcome practically, with greater or with less success, according to the intellect and virtue of the individual; but it can hardly be pretended that any one will be the less qualified for dealing with them, from possessing an ultimate standard to which conflicting rights and duties can be referred. If utility is the ultimate source of moral obligations, utility may be invoked to decide between them when their demands are incompatible. Though the application of the standard may be difficult, it is better than none at all; while in other systems, the moral laws all claiming independent authority, there is no common umpire entitled to interfere between them; their claims to precedence one over another rest on little better than sophistry, and unless determined, as they generally are, by the unacknowledged influence of considerations of utility, afford a free scope for the action of personal desires and partialities. We must remember that only in these cases of conflict between secondary principles is it requisite that first principles should be appealed to. There is no case of moral obligation in which some secondary principle is not involved; and if only one, there can seldom be any real doubt which one it is, in the mind of any person by whom the principle itself is recognised.

Chapter III Of the Ultimate Sanction of the Principle of Utility

The question is often asked, and properly so, in regard to any supposed moral standard — What is its sanction? what are the motives to obey it? or more specifically, what is the source of its obligation? whence does it derive its binding force? It is a necessary part of moral philosophy to provide the answer to this question; which, though frequently assuming the shape of an objection to the utilitarian morality, as if it had some special applicability to that above others, really arises in regard to all standards. It arises, in fact, whenever a person is called on to *adopt* a standard, or refer morality to any basis on which he has not been accustomed to rest it. For the customary morality, that which education and opinion have consecrated, is the only one which presents itself to the mind with the feeling of being *in itself* obligatory; and when a person is asked to believe that this morality *derives* its obligation from some general principle round which custom has not thrown the same halo, the assertion is to him a paradox; the supposed corollaries seem to have a more binding force than the original theorem;

the superstructure seems to stand better without, than with, what is represented as its foundation. He says to himself, I feel that I am bound not to rob or murder, betray or deceive; but why am I bound to promote the general happiness? If my own happiness lies in something else, why may I not give that the preference?

If the view adopted by the utilitarian philosophy of the nature of the moral sense be correct, this difficulty will always present itself, until the influences which form moral character have taken the same hold of the principle which they have taken of some of the consequences — until, by the improvement of education, the feeling of unity with our fellow-creatures shall be (what it cannot be denied that Christ intended it to be) as deeply rooted in our character, and to our own consciousness as completely a part of our nature, as the horror of crime is in an ordinarily well brought up young person. In the meantime, however, the difficulty has no peculiar application to the doctrine of utility, but is inherent in every attempt to analyse morality and reduce it to principles; which, unless the priniciple is already in men's minds invested with as much sacredness as any of its applications, always seems to divest them of a part of their sanctity.

The principle of utility either has, or there is no reason why it might not have, all the sanctions which belong to any other system or morals. Those sanctions are either external or internal. Of the external sanctions it is not necessary to speak at any length. They are, the hope of favour and the fear of displeasure, from our fellow-creatures or from the Ruler of the Universe along with whatever we may have of sympathy or affection for them, or of love and awe of Him, inclining us to do His will independently of selfish consequences. There is evidently no reason why all these motives for observance should not attach themselves to the utilitarian morality, as completely and as powerfully as to any other. Indeed, those of them which refer to our fellow-creatures are sure to do so, in proportion to the amount of general intelligence; for whether there be any other ground of moral obligation than the general happiness or not, men do desire happiness; and however imperfect may be their own practice, they desire and commend all conduct in others towards themselves, by which they think their happiness is promoted. With regard to the religious motive, if men believe, as most profess to do, in the goodness of God, those who think that conduciveness to the general happiness is the essence, or even only the criterion of good, must necessarily believe that it is also that which God approves. The whole force therefore of external reward and punishment, whether physical or moral, and whether proceeding from God or from our fellow men, together with all that the capacities of human nature admit of disinterested devotion to either, become available to enforce the utilitarian morality, in proportion as that morality is recognised; and the more powerfully, the more the appliances of education and general cultivation are bent to the purpose.

So far as to external sanctions. The internal sanction of duty, whatever our standard of duty may be, is one and the same — a feeling in our own mind; a pain, more or less intense, attendant on violation of duty, which in properly cultivated moral natures rises, in the more serious cases, into shrinking from it as an impossibility. This feeling, when disinterested, and connecting itself with the pure idea of duty, and not with some particular form of it, or with any of the merely accessory circumstances, is the essence of Conscience; though in that complex phenomenon as it actually exists, the simple fact is in general all encrusted over with collateral associations, derived from sympathy, from love, and still more from fear; from all the forms of religious feeling; from the recollections of childhood and of all our past life; from self-esteem, desire of the esteem of others, and occasionally even self-abasement. This extreme complication is, I apprehend, the origin of the sort of mystical character which, by a tendency of the human mind of which there are many other examples, is apt to be attributed to the idea of moral obligation, and which leads people to believe that the idea cannot possibly attach itself to any other objects than those which, by a supposed mysterious law, are found in our present experience to excite it. Its binding force, however, consists in the existence of a mass of feeling which must be broken through in order to do what violates our standard of right, and which, if we do nevertheless violate that standard, will probably have to be encountered afterwards in the form of remorse. Whatever theory we have of the nature or origin of conscience, this is what essentially constitutes it.

The ultimate sanction, therefore, of all morality (external motives apart) being a subjective feeling in our own minds, I see nothing embarrassing to those whose standard is utility, in the question, what is the sanction of that particular standard? We may answer, the same as of all other moral standards—the conscientious feelings of mankind. Undoubtedly this sanction has no binding efficacy on those who do not possess the feelings it appeals to; but neither will these persons be more obedient to any other moral principle than to the utilitarian one. On them morality of any kind has no hold but through the external sanctions. Meanwhile the feelings exist, a fact in human nature, the reality of which, and the great power with which they are capable of acting on those in whom they have been duly cultivated, are proved by experience. No reason has ever been shown why they may not be cultivated to as great intensity in connexion with the utilitarian, as with any other rule of morals.

There is, I am aware, a disposition to believe that a person who sees in moral obligation a transcendental fact, an objective reality belonging to the province of "Things in themselves," is likely to be more obedient to it than one who believes it to be entirely subjective, having its seat in human consciousness only. But whatever a person's opinion may be on this point of Ontology, the force he is really urged by is his own subjective feeling, and is exactly measured by its strength. No one's belief that duty is an objective reality is stronger than the belief that God is so; yet the belief in God, apart from the expectation of actual reward and punishment, only operates on conduct through, and in proportion to, the subjective religious feeling. The sanction, so far as it is disinterested, is always in the mind itself; and the notion therefore of the transcendental moralists must be, that this sanction will not exist *in* the mind unless it is believed to have its root out of the mind; and that if a person is able to say to himself, This which is restraining me, and which is called my conscience, is only a feeling in my own mind, he may possibly draw the conclusion that when the feeling ceases the obligation ceases, and that if he find the feeling inconvenient, he may disregard it, and endeavour to get rid of it. But is this danger confined to the utilitarian morality? Does the belief that moral obligation has its seat outside the mind make the feeling of it too strong to be got rid of? The fact is so far otherwise, that all moralists admit and lament the ease with which, in the generality of minds, conscience can be silenced or stifled. The question, Need I obey my conscience? is quite as often put to themselves by persons who never heard of the principle of utility, as by its adherents. Those whose conscientious feelings are so weak as to allow of their asking this question, if they answer it affirmatively, will not do so because they believe in the transcendental theory, but because of the external sanctions.

It is not necessary, for the present purpose, to decide whether the feeling of duty is innate or implanted. Assuming it to be innate, it is an open question to what objects it naturally attaches itself; for the philosophic supporters of that theory are now agreed that the intuitive perception is of principles of morality and not of the details. If there be anything innate in the matter, I see no reason why the feeling which is innate should not be that of regard to the pleasures and pains of others. If there is any principle of morals which is intuitively obligatory, I should say it must be that. If so, the intuitive ethics would coincide with the utilitarian, and there would be no further quarrel between them. Even as it is, the intuitive moralists, though they believe that there are other intuitive moral obligations, do already believe this to be one; for they unanimously hold that a large *portion* of morality turns upon the consideration due to the interests of our fellow-creatures. Therefore, if the belief in the transcendental origin of moral obligation gives any additional efficacy to the internal sanction, it appears to me that the utilitarian principle has already the benefit of it.

On the other hand, if, as is my own belief, the moral feelings are not innate, but acquired, they are not for that reason the less natural. It is natural to man to speak, to reason, to build cities, to cultivate the ground, though these are acquired faculties. The moral feelings are not indeed a part of our nature, in the sense of being in any perceptible degree present in all of us; but this, unhappily, is a fact admitted by those who believe the most strenuously in their transcendental origin. Like the other acquired capacities above referred to, the moral faculty, if not a part of our nature, is a natural outgrowth from it; capable, like them, in a certain small degree, of springing up spontaneously; and susceptible of being brought by cultivation to a high degree of development. Unhappily it is also susceptible, by a sufficient use of the external sanctions and of the force of early impressions, of being cultivated in almost any direction: so that there is hardly anything so absurd or so mischievous that it may not, by means of these influences, be made to act on the human mind with all the authority of conscience. To doubt that the same potency might be given by the same means to the principle of utility, even if it had no foundation in human nature, would be flying in the face of all experience.

But moral associations which are wholly of artificial creation, when intellectual culture goes on, yield by degrees to the dissolving force of analysis: and if the feeling of duty, when associated with utility, would appear equally arbitrary; if there were no leading department of our nature, no powerful class of sentiments, with which that association would harmonise, which would make us feel it congenial, and incline us not only to foster it in others (for which we have abundant interested motives), but also to cherish it in ourselves; if there were not, in short, a natural basis of sentiment for utilitarian morality, it might well happen that this association also, even after it had been implanted by education, might be analysed away.

But there *is* this basis of powerful natural sentiment; and this it is which, when once the general happiness is recognised as the ethical standard, will constitute the strength of the utilitarian morality. This firm foundation is that of the social feelings of mankind; the desire to be in unity with our fellow creatures, which is already a powerful principle in human nature, and happily one of those which tend to become stronger, even without express inculcation, from the influences of advancing civilisation. The social state is at once so natural, so necessary, and so habitual to man, that, except in some unusual circumstances or by an effort of voluntary abstraction, he never conceives himself otherwise than as a member of a body; and this association is riveted more and more, as mankind are further removed from the stage of savage independence. Any condition, therefore, which is essential to a state of society, becomes more and more an inseparable part of every person's conception of the state of things which he is born into, and which is the destiny of a human being. Now, society between human beings, except in the relation of master and slave, is manifestly impossible on any other footing than that the interests of all are to be consulted. Society between equals can only exist on the understanding that the interests of all are to be regarded equally. And since in all states of civilisation, every person, except an absolute monarch, has equals, every one is obliged to live on these terms with somebody; and in every age some advance is made towards a state in which it will be impossible to live permanently on other terms with anybody. In this way people grow up unable to conceive as possible to them a state of total disregard of other people's interests. They are under a necessity of conceiving themselves as at least abstaining from all the grosser injuries, and (if only for their own protection) living in a state of constant protest against them. They are also familiar with the fact of co-operating with others, and proposing to themselves a collective, not an individual interest as the aim (at least for the time being) of their actions. So long as they are co-operating, their ends are identified with those of others; there is at least a temporary feeling that the interests of others are their own interests. Not only does all strengthening of social ties, and all healthy growth of society, give to each individual a stronger personal interest in practically consulting the welfare of others; it also leads him to identify his *feelings* more and more with their good, or at least with an even greater degree of practical consideration for it. He comes, as though instinctively, to be conscious of himself as a being who *of course* pays regard to others. The good of others becomes to him a thing naturally and necessarily to be attended to, like any of the physical conditions of our existence. Now, whatever amount of this feeling a person has, he is urged by the strongest motives both of interest and of sympathy to demonstrate it, and to the utmost of his power encourage it in others; and even if he has none of it himself, he is as greatly interested as any one else that others should have it. Consequently the smallest germs of the feeling are laid hold of and nourished by the contagion of sympathy and the influences of education; and a complete web of corroborative association is woven round it, by the powerful agency of the external sanctions. This mode of conceiving ourselves and human life, as civilisation goes on, is felt to be more and more natural. Every step in political improvement renders it more so, by removing the sources of opposition of interest, and levelling those inequalities of legal privilege between individuals or classes, owing to which there are large portions of mankind whose happiness it is still practicable to disregard. In an improving state of the human mind, the influences are constantly on the increase, which tend to generate in each individual a feeling of unity with all the rest; which, if perfect, would make him never think of, or desire, any beneficial condition for himself, in the benefits of which they are not included. If we now suppose this feeling of unity to be taught as a religion, and the whole force of education, of institutions, and of opinion, directed, as it once was in the case of religion, to make every person grow up from infancy surrounded on all sides both by the profession and the practice of it, I think that no one, who can realise this conception, will feel any misgiving about the sufficiency of the ultimate sanction for the Happiness morality. To any ethical student who finds the realisation difficult, I recommend, as a means of facilitating it, the second of M. Comte's two principal works, the *Traité de politique positive*. I entertain the strongest objections to the system of politics and morals set forth in that treatise; but I think it has superabundantly shown the possibility of giving to the service of humanity, even without the aid of belief in a Providence, both the psychological power and the social efficacy of a religion; making it take hold of human life, and colour all thought, feeling, and action, in a manner of which the greatest ascendancy ever exercised by any religion may be but a type and foretaste; and of which the danger is, not that it should be insufficient, but that it should be so excessive as to interfere unduly with human freedom and individuality.

Neither is it necessary to the feeling which constitutes the binding force of the utilitarian morality on those who recognise it, to wait for those social influences which would make its obligation felt by mankind at large. In the comparatively early state of human advancement in which we now live, a person cannot indeed feel that entireness of sympathy with all others, which would make any real discordance in the general direction of their conduct in life impossible; but already a person in whom the social feeling is at all developed, cannot bring himself to think of the rest of his fellow-creatures as struggling rivals with him for the means of happiness, whom he must desire to see defeated in their object in order that he may succeed in his. The deeply rooted conception which every individual even now has of himself as a social being, tends to make him feel it one of his natural wants that there should be harmony between his feelings and aims and those of his fellow-creatures. If differences of opinion and of mental culture make it impossible for him to share many of their actual feelings—perhaps make him denounce and defy those feelings—he still needs to be conscious that his real aim and theirs do not conflict; that he is not opposing himself to what they really wish for, namely their own good, but is, on the contrary, promoting it. This feeling in most individuals is much inferior in strength to their selfish feelings, and is often wanting altogether. But to those who have it, it possesses all the characters of a natural feeling. It does not present itself to their minds as a superstition of education, or a law despotically imposed by the power of society, but as an attribute which it would not be well for them to be without. This conviction is the ultimate sanction of the greatest happiness morality. This it is which makes any mind, of well-developed feelings, work with, and not against, the outward motives to care for others, afforded by what I have called the external sanctions; and when those sanctions are wanting, or act in an opposite direction, constitutes in itself a powerful internal binding force, in proportion to the sensitiveness and thoughtfulness of the character; since few but those whose mind is a moral blank, could bear to lay out their course of life on the plan of paying no regard to others except so far as their own private interest compels.

Chapter IV Of What Sort of Proof the Principle of Utility Is Susceptible

It has already been remarked, that questions of ultimate ends do not admit of proof, in the ordinary acceptation of the term. To be incapable of proof by reasoning is common to all first principles; to the first premises of our knowledge, as well as to those of our conduct. But the former, being matters of fact, may be the subject of a direct appeal to the faculties which judge of fact—namely, our senses, and our internal consciousness. Can an appeal be made to the same faculties on questions of practical ends? Or by what other faculty is cognisance taken of them?

Questions about ends are, in other words, questions about what things are desirable. The utilitarian doctrine is, that happiness is desirable, and the only thing desirable, as an end; all other things being only desirable as means to that end. What ought to be required of this doctrine—what conditions is it requisite that the doctrine should fulfil—to make good its claim to be believed?

The only proof capable of being given that an object is visible, is that people actually see it. The only proof that a sound is audible, is that people hear it: and so of the other sources of our experience. In like manner, I apprehend, the sole evidence it is possible to produce that anything is desirable, is that people actually do desire it. If the end which the utilitarian doctrine proposes to itself were not, in theory and in practice, acknowledged to be an end, nothing could ever convince any person that it was so. No reason can be given why the general happiness is desirable, except that each person, so far as he believes it to be attainable, desires his own happiness. This, however, being a fact, we have not only all the proof which the case admits of, but all which it is possible to require, that happiness is a good: that each person's happiness is a good to that person, and the general happiness, therefore, a good to the aggregate of all persons. Happiness has made out its title as *one* of the ends of conduct, and consequently one of the criteria of morality.

But it has not, by this alone, proved itself to be the sole criterion. To do that, it would seem, by the same rule, necessary to show, not only that people desire happiness, but that they never desire anything else. Now it is palpable that they do desire things which, in common language, are decidedly distinguished from happiness. They desire, for example, virtue, and the absence of vice, no less really than pleasure and the absence of pain. The desire of virtue is not as universal, but is as authentic a fact, as the desire of happiness. And hence the opponents of the utilitarian standard deem that they have a right to infer that there are other ends of human action besides happiness, and that happiness is not the standard of approbation and disapprobation.

But does the utilitarian doctrine deny that people desire virtue, or maintain that virtue is not a thing to be desired? The very reverse. It maintains not only that virtue is to be desired, but that it is to be desired disinterestedly, for itself. Whatever may be the opinion of utilitarian moralists as to the original conditions by which virtue is made virtue; however they may believe (as they do) that actions and dispositions are only virtuous because they promote another end than virtue; yet this being granted, and it having been decided, from considerations of this description, what *is* virtuous, they not only place virtue at the very head of the things which are good as means to the ultimate end, but they also recognise as a psychological fact the possibility of its being, to the individual, a good in itself, without looking to any end beyond it; and, hold, that the mind is not in a right state, not a state conformable to Utility, not in the state most conducive to the general happiness, unless it does love virtue in this manner—as a thing desirable in itself, even although, in the individual instance, it should not produce those other desirable consequences which it tends to produce, and on account of which it is held to be virtue. This opinion is not, in the smallest degree, a departure from the Happiness principle. The ingredients of happiness are very various, and each of them is desirable in itself, and not merely when considered as swelling an aggregate. The principle of utility does not mean that any given pleasure, as music, for instance, or any given exemption from pain, as for example health, is to be looked upon as means to a collective something termed happiness, and to be desired on that account. They are desired and desirable in and for themselves; besides being means, they are a part of the end. Virtue, according to the utilitarian doctrine, is not naturally and originally part of the end, but it is capable of becoming so; and in those who love it disinterestedly it has become so, and is desired and cherished, not as a means to happiness, but as a part of their happiness.

To illustrate this farther, we may remember that virtue is not the only thing, originally a means, and which if it were not a means to anything else, would be and remain indifferent, but which by association with what it is a means to, comes to be desired for itself, and that too with the utmost intensity. What, for example, shall we say of the love of money? There is nothing originally more desirable about money than about any heap of glittering pebbles. Its worth is solely that of the things which it will buy; the desires for other things than itself, which it is a means of gratifying. Yet the love of money is not only one of the strongest moving forces of human life, but money is, in many cases, desired in and for itself; the desire to possess it is often stronger than the desire to use it, and goes on increasing when all the desires which point to ends beyond it, to be compassed by it, are falling off. It may, then, be said truly, that money is desired not for the sake of an end, but as part of the end. From being a means to happiness, it has come to be itself a principal ingredient of the individual's conception of happiness. The same may be said of the majority of the great objects of human life—power, for example, or fame; except that to each of these there is a certain amount of immediate pleasure annexed, which has at least the semblance of being naturally inherent in them; a thing which cannot be said of money. Still, however, the strongest natural attraction, both of power and of fame, is the immense aid they give to the attainment of our other wishes; and it is the strong association thus generated between them and all our objects of desire, which gives to the direct desire of them the intensity it often assumes, so as in some characters to surpass in strength all other desires. In these cases the means have become a part of the end, and a more important part of it than any of the things which they are means to. What was once desired as an instrument for the attainment of happiness, has come to be desired for its own sake. In being desired for its own sake it is, however, desired as *part* of happiness. The person is made, or thinks he would be made, happy by its mere possession; and is made unhappy by failure to obtain it. The desire of it is not a different thing from the desire of happiness, any more than the love of music, of the desire of health. They are included in happiness. They are some of the elements of which the desire of happiness is made up. Happiness is not an abstract idea, but a concrete whole; and these are some of its parts. And the utilitarian standard sanctions and approves their being so. Life would be a poor thing, very ill provided with sources of happiness, if there were not this provision of nature, by which things originally indifferent, but conducive to, or otherwise associated with, the satisfaction of our primitive desires, become in themselves sources of pleasure more valuable than the primitive pleasures, both in permanency, in the space of human existence that they are capable of covering, and even in intensity.

Virture, according to the utilitarian conception, is a good of this description. There was no original desire of it, or motive to it, save its conduciveness to pleasure, and especially to protection from pain. But through the association thus formed, it may be felt a good in itself, and desired as such with as great intensity as any other good; and with this difference between it and the love of money, of power, or of fame, that all of these may, and often do, render the individual noxious to the other members of society to which he belongs, whereas there is nothing which makes him so much a blessing to them as the cultivation of the disinterested love of virtue. And consequently, the utilitarian standard, while it tolerates and approves those other acquired desires, up to the point beyond which they would be more injurious to the general happiness than promotive of it, enjoins and requires the cultivation of the love of virtue up to the greatest strength possible, as being above all things important to the general happiness.

It results from the preceding considerations, that there is in reality nothing desired except happiness. Whatever is desired otherwise than as a means to some end beyond itself, and ultimately to happiness, is desired as itself a part of happiness, and is not desired for itself until it has become so. Those who desire virtue for its own sake, desire it either because the consciousness of it is a pleasure, or because the consciousness of being without it is a pain, or for both reasons united; as in truth the pleasure and pain seldom exist separately, but almost always together, the same person feeling pleasure in degree of virtue attained, and pain in not having attained more. If one of these give him no pleasure, and the other no pain, he would not love or desire virtue, or would desire it only for the other benefits which it might produce to himself or to persons whom he cared for.

We have now, then, an answer to the question, of what sort of proof the principle of utility is susceptible. If the opinion which I have now stated is psychologically true — if human nature is so constituted as to desire nothing which is not either a part of happiness or a means of happiness, we can have no other proof, and we require no other, that these are the only things desirable. If so, happiness is the sole end of human action, and the promotion of it the test by which to judge of all human conduct; from whence it necessarily follows that it must be the criterion of morality, since a part is included in the whole.

And now to decide whether this is really so; whether mankind do desire nothing for itself but that which is a pleasure to them or of which the absence is a pain; we have evidently arrived at a question of fact and experience, dependent, like all similar questions, upon evidence. It can only be determined by practised self-consciousness and self-observation, assisted by observation of others. I believe that these sources of evidence, impartially consulted, will declare that desiring a thing and finding it pleasant, aversion to it and thinking of it as painful, are phenomena entirely inseparable, or rather two parts of the same phenomenon; in strictness of language, two different modes of naming the same psychological fact: that to think of an object as desirable (unless for the sake of its consequences), and to think of it as pleasant, are one and the same thing; and that to desire anything, except in proportion as the idea of it is pleasant, is a physical and metaphysical impossibility.

So obvious does this appear to me, that I expect it will hardly be disputed: and the objection made will be, not that desire can possibly be directed to anything ultimately except pleasure and exemption from pain, but that the will is a different thing from desire; that a person of confirmed virtue, or any other person whose purposes are fixed, carries out his purposes without any thought of the pleasure he has in contemplating them, or expects to derive from their fulfilment; and persists in acting on them, enough though these pleasures are much diminished, by changes in his character or decay of his passive sensibilities, or are outweighed by the pains which the pursuit of the purposes may bring upon him. All this I fully admit, and have stated it elsewhere, as positively and emphatically as any one. Will, the active phenomenon, is a different thing from desire, the state of passive sensibility, and though originally an offshoot from it, may in time take root and detach itself from the parent stock; so much so, that in the case of an habitual purpose, instead of willing the thing because we desire it, we often desire it only because we will it. This, however, is but an instance of that familiar fact, the power of habit, and is nowise confined to the case of virtuous actions. Many indifferent things, which men originally did from a motive of some sort, they continue to do from habit. Sometimes this is done unconsciously, the consciousness coming only after the action; at other times with conscious volition, but volition which has become habitual, and is put in operation by the force of habit, in opposition perhaps to the deliberate preference, as often happens with those who have contracted habits of vicious or hurtful indulgence. Third and last comes the case in which the habitual act of will in the individual instance is not in contradiction to the general intention prevailing at other times, but in fulfilment of it; as in the case of the person of confirmed virtue, and of all who pursue deliberately and consistently any determinate end. The distinction between will and desire thus understood is an authentic and highly important psychological fact; but the fact consists solely in this—that will, like all other parts of our constitution, is amenable to habit, and that we may will from habit what we no longer desire for itself, or desire only because we will it. It is not the less true that will, in the beginning, is entirely produced by desire; including in that term the repelling influence of pain as well as the attractive one of pleasure. Let us take into consideration, no longer the person who has a confirmed will to do right, but him in whom that virtuous will is still feeble, conquerable by temptation, and not to be fully relied on; by what means can it be strengthened? How can the will to be virtuous, where it does not exist in sufficient force, be implanted or awakened? Only by making the person *desire* virtue—by making him think of it in a pleasurable light, or of its absence in a painful one. It is by associating the doing right with pleasure, or the doing wrong with pain, or by eliciting and impressing and bringing home to the person's experience the pleasure naturally involved in the one or the pain in the other, that it is possible to call forth that will to be virtuous, which, when confirmed, acts without any thought of either pleasure or pain. Will is the child of desire, and passes out of the dominion of its parent only to come under that of habit. That which is the result of habit affords no presumption of being intrinsically good; and there would be no reason for wishing that the purpose of virtue should become independent of pleasure and pain, were it not that the influence of the pleasurable and painful associations which prompt to virtue is not sufficently to be depended on for unerring constancy of action until it has acquired the support of habit. Both in feeling and in conduct, habit is the only thing which imparts certainty; and it is because of the importance to others of being able to rely absolutely on one's feelings and conduct, and to oneself of being able to rely on one's own, that the will to do right ought to be cultivated into this habitual independence. In other words, this state of the will is a means to good, not intrinsically a good; and does not contradict the doctrine that nothing is a good to human beings but in so far as it is either itself pleasurable, or a means of attaining pleasure or averting pain.

But if this doctrine be true, the principle of utility is proved. Whether it is so or not, must now be left to the consideration of the thoughtful reader.

B. From *On Liberty*

Introductory

The subject of this essay is not the so-called "liberty of the will," so unfortunately opposed to the misnamed doctrine of philosophical necessity; but civil, or social liberty; the nature and limits of the power which can be legitimately exercised by society over the individual. A question seldom stated, and hardly ever discussed in general terms, but which profoundly influences the practical controversies of the age by its latent presence, and is likely soon to make itself recognized as the vital question of the future. It is so far from being new that, in a certain sense, it has divided mankind almost from the remotest ages; but in the stage of progress into which the more civilized portions of the species have now entered, it presents itself under new conditions and requires a different and more fundamental treatment.

The struggle between liberty and authority is the most conspicuous feature in the portions of history with which we are earliest familiar, particularly in that of Greece, Rome, and England. But in old times this contest was between subjects, or some classes of subjects, and the government. By liberty was meant protection against the tyranny of the political rulers. The rulers were conceived (except in some of the popular governments of Greece) as in a necessarily antagonistic position to the people whom they ruled. They consisted of a governing One, or a governing tribe or caste, who derived their authority from inheritance or conquest, who, at all events, did not hold it at the pleasure of the governed, and whose supremacy men did not venture, perhaps did not desire, to contest, whatever precautions might be taken against its oppressive exercise. Their power was regarded as necessary, but also as highly dangerous; as a weapon which they would attempt to use against their subjects, no less than against external enemies. To prevent the weaker members of the community from being preyed upon by innumerable vultures, it was needful that there should be an animal of prey stronger than the rest, commissioned to keep them down. But as the king of the vultures would be no less bent upon preying on the flock than any of the minor harpies, it was indispensable to be in a perpetual attitude of defense against his beak and claws. The aim, therefore, of patriots was to set limits to the power which the ruler should be suffered to exercise over the community; and this limitation was what they meant by liberty. It was attempted in two ways. First, by obtaining a recognition of certain immunities, called political liberties or rights, which it was to be regarded as a breach of duty in the ruler to infringe, and which if he did infringe, specific resistance or general rebellion was held to be justifiable. A second, and generally a later, expedient was the establishment of constitutional checks by which the consent of the community, or of a body of some sort, supposed to represent its interests, was made a necessary condition to some of the more important acts of the governing power. To the first of these modes of limitation, the ruling power, in most European countries, was compelled, more or less, to submit. It was not so with the second; and, to attain this, or, when already in some degree possessed, to attain it more completely, became everywhere the principal object of the lovers of liberty. And so long as mankind were content to combat one enemy by another, and to be ruled by a master on condition of being guaranteed more or less efficaciously against his tyranny, they did not carry their aspirations beyond this point.

A time, however, came, in the progress of human affairs, when men ceased to think it a necessity of nature that their governors should be an independent power opposed in interest to themselves. It appeared to them much better that the various magistrates of the state should be their tenants or delegates, revocable at their pleasure. In that way alone, it seemed, could they have complete security that the powers of government would never be abused to their disadvantage. By degrees this new demand for elective and temporary rulers became the prominent object of the exertions of the popular party wherever any such party existed, and superseded, to a considerable extent, the previous efforts to limit the power of rulers. As the struggle proceeded for making the ruling power emanate from the periodical choice of the ruled, some persons began to think that too much importance had been attached to the limitation of the power itself. *That* (it might seem) was a resource against rulers whose interests were habitually opposed to those of the people. What was now wanted was that the rulers should be identified with the people, that their interest and will should be the interest and will of the nation. The nation did not need to be protected against its own will. There was no fear of its tyrannizing over itself. Let the rulers be effectually responsible to it, promptly removable by it, and it could afford to trust them with power of which it could itself dictate the use to be made. Their power was but the nation's own power, concentrated and in a form convenient for exercise. This mode of thought, or rather perhaps of feeling, was common among the last generation of European liberalism, in the Continental section of which it still apparently predominates. Those who admit any limit to what a government may do, except in the case of such governments as they think ought not to exist, stand out as brilliant exceptions among the political thinkers of the Continent. A similar tone of sentiment might by this time have been prevalent in our own country if the circumstances which for a time encouraged it had continued unaltered.

But, in political and philosophical theories as well as in persons, success discloses faults and infirmities which failure might have concealed from observation. The notion that the people have no need to limit their power over themselves might seem axiomatic, when popular government was a thing only dreamed about, or read of as having existed at some distant period of the past. Neither was that notion necessarily disturbed by such temporary aberrations as those of the French Revolution, the worst of which were the work of a usurping few, and which, in any case, belonged, not to the permanent working of popular institutions, but to a sudden and convulsive outbreak against monarchical and aristocratic despotism. In time, however, a democratic republic came to occupy a large portion of the earth's surface and made itself felt as one of the most powerful members of the community of nations; and elective and responsible government became subject to the observations and criticisms which wait upon a great existing fact. It was now perceived that such phrases as "self-government," and "the power of the people over themselves," do not express the true state of the case. The "people" who exercise the power are not always the same people with those over whom it is exercised; and the "self-government" spoken of is not the government of each by himself, but of each by all the rest. The will of the people, moreover, practically means the will of the most numerous or the most active *part* of the people—the majority, or those who succeed in making themselves accepted as the majority; the people, consequently, *may* desire to oppress a part of their number, and precautions are as much needed against this as against any other abuse of power. The limitations, therefore, of the power of government over individuals loses none of its importance when the holders of power are regularly accountable to the community, that is, to the strongest party therein. This view of things, recommending itself equally to the intelligence of thinkers and to the inclination of those important classes in European society to whose real or supposed interests democracy is adverse, has had no difficulty in establishing itself; and in political speculations "the tyranny of the majority" is now generally included among the evils against which society requires to be on its guard.

Like other tyrannies, the tyranny of the majority was at first, and is still vulgarly, held in dread, chiefly as operating through the acts of the public authorities. But reflecting persons perceived that when society is itself the tyrant—society collectively over the separate individuals who compose it—its means of tyrannizing are not restricted to the acts which it may do by the hands of its political functionaries. Society can and does execute its own mandates; and if it issues wrong mandates instead of right, or any mandates at all in things with which it ought not to meddle, it practices a social tyranny more formidable than many kinds of political oppression, since, though not usually upheld by such extreme penalties, it leaves fewer means of escape, penetrating much more deeply into the details of life, and enslaving the soul itself. Protection, therefore, against the tyranny of the magistrate is not enough; there needs protection also against the tyranny of the prevailing opinion and feeling, against the tendency of society to impose, by other means than civil penalties, its own ideas and practices as rules of conduct on those who dissent from them; to fetter the development and, if possible, prevent the formation of any individuality not in harmony with its ways, and compel all characters to fashion themselves upon the model of its own. There is a limit to the legitimate interference of collective opinion with individual independence; and to find that limit, and maintain it against encroachment, is as indispensable to a good condition of human affairs as protection against political despotism.

But though this proposition is not likely to be contested in general terms, the practical question where to place the limit—how to make the fitting adjustment between individual independence and social control—is a subject on which nearly everything remains to be done. All that makes existence valuable to anyone depends on the enforcement of restraints upon the actions of other people. Some rules of conduct, therefore, must be imposed—by law in the first place, and by opinion on many things which are not fit subjects for the operation of law. What these rules should be is the principal question in human affairs. . . .

The object of this essay is to assert one very simple principle, as entitled to govern absolutely the dealings of society with the individual in the way of compulsion and control, whether the means used by physical force in the form of legal penalties or the moral coercion of public opinion. That principle is that the sole end for which mankind are warranted, individually or collectively, in interfering with the liberty of action of any of their number is self-protection. That the only purpose for which power can be rightfully exercised over any member of a civilized community, against his will, is to prevent harm to others. His own good, either physical or moral, is not a sufficient warrant. He cannot rightfully be compelled to do or forbear because it will be better for him to do so, because it will make him happier, because, in the opinions of others, to do so would be wise or even right. These are good reasons for remonstrating with him, or reasoning with him, or persuading him, or entreating him, but not for compelling him or visiting him with any evil in case he do otherwise. To justify that, the conduct from which it is desired to deter him must be calculated to produce evil to someone else. The only part of the conduct of anyone for which he is amenable to society is that which concerns others. In the part which merely concerns himself, his independence is, of right, absolute. Over himself, over his own body and mind, the individual is sovereign.

It is, perhaps, hardly necessary to say that this doctrine is meant to apply only to human beings in the maturity of their faculties. We are not speaking of children or of young persons below the age which the law may fix as that of manhood or womanhood. Those who are still in a state to require being taken care of by others must be protected against their own actions as well as against external injury. For the same reason we may leave out of consideration those backward states of society in which the race itself may be considered as in its nonage. The early difficulties in the way of spontaneous progress are so great that there is seldom any choice of means for overcoming them; and a ruler full of the spirit of improvement is warranted in the use of any expedients that will attain an end perhaps otherwise unattainable. Despotism is a legitimate mode of government in dealing with barbarians, provided the end be their improvement and the means justified by actually effecting that end. Liberty, as a principle, has no application to any state of things anterior to the time when mankind have become capable of being improved by free and equal discussion. Until then, there is nothing for them but implicit obedience to an Akbar or a Charlemagne, if they are so fortunate as to find one. But as soon as mankind have attained the capacity of being guided to their own improvement by conviction or persuasion (a period long since reached in all nations with whom we need here concern ourselves), compulsion, either in the direct form or in that of pains and penalties for non-compliance, is no longer admissible as a means to their own good, and justifiable only for the security of others.

It is proper to state that I forgo any advantage which could be derived to my argument from the idea of abstract right as a thing independent of utility. I regard utility as the ultimate appeal on all ethical questions; but it must be utility in the largest sense, grounded on the permanent interests of man as a progressive being. Those interests, I contend, authorize the subjection of individual spontaneity to external control only in respect to those actions of each which concern the interest of other people. If anyone does an act hurtful to others, there is a *prima facie* case for punishing him by law or, where legal penalties are not safely applicable, by general disapprobation. There are also many positive acts for the benefit of others which he may rightfully be compelled to perform, such as to give evidence in a court of justice, to bear his fair share in the common defense or in any other joint work necessary to the interest of the society of which he enjoys the protection, and to perform certain acts of individual beneficence, such as saving a fellow creature's life or interposing to protect the defenseless against ill usage — things which whenever it is obviously a man's duty to do he may rightfully be made responsible to society for not doing. A person may cause evil to others not only by his actions but by his inaction, and in either case he is justly accountable to them for the injury. The latter case, it is true, requires a much more cautious exercise of compulsion than the former. To make anyone answerable for doing evil to others is the rule; to make him answerable for not preventing evil is, comparatively speaking, the exception. Yet there are many cases clean enough and grave enough to justify that exception. In all things which regard the external relations of the individual, he is *de jure* amenable to those whose interests are concerned, and, if need be, to society as their protector. There are often good reasons for not holding him to the responsibility; but these reasons must arise from the special expediencies of the case: either because it is a kind of case in which he is on the whole likely to act better when left to his own discretion than when controlled in any way in which society have it in their power to control him; or because the attempt to exercise control would produce other evils, greater than those which it would prevent. When such reasons as these preclude the enforcement of responsibility, the conscience of the agent himself should step into the vacant judgment seat and protect those interests of others which have no external protection; judging himself all the more rigidly, because the case does not admit of his being made accountable to the judgment of his fellow creatures.

But there is a sphere of action in which society, as distinguished from the individual, has, if any, only an indirect interest: comprehending all that portion of a person's life and conduct which affects only himself or, if it also affects others, only with their free, voluntary, and undeceived consent and participation. When I say only himself, I mean directly and in the first instance; for whatever affects himself may affect others through himself; and the objection which may be grounded on this contingency will receive consideration in the sequel. This, then, is the appropriate region of human liberty. It comprises, first, the inward domain of consciousness, demanding liberty of conscience in the most comprehensive sense, liberty of thought and feeling, absolute freedom of opinion and sentiment on all subjects, practical or speculative, scientific, moral, or theological. The liberty of expressing and publishing opinions may seem to fall under a different principle, since it belongs to that part of the conduct of an individual which concerns other people, but, being almost of as much importance as the liberty of thought itself and resting in great part on the same reasons, is practically inseparable from it. Secondly, the principle requires liberty of tastes and pursuits, of framing the plan of our life to suit our own character, of doing as we like, subject to such consequences as may follow, without impediment from our fellow creatures, so long as what we do does not harm them, even though they should think our conduct foolish, perverse, or wrong. Thirdly, from this liberty of each individual follows the liberty, within the same limits, of combination among individuals; freedom to unite for any purpose not involving harm to others: the persons combining being supposed to be of full age and not forced or deceived.

· · · · · · · ·

Of the Liberty of Thought and Discussion

The time, it is to be hoped, is gone by when any defense would be necessary of the "liberty of the press" as one of the securities against corrupt or tyrannical government. No argument, we may suppose, can now be needed against permitting a legislature or an executive, not identified in interest with the people, to prescribe opinions to them and determine what doctrines or what arguments they shall be allowed to hear. This aspect of the question, besides, has been so often and so triumphantly enforced by preceding writers that it needs not be specially insisted on in this place. Though the law of England, on the subject of the press, is as servile to this day as it was in the time of the Tudors, there is little danger of its being actually put in force against political discussion except during some temporary panic when fear of insurrection drives ministers and judges from their propriety; and, speaking generally, it is not, in constitutional countries, to be apprehended that the government, whether completely responsible to the people or not, will often attempt to control the expression of opinion, except when in doing so it makes itself the organ of the general intolerance of the public. Let us suppose, therefore, that the government is entirely at one with the people, and never thinks of exerting any power of coercion unless in agreement with what it conceives to be their voice.

But I deny the right of the people to exercise such coercion, either by themselves or by their government. The power itself is illegitimate. The best government has no more title to it than the worst. It is as noxious, or more noxious, when exerted in accordance with public opinion than when in opposition to it. If all mankind minus one were of one opinion, mankind would be no more justified in silencing that one person than he, if he had the power, would be justified in silencing mankind. Were an opinion a personal possession of no value except to the owner, if to be obstructed in the enjoyment of it were simply a private injury, it would make some difference whether the injury was inflicted only on a few persons or on many. But the peculiar evil of silencing the expression of an opinion is that it is robbing the human race, posterity as well as the existing generation—those who dissent from the opinion, still more than those who hold it. If the opinion is right, they are deprived of the opportunity of exchanging error for truth; if wrong, they lose, what is almost as great a benefit, the clearer perception and livelier impression of truth produced by its collision with error.

It is necessary to consider separately these two hypotheses, each of which has a distinct branch of the argument corresponding to it. We can never be sure that the opinion we are endeavoring to stifle is a false opinion; and if we were sure, stifling it would be an evil still.

First, the opinion which it is attempted to suppress by authority may possibly be true. Those who desire to suppress it, of course, deny its truth; but they are not infallible. They have no authority to decide the question for all mankind and exclude every other person from the means of judging. To refuse a hearing to an opinion because they are sure that it is false is to assume that *their* certainty is the same thing as *absolute* certainty. All silencing of discussion is an assumption of infallibility. Its condemnation may be allowed to rest on this common argument, not the worse for being common.

Unfortunately for the good sense of mankind, the fact of their fallibility is far from carrying the weight in their practical judgment which is always allowed to it in theory; for while everyone well knows himself to be fallible, few think it necessary to take any precautions against their own fallibility, or admit the sup-position that any opinion of which they feel very certain may be one of the examples of the error to which they acknowledge themselves to be liable. Absolute princes, or others who are accustomed to unlimited deference, usually feel this complete confidence in their own opinions on nearly all subjects. People more happily situated, who sometimes hear their opinions disputed and are not wholly unused to be set right when they are wrong, place the same unbounded reliance only on such of their opinions as are shared by all who surround them, or to whom they habitually defer; for in proportion to a man's want of confidence in his own solitary judgment does he usually repose, with implicit trust, on the infallibility of "the world" in general. And the world, to each individual, means the part of it with which he comes in contact: his party, his sect, his church, his class of society; the man may be called, by comparison, almost liberal and large-minded to whom it means anything so comprehensive as his own country or his own age. Nor is his faith in this collective authority at all shaken by his being aware that other ages, countries, sects, churches, classes, and parties have thought, and even now think, the exact reverse. He devolves upon his own world the responsibility of being in the right against the dissentient worlds of other people; and it never troubles him that mere accident has decided which of these numerous worlds is the object of his reliance, and that the same causes which make him a churchman in London would have made him a Buddhist or a Confucian in Peking. Yet it is as evident in itself, as any amount of argument can make it, that ages are no more infallible than individuals — every age having held many opinions which subsequent ages have deemed not only false but absurd; and it is as certain that many opinions, now general, will be rejected by future ages, as it is that many, once general, are rejected by the present.

The objection likely to be made to this argument would probably take some such form as the following. There is no greater assumption of infallibility in forbidding the propagation of error than in any other thing which is done by public authority on its own judgment and responsibility. Judgment is given to men that they may use it. Because it may be used erroneously, are men to be told that they ought not to use it at all? To prohibit what they think pernicious is not claiming exemption from error, but fulfilling the duty incumbent on them, although fallible, of acting on their conscientious conviction. If we were never to act on our opinions, because those opinions may be wrong, we should leave all our interests uncared for, and all our duties unperformed. An objection which applies to all conduct can be no valid objection to any conduct in particular. It is the duty of governments, and of individuals, to form the truest opinions they can; to form them carefully, and never impose them upon others unless they are quite sure of being right. But when they are sure (such reasoners may say), it is not conscientiousness but cowardice to shrink from acting on their opinions and allow doctrines which they honestly think dangerous to the welfare of mankind, either in this life or in another, to be scattered abroad without restraint, because other people, in less enlightened times, have persecuted opinions now believed to be true. Let us take care, it may be said, not to make the same mistake; but governments and nations have made mistakes in other things which are not denied to be fit subjects for the exercise of authority: they have laid on bad taxes, made unjust wars. Ought we therefore to lay on no taxes and, under whatever provocation, make no wars? Men and governments must act to the best of their ability. There is no such thing as absolute certainty, but there is assurance sufficient for the purposes of human life. We may, and must, assume our opinion to be true for the guidance of our own conduct; and it is assuming no more when we forbid bad men to pervert society by the propagation of opinions which we regard as false and pernicious.

I answer, that it is assuming very much more. There is the greatest difference between presuming an opinion to be true because, with every opportunity for contesting it, it has not been refuted, and assuming its truth for the purpose of not permitting its refutation. Complete liberty of contradicting and disproving our opinion is the very condition which justifies us in assuming its truth for purposes of action; and on no other terms can a being with human faculties have any rational assurance of being right.

When we consider either the history of opinion or the ordinary conduct of human life, to what is it to be ascribed that the one and the other are no worse than they are? Not certainly to the inherent force of the human understanding, for on any matter not self-evident there are ninety-nine persons totally incapable of judging of it for one who is capable; and the capacity of the hundredth person is only comparative, for the majority of the eminent men of every past generation held many opinions now known to be erroneous, and did or approved numerous things which no one will now justify. Why is it, then, that there is on the whole a preponderance among mankind of rational opinions and rational conduct? If there really is this preponderance—which there must be unless human affairs are, and have always been, in an almost desperate state—it is owing to a quality of the human mind, the source of everything respectable in man either as an intellectual or as a moral being, namely, that his errors are corrigible. He is capable of rectifying his mistakes by discussion and experience. Not by experience alone. There must be discussion to show how experience is to be interpreted. Wrong opinions and practices gradually yield to fact and argument; but facts and arguments, to produce any effect on the mind, must be brought before it. Very few facts are able to tell their own story, without comments to bring out their meaning. The whole strength and value, then, of human judgment depending on the one property, that it can be set right when it is wrong, reliance can be placed on it only when the means of setting it right are kept constantly at hand. In the case of any person whose judgment is really deserving of confidence, how has it become so? Because he has kept his mind open to criticism of his opinions and conduct. Because it has been his practice to listen to all that could be said against him; to profit by as much of it as was just, and to expound to himself, and upon occasion to others, the fallacy of what was fallacious. Because he has felt that the only way in which a human being can make some approach to knowing the whole of a subject is by hearing what can be said about it by persons of every variety of opinion, and studying all modes in which it can be looked at by every character of mind. No wise man ever acquired his wisdom in any mode but this; nor is it in the nature of human intellect to become wise in any other manner. The steady habit of correcting and completing his own opinion by collating it with those of others, so far from causing doubt and hesitation in carrying it into practice, is the only stable foundation for a just reliance on it; for, being cognizant of all that can, at least obviously, be said against him, and having taken up his position against all gainsayers—knowing that he has sought for objections and difficulties instead of avoiding them, and has shut out no light which can be thrown upon the subject from any quarter—he has a right to think his judgment better than that of any person, or any multitude, who have not gone through a similar process.

. . . .

Let us now pass to the second division of the argument, and dismissing the supposition that any of the received opinions may be false, let us assume them to be true and examine into the worth of the manner in which they are likely to be held when their truth is not freely and openly canvassed. However unwillingly a person who has a strong opinion may admit the possibility that his opinion may be false, he ought to be moved by the consideration that, however true it may be, if it is not fully, frequently, and fearlessly discussed, it will be held as a dead dogma, not a living truth.

There is a class of persons (happily not quite so numerous as formerly) who think it enough if a person assents undoubtingly to what they think true, though he has no knowledge whatever of the grounds of the opinion and could not make a tenable defense of it against the most superficial objections. Such persons, if they can once get their creed taught from authority, naturally think that no good, and some harm, comes of its being allowed to be questioned. Where their influence prevails, they make it nearly impossible for the received opinion to be rejected wisely and considerately, though it may still be rejected rashly and ignorantly; for to shut out discussion entirely is seldom possible, and when it once gets in, beliefs not grounded on conviction are apt to give way before the slightest semblance of an argument. Waiving, however, this possibility—assuming that the true opinion abides in the mind, but abides as a prejudice, a belief independent of, and proof against, argument—this is not the way in which truth ought to be held by a rational being. This is not knowing the truth. Truth, thus held, is but one superstition the more, accidentally clinging to the words which enunciate a truth.

If the intellect and judgment of mankind ought to be cultivated, a thing which Protestants at least do not deny, on what can these faculties be more appropriately exercised by anyone than on the things which concern him so much that it is considered necessary for him to hold opinions on them? If the cultivation of the understanding consists in one thing more than in another, it is surely in learning the grounds of one's own opinions. Whatever people believe, on subjects on which it is of the first importance to believe rightly, they ought to be able to defend against at least the common objections. But, someone may say, "Let them be *taught* the grounds of their opinions. It does not follow that opinions must be merely parroted because they are never heard controverted. Persons who learn geometry do not simply commit the theorems to memory, but understand and learn likewise the demonstrations; and it would be absurd to say that they remain ignorant of the grounds of geometrical truths because they never hear anyone deny and attempt to disprove them." Undoubtedly; and such teaching suffices on a subject like mathematics, where there is nothing at all to be said on the wrong side of the question. The peculiarity of the evidence of mathematical truths is that all the argument is on one side. There are no objections, and no answers to objections. But on every subject on which difference of opinion is possible, the truth depends on a balance to be struck between two sets of conflicting reasons. Even in natural philosophy, there is always some other explanation possible of the same facts; some geocentric theory instead of heliocentric, some phlogiston instead of oxygen; and it has to be shown why that other theory cannot be the true one; and until this is shown, and until we know how it is shown, we do not understand the grounds of our opinion. But when we turn to subjects infinitely more complicated, to morals, religion, politics, social relations, and the business of life, three-fourths of the arguments for every disputed opinion consist in dispelling the appearances which favor some opinion different from it. The greatest orator, save one, of antiquity, has left it on record that he always studies his adversary's case with as great, if not still greater, intensity than even his own. What Cicero practiced as the means of forensic success requires to be imitated by all who study any subject in order to arrive at the truth. He who knows only his own side of the case knows little of that. His reasons may be good, and no one may have been able to refute them. But if he is equally unable to refute the reasons on the opposite side, if he does not so much as know what they are, he has no ground for preferring either opinion. The rational position for him would be suspension of judgment, and unless he contents himself with that, he is either led by authority or adopts, like the generality of the world, the side to which he feels most inclination. Nor is it enough that he should hear the arguments of adversaries from his own teachers, presented as they state them, and accompanied by what they offer as refutations. That is not the way to do justice to the arguments or bring them into real contact with his own mind. He must be able to hear them from persons who actually believe them, who defend them in earnest and do their very utmost for them. He must know them in their most plausible and persuasive form; he must feel the whole force of the difficulty which the true view of the subject has to encounter and dispose of, else he will never really possess himself of the portion of truth which meets and removes that difficulty. Ninety-nine in a hundred of what are called educated men are in this condition, even of those who can argue fluently for their opinions. Their conclusion may be true, but it might be false for anything they know; they have never thrown themselves into the mental position of those who think differently from them, and considered what such persons may have to say; and, consequently, they do not, in any proper sense of the word, know the doctrine which they themselves profess. . . .

We have now recognized the necessity to the mental well-being of mankind (on which all their other well-being depends) of freedom of opinion, and freedom of the expression of opinion, on four distinct grounds, which we will now briefly recapitulate:

First, if any opinion is compelled to silence, that opinion may, for aught we can certainly know, be true. To deny this is to assume our own infallibility.

Secondly, though the silenced opinion be an error, it may, and very commonly does, contain a portion of truth; and since the general or prevailing opinion on any subject is rarely or never the whole truth, it is only by the collision of adverse opinions that the remainder of the truth has any chance of being supplied.

Thirdly, even if the received opinion be not only true, but the whole truth; unless it is suffered to be, and actually is, vigorously and earnestly contested, it will, by most of those who receive it, be held in the manner of a prejudice, with little comprehension or feeling of its rational grounds. And not only this, but, fourthly, the meaning of the doctrine itself will be in danger of being lost or enfeebled, and deprived of its vital effect on the character and conduct; the dogma becoming a mere formal profession, inefficacious for good, but cumbering the ground and preventing the growth of any real and heartfelt conviction from reason or personal experience.

. . . .

Of Individuality, as One of the Elements of Well-Being

Such being the reasons which make it imperative that human beings should be free to form opinions and to express their opinions without reserve; and such the baneful consequences to the intellectual, and through that to the moral nature of man, unless this liberty is either conceded or asserted in spite of prohibition; let us next examine whether the same reasons do not require that men should be free to act upon their opinions—to carry these out in their lives without hindrance, either physical or moral, from their fellow men, so long as it is at their own risk and peril. This last proviso is of course indispensable. No one pretends that actions should be as free as opinions. On the contrary, even opinions lose their immunity when the circumstances in which they are expressed are such as to constitute their expression a positive instigation to some mischievous act. An opinion that corn dealers are starvers of the poor, or that private property is robbery, ought to be unmolested when simply circulated through the press, but may justly incur punishment when delivered orally to an excited mob assembled before the house of a corn dealer, or when handed about among the same mob in the form of a placard. Acts, of whatever kind, which without justifiable cause do harm to others may be, and in the more important cases absolutely require to be, controlled by the unfavorable sentiments, and, when needful, by the active interference of mankind. The liberty of the individual must be thus far limited; he must not make himself a nuisance to other people. But if he refrains from molesting others in what concerns them, and merely acts according to his own inclination and judgment in things which concern himself, the same reasons which show that opinion should be free prove also that he should be allowed, without molestations, to carry his opinions into practice at his own cost. That mankind are not infallible; that their truths, for the most part, are only half-truths; that unity of opinion, unless resulting from the fullest and freest comparison of opposite opinions, is not desirable, and diversity not an evil, but a good, until mankind are much more capable than at present of recognizing all sides of the truth, are principles applicable to men's modes of action not less than to their opinions. As it is useful that while mankind are imperfect there should be different opinions, so it is that there should be different experiments of living; that free scope should be given to varieties of character, short of injury to others; and that the worth of different modes of life should be proved practically, when anyone thinks fit to try them. It is desirable, in short, that in things which do not primarily concern others individuality should assert itself. Where not the person's own character but the traditions or customs of other people are the rule of conduct, there is wanting one of the principal ingredients of human happiness, and quite the chief ingredient of individual and social progress.

. . . .

Having said that individuality is the same thing with development, and that it is only the cultivation of individuality which produces, or can produce, well-developed human beings, I might here close the argument; for what more or better can be said of any condition of human affairs than that it brings human beings themselves nearer to the best thing they can be? Or what worse can be said of any obstruction to good than that it prevents this? Doubtless, however, these considerations will not suffice to convince those who most need convincing; and it is necessary further to show that these developed human beings are of some use to the undeveloped—to point out to those who do not desire liberty, and would not avail themselves of it, that they may be in some intelligible manner rewarded for allowing other people to make use of it without hindrance.

In the first place, then, I would suggest that they might possibly learn something from them. It will not be denied by anybody that originality is a valuable element in human affairs. There is always need of persons not only to discover new truths and point out when what were once truths are true no longer, but also to commence new practices and set the example of more enlightened conduct and better taste and sense in human life. This cannot well be gainsaid by anybody who does not believe that the world has already attained perfection in all its ways and practices. It is true that this benefit is not capable of being rendered by everybody alike; there are but few persons, in comparison with the whole of mankind, whose experiments, if adopted by others, would be likely to be any improvement on established practice. But these few are the salt of the earth; without them, human life would become a stagnant pool. Not only is it they who introduce good things which did not before exist; it is they who keep the life in those which already exist. If there were nothing new to be done, would human intellect cease to be necessary? Would it be a reason why those who do the old things should forget why they are done, and do them like cattle, not like human beings? There is only too great a tendency in the best beliefs and practices to degenerate into the mechanical; and unless there were a succession of persons whose ever-recurring originality prevents the grounds of those beliefs and practices from becoming merely traditional, such dead matter would not resist the smallest shock from anything really alive, and there would be no reason why civilization should not die out, as in the Byzantine Empire. . . .

I have said that it is important to give the freest scope possible to uncustomary things, in order that it may in time appear which of these are fit to be converted into customs. But independence of action and disregard of custom are not solely deserving of encouragement for the chance they afford that better modes of action, and customs more worthy of general adoption, may be struck out; nor is it only persons of decided mental superiority who have a just claim to carry on their lives in their own way. There is no reason that all human existence should be constructed on some one or some small number of patterns. If a person possesses any tolerable amount of common sense and experience, his own mode of laying out his existence is the best, not because it is the best in itself, but because it is his own mode. Human beings are not like sheep; and even sheep are not undistinguishably alike. A man cannot get a coat or a pair of boots to fit him unless they are either made to his measure or he has a whole warehouseful to choose from; and is it easier to fit him with a life than with a coat, or are human beings more like one another in their whole physical and spiritual con-formation than in the shape of their feet? If it were only that people have diversities of taste, that is reason enough for not attempting to shape them all after one model. But different persons also require different conditions for their spiritual development; and can no more exist healthily in the same moral than all the variety of plants can in the same physical, atmosphere and climate. The same things which are helps to one person toward the cultivation of his higher nature are hindrances to another. The same mode of life is a healthy excitement to one, keeping all his faculties of action and enjoyment in their best order, while to another it is a distracting burden which suspends or crushes all internal life. Such are the differences among human beings in their sources of pleasure, the susceptibilities of pain, and the operation on them of different physical and moral agencies that, unless there is a corresponding diversity in their modes of life, they neither obtain their fair share of happiness, nor grow up to the mental, moral, and aesthetic stature of which their nature is capable. . . .

Ethics Founded on Reason

·IMMANUEL KANT·

In this excerpt from his Groundwork of the Metaphysics of Morals, *Kant (1724–1804) tries to show that ethics is founded on reason, not on inclinations. It is acting from duty, not from inclination, that endows an action with moral value. But what is the source of the duties that structure the moral life? These are founded on reason. The universalizability criterion provides a logical test for determining whether an action is morally permissible.*

Chapter 1
Passage from Ordinary Rational Knowledge of Morality
to Philosophical Knowledge

[The Good Will]

It is impossible to conceive anything at all in the world, or even out of it, which can be taken as good without qualification, except a **good will**. Intelligence, wit, judgement, and any other *talents* of the mind we may care to name, or courage, resolution, and constancy of purpose, as qualities of *temperament*, are without doubt good and desirable in many respects; but they can also be extremely bad and hurtful when the will is not good which has to make use of these gifts of nature, and which for this reason has the term "*character*" applied to its peculiar quality. It is exactly the same with *gifts of fortune*. Power, wealth, honour, even health and that complete well-being and contentment with one's state which goes by the name of "*happiness*", produce boldness, and as a consequence often overboldness as well, unless a good will is present by which their influence on the mind—and so too the whole principle of action—may be corrected and adjusted to universal ends; not to mention that a rational and impartial spectator can never feel approval in contemplating the uninterrupted prosperity of a being graced by no touch of a pure and good will, and that consequently a good will seems to constitute the indispensable condition of our very worthiness to be happy.

Some qualities are even helpful to this good will itself and can make its task very much easier. They have none the less no inner unconditioned worth, but rather presuppose a good will which sets a limit to the esteem in which they are rightly held and does not permit us to regard them as absolutely good. Moderation in affections and passions, self-control, and sober reflexion are not only good in many respects; they may even seem to constitute part of the *inner* worth of a person. Yet they are far from being properly described as good without qualification (however unconditionally they have been commended by the ancients). For without the principles of a good will they may become exceedingly bad; and the very coolness of a scoundrel makes him, not merely more dangerous, but also immediately more abominable in our eyes than we should have taken him to be without it.

[The Good Will and Its Results]

A good will is not good because of what it effects or accomplishes—because of its fitness for attaining some proposed end: it is good through its willing alone—that is, good in itself. Considered in itself it is to be esteemed beyond comparison as far higher than anything it could ever bring about merely in order to favour some inclination or, if you like, the sum total of inclinations. Even if, by some special disfavour of destiny or by the niggardly endowment of step-motherly nature, this will is entirely lacking in power to carry out its intentions; if by its utmost effort it still accomplishes nothing, and only good will is left (not, admittedly, as a mere wish, but as the straining of every means so far as they are in our control); even then it would still shine like a jewel for its own sake as something which has its full value in itself. Its usefulness or fruitlessness can neither add to, nor subtract from, this value. Its usefulness would be merely, as it were, the setting which enables us to handle it better in our ordinary dealings or to attract the attention of those not yet sufficiently expert, but not to commend it to experts or to determine its value.

[The Good Will and Duty]

We have now to elucidate the concept of a will estimable in itself and good apart from any further end. This concept, which is already present in a naturally sound understanding and requires not so much to be taught as merely to be clarified, always holds the highest place in estimating the total worth of our actions and constitutes the condition of all the rest. We will therefore take up the concept of **duty**, which includes that of a good will, exposed, however, to certain subjective limitations and obstacles. These, so far from hiding a good will

ETHICS FOUNDED
ON REASON

or disguising it, rather bring it out by contrast and make it shine forth more brightly.

[The Motive of Duty]

I will here pass over all actions already recognized as contrary to duty, however useful they may be with a view to this or that end; for about these the question does not even arise whether they could have been done *for the sake of duty* inasmuch as they are directly opposed to it. I will also set aside actions which in fact accord with duty, yet for which men have *no immediate inclination*, but perform them because impelled to do so by some other inclination. For there it is easy to decide whether the action which accords with duty has been done *from duty* or from some purpose of self-interest. This distinction is far more difficult to perceive when the action accords with duty and the subject has in addition an *immediate* inclination to the action. For example, it certainly accords with duty that a grocer should not overcharge his inexperienced customer; and where there is much competition a sensible shopkeeper refrains from so doing and keeps to a fixed and general price for everybody so that a child can buy from him just as well as anyone else. Thus people are served *honestly;* but this is not nearly enough to justify us in believing that the shopkeeper has acted in this way from duty or from principles of fair dealing; his interests required him to do so. We cannot assume him to have in addition an immediate inclination towards his customers, leading him, as it were out of love, to give no man preference over another in the matter of price. Thus the action was done neither from duty nor from immediate inclination, but solely from purposes of self-interest.

On the other hand, to preserve one's life is a duty, and besides this every one has also an immediate inclination to do so. But on account of this the often anxious precautions taken by the greater part of mankind for this purpose have no inner worth, and the maxim of their action is without moral content. They do protect their lives *in conformity with duty,* but not *from the motive of duty.* When, on the contrary, disappointments and hopeless misery have quite taken away the taste for life; when a wretched man, strong in soul and more angered at his fate than faint-hearted or cast down, longs for death and still preserves his life without loving it—not from inclination or fear but from duty; then indeed his maxim has a moral content.

To help others where one can is a duty, and besides this there are many spirits of so sympathetic a temper that, without any further motive of vanity or self-interest, they find an inner pleasure in spreading happiness around them and can take delight in the contentment of others as their own work. Yet I maintain that in such a case an action of this kind, however right and however amiable it may be, has still no genuinely moral worth. It stands on the same footing as other inclinations—for example, the inclination for honour, which if fortunate enough to hit on something beneficial and right and consequently honourable, deserves praise and encouragement, but not esteem; for its maxim lacks moral content, namely, the performance of such actions, not from inclination, but *from duty.* Suppose then that the mind of this friend of man was overclouded by sorrows of his own which extinguished all sympathy with the fate of others, but that he still had power to help those in distress, though no longer stirred by the need of others because sufficiently occupied with his own; and suppose that, when no longer moved by any inclination, he tears himself out of this deadly insensibility and does the action without any inclination for the sake of duty alone; then for the first time his action has its genuine moral worth. Still further: if nature had implanted little sympathy in this or that man's heart; if (being in other respects an honest fellow) he were cold in temperament and indifferent to the sufferings of others — perhaps because, being endowed with the special gift of patience and robust endurance in his own sufferings, he assumed the like in others or even demanded it; if such a man (who would in truth not be the worst product of nature) were not exactly fashioned by her to be a philanthropist, would he not still find in himself a source from which he might draw a worth far higher than any that a good-natured termperament can have? Assuredly he would. It is precisely in this that the worth of character begins to show — a moral worth and beyond all comparison the highest — namely that he does good, not from inclination, but from duty.

To assure one's own happiness is a duty (at least indirectly); for discontent with one's state, in a press of cares and amidst unsatisfied wants, might easily become a great *temptation to the transgression of duty.* But here also, apart from regard to duty, all men have already of themselves the strongest and deepest inclination towards happiness, because precisely in this Idea of happiness there is combined the sum total of inclinations. The prescription for happiness is, however, often so constituted as greatly to interfere with some inclinations, and yet men cannot form under the name of "happiness" any determinate and assured conception of the satisfaction of all inclinations as a sum. Hence it is not to be wondered at that a single inclination which is determinate as to what it promises and as to the time of its satisfaction may outweigh a wavering Idea; and that a man, for example, a sufferer from gout, may choose to enjoy what he fancies and put up with what he can — on the ground that on balance he has here at least not killed the enjoyment of the present moment because of some possibly groundless expectations of the good fortune supposed to attach to soundness of health. But in this case also, when the universal inclination towards happiness has failed to determine his will, when good health, at least for him, has not entered into his calculations as so necessary, what remains over, here as in other cases, is a law — the law of furthering his happiness, not from inclination, but from duty — and in this for the first time his conduct has a real moral worth.

It is doubtless in this sense that we should understand too the passages from Scripture in which we are commanded to love our neighbour and even our enemy. For love out of inclination cannot be commanded; but kindness done from duty — although no inclination impels us, and even although natural and unconquerable disinclination stands in our way — is *practical,* and not *pathological,* love, residing in the will and not in the propensions of feeling, in principles of action and not of melting compassion; and it is this practical love alone which can be an object of command.

ETHICS FOUNDED
ON REASON

Chapter II
Passage from Popular Moral Philosophy to a Metaphysic of Morals
[Imperatives in General]

Everything in nature works in accordance with laws. Only a rational being has the power to act *in accordance with his idea* of laws — that is, in accordance with principles — and only so has he a *will*. Since *reason* is required in order to derive actions from laws, the will is nothing but practical reason. If reason infallibly determines the will, then in a being of this kind the actions which are recognized to be objectively necessary are also subjectively necessary — that is to say, the will is then a power to choose *only that* which reason independently of inclination recognizes to be practically necessary, that is, to be good. But if reason solely by itself is not sufficient to determine the will; if the will is exposed also to subjective conditions (certain impulsions) which do not always harmonize with the objective ones; if, in a word, the will is not *in itself* completely in accord with reason (as actually happens in the case of men); then actions which are recognized to be objectively necessary are subjectively contingent, and the determining of such a will in accordance with objective laws is *necessitation*. That is to say, the relation of objective laws to a will not good through and through is conceived as one in which the will of a rational being, although it is determined by principles of reason, does not necessarily follow these principles in virtue of its own nature.

The conception of an objective principle so far as this principle is necessitating for a will is called a command (or reason), and the formula of this command is called an **Imperative**.

All imperatives are expressed by an *"ought" (Sollen)*. By this they mark the relation of an objective law of reason to a will which is not necessarily determined by this law in virtue of its subjective constitution (the relation of necessitation). They say that something would be good to do or to leave undone; only they say it to a will which does not always do a thing because it has been informed that this is a good thing to do. The practically *good* is that which determines the will by concepts of reason, and therefore not by subjective causes, but objectively — that is, on grounds valid for every rational being as such. It is distinguished from the *pleasant* as that which influences the will, not as a principle of reason valid for every one, but solely through the medium of sensation by purely subjective causes valid only for the senses of this person or that.

A perfectly good will would thus stand quite as much under objective laws (laws of the good), but it could not on this account be conceived as *necessitated* to act in conformity with law, since of itself, in accordance with its subjective constitution, it can be determined only by the concept of the good. Hence for the *divine* will, and in general for a *holy* will, there are no imperatives: *"I ought"* is here out of place, because *"I will"* is already of itself necessarily in harmony with the law. Imperatives are in consequence only formulae for expressing the relation of objective laws of willing to the subjective imperfection of the will of this or that rational being—for example, of the human will.

[Classification of Imperatives]

All *imperatives* command either *hypothetically* or *categorically*. Hypothetical imperatives declare a possible action to be practically necessary as a means to the attainment of something else that one wills (or that one may will). A categorical imperative would be one which represented an action as objectively necessary in itself apart from its relation to a further end.

Every practical law represents a possible action as good and therefore as necessary for a subject whose actions are determined by reason. Hence all imperatives are formulae for determining an action which is necessary in accordancce with the principle of a will in some sense good. If the action would be good solely as a means *to something else*, the imperative is *hypothetical*; if the action is represented as good *in itself* and therefore necessary, in virtue of its principle, for a will which of itself accords with reason, then the imperative is *categorical*.

An imperative therefore tells me which of my possible actions would be good; and it formulates a practical rule for a will that does not perform an action straight away because the action is good—whether because the subject does not always know that it is good or because, even if he did know this, he might still act on maxims contrary to the objective principles of practical reason.

A hypothetical imperative thus says only that an action is good for some purpose or other, either *possible* or *actual*. In the first case it is a **problematic** practical principle; in the second case an **assertoric** practical principle. A categorical imperative, which declares an action to be objectively necessary in itself without reference to some purpose—that is, even without any further end—ranks as an **apodeictic** practical principle.

Everything that is possible only through the efforts of some rational being can be conceived as a possible purpose of some will; and consequently there are in fact innumerable principles of action so far as action is thought necessary in order to achieve some possible purpose which can be effected by it. All sciences have a practical part consisting of problems which suppose that some end is possible for us and of imperatives which tell us how it is to be attained. Hence the latter can in general be called imperatives of **skill**. Here there is absolutely no question about the rationality or goodness of the end, but only about what must be done to attain it. A prescription required by a doctor in order to cure his man completely and one required by a poisoner in order to make sure of killing him are of equal value so far as each serves to effect its purpose perfectly. Since in early youth we do not know what ends may present themselves to us in the course of life, parents seek above all to make their children learn things *of many kinds*; they provide carefully for *skill* in the use of means to all sorts of *arbitrary* ends, of none of which can they be certain that it could not in the future become an actual purpose of their ward, while it is always *possible* that he might adopt it. Their care in this matter is so great that they commonly neglect on this account to form and correct the judgement of their children about the worth of things which they might possibly adopt as ends.

There is, however, *one* end that can be presupposed as actual in all rational beings (so far as they are dependent beings to whom imperatives apply); and thus there is one purpose which they not only *can* have, but which we can assume with certainty that they all *do* have by a natural necessity—the purpose, namely, of *happiness*. A hypothetical imperative which affirms the practical necessity of an action as a means to the furtherance of happiness is **assertoric**. We may represent it, not simply as necessary to an uncertain, merely possible purpose, but as necessary to a purpose which we can presuppose a priori and with certainty to be present in every man because it belongs to his very being. Now skill in the choice of means to one's own greatest well-being can be called *prudence* in the narrowest sense. Thus an imperative concerned with the choice of means to one's own happiness—that is, a precept of prudence—still remains *hypothetical*; an action is commanded, not absolutely, but only as a means to a further purpose.

Finally, there is an imperative which, without being based on, and conditioned by, any further purpose to be attained by a certain line of conduct, enjoins this conduct immediately. This imperative is **categorical**. It is concerned, not with the matter of the action and its presumed results, but with its form and with the principle from which it follows; and what is essentially good in the action consists in the mental disposition, let the consequences be what they may. This imperative may be called the imperative of **morality**.

Willing in accordance with these three kinds of principle is also sharply distinguished by a *dissimilarity* in the necessitation of the will. To make this dissimilarity obvious we should, I think, name these kinds of principle most appropriately in their order if we said they were either *rules* of skill or *counsels* of prudence or *commands (laws)* of morality. For only *law* carries with it the concept of an *unconditioned*, and yet objective and so universally valid, *necessity*; and commands are laws which must be obeyed—that is, must be followed even against inclination. *Counsel* does indeed involve necessity, but necessity valid only under a subjective and contingent condition—namely, if this or that man counts this or that as belonging to his happiness. As against this, a categorical imperative is limited by no condition and can quite precisely be called a command, as being absolutely, although practically, necessary. We could also call imperatives of the first kind *technical* (concerned with art); of the second kind *pragmatic* (concerned with well-being); of the third kind *moral* (concerned with free conduct as such—that is, with morals).

[How Are Imperatives Possible?]

The question now arises "How are all these imperatives possible?" This question does not ask how we can conceive the execution of an action commanded by the imperative, but merely how we can conceive the necessitation of the will expressed by the imperative in setting us a task. How an imperative of skill is possible requires no special discussion. Who wills the end, wills (so far as reason has decisive influence on his actions) also the means which are indispensably necessary and in his power. So far as willing is concerned, this proposition is analytic: for in my willing of an object as an effect there is already conceived the causality of myself as an acting cause—that is, the use of means; and from the concept of willing an end the imperative merely extracts the concept of actions necessary to this end. (Synthetic propositions are required in order to determine the means to a proposed end, but these are concerned, not with the reason for performing the act of will, but with the cause which produces the object.) That in order to divide a line into two equal parts on a sure principle I must from its ends describe two intersecting arcs—this is admittedly taught by mathematics only in synthetic propositions; but when I know that the aforesaid effect can be produced only by such an action, the proposition "If I fully will the effect, I also will the action required for it" is analytic; for it is one and the same thing to conceive something as an effect possible in a certain way through me and to conceive myself as acting in the same way with respect to it.

If it were only as easy to find a determinate concept of happiness, the imperatives of prudence would agree entirely with those of skill and would be equally analytic. For here as there it could alike be said "Who wills the end, wills also (necessarily, if he accords with reason) the sole means which are in his power." Unfortunately, however, the concept of happiness is so indeterminate a concept that although every man wants to attain happiness, he can never say definitely and in unison with himself what it really is that he wants and wills. The reason for this is that all the elements which belong to the concept of happiness are without exception empirical—that is, they must be borrowed from experience; but that none the less there is required for the Idea of happiness an absolute whole, a maximum of well-being in my present, and in every future, state. Now it is impossible for the most intelligent, and at the same time most powerful, but nevertheless finite, being to form here a determinate concept of what he really wills. Is it riches that he wants? How much anxiety, envy, and pestering might he not bring in this way on his own head! Is it knowledge and insight? This might perhaps merely give him an eye so sharp that it would make evils at present hidden from him and yet unavoidable seem all the more frightful, or would add a load of still further needs to the desires which already give him trouble enough. Is it long life? Who will guarantee that it would not be a long misery? Is it at least health? How often has infirmity of body kept a man from excesses into which perfect health would have let him fall—and so on. In short, he has no principle by which he is able to decide with complete certainty what will make him truly happy, since for this he would require omniscience. Thus we cannot act on determinate principles in order to be happy, but only on empirical counsels, for example, of diet, frugality, politeness, reserve, and so on—things which experience shows contribute most to well-being on the average. From this it follows that imperatives of prudence, speaking strictly, do not command at all—that is, cannot exhibit actions objectively as practically *necessary*; that they are rather to be taken as recommendations (*consilia*), than as commands (*praecepta*), of reason; that the problem of determining certainly and universally what action will promote the happiness of a rational being is completely insoluble;

ETHICS FOUNDED
ON REASON

and consequently that in regard to this there is no imperative possible which in the strictest sense could command us to do what will make us happy, since happiness is an Ideal, not of reason, but of imagination — an Ideal resting merely on empirical grounds, of which it is vain to expect that they should determine an action by which we could attain the totality of a series of consequences which is in fact infinite. Nevertheless, if we assume that the means to happiness could be discovered with certainty, this imperative of prudence would be an analytic practical proposition; for it differs from the imperative of skill only in this — that in the latter the end is merely possible, while in the former the end is given. In spite of this difference, since both command solely the means to something assumed to be willed as an end, the imperative which commands him who wills the end to will the means is in both cases analytic. Thus there is likewise no difficulty in regard to the possiblity of an imperative of prudence.

As against this, the question "How is the imperative of *morality* possible?" is the only one in need of a solution; for it is in no way hypothetical, and consequently we cannot base the objective necessity which it affirms on any presupposition, as we can with hypothetical imperatives. Only we must never forget here that it is impossible to settle *by an example*, and so empirically, whether there is any imperative of this kind at all: we must rather suspect that all imperatives which seem to be categorical may none the less be covertly hypothetical. Take, for example, the saying "Thou shalt make no false promises." Let us assume that the necessity for this abstention is no mere advice for the avoidance of some further evil — as it might be said "You ought not to make a lying promise lest, when this comes to light, you destroy your credit." Let us hold, on the contrary, that an action of this kind must be considered as bad in itself, and that the imperative of prohibition is therefore categorical. Even so, we cannot with any certainty show by an example that the will is determined here solely by the law without any further motive, although it may appear to be so; for it is always possible that fear of disgrace, perhaps also hidden dread of other risks, may unconsciously influence the will. Who can prove by experience that a cause is not present? Experience shows only that it is not perceived. In such a case, however, the so-called moral imperative, which as such appears to be categorical and unconditioned, would in fact be only a pragmatic prescription calling attention to our advantage and merely bidding us take this into account.

We shall thus have to investigate the possiblity of a *categorical* imperative entirely a priori, since here we do not enjoy the advantage of having its reality given in experience and so of being obliged merely to explain, and not to establish, its possibility. So much, however, can be seen provisionally — that the categorical imperative alone purports to be a practical **law**, while all the rest may be called *principles* of the will but not laws; for an action necessary merely in order to achieve an arbitrary purpose can be considered as in itself contingent, and we can always escape from the precept if we abandon the purpose; whereas an unconditioned command does not leave it open to the will to do the opposite at its discretion and therefore alone carries with it that necessity which we demand from a law.

In the second place, with this categorical imperative or law of morality the reason for our difficulty (in comprehending its possibility) is a very serious one. We have here a synthetic a priori practical proposition; and since in theoretical knowledge there is so much difficulty in comprehending the possiblity of propositions of this kind, it may readily be gathered that in practical knowledge the difficulty will be no less.

[The Formula of Universal Law]

In this task we wish first to enquire whether perhaps the mere concept of a categorical imperative may not also provide us with the formula containing the only proposition that can be a categorical imperative; for even when we know the purport of such an abolute command, the question of its possibility will still require a special and troublesome effort, which we postpone to the final chapter.

When I conceive a *hypothetical* imperative in general, I do not know beforehand what it will contain — until its condition is given. But if I conceive a *categorical* imperative, I know at once what it contains. For since besides the law this imperative contains only the necessity that our maxim should conform to this law, while the law, as we have seen, contains no condition to limit it, there remains nothing over to which the maxim has to conform except the universality of a law as such; and it is this conformity alone that the imperative properly asserts to be necessary.

There is therefore only a single categorical imperative and it is this: *"Act only on that maxim through which you can at the same time will that it should become a universal law."*

Now if all imperatives of duty can be derived from this one imperative as their principle, then even although we leave it unsettled whether what we call duty may not be an empty concept, we shall still be able to show at least what we understand by it and what the concept means.

[The Formula of the Law of Nature]

Since the universality of the law governing the production of effects constitutes what is properly called *nature* in its most general sense (nature as regards its form) — that is, the existence of things so far as determined by universal laws — the universal imperative of duty may also run as follows: *"Act as if the maxim of your action were to become through your will a* Universal Law of Nature.*"*

[Illustrations]

We will now enumerate a few duties, following their customary division into duties towards self and duties towards others and into perfect and imperfect duties.

1. A man feels sick of life as the result of a series of misfortunes that has mounted to the point of despair, but he is still so far in possession of his reason as to ask himself whether taking his own life may not be contrary to his duty to himself. He now applies the test "Can the maxim of my action really become a universal law of nature?" His

maxim is "From self-love I make it my principle to shorten my life if its continuance threatens more evil than it promises pleasure." The only further question to ask is whether this principle of self-love can become a universal law of nature. It is then seen at once that a system of nature by whose law the very same feeling whose function (*Bestimmung*) is to stimulate the furtherance of life should actually destroy life would contradict itself and consequently could not subsist as a system of nature. Hence this maxim cannot possibly hold as a universal law of nature and is therefore entirely opposed to the supreme principle of all duty.

2. Another finds himself driven to borrowing money because of need. He well knows that he will not be able to pay it back; but he sees too that he will get no loan unless he gives a firm promise to pay it back within a fixed time. He is inclined to make such a promise; but he has still enough conscience to ask "Is it not unlawful and contrary to duty to get out of difficulties in this way?" Supposing, however, he did resolve to do so, the maxim of his action would run thus: "Whenever I believe myself short of money, I will borrow money and promise to pay it back, though I know that this will never be done." Now this principle of self-love or personal advantage is perhaps quite compatible with my own entire future welfare; only there remains the question "Is it right?" I therefore transform the demand of self-love into a universal law and frame my question thus: "How would things stand if my maxim became a universal law?" I then see straight away that this maxim can never rank as a universal law and be self-consistent, but must necessarily contradict itself. For the universality of a law that every one believing himself to be in need may make any promise he pleases with the intention not to keep it would make promising, and the very purpose of promising, itself impossible, since no one would believe he was being promised anything, but would laugh at utterances of this kind as empty shams.

3. A third finds in himself a talent whose cultivation would make him a useful man for all sorts of purposes. But he sees himself in comfortable circumstances, and he prefers to give himself up to pleasure rather than to bother about increasing and improving his fortunate natural aptitudes. Yet he asks himself further "Does my maxim of neglecting my natural gifts, besides agreeing in itself with my tendency to indulgence, agree also with what is called duty?" He then sees that a system of nature could indeed always subsist under such a universal law, although (like the South Sea Islanders) every man should let his talents rust and should be bent on devoting his life solely to idleness, indulgence, procreation, and, in a word, to enjoyment. Only he cannot possibly **will** that this should become a universal law of nature or should be implanted in us as such a law by a natural instinct. For as a rational being he necessarily wills that all

his powers should be developed, since they serve him, and are given him, for all sorts of possible ends.

4. Yet a *fourth* is himself flourishing, but he sees others who have to struggle with great hardships (and whom he could easily help); and he thinks "What does it matter to me? Let every one be as happy as Heaven wills or as he can make himself; I won't deprive him of anything; I won't even envy him; only I have no wish to contribute anything to his well-being or to his support in distress!" Now admittedly if such an attitude were a universal law of nature, mankind could get on perfectly well—better no doubt than if everybody prates about sympathy and good will, and even takes pains, on occasion, to practise them, but on the other hand cheats where he can, traffics in human rights, or violates them in other ways. But although it is possible that a universal law of nature could subsist in harmony with this maxim, yet it is impossible to **will** that such a principle should hold everywhere as a law of nature. For a will which decided in this way would be at variance with itself, since many a situation might arise in which the man needed love and sympathy from others, and in which, by such a law of nature sprung from his own will, he would rob himself of all hope of the help he wants for himself.

[The Canon of Moral Judgement]

These are some of the many actual duties—or at least of what we take to be such—whose derivation from the single principle cited above leaps to the eye. We must *be able to will* that a maxim of our action should become a universal law—this is the general canon for all moral judgement of action. Some actions are so constituted that their maxim cannot even be *conceived* as a universal law of nature without contradiction, let alone be *willed* as what *ought* to become one. In the case of others we do not find this inner impossibility, but it is still impossible to *will* that their maxim should be raised to the universality of a law of nature, because such a will would contradict itself. It is easily seen that the first kind of action is opposed to strict or narrow (rigorous) duty, the second only to wider (meritorious) duty; and thus that by these examples all duties—so far as the type of obligation is concerned (not the object of dutiful action)—are fully set out in their dependence on our single principle.

If we now attend to ourselves whenever we transgress a duty, we find that we in fact do not will that our maxim should become a universal law—since this is impossible for us—but rather that its opposite should remain a law universally; we only take the liberty of making an *exception* to it for ourselves (or even just for this once) to the advantage of our inclination. Consequently if we weighed it all up from one and the same point of view—that of reason—we should find a contradiction in our own will, the contradiction that a certain principle should be objectively necessary as a universal law and yet subjectively should not hold universally but should admit of exceptions. Since, however, we first consider our action from the point of view of a will wholly in accord with reason, and then consider precisely the same action from the point of view of a will affected by inclination, there is here actually no contradiction, but rather an opposition of inclination to the precept of reason (*antagonismus*), whereby the universality of the principle (*universalitas*) is turned into a mere generality (*generalitas*) so that the practical principle of reason may meet our maxim half-way. This procedure, though in our own impartial judgement it cannot be justified, proves none the less that we in fact recognize the validity of the categorical imperative and (with all respect for it) merely permit ourselves a few exceptions which are, as we pretend, inconsiderable and apparently forced upon us.

We have thus at least shown this much — that if duty is a concept which is to have meaning and real legislative authority for our actions, this can be expressed only in categorical imperatives and by no means in hypothetical ones. At the same time — and this is already a great deal — we have set forth distinctly, and determinately for every type of application, the content of the categorical imperative, which must contain the principle of all duty (if there is to be such a thing at all). But we are still not so far advanced as to prove a priori that there actually is an imperative of this kind — that there is a practical law which by itself commands absolutely and without any further motives, and that the following of this law is duty.

[The Formula of the End in Itself]

The will is conceived as a power of determining oneself to action *in accordance with the idea of certain laws*. And such a power can be found only in rational beings. Now what serves the will as a subjective ground of its self-determination is an *end*; and this, if it is given by reason alone, must be equally valid for all rational beings. What, on the other hand, contains merely the ground of the possibility of an action whose effect as an end is called a *means*. The subjective ground of a desire is an *impulsion (Triebfeder)*; the objective ground of a volition is a *motive (Bewegungsgrund)*. Hence the difference between subjective ends, which are based on impulsions, and objective ends, which depend on motives valid for every rational being. Practical principles are *formal* if they abstract from all subjective ends; they are *material*, on the other hand, if they are based on such ends and consequently on certain impulsions. Ends that a rational being adopts arbitrarily as *effects* of his action (material ends) are in every case only relative; for it is solely their relation to special characteristics in the subject's power of appetition which gives them their value. Hence this value can provide no universal principles, no principles valid and necessary for all rational beings and also for every volition — that is, no practical laws. Consequently all these relative ends can be the ground only of hypothetical imperatives.

Suppose, however, there were something *whose existence* has *in itself* an absolute value, something which as *an end in itself* could be a ground of determinate laws; then in it, and in it alone, would there be the ground of a possible categorical imperative — that is, of a practical law.

Now I say that man, and in general every rational being, *exists* as an end in himself, *not merely as a means* for arbitrary use by this or that will: he must in all his actions, whether they are directed to himself or to other rational beings, always be viewed *at the same time as an end.* All the objects of inclination have only a conditioned value; for if there were not these inclinations and the needs grounded on them, their object would be valueless. Inclinations themselves, as sources of needs, are so far from having an absolute value to make them desirable for their own sake that it must rather be the universal wish of every rational being to be wholly free from them. Thus the value of all objects that can *be produced* by our action is always conditioned. Beings whose existence depends, not on our will, but on nature, have none the less, if they are non-rational beings, only a relative value as means and are consequently called *things.* Rational beings, on the other hand, are called *persons* because their nature already marks them out as ends in themselves—that is, as something which ought not to be used merely as a means—and consequently imposes to that extent a limit on all arbitrary treatment of them (and is an object of reverence). Persons, therefore, are not merely subjective ends whose existence as an effect of our actions has a value *for us:* they are *objective ends*—that is, things whose existence is in itself an end, and indeed an end such that in its place we can put no other end to which they should serve *simply* as means; for unless this is so, nothing at all of *absolute* value would be found anywhere. But if all value were conditioned—that is, contingent—then no supreme principle could be found for reason at all.

If then there is to be a supreme practical principle and—so far as the human will is concerned—a categorical imperative, it must be such that from the idea of something which is necessarily an end for every one because it is an *end in itself* it forms an *objective* principle of the will and consequently can serve as a practical law. The ground of this principle is: *Rational nature exists as an end in itself.* This is the way in which a man necessarily conceives his own existence; it is therefore so far a *subjective* principle of human actions. But it is also the way in which every other rational being conceives his existence on the same rational ground which is valid also for me; hence it is at the same time an *objective* principle, from which, as a supreme practical ground, it must be possible to derive all laws for the will. The practical imperative will therefore be as follows: *Act in such a way that you always treat humanity, whether in your own person or in the person of any other, never simply as a means, but always at the same time as an end.* We will now consider whether this can be carried out in practice.

[Illustrations]

Let us keep to our previous examples.

First, as regards the concept of necessary duty to oneself, the man who contemplates suicide will ask "Can my action be compatible with the Idea of humanity *as an end in itself?*" If he does away with himself in order to escape from a painful situation, he is making use of a person merely as a *means* to maintain a tolerable state of affairs till the end of his life. But man is not a thing—not something to be used *merely* as a means: he must always in all his actions be regarded as an end in himself. Hence I cannot dispose of man in my person by maiming, spoiling, or killing. (A more precise determination of this principle in order to avoid all misunderstanding—for example, about having limbs amputated to save myself or about exposing my life to danger in order to preserve it, and so on—I must here forgo: this question belongs to morals proper.)

Secondly, so far as necessary or strict duty to others is concerned, the man who has a mind to make a false promise to others will see at once that he is intending to make use of another man *merely as a means* to an end he does not share. For the man whom I seek to use for my own purposes by such a promise cannot possibly agree with my way of behaving to him, and so cannot himself share the end of the action. This incompatibility with the principle of duty to others leaps to the eye more obviously when we bring in examples of attempts on the freedom and property of others. For then it is manifest that a violator of the rights of man intends to use the person of others merely as a means without taking into consideration that, as rational beings, they ought always at the same time to be rated as ends—that is, only as beings who must themselves be able to share in the end of the very same action.

Thirdly, in regard to contingent (meritorious) duty to oneself, it is not enough that an action should refrain from conflicting with humanity in our own person as an end in itself: it must also *harmonize with this end*. Now there are in humanity capacities for greater perfection which form part of nature's purpose for humanity in our person. To neglect these can admittedly be compatible with the *maintenance* of humanity as an end in itself, but not with the *promotion* of this end.

Fourthly, as regards meritorious duties to others, the natural end which all men seek is their own happiness. Now humanity could no doubt subsist if everybody contributed nothing to the happiness of others but at the same time refrained from deliberately impairing their happiness. This is, however, merely to agree negatively and not positively with *humanity as an end in itself* unless every one endeavours also, so far as in him lies, to further the ends of others. For the ends of a subject who is an end in himself must, if this conception is to have its *full* effect in me, be also, as far as possible, *my* ends.

[The Formula of Autonomy]

This principle of humanity, and in general of every rational agent, *as an end in itself* (a principle which is the supreme limiting condition of every man's freedom of action) is not borrowed from experience; firstly, because it is universal, applying as it does to all rational beings as such, and no experience is adequate to determine universality; secondly, because in it humanity is conceived, not as an end of man (subjectively)—that is, as an object which, as a matter of fact, happens to be made an end—but as an objective end—one which, be our ends what they may, must, as a law, constitute the supreme limiting condition of all subjective ends and so must spring from pure reason. That is to say, the ground for every enactment of practical law lies *objectively in the rule* and in the form of universality which (according to our first principle) makes the rule capable of being a law (and indeed a law of nature); *subjectively*, however, it lies in the *end*; but (according to our second principle) the subject of all ends is to be found in every rational being as an end in himself. From this there now follows our third practical principle for the will—as the supreme condition of the will's conformity with universal practical reason—namely, the Idea *of the will of every rational being as a will which makes universal law.*

By this principle all maxims are repudiated which cannot accord with the will's own enactment of universal law. The will is therefore not merely subject to the law, but is so subject that it must be considered as also *making the law* for itself and precisely on this account as first of all subject to the law (of which it can regard itself as the author).

[The Exclusion of Interest]

Imperatives as formulated above—namely, the imperative enjoining conformity of actions to universal law on the analogy of a *natural order* and that enjoining the universal *supremacy* of rational beings in themselves *as ends*—did, by the mere fact that they were represented as categorical, exclude from their sovereign authority every admixture of interest as a motive. They were, however, merely *assumed* to be categorical because we were bound to make this assumption if we wished to explain the concept of duty. That there were practical propositions which commanded categorically could not itself be proved, any more than it can be proved in this chapter generally; but one thing could have been done—namely, to show that in willing for the sake of duty renunciation of all interest, as the specific mark distinguishing a categorical from a hypothetical imperative, was expressed in the very imperative itself by means of some determination inherent in it. This is what is done in the present third formulation of the principle—namely, in the Idea of the will of every rational being as *a will which makes universal law.*

Once we conceive a will of this kind, it becomes clear that while a will *which is subject to law* may be bound to this law by some interest, nevertheless a will which is itself a supreme lawgiver cannot possibly as such depend on any interest; for a will which is dependent in this way would itself require yet a further law in order to restrict the interest of self-love to the condition that this interest should itself be valid as a universal law.

Thus the *principle* that every human will is *a will which by all its maxims enacts universal law*—provided only that it were right in other ways—would be *well suited* to be a categorical imperative in this respect: that precisely because of the idea of making universal law it is *based on no interest* and consequently can alone among all possible imperatives be *unconditioned.* Or better still—to convert the proposition—if there is a categorical imperative (that is, a law for the will of every rational being), it can command us only to act always on the maxim of such a will in us as can at the same time look upon itself as making universal law; for only then is the practical principle and the imperative which we obey unconditioned, since it is wholly impossible for it to be based on any interest.

We need not now wonder, when we look back upon all the previous efforts that have been made to discover the principle of morality, why they have one and all been bound to fail. Their authors saw man as tied to laws by his duty, but it never occurred to them that he is subject only to *laws which are made by himself* and yet are *universal*, and that he is bound only to act in accordance with a will which is his own but has for its natural purpose the function of making universal law. For when they thought of man merely as subject to a law (whatever it might be), the law had to carry with it some interest in order to attract or compel, because it did not spring as a law from *his own* will: in order to conform with the law his will had to be necessitated by *something else* to act in a certain way. This absolutely inevitable conclusion meant that all the labour spent in trying to find a supreme principle of duty was lost beyond recall; for what they discovered was never duty, but only the necessity of acting from a certain interest. This interest might be one's own or another's; but on such a view the imperative was bound to be always a conditioned one and could not possibly serve as a moral law. I will therefore call my principle the principle of the **Autonomy** of the will in contrast with all others, which I consequently class under **Heteronomy**.

[The Formula of the Kingdom of Ends]

The concept of every rational being as one who must regard himself as making universal law by all the maxims of his will, and must seek to judge himself and his actions from this point of view, leads to a closely connected and very fruitful concept—namely, that of a *kingdom of ends.*

I understand by a "*kingdom*" a systematic union of different rational beings under common laws. Now since laws determine ends as regards their universal validity, we shall be able—if we abstract from the personal differences between rational beings, and also from all the content of their private ends—to conceive a whole of all ends in systematic conjunction (a whole both of rational beings as ends in themselves and also of the personal ends which each may set before himself); that is, we shall be able to conceive a kingdom of ends which is possible in accordance with the above principles.

For rational beings all stand under the *law* that each of them should treat himself and all others, *never merely as a means,* but always *at the same time as an end in himself.* But by so doing there arises a systematic union of rational beings under common objective laws—that is, a kingdom. Since these laws are directed precisely to the relation of such beings to one another as ends and means, this kingdom can be called a kingdom of ends (which is admittedly only an Ideal).

A rational being belongs to the kingdom of ends as a *member,* when, although he makes its universal laws, he is also himself subject to these laws. He belongs to it as its *head,* when as the maker of laws he is himself subject to the will of no other.

A rational being must always regard himself as making laws in a kingdom of ends which is possible through freedom of the will—whether it be as member or as head. The position of the latter he can maintain, not in virtue of the maxim of his will alone, but only if he is a completely independent being, without needs and with an unlimited power adequate to his will.

Thus morality consists in the relation of all action to the making of laws whereby alone a kingdom of ends is possible. This making of laws must be found in every rational being himself and must be able to spring from his will. The principle of his will is therefore never to perform an action except on a maxim such as can also be a universal law, and consequently such *that the will can regard itself as at the same time making universal law by means of its maxim*. Where maxims are not already by their very nature in harmony with this objective principle of rational beings as makers of universal law, the necessity of acting on this principle is practical necessitation—that is, *duty*. Duty does not apply to the head in a kingdom of ends, but it does apply to every member and to all members in equal measure.

The practical necessity of acting on this principle—that is, duty—is in no way based on feelings, impulses, and inclinations, but only on the relation of rational beings to one another, a relation in which the will of a rational being must always be regarded as *making universal law*, because otherwise he could not be conceived as *an end in himself*. Reason thus relates every maxim of the will, considered as making universal law, to every other will and also to every action towards oneself: it does so, not because of any further motive or future advantage, but from the Idea of the *dignity* of a rational being who obeys no law other than that which he at the same time enacts himself.

[The Dignity of Virtue]

In the kingdom of ends everything has either a *price* or a *dignity*. If it has a price, something else can be put in its place as an *equivalent*; if it is exalted above all price and so admits of no equivalent, then it has a dignity.

What is relative to universal human inclinations and needs has a *market price*; what, even without presupposing a need, accords with a certain taste—that is, with satisfaction in the mere purposeless play of our mental powers—has a *fancy price (Affektionspreis)*; but that which constitutes the sole condition under which anything can be an end in itself has not merely a relative value—that is, a price—but has an intrinsic value—that is, *dignity*.

Now morality is the only condition under which a rational being can be an end in himself; for only through this is it possible to be a law-making member in a kingdom of ends. Therefore morality, and humanity so far as it is capable of morality, is the only thing which has dignity. Skill and diligence in work have a market price; wit, lively imagination, and humour have a fancy price; but fidelity to promises and kindness based on principle (not on instinct) have an intrinsic worth. In default of these, nature and art alike contain nothing to put in their place; for their worth consists, not in the effects which result from them, not in the advantage or profit they produce, but in the attitudes of mind—that is, in the maxims of the will—which are ready in this way to manifest themselves in action even if they are not favoured by success. Such actions too need no recommendation from any subjective disposition or taste in order to meet with immediate favour and approval; they need no immediate propensity or feeling for themselves; they exhibit the will which performs them as an object of im-mediate reverence; nor is anything other than reason required to *impose* them upon the will, not to *coax* them from the will—which last would anyhow be a contradiction in the case of duties. This assessment reveals as dignity the value of such a mental attitude and puts it infinitely above all price, with which it cannot be brought into reckoning or comparison without, as it were, a profanation of its sanctity.

What is it then that entitles a morally good attitude of mind—or virtue—to make claims so high? It is nothing less than the *share* which it affords to a rational being *in the making of universal law*, and which therefore fits him to be a member in a possible kingdom of ends. For this he was already marked out in virtue of his own proper nature as an end in himself and consequently as a maker of laws in the kingdom of ends—as free in respect of all laws of nature, obeying only those laws which he makes himself and in virtue of which his maxims can have their part in the making of universal law (to which he at the same time subjects himself). For nothing can have a value other than that determined for it by the law. But the law-making which determines all value must for this reason have a dignity—that is, an unconditioned and incomparable worth—for the appreciation of which, as necessarily given by a rational being, the word *"reverence"* is the only becoming expression. *Autonomy* is therefore the ground of the dignity of human nature and of every rational nature.

[Review of the Formulae]

The aforesaid three ways of representing the principle of morality are at bottom merely so many formulations of precisely the same law, one of them by itself containing a combination of the other two. There is nevertheless a difference between them, which, however, is subjectively rather than objectively practical; that is to say, its purpose is to bring an Idea of reason nearer to intuition (in accordance with a certain analogy) and so nearer to feeling. All maxims have, in short,

1. a *form*, which consists in their universality; and in this respect the formula of the moral imperative is expressed thus: "Maxims must be chosen as if they had to hold as universal laws of nature";

2. a *matter*—that is, an end; and in this respect the formula says: "A rational being, as by his very nature an end and consequently an end in himself, must serve for every maxim as a condition limiting all merely relative and arbitrary ends";

3. a *complete determination* of all maxims by the following formula, namely: "All maxims as proceeding from our own making of law ought to harmonize with a possible kingdom of ends as a kingdom of nature." This progression may be said to take place through the categories of the *unity* of the form of will (its universality); of the *multiplicity* of its matter (its objects—that is, its ends); and of the *totality* or completeness of its systems of ends. It is, however, better if in moral *judgement* we proceed always in accordance with the strictest method and take as our basis the universal formula of the categorical imperative; *"Act on the maxim which can at the same time be made a universal law."* If, however, we wish also to secure accep-

tance for the moral law, it is very useful to bring one and the same action under the above-mentioned three concepts and so, as far as we can, to bring the universal formula nearer to intuition.

[Review of the Whole Argument]

We can now end at the point from which we started out at the beginning—namely, the concept of an unconditionally good will. The *will* is *absolutely good* if it cannot be evil—that is, if its maxim, when made into a universal law, can never be at variance with itself. This principle is therefore also its supreme law: "Act always on that maxim whose universality as a law you can at the same time will." This is the one principle on which a will can never be at variance with itself, and such an imperative is categorical. Because the validity of the will as a universal law for possible actions is analogous to the universal interconnexion of existent things in accordance with universal laws—which constitutes the formal aspect of nature as such—we can also express the categorical imperative as follows: *"Act on that maxim which can at the same time have for its object itself as a universal law of nature."* In this way we provide the formula for an absolutely good will.

Rational nature separates itself out from all other things by the fact that it sets itself an end. An end would thus be the matter of every good will. But in the Idea of a will which is absolutely good—good without any qualifying condition (namely, that it should attain this or that end)—there must be complete abstraction from every end that has to be *produced* (as something which would make every will only relatively good). Hence the end must here be conceived, not as an end to be produced, *but as a self-existent* end. It must therefore be conceived only negatively—that is, as an end against which we should never act, and consequently as one which in all our willing we must never rate *merely* as a means, but always at the same time as an end. Now this end can be nothing other than the subject of all possible ends himself, because this subject is also the subject of a will that may be absolutely good; for such a will cannot without contradiction be subordinated to any other object. The principle "So act in relation to every rational being (both to yourself and to others) that he may at the same time count in your maxim as an end in himself" is thus at bottom the same as the principle "Act on a maxim which at the same time contains in itself its own universal validity for every rational being." For to say that in using means to every end I ought to restrict my maxim by the condition that it should also be universally valid as a law for every subject is just the same as to say this—that a subject of ends, namely, a rational being himself, must be made the ground for all maxims of action, never *merely* as a means, but as a supreme condition restricting the use of every means—that is, always also as an end.

Now from this it unquestionably follows that every rational being, as an end in himself, must be able to regard himself as also the maker of universal law in respect of any law whatever to which he may be subjected: for it is precisely the fitness of his maxims to make universal law that marks him out as an end in himself. It follows equally that this dignity (or prerogative) of his above all the

ETHICS FOUNDED
ON REASON

mere things of nature carries with it the necessity of always choosing his maxims from the point of view of himself—and also of every other rational being—as a maker of law (and this is why they are called persons). It is in this way that a world of rational beings (*mundus intelligibilis*) is possible as a kingdom of ends—possible, that is, through the making of their own laws by all persons as its members. Accordingly every rational being must so act as if he were through his maxims always a law-making member in the universal kingdom of ends. The formal principle of such maxims is "So act as if your maxims had to serve at the same time as a universal law (for all rational beings)." Thus a kingdom of ends is possible only on the analogy of a kingdom of nature; yet the kingdom of ends is possible only through maxims—that is, self-imposed rules—while nature is possible only through laws concerned with causes whose action is necessitated from without. In spite of this difference, we give to nature as a whole, even although it is regarded as a machine, the name of a "kingdom of nature" so far as—and for the reason that—it stands in a relation to rational beings as its ends. Now a kingdom of ends would actually come into existence through maxims which the categorical imperative prescribes as a rule for all rational beings, *if these maxims were universally followed*. Yet even if a rational being were himself to follow such a maxim strictly, he cannot count on everybody else being faithful to it on this ground, nor can he be confident that the kingdom of nature and its purposive order will work in harmony with him, as a fitting member, towards a kingdom of ends made possible by himself—or, in other words, that it will favour his expectation of happiness. But in spite of this the law "Act on the maxims of a member who makes universal laws for a merely possible kingdom of ends" remains in full force, since its command is categorical. And precisely here we encounter the paradox that without any further end or advantage to be attained the mere dignity of humanity, that is, of rational nature in man—and consequently that reverence for a mere idea—should function as an inflexible precept for the will; and that it is just this freedom from dependence on interested motives which constitutes the sublimity of a maxim and the worthiness of every rational subject to be a law-making member in the kingdom of ends; for otherwise he would have to be regarded as subject only to the law of nature—the law of his own needs. Even if it were thought that both the kingdom of nature and the kingdom of ends were united under one head and that thus the latter kingdom ceased to be a mere Idea and achieved genuine reality, the Idea would indeed gain by this the addition of a strong motive, but never any increase in its intrinsic worth; for, even if this were so, it would still be necessary to conceive the unique and absolute lawgiver himself as judging the worth of rational beings solely by the disinterested behaviour they prescribed to themselves in virtue of this idea alone. The essence of things does not vary with their external relations; and where there is something which, without regard to such relations, constitutes by itself the absolute worth of man, it is by this that man must also be judged by everyone whatsoever—even by the Supreme Being. Thus *morality* lies in the relation of actions to the autonomy of the will—that is, to a possible making of universal law by means of its maxims. An action which is compatible with the autonomy of the will is *permitted*; one which does not harmonize with it is *forbidden*. A will whose maxims necessarily accord with the laws of autonomy is a *holy*, or absolutely good, will. The dependence of a will not absolutely good on the principle of autonomy (that is, moral necessitation) is *obligation*. Obligation can thus have no reference to a holy being. The objective necessity to act from obligation is called *duty*.

From what was said a little time ago we can now easily explain how it comes about that, although in the concept of duty we think of subjection to the law, yet we also at the same time attribute to the person who fulfils all his duties a certain sublimity and *dignity*. For it is not in so far as he is *subject* to the law that he has sublimity, but rather in so far as, in regard to this very same law, he is at the same time its *author* and is subordinated to it only on this ground. We have also shown above how neither fear nor inclination, but solely reverence for the law, is the motive which can give an action moral worth. Our own will, provided it were to act only under the condition of being able to make universal law by means of its maxims—this ideal will which can be ours is the proper object of reverence; and the dignity of man consists precisely in his capacity to make universal law, although only on condition of being himself also subject to the law he makes.

Morality and Human Nature

· ARISTOTLE ·

In these passages from The Nicomachean Ethics, *Aristotle (384–322 B.C.) presents several of his central views on ethics. He argues that we can discover what a good life is for human beings by considering what the function of human beings is. This function is to be found in reasoning well. Aristotle also defends his Doctrine of the Mean, which is intended to explain which character traits (virtues) best promote human flourishing.*

Book I

Every art and every inquiry, and similarly every action and pursuit, is thought 1
to aim at some good; and for this reason the good has rightly been declared to 1094ᵃ
be that at which all things aim. But a certain difference is found among ends;
some are activities, others are products apart from the activities that produce
them. Where there are ends apart from the actions, it is the nature of the products
to be better than the activities. Now, as there are many actions, arts, and sciences,
their ends also are many; the end of the medical art is health, that of shipbuilding
a vessel, that of strategy victory, that of economics wealth. But where such arts
fall under a single capacity—as bridlemaking and other arts concerned with the

equipment of horses fall under the art of riding, and this and every military action under strategy, in the same way other arts fall under yet others — in all of these the ends of the master arts are to be preferred to all the subordinate ends; for it is for the sake of the former that the latter are pursued. It makes no difference whether the activities themselves are the ends of the actions, or something else apart from the activities, as in the case of the sciences just mentioned.

2   If, then, there is some end of the things we do, which we desire for its own sake (everything else being desired for the sake of this), and if we do not choose everything for the sake of something else (for at that rate the process would go on to infinity, so that our desire would be empty and vain), clearly this must be the good and the chief good. Will not the knowledge of it, then, have a great influence on life? Shall we not, like archers who have a mark to aim at, be more likely to hit upon what is right? If so, we must try, in outline at least, to determine what it is, and of which of the sciences or capacities it is the object. It would seem to belong to the most authoritative art and that which is most truly the master art. And politics appears to be of this nature; for it is this that ordains 1094ᵇ which of the sciences should be studied in a state, and which each class of citizens should learn and up to what point they should learn them; and we see even the most highly esteemed of capacities to fall under this, e.g. strategy, economics, rhetoric; now, since politics uses the rest of the sciences, and since, again, it legislates as to what we are to do and what we are to abstain from, the end of this science must include those of the others, so that this end must be the good for man. For even if the end is the same for a single man and for a state, that of the state seems at all events something greater and more complete whether to attain or to preserve; though it is worth while to attain the end merely for one man, it is finer and more godlike to attain it for a nation or for city-states. These, then, are the ends at which our inquiry aims, since it is political science, in one sense of that term.

3   Our discussion will be adequate if it has as much clearness as the subject-matter admits of, for precision is not to be sought for alike in all discussions, any more than in all the products of the crafts. Now fine and just actions, which political science investigates, admit of much variety and fluctuation of opinion, so that they may be thought to exist only by convention, and not by nature. And goods also give rise to a similar fluctuation because they bring harm to many people; for before now men have been undone by reason of their wealth, and others by reason of their courage. We must be content, then, in speaking of such subjects and with such premises to indicate the truth roughly and in outline, and in speaking about things which are only for the most part true and with premises of the same kind to reach conclusions that are no better. In the same spirit, therefore, should each type of the statement be *received;* for it is the mark of an educated man to look for precision in each class of things just so far as the nature of the subject admits; it is evidently equally foolish to accept probable reasoning from a mathematician and to demand from a rhetorician scientific proofs.

Now each man judges well the things he knows, and of these he is a good 1095ᵃ judge. And so the man who has been educated in a subject is a good judge of that subject, and the man who has received an all-around education is a good judge in general. Hence a young man is not a proper hearer of lectures on political science; for he is inexperienced in the actions that occur in life, but its discussions start from these and are about these; and, further, since he tends to follow his passions, his study will be vain and unprofitable, because the end aimed at is not knowledge but action. And it makes no difference whether he is young in years or youthful in character; the defect does not depend on time, but on his living, and pursuing each successive object, as passion directs. For to such persons, as to the incontinent, knowledge brings no profit; but to those who desire and act in accordance with a rational principle knowledge about such matters will be of great benefit.

These remarks about the student, the sort of treatment to be expected, and the purpose of the inquiry, may be taken as our preface.

Let us resume our inquiry and state, in view of the fact that all knowledge 4 and every pursuit aims at some good, what it is that we say political science aims at and what is the highest of all goods achievable by action. Verbally there is very general agreement; for both the general run of men and people of superior refinement say that it is happiness, and identify living well and doing well with being happy; but with regard to what happiness is they differ, and the many do not give the same account as the wise. For the former think it is some plain and obvious thing, like pleasure, wealth, or honour; they differ, however, from one another—and often even the same man identifies it with different things, with health when he is ill, with wealth when he is poor; but, conscious of their ignorance, they admire those who proclaim some great ideal that is above their comprehension. Now some thought that apart from these many goods there is another which is self-subsistent and causes the goodness of all these as well. To examine all the opinions that have been held were perhaps somewhat fruitless; enough to examine those that are most prevalent or that seem to be arguable.

Let us not fail to notice, however, that there is a difference between arguments from and those to the first principles. For Plato, too, was right in raising this question and asking, as he used to do, "are we on the way from or to the first principles?" There is a difference, as there is in a racecourse between the course from the judges to the turning-point and the way back. For, while we must begin 1095ᵇ with what is known, things are objects of knowledge in two senses—some to us, some without qualification. Presumably, then, *we* must begin with things known to *us*. Hence any one who is to listen intelligently to lectures about what is noble and just and, generally, about the subjects of political science must have been brought up in good habits. For the fact is the starting-point, and if this is sufficiently plain to him, he will not at the start need the reason as well; and the man who has been well brought up has or can easily get starting-points. And as for him who neither has nor can get them, let him hear the words of Hesiod:

> Far best is he who knows all things himself;
> Good, he that hearkens when men counsel right;
> But he who neither knows, nor lays to heart
> Another's wisdom, is a useless wight.

5   Let us, however, resume our discussion from the point at which we digress. To judge from the lives that men lead, most men, and men of the most vulgar type, seem (not without some ground) to identify the good, or happiness, with pleasure; which is the reason why they love the life of enjoyment. For there are, we may say, three prominent types of life—that just mentioned, the political, and thirdly the contemplative life. Now the mass of mankind are evidently quite slavish in their tastes, preferring a life suitable to beasts, but they get some ground for their view from the fact that many of those in high places share the tastes of Sardanapallus. A consideration of the prominent types of life shows that people of superior refinement and of active disposition identify happiness with honour; for this is, roughly speaking, the end of the political life. But it seems too superficial to be what we are looking for, since it is thought to depend on those who bestow honour rather than on him who receives it, but the good we divine to be something proper to a man and not easily taken from him. Further, men seem to pursue honour in order that they may be assured of their goodness; at least it is by men of practical wisdom that they seek to be honoured, and among those who know them, and on the ground of their virtue; clearly, then, according to them, at any rate, virtue is better. And perhaps one might even suppose this to be, rather than honour, the end of the political life. But even this appears some-what incomplete; for possession of virtue seems actually compatible with being

1096ª asleep, or with lifelong inactivity, and, further, with the greatest sufferings and misfortunes; but a man who was living so no one would call happy, unless he were maintaining a thesis at all costs. Third comes the contemplative life, which we shall consider later. But enough of this; for the subject has been sufficiently treated even in the current discussions.

The life of money-making is one undertaken under cumpulsion, and wealth is evidently not the good we are seeking; for it is merely useful and for the sake of something else. And so one might rather take the aforenamed objects to be ends; for they are loved for themselves. But it is evident that not even these are ends; yet many arguments have been thrown away in support of them. Let us leave this subject, then.

. . . .

7   Let us again return to the good we are seeking, and ask what it can be. It seems different in different actions and arts; it is different in medicine, in strategy, and in the other arts likewise. What then is the good of each? Surely that for whose sake everything else is done. In medicine this is health, in strategy victory, in architecture a house, in any other sphere something else, and in every action and pursuit the end; for it is for the sake of this that all men do whatever else they do. Therefore, if there is an end for all that we do, this will be the good

achievable by action, and if there are more than one, these will be the goods achievable by action.

So the argument has by a different course reached the same point; but we must try to state this even more clearly. Since there are evidently more than one end, and we choose some of these (e.g. wealth, flutes, and in general instruments) for the sake of something else, clearly not all ends are final ends; but the chief good is evidently something final. Therefore, if there is only one final end, this will be what we are seeking, and if there are more than one, the most final of these will be what we are seeking. Now we call that which is in itself worthy of pursuit more final than that which is worthy of pursuit for the sake of something else, and that which is never desirable for the sake of something else more final than the things that are desirable both in themselves and for the sake of that other thing, and therefore we call final without qualification that which is always desirable in itself and never for the sake of something else.

Now such a thing happiness, above all else, is held to be; for this we choose 1097ᵇ always for itself and never for the sake of something else, but honour, pleasure, reason, and every virtue we choose indeed for themselves (for if nothing resulted from them we should still choose each of them), but we choose them also for the sake of happiness, judging that by means of them we shall be happy. Happiness, on the other hand, no one chooses for the sake of these, nor, in general, for anything other than itself.

From the point of view of self-sufficiency the same result seems to follow; for the final good is thought to be self-sufficient. Now by self-sufficient we do not mean that which is sufficient for a man by himself, for one who lives a solitary life, but also for parents, children, wife, and in general for his friends and fellow citizens, since man is born for citizenship. But some limit must be set to this; for if we extend our requirement to ancestors and descendants and friends' friends we are in for an infinite series. Let us examine this question, however, on another occasion; the self-sufficient we now define as that which when isolated makes life desirable and lacking in nothing; and such we think happiness to be; and further we think it most desirable of all things, without being counted as one good thing among others—if it were so counted it would clearly be made more desirable by the addition of even the least of goods; for that which is added becomes an excess of goods, and of goods the greater is always more desirable. Happiness, then, is something final and self-sufficient, and is the end of action.

Presumably, however, to say that happiness is the chief good seems a platitude, and a clearer account of what it is is still desired. This might perhaps be given, if we could first ascertain the function of man. For just as a flute-player, a sculptor, or any artist, and, in general, for all things that have a function or activity, the good and the "well" is thought to reside in the function, so would it seem to be for man, if he has a function. Have the carpenter, then, and the tanner certain functions or activities, and has man none? Is he born without a function? Or as eye, hand, foot, and in general each of the parts evidently has a function, may one lay it down that man similarly has a function apart from all these? What

then can this be? Life seems to be common even to plants, but we are seeking
1098ᵃ what is peculiar to man. Let us exclude, therefore, the life of nutrition and growth.
Next there would be a life of perception, but *it* also seems to be common even
to the horse, the ox, and every animal. There remains, then, an active life of the
element that has a rational principle; of this, one part has such a principle in
the sense of being obedient to one, the other in the sense of possessing one and
exercising thought. And, as "life of the rational element" also has two meanings,
we must state that life in the sense of activity is what we mean; for this seems
to be the more proper sense of the term. Now if the function of man is an activity
of soul which follows or implies a rational principle, and if we say "a so-and-so"
and "a good so-and-so" have a function which is the same in kind, e.g. a
lyre-player and a good lyre-player, and so without qualification in all cases,
eminence in respect of goodness being added to the name of the function (for
the function of a lyre-player is to play the lyre, and that of a good lyre-player
is to do so well): if this is the case, [and we state the function of man to be a
certain kind of life, and this to be an activity or actions of the soul implying a
rational principle, and the function of a good man to be the good and noble
performance of these, and if any action is well performed when it is performed
in accordance with the appropriate excellence: if this is the case,] human good
turns out to be activity of soul in accordance with virtue, and if there are more
than one virtue, in accordance with the best and most complete.

But we must add "in a complete life." For one swallow does not make a
summer, nor does one day: and so too one day, or a short time, does not make
a man blessed and happy.

Let this serve as an outline of the good; for we must presumably first sketch
it roughly, and then later fill in the details. But it would seem that any one is
capable of carrying on and articulating what has once been well outlined, and
that time is a good discoverer or partner in such a work; to which facts the
advances of the arts are due; for any one can add what is lacking. And we must
also remember what has been said before, and not look for precision in all things
alike, but in each class of things such precision as accords with the subject-matter,
and so much as is appropriate to the inquiry. For a carpenter and a geometer
investigate the right angle in different ways; the former does so in so far as the
right angle is useful for his work, while the latter inquires what it is or what
sort of thing it is; for he is a spectator of the truth. We must act in the same
way, then, in all other matters as well, that our main task may not be subordinated
to minor questions. Nor must we demand the cause in all matters alike; it is
1098ᵇ enough in some cases that the *fact* be well established, as in the case of the first
principles; the fact is the primary thing or first principle. Now of first principles
we see some by induction, some by perception, some by a certain habituation,
and others too in other ways. But each set of principles we must try to investigate
in the natural way, and we must take pains to state them definitely, since they
have a great influence on what follows. For the beginning is thought to be more
than half of the whole, and many of the questions we ask are cleared up by it.

We must consider it, however, in the light not only of our conclusion and our 8
premisses, but also of what is commonly said about it; for with a true view all
the data harmonize, but with a false one the facts soon clash. Now goods have
been divided into three classes, and some are described as external, others as
relating to soul or to body; we call those that relate to soul most properly and
truly goods, and psychical actions and activites we class as relating to soul.
Therefore our account must be sound, at least according to this view, which is
an old one and agreed on by philosophers. It is correct also in that we identify
the end with certain actions and activities; for thus it falls among goods of the
soul and not among external goods. Another belief which harmonizes with our
account is that the happy man lives well and does well; for we have practically
defined happiness as a sort of good life and good action. The characteristics that
are looked for in happiness seem also, all of them, to belong to what we have
defined happiness as being. For some identify happiness with virtue, some with
practical wisdom, others with a kind of philosophic wisdom, others with these,
or one of these, accompanied by pleasure or not without pleasure; while others
include also external prosperity. Now some of these views have been held by
many men and men of old, others by a few eminent persons; and it is not
probable that either of these should be entirely mistaken, but rather that they
should be right in at least some one respect or even in most respects.

With those who identify happiness with virtue or some one virtue our account
is in harmony; for to virtue belongs virtuous activity. But it makes, perhaps, no
small difference whether we place the chief good in possession or in use, in state
of mind or in activity. For the state of mind may exist without producing any good
result, as in a man who is asleep or in some other way quite inactive, but the 1099ᵃ
activity cannot; for one who has the activity will of necessity be acting, and acting
well. And as in the Olympic Games it is not the most beautiful and the strongest
that are crowned but those who compete (for it is some of these that are victori-
ous), so those who act win, and rightly win, the noble and good things in life.

Their life is also in itself pleasant. For pleasure is a state of *soul*, and to each
man that which he is said to be a lover of is pleasant; e.g. not only is a horse
pleasant to the lover of horses, and a spectacle to the lover of sights, but also in
the same way just acts are pleasant to the lover of justice and in general virtuous
acts to the lover of virtue. Now for most men their pleasures are in conflict with
one another because these are not by nature pleasant, but the lovers of what is
noble find pleasant the things that are by nature pleasant; and virtuous actions
are such, so that these are pleasant for such men as well as in their own nature.
Their life, therefore, has no further need of pleasure as a sort of adventitious
charm, but has its pleasure in itself. For, besides what we have said, the man
who does not rejoice in noble actions is not even good; since no one would call
a man just who did not enjoy acting justly, nor any man liberal who did not
enjoy liberal actions; and similarly in all other cases. If this is so, virtuous actions
must be in themselves pleasant. But they are also *good* and *noble*, and have each
of these attributes in the highest degree, since the good man judges well about

these attributes; his judgement is such as we have described. Happiness then is the best, noblest, and most pleasant thing in the world, and these attributes are not severed as in the inscription at Delos —

> Most noble is that which is justest, and best is health;
> But pleasantest is it to win what we love.

For all these properties belong to the best activities; and these, or one — the best — of these, we identify with happiness.

1099^b Yet evidently, as we said, it needs the external goods as well; for it is impossible, or not easy, to do noble acts without the proper equipment. In many actions we use friends and riches and political power as instruments; and there are some things the lack of which takes the lustre from happiness, as good birth, goodly children, beauty; for the man who is very ugly in appearance or ill-born or solitary and childless is not very likely to be happy, and perhaps a man would be still less likely if he had thoroughly bad children or friends or had lost good children or friends by death. As we said, then, happiness seems to need this sort of prosperity in addition; for which reason some identify happiness with good fortune, though others identify it with virtue.

· · · · · · · ·

13 Since happiness is an activity of soul in accordance with perfect virtue, we must consider the nature of virtue; for perhaps we shall thus see better the nature of happiness. The true student of politics, too, is thought to have studied virtue above all things; for he wishes to make his fellow citizens good and obedient to the laws. As an example of this we have the lawgivers of the Cretans and the Spartans, and any others of the kind that there may have been. And if this inquiry belongs to political science, clearly the pursuit of it will be in accordance with our original plan. But clearly the virtue we must study is human virtue; for the good we were seeking was human good and the happiness human happiness. By human virtue we mean not that of the body but that of the soul; and happiness also we call an activity of soul. But if this is so, clearly the student of politics must know somehow the facts about soul, as the man who is to heal the eyes or the body as a whole must know about the eyes or the body; and all the more since politics is more prized and better than medicine; but even among doctors the best educated spend much labour on acquiring knowledge of the body. The student of politics, then, must study the soul, and must study it with these objects in view, and do so just to the extent which is sufficient for the questions we are discussing; for further precision is perhaps more laborious than our purposes require.

Some things are said about it, adequately enough, even in the discussions outside our school, and we must use these; e.g. that one element in the soul is irrational and one has a rational principle. Whether these are separated as the parts of the body or of anything divisible are, or are distinct by definition but by nature inseparable, like convex and concave in the circumference of a circle, does not affect the present question.

Of the irrational element one division seems to be widely distributed, and vegetative in its nature, I mean that which causes nutrition and growth; for it is this kind of power of the soul that one must assign to all nurslings and to embryos, and this same power to full-grown creatures; this is more reasonable than to assign some different power to them. Now the excellence of this seems to be common to all species and not specifically human; for this part or faculty seems to function most in sleep, while goodness and badness are least manifest in sleep (whence comes the saying that the happy are no better off than the wretched for half their lives; and this happens naturally enough, since sleep is an inactivity of the soul in that respect in which it is called good or bad), unless perhaps to a small extent some of the movements actually penetrate to the soul, and in this respect the dreams of good men are better than those of ordinary people. Enough of this subject, however; let us leave the nutritive faculty, alone, since it has by its nature no share in human excellence. 1102ᵇ

There seems to be also another irrational element in the soul—one which in a sense, however, shares in a rational principle. For we praise the rational principle of the continent man and of the incontinent, and the part of their soul that has such a principle, since it urges them aright and towards the best objects; but there is found in them also another element naturally opposed to the rational principle, which fights against and resists that principle. For exactly as paralysed limbs when we intend to move them to the right turn on the contrary to the left, so is it with the soul; the impulses of incontinent people move in contrary directions. But while in the body we see that which moves astray, in the soul we do not. No doubt, however, we must none the less suppose that in the soul too there is something contrary to the rational principle, resisting and opposing it. In what sense it is distinct from the other elements does not concern us. Now even this seems to have a share in a rational principle, as we said; at any rate in the continent man it obeys the rational principle—and presumably in the temperate and brave man it is still more obedient; for in him it speaks, on all matters, with the same voice as the rational principle.

Therefore the irrational element also appears to be twofold. For the vegetative element in no way shares in a rational principle, but the appetitive and in general the desiring element in a sense shares in it, in so far as it listens to and obeys it; this is the sense in which we speak of "taking account" of one's father or one's friends, not that in which we speak of "accounting" for a mathematical property. That the irrational element is in some sense persuaded by a rational principle is indicated also by the giving of advice and by all reproof and exhor- 1103ᵃ tation. And if this element also must be said to have a rational principle, that which has a rational principle (as well as that which has not) will be twofold, one subdivision having it in the strict sense and in itself, and the other having a tendency to obey as one does one's father.

Virtue too is distinguished into kinds in accordance with this difference; for we say that some of the virtues are intellectual and others moral, philosophic wisdom and understanding and practical wisdom being intellectual, liberality and temperance moral. For in speaking about a man's character we do not say that he is wise or has understanding but that he is good-tempered or temperate; yet we praise the wise man also with respect to his state of mind; and of states of mind we call those which merit praise virtues.

Book II

1   Virtue, then, being of two kinds, intellectual and moral, intellectual virtue in the main owes both its birth and its growth to teaching (for which reason it requires experience and time), while moral virtue comes about as a result of habit, whence its name (ἠθική) is one that is formed by a slight variation from the word ἔθος (habit). From this it is also plain that none of the moral virtues arises in us by nature; for nothing that exists by nature can form a habit contrary to its nature. For instance the stone which by nature moves downwards cannot be habituated to move upwards, not even if one tries to train it by throwing it up ten thousand times; nor can fire be habituated to move downwards, nor can anything else that by nature behaves in one way be trained to behave in another. Neither by nature, then, nor contrary to nature do the virtues arise in us; rather we are adapted by nature to receive them, and are made perfect by habit.

Again, of all the things that come to us by nature we first acquire the potentiality and later exhibit the activity (this is plain in the case of the senses; for it was not by often seeing or often hearing that we got these senses, but on the contrary we had them before we used them, and did not come to have them by using them); but the virtues we get by first exercising them, as also happens in the case of the arts as well. For the things we have to learn before we can do them, we learn by doing them, e.g. men become builders by building and lyre-players by playing the lyre; so too we become just by doing just acts, temperate by doing temperate acts, brave by doing brave acts.

1103ᵇ   This is confirmed by what happens in states; for legislators make the citizens good by forming habits in them, and this is the wish of every legislator, and those who do not effect it miss their mark, and it is in this that a good constitution differs from a bad one.

Again, it is from the same causes and by the same means that every virtue is both produced and destroyed, and similarly every art; for it is from playing the lyre that both good and bad lyre-players are produced. And the corresponding statement is true of builders and of all the rest; men will be good or bad builders as a result of building well or badly. For if this were not so, there would have been no need of a teacher, but all men would have been born good or bad at their craft. This, then, is the case with the virtues also; by doing the acts that we do in our transactions with other men we become just or unjust, and by doing the acts that we do in the presence of danger, and being habituated to feel fear or confidence, we become brave or cowardly. The same is true of appetites and feelings of anger; some men become temperate and good-tempered, others self-indulgent and irascible, by behaving in one way or the other in the appropriate circumstances. Thus, in one word, states of character arise out of like activites. This is why the activites we exhibit must be of a certain kind; it is because the states of character correspond to the differences between these. It makes no small difference, then, whether we form habits of one kind or of another from our very youth; it makes a very great difference, or rather *all* the difference.

Since, then, the present inquiry does not aim at theoretical knowledge like the others (for we are inquiring not in order to know what virtue is, but in order to become good, since otherwise our inquiry would have been of no use), we must examine the nature of actions, namely how we ought to do them; for these determine also the nature of the states of character that are produced, as we have said. Now, that we must act according to the right rule is a common principle and must be assumed — it will be discussed later, i.e. both what the right rule is, and how it is related to the other virtues. But this must be agreed upon beforehand, that the whole account of matters of conduct must be given in outline and not precisely, as we said at the very beginning that the accounts we demand must be in accordance with the subject-matter; matters concerned with conduct and questions of what is good for us have no fixity, any more than matters of health. The general account being of this nature, the account of particular cases is yet more lacking in exactness; for they do not fall under any art or precept but the agents themselves must in each case consider what is appropriate to the occasion, as happens also in the art of medicine or of navigation.

But though our present account is of this nature we must give what help we can. First, then, let us consider this, that it is the nature of such things to be destroyed by defect and excess, as we see in the case of strength and of health (for to gain light on things imperceptible we must use the evidence of sensible things); both excessive and defective exercise destroys the strength, and similarly drink or food which is above or below a certain amount destroys the health, while that which is proportionate both produces and increases and preserves it. So too is it, then, in the case of temperance and courage and the other virtues. For the man who flies from and fears everything and does not stand his ground against anything becomes a coward, and the man who fears nothing at all but goes to meet every danger becomes rash; and similarly the man who indulges in every pleasure and abstains from none becomes self-indulgent, while the man who shuns every pleasure, as boors do, becomes in a way insensible; temperance and courage, then, are destroyed by excess and defect and preserved by the mean.

But not only are the sources and causes of their origination and growth the same as those of their destruction, but also the sphere of their actualization will be the same; for this is also true of things which are more evident to sense, e.g. of strength; it is produced by taking much food and undergoing much exertion, and it is the strong man that will be most able to do these things. So too is it with the virtues; by abstaining from pleasures we become temperate, and it is when we have become so that we are most able to abstain from them; and similarly too in the case of courage; for by being habituated to despise things that are terrible and to stand our ground against them we become brave, and it is when we have become so that we shall be most able to stand our ground against them.

2

1104ᵃ

1104ᵇ

<u>3</u>   We must take as a sign of states of character the pleasure or pain that ensues on acts; for the man who abstains from bodily pleasures and delights in this very fact is temperate, while the man who is annoyed at it is self-indulgent, and he who stands his ground against things that are terrible and delights in this or at least is not pained is brave, while the man who is pained is a coward. For moral excellence is concerned with pleasures and pains; it is on account of the pain that we abstain from noble ones. Hence we ought to have been brought up in a particular way from our very youth, as Plato says, so as both to delight in and to be pained by the things that we ought; for this is the right education.

Again, if the virtues are concerned with actions and passions, and every passion and every action is accompanied by pleasure and pain, for this reason also virtue will be concerned with pleasures and pains. This is indicated also by the fact that punishment is inflicted by these means; for it is a kind of cure, and it is the nature of cures to be effected by contraries.

Again, as we said but lately, every state of soul has a nature relative to and concerned with the kind of things by which it tends to be made worse or better; but it is by reason of pleasures and pains that men become bad, by pursuing and avoiding these—either the pleasures and pains they ought not or when they ought not or as they ought not, or by going wrong in one of the other similar ways that may be distinguished. Hence men even define the virtues as certain states of impassivity and rest; not well, however, because they speak absolutely, and do not say "as one ought" and "as one ought not" and "when one ought or ought not," and the other things that may be added. We assume, then, that this kind of excellence tends to do what is best with regard to pleasures and pains, and vice does the contrary.

The following facts also may show us that virtue and vice are concerned with these same things. There being three objects of choice and three of avoidance, the noble, the advantageous, the pleasant, and their contraries, the base, the injurious, the painful, about all of these the good man tends to go right and the bad man to go wrong, and especially about pleasure; for this is common to the animals, and also it accompanies all objects of choice; for even the noble and the advantageous appear pleasant.

1105ᵃ   Again, it has grown up with us all from our infancy; this is why it is difficult to rub off this passion, engrained as it is in our life. And we measure even our actions, some of us more and others less, by the rule of pleasure and pain. For this reason, then, our whole inquiry must be about these; for to feel delight and pain rightly or wrongly has no small effect on our actions.

Again, it is harder to fight with pleasure than with anger, to use Heraclitus' phrase, but both art and virtue are always concerned with what is harder; for even the good is better when it is harder. Therefore for this reason also the whole concern both of virtue and of political science is with pleasures and pains; for the man who uses these well will be good, he who uses them badly bad.

That virtue, then, is concerned with pleasure and pains, and that by the acts from which it arises it is both increased and, if they are done differently, destroyed, and that the acts from which it arose are those in which it actualizes itself — let this be taken as said.

The question might be asked, what we mean by saying that we must become 4 just by doing just acts, and temperate by doing temperate acts; for if men do just and temperate acts, they are already just and temperate, exactly as, if they do what is in accordance with the laws of grammar and of music, they are grammarians and musicians.

Or is this not true even of the arts? It is possible to do something that is in accordance with the laws of grammar, either by chance or at the suggestion of another. A man will be a grammarian, then, only when he has both done something grammatical and done it grammatically; and this means doing it in accordance with the grammatical knowledge in himself.

Again, the case of the arts and that of the virtues are not similar; for the products of the arts have their goodness in themselves, so that it is enough that they should have a certain character, but if the acts that are in accordance with the virtues have themselves a certain character it does not follow that they are done justly or temperately. The agent also must be in a certain condition when he does them; in the first place he must have knowledge, secondly he must choose the acts, and choose them for their own sakes, and thirdly his action must proceed from a firm and unchangeable character. These are not reckoned 1105^b in as conditions of the possession of the arts, except the bare knowledge; but as a condition on the possession of the virtues knowledge has little or no weight, while the other conditions count not for a little but for everything, i.e. the very conditions which result from often doing just and temperate acts.

Actions, then, are called just and temperate when they are such as the just or the temperate man would do; but it is not the man who does these that is just and temperate, but the man who also does them *as* just and temperate men do them. It is well said, then, that it is by doing just acts that the just man is produced, and by doing temperate acts the temperate man; without doing these no one would have even a prospect of becoming good.

But most people do not do these, but take refuge in theory and think they are being philosophers and will become good in this way, behaving somewhat like patients who listen attentively to their doctors, but do none of the things they are ordered to do. As the latter will not be made well in body by such a course of treatment, the former will not be made well in soul by such a course in philosophy.

Next we must consider what virtue is. Since things that are found in the soul 5 are of three kinds — passions, faculties, states of character, virtue must be one of these. By passions I mean appetite, anger, fear, confidence, envy, joy, friendly feeling, hatred, longing, emulation, pity, and in general the feelings that are accompanied by pleasure or pain; by faculties the things in virtue of which we are said to be capable of feeling these, e. g. of becoming angry or being pained or feeling pity; by states of character the things in virtue of which we stand well or badly with reference to the passions, e.g. with reference to anger we stand badly if we feel it violently or too weakly, and well if we feel it moderately; and similarly with reference to the other passions.

Now neither the virtues nor the vices are *passions*, because we are not called good or bad on the ground of our passions, but are so called on the ground of our virtues and our vices, and because we are neither praised nor blamed for our passions (for the man who feels fear or anger is not praised, nor is the man who simply feels anger blamed, but the man who feels it in a certain way), but for our virtues and our vices we *are* praised or blamed.

1106ᵃ Again, we feel anger and fear without choice, but the virtues are modes of choice or involve choice. Further, in respect of the passions we are said to be moved, but in respect of the virtues and the vices we are said not to be moved but to be disposed in a particular way.

For these reasons also they are not *faculties*; for we are neither called good nor bad, nor praised nor blamed, for the simple capacity of feeling the passions; again, we have the faculties by nature, but we are not made good or bad by nature; we have spoken of this before.

If, then, the virtues are neither passions nor faculties, all that remains is that they should be *states of character*.

Thus we have stated what virtue is in respect of its genus.

6 We must, however, not only describe virtue as a state of character, but also say what sort of state it is. We may remark, then, that every virtue or excellence both brings into good condition the thing of which it is the excellence and makes the work of that thing be done well; e.g. the excellence of the eye makes both the eye and its work good; for it is by the excellence of the eye that we see well. Similarly the excellence of the horse makes a horse both good in itself and good at running and carrying its rider and at awaiting the attack of the enemy. Therefore, if this is true in every case, the virtue of man also will be the state of character which makes a man good and which makes him do his own work well.

How this is to happen we have stated already, but it will be made plain also by the following consideration of the specific nature of virtue. In everything that is continuous and divisible it is possible to take more, less, or an equal amount, and that either in terms of the thing itself or relatively to us; and the equal is an intermediate between excess and defect. By the intermediate in the object I mean that which is equidistant from each of the extremes, which is one and the same for all men; by the intermediate relatively to us that which is neither too much nor too little—and this is not one, nor the same for all. For instance, if ten is many and two is few, six is the intermediate, taken in terms of the object; for it exceeds and is exceeded by an equal amount; this is intermediate according to arithmetical proportion. But the intermediate relatively to us is not to be taken

1106ᵇ so; if ten pounds are too much for a particular person to eat and two too little, it does not follow that the trainer will order six pounds; for this also is perhaps too much for the person who is to take it, or too little—too little for Milo, to much for the beginner in athletic exercises. The same is true of running and wrestling. Thus a master of any art avoids excess and defect, but seeks the intermediate and chooses this—the intermediate not in the object but relatively to us.

If it is thus, then, that every art does its work well—by looking to the intermediate and judging its works by this standard (so that we often say of good works of art that it is not possible either to take away or to add anything, implying that excess and defect destroy the goodness of works of art, while the mean preserves it; and good artists, as we say, look to this in their work), and if, further, virtue is more exact and better than any art, as nature also is, then virtue must have the quality of aiming at the intermediate. I mean moral virtue; for it is this that is concerned with passions and actions, and in these there is excess, defect, and the intermediate. For instance, both fear and confidence and appetite and anger and pity and in general pleasure and pain may be felt both too much and too little, and in both cases not well; but to feel them at the right times, with reference to the right objects, towards the right people, with the right motive, and in the right way, is what is both intermediate and best, and this is characteristic of virtue. Similarly with regard to actions also there is excess, defect, and the intermediate. Now virtue is concerned with passions and actions, in which excess is a form of failure, and so is defect, while the intermediate is praised and is a form of success; and being praised and being successful are both characteristics of virtue. Therefore virtue is a kind of mean, since, as we have seen, it aims at what is intermediate.

Again, it is possible to fail in many ways (for evil belongs to the class of the unlimited, as the Pythagoreans conjectured, and good to that of the limited), while to succeed is possible only in one way (for which reason also one is easy and the other difficult—to miss the mark easy, to hit it difficult); for these reasons also, then, excess and defect are characteristic of vice, and the mean of virtue;

For men are good in but one way, but bad in many.

Virtue, then, is a state of character concerned with choice, lying in a mean, 1107ᵃ i.e., the mean relative to us, this being determined by a rational principle, and by that principle by which the man of practical wisdom would determine it. Now it is a mean between two vices, that which depends on excess and that which depends on defect; and again it is a mean because the vices respectively fall short of or exceed what is right in both passions and actions, while virtue both finds and chooses that which is intermediate. Hence in respect of its substance and the definition which states its essence virtue is a mean, with regard to what is best and right an extreme.

But not every action nor every passion admits of a mean; for some have names that already imply badness, e. g. spite, shamelessness, envy, and in the case of actions adultery, theft, murder, for all of these and suchlike things imply by their names that they are themselves bad, and not the excesses or deficiencies of them. It is not possible, then, ever to be right with regard to them; one must always be wrong. Nor does goodness or badness with regard to such things depend on committing adultery with the right woman, at the right time, and in the right way, but simply to do any of them is to go wrong. It would be equally absurd, then, to expect that in unjust, cowardly, and voluptuous action there should be a mean, an excess, and a deficiency; for at that rate there would be a mean of excess and of deficiency, an excess of excess, and a deficiency of deficiency. But as there is no excess and deficiency of temperance and courage because what is intermediate is in a sense an extreme, so too of the actions we have mentioned there is no mean nor any excess and deficiency, but however they are done they are wrong; for in general there is neither a mean of excess and deficiency, nor excess and deficiency of a mean.

7   We must, however, not only make this general statement, but also apply it to the individual facts. For among statements about conduct those which are general apply more widely, but those which are particular are more genuine, since conduct has to do with individual cases, and our statements must harmonize with the facts in these cases. We may take these cases from our table. With regard to

1107ᵇ feelings of fear and confidence courage is the mean; of the people who exceed, he who exceeds in fearlessness has no name (many of the states have no name), while the man who exceeds in confidence is rash, and he who exceeds in fear and falls short in confidence is a coward. With regard to pleasures and pains—not all of them, and not so much with regard to the pains—the mean is temperance, the excess self-indulgence. Persons deficient with regard to the pleasures are not often found; hence such persons also have received no name. But let us call them "insensible."

With regard to giving and taking of money the mean is liberality, the excess and the defect prodigality and meanness. In these actions people exceed and fall short in contrary ways; the prodigal exceeds in spending and falls short in taking, while the mean man exceeds in taking and falls short in spending. . . . With regard to money there are also other dispositions—a mean, magnificence (for the magnificent man differs from the liberal man; the former deals with large sums, the latter with small ones), an excess, tastelessness and vulgarity, and a deficiency, niggardliness; these differ from the states opposed to liberality. . . .

With regard to honour and dishonour the mean is proper pride, the excess is known as a sort of "empty vanity," and the deficiency is undue humility; and as we said liberality was related to magnificence, differing from it by dealing with small sums, so there is a state similarly related to proper pride, being concerned with small honours while that is concerned with great. For it is possible to desire honour as one ought, and more than one ought, and less, and the man who exceeds in his desires is called ambitious, the man who falls short unambitious, while the intermediate person has no name. The dispositions also are nameless, except that that of the ambitious man is called ambition. Hence the people who are at the extremes lay claim to the middle place; and we ourselves sometimes call the intermediate person ambitious and sometimes unambitious, and sometimes praise the ambitious man and sometimes the unambitious. . . . [N]ow let us speak of the remaining states according to the method which has been indicated.

1108ᵃ   With regard to anger also there is an excess, a deficiency, and a mean. Although they can scarcely be said to have names, yet since we call the intermediate person good-tempered let us call the mean good temper; of the persons at the extremes let the one who exceeds be called irascible, and his vice irascibility, and the man who falls short an inirascible sort of person, and the deficiency inirascibility.

There are also three other means, which have a certain likeness to one another, but differ from one another: for they are all concerned with intercourse in words and actions, but differ in that one is concerned with truth in this sphere, the other two with pleasantness; and of this one kind is exhibited in giving amusement, the other in all the circumstances of life. We must therefore speak of these too, that we may the better see that in all things the mean is praiseworthy, and the extremes neither praiseworthy nor right, but worthy of blame. Now most of these states also have no names, but we must try, as in the other cases, to invent names ourselves so that we may be clear and easy to follow. With regard to truth, then, the intermediate is a truthful sort of person and the mean may be called truthfulness, while the pretence which exaggerates is boastfulness and the person characterized by it a boaster, and that which understates is mock modesty and the person characterized by it mock-modest. With regard to pleasantness in the giving of amusement the intermediate person is ready-witted and the disposition ready wit, the excess is buffoonery and the person characterized by it a buffoon, while the man who falls short is a sort of boor and his state is boorishness. With regard to the remaining kind of pleasantness, that which is exhibited in life in general, the man who is pleasant in the right way is friendly and the mean is friendliness, while the man who exceeds is an obsequious person if he has no end in view, a flatterer if he is aiming at his own advantage, and the man who falls short and is unpleasant in all circumstances is a quarrelsome and surly sort of person.

There are also means in the passions and concerned with the passions; since shame is not a virtue, and yet praise is extended to the modest man. For even in these matters one man is said to be intermediate, and another to exceed, as for instance the bashful man who is ashamed of everything; while he who falls short or is not ashamed of anything at all is shameless, and the intermediate person is modest. Righteous indignation is a mean between envy and spite, and these states are concerned with the pain and pleasure that are felt at the fortunes 1108^b of our neighbours; the man who is characterized by righteous indignation is pained at undeserved good fortune, the envious man, going beyond him, is pained at all good fortune, and the spiteful man falls so far short of being pained that he even rejoices. . . .

There are three kinds of disposition, then, two of them vices, involving excess 8 and deficiency respectively, and one a virtue, viz. the mean, and all are in a sense opposed to all; for the extreme states are contrary both to the intermediate state and to each other, and the intermediate to the extremes; as the equal is greater relatively to the less, less relatively to the greater, so the middle states are excessive relatively to the deficiencies, deficient relatively to the excesses, both in passions and in actions. For the brave man appears rash relatively to the coward, and cowardly relatively to the rash man; and similarly the temperate man appears self-indulgent relatively to the insensible man, insensible relatively to the self-indulgent, and the liberal man prodigal relatively to the mean man, mean relatively to the prodigal. Hence also the people at the extremes push the intermediate man each over to the other, and the brave man is called rash by the coward, cowardly by the rash man, and correspondingly in the other cases.

These stages being thus opposed to one another, the greatest contrariety is that of the extremes to each other, rather than to the intermediate; for these are further from each other than from the intermediate, as the great is further from the small and the small from the great than both are from the equal. Again, to the intermediate some extremes show a certain likeness, as that of rashness to courage and that of prodigality to liberality; but the extremes show the greatest unlikeness to each other; now contraries are defined as the things that are furthest from each other, so that things that are further apart are more contrary.

1109ª To the mean in some cases the deficiency, in some the excess is more opposed; e. g. it is not rashness, which is an excess, but cowardice, which is a deficiency, that is more opposed to courage, and not insensibility, which is a deficiency, but self-indulgence, which is an excess, that is more opposed to temperance. This happens from two reasons, one being drawn from the thing itself; for because one extreme is nearer and liker to the intermediate, we oppose not this but rather its contrary to the intermediate. E.g., since rashness is thought liker and nearer to courage, and cowardice more unlike, we oppose rather the latter to courage; for things that are further from the intermediate are thought more contrary to it. This, then, is one cause, drawn from the thing itself; another is drawn from ourselves; for the things to which we ourselves more naturally tend seem more contrary to the intermediate. For instance, we ourselves tend more naturally to pleasures, and hence are more easily carried away towards self-indulgence than towards propriety. We describe as contrary to the mean, then, rather the directions in which we more often go to great lengths; and therefore self-indulgence, which is an excess, is the more contrary to temperance.

9 That moral virtue is a mean, then, and in what sense it is so, and that it is a mean between two vices, the one involving excess, the other deficiency, and that it is such because its character is to aim at what is intermediate in passions and in actions, has been sufficiently stated. Hence also it is no easy task to be good. For in everything it is no easy task to find the middle, e. g. to find the middle of a circle is not for every one but for him who knows; so, too, any one can get angry—that is easy—or to give or spend money; but to do this to the right person, to the right extent, at the right time, with the right motive, and in the right way, *that* is not for every one, nor is it easy; wherefore goodness is both rare and laudable and noble.

Hence he who aims at the intermediate must first depart from what is the more contrary to it, as Calypso advises—

Hold the ship out beyond that surf and spray.

For of the extremes one is more erroneous, one less so; therefore, since to hit the means is hard in the exteme, we must as a second best, as people say, take the least of the evils; and this will be done best in the way we describe.

But we must consider the things towards which we ourselves also are easily 1109ᵇ carried away; for some of us tend to one thing, some to another; and this will be recognizable from the pleasure and the pain we feel. We must drag ourselves away to the contrary extreme; for we shall get into the intermediate state by drawing well away from error, as people do in straightening sticks that are bent.

Now in everything the pleasant or pleasure is most to be guarded against; for we do not judge it impartially. We ought, then, to feel towards pleasure as the elders of the people felt towards Helen, and in all circumstances repeat their saying; for if we dismiss pleasure thus we are less likely to go astray. It is by doing this, then, (to sum the matter up) that we shall best be able to hit the mean.

But this is no doubt difficult, and especially in individual cases; for it is not easy to determine both how and with whom and on what provocation and how long one should be angry; for we too sometimes praise those who fall short and call them good-tempered, but sometimes we praise those who get angry and call them manly. The man, however, who deviates little from goodness is not blamed, whether he do so in the direction of the more or of the less, but only the man who deviates more widely; for *he* does not fail to be noticed. But up to what point and to what extent a man must deviate before he becomes blameworthy it is not easy to determine by reasoning, any more than anything else that is perceived by the senses; such things depend on particular facts, and the decision rests with perception. So much, then, is plain, that the intermediate state is in all things to be praised, but that we must incline sometimes towards the excess, sometimes towards the deficiency; for so shall we most easily hit the mean and what is right.

. . . .

Book X

If happiness is activity in accordance with virtue, it is reasonable that it should 7 be in accordance with the highest virtue; and this will be that of the best thing in us. Whether it be reason or something else that is this element which is thought to be our natural ruler and guide and to take thought of things noble and divine, whether it be itself also divine or only the most divine element in us, the activity of this in accordance with its proper virtue will be perfect happiness. That this activity is contemplative we have already said.

Now this would seem to be in agreement both with what we said before and with the truth. For, firstly, this activity is the best (since not only is reason the best thing in us, but the objects of reason are the best of knowable objects); and, secondly, it is the most continuous, since we can contemplate truth more continuously than we can *do* anything. And we think happiness has pleasure mingled with it, but the activity of philosophic wisdom is admittedly the pleasantest of virtuous activities; at all events the pursuit of it is thought to offer pleasures marvellous for their purity and their enduringness, and it is to be expected that those who know will pass their time more pleasantly than those who inquire. And the self-sufficiency that is spoken of must belong most to the contemplative activity. For while a philosopher, as well as a just man or one possessing any other virtue, needs the necessaries of life, when they are sufficiently equipped with things of that sort the just man needs people towards whom and with whom he shall act justly, and the temperate man, the brave man, and each of the others is in the same case, but the philosopher, even when by himself, can contemplate truth, and the better the wiser he is; he can perhaps do so better if he has fellow-workers, but still he is the most self-sufficient. And this activity 1177ᵇ alone would seem to be loved for its own sake; for nothing arises from it apart from the contemplating, while from practical activities we gain more or less apart from the action. And happiness is thought to depend on leisure; for we are busy that we may have leisure, and make war that we may live in peace. Now the activity of the practical virtues is exhibited in political or military affairs, but the actions concerned with these seem to be unleisurely. Warlike actions are completely so (for no one chooses to be at war, or provokes war, for the sake of being at war; any one would seem absolutely murderous if he were to make enemies of his friends in order to bring about battle and slaughter); but the action of the statesman is also unleisurely, and — apart from the political action itself — aims at despotic power and honours, or at all events happiness, for him and his fellow citizens — a happiness different from political action, and evidently sought as being different. So if among virtuous actions political and military actions are distinguished by nobility and greatness, and these are unleisurely and aim at an end and are not desirable for their own sake, but the activity of reason, which is contemplative, seems both to be superior in serious worth and to aim at no end beyond itself, and to have its pleasure proper to itself (and this augments the activity), and the self-sufficiency, leisureliness, unweariedness (so far as this is possible for man), and all the other attributes ascribed to the supremely happy man are evidently those connected with this activity, it follows that this will be the complete happiness of man, if it be allowed a complete term of life (for none of the attributes of happiness is *in*complete).

But such a life would be too high for man; for it is not in so far as he is man that he will live so, but in so far as something divine is present in him; and by so much as this is superior to our composite nature is its activity superior to that which is the exercise of the other kind of virtue. If reason is divine, then, in comparision with man, the life according to it is divine in comparison with human life. But we must not follow those who advise us, being men, to think of human things, and, being mortal, of mortal things, but must, so far as we can, make ourselves immortal, and strain every nerve to live in accordance with 1178ᵃ the best thing in us; for even if it be small in bulk, much more does it in power and worth surpass everything. This would seem, too, to be each man himself, since it is the authoritative and better part of him. It would be strange, then, if he were to choose not the life of his self but that of something else. . . . [T]hat which is proper to each thing is by nature best and and most pleasant for each thing; for man, therefore, the life according to reason is best and pleasantest, since reason more than anything else *is* man. This life therefore is also the happiest.

But in a secondary degree the life in accordance with the other kind of virtue 8 is happy; for the activities in accordance with this befit our human estate. Just and brave acts, and other virtuous acts, we do in relation to each other, observing our respective duties with regard to contracts and services and all manner of actions and with regard to passions; and all of these seem to be typically human. Some of them seem even to arise from the body, and virtue of character to be in many ways bound up with the passions. Practical wisdom, too, is linked to virtue of character, and this to practical wisdom, since the principles of practical wisdom are in accordance with the moral virtues and rightness in morals is in accordance with practical wisdom. Being connected with the passions also, the moral virtues must belong to our composite nature; and the virtues of our composite nature are human; so, therefore, are the life and the happiness which correspond to these. The excellence of the reason is a thing apart; we must be content to say this much about it, for to describe it precisely is a task greater than our purpose requires. It would seem, however, also to need external equipment but little, or less than moral virtue does. Grant that both need the necessaries, and do so equally, even if the statesman's work is the more concerned with the body and things of that sort; for there will be little difference there; but in what they need for the exercise of their activities there will be much difference. The liberal man will need money for the doing of his liberal deeds, and the just man too will need it for the returning of services (for wishes are hard to discern, and even people who are not just pretend to wish to act justly); and the brave man will need power if he is to accomplish any of the acts that correspond to his virtue, and the temperate man will need opportunity; for how else is either he or any of the others to be recognized? It is debated, too, whether the will or the deed is more essential to virtue, which is assumed to involve both; it is surely clear that its perfection involves both; but for deeds many things are needed, and more, the greater and nobler the deeds are. But the man who is contemplating 1178ᵇ the truth needs no such thing, at least with a view to the exercise of his activity; indeed they are, one may say, even hindrances, at all events to his contemplation; but in so far as he is a man and lives with a number of people, he chooses to do virtuous acts; he will therefore need such aids to living a human life.

But that perfect happiness is a contemplative activity will appear from the following consideration as well. We assume the gods to be above all other beings blessed and happy; but what sort of actions must we assign to them? Acts of justice? Will not the gods seem absurd if they make contracts and return deposits, and so on? Acts of a brave man, then, confronting dangers and running risks because it is noble to do so? Or liberal acts? To whom will they give? It will be strange if they are really to have money or anything of the kind. And what would their temperate acts be? Is not such praise tasteless, since they have no bad appetites? If we were to run through them all, the circumstances of action would be found trivial and unworthy of gods. Still, every one supposes that they *live* and therefore that they are active; we cannot suppose them to sleep like Endymion. Now if you take away from a living being action, and still more production, what is left but contemplation? Therefore the activity of God, which surpasses all others in blessedness, must be contemplative; and of human activities, therefore, that which is most akin to this must be most of the nature of happiness.

This is indicated, too, by the fact that the other animals have no share in happiness, being completely deprived of such activity. For while the whole life of the gods is blessed, and that of men too in so far as some likeness of such activity belongs to them, none of the other animals is happy, since they in no way share in contemplation. Happiness extends, then, just so far as contemplation does, and those to whom contemplation more fully belongs are more truly happy, not as a mere concomitant but in virtue of the contemplation; for this is in itself precious. Happiness, therefore, must be some form of contemplation.

But, being a man, one will also need external prosperity; for our nature is not self-sufficient for the purpose of contemplation, but our body also must be healthy 1179ᵃ and must have food and other attention. Still, we must not think that the man who is to be happy will need many things or great things, merely because he cannot be supremely happy without external goods; for self-sufficiency and action do not involve excess, and we can do noble acts without ruling earth and sea; for even with moderate advantages one can act virtuously (this is manifest enough; for private persons are thought to do worthy acts no less than despots—indeed even more); and it is enough that we should have so much as that; for the life of the man who is active in accordance with virtue will be happy. Solon, too, was perhaps sketching well the happy man when he described him as moderately furnished with externals but as having done (as Solon thought) the noblest acts, and lived temperately; for one can with but moderate possessions do what one ought. Anaxagoras also seems to have supposed the happy man not to be rich nor a despot, when he said that he would not be surprised if the happy man were to seem to most people a strange person; for they judge by externals, since these are all they perceive. The opinions of the wise seem, then, to harmonize with our arguments. But while even such things carry some conviction, the truth in practical matters is discerned from the facts of life; for these are the decisive factor. We must therefore survey what we have already said, bringing it to the test of the facts of life, and if it harmonizes with the facts we must accept it, but if it clashes with them we must suppose it to be mere theory. Now he who exercises his reason and cultivates it seems to be both in the best state of mind and most dear to the gods. For if the gods have any care for human affairs, as they are thought to have, it would be reasonable both that they should delight in that which was best and most akin to them (i.e. reason) and that they should reward those who love and honour this most, as caring for the things that are dear to them and acting both rightly and nobly. And that all these attributes belong most of all to the philosopher is manifest. He, therefore, is the dearest to the gods. And he who is that will presumably be also the happiest; so that in this way too the philosopher will more than any other be happy.

Suggestions for Further Reading

Gilbert Harman, *The Nature of Morality*. New York, Oxford University Press, 1977.

Thomas Nagel, *Mortal Questions*. London, Cambridge University Press, 1979.

Derek Parfit, *Reason and Persons*. New York, Oxford University Press, 1984.

John Rawls, *A Theory of Justice*. Cambridge, Massachusetts, Harvard University Press, 1971.

J. J. C. Smart and Bernard Williams, *Utilitarianism: For and Against*. London, Cambridge University Press, 1973.

Bernard Williams, *Morality*. New York, Harper Torchbooks, 1972.

·G·L·O·S·S·A·R·Y·

a posteriori   A proposition that can be known or justified only by sense experience. An *a posteriori* argument is an argument in which at least one premiss is an *a posteriori* proposition.

a priori   A proposition that can be known or justified independent of sense experience. An *a priori* proposition can be known or justified by reason alone (once you grasp the constituent concepts). Truths of mathematics and definitions are often thought to be *a priori*. An *a priori* argument is an argument in which all the premisses are *a priori* propositions. The ontological argument for the existence of God was supposed to be an *a priori* argument.

abduction   A form of nondeductive inference, also known as inference to the best explanation. The Surprise Principle and the Only Game in Town Fallacy are relevant to deciding how strong an abductive inference is.

altruism   *See* psychological egoism.

analogy arguments   A nondeductive inference in which one infers that a target object *T* has some characteristic, on the ground that *T* is similar to some other object *A* (the analog), and *A* is known to possess that characteristic. Example: "Other galaxies probably contain life, since they are quite similar to our own galaxy and our own galaxy contains life." The strength of analogy arguments is relevant to the argument from design and to the problem of other minds.

analytic   An analytic sentence is one whose truth or falsehood is deductively entailed by definitions. Many philosophers have held that mathematical statements are analytic. If a sentence is not analytic, it is synthetic.

argument from evil   An argument that claims that the existence of evil shows either that there is no God or that God cannot be all-powerful, all-knowing, and all-good.

axiom   In mathematics, a starting assumption from which theorems are deduced.

begging the question   An argument begs the question when one would not accept the premisses unless one already believed the conclusion.

behaviorism   *See* logical behaviorism; methodological behaviorism.

bias   *See* sample bias.

birthday fallacy   The error in reasoning that one would make in thinking that "everyone has a birthday" deductively implies that "there is a single day on which everyone was born."

categorical imperative   An imperative (a command) that is unconditional (no if's). In contrast, a hypothetical imperative is a command of the form "If you have goal *G*, then do action *A*." Kant thought that moral rules (such as "Do not lie") take the form of categorical imperatives. In contrast, rules of prudence (such as "Stop smoking if you want to be healthy") are hypothetical.

causal argument for the existence of God   An argument that Descartes gives in the *Meditations* for the claim that God exists and is no deceiver: Since I have an idea of a perfect being, the cause of that idea must be a perfect being.

circularity   *See* begging the question.

clarity and distinctness criterion   Descartes maintained that if a belief is clear and distinct, then it cannot fail to be true. The reason that clear and distinct ideas must be true is that God exists and is no deceiver.

compatibilism The thesis that free will and determinism are compatible. Soft determinism is a version of compatibilism. Hard determinism and libertarianism are incompatibilist theories.

compatibility Two propositions are compatible if the truth of one would not rule out the truth of the other. Example: (1) This shirt is blue: (2) this shirt is torn. (1) and (2) are compatible. This does not mean that either is true.

conditional An if/then statement. The "if" clause is called the antecedent; the "then" clause is called the consequent.

consequentialism A kind of ethical theory that holds that the ethical properties of an action (its rightness or wrongness, its justness or unjustness, and so on) can be determined by seeing what consequences the action would have if it were performed. Utilitarianism is a consequentialist doctrine. Kant's theory is not.

conservation law A law in physics that says that some quantity (such as matter or mass/energy) can neither increase nor decrease in a closed system.

contingent A being is contingent if it exists in some, but not all possible worlds; a proposition is contingent if it is true in some, but not all possible worlds. You are an example of a contingent thing—though you exist in the actual world, you could have failed to exist.

conventionalism Trivial semantic conventionalism holds that a true *sentence* might have been false if we had defined our terms differently. For example "Dogs have four legs" might have been false if we had used the word "dog" to refer to fish. A substantive conventionalism holds that a true *proposition* might have been false if we (or someone) had adopted different conventions. For example, the following is a substantive conventionalist claim (and a false one): Dogs might have lacked four legs if we had used the word "dog" to refer to fish. *See* ethical conventionalism.

counterexample A counterexample to a generalization is an object that refutes the generalization. A rotten apple in the barrel is a counterexample to the claim "All the apples in this barrel are unspoiled."

deductive validity An argument is deductively valid because of the logical form it has. A deductively valid argument is one in which the premisses absolutely guarantee that the conclusion must be true.

descriptive/normative distinction A descriptive claim says what is the case without commenting on whether that is good or bad. A normative claim says whether something should be the case, or whether it is good or bad. "Drunk drivers kill thousands of people every year" is a descriptive claim; "It is a national disgrace that drunk driving is so lightly punished" is a normative claim.

the design argument An *a posteriori* argument that God exists, advanced by Aquinas and Paley, criticized by Hume. The argument claims that some feature of the world (such as the simplicity of its laws or the fact that organisms are intricate and well-adapted) should be explained by postulating the existence of an intelligent designer—namely, God.

determinism The thesis that a complete description of the causal facts at one time uniquely determines what must happen next. There is only one possible future, given a complete description of the present. Newtonian physics says that the behavior of physical objects is deterministic. *See* indeterminism.

divine command theory The theory that ethical statements are made true or false by God's decreeing how we should act.

dualism   The thesis that the mind and the body are two distinct entities. Dualists claim that a person's mind is made of a nonphysical substance. Dualism rejects materialism.

egoism   *See* psychological egoism.

emotivism   A theory about how ethical statements are used. Such statements are never true or false; rather, they merely allow the speaker to express feelings and attitudes. Emotivism accepts ethical subjectivism.

empirical   *See a posteriori.*

epistemology   The branch of philosophy concerned with concepts such as knowledge and rational justification.

equivocation, fallacy of   An argument commits this fallacy when it uses a term with one meaning for part of the argument and then shifts to another meaning for the rest of the argument. Example: "I put my money in the bank. A bank is a side of a river. Hence, I put my money in the side of a river." Arguments that commit this fallacy should be clarified so that the terms in them are used with a single meaning throughout.

ethical conventionalism   The thesis that ethical statements are made true by someone's say-so. The divine command theory, ethical relativism, and Sartre's version of existentialism are conventionalist theories. *See* conventionalism.

ethical realism   The thesis that some ethical statements are true and are true independently of anyone's thinking or saying that they are.

ethical relativism   The thesis that an ethical statement is true or false in a society because of the norms adopted in that society. Ethical relativism is a normative, not a descriptive thesis.

ethical subjectivism   The thesis that there are no ethical facts, only ethical opinions. Ethical statements are neither true nor false.

evil   *See* argument from evil; theodicy.

existentialism   A twentieth-century philosophical movement that places great weight on the fact that individuals are free and so must take responsibility for how they live their lives. In Sartre's version of existentialism, each person creates ethical facts for himself or herself, by a free decision.

fallacy   An error in reasoning.

falsifiability   *See* strong falsifiability.

fatalism   The theory expressed by the slogan "Whatever will be, will be" (*que sera, sera*). According to this theory, what happens to us does not depend on what we think or want or try to do. Oedipus, the myth says, was fated to kill his father and marry his mother. Fatalism and determinism are different.

foundationalism   The view that all the propositions we know to be true can be divided into two categories. First, there are the foundational propositions, which have some special property (such as indubitability) that explains why we know them to be true. Second, there are the superstructural propositions, which we know because they bear some special relationship (such as deductive implication) to the foundational propositions. Sometimes foundationalism is understood as a thesis about justified belief, not knowledge.

functionalism   The theory in the mind/body problem that says that psychological properties (types) are not identical with physical properties because psychological properties are multiply realizable. In addition, functionalism maintains that psychological properties are to be understood in terms of their causal roles.

genetic fallacy   The mistake of thinking that a statement cannot be true simply because there is a causal explanation for why people believe that it is true.

hard determinism   The incompatibilist doctrine that holds that human actions are un-free because they are causally determined.

identity theory   The thesis that the mind and the brain are identical. Also, that psychological properties are identical with physical properties.

if and only if   "*X* is true if and only if *Y* is true" means that the truth of *X* is both necessary and sufficient for the truth of *Y*. "*X* if and only if *Y*" means that *X* and *Y* are either both true or both false.

incompatibilism   *See* compatibilism.

incorrigibility of the mental, thesis of the   This thesis claims that we cannot be mistaken in the beliefs we have about the contents of our own minds. If you believe that you believe *P* or want *Q* to be true, then it must be true that you believe *P* or want *Q* to be true.

independent   Two propositions are logically independent of each other if the truth or falsity of one does not deductively imply the truth or falsity of the other. It was discovered in the eighteenth and nineteenth centuries that Euclid's parallel postulate is independent of the other axioms and postulates of his system of geometry.

indeterminism   The thesis that even a complete description of the present does not uniquely determine what will happen next. There is more than one possible future, each with its own probability of coming true, given a complete description of the present. The Quantum Theory says that nature is indeterministic.

induction   A nondeductive argument in which characteristics of individuals not in a sample are inferred from the characteristics of individuals in the sample. The strength of an inductive inference is influenced by sample size and sample bias.

is/ought gap   Hume argued that ethical statements concerning what *ought* to be the case cannot be deduced from statements that describe only what *is* the case.

JTB theory   The theory that knowledge is justified true belief. In other words, the theory advances the following proposal: For any person *S* and any proposition *p*, *S* knows that *p* if and only if (1) *S* believes that *p*; (2) *p* is true; (3) *S* is justified in believing that *p*.

KK principle   This principle says that if *S* knows that *p*, then *S* knows that *S* knows that *p*. The principle is rejected by the reliability theory of knowledge.

law   A scientific law is a proposition that is general (it concerns *all* objects of a certain kind), which does not refer to any individual, place, or time, and which has a kind of necessity called "nomological necessity." The term is often reserved for *a posteriori* propositions satisfying these conditions.

Leibniz's Law   If *a* and *b* are identical, then they must have all the same properties. Mind/body dualists defend their view by attempting to find some property that the mind has but that the body lacks; they thereby appeal to Leibniz's Law.

libertarianism   The incompatibilist doctrine that holds that some human actions are not causally determined, since they are free.

logical behaviorism   The thesis that the meanings of mentalistic terms can be given in exclusively behavioral terms.

logical form   The logical form of an argument is what makes it deductively valid or deductively invalid. *See* deductive validity.

materialism   The thesis that every object is a physical object. The mind/brain identity theory and functionalism are materialistic theories about the mind. Both reject the dualist claim that minds are made of an immaterial substance.

mentalism   The view that mental states are inner causes of outward behavior. Beliefs and desires are "inside" the subject; they cause behavior, which is more directly observable by others.

method of doubt The method that Descartes used to determine which propositions are foundational. If it is possible to doubt the proposition, then it fails the test. To see if it is possible to doubt the proposition, see if you can construct a story in which the proposition is false even though you believe that it is true.

methodological behaviorism The view that science should not talk about the inner states of organisms when it attempts to explain behavior. Methodological behaviorism rejects mentalism.

mind/brain identity theory *See* identity theory.

multiple realizability A property (type) is multiply realizable if the tokens that fall under the type need have nothing in common physically. *Being a mousetrap* is multiply realizable. Functionalism claims that psychological properties are multiply realizable.

mutually exclusive Two categories are mutually exclusive when nothing can fall in both of them. Being a triangle and being a circle are mutually exclusive.

naturalistic fallacy G. E. Moore argued that the ethical properties of an action — for example, its being morally obligatory — are not identical with any "naturalistic" properties of the action. A naturalistic property is a property that might be studied in a natural science. To deny this, Moore held, is to commit the naturalistic fallacy.

necessary A being is necessary if it must exist, no matter what the world is like. A proposition is necessary if it must be true, no matter what the world is like. Necessary beings exist in all possible worlds; a necessary proposition is true in all possible worlds. It is customary to distinguish three kinds of necessary propositions — ones that are logically necessary (such as "Bachelors must be unmarried"), ones that are nomologically necessary (such as "Nothing can move faster than the speed of light"), and ones that are circumstantially necessary (such as "The bomb had to explode").

necessary condition "X is a necessary condition for Y, means that if Y is true, then so is X. See sufficient condition.

normative claim *See* descriptive/normative distinction.

objective A proposition is objective if it is true or false independently of anyone's believing it or thinking about it.

observation An observational proposition is one you come to believe via the "direct" testimony of sense experience (sight, hearing, taste, touch, smell). One philosophical question about observation concerns what "direct" means in this definition.

omnipresent A being is omnipresent if it exists at all times — past, present, and future.

Only Game in Town Fallacy The error of thinking that you are obliged to believe a proposed explanation just because it is the only explanation that has been proposed.

ontological argument An *a priori* argument for the existence of God, proposed by Saint Anselm. It attempts to show that the definitiion of the concept of God entails that God exists, necessarily.

other minds, problem of This is the problem of explaining how we know that other individuals have minds and how we know what the contents of those minds are.

physicalism *See* materialism.

positivism The philosophical view that sentences about God, morality, aesthetics, and metaphysics are meaningless and are shown to be so by the testability theory of meaning.

possible *See* necessary and contingent.

pragmatism In this book, the philosophical theory that claims that the usefulness of a belief is what makes it reasonable to believe. Pragmatists also proposed a theory about what truth is. One version of this theory is that a true belief is one that is useful (in some sense that requires clarification). Another holds that a proposition is true if it would be contained in the set of beliefs an inquirer would have after an infinite time spent inquiring. *See* truth.

Principle of the Common Cause   A principle governing abductive inference. It asserts that when two or more objects exhibit an intricate series of similarities, the similarities should be explained by postulating a common cause; this is preferable to the separate cause explanation, according to which each object obtained its characteristics independently. Example: Two students hand in identical essays in a philosophy class. It is more plausible to explain this as the result of plagiarism than to think that each student worked independently. The Common Cause Principle is an application of the Surprise Principle.

Principle of Parsimony   Otherwise known as Ockham's razor. This principle says that an explanation that postulates fewer entities or processes is preferable to one that postulates more.

Principle of the Uniformity of Nature   The thesis that the future will resemble the past. Hume believed that all inductive arguments presuppose that this principle is true.

proposition   That which is expressed by a true or false declarative sentence. Though the sentence "lemons are yellow" is part of the English language, the proposition that this sentence expresses is no more a part of English than it is a part of any other human language. A variety of philosophical theories maintain that some declarative sentences do not express propositions (though they may seem to). For example, ethical subjectivism says that ethical statements are neither true nor false. Logical positivism maintains that the statement "God exists" is neither true nor false.

propositional attitudes   Consider the following statements: "S believes that lemons are yellow," "S wants to drink a cup of coffee," "S doubts that it will rain." In each of these, a subject, S, is said to have an attitude — believing, desiring, or doubting — toward a proposition.

psychological egoism   The claim that people always put their self-interest ahead of the welfare of others. Sometimes the doctrine is given a more extreme formulation — that people only care about their own interests, never about the welfare of others.

random   A sampling process is random when each object in the population from which the sample is drawn has the same probability of being drawn.

realism   *See* ethical realism.

reductio ad absurdum   A deductively valid form of argument in which one proves that P is true by showing that (1) if P were false, A would have to be true, and (2) A is false.

redundancy theory of truth   This theory claims that to say that a statement is true is to do nothing more than assert that statement: "It's true that lemons are yellow" is just a long-winded way of saying that lemons are yellow.

reference   *See* sense and reference.

relativism   *See* ethical relativism.

relativity   The truth or falsity of a proposition p is a relative matter if p's truth or falsehood depends on an arbitrary choice. Example: Sue and Mary are walking side by side. Is Sue to the left of Mary? That depends on (is relative to) a choice of point of view. There are several equally correct choices. Whether it's true or false that Sue is to the left of Mary depends on that (arbitrary) choice.

reliability theory of knowledge   A theory that exploits the analogy between a thermometer's reliably representing the temperature and a subject's knowing a proposition to be true. The theory says that S knows that p if and only if (1) S believes that p; (2) p is true; and (3) in the circumstances that S occupies, S would not have believed that p unless p were true.

sample bias An inductive inference is weakened by having a biased sample. If you want to know what percentage of Americans believes in God, do not conduct your survey by using church membership lists. To do so would probably bias your sample.

sample size An inductive inference is made stronger by increasing its sample size. In telephone surveys, your conclusion about the population sampled is on firmer ground if you call more people than if you call fewer.

sense and reference Two terms in a language may refer to a single object, even though they have different meanings (senses). An example: "The inventor of bifocals" and "the first U.S. ambassador to France" have different senses, though both refer to the same person, namely, Benjamin Franklin. Frege held that terms with the same sense must have the same reference.

skepticism The thesis that knowledge (or rational justification) is unobtainable. Descartes tried to refute skepticism about knowledge; Hume was a skeptic about the rational justifiability of induction.

soft determinism The compatibilist thesis that human actions are both free and causally determined.

solipsism The thesis that the only thing that exists is my mind and its contents.

strong falsifiability A hypothesis is strongly falsifiable if it deductively implies an observation sentence. "Falsifiable" does not mean *false*.

subjective A proposition is subjective if its truth or falsehood depends on what occurs in the mind of some subject. *See* objective.

subjectivism *See* ethical subjectivism.

sufficient condition "X is a sufficient condition for Y" means that if X is true, so is Y. *See* necessary condition.

Surprise Principle A principle governing abductive inference. An observation O strongly favors one hypothesis (H_1) over another (H_2) when two conditions are satisfied, but not otherwise: (1) If H_1 were true, we would expect O ; (2) if H_2 were true, we would not expect O.

synthetic *See* analytic.

teleology An object is described in a teleological fashion when it is described in terms of its goals, purposes, or ends.

testability theory of meaning A positivist doctrine, which says that a meaningful sentence must either be analytic or empirical. One way that positivists proposed to understand what it means to be empirical is in terms of strong falsifiability.

theodicy The attempt to reconcile the existence of evil in the world with the idea that God exists and is all-powerful, all-knowing, and all-good.

theorem *See* axiom.

truth In this book, it is assumed that, for most propositions, whether they are true is quite independent of the question of whether anyone believes them or thinks about them. The idea that truth is independent of psychological facts or capacities is sometimes termed a realist theory of truth. *See* redundancy theory of truth.

type/token distinction A type is a property or characteristic. The individual items that populate the world are termed "tokens." A given token falls under many types. So, for example, you are a token of the type *human being* and a token of the type *object on the surface of the earth*. The type/token distinction is important to functionalism's critique of the mind/brain identity theory.

universalizability criterion Kant thought that the ethical permissibility of an action could be determined by seeing if it passes the universalizability test: See if it is possible for the action to be universal (performed by everyone) or if it is possible for a rational agent to will (intend) that the action be universal.

utilitarianism   The ethical theory that the action you should perform in a given situation is the one that would promote the greatest good for the greatest number of individuals. Hedonistic utilitarianism equates good with the feeling of happiness and the absence of the feeling of pain. Preference utilitarianism says that the good to be maximized is the satisfaction of preferences. Utilitarian theories also are distinguished by whether they are act or rule utilitarian. An act utilitarian says that it is the consequences of the token action under consideration that need to be considered. A rule utilitarian says that it is the long-term effects of a type of action that are relevant to deciding whether to perform a token act of that type.

validity   *See* deductive validity.

verifiability   *See* testability theory of meaning.

vitalism   The theory that living things differ from nonliving things because they possess a special immaterial substance — an *élan vital* — that animates them with life. Vitalism and dualism both reject materialism.

·S·O·U·R·C·E·S·

Philosophy of Religion

Saint Thomas Aquinas, "Five Ways to Prove that God Exists." From *The Basic Writings of St. Thomas Aquinas*, Anton C. Pegis (ed.), New York: Doubleday & Co., 1955.

William Paley, "The Design Argument." From *Natural Theology*, 1805.

David Hume, "Critique of the Design Argument." From *Dialogues Concerning Natural Religion*, edited by Norman Kemp Smith. Walton-On-Thames, England: Thomas Nelson and Sons Ltd., 1947.

St. Anselm and Gaunilo, "The Ontological Argument," translated by Arthur C. McGill. From *The Many-Faced Argument*, edited by John H. Hick and Arthur C. McGill. New York: Macmillan, 1968. Copyright © 1967 John H. Hick and Arthur C. McGill.

Alfred Jules Ayer, "Religious Discourse Is Meaningless." From *Language, Truth and Logic*, by Alfred Jules Ayer. New York: Dover Books, 1936, pp. 114–120.

Ernest Nagel, "Philosophical Concepts of Atheism," in J.E. Fairchild (ed.), *Basic Beliefs; The Religious Philosophies of Mankind*. Dobbs Ferry, NY: Sheridan House, Inc., 1959.

Theory of Knowledge

Plato, "Knowledge and True Belief." From *The Theaetetus, The Collected Dialogues of Plato*, translated by F. M. Cornford. Andover, Hants, England: Routledge, a division of Routledge, Chapman & Hall Ltd. 1961, pp. 905–908, pp. 914–919.

René Descartes, "Meditations on First Philosophy," translated by Donald Cress. Indianapolis: Hackett Publishing Co., 1979, pp. 13–56. Reprinted with permission of Hackett Publishing Company, Inc.

David Hume, "Induction Cannot Be Rationally Justified." From *An Inquiry Concerning Human Understanding*, edited by Charles W. Hendel. New York: Macmillan, 1957, pp. 40–53. Copyright © 1985 by Macmillan Publishing Company; copyright 1951.

Philosophy of Mind

Bertrand Russell, "Other Minds Are Known by Analogy from One's Own Case." From *Human Knowledge: Its Scopes and Limits*. London: Unwin Hyman Ltd., 1948, pp. 482–486. Reproduced with kind permission of Unwin Hyman Ltd.

J.J.C. Smart, "Mental Processes Are Physical." From "Sensations and Brain Processes," *Philosophical Review*, 1959, LXVIII, pp. 141–156.

A.M. Turing, "Computing Machinery and Intelligence." From *Mind*, volume 59 (1950), pp. 433–460 by permission of Oxford University Press.

David Hume, "Of Liberty and Necessity." From *An Inquiry Concerning Human Understanding*, edited by Charles W. Hendel. New York: Macmillan, 1957, pp. 90–111. Copyright © 1985 by Macmillan Publishing Company; copyright 1951.

C.A. Campbell, "Has the Self 'Free Will'?" From *On Selfhood and Godhood*. London: Unwin Hyman Ltd., 1957, pp. 158–165, 167–179. Reproduced with kind permission of Unwin Hyman Ltd.

Ethics

Plato, "Critique of the Divine Command Theory." From *The Euthyphro,* in *The Trial and Death of Socrates,* translated by G. M. A. Grube. Indianapolis: Hackett Publishing Co., 1975, pp. 5–22. Reprinted with permission of Hackett Publishing Company, Inc.

Jean-Paul Sartre, "Existentialism." From *Existentialism,* translated by Bernard Frechtman. New York: Philosophical Library, 1947, pp. 14–39.

John Stuart Mill, "Defence of Utilitarianism." From *Utilitarianism,* 1861.

Immanuel Kant, "Ethics Founded on Reason." From *Groundwork of the Metaphysics of Morals,* translated by H.J. Paton. London: Unwin Hyman Ltd., 1956, pp. 61–62, 64–67, 74, 80–92, 95–107. Reproduced with kind permission of Unwin Hyman Ltd.

Aristotle, "Morality and Human Nature." From *The Nicomachean Ethics,* translated by W.D. Ross, Oxford: Oxford University Press, 1925, pp. 1094a1–1096a10, 1097a15–1099b8, 1102a5–1109b27, 1177a11–1179a132.

·I·N·D·E·X·

A

A posteriori and *a priori*, 75, 78, 84, 160 , 163, 175, 276, 299
Abductive arguments, 8*ff.*
  design argument and, 55
  differs from induction, 23
  existence of God and, 36, 52, 69
  explain observations, 23, 52, 65, 68, 268
  other minds and, 260
  not deductively valid, 24
  standards for evaluating, 26–31
Aboutness, 253
Adaptation, 62, 65
  See also Function
Aesthetics, 400
Allen, W., 420
Altruism, 318*ff.*
Ambiguity of necessity, 166, 314
Analogy, 51
  design argument and, 53
  other minds and, 259–260
Analytic and synthetic statements, 84
Anselm, 76*ff.*, 97, 118*ff.*
Aquinas, T., 36–50, 67, 97, 106*ff.*
Arguments
  good, 8
  premises and conclusion of, 8
  See also Deductive; Inductive; Abductive
Aristotle, 38, 47, 107, 319
  ethical views of, 440*ff.*, 527*ff.*
Armstrong, D., 161
Astrology, 31
Atheism, 48, 126*ff.*
Auxiliary assumptions, 86, 88–89, 96, 187
Axioms, 8, 147
Ayer, A., 91, 121*ff.*

B

Begging the Question. *See* Circularity

B

Behaviorism
  computers and, 334*ff.*
  logical, 258*ff.*, 287
  methodological, 268*ff.*, 287
  nature/nurture problem and, 273–274
  novel behaviors and, 270*ff.*
  pain and, 266
Belief
  the will and, 95
  truth and, 15
  two reasons for, 92
  See also Arguments
Birthday fallacy, 39, 49, 284
Black, M., 182
Block, N., 284
Bogart, H., 388
Brainwashing, 291

C

Campbell, C., 301, 307, 370*ff.*
Category mistakes, 261
Causality
  apportioning causal responsibility, 325
  existence of God and, 37, 47, 155
  explanation and, 71
  functionalism and, 285
  moral responsibility and, 312
  necessary/sufficient conditions and, 292
  transitivity and, 290
  between mind and matter, 256
  inside of space and time, 73
  See also Explanation; Principle of Common Cause
Certainty, 45–46
  knowledge and, 148, 171
  science and, 57, 69, 74
Chance, 293
  See also Probability
Chimps, 60

Chomsky, N., 271
Circularity, 14–15, 156, 182, 255
Circumstantial necessity, 164
Clarity and distinctness, 154, 157, 159
Clifford, W., 99
Coercion, 306, 315
Compatibilism, 299, 308*ff.*
Compulsions, 291, 304
Computers
  freedom and, 289
  minds and, 283, 334*ff.*
Conditionals, 11, 14
Consequentialism, 433
Conventionalism, 388, 407*ff.*
Converse and contrapositive, 14
Correlation, 278
Counterexample, 143
Counterinduction, 183
Creationism. *See* Evolution

D

Darwin, C., 56, 59, 63, 130
Decision theory, 94*ff.*
Deductive
  arguments, 8
  invalidity, 10–13
  justification of a theory, 26
  validity, 9–11, 18–19, 100, 147
Definitions
  a priori status of, 76
  existence of thing defined and, 76,
    82, 83
  provide necessary and sufficient
    conditions, 140
  versus examples, 2, 7
Dennett, D., 266
Descartes, R., 66, 147*ff.*, 196*ff.*, 307
  Hume and, 173, 185
Design Argument, 49*ff.*
  local and global, 50
  See also Evolution
Determinism, 293
  causality and, 296
  hard and soft, 300
Dewey, J., 98
Dirty hands, 427
Dispositions, 265
Divine Command theory, 409*ff.*
Dixon, J., 31

Dostoyevsky, F., 386
Doubt
  dualism and, 251
  method of, 148
  See also Certainty
Dreams, 149
Dretske, F., 296
Dualism, 3, 248*ff.*, 262, 277, 285, 287

E

Egoism, 318*ff.*, 390
Einstein, A., 77, 169
Emotivism, 391
Epistemology, 138*ff.*
Error, 158
  See also Skepticism; Knowledge
Essential property, 257
Ethical relativism. *See* Relativity
Ethics
  normative and meta, 386
  truth and opinion in, 387
  See also Aristotle; Kant; Relativity;
    Subjectivism; Utilitarianism
Euclid, 147, 153
Evidence versus prudence, 92
  See also Abductive; Prediction
Evil
  existence of God and, 100*ff.*
  demon, 150
  soul-building and, 102
  two kinds of, 101
Evolution
  creationism and, 56*ff.*
  human beings and, 63–64
  linguistic, 61
  two part theory of, 58
Existentialism, 414–415
Expectation, 93
Experience machines, 419
Explanation, 70*ff.*
  ethics and, 404–405
  local and global, 71
  minimal and deep, 272
  See also Abduction

F

Falsifiability, 85
Fatalism, 297
Fodor, J., 281

Form. *See* Logical form
Foundationalism, 147, 150, 174, 185,
    188–189
Freedom
    chance and, 295
    could-not-have-done-otherwise and,
        290, 305, 313, 356*ff.*, 370*ff.*
    distant causation and, 290, 296, 312
    of the will, 103, 248, 289*ff.*
    political 302, 498*ff.*
    unfreedom and, 291
Frege, G., 254–255, 394, 398
Freud, S., 97, 152
Function, 56, 310, 317
    See also Goal-directed systems
Functionalism, 281*ff.*

G

Gambling
    expected pay-offs in, 93*ff.*
    inductive inference and, 20
    knowledge and, 143
Gaunilo, 79, 118*ff.*
Gene. *See* Mendel; Nature/Nuture
Genetic fallacy, 392, 398
Gettier, E., 143
Goal-directed systems, 49, 442
God
    concept of, 37, 66, 68
    evil and existence of, 100*ff.*
    explanation of, 69
    knowledge and, 154
Good, I., 187
Goodness, 441
Gould, S., 63
Gremlins, 31

H

Happiness, 419*ff.*, 444
Harman, G., 399*ff.*
Hitler, A., 105
Holmes, S., 21, 68, 86
Human nature, 443*ff.*
    See also Innateness
Hume, D., 50, 53
    Descartes and, 173–174, 185
    on design argument, 53–55, 67,
        111*ff.*
    on freedom. 303, 311, 356*ff.*

on induction, 138, 171*ff.*, 236*ff.*
on is/ought, 395*ff.*, 403
on miracles, 91
on moral facts, 407
on role of reason in action, 431
Huxley, A., 420

I

Identity, 75, 250, 277, 393
Ignorance, 69
    See also Knowledge
Imperatives, hypothetical and categori-
    cal, 432
Imperialism, 412
Incorrigibility Thesis, 152, 302
Indubitability, 149
    See also Doubt; Certainty; Incorrigi-
        bility Thesis
Inductive arguments, 8
    design argument and, 54–55
    differs from abduction, 23–24
    generalizations and predictions in,
        175
    Newton on, 279
    other minds and, 259*ff.*
    reliability of, 180
    strength of, 22
    See also Analogy; Hume; Principle of
        Uniformity of Nature
Infinity, 37
Innateness, 76, 443
    See also Nature/Nuture
Instrumental reason, 431
Introspection. *See* Incorrigibility thesis
Islands, 79
Inverted spectrum problem, 288
Investment swindle, 30

J

James, W., 98, 319
Justice, 423

K

KK-Principle, 165
Kant, I.,
    on determinism, 299
    on ethics 431*ff.*, 506*ff.*
    view that existence not a predicate,
        81, 129

Knowledge
  as internally certifiable, 160
  JTB theory of, 142
  object, propositional, and know-
    how, 139
  reliability theory of, 160*ff.*
  versus justified belief, 171
  versus true belief, 3, 141
  See also Skepticism

L

Laplace, P., 133
Laws
  necessity and, 163
  conservation, 42, 256
  moral, 432*ff.*
  scientific, 20
Leibniz, G., 72, 250
Liberalism and conservatism, 426
Libertarianism, 301, 370*ff.*
Locke, J., 305, 314
Logical
  form, 9, 80
  positivism. *See* Positivism
  possibility, 163
Loyalty, 429

M

Macbeth, 149
Materialism, 276
Mathematics, 43, 84, 147, 150
Mean, Doctrine of, 445
Meaning
  of mentalistic vocabulary, 264
  reference and, 254, 331, 394
  testability theory of, 83*ff.*
Mendel, G., 23, 55, 84, 268
Mentalism, 259, 269, 287
Mill, J., 417*ff.*, 471*ff.*
Mind/Brain Identity Theory, 3, 249,
    276*ff.*, 285, 287, 331*ff.*, 393
Miracles, 90
Monod, J., 67
Moore, G., 393
Morality. *See* Ethics
Motion
  existence of God and, 37–38
  laws of, 432
Multiple realizability, 282

Mutation, 59
Mutually Exclusive, 9

N

Nagel, E., 126*ff.*
Names, 62, 408
  differ from things named, 44
Natural selection, 58–59, 74
Naturalistic fallacy, 390*ff.*
Nature/Nuture problem, 273–274
Necessary and sufficient conditions,
    140, 292–293
Necessity
  ambiguity of, 166, 314
  circumstantial, 164
  contingency and, 39, 78
  kinds of, 163
  mathematics and, 43
  versus certainty, 45
Neptune, 87
Newton, I., 20–21, 38, 279, 432
Nomological possibility, 163
Numbers, 45

O

Objective versus subjective, 4, 294,
    391, 401, 409
Obligations, 440
Observation
  abduction and, 23
  in ethics, 398*ff.*
  testability and, 85, 269
  theory-ladenness of, 400
Oedipus, 252, 297
Omnipresence, 41
Only game in town fallacy, 31, 69, 73
Ontological argument, 75*ff.*
Other minds, problem of, 259, 327*ff.*

P

Pain, 266, 286
Paley, W., 50*ff.*, 62, 67, 97,
    108–111
Panda's thumb, 63
Parsimony, Principle of, 133, 279,
    330, 404
Pascal, B., 92*ff.*
Pasteur, L., 67
Peirce, C., 9, 98

Perfection, 47, 79, 155
Philosophy, nature of, 2–7
Phobias, 275
Place, U., 277
Plato, 141, 191*ff.*, 409, 450*ff.*
Pleasures, higher and lower, 420
Popper, K., 85
Population explosion, 430
Positivism, 83, 121*ff.*
Possibility
   of error, and knowledge, 144, 158
   three kinds of, 163
   versus conceivability, 77–78
Possible worlds, 39–41, 72
Pragmatism, 98
Prediction, 20, 24–25, 27, 33, 174
Predictive equivalence, 66–67, 419
Principle of the common cause, 61,
   67, 279
Principle of the Uniformity of Nature,
   176, 179, 186
Probability, 294
   See also Randomness
Proposition
   -al knowledge, 139
   -al attitudes, 252
   necessary and contingent -s, 44
   versus sentence, 409
Punishment, 423
Putnam, H., 281
Python, M., 29

Q
Quantam mechanics, 294

R
Randomness, 22, 51
Realism, 388
Reciprocal illumination, 418
Reductionism, 395–396
Reference. *See* Meaning
Reichenbach, H., 61
Relativity
   in ethics, 389–390, 411
   of the evidence relation, 187
   of knowledge, 168
   of simultaneity, 169
Reliability, 161*ff.*
   degree of, 180

Representation, 155
Research programs, 269
Responsibility, moral and causal,
   312–313
Right, theory of the, 441
Rules of inference, 180
Russell, B., 143, 327*ff.*
Ryle, G., 258*ff.*

S
Sampling. *See* Inductive arguments
Sartre, J., 389, 414, 463*ff.*
Sense. *See* meaning
Sets, 45
Side effects of action, 321*ff.*
Similarity
   abductive inferences and, 62
   analogy and, 54
   two kinds of, 62
Singer, P., 430
Skepticism, 3, 138, 144, 145, 158,
   164, 172, 188
Skinner, B., 268*ff.*
Smart, J., 277, 330*ff.*
Snyder, A., 296
Sober, A., 139
Sober, S., 28
Solipsism, 328
Soul, immortality of, 250
Species, evolotion of, 59–60
Spontaneous generation, 64, 67
Strawson, P., 181
Subjectivism, 388, 391, 396, 404
Surprise Principle, 26–31
   competing hypotheses and, 29,
     65–66
   evolution and, 65
   mind/body problem and, 267
   miracles and, 90
   principles of the common cause
     and, 61

T
Testing hypotheses
   in ethics, 400
   role of auxiliary assumptions in,
     86–90
   See also Abductive; Prediction; Sur-
     prise Principle

Theodicy, 101
Thermodynamics, 57
Thermometers, 161*ff.*
Thought experiments, 400
Tolerance, 425
Transitivity, 290
Tree of life, 60
Truth
    as redundancy, 17–18
    knowledge and, 141, 172
    versus belief, 15
    versus validity, 10
    See also wishful thinking
Turing, A., 334*ff.*
Type/token distinction, 281, 285, 424,
    436

U

Universalizability criterion, 434
Universals of culture, 412

Utilitarianism, 133, 393, 416*ff.*, 471*ff.*
    act versus rule, 424
    hedonistic versus preference, 421
Utility comparisons, 421

V

Validity. *See* Deductive validity
Values in science, 403
Vegetarianism, 430
Vestigial organs, 63
Vitalism, 277, 279–280
Vulcan, 87

W

Weather vanes, 308*ff.*
Wishful thinking, 16, 98, 153, 416

Z

Zebras, 59